D0282623

HIGH
WIRE ACT

TED
ROGERS
AND THE EMPIRE
THAT DEBT BUILT

CAROLINE VAN HASSELT

John Wiley & Sons Canada, Ltd.

inaccuracies by checking with multiple sources. Where there are differences in recollection, I've either noted it within the text or in the endnotes.

In chronicling the RCI story, I interviewed nearly 200 people. Many people spoke to me on the condition of anonymity and have not been quoted. Though their names cannot be mentioned here, I want them to know that I am deeply appreciative of their input and feedback. I thank everyone, who spoke on and off the record, for sharing and reliving their experiences with me. Their insights and contributions are imbedded throughout the book. I owe special thanks to Marc Belzberg, Robi Blumenstein, Philippe de Gaspé Beaubien, Gar Emerson, Nick Hamilton-Piercy, Nick Kauser, Doug Kirk, Robin Korthals, David Masotti, Craig McCaw, Brian Roberts, Loretta Rogers, John A. Tory, Burke van Valkenberg and Colin Watson.

Since Rogers is easily one of Canada's most written about business leaders, I am indebted to all of the journalists before me who have covered RCI. All interviews are mine unless otherwise noted. The only person who declined to be interviewed was BCE's Michael Sabia. Through his spokesman Ron Alepian, Sabia said he didn't want "his words to appear in a book for posterity" because his comments about Rogers "might change."

I also thank Paul McLaughlin for his early encouragement and constructive feedback and give honorable mentions to Kevin Bell, Rachel Layne, Sara Monahan, Kathie O'Donnell and Rob Wells for their support—not to mention occasional access to the Bloomberg terminal. I am immensely grateful to Louise Ross, who cheerfully transcribed last-minute interview tapes, Jim Harrison, who provided valuable feedback, and Jennifer Garbin, who completed her Master of Divinity degree to become a reverend, while helping me transcribe interviews. Jennifer kept me laughing and always allowed me to bend her ear. Heather Wilson at the Joseph L. Rotman School of Management at the University of Toronto was a godsend. She unearthed decades-old articles, CRTC transcripts and obscure documents. I also thank the librarians at the CRTC, the Cable Center in Denver and the Minneapolis Public Library for their assistance. For his sage counsel, I thank David Steinberg. Brian Rogers (no relation to Ted), who provided enthusiastic and helpful feedback on the manuscript, was wonderful and kept me out of trouble.

Throughout, Tanya Crowell and Natasha Turner kept me physically healthy as I, in their words, obsessed over this book. I also thank Dr. Yvonne Verbeeten for her watchful care.

Kevin Doyle, one of Canada's most gifted and accomplished editors, who was Bloomberg Canada's bureau chief and editor of *Maclean's* magazine, has been an inspiration and mentor to me. Without his support in the early days of this project, it is unlikely that I would have pursued this adventure. He was a joy to work both for and with. I owe him a debt of gratitude.

I am especially grateful to Don Loney, who supported me and embraced this book from the start, Pamela Vokey for her superb editorial counsel, and Jennifer Smith, the publisher at Wiley Canada, for her wholehearted commitment and enthusiasm. This book would not have been possible without the dedication and help of the talented team at Wiley.

I must thank my family, especially my mother, for their support and continual laughter. My parents, who came to Canada as penniless European immigrants to carve out a new life, have always been my inspiration. My deepest sorrow is that my father, a spiritually strong man and my greatest supporter, died of prostate cancer before I could complete this book.

Lastly, I give heartfelt thanks to Theresa Tedesco, a dear friend, for her enduring friendship, cheerful encouragement, and wise counsel over the years. With enormous patience and sensitivity, she helped me see this book through to its fruition and saved me from myself. It was her idea that I write this book and without her unwavering support, it would never have been written.

While the players in the political, regulatory and commercial arenas have changed, Ted Rogers has remained the one constant in the communications industry for almost 50 years. Indeed, the words of another outsized historical figure Theodore Roosevelt seem to be as apt today about Rogers, unbeaten and unbowed, as they were when Roosevelt spoke of the Man in the Arena in his famous *Citizenship in a Republic* speech at the Sorbonne in Paris in 1910:

> It is not the critic who counts: not the man who points out how the strong man stumbles or where the doer of deeds could have done better. The credit belongs to the man who is actually in the arena, whose face is marred by dust and sweat and blood, who strives valiantly, who errs and comes up short again and again, because there is no effort without error or shortcoming, but who knows the great enthusiasms, the great devotions, who spends himself for a worthy cause; who, at the best, knows, in the end, the triumph of high achievement, and who, at the worst, if he fails, at least he fails while daring greatly, so that his place shall never be with those cold and timid souls who knew neither victory nor defeat.

Caroline Van Hasselt.
August, 2007.

Not Your Average Cable Guy

"I've got a belief and a faith, and an ego, that tells me that we can succeed no matter what we try."

—Ted Rogers

It was early December 2005. Geoff Beattie, the *consigliore* for the world's ninth-richest man, Lord Kenneth Thomson of Fleet, telephoned Ted Rogers, the irrepressible founder of Canada's biggest cable and wireless company, Rogers Communications Inc. (RCI). Rogers refused to take his call as he was immersed in budget meetings and didn't want to be disturbed. Beattie was taken aback. He was merely making a courtesy call to Rogers to give him a heads-up before his big news was splashed all over the media.

After three arduous years of often-heated talks, Beattie had finally convinced Rogers' long-time archrival, BCE Inc., to offload most of its stake in Canada's media giant, Bell Globemedia (BGM), to Bell's minority partner Woodbridge Co., the Thomson family's private holding company.

BCE, once Canada's most powerful conglomerate, agreed to reduce its 68.5-percent stake to 20 percent in the Bell-Thomson joint venture, which owns *The Globe and Mail* newspaper; Canada's largest private television broadcaster, CTV Inc.; several specialty channels, including The Sports Network (TSN); and a 15-percent stake in Maple Leaf Sports and Entertainment, the owner of two of Toronto's four pro sports teams—the Maple Leafs and the Raptors—as well as the Air Canada Centre. Thomson, a die-hard Leafs fan, had agreed to raise Woodbridge's stake to 40 percent, gaining effective control of the company, and bringing in two new partners, each with 20 percent: Ontario Teachers' Pension Plan and Torstar Corp., owner of Canada's largest daily newspaper, the *Toronto Star*.

Beattie had worked on this deal since 2002 when BCE's newly installed CEO, Michael Sabia, the Yale-educated former bureaucrat, called BGM, his predecessor's $4-billion answer to AOL's stupendous US$165-billion takeover of old media behemoth Time Warner, a non-core strategic asset. For the next three years, to Beattie's frustration—prompting him to codename the deal Project Odyssey—Sabia dithered, fearing Woodbridge would flip its stake to Ted Rogers—the worst possible outcome for Ma Bell, which has watched this pesky cable guy not just invade its turf but at times beat it at its own game. Sabia couldn't risk that sort of humiliation for himself or his beleaguered company. He decided he'd better play it safe and hold onto 20 percent, a sort of schmuck insurance to ensure Bell still had access to content and, more importantly, isolate Rogers. Ironically, Sabia threatened to bring in other partners, implicitly referring to Rogers, when talks at one point derailed. Rogers' shadow had loomed so large that he influenced the deal, even though he wasn't even at the negotiating table.

When Beattie reached Rogers, the 72-year-old cable billionaire cackled, half jokingly, "Is there an anti-Rogers clause?"

Fair enough question. After all, Rogers wields control over Canada's second-largest telecommunications company by revenue, behind the 900-pound gorilla BCE and ahead of western Canadian upstart Telus Corp. He owns Canada's largest wireless phone company, its biggest cable television monopoly, one of its largest radio networks, a national chain of video stores, most of its consumer magazines, including *Maclean's* and *Chatelaine*, and the country's only nationally televised shopping service, The Shopping Channel. He is the owner of Canada's only Major League Baseball team, the Toronto Blue Jays, and the taxpayer-built stadium in which they play. His name is now emblazoned in gigantic red letters on all corners of the façade of the Rogers Centre, formerly the SkyDome.

For 50 years, Rogers has been a pervasive force in the lives of Canadians. In the clubby business community, he's known simply as Ted. But, to the millions of Canadians, who subscribe to his cable and Internet service, rent his videos and use his wireless network, he's known as Rogers. Either way, he's clawed his way to the top in an industry dominated by Bell Canada, the greatest monopoly of them all, in a country whose government doesn't foster entrepreneurial spirit. He's the only cable guy in North America that owns a wireless company. He played in the U.S. sandbox long enough to build key alliances south of the border and a tougher and stronger company in Canada for the time spent there. "He has everything you could ever want in one company," says Comcast Corp.'s CEO Brian Roberts, whose family is close to the Rogers clan. "Ted has not missed an opportunity to keep his company in the forefront and, for that matter, keep Canada in the forefront."

The empire Ted Rogers has built, assembled and almost lost (no less than three times) began in 1960 at a tiny FM radio station, near the heart of Toronto's financial district, years before the country's largest banks raised their lofty towers. As a young, aspiring law student, Rogers cajoled his way into partnering with legendary media baron John Bassett to win the license for Toronto's first private TV station, CFTO, the jewel in the CTV Network's broadcast crown. Rogers bought his first cable TV system in 1967, the year of Canada's centennial. Joining him shortly thereafter for the ride was the keeper of the flame, Phil Lind. The two most unlikely of partners spent the next four decades outmaneuvering most of Canada's other cable pioneers. Certainly, they've outlasted them. Together, they are still stirring up trouble. A $100 investment in RCI shares in 1985 now would be worth more than $4,000—that's if investors were able to stomach the ride. Most of them couldn't. RCI was no "widows-and-orphans stock" like Bell. The real winners, until recently, were RCI debt holders.

Ted Rogers' appetite for risk is unparalleled in Canada. Debt doesn't scare him. He's been blessed with exceptionally good luck and intelligence enough to put it to good use. He goes after what he wants. Rarely does he lose. In the 28 years since his first major coup in 1979, when he snared Canadian Cablesystems Ltd., a company twice the size of his own, Rogers has scared up vertiginous mountains of debt, recycling with junk-bond guru Michael Milken's help a staggering $30 billion of debt—the size of Nova Scotia's economic engine. Put another way, he spent $1.3 billion a year—borrowing from his bankers to finance acquisitions, issuing bonds to wipe the loan-slate clean, borrowing again to build or upgrade his cable and wireless networks, selling more bonds to pay off his loans and so on—a perpetual financing circle built on the backs of his often-unforgiving subscribers. Skeptics feared he'd self-implode, and while he's come close, he never has, and in 2004 he pulled off in rapid-fire succession two multi-billion-dollar deals to fortify his national wireless company.

All the while, BCE's Michael Sabia sat on the sidelines worrying through his corporate makeover of the once mighty Bell, missing the opportunity of a lifetime to thwart Rogers' ambitions to be No. 1 in wireless. What's more, Ted Rogers even invited Sabia to make a joint bid where they'd divvy up the assets. Bell took a pass. What a blunder.

In 2006, Sabia watched as Ted Rogers, grinning from ear to ear, held up a blue-and-white Toronto Maple Leafs hockey jersey, a symbol of his new relationship with Maple Leaf Sports and Entertainment. Rogers' surname was emblazoned on the back of the jersey, above, fittingly enough, a big, blue numeral "1." In a major coup, Rogers replaced Bell for a major telecom contract at Canada's hockey shrine and condominium complex. (The ground war between them is such that Bell once wanted MLSE to sign a wireless contract stating they'd cover the Air Canada Centre as long as MLSE didn't allow in any Rogers signals—preventing a Rogers cellphone from working in the ACC.) RCI also replaced Bell as a major corporate sponsor.

Rogers' good friend and neighbor Larry Tanenbaum helped broker the deal. The two men once aspired to create a sporting "convergence" of the Leafs, Raptors and Blue Jays, with their own digital cable TV channel—modeled after the powerhouse Yankees Entertainment and Sports (YES) Network. They keep talking about bringing a National Football League franchise to Toronto, a possible way–if the stars align properly—to dust off their old media/sports strategy. Tanenbaum needs a loyal ally in his camp against Woodbridge if he chooses to vie for ownership. With Woodbridge's genteel owner Ken Thomson now dead, there's a distinct possibility the gloves will come off. There's no love lost between Geoff Beattie and Tanenbaum. Still, neither of them actually wants a collaboration with Ted Rogers, given his history of devouring his partners.

And neither does Sabia, although he didn't have much say in the matter. Ma Bell is bleeding customers to the cable guys in a business it monopolized for more than a century. Sabia faced the difficult task of making up decades of lost ground for his predecessors' inability, or unwillingness, to take on risks at a time when rapid changes in technology were demanding it. Technology has evolved so quickly in the past decade that the lines of demarcation between the telecom, wireless and cable industries have blurred. For its part, after years of fighting a monolithic giant, Rogers is starting to look like one of them, which paradoxically enough is his biggest fear and may well be his unintended legacy. In this new millennium, the phone companies are facing stiff opposition from the cable guys, parvenus who have finally gained credibility after decades of overly hyped promises, in an all-out war for control of your digital home.

RCI's story is unique in Canada. No other business leader north of the 49th has rolled the dice as often and won. No other industry—food, textile, real estate, oil, gold or pharmaceuticals—has changed as rapidly as telecom has. And few of Canada's successful entrepreneurs, including Galen Weston, Laurent Beaudoin, Ron Southern, brothers Wallace and the late Harrison McCain, James Pattison and the late K.C. Irving, have bet their businesses as often as Ted Rogers has. For the most part, they played within their industry segment. Only the Thomson family—Canada's richest—has successfully shifted out of and into diverse industries from newspapers to North Sea oil to electronic media and prospered.

"It's very seldom you see an entrepreneur willing to bet virtually his business three or four times in his career. Most of them have bet big-time, maybe once or twice. Ted has done it five or six times. If you weren't willing to bet many times on telecom, and you weren't Bell Canada, you stayed for one or two rounds, and then, you walked out with your money, but Ted didn't," says Jean Monty, BCE's former chief executive officer. Monty bet big when he created Bell Globemedia—and paid the ultimate price when his board fired him.

ACT ONE

RADIO

CHAPTER 1

3BP

*"The world has so far seen only a fraction of what is in store
for radio owners now and in the future."*

—E. S. Rogers Sr., 1930

EDWARD SAMUEL (TED) ROGERS JR. was born on May 27, 1933 to parents
Edward Samuel Rogers and Velma Melissa Taylor, indisputably one of Toronto's
dynamic, young power couples of their time.

Rogers Sr., more familiarly known as "Ted" just as his son would be, was
a month shy of his 33rd birthday when his son was born. At six feet, he was a
handsome man with piercing blue eyes who exuded the easy self assuredness
that wealth bred and sharp intellect fostered. His 27-year-old wife was a svelte
five feet eight inches, poised and strikingly beautiful with copper hair and green
eyes, rather similar in appearance—and some would say, character, given her
flair, charisma and combativeness—to film star Katharine Hepburn. She was
the fourth-eldest of six children raised in a Baptist family in the small southern
Ontario town of Woodstock, 160 kilometers west of Toronto.

Velma was pursuing a nursing degree, then considered one of the few
acceptable professions for women, at the University of Toronto when she met
Rogers at a social function. Rogers, six years her senior, had dropped out of the
university's electrical engineering program after his second year to devote all
of his energies to making radio accessible to the masses. They courted for five
years, during which time he invented the world's first light-socket-powered radio,
built his own radio manufacturing company, founded Toronto radio station
CFRB, co-founded CKOK in Windsor, Ontario, and in 1930, the year he finally
did marry, won one of the four licenses issued by the Canadian government to
experiment with television.

The couple married on February 1, 1930, four months before Rogers' 30th birthday, in two quiet family ceremonies, the first at the Bloor Street Baptist Church in Toronto, and the second at a Quaker meeting house in Newmarket, northeast of Toronto, the roots of the Rogers clan in Canada. Their son would be christened a Baptist and become an Anglican, although an infrequent churchgoer. "I go but not enough," says Ted Rogers. "I find it a little upper scale for me. I probably would be into not so much listening to great choruses, but participating more … and that means more Baptist oriented."

The family's Quaker roots run deep. Rogers' forebears introduced the practice of the Religious Society of Friends, better known as Quakerism, to Ontario when the family patriarch, Timothy Rogers, a devout Quaker millwright from Connecticut, fled the United States in the early 1800s to escape political persecution for harboring escaped slaves. He settled his family in what became Newmarket, just north of the City of York (as Toronto was then called), and helped colonize the area with Quakers from New England.

Pioneering has long coursed through the family's blood.

Edward S. Rogers Sr. was born on June 21, 1900 into a family of wealth and privilege. His grandfather Samuel and his great-uncle Elias made their money in oil and coal, virtually dominating the industrial era in Toronto at the turn of the century. Samuel founded the eponymous oil, kerosene- and fuel-distribution company Samuel Rogers Co. in 1881, which he merged with his Hamilton and Ottawa outlets to form Toronto-based Queen City Oil Co. To fund its expansion, he sold 80 percent of Queen City Oil to John D. Rockefeller's Standard Oil Co., becoming an affiliate of the New York giant. Queen City was one of the four affiliates that were folded into Imperial Oil Co. in 1899 after the U.S. oil company acquired a majority stake in Imperial Oil. In 1911, when the U.S. Supreme Court broke up the Standard Oil monopoly, Imperial was allotted to Standard Oil of New Jersey, which today is known as Exxon Mobil Corp. Samuel's sons, Albert and Joseph, sold the family's remaining stake in Queen City to Imperial in 1912 and were directors of the board until their deaths. For his part, Samuel's brother Elias founded the Elias Rogers Co., which owned two giant coal and lumber yards on the Esplanade near Church St. in downtown Toronto.

Radio, as we know it today, was in its infancy when Edward Samuel Rogers was growing up. At the turn of the twentieth century, the radio existed only in the minds of inventors, many of whom either had a hand in, or claimed credit for, its invention during the years between German scientist Heinrich Hertz' discovery of radio waves in 1887 to Canadian entrepreneur Edward S. Rogers'

introduction of the electric radio in 1925. Hertz deduced the existence of radio waves two decades after Scottish physicist James Clerk Maxwell predicted them mathematically, although he immediately dismissed the idea of his discovery holding any practical purposes. Italian physicist Guglielmo Marconi then proved him wrong by harnessing the power of the "Hertzian waves" to transmit Morse code communications. A pragmatist, Marconi was far more interested in making money than in pursuing wireless telephony. He left the early experiments in wireless telephony to Canadian-born U.S. professor Reginald A. Fessenden and later the controversial U.S. inventor Lee de Forest.

Indeed, contrary to popular belief, Marconi didn't invent the radio. The courts ultimately settled the issue. Serbian-born American Nikola Tesla is the acknowledged father of the modern radio, having created a theoretical model that he patented in 1893. While Tesla strove to make absolutely sure his system would work, Marconi forged ahead, attracting investors to his Marconi Wireless Telegraph Co. Tesla fought Marconi in the courts for patent infringement. Finally, in October 1945, the U.S. Supreme Court ruled in Tesla's favor, stating there was nothing in Marconi's work that had not already been discovered by Tesla. Unfortunately, Tesla didn't live to see his life's work vindicated. He had died nine months earlier, impoverished and forgotten at age 86.

On Christmas Eve in 1906, when Rogers Sr. was just six years old, Reginald Fessenden tapped out the Morse code "CQ, CQ, CQ"—the general call to all wireless operators within range—from his workshop on the isolated, barren shoals of Brant Rock, Massachusetts to alert ships at sea to expect an important transmission. Standing in front of a microphone, Fessenden then spoke, introducing a short Christmas concert. Astonished telegraphers aboard banana boats for the United Fruit Co. along the Atlantic coast and as far away as the West Indies couldn't believe they had just heard the unimaginable: the sound of a human voice.

After playing a phonographic recording of Handel's *Largo*, Fessenden played the carol *O Holy Night*, on his violin, singing the last verse. His wife, Helen, and secretary, Miss Bent, were then to read passages from the Bible when they froze with stage fright in front of the microphone, forcing Fessenden to fill the momentary silence with the Christmas story from the book of Luke. Then he signed off with a hearty "Merry Christmas," asking any listeners to write him. Fessenden, the father of AM radio, had just aired the world's first-ever radio broadcast. He repeated the program on that New Year's Eve.

The cigar-chomping Fessenden sent the first-ever wireless transmission of the human voice—his own—six years earlier in 1900, while working for the U.S. Weather Bureau. He rebuilt the high-frequency alternator he commissioned General Electric Co. to construct, to transmit a pure continuous wave (CW)—combining sound waves with radio waves in the ether and sending them to a receiver where the radio waves are removed so that listeners hear only the original sound, exactly how radio works today. Marconi, establishing himself as an industrial titan, ridiculed Fessenden's CW theory, promoting a so-called whiplash effect—a damning indictment that impeded the evolution of radio for a decade. In 1916, Marconi finally admitted his own system couldn't transmit voices properly, and ironically he acquired Fessenden's patents.

Unlike Marconi and Dr. Lee de Forest, a U.S. inventor and self-promoter who was implicated in a stock fraud scandal, Fessenden wasn't a showman. The professor was the most at ease in his laboratory, and never reaped any financial reward until very late in life after winning lengthy, bitter court fights.

De Forest in particular was at the time garnering the extensive press coverage. He was widely embraced by the U.S. media as the "Father of Radio" upon his death in 1961. De Forest orchestrated a series of what were later described as "public stunts," including the broadcast of opera from the Eiffel Tower in 1908 and of tenor Enrico Caruso from New York's Metropolitan Opera House in 1910. De Forest, who built upon the work of Fessenden and British Marconi Co. executive Sir John Ambrose Fleming, invented the Audion tube, a noted breakthrough in the field of radio because the triode vacuum tube made it possible to amplify radio signals. U.S. inventor Edwin Howard Armstrong, the father of FM radio, then made the de Forest tube into a transmitter as well as a receiver that not only amplified radio signals but also generated them, which became one of the most important advances in radio.

Young Ted Rogers Sr. avidly followed the exploits of these pioneers. With some trial and error, and the help of his older brother J. Elsworth, Rogers built his own crystal set, or radio receiver, using coils, condensers and a thin springy wire, known as cat's whisker, to make contact with galena (lead ore) crystals, in the bedroom of the family's comfortable Rosedale home. The two boys took the earpiece off the rarely used family telephone, connected it to their contraption and heard their first signal from naval station NAA in Arlington, Virginia. Their father was impressed enough to buy them a proper set of radio headphones.

Radio became an obsession. Radiotelephony, while we take it for granted today, was magical, the stuff of science fiction, when 11-year-old Rogers was introduced in his grade-school science class to the idea of sending messages through the air without wires. He taught himself Morse code and spent virtually all of his spare time perfecting his crystal set and reading up on the latest innovations. Radio became his obsession. The possibilities of radiotelephony seemed endless. Radio opened up a whole new world to him, one beyond the provincial confines of Toronto. He hauled his half-kilowatt spark transmitter up to the family's cottage at Pointe au Baril on Georgian Bay, where he heard the telegraph reports on the sinking of the luxury passenger ship RMS *Titanic* in April 1912.

Thanks to this obsession, Rogers became something of a celebrity in his pubescence. On July 21, a month after his 13th birthday, "Teddy" Rogers and his school chum "Davy" Johnston were featured in the *Toronto Telegram* as "Real Marconis" after they picked up a message, transmitting from Cape Cod, Massachusetts, that the transatlantic passenger liner SS *Haverford* had run aground off Queenstown, Ireland. The newspaper described Rogers' telegraph set and the maze of wires running up his home's chimney to serve as an antenna as "probably the very best amateur wireless apparatus in the province." At the family's Georgian Bay cottage, the enterprising young radio enthusiast picked up faint German radio signals declaring the start of the First World War and broke the news to the local community long before it made the newspapers. He spent three summers working as a telegraph operator for Canadian Marconi Wireless Telegraph Co. aboard passenger vessels on the Great Lakes.

In 1919, after the wartime ban on amateur telegraphy was lifted, Rogers purchased one of the country's first amateur licenses for radiotelephony, for the cost of $1. He was assigned the call letters 3BP—which became forever intertwined with his name. Years later, he had a special gold signet ring made with 3BP inscribed on its face.

At 21, Rogers was the first Canadian radio amateur, or ham operator, to send a radio signal across the ocean to Europe. He merited the front page of the *Toronto Star* for telegraphing a message from Newmarket, where he had erected a 100-foot-high aerial, across the Atlantic to Ardrossan, Scotland, near Glasgow, as part of a contest organized by the American Radio Relay League to see how far a low-power amateur signal could carry wavelengths shorter than 200 meters. The power output could not go beyond 1 kW. Two decades earlier, Marconi had used a spark gap transmitter; this time, amateurs were using tube transmitters. Rogers was the only Canadian among 27 selected contestants, most of whom were located along the eastern seaboard. While amateurs demonstrated that ionospheric refraction could enable worldwide communication by short waves, skeptics were surprised that Rogers succeeded, because, unlike the majority of his competitors, he had to first transmit overland almost 1,000 kilometers before even crossing the ocean.

The contest proved that short-wave low frequencies could be transmitted over long distances. By moving short wave onto lower frequencies, higher frequencies were freed up, making it possible for the eventual transmission of television, FM radio, radar, microwave networks and satellite relays.

Rogers dropped out of university to join radio manufacturer Canadian Radio Corp., a division of Canadian General Electric Co.'s Canadian Independent

Telephone Co., CITCO, as a technician. When CITCO was forced to file for bankruptcy in 1923, Albert Rogers financed his son's purchase of the company's radio holdings to form Rogers Radio Co. His dad, still the president of Imperial Oil, gave his son office space down the hall from his own in the oil company's Church St. building. The 23-year-old Rogers now found himself the owner of a radio manufacturer, but what he really needed was a marketable product, a radio that was both affordable and accessible to the masses.

The radio in 1920 was in much the same position as the personal computer was in 1982 and the Internet was in 1992. A lot of people were experimenting with it, but it was not yet ready for prime time. The radio sets of the twenties were expensive and inconvenient; they were powered by short-lived wet lead-acid batteries, which leaked and interfered with sound quality, emitting a constant annoying hum—not that there was much to listen to. Radio stations were in their infancy. The world's first regularly scheduled programs—weather reports and the playing of gramophone records—were broadcast in 1919 from station CFCF in Montreal, then known as XWA, an experimental radio station owned by Marconi Wireless Telegraph Co. of Canada. In the United States, WWJ Detroit went on the air in August 1920, and Westinghouse Electric Co.'s KDKA in Pittsburgh, Pennsylvania, the first government-licensed U.S. radio station, began broadcasting news, sports, music and commercials three months later.

Rogers wanted to eliminate the need for batteries altogether by creating an electric radio. After all, other household items were already powered by electricity. The electric toaster was invented in 1909, although it toasted only on one side and required constant vigilance. The electric iron, invented in France in 1882, emerged in the United States in 1910. So, why not the radio? The problem was with the vacuum tube, the most vital component of the radio. Many engineers before Rogers had tried and failed to develop a tube that could eliminate the heat and incessant hum caused by the flow of alternating current (AC) through the device.

Rogers was not a man to be easily discouraged. He traveled to Pittsburgh to visit the Westinghouse Electronics Research Laboratory, where he met American inventor Frederick S. McCullough, who was attracting widespread attention in U.S. technical journals for his attempts to create his own AC tube. Rogers spent several weeks working alongside McCullough, but decided he would be better off working on his own. The 24-year-old astutely bought, with his father's money, the Canadian rights to McCullough's experimental AC tube for $10,000 to avoid any possible future litigation.

If the young man wanted to achieve success, he had to do without the backing of the big boys. Radio manufacturers had no interest in making the capital investment necessary to retool their plants and redesign radio sets.

Battery makers were even less keen, because they feared an electric radio would drive them out of business. No one wanted to upset the apple cart—U.S. sales of radio receivers had exploded, jumping to 3 million in 1924 from 500,000 in 1923.

Rogers worked relentlessly, often well into the night, to make improvements to the McCullough AC tube, achieving success on August 1, 1924. He called his AC tube 15S—the world's first AC Simple Rectifier Tube. He protected the five-inch cathode filament with insulation that shielded the input and output circuits of the tube from heat, eliminating the AC hum that drowned out sound from the set's speakers. By perfecting the amplifying tube, Rogers would make possible an electric radio for the home. On April 8, 1925, he built the world's first radio to operate from a 110-volt household electric light socket, a year before "batteryless" radios, as he called them (just as the car was called the "horseless" carriage when it was introduced), were introduced in the United States and two years before they appeared in Europe.

After developing this revolutionary tube, he and his brother, Elsworth, started a new company to make radio receivers. Their father financed the operations through a holding company incorporated as Standard Radio Manufacturing Co. Standard controlled both Rogers Radio Tube Co. and Rogers Batteryless Radio Co. Rogers displayed his first "Rogers Batteryless Radio" receivers in August 1925 just in time to be displayed at the annual Canadian National Exhibition under the catchy slogan "Just Plug In—Then Tune In"—a marketing strategy his son would later intentionally imitate.

Canada's youngest industrialist of his time made three astute decisions: *secure the patents, start a radio station* and *form an alliance.* He acquired de Forest's radio patents in Canada to protect his invention from any possible future lawsuits by the notoriously litigious U.S. inventor. To drum up interest in his batteryless radio receivers, and out of his own frustration over the poor quality of sound and programming emanating from Toronto's five radio stations, Rogers decided he needed his own broadcast station.

Using the tubes he had developed, Rogers built the world's first radio broadcasting station powered by electricity rather than batteries or motorized direct current converters: CFRB. The government assigns the first two call letters. The last two represent "Rogers Batteryless"—and, over time, whenever the station wanted to strike a sympathetic cord with the public, or more importantly with the regulators, it would refer to itself as "Canada's First Rogers Batteryless" station. The station went live in 1927, the same year the Toronto Maple Leafs hockey franchise was created. Listeners were astounded at the clarity of the station's inaugural broadcast on February 19th. CFRB's signal was so clear and so strong—thanks to two powerful 100-foot transmitters Rogers erected 40 kilometers north of Toronto in Aurora—that its programming was heard as far away as Honolulu, Hawaii.

The station quickly earned a reputation for quality, using more live talent than any other station in the country, and airing live broadcasts during the peak evening listening hours and recorded music during the day. In 1929, CFRB fed its first network show—Guy Lombardo and his Royal Canadians—to a 28-year-old William S. Paley's recently acquired CBS network.

By 1928, with just over 4 percent of the population, or some 400,000 Canadians, owning battery-operated radios, Rogers saw a market ripe for the picking. With demand outstripping what his Chestnut Street factory in downtown Toronto could produce, he formed an alliance with the then-emerging industry leader, Chicago-based Grigsby-Grunow Co., to manufacture radios under the name Rogers-Majestic in a new modernized facility. The new company, Rogers-Majestic Corp., built the factory for $300,000 in an industrial park at the northwest corner of Bathurst and Fleet streets. While the U.S. firm failed to survive the Great Depression, Rogers held the trademark and exclusive manufacturing rights for the Majestic brand in Canada. His invention would spark the radio boom that would engulf North America in the twenties and thirties.

A hard worker and a hard drinker, Rogers was in the prime of his life when he died on Saturday, May 6, 1939, three days after undergoing emergency surgery for what probably was a ruptured abdominal aortic aneurysm. His wife, Velma, found him in the late evening hours buckled over in the bathroom; the walls were splattered, and the ceiling dripped, with blood that he had spewed from his mouth after the aneurysm burst. Just as he seemed to be recovering in hospital, he suffered another aneurysm, which killed him. The son who bears his name was not yet six years old.

When the funeral wreath was hung on the front door, everyone mistakenly thought Velma had died because she had suffered a heart attack four years earlier. For Velma, in shock and consumed by grief, alcohol became her succor. "She told me that when [her husband] died, people and friends would drop in and try to give [her] some support and when they were there, they'd say, 'Why don't you have a drink? You'll feel much better,' and there'd be too many people dropping in and telling her to have a drink," recalls Loretta Rogers, who married Ted in 1963.

"She was just stunned. It was too much for her," remembers Ann "Rooney" Graham, Velma's daughter from her subsequent marriage to Toronto lawyer John W. Graham. "She had a child …"—Ann pauses—"and then, she had this husband who left her, who she adored. He worked like Ted does. He worked all the time. He had his laboratory in the basement in the house we lived in.

Four months before the outbreak of the Second World War, Velma found herself alone with a sickly five-year-old boy, and under pressure to sell her late husband's sprawling business. Had he lived, Edward S. Rogers might well have become Canada's equivalent to his contemporary, U.S. media icon William S. Paley. Rogers was too young to have built up much life insurance, or other liquid assets. He left what easily can be considered a sizeable fortune for Depression-era Canada: $384,243 worth in property, stocks, assets and cash—in today's dollars, $5.12 million. However, the bulk of his estate was tied up in his companies, which were either sold or shuttered by Velma's brother-in-law, Elsworth.

The Rogers clan did little to support the young widow or protect her son's inheritance. Velma moved to Windsor, Ontario, where her younger brother, Dr. Allan Taylor, a family practitioner, and his family took care of her and her young son. Velma, who had pawned her jewelry and other personal possessions during the Great Depression to help keep her husband's businesses afloat, had been left with enough money to live comfortably, but she would never forget, nor for that matter let anyone else forget, let alone forgive, that her child's birthright had been stolen from him. The only tangible item that her son had from his father's legacy was his 3BP signet ring.

Elsworth Rogers, who had been treasurer of his brother's business, took over the presidency after his brother's death. In less than two years, he sold all of the company's manufacturing assets to Small Electric Motors Co., run by chartered accountant W. C. Thornton (Winks) Cran, a British émigré. Cran would years later unwittingly treat Ted Rogers with enough disdain to fuel the teenager's desire for retribution. In 1945, soon after the war ended, Cran sold the merged company to Dutch giant Philips Electronics Ltd., which used the Rogers-Majestic brand name on radios, stereos, televisions and other home appliances until the brand was discontinued in 1964.

Elsworth renamed Rogers-Majestic as Standard Radio Ltd., which became the parent of Rogers Radio Broadcasting Co., the holding company that held the license for CFRB. In 1946, he urged Velma to sell her late husband's shares in Standard Radio. Soon afterwards, Canadian company Argus Corp. acquired shares in Standard Radio, taking control of CFRB. The previous year, Edward Plunket (E. P.) Taylor and a group of like-minded industrialists had pooled their resources to create Argus, a closed-end investment holding company modeled after a U.S. company, Atlas Corp. (which itself took a sizeable initial stake in

Argus). In the span of a year, Argus had acquired significant shareholdings in five companies, which accounted for 80 percent of its approximately $13.5 million of assets. The companies included Canadian Breweries Ltd., Massey-Harris Co. (later Massey-Ferguson) and Dominion Stores Ltd. Taylor's minority partners were Lt. Col. Eric Phillips, Wallace McCutcheon and John A. (Bud) McDougald—all the business greats of their day.

Ted Rogers recalls the day when he lost his heritage. He was eight years old, clutching his mother's hand as she stood in a telephone booth near the family cottage in Shanty Bay, Ontario, on Lake Simcoe. He remembers her reluctantly acquiescing to his uncle's wishes to sell her stake in her late husband's businesses. "He hated my mother. My mother hated him," Ted Rogers states emphatically. "He had only ever worked for his father and his younger brother. According to my mother, my uncle Elsworth was always teasing my father, always pulling him down, envious, and when he died of course he was always trying to get my mother to sign things and she wouldn't." Until he finally wore her down.

"I would send Christmas cards to him when I was in boarding school, but I never got an answer," says Rogers. "I went to him a couple of times. One time I said, 'We've got to buy this place back,' and Elsworth still had some shares, the right kind of shares—voting shares—and he says, 'Ted, I'm too old and I'm too sick and I'm too tired.' I'll never forget it—too old, too sick and too tired," he recalls, nodding his head laterally, still incredulous at his uncle's response decades later. Those words are not in Ted Rogers' lexicon.

The loss of his father would haunt Ted Rogers his entire life. His mother's grief would leave an indelible scar on the young boy. He has no distinct memories of his father. Together, he and his mother pasted the many newspaper clippings, letters and mementoes documenting his life and tragic death into a voluminous scrapbook. The bedtime stories he heard as a child were of his father's adventures:

Wireless Wizard Has Performed Big Feat: Amateur at Newmarket Establishes Transatlantic Communication— Interesting Test

There's a young chap up in Newmarket who possesses both qualities of enthusiastic persistence and native talent in so high a degree that as a radio engineer he may some day break in to the class of Nikola Tesla and Alexanderson, to each of whom can be correctly applied the expression "electrical wizard ... This exploit marks him as the leader among Canadian wireless amateurs, no other of whom has been successful.

Ted Rogers is an expert operator and is filled with unbounded enthusiasm for the wireless game.

I have got a spark coil up here and have more fun than a picnic with it. Got my doorknob and part of the floor electrified; make the fellows jump like everything. My room at the present time is a mass of wires.

Early Saturday, E. S. Rogers, of Toronto, succeeded in establishing what is thought to be the first amateur radio station conversation with England. The working was on 100 metres and constitutes a record for Canada and British amateur stations as far as known.

Toronto inventor turned "hopeless" tube into commercial success.

He was a young man who declined to let obstacles stand in the way of success. Like the inventor of the telephone and the electric light, Ted Rogers often burned the midnight oil before he worked out the problem, which had baffled older heads. Young folks and old were thrilled by his success. It provides a lesson for other young men inclined to the defeatist attitude.

Ted will always be remembered as a shy, modest and unassuming young genius, who, at our conventions and meetings, could barely be persuaded to rise and accept, with a bow, the tribute of his admirers.

You know, genius has often been described as an infinite capacity for taking pains. And, that describes Ted Rogers.

On June 19, 1941, Velma wed a dashing soldier, John Webb Graham. At 35, she had several suitors but she purposely chose a man six years her junior, intuitively knowing the young lawyer would take care of her son if anything should happen to her. "She wasn't expected to live when she married my father. She was sick with alcoholism and the shock of Mr. Rogers dying just sent her over the edge, and there was nobody to help in those days," explains her daughter, Ann, during an interview. "She had a definite plan in mind. She literally chose him. She had been engaged many times after Mr. Rogers died. It wasn't a long time."

"You mean it was a quick marriage before she broke the engagement again," interjects Loretta Rogers.

"That's right," laughs Ann. "But, she chose Father because she felt he had the steadfastness, the common sense and the intelligence to deal with Ted and to help him."

Rogers was barely eight when his mother remarried. He tried to follow her and his new father into the newlyweds' car after the wedding reception. Startled family friends pulled him back, lightly admonishing him. "You can't go. They're going on their honeymoon." Annoyed, Rogers retorted, "Don't sons always go on the honeymoons?"

Ann Graham was born two years later, in 1943. Velma christened her daughter Ann and then, so as not to confuse her daughter with her niece Ann, who was born just a month earlier, she nicknamed her "Rooney" after the popular song *Little Annie Rooney Is My Sweetheart.* She never expected to have another child because she had been so ill while pregnant with her firstborn. She had been warned by her doctors not to have any more children after contracting the measles during her first pregnancy, an illness that left her son with lifelong vision problems. "She never did what she was told," says Loretta matter-of-factly.

Velma could not have met a better match than John W. Graham. Of Irish descent, he was a dark-haired, moustached gentleman with soulful, intelligent brown eyes. He graduated from Upper Canada College—where the elite and privileged sent their boys—the University of Toronto and York University's Osgood Hall Law School. He was called to the bar of Ontario in 1936. The son of Toronto's second chief coroner shared a common bond with the young Rogers, having lost his own father at a young age, 14.

As a student and into his late 20s, Graham served with the Governor General's Body Guard and later, the Governor General's Horse Guards, whose motto is *nullis secundus*, second to none. In 1939, after Canada joined England and France in declaring war on Germany, the 27-year-old reservist was part of the Third Armoured Reconnaissance Regiment in the Royal Canadian Armoured Corps (Cavalry) from 1939 until 1946 at home and abroad, in Italy and northwest Europe. He rose through the ranks, becoming a major before retiring from the military when the war ended.

After the war, Graham joined the Toronto law firm of Daly, Thistle, Judson & McTaggart. In 1949, he left to become the general counsel of Imperial Life Assurance Co., where he stayed for the next 10 years until he returned to private practice. He formed the law firm of Payton, Biggs & Graham, where he specialized in insurance, tax and estate planning law—areas in which Ted Rogers would subsequently excel at in protecting his family and his business empire. In 1959, Graham would right a wrong committed by the Rogers Estate and come up with enough money to help give the young Ted Rogers his start in business.

When he returned home from the war, Graham was a stranger to his family, an alcoholic wife and two young children. His daughter was barely three; his stepson was on the verge of manhood, then 12, boarding at Upper Canada College, a prestigious private boys' school. He became the family's rock. Graham helped Velma seek the necessary help to overcome her dependence on alcohol. She overcame the rigid mores of the time to join Alcoholics Anonymous in the late forties, becoming one of its first female members in Toronto. She entertained AA co-founder Bill "the New York broker" Wilson in her home, and for several years, until her first diagnosis of cancer in 1961, she took in and dried out inebriated strangers in her home at 405 Glenayr Road in Toronto's tony Forest Hill, an old-moneyed neighborhood of tree-lined streets and mansions.

From all accounts, Graham was a gentleman in the truest sense of the word. He was a considerate, patient man with strong moral principles and a wonderfully keen sense of humor. He took his rambunctious stepson, who had already been left to his own devices at preparatory school, under his wing upon his return from the war. "John was a great person. He knew everything. He was a great historian. He inspired you to think of these things," says Rogers. "I respected him. It grew, as I got older; in the early days, probably not. He took me down to Washington for a week one time in the car. He was very good at that, spending time with me. He was a very thoughtful man. He did a better job with me than I've done with any of my children."

"He was the one who kept Ted moving forward because Ted would get himself into all sorts of jams and messes," says Toby Hull, Rogers' best friend and a long-time Rogers Communications Inc. (RCI) director. "Ted, sometimes, is pretty tough on people, and John would be the one who would come in and put everything back together, smooth things out. John was a very respectable, a very likeable individual and very proper. He had tremendous control of the English language. He was a lot of things Ted wasn't, so it was a great combination. John Graham taught Ted a lot. He was a great negotiator, because he would negotiate from a different plane than Ted would. Ted would be more of a rough diamond; John was very diplomatic, very smooth and no-nonsense."

The lawyer and Second World War veteran was, until his death, a voice of reason within RCI. He was the stabilizing factor that held together the management team. Where his stepson was often mercurial, John Graham was cerebral and rational. He kept his stepson in check, and when that wasn't possible, Graham was usually the one to repair the damage his stepson wreaked. Rogers' longest-serving lieutenant, Phil Lind, calls Graham the company's "conscience." Graham, Lind says, was "universally respected for his integrity, his decency, and civility." There wasn't a day that Rogers didn't talk to his second father, or seek his counsel.

Velma never allowed the memory of her first husband to fade, even after she remarried. "Everything in the house was his," says her daughter, Ann Graham. "You would look and there'd be the picture of the boat they had together, the painting that they bought together. His huge portrait hung in our upper hall for years over the original tube collection. I mean, it was a monument. [Ted's] father was way more important than my father was. He was the only presence. He was *the* presence."

Rogers, who grew up surrounded by his father's ghost, didn't think anything of it until one day it occurred to him how hurtful it must be to his stepfather to have this constant reminder of his wife's first and true love so prominently displayed in the house. He suggested to his stepfather that they should take the portrait down, or hang it elsewhere. Rogers says his stepfather told him to leave everything the way it was to honor the memory of his father and out of respect for his mother, since the portrait meant so much to her.

Velma was more than a mother to Rogers; she was his partner, best friend and loyal confidante until her painful death from cancer in 1971. When she became too ill to get out of bed, Rogers held board of directors meetings in her bedroom, everyone gathered around her bed. She shaped the boy into the man he became. She imbued in him by her sheer force of personality the zealous drive to rebuild what had been lost, to never give up. She instilled in him the importance of remembering his lost heritage and to pay homage to everything his father had achieved. The young boy wanted nothing more than to please her. "When I was eight she told me what was expected, and you go on from there. Well, not expected, but what we would like to see, and this is your destiny, this is your mission," says Rogers.

A shrewd stock investor, Velma spent hours reading the business papers and studying the stock tables. She used her profits to pay for her children's private schooling and their clothes. "She was very smart with the [stock] market," says her daughter, Ann. "There wasn't a lot of money but there was enough money for her; give her a dollar and she could make five. I can remember Mother in bed and she'd have her breakfast in bed and she'd have the newspaper, market pages out, and she'd scan the market pages and look at them, talk to her broker and then make a deal, and that's how my education was paid for, our education was paid for, how I dressed, how Ted dressed."

One day after a particularly successful trade in the stock market, Velma walked into the den where her husband and his friend were sitting, arched one of her finely shaped eyebrows at them and asked, "Well, what have you fools done today? This is what I've done. Can you match it?"

Sitting in the sunroom at Rogers' Frybrook home, Velma's daughter and daughter-in-law, who insisted on speaking together, reminisced fondly what a trailblazer Velma was in her day.

"She liked to play in a man's world," says Ann. "She inspired Ted. I remember, she was sitting for hours and hours and hours and he'd talk business and business and business."

"Their favorite subject," comments Loretta dryly.

"She was a remarkable woman. She taught Ted everything he knows—unfortunately, for some of us," Ann smiles. "But, she really pounded. She was a Gemini, like him, and she was very determined that he would bring his father's name back into everyday Canadian life as it had been. She taught him how to fight, because when he was younger, he had been very ill as a child, so when he finished high school, and he was home, they used to get into these little discussions, and the discussions would get a little more heated, and I, of course, would be hiding; the doors would be slamming and then the next thing I'd hear was laughter. The two of them were sitting in there, laughing, and having a wonderful time. They can't remember their argument. It's all gone and they moved on. And, that's the way Ted still is. He moves on."

"She used to get mad at Ted," remarks Loretta.

"Oh, terribly mad," concurs Ann. "Poor Ted. I can remember Ted walking out of the house all dressed up; they used to wear what were 'zoot suits,' all black and grey, and there were pink highlights in the shirt. Ted thought he was really cool with this outfit on, and he and Mother had had a particularly bad one, and her dressing room window was directly over the front door, and so he went out the front door and slammed the door. She had just given him a car—and he said, 'I'm going to be gambler' and drove off. Well, in those days, Forest Hill used to have its own police force and fire department, and Mother just picked up the phone, called the police, gave them his license plate number and told them to 'pick him up and put him in jail, please. He needs to cool off a little bit.' She would do that to him regularly."

Rogers spent a summer working as a caddie, toting golf bags at Bigwin Inn on Lake of Bays, once billed as the most luxurious and largest summer resorts in North America. He bought his first car while working up at Bigwin Inn, a beat-up 1932 Chevrolet with an old wooden steering wheel. "It was just a piece of nuts and bolts," laughs schoolmate Bill Boultbee, "and he drove up to his driveway and proud as punch went in and told his mother to look out [to] the driveway and see what he had, and she looked and said, 'Ted, I'm going to give you one half-hour to get that off the driveway. Get rid of it. I don't want my neighbors to see this car.' He was quite hurt about it all. He had taken a day or two off work and came down in the car and then he had to sell the car and take the train back. It was just not the right kind of car for a Forest Hill village house.

"Ted was in awe of his mother," he continues. "He worshipped his mother. She was a very beautiful woman. She was, sort of, like a mother to me. We'd be together a lot, Ted and I, on the weekends. We were sort of gangly; we didn't have anything else to do and we'd go off and go to a bowling alley, or something, on a Friday, or I'd just stay the weekends at the house, and Velma Graham felt like a mother. She'd give us advice. I can remember her saying things like 'Now remember, you two boys, that if you go out on a date, you must always phone the girl the next day and tell her how much you enjoyed the date.' Velma was very sticky on manners. She taught us a lot about protocol."

CHAPTER 2

Club 405

"Ted's signature was 'Now, here's Peter Appleyard, brought to you by Rogers Worldwide Broadcasting.' That was Club 405: Rogers Worldwide Broadcasting."

—Burke van Valkenburg

FRAIL, PALE-SKINNED WITH REDDISH-BLOND HAIR and wonky blue eyes, Rogers was cosseted by women until he was eight years old and sent to board at the private boys school Upper Canada College (UCC), four blocks from his Forest Hill home. He hated living away from home. He was a shy boy who craved attention. Live-ins, as they were known, were allowed to go home only twice a semester, and while he missed his mother terribly, he says his formative school years toughened him.

He had had a rough start in life, losing his father so young, and plagued with health problems that failed to dim his spirit. As a child, he suffered from what was believed to be celiac disease, a digestive disorder that interferes with absorption of nutrients from food. From the time he was one until he was 13, he wore eyeglasses, strapped around his face. Teased mercilessly because of an eye patch he wore much like a pirate to correct a lazy eye, he developed an "I'll show them" attitude. He wore thick-lensed bottle-like glasses. When he was 13, his mother took him to New York to visit optometrist Dr. Harold M. Peppard, who had taken over the practice of famous ophthalmologist Dr. William H. Bates and built upon his work to author in 1940 *Better Eyesight without Glasses*. He taught Rogers the Bates Method of special eye exercises to correct his poor eyesight, a technique that worked. Rogers did not wear eyeglasses again until he was 33. To strengthen his ankles, he took tap-dancing lessons.

Called by his middle name "Samuel" rather than Ted, the boys nicknamed him "Bones Rogers" because he was so scrawny his ribs showed. David Walker, a UCC classmate and son of a Progressive Conservative senator, remembers visiting the school's infirmary one day to see his family doctor and UCC physician Dr. Wilson McTavish when Rogers "lurched out" the door. "He looked delirious, and the doctor didn't expect him to live."

Rogers didn't have the build or stamina to play team sports, one of the reasons why he never became an avid fan of team sports, nor developed an easy bond with other men. Of all the sports that he could have played, he chose perhaps the toughest: boxing. The half-blind eight-year-old took up boxing and stayed at it for five years until he finally won his weight class. "I didn't have the big muscles the other guys had, but I had longer arms," quips Rogers. "I didn't pack the punch the other guys did, but I got more punches in.

"You have to overcome early losses, and just keep at it, and keep at it and keep at it," he adds. "That's what my dad did in his inventions. If it didn't work, he tried this combination and that combination and on and on and on until finally [he] hit it."

His schoolmates, many of whom remain friends with Rogers even though they've gone their separate ways, remember him as a fun loving, though unremarkable, boy who always made them laugh. Whatever he may have lacked in physique, he more than compensated for with his quick wit and sharp retorts. "If somebody said something to him, he'd make a crack back at him. 'You're not so great yourself. You're not an oil painting,'" says Bill "Bugs" Boultbee.

The young boy had a propensity for getting himself into trouble. Just like his father, who took his crystal set with him while attending Pickering College—the school his father, Albert, had built in Newmarket, Ontario—Ted Rogers, though considerably younger, set up his own crystal set in his tiny cubicle by the window in his dormitory. But, unlike in his father's era, UCC frowned on such behavior. "They would always be confiscated," says Rogers. "When I was in junior school, you were in dorms and I was on the side of the dorm that had a window, thank goodness, and I snuck the wire out the window. The principal's garden was down below and he rarely went out there, so I dropped the wire out and had it running along a couple of trees. There was great reception until one day, he happened to pick an apple from one of the trees," he laughs, his voice trailing off before he continues, grimacing at the memory. "You're moved from the window over to the other side [of the dorm], and now you don't have a window. So, I then, after a while, got it; there's linoleum between the cells, as I called them, and with a knife, you could put the wire under the linoleum and then out the window. I had an antenna inside, and at one point, I had it hooked up to the bed springs."

He showed an early proficiency as a gambler. When in middle school, he ran a crown and anchor game, a fast-paced dice game where the advantage always lies with the banker, not the players. Rogers naturally was the banker.

Being a bit of a prankster made him the center of attention. He made the boys laugh, and they liked him. He started the college's Commerce Club, inviting in businessmen, including his stepfather, to speak to members. Rogers managed to talk his way out of joining the school's battalion by drawing upon his Quaker roots, a stance that drew him to the attention of the adjutant, Toby Hull, who remembers having to chastise Rogers. "I had to call him up and tell him it was unacceptable that he'd missed all these drills," recalls Hull. "He said, with a straight face, that his religion did not allow him to serve in the army. So, he got exempted."

After the nightly roll call, he and a few friends would sneak out of Seaton House to go over to his house where they would listen to music and drink bottles of beer that he had stashed with ice in the washing machine, the least likely place his mother would look. "'What happens when your mom comes to do the laundry?' He said, 'She doesn't,'" says Richard Wilson, whose ground floor window was used as the means of escape. "On our way back one night we got picked up by the Forest Hill police. They said it wasn't safe to be out and they'd drive us home, over to my house. They dropped us at the front door and we had to make like we were going in, and then high-tailed it back to UCC and back through my window."

Rogers was no scholar. He was much too busy for schoolwork. He tried selling encyclopaedias—much like the media mogul Jack Kent Cooke did during the Great Depression—but quit that endeavor when he only managed to sell one set. He was more apt to spend his school recesses calling stockbrokers, or scampering off to CFRB to watch live radio shows, than studying. His parents chastised him for his low grades, but even when he did achieve top marks, the rebellious youth declared, "There. I've shown you, and now I'll go back to believing that if you get fifty percent, you'll get ahead just as fast as the person who gets ninety percent." He flunked his year, failed to win his matriculation, and had to spend a year at a cram school, Dominion Business College on Bloor St., making up grades before entering university. French was his downfall. Says Boultbee, "We were never taught conversational French, which would have made it much more alive for him."

The one thing Rogers did excel at was public speaking, mastering the art of debate. In his last year at UCC, he won the Wallace Rankin Nesbitt Cup for extemporaneous speaking. He spoke in favor of state medicine, a topic he still loves to debate if given the chance. "I used to compete in speaking contests against him, which he always won," laughs David Walker. "I think he won every year. He was in a league by himself, even then."

The lanky teenager started his very first company with school chum Richard Hoyt Dameron while they were in high school. They called it Music Services. Rogers' stepfather even incorporated the company with the stated purpose of "supplying orchestras and sound systems." The pair rifled off letters promoting their band trios or quartets to high schools, university fraternities and sororities, and clubs and associations as diverse as the Royal Order of Moose, Alcoholics Anonymous and the Diamond Boxing Club.

They held auditions for prospective clients in the studios of CFRB, a place where Rogers would loiter, feeling close to his unknown father but also gleaning the inner workings of a broadcast station. The staff doted upon the founder's kid. He attempted to start his own radio program and along with three schoolmates worked on scripts and prepared demos for a weekly program they called "Quizzical Pranksters." It never aired. He brought his bands into the studio until CFRB's chief engineer, Clive Eastwood, complained to his boss, Harry Sedgwick, that they couldn't keep letting him use it for free while charging others rent.

Rogers was booking dance halls as far south as Windsor, Ontario, where he spent a summer working at his dad's old radio station CKLW, to as far north as the village of Baysville, in the heart of Muskoka cottage country, where he just happened to have a girlfriend. As word spread, his bands were engaged to play at private house parties. Rogers would dutifully wait in the kitchen until their performances were over. Just before their performances, Rogers would show up, step up to the microphone and introduce the band, not by their names but by the instruments they played: trumpet, drums, piano and vibes.

Canadian music icon Peter Appleyard, a world-renowned jazz musician, was one of Rogers' first bookings. His first gig playing the vibes in North America was at a tiny hamburger joint in Baysville in Rogers' band. A native of Cleethorpes, England, Appleyard quit a gig in Bermuda where he played the drums for the chance to play the vibraphone at the Lichee Gardens restaurant in Toronto's Chinatown. Only after he arrived in Toronto did the union tell him he couldn't work as a musician until he had lived in Canada for a year—a restriction that, he learned years later, didn't exist. "The man said, 'What do you play? Where are you from?' I said, 'Well, I play the drums and I'm from England.' He said, 'We don't need you here.' That was my 'Welcome to Canada.'"

Appleyard bided his time working odd jobs, including selling tobacco at Simpson's department store Simpson's and manning the front desk nights at the King Edward Hotel. Rogers found him at Simpson's selling men's shirts and offered him a job playing the vibes in his band. With just three months left to serve before receiving his union card, Appleyard was worried he'd be fined by the union if they ever found out. But Rogers was persuasive, chuckles Appleyard. "He said, 'Oh, don't worry. We'll pay you thirty-five dollars for the Friday and Saturday night, plus all the food you can eat and all the beer you can drink.' Well, I didn't drink in those days. I said, 'Oh heck, I'll do it.' He said, 'They'll never find out.' Well, they did. I was fined several hundred dollars."

Rogers was plugged into the heart of Toronto's music scene, and he'd recruit his friends to help him out. "A lot of the up-and-coming musicians would go through Ted," says Boultbee. "Sometimes, we'd work together on a New Year's Eve, and we'd float around the city, checking where the bands were, seeing if everything was going well. We were sort of strange like that. We didn't have to go out with girls. New Year's Eve was a working time for Ted."

He was the first person to bring a black person into Toronto's exclusive Granite Club. The late bass player Al Mercury played in one of Rogers' bands. "Ted went to bat for him," says long-time friend Burke van Valkenburg. "They appeared at the door, and they were refused entry, and Ted, being Ted, said, 'If that man doesn't come in to play for this dance, nobody goes in. I'll cancel the party.' Well, they weren't quite sure to how to handle that. So, in he came."

Rogers organized the music for his high school graduation party in June 1951 at Rosedale's Mooredale House, a mansion that had been converted into a community center. The crowd grew quiet as Rogers strode to the microphone to introduce a special guest, Billy Daniels, who had become world renowned for his hit song *That Old Black Magic*. The very next year Daniels made history by becoming the first African-American to host an American network TV program. Daniels was in Toronto for a week performing at the Casino, a burlesque theater on Queen St. across from the old City Hall, and slipped out during his act that evening to sing a set at Mooredale. Only he didn't make it back in time for the start of the second half. The showgirls were left trying to keep the audience entertained as best they could until the owner of the Casino tracked Daniels down just as Rogers was on stage graciously thanking him for coming. Rogers reached into his jacket for what Daniels assumed was a check for his performance only to be presented with a pair of UCC cufflinks. Once offstage, nearby witnesses recall the two men exchanging some heated words.

"It was clear there was a misunderstanding over how much he'd be paid," says fellow UCC alumnus William Crossin, who five decades later still shakes his head in awe at Rogers' chutzpah. "I remember thinking after the dance, he's either going to make a million dollars or go to jail."

The union reps eventually caught up to Rogers. One night after checking up on his band at the Palace Pier, he headed back to the car his parents bought him, a 1949 red two-door Plymouth. As he reached into his blazer for the keys, two men accosted him, roughing him up. Rogers, despite his boxing skills, was too surprised and too astute to fight back. "I'll never forget the sound of that man's voice," says Rogers. "He was warning me off. He was with the union and we weren't carded. He knew who I was. He knew I eventually would want to go into radio, and if I didn't give up the orchestra, the union would make things difficult for me in the future."

His bands weren't the idle whimsies of a misspent youth; they were his stepping-stones into the world of entertainment.

Rogers' friends called his home at 405 Glenayr, in Toronto's upper crust Forest Hill neighborhood, Club 405. The family had a state-of-the-art sound system and piano in the basement's recreation room, where Rogers hosted numerous parties. One of the walls was brightened with a mural of a woman, dressed in dancing garb, giving the recreation room a Roaring Twenties feel. When his parents were out of town, Rogers and his friends would take over the whole house. If 50 people were invited, 100 would inevitably show up. His bands played there often. Rogers always got up to put on a tap dance, showing off something he had just learnt. "It shows you how hard-pressed I was to have everybody look at me," quips Rogers. The next day, he'd throw a clean-up party.

"We used to make-believe we were broadcasting the bands," says van Valkenburg. "All through the forties and fifties, bands from across North America would play in the Rainbow Room in the Roosevelt Hotel in New York City, and you'd hear them being introduced on the radio: 'Here's the Benny Goodman Orchestra, brought to you by NBC.' So, Ted's signature was 'Now, here's Peter Appleyard, brought to you by Rogers Worldwide Broadcasting.' That was Club 405: Rogers Worldwide Broadcasting."

Rogers had been introduced to politics at age 12 when John Graham, his stepfather, or second father as he prefers to call him, took him to a Progressive Conservative (PC) Party meeting in 1945 to support returning war hero and Graham's fellow Sigma Chi brother Lawrence W. Skey, who went on to win the Toronto riding of Trinity for the Tories in the June 1945 federal election.

German and Scottish ancestry, the jowl-wagging Diefenbaker called himself "Mr. Canada" and sincerely believed in "One Canada, One Nation"—striking a patriotic cord in Rogers. Diefenbaker was the archetypal underdog who never quit, losing five times before winning a public berth. The two men, separated in age by almost four decades, were very much alike. Both in their day were branded as odd, or even nuts. Diefenbaker was regarded as a renegade, a cowboy, in much the same way as Rogers enjoys being perceived. Both were underestimated in contests with the entrenched leaders of their day, one in politics and the other in business.

Rogers chaired the Youth for Diefenbaker committee, orchestrating a nationwide campaign to bring out the youth vote for him at the 1956 leadership convention in Ottawa. UCC pal Henry (Hal) Jackman, who parlayed his inheritance into a multi-billion-dollar financial, insurance and investment empire, was his assistant. His runner was Brian Mulroney, who almost 30 years later became Canada's 18th prime minister. They nicknamed themselves "Rogers' Raiders."

Rogers asked Mulroney, then 17 years old, to be vice chairman of the youth campaign in the Maritime provinces, where the youngster was attending St. Francis Xavier University in Antigonish, Nova Scotia. "I was always impressed by Ted, but never surprised by his ambition or vision, because I had seen it earlier in 1956, when he came to talk to me about how John Diefenbaker was going to be the next prime minister of Canada at a time when that statement alone would be legitimate grounds for questioning your sanity," says Mulroney. The Liberals were solidly entrenched, having held power for the past 22 years. Diefenbaker was a no-name Member of Parliament (MP) from Saskatchewan.

Mulroney recalls reporting for duty at Rogers' campaign headquarters, a hotel suite at the Chateau Laurier in Ottawa, on a bitterly cold winter day in December 1956.

"What do you want me to do?" Mulroney asked the 23-year-old Rogers.

"I want you to put these Diefenbaker posters all over town," Rogers replied.

Mulroney, feeling as if he had been summoned to greatness, went out into the subzero weather and put up all the posters Rogers had handed him and marched back into the office. "Well Ted, I got it all done. What do I do now?"

"You put up more posters."

"So, I went off and did that," recalls Mulroney. "He ran us like an army.

"Ted was very stylish. He never wore sports jackets. We did. He always wore suits. I was very impressed with Ted. What I remember best about him is that he always had a brown leather briefcase. He carried it everywhere, and it was jammed with stuff—meeting notes, agendas, travel schedules. I had never seen this before, and I figured this has got to be one important guy," Mulroney says. "He was a going concern, believe me."

Diefenbaker won the PC leadership handily, defeating fellow MPs Donald Fleming and Davie Fulton. Dief the Chief, as he was called, was a great orator who, on the campaign trail with his circus-barker energy and theatrical performances, won the hearts of Canadians. The Liberals underestimated the Chief. He defeated them in the 1957 federal election to become prime minister of a minority government. The next year he solidified his party's grip on power by taking 208 of the 265 parliamentary seats to form the then-largest-ever majority government. But he lost the next two elections and, when he refused to resign as leader of the PC Party, party president Dalton Camp mounted a successful, albeit tumultuous, public campaign to force a leadership review in 1967. At the convention held at hockey shrine Maple Leaf Gardens in Toronto, Rogers, in the throes of building his nascent empire, passionately defended Diefenbaker when everyone around him was fast and ready to knife the fallen leader. Says Mulroney, "Ted Rogers was completely loyal to Diefenbaker. He never faltered. He was with Diefenbaker right to the end."

CHAPTER 3

Rogers, Bassett and the BBG

"I've never heard of you. Why should I talk to you?"

—John Bassett

IN HIS DORMITORY ROOM AT SEATON HOUSE, Ted Rogers hid a seven-inch television set in his closet, rigging it up to a home-made antenna he put on the roof and then audaciously charged his dorm mates a small viewing fee to watch Milton Berle's *Texaco Star Theater*, drama programs on *The Actors' Studio* and Ed Sullivan's *Toast of the Town*. It was his first communications network, as he likes to call it, laughing at how one night his antenna blew over and crashed through a junior housemaster's window, causing quite a ruckus and putting an end to his fledgling empire.

His dormitory room became a popular hangout, since few people, let alone teenagers, owned TV sets back then. Fewer than 70,000 of the 14 million Canadians in 1950 had television sets—and, they were all watching U.S. programs. In the United States, more than 12 million people, or 7 percent of the population, owned a TV. In 1950, the start of the Golden Era of Television—when the TV became what radio had been, the central medium of entertainment and diversion in virtually every home—the United States already had five broadcast networks: American Broadcasting Co. (ABC), Columbia Broadcasting System Inc. (CBS), DuMont Television Network, National Broadcasting Co. (NBC) and Westinghouse Electric Corp. Canada had none. The country was already running behind. The clash between technology and Canadian nationalism has lasted ever since.

Competition flourished in the United States, where broadcasters offered an array of programming, from game shows, westerns and soap operas to vaudeville and variety shows: *I Love Lucy*, *The Lone Ranger*, *Hopalong Cassidy*,

Gunsmoke, The Honeymooners, American Bandstand and *The Adventures of Ozzie and Harriet.*

American television built Canadian audiences. U.S. border stations—WBEN (now WIVB) Buffalo, WROC Rochester, WHEN and WSYR Syracuse, and WWJ, WXYZ and WJBK Detroit—all signed on between 1947 and 1950. Their signals invaded southern Ontario. KING Seattle captured viewers in Vancouver. WBEN from Buffalo drew more than 50,000 regular viewers in southern Ontario.

Canada entered the age of television in 1952 when, on September 6, the state-funded Canadian Broadcasting Corp. (CBC) went on the air in Montreal and two days later, in Toronto—despite the fact that Ottawa issued four TV licenses to private broadcasters as early as 1930. In 1936, the year Germany televised the Berlin Olympics—one of the world's first major broadcasts—Canada revised its broadcasting laws, replacing the Canadian Radio Broadcasting Commission with the more autonomous Canadian Broadcasting Corp., which was modeled after the British Broadcasting Corp. (BBC). In emulating the BBC, the politicians made the public broadcaster the industry's regulator, bestowing upon it the ultimate power to grant or deny private sector broadcast licenses, and consequently stymieing the industry's development. One of the CBC's first regulatory acts was to prevent private radio broadcasters, including Rogers' father, from developing the medium of television. Instead of filling the void, the CBC, lacking initiative and foresight—and then financially constrained once Ottawa tightened its purse strings during the Second World War—was content to watch other countries develop this exciting new medium.

The TV mania sweeping postwar America took Canada by storm. As sales of television sets soared, Canadians had little else to watch except U.S. programs. Even the CBC—once it got on the air—broadcast American shows to fill its time slots. In order to develop a TV service across Canada as quickly as possible, the CBC was authorized to build stations in major cities and to create a program network linking those stations. The CBC only began to award private licenses when it lacked the funds to expand beyond Canada's major urban centers. The private stations, though, were CBC affiliates, obliged to carry CBC national programming. Unlike in the United States, where competition flourished among privately owned networks, there were no competitive stations in Canada. With the public outcry for more diverse programming mounting, the governing Liberals decided to study the problem by creating a royal commission. The Fowler Royal Commission on Broadcasting, chaired by lawyer Robert M. Fowler, advocated, among other things, the creation of a new regulatory body to remove the inherent conflict of interest of the CBC being both a broadcaster and a regulator.

Canada would not attain some semblance of competition until John Diefenbaker's Tories ousted the Liberals. Diefenbaker found it intolerable that the CBC was empowered to be "litigant and judge, investigator and jury."

In 1958, acting on the Fowler Commission's findings, his government swiftly passed a new *Broadcasting Act,* which established an independent regulatory body, the Board of Broadcast Governors (BBG). The BBG, which was comprised of three full-time and 12 part-time members, was later attacked for its lack of broadcasting knowledge and its political ties to the Conservative Party. The newly created organization promptly announced its intention to issue private TV licenses in eight cities, including Toronto, the country's fastest growing and most lucrative advertising market.

On October 8, 1959, the BBG announced that the public hearings in Toronto would begin on March 17, 1960. The business and entertainment worlds—the crème de la crème of Toronto's who's who—including newspaper publisher John W. H. Bassett, media baron Roy H. Thomson, business tycoon E. P. Taylor, broadcaster Foster Hewitt, and cultural icon Mavor Moore, raced to form consortiums.

Ted Rogers, now 26, desperately wanted to be part of the action. He was flunking law school and trying to find a path to fullfil his expected destiny. He wasn't cash poor, but he didn't have the kind of money at his disposal to just go off and buy his way into the business. He didn't have any business connections.

In his second year of law at the esteemed Osgoode Hall, Rogers failed two subjects and, after shakily writing the supplemental exams—he prepared for the wrong examination after confusing the dates—Rogers wrote to the dean of law, pleading for admittance into third year. He blamed his poor grades on a nervous stomach and promised to do better if he wasn't kicked out. Indeed, the highly strung young man had been suffering acute stomach pain that left him anxious, perspiring excessively and for periods of time in great discomfort. He was hospitalized for tests, and when they couldn't find anything wrong, he was told he had a nervous stomach. While he barely passed Constitutional Law, the faculty gave him Equity, permitting him to enter third year.

"I used to take coffee in to him, while he was writing exams," says van Valkenburg, adding that he wasn't passing along any crib sheets. "He just needed a cup of coffee; he had health problems when he was younger, and I guess, he needed coffee to keep going. They made a special dispensation for him, and they seemed to get to know me. I'd knock and say, 'Well, I've got Ted's coffee.' 'He'll be out in five minutes.' And, they'd let him go out and he'd drink it out in the hallway."

Enter John Graham. He came through with the money and connections to launch his stepson's career. He had just spent the better part of the past two years battling to liquefy part of the estate left by his stepson's late father. The estate held shares—worth potentially half a million dollars—in CKLW Radio and its sister station, CKLW-TV, a CBC affiliate, in Windsor, just across the Detroit River from Detroit, Michigan, through two companies controlled by a voting trust created after Rogers' death. The voting trust members included Rogers' brother, Elsworth; his cousin, Samuel, the family's long-time lawyer; Samuel's son, Allen; CFRB's general manager, Harry Sedgwick; and Sedgwick's brother and CFRB lawyer, Joseph. Velma Graham, through her husband's estate, was left conspicuously absent.

When the majority shareholders, the Rogers-Sedgwick Group, decided to sell the broadcasting stations to Famous Players Canadian Corp., they excluded the minority stakeholder, the Rogers estate, in the deal. After the regulator, the CBC Board of Governors, denied their application to sell to an American-controlled company, they dissolved their voting trust—a tactic cleverly designed to make a foreign sale more palatable to the regulators since now they would be selling their individual shareholdings separately. They found another buyer—U.S. broadcaster General Tire and Rubber Co.'s RKO/General, which agreed to pay $500 per unit. For its part, RKO promised at the regulatory hearing not to interfere with the Canadian management of the stations. Their ploy worked. In 1956, the CBC Board of Governors approved the sale. The CBC also said that future foreign ownership of Canadian broadcasters should be limited to 20 percent—a policy directive, not then enacted into law, which would make it virtually impossible for the estate to sell its shares to RKO.

The Rogers-Sedgwick group promised Graham that a "Mister Caesar" would emerge to buy out them at the same price, but an offer never materialized. Instead of suing, a sure way to scare off a potential buyer, Graham managed to persuade RKO to agree to buy the rest of the shares if he could secure the necessary regulatory approval, a feat easier said than done. He enlisted the help of his political friends and acquaintances, including former Liberal cabinet minister Paul Martin Sr., father of Canada's 21st prime minister, from the riding of Essex-Windsor, the home of CKLW's broadcast facilities, and Tory senator William Brunt.

Graham, known for his command of and precise use of the English language, called upon the newly created BBG in one of its earliest public hearings to rectify the "injustice," as he described it, that had befallen the Rogers estate by the previous regulator's decision that prevented the minority from tendering their shares into the RKO bid. Graham won the day. The BBG permitted the transaction, which meant the otherwise worthless shares were sold at the agreed-upon $500 per unit price for total cash proceeds of $400,000—enough to get his stepson started.

Ted Rogers enjoys talking about his exploits, although he appears rather sheepish when asked to recall the infamous anecdote of him cornering Canada's leader John Diefenbaker at the men's urinals—actually, the one commode in the executive washroom of the Prime Minister's Office in the Langevin Block on Parliament Hill in Ottawa.

"I only went to see him once, and I said to him, 'I don't come here; I don't bother you, but this is important to me.' So, I'm given five minutes. He starts ... he tells me a joke and just as he's finishing the joke, I think, 'Gosh, I've got about two minutes left,' and he says, 'Ted, I'm just going to go to the washroom.'

"So, he gets up and goes into the washroom. I realize it's now a minute and three-quarters, and they'll be pounding on the door, and so I follow him into the washroom. I said, 'Prime Minister, I wouldn't do this, but it's important to me and here's the pitch.' I gave him the pitch as he was doing his business, and afterwards, for years, he would tease me and say, 'You're the only fellow ever, who had the nerve to walk into the washroom of the Prime Minister as he was doing his thing.'" Rogers shakes his head, abashed at and proud of his audacity, at the same time. "I had to do it." His destiny hinged on it. To this day, he won't say what "it" was—what he pitched to Diefenbaker. Rogers felt then, and believes today, that he faced a situation that would either make or break his destiny. Only the Chief, in power from June 1957 until April 1963, could help him. Ted has never said what he asked of Diefenbaker, although Peter Newman, in reporting the incident in a 1994 Maclean's story, said it took place in 1961 over a policy decision.

Rogers felt, as many did, that applicants who owned radio stations held an edge over others vying for a television license. He was hell-bent on buying CFRB. He was intent on owning his dad's old station. He had spent so much time there over the years that he was allowed to roam the facilities freely. The staff knew him well. They drew him into—as much as he insinuated himself in—the station's plans to apply for the TV license until Thornton Cran returned from England in 1959 to spearhead the TV application for Argus, the station's ultimate parent.

Since he already had one member of the Rogers clan in his pocket—Elsworth was on the board of directors—Cran certainly didn't need the founder's son, a 26-year-old know-it-all who wanted to run the show, involved. Cran had CFRB staffers remove the pictures of Rogers Sr. from the walls and barred Junior from the premises. Rogers' quest for a television license had suddenly become personal. Cran embodied the larger-than-life enemy that motivated Rogers to pursue a license. "I immediately, of course, disliked him and said, 'I am going to compete with you on the TV license—and, I know everything you're planning to do,'" says Rogers. "If they had a loveable guy in there, it would have been a lot harder for me to mount the campaign."

Unlike Harry Sedgwick, who treated Rogers with fondness, Cran showed him disdain, never making time for the boy who spent hours hanging out at the radio station, soaking up the atmosphere and proudly admiring the photos of his dad. "Cran took my father's pictures down, and threw me out," says Rogers. "It was really quite a personal thing between him and me."

Rogers needed a partner. John Graham had just established his own law practice, Payton, Biggs & Graham, and through one of his partners, introduced Rogers to Joel Aldred, a radio and TV announcer who had made it big in Hollywood. A decorated veteran of the Second World War, Aldred served in the Royal Canadian Air Force, rising to the rank of wing commander, and did most of the stunt flying in Warner Bros.' 1942 movie *Captains of the Clouds*, starring James Cagney and Alan Hale. After the war, he worked for the CBC until getting fired for criticizing the broadcaster's overly artsy programming. He subsequently became an announcer for CBS and NBC on several popular U.S. television programs, including *The Dinah Shore Show*, *The Bob Hope Show* and *The Perry Como Show*. He was the voice in all of the automaker General Motors Corp. and consumer-products maker Procter & Gamble Co. advertisements. He also did hundreds of commercials for cigarette-maker Rothmans of Pall Mall and hosted the fifties' dramatic-anthology television series *Studio 57*. His voice was in such high demand that, in 1956, *Maclean's* magazine called him "The Man with the $100,000 Voice."

Aldred was also a stalwart Tory, lending his face and his voice to the Conservative Party's efforts. He was a good friend of Diefenbaker's, having known him since 1948. He had been the party's master of ceremonies in 1957 at Toronto's Massey Hall, the night Diefenbaker kicked off his election campaign as Tory leader. He even met Rogers briefly that evening when, after Diefenbaker's speech, Rogers clasped his hand before striding into the mayhem to have his picture taken with the Chief.

Aldred was also seeking partners when John Graham set up a meeting with his stepson. They joined forces, thinking the other was rich. Laughs Rogers, "Joel thought I had money, and I thought he had money." They agreed that the best way to win the TV license was to own a broadcast station like CFRB. Each undertook to secure a line of credit for just over $1 million, enough to make a takeover offer for CFRB's parent, Standard Broadcasting Co., the publicly traded holding company.

Rogers was determined to buy his dad's radio station. One day, while he was still a law student, he showed up on Argus' doorstep with a check for $1 million drawn from a bank line of credit. Burke van Valkenburg was with him. "We walked down King Street into Argus Corp. with this million-dollar cheque. He handed it to me, and I held it and said, 'It's a million dollars, Ted!' It was kind of a special moment, but he did get a nasty reception. Ted said, 'I want to buy CFRB back from you.' They said, 'It's not for sale. Get out. Your money's no good here, Ted.' They threw us out," says van Valkenburg.

Rogers refused to borrow money from his mother and stepfather. When they suggested they lend him $400,000 from his father's estate, Rogers declined the offer. He didn't want his mother to be left penniless if his venture failed. Instead, he decided to borrow the money against the estate.

Taking along his old school chum Toby Hull, Rogers met with a trust officer from National Trust Co.'s predecessor, Victoria & Grey Trust Co. (V&G), where the Rogers estate was being managed. Hull, a year older than Rogers, had bypassed university to become an insurance agent like his father. In their Sunday best, the two young men sat on the edge of their chairs while the trust officer austerely declined their proposal. He expressed concern that if Rogers died before his mother, then V&G would end up fighting the estate to recover its loan. Just as Rogers was about to respond, Hull swiftly kicked his shin and interjected, "Look, that's a reasonable problem. I'm sure it's a big problem, but is that the only reluctance you have in making the loan, the only reluctance?"

"Yes."

"Okay, thank you for your time. Ted, let's leave," Hull said. Rogers was aghast.

On their way out the door, Hull quietly proposed to Rogers a way to appease the trust officer. If Rogers took out a life insurance medical policy to protect the loan, V&G would have no reason to refuse his request. "If you die first, they get the $400,000," he said.

Hull picks up the story. "So, we go get the medical done; we pushed to get it done. We go back, and Ted pulls out the policy and reminds them that this was their only issue. They were dumbfounded. They said, 'How do we know you'll pay the premiums?' Ted told them, 'I'll prepay it from their advance. What's your next problem?'"

He got his loan. While commonplace today, key-person life insurance was a rather novel concept in 1959. Ever since then, Rogers continually updates his key-person Lloyd's of London life insurance policy to protect his family's estate in the event of his death. "He's got every bank and financial institution there ever was stamped on the back on his life insurance policy. He moves them around, and he's still moving them around. Banks change. Some of the loans are big, so consortiums are formed. He's always been a big believer in sharing his liabilities, and making sure there's liquidity at death, and one of the simplest ways [of doing that] is through a life insurance policy," says Hull, who parlayed his work for Rogers into a successful Toronto-based insurance agency catering to communications and media companies. He's been a company director ever since.

John W. H. Bassett, the publisher of the *Toronto Telegram*, then one of Toronto's three daily newspapers, was seeking outside partners after media baron Roy H. Thomson withdrew from their partnership. The BBG, concerned as it was of media concentration, forewarned Thomson it wasn't prepared to award a television franchise to him because of his vast radio and TV assets.

Bassett, known as Big John, was a tall, debonair, blond-haired newspaperman of Irish descent, who easily charmed retailing imperator John David Eaton, six years his senior, with his wit and carousing to join the ranks of Toronto's powerful business elite. In 1952, Bassett, 37, persuaded Eaton, Canada's richest man, to help him buy the *Telegram* from the estate of George McCullagh, the founder of *The Globe and Mail*, who had committed suicide at age 47 earlier that year. Although ownership of the *Telegram* was vested in a trust for the benefit of McCullagh's sons, Bassett exercised sole power over the voting shares. Bassett and Eaton created Baton Broadcasting Co., a contraction of their surnames, for their television application. Bassett, a Progressive Conservative Party insider, who ran unsuccessfully for election twice, was well connected with the Diefenbaker government.

Rogers had never previously met Bassett, despite their common political stripes. The two men, separated in age by 18 years, moved in very different social circles. Rogers, with his *carpe diem* outlook on life, had already approached—and been flatly rejected by—virtually every other business leader and banker in his quest to pull together a group for a private television franchise. He picked up the phone, and cold-called Bassett.

"Hi. I'm Ted Rogers. I'm interested in the Toronto television license."

"I've never heard of you. Why should I talk to you?" retorted Bassett, who always answered his own phone.

Rogers played up his roots, emphasized his partnership with the renowned Joel Aldred and dropped the names of some mutual political acquaintances. He held his breath for Bassett's response. "Macy's doesn't talk to Gimbels," Bassett roared. Rogers kept right on talking until he managed to persuade Bassett to at least meet with him and Aldred. He explained that he was intimately familiar with the details of CFRB's application and had been actively involved in its preparation until Cran had barred him from the radio station. Argus intended to apply for the license using the name Rogers Radio Broadcasting Co., the parent of radio station CRFB, rather than Standard Radio, the publicly traded entity overtop Rogers Radio. Cran planned to rely on the station's superb track record in the radio business and play up the founder's name to curry favor with the governors, which irritated Ted Rogers, whose only claim to his lost heritage was his blood. He intended to downplay the ownership of mighty Argus as much as possible.

Bassett, believing his biggest challenge would come from CFRB, invited Rogers and Aldred to see him the next day at the *Telegram*. When they got down to the brass tacks, Rogers brazenly said, "We'll merge with you fifty-fifty."

"You guys have a hell of a nerve. You're suffering from the disease of self-importance. You're going to get thirty-seven percent," retorted Bassett. Rogers never expected that Bassett would offer them as much as that. He was so relieved he says he just wanted to hightail it out of there before Bassett changed his mind. In his memoirs, Bassett's lawyer, Eddie Goodman, described Aldred and Rogers as having "more confidence and ambition than Planters had peanuts."

"Bassett wouldn't think of Ted as anything but a kid," recalled the late Eddie Goodman. "He would have been interested in him because of Ted's father. Ted makes it carry a lot of credence, justifiably so. I was closer to Ted than John was. They were two of the most impossible people in the world. They were both determined and ambitious. I was not much older than Ted. I thought he was pretty clever and a little nuts."

Rogers, who says that he was mistaken once for one of Bassett's sons at a Baton shareholders' meeting because they were both tall, "fast-moving" men, although he clarifies that Bassett, a renowned womanizer, "was much more with the women than me," explains why he and Bassett hit it off: "We're both bullshitters, and it takes one to know one."

Bassett had a big impact on Rogers. "Ted picked up some of John's wonderful *joie de vivre*, and just his general way of dealing with people, shaking hands and greeting people," says Trevor Eyton, a Conservative appointee to Canada's Senate, who articled with Rogers at law firm Torys LLP. "Ted's got a big personality. He's the kind of person who walks into the room and he fills the space. He's got big ideas and he's got a big voice."

In December 1959, three months before the March hearings, Bassett renamed Baton Broadcasting. The new moniker was Baton Aldred Rogers Broadcasting Ltd. to reflect his partners. Rogers, 26, was the youngest member of Bassett's consortium, which included broadcaster Foster Hewitt, Canada's legendary voice of hockey who made famous the "He shoots; He scores" phrase and owner of Toronto radio station CKFH 1430; movie-theater impresario Paul Nathanson of Sovereign Films Distributors; a company called Heathcourt Boulevard Investments, which held Goodman's contract; and lawyer Charles Dubin, who three decades later became the Chief Justice of Ontario. Bassett included Nathanson, a Liberal, to make his bid appear less Tory blue. Nor did it hurt that Paul Martin Sr., a former Liberal cabinet minister, was Nathanson's lawyer.

The BBG began its hearings for private TV licenses in Vancouver and moved eastward across the country. Rogers did reconnaissance for the Baton team at the hearings in Winnipeg. This was his first exposure to the regulatory process. He reported back to Bassett and Aldred his belief that the single, most important factor to winning the governors' approval was in the question-and-answer period. "To me, this is the area where the board separates the men from the boys," he told them. "The answers must come instantly without reference to notes. We must give facts—and every fact supported by its source. We must not be afraid of appearing too much like Madison Ave. We must be extremely professional, well organized and use the most modern visual devices to put across our case. We must at all times be humble—sincere, industrious, imbued with the challenge, confident that we can do a job—but always be humble." Bassett, with all of his pre-decision boasting of the license being "in the bag"—something Eddie Goodman tried hard to restrain—was not anyone's personification of the word humble.

On St. Patrick's Day, 1960, Ted Rogers participated in his first-ever BBG hearing. The day did not start off well. Overnight, the Toronto had been hit with a major snowstorm. The city was knee-deep in snow. The streets were gridlocked and people could barely get to Union Station, the venue for the hearings. As part of its presentation, Baton Aldred Rogers intended to dazzle the governors with a closed-circuit television presentation of news, entertainment and sports programming. None of the other applicants had thought of actually using the medium for which they were seeking a license. Baton went to the trouble of having Bell lay eight kilometers of coaxial cable to connect the 13 TV monitors in the Oak Room at Union Station with the Meridian Video Tape Centre in east-end Toronto. Rogers was given the job of pressing the button to signal Meridian to send the video feed. His cue came when John Bassett said, "Others have promised, Mr. Chairman, but we want to show you what we have done." Rogers pushed the button and blew a fuse. The Oak Room was plunged into darkness.

"Mr. Chairman, show business has to deal with the unexpected eventualities and while we had not scheduled this brief interlude and while there are no commercials to roll, I'm sure Joel Aldred will get the show back on the road," Bassett continued. Four minutes later, the lights came back on. In addition to their many pledges of Canadian content (which were later ignored), one of the key selling points was the all-Canadian composition of their consortium. Bassett proudly promised to keep his shareholder group Torontonian, another pledge he later broke.

The hearings set the benchmark for all future regulatory presentations. Words like "public service," "community interest," "cultural fabric" and "educational responsibility" were "studded like sequins through briefs and submission," wrote journalist and author Pierre Berton in his *Toronto Star* column, saying he had never before seen so many "distinguished Canadians" under one roof. "One heard practically nothing about Old Movies, TV Westerns, rock 'n' roll or Mighty Mouse. The accent was on Canadianism and the Arts. Buffalo was the wicked villain and everybody … was trying to out-CBC the CBC."

The 15-member Board of Broadcast Governors knew next to nothing about television. Twelve were prominent Tories, and after the hearing from nine applicants—including Jack Kent Cooke, Maclean Hunter Publishing Co., Southam, the *Toronto Star* and Spencer W. Caldwell (who later formed the CTV Network)—the BBG took only three days to wade through the applications and award the license to Baton. The board's decision—made with unseemly haste and unsupported by any announced reasons—sparked howls of protest from the losers, the public and politicians. The governors were accused of listening more to their political masters than they did to the applicants. In a letter to *The Globe and Mail*, Joseph Sedgwick, CFRB's lawyer, said the decision appeared "not to be explained by any ordinary process of thought or reason."

Joel Aldred oversaw the building of the CFTO-TV studios in Scarborough, northeast of Toronto, and hired most of the station's top management, including program director Rai Purdy, a former CFRB announcer who worked for Thomson Corp.'s Scottish Television Ltd.; station manager Charles Baldour from NBC in Hollywood; and comptroller Burgess Kayajanian, a former NBC accountant.

Aldred, who spared no expense, almost bankrupted the fledgling station. He spent $4.5 million—two-and-a-half times the budget—to build studios that rivalled those in Hollywood, and hired more than 400 staff members, more than any other TV station in North America. In what would prove to be a far-sighted move, he equipped the station for color, even though Canada would not permit color broadcasts for another six years. On December 31, 1960 at ten at night, CFTO-TV (Channel 9) made broadcasting history: Toronto's first private TV station. They broadcast a charity telethon non-stop for 18 hours with more than a thousand volunteers turning out to help. Aldred hosted the event. At midnight, the founders, a beaming Ted Rogers and the team who built Channel 9 and put it on the air gathered outside the station to celebrate the launch, ushering in 1961 with fireworks and champagne. There would soon be fireworks of another kind.

Before long, CFTO-TV was hemorrhaging money. Bassett and Aldred, both war veterans and both with formidable egos, clashed continually. Finally, when Aldred was away on vacation, John Bassett simply moved into his office and promptly fired 58 people. Within months of CFTO-TV going on the air, Bassett, who had 51-percent voting control of the TV franchise through the Telegram, exercised his power, sweeping out the entire executive management and production team, who had been part of the application process.

In late July 1961, Bassett, desperate for a new source of capital, negotiated a refinancing package with American Broadcasting-Paramount Theaters Inc., owner of the ABC TV network. The federal government permitted non-Canadians to own as much as 25 percent of the voting stock in a Canadian TV station. ABC agreed to buy 25 percent—the permissible amount by law—of the common equity in Baton Aldred Rogers (representing 18.9 percent of its voting stock) for $300,000 as well as invest in $2 million of debentures. The U.S. giant not only would inject fresh capital into the ailing TV station, but also refinance the shareholder group. The *Telegram*, owned by Bassett and Eaton, would recover its entire investment, while retaining control of the TV station.

In order to accommodate his new American partner, Bassett had to get rid of one of his partners, dilute their interest or both. Aldred, Rogers and John Graham tried to pull together their own alternative financing package with the Peacock Network, National Broadcasting Co. (NBC), but they were too late. Rogers recalls being summoned to a shareholders' meeting in August 1961 at Bassett's house at 11 at night. The others—from the *Telegram*, the Eaton Trust and ABC—were already there. Joel Aldred was in Montreal. Bassett stood on the hallway stairs and announced the terms of the proposed contract with ABC, deliberately cutting out Aldred and Ted Rogers. "We're not open to negotiation. He's fired. As for you," he pointed at Rogers, "if you want to stay in, it's going to cost you $500,000."

Bassett asked John Graham to break the news to Aldred. Graham, accompanied by Rogers, went into an upstairs bedroom and called Aldred, who was staying at the Hotel Bonaventure in Montreal. An inebriated Aldred angrily shouted obscenities into the phone. When they went back downstairs, Bassett asked Graham what Aldred had said. Graham translated his "tell him to go to hell" into "Joel said that he appreciated being informed of your views, and he said to tell you that he will give them due consideration."

"I'll tell you how long he has to think about it," Bassett replied. Bassett gave them until three the next afternoon to sign the necessary documentation. "Finish your drink and get out," Rogers recalls Bassett saying.

"It was sort of like the Japanese surrendering at Tokyo Bay," says Rogers.

Bassett's deal with ABC required regulatory approval. The BBG endorsed the sale of stock to ABC so long as no other Canadian company emerged to match ABC's offer. They gave Canadian companies until September 25 to match ABC's offer. No other offer was forthcoming. BBG chairman Andrew Stewart and future Liberal senator Eugene Forsey cast the only dissenting votes, fearing if they permitted one U.S. broadcaster into the country others would follow and, before long, the Americans would be wielding control of Canada's private TV stations. With the Liberal opposition in Ottawa fueling a growing anti-Americanism backlash, the BBG reversed its decision, angering the Bassett team. "How could you sons of bitches go back on yourselves?" Eddie Goodman remembers thinking.

With CFTO headed for bankruptcy, Bassett and his lawyers went back to the drawing board. This time, they purposely structured a transaction that involved no equity to sidestep the regulatory process altogether. ABC acquired the $2-million-plus of debentures. The U.S. giant also acquired specially created irrevocable and irredeemable participating debentures, as good as permanent stock, entitling the network to a 25-percent share of CFTO-TV's future profits. Since no stock would be involved, Bassett was not obliged to reveal the details, which prompted the BBG to seek parliamentary changes granting them the authority to request such disclosures, although the regulator was lambasted in the press because it already had the power under the Broadcasting Act to demand from licensees information "regarding their financial affairs" and chose not to exercise it. While the transaction was legal, Bassett was accused of violating the spirit of the board's position. (Later, Baton bought out ABC.)

Joel Aldred, pocketing $200,000, was out. Bassett permitted Rogers to remain a minority owner with 10 percent and allowed him to keep his FM radio antenna on the CFTO TV tower. By then, Rogers was the proud owner of CHFI-FM.

In his last year of law school, Rogers needed to find an articling job with a law firm. Rogers booked an appointment to see Roy Thomson's lawyer, J.S.D. Tory, who only agreed to see him because he thought Rogers was looking for partners on behalf of Baton Aldred Rogers for the TV bid. (Tory first acted for Thomson in his failed attempt to buy *The Globe and Mail* newspaper.) Rogers arrived at Tory's offices the next day at 10 in the morning. Less than five minutes into the meeting, Tory realized he had been duped, and immediately phoned his son John A., asking him to come into his office where he proceeded to introduce him to Rogers. John A. Tory, then 29, was responsible for hiring the one or two articling students the small firm accepted each year. Although he had already hired his quota for the year, his father told him to take Rogers to lunch. Tory rounded up his twin brother, Jim, and, by 10:30, the three men were sitting down for lunch. Rogers impressed the pair with his tenacity and earnestness. They liked him. He seemed a whole lot smarter than his school records indicated. They took a risk. Since Tory was already mentoring an articling student, Rogers was assigned to Jim, not the firm as was the custom then. "Ted Rogers would probably have not been on our list to interview, but we did hire him. Whether we would have kept him is another question," quips John A. Tory. "He wasn't around very much."

Rogers divided his time between articling, reading well into the night reams of documentation on corporate acquisitions, working on the TV license application, and trying to cobble enough money together to buy a radio station. "He wasn't a brilliant student, but he's got a brilliant mind. He will look at anything that somebody does that he thinks is clever and use it in his own business," says Tory.

Trevor Eyton was also articling at the law firm. The two men—both tall in stature, although Eyton, a former footballer, is more athletic than Rogers—shared the same office, each in tiny cubicles surrounded by mountains of paperwork. Eyton already knew Rogers from the many Sigma Chi parties Rogers threw while they were both university undergraduates. "Even then he was a big personality," recalls Eyton, a Delta Theta brother. "He was outrageous and amusing and ... big. You always knew where Ted was. You could hear him. He was always organizing things; he was just fun. He was lots of fun to be around.

"He was always busy on twenty different projects, and in between and along the way, he packed in a little bit of law school. Everybody else was tormented by the bar admission exam and working eighteen hours a day, and as far as I could tell, he was working eight minutes a day, but he got through even in spite of all of his projects.

"Ted is the sort of person who will pitch in whenever anything needs to get done. It doesn't matter what it is. It could be carrying cartons up from the basement, or going off to the library to get a book, or writing a brief, or going to court. If it needs to be done, Ted will pitch in," says Eyton. "I'm sure I put in more hours working on the law than Ted, but on the other hand, he was always there and always ready to help at any level."

At the end of the articling period, Jim Tory refused to sign the necessary form stating that Rogers had articled for him on a "full-time" basis. He relented only at his brother's urging and after Rogers promised to get down on his knees and shine his shoes whenever Jim Tory wanted—at any time in any place for the rest of his life. True to his word, Rogers did shine Jim Tory's shoes on several occasions over the years, including some swank black-tie dinners.

In 1963, two years before the death of their father, who had been quite ill for several years already, the Tory twins set up their own law practice with two University of Toronto fraternity brothers, William DesLauriers and Art Binnington. Hanging up the shingle Tory Tory DesLauriers & Binnington, the venture quickly became one of Canada's most prestigious law firms, and is now known simply as Torys LLP. Rogers would become one of the firm's clients after John A. Tory left in 1973 to become a full-time consigliere to the late Lord Ken Thomson and his family.

CHAPTER 4

680 Radio

"Ted did not like dead air."

—Ray Cook

RIDING ON BIG JOHN BASSETT'S COATTAILS, Rogers could call himself a TV broadcaster, but the fresh-faced law student was just a minority stakeholder in CFTO, a stepping stone on the path to restoring his family's name in the world of broadcasting. With Aldred immersed in the task of building CFTO's studios, Rogers hunted for radio and TV assets. With his stepfather's help, he went after CKLW radio and TV in Windsor, which he felt should have been his birthright. He made an offer to buy a 50-percent stake in the Windsor stations from their U.S. parent, RKO General Inc., which showed him the door. Of the five AM stations in Toronto, only one was for sale: Jack Kent Cooke's CKEY 580. Cooke, en route to California, where he'd buy the Los Angeles basketball franchise and go on to become a U.S. media and sports mogul, was asking for too much money.

FM, considered throwaway bandwidth, was only just emerging. The acronym stands for frequency modulation, which improved both the quality of broadcasting with high-fidelity sound and later played a major role in making cellular possible. While U.S. stations were experimenting with stereophonic transmission, only a handful of AM-owned FM stations existed in Canada, and they only offered a few hours of separate programming, if that. Canada had just one stand-alone FM station: CHFI-FM.

Edward J. Piggott founded CHFI 98.1 FM in 1957. Piggott wasn't interested in being a broadcaster. The 52-year-old entrepreneur was just looking for a cheaper and more efficient way of piping background, or "elevator," music to his customers than over the telephone lines. Piggott peddled soft music, so-called

Muzak, for a fee to factories, restaurants, offices and apartment buildings. He applied four times for an FM license before the CBC Board of Governors finally granted him one. He hired Donald E. Wright as the station's general manager, chief announcer and sole programmer. Wright, 46, a pioneer in AM radio, was a Saskatchewan native who had produced the popular fifties' radio quiz show *Mother Parker's Musical Mysteries* and helped start Canadian Press' radio service, which later became Broadcast News.

On February 1, 1957, CHFI—the call letters stood for High Fidelity—began broadcasting 18 hours a day on 98.1 kHz from 13 Adelaide St. East in downtown Toronto, just east of Yonge St. and north of the King Edward Hotel. Piggott beamed his elevator music on a mere 340 watts from the neighboring 23-storey Imperial Life Assurance Building. Wright dubbed the fledgling station's supper-hour program *Candlelight Music*, which was billed in the newspaper program guides as "Your Invitation to Cocktails." He also introduced the popular Sunday afternoon program *Front Row Centre*, during which he played music from Broadway shows. But, the quality of the sound was atrocious, with an annoying hum throughout.

In September 1960, Rogers heard from one of CFTO's consulting engineers, Donald B. Williamson, that Piggott was interested in selling CHFI-FM. Ten days later, on September 30, Rogers paid Piggott $100,000 to acquire CHFI-FM, a studio/control room no bigger than an oversized walk-in closet with six desks, a couple of typewriters and an adding machine in the Adelaide St. three-storey walk-up above a greasy-spoon diner and a tobacco shop.

Just before midnight, the law student checked out the premises. The place was as different from CFRB's gleaming, polished studios as one could imagine. CHFI-FM occupied the back half of the second floor, and the entire third floor. A jeweler was among the other second-floor tenants at the front of the building. The entrance was between the diner and the wholesale tobacconist. Rogers raced up the stairs to the second floor, walked down the hallway, and headed up the additional three steps onto the split-level landing to the studio. He'd have his office on the third floor with sales and accounting.

"The equipment was homemade. We threw it all out. It was junk," says Ray Cook, now 65, a former CHFI technician who joined the station shortly after Rogers acquired CHFI from Piggott and was there for 13 years, installing and maintaining CHFI's radio and transmission equipment. The toilets in the women's washroom, located on the third floor, habitually broke down and overflowed, seeping through the walls into the main floor tobacconist. "I'd see them down there wiping the tobacco off, and putting it back on the shelf," recalls Cook. "Those poor guys, we drowned the tobacco shop out so often they finally built a special tin roof over their tobacco to save their stock. Eventually, they moved. I would know when I went in the front door whether the can was working or not." More often than not, rummies sought shelter at the station; women came to work Monday morning to find a drunk passed out in the washroom.

The conditions were so appalling that Rogers' first financial officer quit. "I asked him why he resigned," recalls Rogers. "He said, 'Well, I couldn't stand it any more. First of all,' he said, 'the building shakes.'

"I said, 'The building only shakes once in a while in the winter from the subway when the ground's frozen. Surely, that's not why.'

"'Well, secondly, you put this plastic over the windows, and I feel asphyxiated.'

"'We put the plastic on the windows, so that you wouldn't get cold. You said you were cold. Do you remember? What's the real reason?'

"'Well, I go downstairs and sit on the toilet, and the cockroaches crawl up my leg.'

"That's when I gave up, and asked where he was going," says Rogers. The financial officer went to work for the federal income tax department across the street.

The offices were fumigated regularly to little avail. One day, radio technicians asked Cook to come into the control studio to watch two cockroaches sitting on top of a record album spinning on the turntable. The place reeked of cigarette smoke and grease from the downstairs diner permeated the carpets, drywall and plaster. "In the summer, it was pretty hot up there and everybody smoked," recalls Rogers, who himself once smoked three packs of Export A cigarettes a day. "Loretta's father and mother came in to see [the station] one day, and they couldn't breathe for all the smoke. They said, 'This is absolutely terrible. You've got to do something about this.' So, I said, 'Alright, we'll put in an exhaust fan that pulls the air out,' and we installed it upstairs and called it the 'Lord Daddy Martonmere Hot Air Fan.'

"They were very tolerant [of me]," he says. "Her father was. I suspect, they probably had a lot of wealthy second-generation types after their daughter who weren't working, were [polo] riding and all this stuff, going to parties all the time. So, they probably thought this was terribly different."

That the place was a dump didn't matter. Rogers was the owner of a radio license, the first step in rebuilding his lost heritage. He had bold dreams. If he couldn't buy his dad's old station outright, he'd do his damnedest to outdo CFRB until he was in a position to acquire it. Until then, he first needed the Board of Broadcast Governors' (BBG) consent to acquire Piggott's license. To win regulatory approval, Rogers decided he needed to show the regulator that he was serious about making Canada's only stand-alone FM station a success. First he'd need to fix it up. He bought new equipment, signed contracts with new talent and negotiated a "contra" arrangement with John Bassett to share each other's personnel and services once CFTO-TV went live. In the first three months, he spent eight hundred dollars to buy new records, on a three-month average 10 times more than Piggott ever spent. He put in a new control room. His sister, Ann Graham, became the station's girl Friday, doing odd jobs and manning the phones at reception. The station manager, Don Wright, renamed the supper-hour show *Candlelight and Wine*. Hosted by the velvety-voiced Don Parrish, *Candlelight and Wine* would become CHFI-FM's mainstay program for the next 25 years.

Rogers' application wasn't the only one before the BBG. The regulator had two others to consider, from powerhouse AM stations CFRB and CHUM, requests that if granted would potentially crush tiny CHFI-FM before it could get started. CFRB had for years ignored its FM frequency, simulcasting its AM programs on FM merely to maintain its license. Now, with the founder's son trying to break into radio business, CFRB—still stinging from losing the private TV license to Bassett and Aldred-Rogers—wanted the right to air its programs on the FM frequency, too. Like Rogers, CFRB also wanted more FM power output.

Wright urged Rogers to move CHFI-FM's transmitter from the Imperial Life roof to the top of the CFTO-TV Channel 9 tower, which was going up in Agincourt, northeast of Toronto, to compete with CFRB-FM's new 200,000-watt transmitter atop the downtown Toronto Bank of Commerce building, then the tallest in the British Commonwealth at 34 storeys. Unbeknownst to John Bassett, whose subsequent anger was quickly diffused, Rogers persuaded the CFTO-TV station engineers to overbuild the Channel 9 tower to a height of 245 meters (816 feet), twice as high as CFRB-FM's antenna, to ensure his radio signal carried far and wide. He also wanted to boost the station's power output from 9,450 watts to a phenomenal 210,000 watts, making CHFI 98.1 FM more powerful than his nemesis' station. Indeed, it was Canada's most powerful FM signal.

CFRB wasn't Rogers' only problem. The late Allan F. Waters, who bought 1050 CHUM-AM in 1954, wanted to break into the market with an FM license to end CHFI's monopoly on 24-hour separate FM broadcasting. Waters made history three years earlier by revamping 1050 CHUM into Canada's first Top 40 24-hour rock station, a move that unseated rival Jack Kent Cooke's CKEY, which had previously ruled the airwaves and ultimately hastened Cooke's departure from Canada. "It was the hottest station in Canada," legendary rocker Rompin' Ronnie Hawkins told the *Toronto Star*. "CHUM was it. Nobody else played rock 'n' roll then." In his pursuit of an FM station, Waters warned the BBG that

Canada was in danger of losing FM frequencies if the federal government didn't encourage the use of FM along the border. At 27 percent, FM penetration in the United States already was more than double that of Canada's.

John Graham was a tower of strength for Rogers at the BBG hearings. Graham intervened, arguing convincingly, given the BBG's ruling against CHUM's application, that the Toronto market could not support two FM giants. Waters offered to forgo a full year's worth of commercial revenue if the regulator gave him immediate approval. In December 1960, the BBG approved the sale of the CHFI-FM license to Rogers, permitted CFRB-FM to transmit at 200,000 watts, and deferred decisions on the other two applications until it had time to assess the market impact of Rogers' request to beam a stronger CHFI-FM signal.

In the spring of 1961, the BBG allowed Rogers to boost the CHFI-FM signal. While it also permitted CFRB to air separate FM programming, it iced CHUM. The BBG wasn't sure Toronto's advertising market was large enough to support a new FM station, especially with a second TV station just getting started. The BBG decided the best approach was to take a wait-and-see position rather than simply permit competition to sort out the winners and the losers. For now—at least until CHUM was allowed to launch 104.5 FM, a classical music station, in 1963—Rogers faced just one competitor: CFRB-FM.

License in hand, Rogers was hardly a threat to CFRB. He owned a radio station that piped Muzak to apartment buildings. He had a powerful transmitter—powerful enough to reach a potential FM audience of 5.5 million listeners across southwestern Ontario and upper New York State—but what good was such transmission capability if people didn't own an FM radio? There was no market. Only one household in six in Metro Toronto had an FM radio. Cars didn't have FM receivers. FM sets were big and pricey—the only ones on the market were monster-sized consoles designed for living rooms, which cost upwards of $600.

Rogers had to create demand for FM out of thin air. First, he needed an affordable product. Second, he had to give people a reason to buy it. Rogers set out to make FM sets more reasonably priced. He shelled out $100,000 to contract Canadian Westinghouse Ltd. in Hamilton, Ontario to manufacture stylish, inexpensive FM table model sets of his own design. He had the slogan "CHFI 98.1—Canada's First Station for Fine Music" embossed in gold on the front, with a red dot on the tuning dial to indicate the spot where listeners could easily find the 98.1 FM frequency. In late August 1961, Rogers unveiled the new tabletop radios at the Canadian National Exhibition, the same forum where his father displayed the world's first electric radio. Through a special promotional campaign, Rogers began selling some 5,000 sets at a reduced price of $39.95, tripling FM penetration in the Toronto area from just 3 percent in 1957 to 15 percent in 1962.

Rogers plastered the CHFI call letters on outdoor billboards, on subway exits, on streetcars and car stickers. He gave potential advertisers free FM radios to demonstrate to them that FM was superior in sound quality to AM. He gave free radios to his friends. His friends even pitched in, selling radios to their neighbors out of the trunks of their cars. CHFI began selling *Candlelight and Wine* record albums to attract listeners. "My billboards were 'Look what CFRB listeners are missing.' Can you believe it?" guffaws Rogers at his own audaciousness.

To drum up excitement for the transformed station, Rogers and Joel Aldred, still his partner, although he spent most of his time at CFTO-TV, celebrated by clinking champagne glasses with 600 broadcasters and advertisers. They took out a full-page ad in the industry trade publication to attract advertisers, featuring a stern-looking, white-haired, tuxedoed waiter bearing a tray of food and the requisite bottle of champagne with the text: "Filet Mignon ... or hash? When they're just about the same price and quantity ... the answer is obvious. Filet Mignon, or FM for short, is the better buy."

Rogers was young, energetic and brimming with enthusiasm. He was the PR man's PR man. He had to be. He didn't have the money to serve filet mignon. He was in a race with CFRB to broadcast stereophonic sound, then just emerging. Even though CHFI-FM boasted of being the first and having a better sound, it wasn't and it didn't. Both CHFI and CFRB began broadcasting in stereo at midnight on August 31, 1961. CHFI's sound quality had static. It wasn't as clean as CFRB's, which was better, although it wasn't perfect either. CFRB spent more than $5,000 for an RCA commercial unit that it upgraded later. Rogers didn't have that kind of money to spare. His chief engineer, Ronald H. Turnpenny, came up with a solution. He fashioned a $300 signal generator into an exciter that, while not perfect, enabled Rogers to go on the air with stereophonic sound the same time CFRB did. "He had all kinds of trouble," recalls Clive Eastwood, now 85, Turnpenny's counterpart at CFRB, who received an engineering award in 1962 for his work in developing multiplex stereophonic standards. "Ours was much better at first, but then they got a commercial one that was available, and it's all been good since."

To the grief of his technicians, Rogers continued piping Muzak into apartment and office buildings primarily to generate cash flow while he tried to build a market for FM. The signals interfered with each other. If the FM signal went quiet at the end of a record, listeners would hear a swishing sound underneath it from the background music. Eventually, it was filtered out. "It really mussed things up," recalls Cook. "There were a lot of headaches in those days." Through sheer hard work, ingenuity and clever marketing, Rogers won the first of many battles to come when CHFI-FM, calling itself "The High Fidelity Music Station," emerged as the clear ratings winner.

Rogers put all of his energy into CHFI-FM. He took up the cause of FM, long the neglected poor sister to the highly coveted AM band. He felt alone in championing FM radio in Canada. No one was working harder than him to bring FM into the home. So, when the U.S. National Association of FM Broadcasters invited Jack Kennedy, the station manager at CFRB-FM, onto its board, Rogers had a conniption fit. No Canadian had ever been tapped to be a director. Rogers protested Kennedy's appointment to the board's president at the industry's Washington DC conference. The board considered and dismissed Rogers' protest against his fellow Canuck, the only other Canadian at the trade show. Half an hour later, Rogers appeared before the board, repeating his earlier protest. Kennedy returned to Toronto unsure if he'd been elected or not. He received a wired confirmation four days later that he was indeed a director.

Vaughn Bjerre was one of Rogers's earliest CHFI-FM hires. The station's general manager, Dr. B.K. Bryam, whom Rogers brought onboard as a consultant, set up an interview for Bjerre with Rogers for 12 o'clock—midnight. "I couldn't believe it," recalls Bjerre. "I've never been hired at 12 midnight! He liked meetings that went on in the evening because they could go on till 12 or one in the morning, and I remember Dr. Byram couldn't stand it because he'd come in at nine in the morning and by midnight, he would be pretty pooped out. He kept on falling asleep during the meetings. But, that should have given me some inkling of what he was like when he hired me at midnight."

Van Valkenburg, who pitched in at CHFI, remembers advising Bjerre, who had a young family, to tell Rogers that he must catch the five-thirty train home every day because otherwise Rogers, just arriving, might keep him there until midnight. "[Rogers] was like Churchill," says van Valkenburg. Bjerre heeded his advice. Rogers always phoned him by five if he wanted to talk to him, although Rogers wouldn't hesitate to call him at home in the middle of the night. "He wasn't bad with me," says Bjerre. "He really didn't expect other people to work like workaholics. He never condemned anybody for not hanging around at night, or on the weekends. But, before he got married, he was particularly bad at working at something at eleven at night or at midnight, and calling you at home, and saying, 'Hey, I've got a great idea. What do you think of this?' It wouldn't be a five-minute conversation. He'd want to talk for an hour or two. I don't know how Loretta ever put up with it."

Still in law school, Rogers often worked through the night, often sleeping on the floor at his friend Toby Hull's nearby life insurance office. Because of his eye problems, Rogers had difficulty parking his car in the underground parking lot, so he had someone else park it for him. He'd park on Adelaide Street right in front of the building, and if he couldn't immediately find someone to park it, he'd leave it there, lights on, and usually forget all about it. Inevitably, he'd get a parking ticket. Since he couldn't be at the station 24/7 because he was either studying or at the CFTO studios, or later articling at Tory's, Rogers left copious memos for his staff, leaving instructions.

Bjerre essentially replaced Don Wright, who left in July 1961, unable to connect with a new high-strung boss 22 years his junior. Even with budgetary constraints, CHFI flourished under Bjerre's guidance. Rogers, who was determined to make his radio station Toronto's best, gave him full rein. They hired a full-time news director and news reporters for Ottawa and Washington DC. They built a new control room. Rogers multiplied the budget for LP recordings tenfold. "We had a pretty good news department for a radio station in Toronto at the time in terms of the numbers of people and equipment," says Bjerre. "It was really astounding, and surpassed anything in Toronto at the time. He put a lot of money into it. We had three cruisers. You could broadcast with portable hand-held transmitters from a site to the news van or [a] news cruiser that would transmit back to the radio station. We had a news network going for a while where we were feeding twelve or fifteen stations across the country. It was quite an operation."

As an owner, Rogers didn't interfere with content decisions. "In the whole time I was there, not once did he ever interfere with the news as to what the content should be. I can remember on one occasion a good friend of his—a very prominent person in Toronto—was arrested, I think it was for drunk driving, and he came to me and he said, 'Do we have to put that on the air?' and I said, 'Yes, we do, Ted, because it's going to be on another station. It's going to be in the paper. It's on the public record and we'll look bad if we didn't run it because people knew you hung out in the same group.' So, he said, 'Okay, I see that.' And, we ran it. That was the one and only time in the ten years I was there that he ever, ever mentioned anything about content."

Every Saturday night, a radio technician hauled the necessary equipment from the station five blocks south to the Royal York Hotel in order to broadcast Moxie Whitney's 12-piece orchestra. In the wintertime, when it was bitterly cold, the technician would take a taxicab, which, in those days, cost about two dollars each way. "I can't remember what we paid the operator, maybe five or ten dollars or something," recalls Bjerre. "He'd have to come in on a Saturday night and do this whole damn thing. Ted would look at the bills and say, 'Well, why are we paying him the cab fare? We're paying him to go there. He's got to supply his own transportation.'

"No, no Ted," Bjerre recalls telling him. "You can't expect him to do that and pay for the cab, or the parking. You've got to pay the four-dollar cab fare."

"This was a subject that would come up periodically over two or three years, and yet, there would be things that would involve several hundred thousand dollars, or a quarter of a million dollars and that wouldn't bother him. You could make some very big decisions on your own without any reference to him, and he'd say, 'Oh, gee, that's great.' But, if you decided to spend four dollars, that could plague him for two or three years. He wouldn't worry, sometimes, about the big things, but would worry about the minutiae."

In spite of his efforts, Rogers was losing money hand-over-fist. With AM stations clearly subsidizing their weak FM sisters, Rogers was at a distinct disadvantage without an AM station. To get a handle on FM's prospects, Rogers asked Dr. Byram, who had conducted audience research for the CBC and CFTO, to study the marketplace. His report illustrated the brutal reality: FM wasn't popular, or economical, despite the apparent inroads it was making south of the border. In Metro Toronto, 60,000 households had FM receivers, compared to 400,000 households with AM radios. No advertiser was going to buy airtime on a stand-alone FM station, since the audiences were too small and limited to the so-called audiophiles, or high-fidelity fanatics. People also tended to listen to FM in the evening in their living rooms, whereas the less expensive AM receivers were everywhere—in bedrooms, kitchens and bathrooms. Byram told Rogers the only way to popularize FM was to play FM music on the AM band. Rogers decided to go AM.

Rogers sought to find a spot on the already overcrowded AM band. His engineering consultant, Don Williamson, whom he hired from CFTO-TV, found three useable AM frequencies: 860, 1190 and 1540. They chose 1540 despite that it's an unfavorable spot on the dial, because it required the least amount of land for an antenna system.

Rogers managed to buy 15 acres of farmland at Highway 10 and Burnhamthorpe Road in Mississauga, then a small bedroom community west of Toronto, for $60,000, in order to erect an AM antenna. This was after the city of Toronto refused to lease him land on the Toronto Islands where CHUM and CKFH already had transmitters, in fear that the Islands might "wind up looking like a Texas oilfield." The Islands were the ideal spot because the broadcast signals could be beamed north over the city with no interference from U.S. signals.

Williamson figured that from the Burnhamthorpe site, they could direct a signal north and east on the 1540 kHz AM band to cover most of the greater Toronto area without interfering or colliding with any other signal. But, they couldn't use 1540 at night because they'd create too much interference with other stations, including WKBW in Buffalo, New York, which was blasting its Top 40 format on the nearby 1520 frequency.

Rogers set off for Ottawa in August 1961, even though Canada's Minister of Transport temporarily had prohibited the BBG from granting new broadcasting licenses in cities with second TV stations, ostensibly to protect the newcomers' share of advertising dollars. Arguably, the government wanted a breather from the spotlight after the controversy surrounding the awarding of private TV licenses. Nevertheless, Rogers implored the BBG to allow him to simulcast CHFI-FM on 1540 AM to promote FM music. He stressed he wasn't asking for a "new" station, but rather he just wanted to extend his current FM service. Since the programs were identical, he argued, he wouldn't be taking advertising dollars away from anyone else. He also reminded the board that Canada stood a good chance of losing its frequencies to U.S. border stations if Canada didn't claim them first. As it was, the U.S. border stations were beaming their signals northward, having erected their towers south of Rochester and Buffalo. "This station must be given a chance to compete," he pleaded. "FM-type programming is our present and our future ... This application should, we submit, be allowed under the Board's paramount policy of encouraging FM in Canada, and ... in fairness, new competition has been allowed, affecting our station. It will not affect the audience or revenue, we believe, of existing AM stations."

Although it commended his application, the BBG denied his request. He was forced to wait. Then, five months later, in January 1962—a month before Rogers was to write his bar exams—William "Bill" Bellman, who co-founded CHQM-AM, Vancouver's first FM radio station in 1959 with fellow broadcaster Jack Stark—submitted an application for the 1540 frequency in Toronto. CHQM, named for Quality Music, was known as the "The Good Music Station," serenading Vancouver with beautiful melodies and warm, personable announcers.

Rogers found himself against a formidable opponent and one, he felt, was in cahoots with his old nemesis CFRB. "That was a very tough year," he recalls. Worse, Bellman unearthed an error in Rogers' application. To his dismay, Rogers had breached the so-called 1 percent field-strength rule, which prevented broadcasters from erecting antennas if more than 1 percent of the population in the primary coverage area was unable to receive other signals. Williamson neglected to factor into his calculations the sudden spurt of growth along Burnhamthorpe Rd. and Highway 10, an area that was then still considered Toronto but later was amalgamated into the ever-expanding city of Mississauga.

Rogers had just two weeks before the next BBG public hearing, scheduled for February 6 in Quebec City, to buy more land and relocate his two antenna towers in order to meet the 1 percent rule. On January 17, 1962, with the help of his stepfather, Rogers made the first of several land purchases to increase the size of the property from 15 to 100 acres. The total cost: $335,000—the equivalent of $2.01 million today.

To prepare for the upcoming hearing, Rogers had his CHFI-FM staff put together a program he could air at the hearing. "We were up against Bellman, who was a brilliant programmer," says Rogers. "I thought the only way we were going to fight him is to be good at programming, so we decided to make up a wonderful tape to play at the BBG. The trouble was we only had one control studio. How can you produce a tape when you're on the air? So, we did it during the news slot from 10 to 10:30 p.m. and we recorded [newscaster] Larry Henderson's [report]. We went from the playback machine direct and plugged it into the line to the transmitter, bypassing the console, and we used the console for producing this wonderful tape for the BBG. So, the second night, we were doing that, and at five minutes after ten [p.m.], the phones started to light up. Somebody answered it, and then said to me, 'Ted, we've got a problem. This fellow says we're playing last night's news tonight. What do we do? Do we stop our production?' I said, 'Just keep the tape going. Let the phones ring. Don't answer them. Let's get this bloody tape produced.' And, we did. In this little control room."

Rogers also had a secret weapon: John Lombardi. Lombardi, an Italian-Canadian grocer and radio impresario, introduced foreign-language programming on Allan Waters' CHUM and later Foster Hewitt's CKFH. Lombardi played lead trumpet in the Benny Palmer Orchestra before he went overseas to fight in the Second World War. After returning home a decorated war hero, Lombardi, the unofficial mayor of Toronto's Little Italy, opened a grocery store, but since none of the radio stations played music that he enjoyed, he convinced Waters and Hewitt to give him his own one-hour show, playing Italian music. They agreed so long as he supplied his own advertising. Lombardi swapped advertising time for salami, cottage cheese, and other produce immigrants made at home and sold at his supermarket. Ted Rogers called him at his home one Saturday evening. "I explained who I was," recalls Rogers. "He wouldn't know my name from a hole in the ground. I mentioned a few names of friends of mine who were friends of his." Lombardi invited him to his house. Rogers arrived with the ever-reliable bottle of champagne. And, when Lombardi's wife asked him why he wasn't married yet, Rogers quipped something to the effect of: "Well, I haven't had time. I just graduated from law school and I want to be a broadcaster just like my father."

On February 6, 1962, at the BBG hearings in Quebec City, Rogers proudly announced that John Lombardi had joined CHFI as a director of the board and would oversee three hours a day of ethnic programming. He aired the tape they had produced, the first stereo programming demonstration the board ever heard. Bellman had also produced tapes, but for his own reasons chose not to play them. Rogers also informed the board he'd solved the 1-percent rule issue. CHFI's auditor, A. J. Little, informed the BBG the radio station had lost $192,000 in the previous year and needed to treble its revenue just to get into the black. "CHFI can not continue long as it is," warned Little. "There is a crying economic need for an AM station."

Former Canadian prime minister Brian Mulroney recalls meeting up with Rogers in the bar at Quebec City's Chateau Frontenac Hotel. Mulroney was studying law at Laval University. He remembers being awestruck, as over drinks, Rogers clearly and passionately explained the difference between AM and FM radio, and why FM was going to become the dominant force in radio broadcasting, how he saw the communications business evolving in Canada, and how he hoped to build a great family enterprise.

"He spelled it out," says Mulroney. "He articulated a view of the future of the industry and the role he saw for himself in that in Canada, which was really amazing. Ted was dreaming of convergence before anyone even knew how to spell it."

Rogers won. The BBG allowed him to sell the value of FM to the AM audience. CHFI went live on the AM dial at 1540 kHz on August 8, 1962, simulcasting its FM programs. Listeners tuning into 1540 AM that morning heard Gerry Herbert's *Sunrise Serenade* already in progress on 98.1 FM. Having just sunk $300,000 into an AM station, Rogers for once enjoyed a trouble-free day, giving Toronto mayor Nathan Phillips a tour of the Adelaide St. East studio. "With the enthusiasm of a boy who has assembled his first electric train set, Mr. Rogers toyed with the dials on a complex radio hookup beside his desk," *The Globe and Mail*'s Marvin Schiff wrote. "To explain the differences in quality between the three types of broadcast CHFI offers—AM, regular FM and stereophonic FM, he switched from one to the other, noting the subtle changes in tonal quality."

Rogers told Schiff: "We intend to woo the housewife with FM quality all day so she will press her husband into purchasing an FM set."

In a half-page 1962 newspaper ad for Canadian General Electric, a suit-and-tie clad Rogers proudly showed off "the heart" of CHFI 1540 AM, its 50-kW transmitter, "the finest on the market today," which had been designed and built at Canadian General Electric's Royce Works plant. "From here, for the first time in Canadian broadcasting history, it becomes 50,000 musical watts of

FM programming … entertaining you at 1540 on your regular radio dial. That's right—it's all yours! From sunrise to sunset …"

CHFI 1540, at the top of the AM bandwidth, was a "daytime-only" 50 kW station because it occupied the same frequency as a so-called clear channel. Under the 1941 multilateral treaty governing radio frequency usage in North America, the United States had already assigned 1540 as a clear channel AM station to KXEL in Waterloo, Iowa. Later, KXEL shared the 1540 with ZNS-1 in the Bahamas. On clear channels, only one station, called the "dominant" station, is permitted to broadcast during night-time hours over wide areas, typically within a 1,207-kilometer radius.

That meant Rogers could only broadcast on 1540 AM from dawn to dusk. In the winter when there are fewer daylight hours, 1540 AM had less than 90 minutes of airtime in the key six to nine in the morning time slot. "It was brutal in the wintertime," recalls Bjerre. "You couldn't get on the air until close to eight o'clock and you'd be off the air at four o'clock."

Rogers ran into trouble. He began to lose big name advertisers, including Coca-Cola and Maxwell House. New advertisers shunned the AM station because of its inconsistent on-air times. Rogers also lacked news programming. All of his major radio competitors in Toronto had ties with U.S. networks. CHUM was tied to Mutual Broadcasting Ltd. Westinghouse Inc. was contractually tied to CKEY. At CFRB, Rogers' father had negotiated a deal with William Paley in 1928 to lock up CBS, a relationship that perseveres to this day. After Foster Hewitt's CKFH negotiated a deal with ABC, Rogers wrote to NBC, appealing to them to link up with CHFI-AM, but NBC declined. He developed his own deals, and many big-time names passed through the station, including Arnold Edinborough, the editor, and eventual owner, of *Saturday Night* magazine, and sports writer Dick Beddoes.

Even so, Rogers was making headway. By the end of 1962, CHFI-1540 had 137,600 listeners. But Rogers was also burning through a lot of cash. He had been in the radio business for just two years and his losses already totalled almost half a million dollars. He didn't expect to break even until 1965, and by then, he reckoned his losses would be even higher. He only had one option: expand his AM station into a 24-hour operation.

As 1962 unfolded, Rogers' relationship with John Bassett unravelled. As he fought to win approval for an AM station, Baton's president William Crampton began questioning John Graham's invoices for legal services, and blamed Rogers for stealing two CFTO engineers, Don Williamson and Ron Turnpenny. Bassett's

Baton Broadcasting withdrew its support for Rogers' long-planned radio studios on the roof of the Royal York Hotel, where his father had had studios. CHFI was destined to stay in the cockroach-infested Adelaide St. building.

Williamson, who wasn't especially well liked, although he was politically well connected and widely regarded as an engineering expert, eventually left. He had co-founded in the late fifties, and then owned outright, CHUC-AM in Cobourg, Ontario, east of Toronto.

The late Ron Turnpenny was known as Rogers' "fireman," as former CHFI engineering consultant Gordon Elder describes him. Rogers relied heavily upon Turnpenny. "He was like a bulldog," remembers Cook. "If Ted said to find something and he put Ron on it, Ron would just latch onto it and wouldn't give up bugging people until he had the answer." Or, as Rogers succinctly puts it: "He got things done. He was a character. I liked him very much."

A British émigré, Turnpenny was a slightly pudgy, belligerent man everyone loved even if he drove him or her nuts. "He was the most miserable s.o.b. you could possibly imagine, but brilliant, and he just cared. He cared for everything," says Russ Holden, 680's traffic reporter and the CHFI station's longest-serving employee (aside from Rogers), having joined part-time in January 1966. Holden recalls the day Turnpenny went ballistic in the control room when he noticed a plastic urinal stuck on the wall. Rick Moranis, who went on to become one of Canada's famous comic actors on SCTV and co-starred in such films as *Ghostbusters* and *Spaceballs*, was working at CHFI-FM and had stuck it on the wall as a joke. "You can't do this in the control room," Turnpenny shouted. (Moranis also was a DJ on CFTR for a couple of years in the seventies under the name Rick Allen.)

As chief engineer, Turnpenny oversaw the designing of the antenna arrays and handled the administrative side of the engineering department, while Cook made it happen. "Ray Cook ran the place. He knew more in his little finger about technology than anybody else in his or her entire lifetime," says Holden. "Ray was the unsung hero."

Cook built a special device for the dashboard of Rogers' car, a Chrysler that he leased, so that Rogers could check CHFI's signal strength wherever he was driving. Car FM receivers were rarities back then. "He was listening all the time," says Cook, adding dryly, "Ted did not like dead air."

Since the car was leased, Cook had to make sure the device could be removed without leaving any marks on the leatherette dashboard. He recalls, "I got matching leatherettes to cover up my box to make it look as if it was built by the company, and I tried to use existing screws, or whatever I could.

"Ted would come in and say, 'Why was the signal down in this area?' and you'd have to explain it was because of shielding. He'd send you a memo, saying,

'I was in this guy's office in this building, and I was astounded at the lack of signal we have inside this building. Why is this?' You'd write back and say, 'Well, you're in a salmon can to start with. It's the shield; there's steel all around it. You can't get signals in this building.' And, he might write back, 'How can we fix it?' If you gave a different answer, he'd probably say, 'You go over and fix it.' I was doing this all the time.

"Ted ran everything like a court case," says Cook. "If he had any dead air, or any problems showed up and he caught wind of it, he was the judge, and you better have the paperwork to back it up, or have an answer, and if you didn't, he just kept hammering at you."

Rogers asked Bill Wright, a tall, young broadcasting engineer with Canadian General Electric Co., a unit of General Electric Co., to find an AM frequency in Toronto that could be used for 24-hour AM broadcasting. Wright knew his mission was doomed before he even began. There simply were no open AM frequencies available anywhere in southern Ontario, mostly because of the many U.S. border stations. Wright suggested five possible frequencies in Toronto, all of which had major drawbacks. Only one of the five had the potential of providing a strong signal — 680.

And, even that frequency wasn't perfect, either. Three other stations were already using the 680 band: CHLO in St. Thomas, 205 kilometers southwest of Toronto; CKGB in Timmins, coincidentally, exactly 680 kilometers north of Toronto; and WRVM in Rochester, New York, across Lake Ontario.

Rogers cut a deal with CHLO's owner, Souwesto Broadcasters Ltd., to move CHLO from 680 to 1410, so that he could turn 680 into a Toronto frequency. He agreed to pay CHLO $150,000 to subsidize its costs for switching to 1410. Until CHLO moved, Rogers planned to share 680 kHz on the AM band. He'd just ask listeners to switch from his daytime 1540 to 680 at night. He needed three decisions to go his way. First, CHLO needed the BBG to approve its move to 1410. Second, Rogers would need permission to broadcast on 680 at night; and, third, once CHLO switched frequencies, Rogers would need a 24-hour broadcasting license for 680.

Rogers was taking a calculated risk. He agreed to pay CHLO a lot of money to subsidize the equipment costs of switching frequencies once the BBG approved the transfer, but he had no certainty that he'd win regulatory approval to take over the 680 frequency.

In June 1963, two months after a spring election that saw Prime Minister Diefenbaker defeated by Lester B. Pearson's Liberal Party, the BBG approved CHLO's move to 1410—which freed up 680—but reserved judgment on Rogers' bid to acquire 680, caving in to pressure from CFRB, which publicly accused Rogers of "trafficking" in broadcast licenses. In a letter to the BBG, CFRB's president W. C. Thornton Cran had written that if CHLO "is being paid or indemnified in any way, that is trafficking in radio licenses which, it is respectfully suggested, the board should not permit."

There was no love lost between Rogers and CFRB. Cran's accusations infuriated Rogers. He jotted in his organizer that he felt it was "a low thing and a shame for CFRB, founded by my father, to oppose his son." John Graham told the BBG that Cran's use of the word "trafficking" had been used carelessly, if not deliberately, and was part of a smear campaign. Rogers admits he despised Cran, the man whom he believes stole his father's radio station from his mother, and then had the audacity to exploit his father's name—his surname, his lost legacy—in a failed attempt to win Toronto's first TV license. Rogers took steps to reclaim the family name with his stepfather's help. They incorporated an entity called Rogers Broadcasting Ltd., knowing that Standard Radio would likely sue them for trademark infringement, which it did. When Standard argued the name similarities created confusion among the public, John Graham petitioned the court, retorting that his stepson had the right to operate a business under his own name like any other entrepreneur. His argument prevailed and the court ordered Standard Radio to stop referring to itself as Rogers Radio Broadcasting.

As for the split frequency, Rogers asked the BBG to cut him some slack. With the AM broadcasters, namely CFRB and CHUM, joining the FM spectrum, Rogers implored the regulator for an equal footing to compete on the AM band. He promised two hours of ethnic programming every night—something no other private broadcaster was doing. Regulators, though, disliked so-called split frequencies—using 680 at night and 1540 during the day—because they felt it was an inefficient use of the airwaves. So, the BBG deferred its decision, and worse, it also refused to hold any more hearings regarding the use of 680 in Toronto, day, night or both, before 1964.

In September 1963, Rogers was aboard the *Queen Elizabeth* on his way to London, England to be married to Loretta Anne Robinson when, on his first day at sea, John Graham cabled him to let him know that George McIlraith, the minister of transport in the new Liberal government, had vetoed the BBG's decision permitting CHLO to vacate 680. Rogers immediately cabled back: "In the face of adversity, I do not believe in standing still—an immediate rebound is more to my liking and in the tradition which has built our radio station."

McIlraith was the first minister ever to reverse a BBG decision—and he exercised his veto power not once but twice in the span of three months. He ordered a new hearing to permit an opposing application from his Liberal bagmen friends at CKSL 1290 in London, 25 kilometers north of St. Thomas. All of a sudden, CKSL now wanted 1410 kHz, even though the frequency had been vacant for the past 20 years. According to *Globe and Mail* columnist Dennis Braithwaite, who dubbed the affair "The Frequency Caper," the BBG often receives 11th-hour interventions like CKSL's but usually gives them little credence. McIlraith seemed to think this intervention was important. Why? It turns out that the biggest shareholder in CKSL was the federal Liberal Party's biggest fundraiser: Captain Joseph Jeffrey, the chairman of London Life Insurance Co. and one of London's wealthiest men. CKSL's president was F. Vincent Regan, another Liberal insider.

McIlraith defended his veto, stating he just wanted to make sure the intervener had time to make an opposing application. Months later, he served up another explanation, declaring that frequencies must be open to public bidding and alleging Rogers had secretly concocted a private deal to finance CHLO's move to another frequency. According to Braithwaite, however, the BBG had been fully apprised of the transaction well in advance of the June 1963 hearing. The media had also reported the details of the deal the day before the hearing began.

On the QE, Rogers began writing a brief for a new application. When Rogers arrived at The Savoy in London, he phoned his stepfather, telling him he wanted to proceed with the application to use 680 kHz at night, regardless of whether or not CHLO was allowed to vacate the frequency. CHLO's owners Souwesto ultimately decided to stay on 680 for the time being, and Capt. Jeffrey's CKSL ended up with the 1410 signal.

In the 10 days before his wedding, Rogers worked like a madman. He sent to his stepfather and Bjerre by airmail a detailed plan to win over the BBG. He was specific as to what he wanted: a brief similar to the one they put together in 1960 bound by a multi-ring glossy binder with a baton on the cover. He wanted 30 glossy sheets with printing on both sides. He wanted every senior staff person at CHFI to make personal contact with the regulators. Graham and Bjerre were dispatched to visit the TV columnists at Toronto's three major newspapers to build support for what he was doing. He fired off a memo chastising CHFI employees for the size of the station's telephone bills and cost of their office supplies. Then, after he mailed that missive, he promptly composed another memo, instructing his staff to deliver Christmas presents early to the station's clients and demand that overdue accounts receivable be brought up to date. Four minutes before he left for the church, Rogers signed the material being sent back to Canada.

CHAPTER 5

"The Hardest Fight of My Life"

*"This whole investment really depends on our and Loretta's
personal faith in your integrity and industry, and we feel
confident that you will devote yourself to the affair of CHFI
with a single-mindedness of purpose."*

—Lord Martonmere

ROGERS MET HIS WIFE, Loretta Anne Robinson, just before Christmas
in 1957, while visiting his university Sigma Chi frat brother Ian Henderson in
the Bahamas. Loretta's parents—Sir John Roland and Maysie Robinson—had
invited Ian Henderson to a dinner party in honor of their daughter. Rogers, 24,
was included in their party because he was a house guest. He was immediately
smitten with Loretta, an 18-year-old, vivacious, diminutive brunette, although
he barely spoke two words to her. He spent most of the evening talking to her
father about politics.

Loretta was born on April 13, 1939 in London, England to a British member
of parliament and an American heiress to the Woolworth fortune. Her father,
John "Jack" Roland Robinson, the eldest son of a solicitor, studied law at Trinity
Hall in Cambridge and was called to the Bar by Lincoln's Inn in 1929. At 24, Jack
Robinson was the youngest member of parliament when he entered the House
of Commons in 1931 as the Conservative member for Widnes. A handsome
young man, Robinson transferred his allegiance to his hometown of Blackpool,
a resort town just north of the industrial city of Liverpool, for the 1935 general
election and won. He held his seat for 33 straight years, the longest unbroken
record ever by a British MP.

On July 9, 1930, Robinson wed socialite Maysie Gasque, the daughter of Maude Meacham and Clarence Warren Gasque, in a society wedding amid royalty at the Anglican church of St. Margaret's, Westminster, the parish church of the British Houses of Parliament, on the grounds in Westminster Abbey on Parliament Square. Clarence Gasque had moved his young family to London from New York to help his brother-in-law, Hubert Templeton Parson, expand the five-and-dime Woolworth store chain in the United Kingdom. Maysie Gasque was an acclaimed pianist, spoke fluent French and Italian, and was an accomplished pilot. Her father died, aged 54, before he saw his only child married. Her uncle, Hubert Parson, walked her down the aisle. Parson became president of Woolworth in 1919 after the company's founder and his mentor, Frank Woolworth, unexpectedly died.

Clarence Gasque shared Parson's penchant for opulence, sparing no expense when he commissioned an obscure coach-builder to build a one-of-a-kind Rolls-Royce Phantom I Brougham de Ville for his wife, Maude. He left instructions that the car's interior was to be finished in his favored Louis XV style, and didn't want to see, or hear about the car, dubbed the "Phantom of Love," until it was finished because he wanted to surprise his wife. Outwardly, the car appeared austere but the interior was beautifully and intricately painted; the ceiling depicted pink roses and Amoretti. The bodywork alone is estimated to have cost about £4,500, or £275,000 (almost $600,000) in current dollars.

They had little chance to enjoy the Rolls, because Gasque died 18 months after it was delivered. His widow put the car into storage in 1937 and, when she died in 1952, it was sold. In 2004, after having just two owners, the Rolls-Royce Gasque Phantom I made its first appearance in three decades, as a new owner purchased it for £500,000 ($1.2 million). Widowed Maude, who originally hailed from Chicago, threw herself into the vegetarian and animal welfare movements, even though she could easily have lived in idle luxury. She traveled around the world speaking at symposiums, advocating spiritual and liberal religious understanding. An eccentric woman, Maude Gasque once whisked her granddaughter away on worldwide excursions, often without her parents' knowledge. Loretta's first trip to Canada was with her father and mother on a rail tour of North America.

Loretta's parents were almost killed in a plane crash in France in the summer of 1939 when she was barely three months old. Her mother, a pilot, was critically injured, and her father had surgeons flown in from Britain to save her. As she recuperated in a French hospital, the authorities, fearing war was imminent, told them to leave. Robinson sent his wife, who still carried a U.S. passport, and his two young children to New York to live with Hubert Parson, who died the following year, and his wife, Maysie, who themselves went to live with the Woolworths.

With the family's assets tied up in Britain because of the war, the Robinsons were obliged to live off the Woolworths. Loretta and her older brother, Richard, spent almost seven years with the Woolworths on Fifth Avenue. But, as soon as she was able, Loretta's mother returned to London to help with the war effort. She aided the British troops in Rome by working as an Italian translator.

In 1940, Loretta's father joined the Royal Air Force (RAF) Volunteer Reserve, where he attained the rank of wing commander, and served in the United Kingdom, Italy and other Mediterranean countries. He was also a liaison to the American Eagle Squadron attached to the RAF and became an officer of the U.S. Legion of Merit, a U.S. armed forces military decoration awarded for exceptional meritorious conduct. Robinson was a frequent speaker in the House of Commons. Since he had an extensive knowledge of American affairs, he was joint deputy chairman and one of the founders of the British-American Parliamentary Group. He was knighted in 1954 and elevated to the peerage as Baron Martonmere in 1964.

From 1964 until 1972, Lord Martonmere served as the governor and commander-in-chief of Bermuda, where he oversaw the establishment of the British colony's parliamentary government and its first constitution. Since he spent more time as governor than anyone else had since the late eighteenth century, Lord Martonmere was enormously popular on the island. He genuinely took an interest in people, rich or poor, and made them feel comfortable in his presence.

While Loretta's father had the common touch, her mother intimidated most people. She was a concert pianist, who never played after she married because her commitments as a wife to a prominent politician meant she couldn't put in the hours of practicing time necessary for a perfect performance. "She scared me actually," says Senator Trevor Eyton. "She was so proper. She was very formidable. She was Lady Martonmere. And, he was jolly." Fortunately for Rogers, Loretta's mother and Velma Rogers Graham—two strong-willed women—got on extremely well with each other.

Loretta bounced between the family homes in Lyford Cay in the Bahamas and Tucker's Town in Bermuda—two of the West Atlantic's most exclusive areas—and in London. She spent her formative years at Graham-Eckles, a private boarding school in Palm Beach, Florida, before attending the esteemed women's school Wellesley College in Massachusetts, arguably the Queen of the Seven Sisters—seven liberal arts women's colleges in the northern United States—and one of only two that stayed all female, but the sun-loving young woman didn't like the school's haughty attitude and transferred to the University of Miami, where she received a Bachelor of Fine Arts degree. A talented painter, Loretta continued her studies in London at the prestigious Byam Shaw School of Art.

Born into a home of wealth and privilege, Loretta is a demure, unassuming, although strong-willed lady who wears her wealth well. She has the gracious manners of a Brit and her voice, deep-toned and earthy from years of smoking, carries a trace of an American accent. She's inseparable from her father, and learned at his knee how to be sociable with people from all walks of life. Among her friends, she's the worst gossip. She's a party girl. On her 60th birthday, celebrated on their custom-made yacht, the *Loretta Anne*, she delighted and astonished her husband and guests by dressing up as a five-year-old Raggedy Ann doll with pigtails and miniskirt. She is a perfect foil to her husband. Unlike him, Loretta can talk on any subject for five minutes, or more if she so chooses. She's blunt and candid with a self-described *que sera sera* attitude. "There's no point worrying over things you can't change," she says.

Rogers ran the business; Loretta ran the family. She was also his sounding board, off of which he crystallized his ideas. She may not be vocal at board meetings, but she doesn't hesitate to speak her mind at home. "Oh, I tell him what I think," she says.

Loretta brought Rogers, renowned for his quick temper, to heel shortly after their honeymoon. He quickly learned not to bring his frustration home. "I established that right away," she says. "I would just say, 'When you are prepared to be civilized, I will speak to you.' I'd go into the bedroom and shut the door. It worked. He stopped it. I should do it more often, because I always got flowers the next day. Sometimes, you need more flowers. I just didn't like fighting."

No one in Toronto hosts more parties than Loretta Rogers. "She does an awful lot for Ted," says Peggy Hull, Toby Hull's first wife and a Seagram. "To this day, Ted tells her that she doesn't entertain enough. There's only one person in all of Toronto that entertains all the time, and that's Loretta Rogers."

After a six-year courtship, on September 25, 1963, Ted Rogers and Loretta Robinson were married at St. Margaret's Church in Westminster, where Loretta's parents had wed. "Oh my God, it was just beautiful," recalls the Matron of Honor, Peggy Hull, who at the time was married to Toby Hull. "Loretta looked beautiful, showing the most happiness I'd ever seen in a bride. It was just a whirlwind with a couple of dinners and parties." While Rogers and his bride were on their honeymoon at the famous Treetops Hotel in Kenya, his stepfather, John Graham, reapplied to the BBG to use 680 at night.

Graham noted to the BBG that its decision to defer Rogers' application to broadcast on 680 kHz in Toronto at night was no longer valid since McIlraith refused to approve CHLO's application to vacate the frequency. He also reminded the regulator that CHFI alone had figured out how to broadcast 680 at night while CHLO used 680 during the day. He also stressed that CHFI, unlike its competitors, started life on the FM band. Unlike his rivals, who had lucrative AM advertising dollars at their disposal to subsidize their FM sisters, Rogers didn't have a 24-hour AM station to finance his fledgling FM operation. He desperately needed this split frequency, 1540 dawn-to-dusk and 680 at night.

Rogers did something many newly married men wouldn't dream of doing: he cut short his honeymoon to head back to Ottawa with his bride to plead his case in person for a split frequency. He grimaces at the memory some 40 years later, although he acknowledges if he had to do it all over again, he still would've cut short their honeymoon. "I feel badly about it," says Rogers. "But, you had to do what you have to do."

He cut short his honeymoon to appear before the BBG to take questions from the BBG counsel, such as: "There will be a period, though, Mr. Rogers, perhaps in the fall and in the springtime when you will have to make this switch in the middle of shaving. This might be inconvenient."

"We actually foresee no problem   I must be frank, the type of listeners who listen to good music, who like a restrained commercial policy and authoritative news and comment, are above average intelligence, and we believe they will have no problem with this," said Rogers.

"Do they have beards?"

"I may say our survey does not disclose how many people have sets in their bathrooms, either," John Graham replied.

"Well, I was thinking of having to run out of the bathroom down to the bedroom to turn the set over because it had gone off. This was inconvenient," the BBG's counsel said.

Cutting his honeymoon short worked. In October 1963, Rogers received permission to broadcast 680 at night with a power of 10 kW. "I remember we couldn't get a very good hotel room in Ottawa," says Rogers. "We got this crummy little room that wasn't heated, and I got a cold. We were applying for 680 night to work with 1540 day, and obviously, it was an idiotic idea," says Rogers. "It's obviously an incredibly foolish idea. The breakfast period and drive period at night are the two prime times in radio, and when you come on in January and February at a quarter to eight in the morning and prime time starts at six, it's a bit of a problem, and when you turn off your station at a quarter to five at night before people even get out of the office for the drive home, this is a real problem. Those were difficult things to do, I guess like beating the Yankees is today."

Less than six months after their wedding, Loretta told her father she wanted to financially back her husband's career. He agreed, albeit reluctantly, to advance to her $450,000—in current dollars, $2.9 million. Lord Martonmere issued a stern warning to his son-in-law: "This whole investment really depends on our and Loretta's personal faith in your integrity and industry, and we feel confident that you will devote yourself to the affair of CHFI with a single-mindedness of purpose."

Loretta was now a full-fledged business partner. She became a director of the parent company, Edward S. Rogers Ltd., the successor company to Aldred Rogers Ltd., and its subsidiary, Rogers Broadcasting Ltd., which owned CHFI. Her father advanced the money on the condition that they never mortgage their Forest Hill home, which they later did, not once but twice, although they never told her parents. She has as much on the line as her husband.

Even as he fought for 680, Rogers was still obsessed with taking over CFRB, that is, until Loretta put an end to it. "I told him he couldn't," she says. "He could have bought it, and I said, 'No. You and your people built up CHFI. They've put so much into it. You can't. That's the one that's yours. That's the one everyone put his or her heart and soul into. The other one was too long ago.' Well, he realized when I put it that way that it wouldn't be fair to anyone to walk away from CHFI."

He put that dream behind him and marched on. CFRB ruled the airwaves. He was bound and determined to challenge its pre-eminence by making CHFI-FM, and its AM sister, if he could only get a decent AM frequency, into Toronto's most listened to and respected radio stations at any cost.

In March 1964, for the 11th time in four years, Rogers appeared before the BBG. This time, he sought permission to beam his FM signal vertically on 210 kW, using so-called effective radiated power (ERP). He was already powering at that voltage on horizontal FM radio waves. Now, he sought vertical polarization, which was just emerging as a way of improving FM signals in apartment buildings and on car radios. FM was growing in popularity, with 40 percent of Torontonians listening to FM radio by the fall of 1964. If reception improved, Rogers hoped to create demand for tabletop FM sets and car radios, which were then expensive extras with disappointing sound quality. As an advertising gimmick, he called it "vertipower."

However, the BBG limited CHFI-FM to 100 kW after the FCC complained. For the next year, Rogers determinedly fought the FCC on the interpretation of the rules since they weren't clear. Was it 100 kW vertically, horizontally or combined? "We got ourselves into a tremendous row with the American government and the FCC," he told the Monetary Times. He retained U.S. lawyers and engineering consultants to fight the FCC. Although aliens are not allowed to intervene on U.S. domestic matters, Rogers' lawyers found a loophole so that he could personally present his case to the U.S. government. He succeeded in getting the FCC's proposed rule-making revoked, which cleared the way for him to reapply to the

BBG. In June 1965—15 months later—Rogers reapplied for, and was granted a month later, 210 kW ERP vertical polarization. Rogers spent a costly $100,000 fighting the regulatory battle. Says Cook, "They allowed the doubling of the power after a great hassle. It's an expensive way to get more power."

His engineers added, with some difficulty, the new rigging to the CFTO-TV tower. "They had antenna problems one night. I think Channel 9 did, too," recalls Loretta Rogers, "but it was icy and they wanted to climb the bloody tower at about two in the morning. So, we put some coffee out, and stayed with the guys for a while. Ted was quite hands on. He was very good when it was small. He knew everyone, and so did I."

Rogers still faced engineering hurdles on the 680 AM front. A full year after being authorized for night-time broadcasting on 680, he still wasn't on the air at night. To attract advertisers, who were growing disillusioned with his promises of increased power and reach, Rogers desperately needed a 24-hour AM station. All of his AM rivals operated on 50 kW. At the very least, he needed to match their power, if not go higher, but his engineers still hadn't figured out how to configure 680's daytime power so that it didn't encroach on the St. Thomas and Rochester 680 signals.

Rogers called industry expert A. Earl Cullum in Dallas on a Saturday afternoon. Cullum served during the Second World War as the communications consultant to U.S. and British military units, for which he received the Presidential Certificate of Merit. Cullum, renowned for solving problems for radio stations, bluntly told Rogers it was impossible. Rogers refused to accept his opinion, insisting Cullum meet with his engineers to discuss the matter. The next day, Ron Turnpenny and Bill Wright, the General Electric consulting engineer, met Cullum in a Dallas motel room. Cullum reiterated it couldn't be done; it was impossible for CHFI-AM to radiate a signal on 680 kHz at 50 kW of power without encroaching on WRVM Rochester. What they were proposing was to create a transmission pattern for 680 that was tighter than anything that existed in the United States. It just wasn't possible at 50 kW. For the next three days, they debated the conundrum. On the plane home, Wright wrote up his report, concluding that the only option was to get Rochester off 680.

"Rogers was certainly imaginative," says Bjerre. "I think one of the things that helped him was that he really had no background in broadcasting, and so he questioned everything—things that had been done for decades in broadcasting that we didn't even think about. This is just the way it's done. He'd question everything.

"He used to drive us crazy at times. Someone like myself, who had been in the business for many, many years, would be doing something, and we'd get into some heated discussions over why we were doing it this way. He would never accept the 'Well, it's always been done this way' logic of it. It sometimes made life a little difficult."

In June 1964, Rogers asked the BBG for a 24-hour 680 radio station, to cover just Metro Toronto. He fought to keep the 1540 daytime signal to blanket southern Ontario. Though he won his 680 application, the BBG denied his request to keep 1540 until he was ready to go live on 680 daytime. Well, he didn't like that decision.

Rogers didn't want to give up 1540. He couldn't afford to. For one thing, his engineers were still working on the transmission site for 680. He was limited to 1 kW of daytime power on 680 kHz to protect the daytime-only St. Thomas and Rochester 680 AM stations. With just 1 kW on 680 day, he reckoned he'd be able to reach a potential audience of 1.7 million people in Metro Toronto. By contrast, with 50 kW on 1540 day, CHFI reached 3.1 million people.

As the engineers worked diligently on designing 680's tower arrays, another problem cropped up. Cullum, who helped craft 680's pattern of transmission, discovered that Ontario Hydro's nearby electricity towers were reradiating the 680 signal, wildly distorting their radiation pattern. "It was a decade of trials and errors," says retired engineer Gordon Elder, now 79 years old. "We were breaking new ground."

While Rogers persuaded Ontario Hydro to lift and insulate the hydro wires, he decided the station might be better off looking for an alternative transmission site. In December 1964, two days after Rogers and Loretta sailed for Bermuda to spend Christmas with Loretta's parents, John Graham bought 106 acres of farmland—well away from the hydro towers—across the road from the 1540 site for $499,431, or roughly $5,000 an acre. Rogers gasped at the price. (But, the property turned out to be extremely valuable. He sold the land to his company five years later at its appraised value of $1.5 million, using it to borrow $1.25 million from the Bank of Montreal to support his fledgling cable business. Two years later, the property doubled in value. Rogers would repeatedly mortgage the site to finance future deals.)

Most radio stations have two-, four- or six-tower arrays—not Rogers'. Over the next year, employing some of the best engineering talent he could find, Rogers erected what looked like a missile launching pad on 107 acres—nine towers, each 94 meters tall, and raised counterpoises, less than a meter from the ground and 21 meters in diameter around each tower. "It was terribly complicated," says Bjerre. "You had to get some very expensive and complicated antenna arrays."

"It was a fantastic engineering feat," Rogers told the *Monetary Times*. "Some of this engineering work is pure research … The 680 engineering installation is unique in this country and one of the most extraordinary in North America."

Rogers recalls other minor problems that cropped up. "We could not get a building permit in Mississauga. So I said to [Ron] Turnpenny, 'Build it anyway. We'll get the building permit somehow.' So, we put the towers up. We put the building up, and the plumbing inspector came in and said to Turnpenny, 'Where is it?'

"'Where's what?'

"'I've got to fill in this form. I've got to write in the building permit number.'

"Turnpenny says, 'Well, actually, it fell down on the floor and the dog ate it.' The guy says, 'What are you talking about? Anyway, you'd have copies of it.'

"Before the night was over, Turnpenny was in jail. And, John Graham had to go and get him out," says Rogers. "Many years later, we were moving 680 over to Grimsby [near Niagara Falls]. I was trying to build thirteen towers. The last thing Grimsby wanted was thirteen towers, so they wouldn't give us the permit. They wouldn't even give us the permit to put a tower up to test it. Turnpenny got an idea, he got a flatbed truck and he put the tower on the truck and then he backed the truck onto the property, so the tower was not on the ground and they couldn't stop the testing. The test passed and the Department of Communications said to the City, you must allow it to happen [to protect the other stations] and so we were able to get the permit. That's what you go through.

"So, when these guys come to me [today] with relatively minor problems, like they can't get this and can't get that … they come to me, and say they couldn't get in this building, which had the equipment; it's owned by somebody else. I said, 'Well just tear down the door. It's simple. And take the stuff out, and move it somewhere else. And, by the time they get the complaint that the door's torn down, what the hell are they going to do about [it]?'"

It was time for Rogers to drop 1540. As far as the BBG was concerned, 680 was technically feasible so Rogers couldn't hold onto 1540 any longer. He had to vacate the frequency. *Globe* columnist Dennis Braithwaite wrote that he expected several bidders. But Rogers already had one lined up, or so he believed. In return for helping him, Rogers had promised John Lombardi the first opportunity to buy 1540 if he ever planned to sell it or move onto another frequency. Lombardi, though, was now reticent about making the purchase. Rogers, charm on full blast, managed to persuade him into making the acquisition. By the end of 1965, Rogers closed the sale of 1540, including the land in Mississauga, to Lombardi, who a year later received the BBG's approval to establish CHIN 1540 AM, Canada's first multilingual radio station, playing primarily Italian music.

"When we got 680 full time, we got off the 1540 frequency, and I just assumed it would go back into the public domain, and Rogers said, 'Oh no, we'll sell that,'" recalls Bjerre. "I said, 'But you've been given 680 and you're getting off 1540. Hell, they're not going to let you sell it.' Well, as sure as hell, he applied to sell it to Johnny Lombardi for his ethnic station and it was approved. It is amazing. Most people would have thought it would just go back into the public domain."

Since first applying for the 1540 frequency in August 1961, Rogers had spent more than $1 million to establish himself in AM radio. In the five years since 1960, Rogers appeared 15 times before the BBG. John Graham was at his side each time, stickhandling the proceedings. "It would almost be a letdown now to hold a hearing without Ted Rogers appearing," BBG vice-chairman Carlyle Allison remarked.

His quest for an AM frequency was enough to drive one to drink, or smoke. For Rogers, it induced him to stop smoking. "I was lying upstairs in bed coughing and spewing, and I just thought I would lose the business if I didn't get out of bed and get to work. So, I stopped smoking," says Rogers, who quit in 1966 at age 33.

On March 28, 1966—a year after he received permission to broadcast on 680—CHFI signed off 1540 AM and began simulcasting its FM programs on 680 AM, 24 hours a day—three years after Rogers first sought the 680 frequency.

CHFI 680 AM was the reverse of most AM stations. During the day, 680 broadcast on 1 kW to protect the daytime St. Thomas and Rochester 680 signals. At night, it jacked up its power, just as its rival stations powered down. AM stations power down at night because if every AM station kept its daytime operating power at night, there'd be massive interference due to an ionospheric phenomenon known as "skywave" propagation. During daylight hours, AM signals travel over the earth's surface, known as "groundwave" propagation. Hence, AM service is generally limited to a radius of no more than 162 kilometers, even for the most powerful stations. At night, AM signals are reflected off the ionosphere, just like a mirror, traveling hundreds of kilometers. As such, Rogers couldn't expand his reach outside Metro Toronto.

The main problem was WRVM 680, right across Lake Ontario in Rochester. The owner was Chicago native Milton Maltz. A former disc jockey, Maltz had served in the United States Navy and worked for the National Security Agency in Washington DC. After buying his first radio station in 1956, Maltz parlayed that investment into Cleveland, Ohio-based Malrite Communications Group Inc., eventually owning several radio and TV stations in major U.S. markets, including New York and Los Angeles. The first time Maltz heard of Ted Rogers was when he received a notice from the FCC saying that Rogers was challenging his right to broadcast on 680.

Technically, WRVM was a sunrise-to-sunset station, but in the wintertime, it began broadcasting at six in the morning, well before sunrise, to cater to morning commuters. Maltz sought help from the FCC, which told him there wasn't anything it could do to help him, other than slow the process, which it did. Maltz later changed the station's call letters to WNYR, transforming it into a country music station billed as the "Clear Channel 680" to garner U.S. regulatory support, even though it technically wasn't a clear channel.

Rogers wouldn't accept that this nondescript radio station in Rochester could wreak such havoc with his plans to expand 680's reach. He felt that the United States had licensed far too many radio stations along the U.S.-Canadian border, creating an overcrowding of frequencies. Rochester had just as many radio stations as Toronto, but population-wise, it was only a third of its size. He hired legal expertise in Washington to work on the file. "I had huge books on the rules," he says. He even bought an 80-acre farm outside of Rochester—that stood vacant for years—to make it more convenient for Maltz to move the station's transmitter. "I owned a farm in Rochester for years," guffaws Rogers.

Rogers tried to negotiate with Maltz, going so far as to get face time with him by boarding Maltz' Detroit-to-DC flight at the stopover in Cleveland and squeezing himself into the open middle seat beside Maltz and his partner. "I decided I would get on this plane and try to talk sense to him," says Rogers. "The plane landed, and I come up the stairs, and they're sitting in the front row with a vacant seat in the middle. I plop down in the middle seat. That night at the hotel, Maltz took his shoe off—like [Soviet Union Premier Nikita] Khrushchev—and pounded the table: 'You're hounding me. You're following me. I can't even get on a plane, and you're beside me.' I said, 'Milton, this is good for both of us.'

"You do what you have to do," says Rogers. "It was in the way."

Since Maltz and Rogers, as radio station owners, were stewards of public licenses belonging to their respective governments, they weren't actually allowed to negotiate with each other—that's why Rogers boarded the plane. "Once we were over international waters, we could chat," recalls Maltz. "Ted just refused to give up. He was driven and determined to get that station on 50,000 watts and nothing was going to stand in his way. We were just kids, crazy kids in the broadcast business."

Maltz remembers Rogers expressing to him his fear he wouldn't live long enough to build the company. He only had until 1972, when he would turn 39, the same age at which his father died. "I've got this thing. I've got to build this company before I hit this wall," Maltz recalls Rogers telling him. "I've got to get this done before I hit that birthday because I don't know if I'm going to make it or not."

"Ah, Ted. You will make it. Just let your mind be the control room to your body, and your mind is great," Maltz told him.

"He was so worried," Maltz recalls. "He was a dynamite guy, a great personality, intelligent and very caring. I was really concerned about him."

In the end, Rogers solved the dilemma by paying the other stations to get off 680. In 1970, seven years after his ill-fated deal with CHLO in St. Thomas, Rogers paid the station to switch to 1570 kHz. Rogers charmed Milton Maltz into starting a Rochester FM station on 101.3 kHz in 1966, allowing him to pull back on his daytime signal to permit CHFI 680 greater range. To prevent his signal from interfering with Maltz' 680, his engineers tuned the signal so that it couldn't be picked up beyond the middle of Lake Ontario. In the mid-seventies, high-rise buildings (eight storeys high) sprang up around the Mississauga 680 transmission site, reradiating the signal so that it interfered quite heavily with Maltz' revamped country music station, WNYR 680 in Rochester. Rogers ultimately relocated the 680 transmitter site to Grimsby, Ontario, on the south shore of Lake Ontario, near Niagara Falls. In spite of the town's backlash to his plans (court approval was sought), Rogers built eight 300-foot towers on an 83-acre site.

In the spring of 1980, Maltz finally vacated 680 altogether and moved to a Canadian clear channel, 990 kHz on the AM band, using a directional antenna to protect a Montreal station already on that frequency. With the help of his stepfather, Rogers orchestrated the deal, which involved Canadian and U.S. governments. The United States was given 990, a Canadian clear channel, in exchange for deleting 680 off of its list of channel assignments. Rogers then powered up 680 to 50,000 watts. In 1984, Rogers moved one more station, paying CKGB Timmins to switch from 680 to 750 kHz.

"I moved more people to another frequency than anybody else in history," laughs Rogers. "We got 680 day, which we planned to, but that was the hardest project I ever had. I worked so hard on that, the hardest of anything in my life. 680 was the hardest fight of my life."

When Rogers learned rival CKEY was going to broadcast live traffic reports from two helicopters, he told his troops to beat them to the punch. Fortunately, Bjerre had just finalized a deal to lease two Hughes 300 choppers for $200,000 a year, but the station didn't have the necessary two-way radios or the antenna installed to handle the trafic reports. Rogers called Ray Cook at home late one night to tell him he had four days to pull it altogether.

"What a hell of a job," sighs Cook. "I worked in the aircraft industry, so I was familiar with what was required, but getting the radio equipment ... I had to borrow equipment from Motorola. I could only get certain types. The lead-time is, like, six months to get radios after you ordered them, and I had four days to get something up. And, the signal was boxed in by the high-rises, so you couldn't get decent reception anywhere, even from the Imperial Life building, so we had to bring the helicopters in close enough—five or six miles—for the antenna to pick up the announcers."

CKEY, which, unlike Rogers, bought its helicopters, failed to meet its scheduled on-air debut after a delay in getting their second chopper in from Montreal. Cook says Maclean Hunter's CKEY attempted to steal the spotlight from CHFI by sending up two announcers in one helicopter to do the rush-hour traffic reports, pretending as if they really had two choppers in the air in different locations.

Cook got the job done. On Thursday, April 18, 1968, CHFI was airing traffic reports from two helicopters, three days before CKEY finally got its second chopper airborne. Even though CFRB had been using one traffic helicopter regularly since 1961, CHFI was Canada's first station to use two. Upon hearing the live traffic reports on CHFI, Rogers was beyond ecstatic. "The first time we had two helicopter reports on the air, one right after the other, before CKEY, Rogers literally was jumping up and down in the hallway. He was so excited," says Russ Holden.

CHFI had been airing its traffic reports for two weeks when Cook just happened to walk into the federal department of transport [DOT] office across the street where three inspectors cornered him. "You know, you're operating two helicopters with no license, and that's illegal," he was told.

Cook stared at them dumbfounded. "I haven't been handling it, but I know there's licenses for ground."

"Yes, but you need another license, a maritime mobile license to broadcast from the helicopters, and you don't have it."

Cook stood there, stunned. His life flashed in front of him. "They might as well have shot me on the spot because I didn't have an answer for them. I could have crawled underneath the counter because one of the things you don't want to do is piss them off because they can yank your license. I thought, oh my God. I can't go back to Ted and say, 'You're off the air.' I had to solve this instantly. Right now. Ted would've killed me if he knew. Nobody knew about the license, and I hadn't been handling it."

Cook recalls asking, "If I get the application in and the money after lunch, can we stay on the air temporarily until we get the license sorted out?" The three inspectors went into an adjoining room and closed the door. When they emerged from their powwow, the DOT manager said, "Get your application in right away."

Cook raced back, heading straight for Vaughn Bjerre's office. The two men huddled. Cook said he'd fill out the form, go to accounting and get the money and then Bjerre could sign off on the application. As Cook did the paperwork, he realized he had another potentially disastrous problem. He had to disclose, truthfully, the wattage of power they were using on their helicopter radios. The regulator only permitted five watts of power. They were using two radios, one that exceeded the allowed range, and was therefore illegal, and the other, below. Playing it safe to ensure the paperwork wouldn't be rejected, Cook jotted down three watts, the lesser of their two radio powers. (For years afterwards, he received flak for putting down the lower number.) Two hours later, he ran across the street and slapped the application down on the counter, along with the money—"because it's really the money they're worried about." The inspectors checked it over and said, "Okay, you can stay on the air."

Cook let out a huge sigh of relief.

"Ted does not know about it, not even to this day. If they had shut us down, everybody would have been in real big trouble, because that's the kind of thing Ted likes to sink his teeth into. He would have gone orbital."

For eight months, CHFI listeners heard a U.S. trucking dispatcher, in a Georgia twang, shouting instructions during 680's traffic reports: "Truck Number Eight, you better get over to ..." CHFI 680's traffic reporters were using the same frequency that belonged to a U.S. heavy-equipment company. Rogers persuaded the U.S. trucking company to stay off the air on the half-hour during the morning and afternoon rush-hour traffic reports until CHFI could find another frequency. However, the DOT kept insisting there weren't any frequencies available. Finally, under Rogers' incessant complaints, the government ran the frequencies through their computers, and lo and behold, managed to find 20 free frequencies.

"It was a zoo. It went on like this every day, with problems," says Cook. "It was like pushing an elephant every day, and Rogers was pushing the elephant, too."

680 CHFI-AM was on a roll. It outbid rival CFRB in 1969 for the right to broadcast two seasons of the Toronto Argonauts football games, a coup for the fledgling station. For the previous 24 years, the Argo games were heard exclusively on CFRB. But, when listeners kept getting confused between CHFI-FM and CHFI-AM, Rogers changed the AM station's call letters in 1971 to 680 CFTR, which stands for "Canada's First Ted Rogers" to honor his late father's accomplishments. After boosting 680's power, he didn't want new listeners to get his stations mixed up. "People used to look for the Argos [his big AM attraction] on FM and for *Candlelight and Wine* on AM," Rogers told *The Globe and Mail*. "We were darned if we were going to have the confusion spread to the new audience."

It was sheer happenstance that they came up with the CFTR call letters. "We ran every combination [of call letters] possible through the computer [at the IBM Centre] and came up with CFTR, and I looked at it and I thought, 'Jesus—TR, Ted Rogers.' We ran the name past him and, of course, he was delighted with it," recalls Bjerre.

They adopted the new call letters on Rogers' late father's birthday, June 21. His mother, Velma, who died some five months later from cancer, lived long enough to see her son fulfill her wishes with this public tribute: "Every time we plug our radios into our wall socket and with the flick of a dial enjoy today's popular music, news and sports programs, we have reason to be grateful to the late Ted Rogers," full-page ads, proclaiming the new CFTR, said. "... [T]here is no better day of the year for CFTR's Ted Rogers to honour his illustrious father, and to pledge to you, the listener, that the same pioneering spirit that started back in the '20s will continue in the '70s right here at the new CFTR." Over the next three decades, Rogers, and his staff, knowing his wishes, timed announcements of the family's sizeable charitable donations, or annual shareholders' meetings, to occur on his deceased father's birthdays.

Bjerre came up with the idea of throwing a party to mark the occasion. On the evening of June 21, 1971, Rogers welcomed 3,000 people, including his bankers and the city's entire advertising community, at Casa Loma, a medieval-styled castle with plush gardens in the heart of city. While the invitation read from 5:30 until 7:30 in the evening, the party lasted until dawn. Trumpeter Bobby Gimby's band performed—broadcast live on CFTR. Pipe bands welcomed guests as they arrived. The station's two traffic helicopters were parked on the Casa Loma lawn. Rogers chartered a Canadian Pacific jet to fly in buyers and advertising agents from Montreal. Most of everything provided was "contra," where they exchanged the goods and services for unused airtime. The champagne—some 1,000 magnums obtained in a contra deal with one of the Canadian vineyards— flowed like Niagara Falls. The bottles were stuck into a gigantic ice sculpture. The station's radio announcers kept the glasses topped up with the champagne, which apparently was horrible, although that didn't stop anyone from drinking it. "A lot of people got terribly drunk," recalls Bjerre. "It was a monumental party, and it was the kind of thing that appealed to Ted, because it was done on a big, magnificent scale, and he liked that kind of thing."

ACT TWO

CABLE

CHAPTER 6

The Cable Guy

"Ted, it's really simple. There's no magic to it. Just give your customers more—more and better. Give them more channels and better reception, and they'll have something to buy."

—Owen Boris

ON A LATE SUMMER EVENING IN 1966, Ted Rogers was standing in the middle of the street outside his Forest Hill home with his friend Burke van Valkenburg. They were staring at the stacked array of six Yagi antennas protruding from his rooftop TV tower. When Loretta's parents bought the newlyweds their beautiful pale-colored two-storey brick-and-stucco house at 3 Frybrook Rd. in 1963, the Christie House, as it was known, came with a 9.1-meter-high pole mounted on the center of the roof right above the front door. Four unsightly guy wires ran to the roof eves to hold the contraption down. The Yagis—unidirectional antennas—strategically pointed in various directions, picking up signals from six different local and stateside channels. "It was big, ugly and highly visible from the driveway," says van Valkenburg, who recalls thinking to himself rather wryly that the house reminded him of one of those tarpapered shacks along the freeway outside of Detroit, the ones with the gigantic TV antennas in the front yards and Cadillacs parked in the driveway.

"Ted, see all these antennas on the top of your house?" pointed out van Valkenburg. "You can get rid of them and hook up to cable television. It's running right past your house."

"Why would I want to bother, Burke?" shot back Rogers.

"Well, because you'll get rid of all of this mess on top of your roof," he answered.

Rogers pondered his comment for a minute before saying, "Burke, I guess we don't know how well off we are."

Not one to be put off, van Valkenburg told him to think it over. Van Valkenburg, an amateur radio enthusiast, was then working as a wholesale radio/television electronics parts salesman and learned from his contacts that people were starting to scramble to get into the cable TV business. "You don't have to do anything with the license," he pleaded, "but, just grab it before somebody else does."

Famous Players Canadian Corp., the U.S.-controlled movie-theater chain, pioneered cable TV in Toronto. The company, through its subsidiary, Metro Cable TV Ltd., offered cable TV service in Forest Hill and Rosedale, two of the city's most affluent neighborhoods where residents could afford to buy color television sets and pay their monthly cable bills. Rogers had a Metro Cable TV cable running right past his home.

Toronto was a forest of antennas. Six-to-twelve-meter-high antennas were mounted on rooftops, all of them pointed south to Buffalo, New York. The building boom in high-rises and color programming spurred demand for cable TV service. With signals ricocheting off apartment buildings, city dwellers saw double, sometimes triple images, of variety show host Ed Sullivan, *Bonanza* actor Lorne Greene or newscaster Walter Cronkite and, while somewhat tolerable in black and white, watching multiple shadows in color was virtually dizzying. Worse, when the skyscrapers went up, distant U.S. signals were blocked out entirely. Cable solved that problem.

Color TV had been available in the United States since 1953, the year the Federal Communications Commission (FCC) set the final standards. An episode of the popular police drama *Dragnet* was the first-ever color program aired. Live colorcasts followed, including the 1954 Tournament of Roses Parade and the 1955 World Series between the New York Yankees and Los Angeles Dodgers. Color TV was slow to gain mass appeal, plagued with rivaling technology standards, much like high-definition TV today. As the technology improved and prices for color sets fell, the only barrier preventing consumers from buying color sets was the sheer lack of color programming. Sales of color TV sets skyrocketed after *Walt Disney's Wonderful World of Color* premiered in December 1961. A year later, *The Flintstones* and *The Jetsons*, both color-animated cartoons, aired.

In 1966, the year NBC went all color, the BBG permitted color broadcasts, 13 years behind the United States. On September 1, 1966, CFTO-TV, the flagship of the newly created CTV Network, aired a one-hour special in color to mark the occasion, with appearances from BBG chairman Andrew Stewart and Canada's secretary of state Judy La Marsh. The CBC, which was dead-set against color, ushered in this new era by showing a previously broadcast colorized black-and-white 30-minute bronco-busting documentary. Rogers' former partner, Joel Aldred, might have blown the budget, but he ensured that CFTO-TV was ready to broadcast in color at the flick of a switch. The CBC didn't switch over to full color until 1974.

Cable took off in Canada as a way of getting U.S. channels. The industry, then called "community antenna television" (CATV), literally an antenna serving a community—the broadcasters pejoratively used the term "cat-vee"—percolated along the border wherever U.S. signals could be pulled out of the air and delivered to the home through coaxial cable. In a CATV system, it's also possible to transmit directly over the cable without receiving any signal from the air—called "cablecasting" or "program origination." The earliest CATV pioneers—plumbers, television salesmen and electricians—emerged across Canada, including Edwin R. (Ed) Jarmain in London, Ontario; George Chandler in Vancouver, British Columbia; Sydney Welsh in Vancouver, British Columbia; Fred Metcalf in Guelph, Ontario; Omar Girard in Magog, Quebec; and Ed Polanski in Thorold, Alberta. The early pioneers started out of their garages. In Montreal, U.K. radio giant Rediffusion built the first cable TV system, using aluminium-sheathed coaxial cable, the first ever produced. It was offering cable TV service in 1951, a year before Canada even had a television network. The company produced its own live news reports and commentaries and mainly broadcast French-language films. By 1966, there were some 300 CATV systems in Canada serving 310,000 subscribers—a level of penetration more than twice that in the United States.

John Graham was urging Ted Rogers to expand into cable. He showed his stepson a business case with financial projections. Rogers was young, combative and moreover obsessed with becoming a radio magnate. He was heard arguing with his stepfather in the CHFI offices posing the same question he later asked van Valkenburg: "Why would I bother?" His interest, however, was piqued enough to learn more. At a cable meeting in Winnipeg, he hooked up with Sydney Welsh's partner, W. Garth Pither. "We sat up all night with the assistance of a little libation and we talked cable television. At the end Ted said, 'Great business, I've got to get into it,'" Pither remarked. "My partners blamed me a little bit for that and said [I] got that guy going."

Many people just didn't consider Toronto a viable cable market at the time because of its plentiful local and U.S. over-the-air broadcast signals. No one was willing to gamble on cable TV until U.S.-controlled Famous Players blazed the trail.

The company got into cable through the back door in 1960 when it introduced Canada's first (and the world's first sustained) pay-television service in Etobicoke, a middle-income west-end Toronto bedroom community, with

Los Angeles-based International Telemeter Corp. Customers fed coins into little boxes attached to their televisions to watch recently released Hollywood movies, specially produced closed-circuit programs, such as First World War songstress Gracie Fields with British comedian Stanley Holloway, Broadway hits, heavyweight boxing matches and away games for the Toronto Maple Leafs delivered via coaxial cable. (Telemeter carried Leafs away-from-home games for $1.50.)

Initially, Famous Players chose London, Ontario, halfway between Toronto and Detroit, as its pay TV test bed and partnered with local cable pioneer Ed Jarmain, who was looking for a new antenna site. Jarmain, an engineer by training and an amateur radio enthusiast, was running his deceased father's dry cleaning business in 1952 when he and his neighbor Frank Gerry, a Philco TV distributor, erected a gigantic common antenna in their adjoining backyards and then lent TV sets to 15 neighbors in order to persuade them to hook up. Thirteen neighbors received crystal-clear reception of TV programs from Cleveland, Ohio; Erie, Pennsylvania; and Detroit, Michigan. (CFPL-TV in London—one of only two privately owned CBC affiliates in Canada—didn't start until November 1953.)

In September 1959, Famous Players and Jarmain became equal partners in London TV Cable Ltd. The cable pioneers faced two major hurdles—the inability to obtain financing, which would be a recurring theme; and the telephone company, which either charged exorbitant fees to string cable on their poles or outright refused requests to do so. In exchange for equity stakes, Famous Players provided the seed money for cable pioneers in communities from Port Alberni on Vancouver Island; Powell River, British Columbia; Medicine Hat, Alberta; Estevan, Saskatchewan; and Winnipeg, Manitoba; to Cornwall, Guelph, Kitchener-Waterloo and Thunder Bay, Ontario.

In 1970, in order to meet the government-mandated Canadian ownership rules, Famous Players was forced out to spin off its cable business. The company that emerged would later become the keystone of Ted Rogers' cable empire.

Van Valkenburg took Rogers to meet Wes Hosick, a radio/TV repairman who was building a CATV system in a small section of the Borough of York, east of Toronto's Humber River. Rogers peppered Hosick with questions, but Loretta Rogers says her husband didn't become fully committed to the concept of cable TV until he was sitting on a beach in Fiji reading about it. "When you're on holiday—mind you, his mind never takes a holiday—you have time to think," she says. Then something else happened to cement his decision to go into cable. Rogers was talking to Metro Cable, trying to get the company to carry CHFI-FM's signal. The company refused him outright because it was already carrying CFRB-FM.

As a Baton director, Rogers had undertaken to take all proposed projects in the communications field to the Baton board. He proposed, at a board meeting, that they enter the cable TV business but John Bassett pooh-poohed the idea. Baton wasn't interested. Rogers called for a meeting of his own company's directors at his home for 11:30 at night. He told them he intended to go to Ottawa the next day and buy a cable license for part of Toronto from the Department of Transport. He went with their blessing. That was the easy part.

Ted Rogers paid $25 in February 1967 for his first cable TV license. Virtually anyone who mailed in an application (or went in person) with the token fee received a license. The federal transport department merely required cable TV applicants to meet certain technical requirements. The licenses, moreover, were not exclusive. The cable pioneers held licenses for territories that overlapped.

In the absence of a regulator, the telephone company was the effective cable-licensing authority. The cable TV pioneers were forced to rely on Bell Canada—or the provincial telephone carriers, depending where the pioneers were based—to build their cable systems because of the phone companies' statutory rights to erect telephone poles and lay conduits across and along public highways.

Ironically, Bell Canada decided who got what in Toronto. Bell had received an order from Metro Cable that totalled 1 million feet of cable. Metro Cable's biggest competitor, York Cablevision Ltd., owned by Vancouver's Sydney Welsh and bankrolled by U.S. giant CBS, had also applied to Bell to lay down cable in all of the areas not already ordered by Metro. According to Ken Easton, a cable engineer and historian, Bell Canada refused to accept orders from the two biggest players that might see Metro Toronto carved into a duopoly, prompting Ma Bell to establish ground rules for all licensees. Bell consequently only accepted orders from companies for a maximum of 1 million feet of cable at $1 a foot on a first-come, first-served basis.

Rogers, publisher Maclean Hunter Ltd., Geoff Conway, Barry Ross and David Graham (no relation to John) all applied to Bell within months. Rogers, as a bit of latecomer, ended up with parts of downtown and east Toronto, which were then considered the least desirable (less affluent) areas. Licensees risked losing their territories if they didn't place their order—along with a $250,000 down payment—with Bell. Bell then refused to take additional orders from licensees until half of their quotas were installed. Bell carved up the city among five players: Metro Cable, York Cablevision, Maclean Hunter, Barry Ross' Coaxial Colourview Ltd. and Rogers. Small cable firms, holding valid licenses, were shut out. In the seventies, they would jostle among each other for ever-increasing territories.

Rogers had to rustle up the money quickly for the required deposit, otherwise he'd lose out to somebody else. His wife, showing steadfast faith in her husband, came through for him. With her father's consent, Loretta loaned Rogers $225,000 against his radio assets—$1.3 million in 2005 dollars. By decade's end, the city had been carved into exclusive territories. But, many of the licensees ended up in areas that weren't contiguous. For the next decade, until the territories were rationalized to conform along the lines of municipal borders—for which Rogers lobbied—the ownership map of Toronto's cable TV market resembled a patchwork quilt of interlocking boundaries.

While waiting for Bell to lay the cable, Rogers acquired his first cable system on June 23, 1967—a 300-subscriber cable TV service in Bramalea, a satellite community 40 kilometers northwest of Toronto that later merged with the neighboring city of Brampton. Using his personal savings, he paid $17,000, or about $56 per subscriber, for 90 percent of Bramalea Telecable from Saskatoon native Clinton Forster's Noram Cable Construction Ltd. Rogers also advanced Noram $65,700 to eliminate its accounts payable. A year later, he purchased Forster's remaining 10 percent and bought 90 percent of Barry Ross' Coaxial Colourview Ltd. to expand his subscriber base in Bramalea. Rogers didn't know Ross. He just showed up on his doorstep one winter's evening brandishing a magnum of champagne. Intrigued, Ross invited him in; they talked, and mere months later, they cut a deal. The late Barry Ross became Rogers Cable TV's general manager.

Rogers didn't stop there. He bought General Broadcasting Sales Ltd., a holding company for his expanding stable of cable licenses, from Canadian author and broadcaster Pierre Berton, and shortened the name to General Broadcast Ltd. In the summer of 1967, Rogers promptly scooped up licenses north and west of the city of Toronto—from Markham, Vaughan, Port Credit, Streetsville and Mississauga, then called the Township of Toronto—all bedroom communities that later evolved into densely populated urban centers.

John Bassett was livid at Rogers when he found out. As a part owner in and director of CFTO-TV, Rogers was prohibited from competing in the television business—and Bassett felt cable was TV. Bassett insisted that the cable licenses belonged to Baton, not Rogers. "We had a real argument," is the way Rogers sums it up three decades later. "They wanted in on the cable and I didn't want to let them in."

John Graham, Rogers and Senator Richard Stanbury, one of Rogers' directors, went to see John Bassett in the *Toronto Telegram* boardroom. Bassett got red in the face and pounded the table, insisting that he would never agree to a deal where he'd put up most of the capital while giving Rogers complete discretion in the company's management, Stanbury recalls. "I hope we can work this out," Bassett declared in his big, booming voice. "Ted, I've always thought of you as a son." According to Rogers, Stanbury whispered, "Yeah, like a son of a bitch."

Rogers stood up. "In many respects, I've thought of you as another father." He recalls saying, "Okay. I'll put all the licenses and Bell contracts … into a company. We'll split it fifty-fifty, but you'll put up two-thirds [of the money]. I'll put up one-third. I'll run it, but you'll put in your own chief financial officer."

Rogers, who knew Bassett liked to control his investments through a CFO, thought he might have gone too far, but after about two hours of discussion, Bassett agreed to Rogers' terms and installed Gordon Ashworth as CFO. Some time afterwards, Rogers worried he had irrevocably damaged their partnership by bidding on some new cable sites with a cheque that Ashworth hadn't co-signed. "I'd broken the rules," says Rogers. "So I wrote a personal cheque and went down to see Bassett." Bassett ripped up the cheque and then hugged him, shouting, "You're my boy!"

"We wouldn't have been in the cable business if it wasn't for Ted," recalled Bassett's lawyer Eddie Goodman. "He was the one that drove it. I drove it through the board. If I had told Bassett, 'What are we doing this for?' Bassett would have thought about it again. Bassett was not hot on cable. He only agreed because Ted wanted it."

Bassett persuaded the Canadian Imperial Bank of Commerce (CIBC), Bank of Nova Scotia (Scotiabank) and the Bank of Montreal (BMO) to extend $6 million in non-revolving credit lines to the newly created Rogers Cable TV Ltd., incorporated on August 4, 1967. Through a company called Glen-Warren Productions Ltd., which held his 50-percent stake in Rogers Cable, Bassett was responsible for the repayment of $4 million, a full two-thirds of arranged credit. Rogers was liable for the remaining third.

With the weight of the Bassett name behind him, Rogers went full-steam ahead. He instructed his engineer, Frank Verkaik, a Dutch émigré who joined Rogers Cable after Famous Players pulled the plug on Telemeter, to build a cable system that could deliver better quality pictures than anyone else's. Verkaik consequently made sure that Bell Canada installed coaxial cable wires that had a 20-channel capacity, not the usual standard fare, although anything beyond 12 channels was then considered futuristic.

On July 1, 1968, Rogers signed his first cable TV customer in downtown Toronto, and within a month, he had 500. He also turned to his cable brethren for advice on how to improve the business. He invited Owen Boris, the founder of Hamilton, Ontario-based Mountain Cablevision Ltd., to his house for lunch to find out how he was managing to attract cable customers on the "mountain," where people with simple 20-foot antennas received fairly good reception. "I have a license for Toronto where people also get good reception with an antenna," Rogers told him. "I'd like to know what you're doing right that is getting subscribers."

"I went to his house, we had lunch," says Boris, "and I said, 'Ted, it's really simple. There's no magic to it. Just give your customers more—more and better. Give them more channels and give them better reception, and they'll have something to buy.' Well, Ted not only took that advice, he went far beyond that."

The year 1968 was momentous for several reasons. Pierre Trudeau, the charismatic Liberal Party leader, was swept into power on a massive wave of public support for the party, called Trudeaumania. He created policies to strengthen Canadian economic nationalism, which spilled over into culture. Canada's communications policies consequently became inextricably linked to "cultural sovereignty," two words absent from the comparable U.S. lexicon.

Rogers joined the cable club just as the regulatory milieu was changing. TV broadcasters had long perceived cable TV owners as a menace. They urged Ottawa to bring this nascent industry to heel before its phenomenal growth—unfettered as it was by anything other than the pace at which the Bell linemen could string up or bury coaxial cable—resulted in their much-ballyhooed demise. By 1970, cable subscriptions had soared 79 percent to 923,811 homes—approaching 1 million households—across Canada from 516,484 homes in 1967, fueled by the public's demand for access to television and a wider choice of programming. (Subscribers paid, on average, $18 for the installation and a $5 monthly fee.) The broadcasters' lobbying efforts paid off.

In 1968, Ottawa folded this budding industry into a new *Broadcasting Act*, which replaced the BBG with an independent federal authority with quasi-judicial status: the Canadian Radio-television Commission (CRTC), now known as the Canadian Radio-television and Telecommunications Commission. It was and is the CRTC's job to carry out and oversee the *Broadcasting Act*'s provisions, including ensuring the broadcasting system is predominantly Canadian and "strengthening Canada's cultural, social and economic structures." The regulator became the licensing authority for all so-called "broadcasting undertakings," including CATV systems and all holders of CATV licenses issued by the Department of Transport.

Since the cable guys at the time were not truly broadcasters, the CRTC a year later designated cable systems "broadcasting receiving undertakings" (later "broadcasting distribution undertakings" or "BDUs"), essentially to legitimize its oversight authority—and setting the stage for a score of future regulatory quagmires, bureaucrat infighting and federal-provincial jurisdictional disputes. Cable was the black swan—bearing the characteristics of both broadcasting and telephony, yet by the very virtue of its wire different from both. Neither fish nor fowl, cable posed an immediate threat to the broadcasters and a latent one to the telephone companies.

The cable owners were not put under the CRTC's purview to "regulate" their networks on behalf of Canadians, or oversee the quality of their service, or to provide a wide variety of programming choice, but to stymie its growth. The first two items on the CRTC's agenda were repatriating the industry by forcing 80 cable companies to shed their foreign parents—kicking out the Yanks, the financial lifeblood for the early cable pioneers—and re-licensing the country's staggering number of cable systems, now as many as 480, with the majority in Bell's backyard, Ontario and Quebec. "Our mandate is not to wire up Canada as fast as possible for American television," said CRTC chairman Pierre Juneau, a close friend of Trudeau's. "We are not trying to find ways of subsidizing cable or cross-subsidizing cable in order to make the American channels available faster than they would otherwise be available."

In the late sixties, the proliferation of new technologies—computers and satellites—animated the talk among regulatory mandarins in Canada and the United States. In response, Trudeau's newly elected Liberal government also created the Department of Communications (DOC) to advance social and economic benefits of communications, which at the time meant getting a Canadian bird in orbit.

Shortly after the formation of the DOC, its minister, Eric Kierans—who declared that communications was "the nerve system of a nation in search of itself"—appointed Deputy Minister Alan Gotlieb to lead a comprehensive study into Canada's $5-billion telecommunications industry and its future prospects, entitled *Instant World*. The landmark 1971 report, the culmination of 8,000 pages worth of background material, anticipated the marriage of computers and communications and delineated the regulatory conundrums of evolving technologies, their economics, the competing interests of shareholders versus customers and the challenges of rolling out new technologies to urban and rural Canadians. The report tied the importance of Canada being at the forefront of communications technology as a means of ensuring its national sovereignty. *Instant World*—expressing concern over Canada's scarce capital resources—in essence, although it did not explicitly say it, chose Bell Canada, the federally regulated leviathan among the provincially owned telephone carriers, as the national champion "in the interest of Canadian sovereignty, to ensure the adequacy of east-west communications, which may be jeopardized by the rapidly developing warfare between the multinational corporate giants in the U.S.," especially since the global market for computers and computer services was "almost totally captive to the U.S.

"Against them, Canada has only one high card to play—the existence of a telecommunications industry that is largely Canadian-owned and has, in one instance, a corporate tie with a Canadian manufacturing undertaking sufficiently large and diversified to benefit from economies of scale in production, research and development."

Also, in 1968 as Rogers was signing up his first cable TV subscriber, Canada's parliament revised Bell's charter, specifically prohibiting it from applying for or becoming a holder of a broadcasting or a cable TV license. In hearings leading up to the charter's revisions, Bell renounced its ability to move into cable TV. Bell Canada's legal counsel, A. Jean de Grandpré, who would go on to build the sprawling Bell empire, dealt away the possibility of entering the cable and broadcasting industries for the right to diversify into telecommunications (as opposed to just telephones) in parliamentary hearings leading up to the revision of its charter. De Grandpré stated the company did not want to be a broadcaster, cable television operator, or "to control in any way the contents of the message … [T]he telephone companies wanted to be common-carriers, pure and simple."

Many industry participants feared Bell would end up controlling the nascent cable industry. "Bell is attempting to control coaxial cable uses and to take over as much of the field as it can," warned G. D. (Doug) Zimmerman, the president of Industrial Wire and Cable Co. at the Standing Committee on Transportation and Communication for the bill amending Bell's charter. "They will end up controlling CATV and, in time, all the other uses that this electronic highway to my house and yours will represent."

The industry's concerns were not far-fetched. The phone companies already owned the cable wires. Bell was charging the cable companies 80 percent of the building costs, while retaining ownership of the cables attached to the Bell poles. For an additional monthly fee, Bell leased back portions of the spectrum to the cable operator. "That's like buying a house and you don't get title, you pay rent—it was just awful," says Robert C. Short, former president of the now-defunct Canadian Cable Television Industry Association and later of Rogers Cable. Another decade would pass before the cable companies won a hard-fought battle for the right to own their own cable networks and the telephone companies were ordered to negotiate "reasonable" pole rentals.

Unlike the broadcasters, Bell Canada ignored the budding cable industry's latent threat even if its research arm saw it coming. Bell Canada, driven to create short-term shareholder value and cheered on by Bay and Wall Streets, became caught up in its global ambitions. For three decades, Bell—supported by the DOC—expounded the "one-wire theory" in which all communications services into the home should be over one wire—and here's the clincher—*controlled and operated by the telephone industry*. Bell held firm to the belief that its natural monopoly, where the public good is best served by one efficient utility, should extend to cable television. It wanted a single integrated network capable of transmitting all voice, visual and data communications. "Bell was a strong enough company that if they wanted to change their charter, they could have," says veteran telecom consultant Ian Angus. "There has never been a federal government that stood up to Bell in any major way. If Bell had in 1968 said, 'No, we want the ability. We don't want to be a TV station, but we would like to carry television signals, they could have got it."

To be sure, coaxial cable, colloquially called coax, had the potential—in the right hands—to bring the *Instant World* one step closer to reality. Coax is a step up from the phone company's century-old wrapped copper pair. It's not as if the telephone companies weren't laying down coax, because they were—the first high capacity long-distance line between Montreal and Toronto was coax—they just never installed it directly into the home. The cable pioneers took coax right into the home because, unlike the copper wire, coaxial cable could carry very high frequencies—the kind of bandwidth hogged by television signals—without any leakage. The majority of the cable pioneers, most famously TCI's Bob Daniels and John Malone, who were reputed to have some of the "crappiest" cable systems around, and Sydney Welsh at Premier Cablevision, were hardware capitalists. They didn't look beyond the monthly cash flow. Just hook up the subscriber and collect the easy money.

The capacity of coaxial cable was like "comparing Niagara Falls to a garden hose," former FCC commissioner Nicholas Johnson told Ralph Lee Smith, author of the seminal book *The Wired Nation*, in 1970. Smith predicted "the stage for a communications revolution was being set," whereby cable wires would one day deliver "audio, video, and facsimile transmissions that can provide newspapers, mail service, banking and shopping facilities, data from libraries and other storage centers, school [curriculum], complete course offerings leading to college degrees, cultural programs, community-originated TV fare, and other forms of information too numerous to specify. In short, every home and office can contain a communications center of a breadth and flexibility to influence every aspect of private and community life.

"This is no dream," he wrote. "The cable could carry it all, and the technology is in existence or soon will be."

Licenses in hand, Rogers was exercised to make his case before Ottawa's bureaucrats, all the while drawing fire from just about everyone along the way. "He kept prodding," recalled the late CRTC chairman Harry J. Boyle. "He didn't seem to know exactly where he was going, but he was going someplace. He had this bug in his bonnet about what cable was going to do, and everybody looked at him in amazement. They didn't want it to happen. But, he was absolutely convinced that cable was the future of the broadcasting industry. He's miles ahead of other people. Ted shone over all of them." He remembered the first time Rogers appeared before the commission to talk about cable. "He sailed into the business case, showing the potential for it, and it terrified the hell out of all of us." In the land of the blind, the one-eyed man was king.

Just as he did with CHFI, Rogers did big things to market his cable service. On the evening of July 20, 1969, at Toronto's new City Hall, Rogers Cable erected a gigantic screen to show pictures of the moon landing of the Apollo spaceship. His vans, bearing the company name, surrounded the entire area. By 1970, he had 26,000 subscribers. Even then, he was cross-promoting his cable TV services with his radio stations in his promotional mailings: "Down come those ugly antennas ... and in goes CABLE TV, bringing you ten great channels ... By the way, you will also receive radio stations CHFI-FM and CKEY-AM on your TV set."

Even though Bassett allowed Rogers to locate his master antenna (cable head-end) on CFTO-TV's tower in Agincourt, Ontario, northeast of Toronto, Rogers entered into protracted negotiations with A.E. LePage's president Gordon Gray for a 20-year lease to perch his cable head-end, as well as the CHFI news and traffic antennas, on top of the new 54-storey TD Bank Tower, at that time the city's highest office tower, a location offering the clearest possible reception for over-the-air TV signals in downtown Toronto. (The head-end is the control center, where incoming TV signals are amplified and processed into a common cable for transmission to customers.) Gray, a chartered accountant, was responsible for assembling the land to construct the TD Centre, which at the time was considered to be one of the country's most complex real estate deals. He says he spent more than a year negotiating the cable head-end lease, or as he exasperatedly describes it, "this bloody document," with the two men finally settling on the terms.

It was almost more difficult than the land deal itself. "It was quite a sporting negotiation; it was very complicated. It had engineering and financial implications," recalls Gray, who came to respect Rogers's intellect. "I loved sparring with him on the negotiations."

No sooner had the antenna gone up when Richard M. (Dick) Thomson, then assistant to TD Bank CEO Al Lambert, ordered it down because the antenna looked "like hell," marring the simplicity of the towers designed by the famed German architect Ludwig Mies van der Rohe. "I knew that Mies liked clean lines, and I thought, my God, if he saw that tower up there, he'd have a fit," recalls Thomson, who asked Gray to tell Rogers to take the tower down. "We wanted to put things on the plaza, and he wouldn't let us. We didn't even put a TD sign on the building.

"Ted phoned me, and said, 'Are you serious?'" says Thomson, who explained the architect's concerns.

"I understand you, Dick," he remembers Rogers saying. "I'll move it."

"That's the kind of guy Ted is. He understood exactly why we were concerned. He knew about architecture. He's got a lot of great taste. He didn't argue. He had the lease. He could have kept it there for several years, but he said, fine, I'll move it."

"He's the ultimate entrepreneur," says Gray, who joined the Rogers board in 1971. "A lot of entrepreneurs aren't detail guys, but Ted is. This is unusual for lawyers. I'm not critical of the profession, but for Ted to have such technical knowledge, such a passion for getting into the details, into the minute details, is unusual. There's not one little niche, or corner of his businesses, that he doesn't totally understand. His knowledge is beyond belief. I tell you, things were never dull at Rogers."

Gray retired as an RCI director in 2001 after 30 years, most of which he served as the board's audit committee chairman. "We'd change year-ends all the time to take advantage of some new tax wrinkle," he laughs. "I would kid him about it all the time. Ted is a master at tax planning. I don't mean tax evasion. He knows every angle that ever was."

CHAPTER 7

Enter Phil Lind, the Banks and the CRTC

"We had all kinds of crazy ideas in the seventies, but they were all prescient. They lasted about four months. We were competing with the broadcasters, and you could never do that as a cable operator. You could never compete. You could never offer anything decent."

—Phil Lind

TED ROGERS FASCINATED PHIL LIND. While he had never met Rogers, he knew plenty about the family. A decade younger than Rogers, Philip Bridgman Lind was born in Toronto on August 20, 1943 into a well-heeled family with early twentieth-century business ties to the Rogers clan. Lind's grandfather, John Grieve Lind, made the long trek to the Yukon before the 1897–98 Klondike Gold Rush and, through hard work and circumstance, he returned home to St. Marys, a small, idyllic town in southwestern Ontario, an extremely wealthy man. His love of the Yukon inspired his descendants to travel there frequently and, more recently, to donate $250,000 to Dawson City's museum. In 1912, he co-founded St. Marys Cement Co. with Alfred Rogers, who ran the coal distributing and lumberyard business his father, Elias, established in Toronto. Elias was Ted Rogers' great granduncle. Both families owned shares in the privately held cement maker for 85 years until 1997, when they decided to sell the company for £164 million ($374 million) to Britain's leading cement company, Blue Circle Industries PLC, a sale that Phil Lind, a company director, reluctantly supported.

Lind was a friend of Rogers' sister, Ann Graham. They were the same age. Whenever they ran into each other at parties, Lind always peppered her with questions about her brother's latest endeavors, recalls Graham. At her 21st birthday party—a spiffy black-tie dance for 100 guests hosted by the Rogers at Frybrook in their as-yet unfurnished living room made up especially for the occasion, with a dramatic tented ceiling—Lind pointedly asked her how he could get a job with her brother.

"I've done everything," he said. "I don't know what else to do."

"Well, why don't you ask him?"

"Oh, I can't do that."

"Alright, Phil, I tell you what. Come with me." She took him by the arm and led him from the room to the backyard entrance into the rose garden, where Rogers was standing. "Ted, Phil Lind has admired you for years and wants a job at your company. Would you please talk to him about it? Because I'm sick and tired of listening to him." She turned on her heel and returned to the dance floor, leaving them to stroll among the rose bushes.

The two men hit it off. They shared similar interests in politics, both being card-carrying Tories. Lind, who attended Upper Canada College and Ridley College, promised Rogers to stay in touch while he completed his undergraduate studies in political science at the University of British Columbia. He then went on to earn a master's degree in sociology from the University of Rochester, New York. In the summers, he worked for the Progressive Conservative Party, becoming assistant national director reporting to Eddie Goodman. One day, Lind was hand-delivering important correspondence to Goodman at the CFTO-TV studios. Goodman, ensconced into a CTV Network board meeting, asked him to stay. Lind, seated among the directors, had found his calling. In that moment, he decided to pursue a career in television broadcasting, where he too might influence decisions.

Lind lined up a job interview at Selkirk Holdings Ltd., a rapidly growing radio and television broadcaster, part owned by newspaper giant Southam Inc. Selkirk's president, J. Stuart MacKay, like many others in the industry at the time, was predicting that Canada would have six or seven national television networks within the next five years, with cable TV bringing viewers 24 to 48 channels—specialty networks devoted to pay television, international coverage, entertainment, news and education.

But soon Lind was to be waylaid by Rogers. "Why don't you come [here], and we'll do some stuff together," he told Lind. "You love programming and we only have a little programming stuff. We've only got a little company, but you're just starting out. You're better off with friends and a little company, instead of with these aristocracy companies." As Lind says, "We've been together ever since."

Lind joined Rogers on October 20, 1969 in the radio company until Rogers put him in charge of the cable TV company's programming, where he immediately became immersed in dealing with regulatory matters. "Rogers made me secretary just so that I could attend the boardroom meetings," he says. "Rogers was the strategic thinker."

Lind is an affable, elegant senior executive, with a common man's touch. Easygoing and graceful, his networking abilities paid huge dividends to Rogers in the company's government relationships. Rogers, more effusive and less refined than Lind, can be just as effective in achieving the same results. "He's Ted's man Friday," says David Colville, retired CRTC vice chairman. "One doesn't go without the other."

He joined the company just as the rapidly growing cable industry was struggling for credibility—and right in time for its first near-death crisis. In July, four months earlier, CRTC chairman Pierre Juneau had ordered John Bassett out of the cable industry in Toronto, a crippling blow to Rogers. Barely a year old, the CRTC was undertaking the massive job of re-licensing the country's cable systems. As part of that process, the CRTC had felt Bassett—the owner of a major Toronto daily, the city's only private TV station and cable TV assets—wielded too much control of Toronto's media. The CRTC, repealing 40 percent of the licenses Rogers had amassed, renewed the remaining Rogers Cable TV licenses for two years (instead of the permissible five) on the condition Bassett divest his stake in the company. "They thought we'd clean out the whole of Ontario. We were really working our way to do that," says Rogers.

His grasping pursuit of cable properties made small cable owners wary of him. "They saw Ted Rogers as big of an enemy as Bell," says veteran industry consultant Ian Angus, who did consulting work in the seventies for many small cable-television owners.

Bassett, through Glen-Warren, owned half of the equity in Rogers Cable. However, more critically to Rogers, Bassett was liable for two-thirds of the debt, which now Rogers somehow had to assume. A frantic Rogers visited Bassett, who did his best to reassure him. "You've done a good job," Rogers recalls Bassett saying. "You and Loretta are good people. We will sell to a strong institution."

Rogers didn't want another partner. He'd hit paydirt with Bassett. He'd never again find a passive investor content with owning just half of the equity while being liable for most of the debt. Rogers proposed that they get the assets valued, and then he'd swap his 10-percent stake in Baton for Glen-Warren's 50-percent stake in Rogers Cable. Bassett agreed, readily buying back Rogers' Baton shares. For his part, Rogers couldn't scrape together all the money he needed to buy out Bassett. He paid him with a note due in 18 months.

He carried on. He had to. He was now the proud father of a 21-month-old baby girl, Lisa Anne, whom he and Loretta had adopted, and a newborn son, Edward Samuel Rogers III, born less than three weeks before Juneau's unexpected edict ordering Bassett's divestiture. No one was more ecstatic than Rogers when his son was born. He was so overjoyed that he broadcast Loretta and their newborn on his community cable channel from her hospital room.

The couple had decided to adopt after being unable to conceive their own children. Rogers says he was devastated upon learning that they couldn't conceive any children. The couple tenaciously pursued various treatments before Rogers eventually was referred to a U.S. marine hospital physician, Dr. C. Alvin Paulsen, whom he credits for their eventual success in producing offspring. (Paulsen later became internationally renowned for his research of male hormones.) Rogers checked himself into the U.S. Public Health Service Hospital (now the Pacific Medical Center) in Seattle, Washington. The next thing they knew, Loretta delivered three infants in the span of three years—from June 1969 to April 1972—during the company's worst-ever crisis.

Rogers was building out his cable systems, all the while fighting with the banks for more borrowing power and searching for new sources of financing in a country where capital was scarce, especially for risky capital-intensive endeavors. The cost to lay cable was then about $5,000 or $6,000 in 1972 per linear mile, not including the cost to connect the cable trunk to the subscriber's TV set. Block by block, the cable was laid. Right behind them, at least in already established residential areas, the cable guy was knocking on the doors, trying to sign up subscribers.

Every month, revenue rose, but costs were rising faster. An average-size, 5,000-subscriber system cost up to half a million to build and generated annual revenues of about $270,000, at $4.50 a month per subscriber. Rogers had already consumed the $6-million credit line from the three-bank consortium. For all the money he was ploughing into the business, he didn't expect to recoup his investment for nine years. Maclean Hunter's Don Hunter, Rogers' friend and next-door neighbor, was more pessimistic, expecting his company to recoup its planned investment in 10 to 15 years. "We're betting we'll get our money back before satellites affect the situation," Hunter told the *Toronto Daily Star*.

At his Muskoka cottage, Rogers ran into Dick Thomson, TD Bank's chief operating officer, and told him he might have to sell his cottage if he didn't raise additional funds soon. In reply, Thomson told him to see his right-hand man, often described as his more intellectual alter ego, Robin Korthals.

Robert W. (Robin) Korthals would figure prominently in Rogers' success, first as his banker, and later as an RCI director for 10 years. The quiet-spoken Venezuelan native, whose Dutch and Scottish parents sent him to boarding school in Canada, joined TD Bank in 1967, became president in 1981 and retired in 1995.

Korthals was one of the few Canadian bankers actually knowledgeable about the fledgling cable TV industry. He structured several financings for small

U.S. cable TV partnerships while working for his previous employer, brokerage house Nesbitt Thomson & Co. In the United States, although cable TV systems were expensive to build, the early pioneers almost immediately recovered some of their original build-out costs once customers paid their installation charges. From then on, subscribers paid with unerring regularity their monthly bill to watch their favorite TV shows. They'd sooner disconnect their phone than their television. A shrewd cable operator might write off his investment over several years, preventing the company from making a profit. Since the cable system snatched broadcasting signals out of the air for free, the owner had a reliable stream of cheap money. "You had a tax-sheltered investment that actually increased in value," Korthals says.

TD Bank was so enthusiastic about cable that it tried to buy an equity stake in Maclean Hunter Cable TV Ltd. in 1969 to help finance the company's growth, a move the CRTC quickly nixed. The regulator was uncomfortable with the long-term implications of allowing banks to take equity positions in its licensees. Recalls Thomson, "That was a blow to us, but we got to know a lot about the cable business, and we saw how good it was."

TD became the banker to Canadian cable pioneers Maclean Hunter, Rogers, David Graham and his partner, Jim Meekison, and the Shaw family. As the Canadians joined the U.S. city franchising wars of the late seventies and early eighties, TD was right behind them. TD, led by Thomson and Korthals, evolved into North America's pre-eminent lender to companies in the cable and telecom industry, a niche rivals greatly envied. "If nothing else, Ted's account has been a great training ground. It never sleeps," Korthals once said.

Korthals asked Rogers what security he had for a loan. Rogers didn't answer. "I thought so, none," Rogers recalls Korthals saying.

"I have a cottage," blurted out a desperate Rogers, who says he was perspiring at that point.

Korthals "looked at me for the longest time and said, 'Keep your cottage.'" Rogers says he was impressed that he "didn't extract that last pound of flesh" from him.

He gave Rogers some breathing room, arranging for the bank to loan Rogers more than $2 million against Rogers Broadcasting, and members of the Rogers family. However, Scotiabank, CIBC and Bank of Montreal refused to release Baton from its guarantees and undertakings associated with their earlier credit arrangement. Of the three, Scotiabank was the most intransigent, prompting Rogers to have the bank removed from the lending consortium, although in later years the bank would become his major lender. In a complex agreement, Bassett renegotiated new terms, stepping in to reassure Rogers' uneasy bankers that Baton would guarantee any amounts over and above their credit line to help Rogers, if need be, complete the build out of the cable system. Baton was eventually released from its guarantees, but only after Rogers' family and friends filled the void. In total, Rogers was in hock for $8.5 million.

A year passed before loan terms were finally reached. Revenue from his cable subscribers was just covering the interest payments on the bank debt. "Rumor, that Ted Rogers, the ambitious and high-flying owner of CHFI and Rogers Cable Television Ltd., has run out of money," wrote *Globe and Mail* television columnist Blair Kirby in August 1970. "I suppose the rumor is false," said Rogers, described as sounding doubtful. "But, I suppose anybody that thinks he's flush today is foolish."

As the winter of 1970 passed into 1971, the outlook remained bleak. If he just had another $1 million, Rogers reckoned he could increase his number of subscribers and stay afloat for another six months, enough time to arrange additional funds through the public or private sale of shares. His bankers wouldn't lend him any more money without additional collateral. It was during this period when Rogers had his loan called—the only one he's ever had called. The Bank of Nova Scotia called it. A decade later, of all ironies, Scotiabank was knocking on his door, begging to lend him money to fund wireless. "I deserved to have it called," recalls Rogers. "I was a smart ass. I was glib and I was not respectful and I paid for it."

The Industrial Development Bank, the federal crown corporation now known as the Business Development Bank, turned him away. He contemplated accepting an offer from Selkirk Holdings Ltd.'s Stuart Mackay to invest $5-million cash for Bassett's 50-percent stake in Rogers Cable. Selkirk then owned three cable TV systems as well as radio and TV stations, including Hamilton's CHCH. If he accepted, Rogers would recover most of his family's collateral and pay off most of his company's debt. However, Mackay expected an equal say in the company, something Rogers was reluctant to surrender. He thanked Mackay, but passed on the offer. Years later, in 1987, Rogers would make a failed takeover run for Selkirk.

Rogers turned to his family for help. His mother, Velma, wife, Loretta, and sister, Ann, all contributed what they could. His stepfather, who wasn't a wealthy man, contributed $5,000 so the company could meet its payroll. He even asked for help from his Aunt Katherine in Winnetka, Illinois. Rogers asked his brother-in-law, Richard Robinson, if he would invest in the company. Rogers scribbled in his daily organizer on December 8, 1970: "Talked to Richard Robinson in his office. Very disappointing. He said he had been too embarrassed to say no, which he had decided … I was smiling and friendly—tried to talk some sense. It was pretty difficult. He was afraid of [the] whole Robinson family being swallowed up."

"There's hardly a name in Canada that I haven't been to looking for money," says Rogers. "I once went out to [Roy] Thomson's summerhouse in Mississauga, looking for money [for CFTO and CHFI]. I didn't get it. I went to the [*Toronto*] *Star* and offered them fifty percent of the company when I was starting the cable business. They said 'no.' Everybody said 'no.' All my relatives said 'no.'"

Rogers and Loretta then did something they promised Loretta's father they would never do when he bought the Frybrook house for them: They mortgaged it for $1.5 million at a 13-percent interest rate.

Rogers had barely been covering the weekly payroll. Once, he paid employees on the Monday, instead of the usual Friday, recalls CHFI mainstay Russ Holden. It was the only time Rogers failed to meet the scheduled payroll. Rogers, as most entrepreneurs in a cash crunch, didn't pay himself until the tide turned. He withheld paying his bills for as long as he could. The accounts payable clerks spent their days taking calls from angry creditors. They were put on shifts and started at seven in the morning in an attempt to work for a few hours before the phones began ringing. Rogers refused to deal with any supplier who wouldn't grant 90 days' credit. He laughs that he had to resort to putting bills into a hat, and paying them on the basis of whichever one he pulled out first. "What else could you do, but laugh at your predicament? Other guys would go and shoot themselves, you know." Phil Lind, who knew Bell's Ontario boss James Thackery from their political work together, asked him for a two-month reprieve from paying their pole charges. If Thackery had not agreed, Bell Canada could have wiped Rogers out.

"It was absolutely, unbelievably frightful," says Hugh Lewis, an English émigré who joined in April 1971 as Rogers' finance director and stayed until 1975. "I was scared to cash my expense cheque for fear it would bounce."

Luckily, "Ted could charm birds off the branches," says Lewis, who relocated to Toronto from Montreal, where he'd been the treasurer at color-TV manufacturer RCA Canada. He was well aware of Rogers' plight; after all, while at RCA, he tried to ease Rogers' financial obligations by waiving the principal payments on his supplier financings. Rogers' job offer came at an opportune time, since RCA was paring its Canadian staff. Also, Lewis wanted to leave Montreal, one of the many Anglophones who would leave the city over the next decade after the October 1970 FLQ terrorist kidnappings and the rising Quebec secessionist movement.

"When [Rogers] set his mind to be agreeable, he was marvellously agreeable and persuasive. The big thing, at least for me, was watching the guy's ideas. Even in my own sphere of knowledge, some of the things that he came up with relative to taxation were astounding. He wouldn't take 'no' for an answer. He would worry problems to death long after everybody else had thrown up their hands, and would finally come up with an answer."

Lewis lent the ailing company a fair degree of creditability with the bankers, since he came from the Canadian subsidiary of a major U.S. corporation. He instituted a policy of openness with the banks that became the company's hallmark trait over the decades. The bankers may not have liked what they heard, but they could rely on being told the brutal truth in a timely manner. Lewis recalls meeting with the company's three bankers a month into his new job and, after several failed pitches to extend their credit, he said, "Well, gentlemen, I came to this meeting with not only suspenders and a belt, but also a piece of string in my pocket. What do you now suggest we do?"

"Well, why don't you have three more sets of keys cut?" one of the bankers replied.

In 1971, John Bassett decided to take Baton Broadcasting public to finance their expansion in radio and TV, a decision that meant he needed Rogers' promissory note off his books immediately lest he again incur the CRTC's wrath. Rogers, up to his eyeballs in debt, needed more time to raise the money. To get a three-month extension, Rogers appeared teary eyed before the Bassett-Eaton trustees and signed away his right to insist on a valuation of the assets. Bassett gave him until July 15, 1971. "They were very good to me. They gave me extension after extension after extension until finally the time comes where there are no more extensions," says Rogers. "We just make it by the skin of our teeth."

TD's Dick Thomson was at his summer cottage on Lake Rosseau in Ontario's heavily forested and lake-rich Muskoka, lunching with his wife and their guests, John A. Tory and his wife, Liz, when Tory suggested they go over and visit Rogers. The three men sat on the dock talking about the bind Rogers was in. "I decided that we would like to try and help," says Thomson. Again, he asked Korthals to figure something out.

Knowing TD was already fully extended to Rogers, Korthals sought another route. He called his friend Gordon Osler, the chairman of UNAS Investments Ltd., a Toronto-based venture capital company, of which Korthals was a director. Osler promised to arrange a meeting with Rogers. When he couldn't get ahold of Rogers, who was out of town, Osler met with John Graham, who succinctly explained their precarious situation and handed over their financial statements. The UNAS team crunched the numbers over the weekend and met with Rogers the day before his three-month deadline was set to expire.

Osler agreed to loan Rogers $2.3 million for three years at 15-percent interest, double the prime rate the banks charged to their best customers, and an option to buy up to 5,000 common shares of Rogers Cable TV, equal to 5 percent of the company's equity, at $45 a share. "It was a lot of money for us," recalls Osler. "It was quite a gamble and Ted has been eternally grateful."

At ten minutes to midnight on a hot and humid July night, Ted and Loretta Rogers signed the necessary paperwork at the Tory law offices in the TD Centre. There was no air-conditioning. Rogers' mother, Velma, who was quite ill with cancer and would die four months later, waited up in bed for them to return home with the news that the company had been pulled back from the brink of bankruptcy. "She was captain of the ship," says Rogers. "We always gathered around her bed for the board meetings."

The next day, Rogers marched over to the *Telegram*'s offices to see Bassett. He brought along a bottle of champagne and a book inscribed "Presentation to J. W. H. Bassett." All of the pages were blank. When Rogers entered the room, he took out his keys and placed them beside the book.

"No more presentations Ted, it's over," hollered Bassett, misunderstanding the gesture.

Rogers persuaded Bassett to open the book. "There's nothing here!" Bassett roared, flipping through the book until he reached the last page, where Rogers had hidden the certified cheque that cleared the note. Just as Bassett reached the last page, his son, Doug, fully aware of Rogers' plan, popped the cork from the champagne bottle. "Jesus Christ! What?" a startled Bassett erupted. Bassett was thrilled. They all embraced. Emotionally drained, Rogers clinked his champagne glass with Big John's in relief tinged with sadness: His 12-year business relationship with Bassett was now over. Says Rogers, "I was out of Baton and he was out of Rogers Cable."

Toronto-Dominion Bank became Rogers' biggest lender, backstopping his every move. Cable TV, after all, was a wonderful business. Canadians were becoming addicted to watching TV. Revenue from cable TV subscribers was recession proof. They'd happily pay their monthly bills for cable TV service—giving the cable guys a monthly stream of cash flow, much like an annuity. The certainty of this monthly cash flow gave them the comfort they needed to lend the cable guys money.

Just as Korthals had recognized earlier, Rogers immediately grasped the potential. Instead of using hard assets to secure debt, he could leverage his business using cash flow. The more he built cash flow, the more he expanded his borrowing capacity, although even his staunchest bankers had their limits.

Rogers, and other daring cable cowboys, only had to await the arrival of junk-bond guru Michael Milken to take this financial alchemy to new plateaus, which prudent business operators would never contemplate. They embraced this self-perpetuating financing circle, one strikingly similar to a nuclear chain reaction. And, much like the physical nuclear chain reaction, which ultimately ends up exploding, many often questioned if Rogers might suffer the same fate with the financial equivalent.

"Robin Korthals was a constant source of strength to us," says Hugh Lewis. "He alone of all the bankers understood what was going on. That's not to say he was a pansy, or an easy pushover, but he was the only one of the bankers who really understood."

In September 1972, Lewis recalls negotiating a new loan package with the banks that would give them "some peace and quiet" for a while. He sent the 50-page-plus document to Rogers to review. Rogers, doing what he loved the best—expanding his business—had not been heavily involved in the negotiations. The next day he stormed into Lewis' office.

"There's no goddamn way I'm going to sign an agreement like this," he blasted. "It's unjust. We can't do this. We can't do this. It's unfair."

"Ted, this really is the best we can do, and if we can't sign this agreement, I think the banks are going to close in on us," Lewis said.

"I'm not going to put up with it! But," Rogers added, "I will allow you to present it to the board of directors."

He was furious that the banks were going to lend him only $75 per subscriber. He believed the company's borrowing power was at least $125 per subscriber. He also wanted released from their control the $3 million of securities that Loretta had pledged as collateral for the cable loan. He had pledged the securities after the bank consortium released Baton from its undertakings. In the end, they all agreed to what subsequently was dubbed the Korthals Formula: The Rogers family would be obliged to maintain its collateral only to the extent that the cable company's borrowings exceeded 12 times its operating profit for the most recent three-month period.

The nine directors, which included Ted's wife, Loretta, convened for lunch in the wood-panelled grand dining room at Toronto's Albany Club, one of the few remaining private political clubs, where the company's directors met regularly until the company became publicly traded. They were there ostensibly to dismiss the loan package. Rogers spent 15 minutes strenuously denouncing the package. Then, just before wrapping up, Rogers said, "But, Hugh has a different view, and I suppose we should listen to him." As Lewis made his pitch, he recalls that Rogers interrupted him repeatedly.

"Well," said Rogers when Lewis finished, "is there any more discussion? I'd like to bring this to a vote, so we can all go home."

Those in favor raised their hands. The vote: nine to one—against Rogers. Even his wife voted against him. "You'll all crazy!" blasted Rogers. "There's no goddamn way I'm going to sign this agreement." Rogers then turned slightly in his chair, leaning in towards John Graham, and quietly whispered, "but you and Hugh can."

"You have to be pretty big to allow your subordinate to carry your board against you," says Lewis. "We did sign the agreement, and the banks left us alone. It was the hinge point. We were dead in the water without it."

Armed with a TV camera, Ted Rogers ventured out onto the roof of the TD Bank Tower, then Toronto's largest tower. Phil Lind was right behind him, lugging the rest of their community channel equipment. They intended to film the Canadian International Air Show, which is held, weather permitting, every Labour Day weekend at the Canadian National Exhibition, the world's biggest fair, colloquially known as "The Ex." With everything ready to go, Rogers was behind the camera, ready to capture the show on film. Lind was standing to the side, scanning the clear blue skies for any signs of aircraft, when they both heard the resonating thunder of jets approaching.

"Phil, where are they?"

"They're coming."

"Where?" roared Rogers.

The jets zoomed past.

"They've gone!"

Rogers was pointing the camera south at Lake Ontario rather than to the west from where the jets were coming in their loop back over the lake to the CNE grounds. "What a dolt I was!" Rogers recalls, admitting he upbraided Lind for their stupidity. "Why didn't you tell me to shoot it as they were coming at us?"

"Well, why didn't you think of it?" Lind fired back.

The two cable guys did just about everything they could to get content to attract subscribers. They were the first to broadcast city council meetings, causing three councillors to lose their jobs in the next election. With Rogers again working as a cameraman, Barry Ross hosted *Over to You*, a phone-in show where subscribers called in with their comments and complaints. Renamed *Ask Us*, Phil Lind became the host. After Rogers acquired Canadian Cablesystems

Ltd., former CCL executive Colin Watson, as the new head of Rogers Cable, joined Lind as a co-host for this quirky customer call-in show where the cable executives were on the hot seat answering complaints, or getting razed by their own employees. *Ask Us* broadcast monthly for almost three decades—its last show aired in 2003.

Rogers Cable's subscribers were mostly in neighborhoods populated with immigrants—Greeks, Italians and Portuguese. Rogers and Lind went knocking on household doors, trying to sell their fledgling cable television service, mostly to housewives who didn't understand a word of what they said.

Rogers remembers, "In 1971, Phil devised a solution to a problem we had in Toronto where our salesmen would go and try to sell them cable and they couldn't speak English so they wouldn't know what we were talking about. We didn't do very well and the banks would be very mad. So Phil got the idea of putting on a few channels of programming in different languages and then we hired some salespeople who spoke those languages and went around and that had a big effect on the company. We were the first in Canada to have more than twelve channels and that started a tradition of multicultural programming, which has lasted through all the years. I think that was a key issue."

Two years before the late Daniel Iannuzzi, publisher of the Italian daily *Corriere Canadese*, began airing multilingual TV programs on Toronto's CityTV (which started in 1972), Lind was sending cable technicians to Italy, Greece, Portugal, Brazil and France to record programs from their hotel TV sets and smuggle the tapes back into Canada, where they were reformatted for broadcast on Rogers Cable's community channel. "We were bad in those days," says Lind, who, as mentioned earlier, started at Rogers Cable in programming, an area in which he excelled. "It wasn't that we couldn't pay for them. They just weren't available. Nothing was available. Portuguese, Greeks and Italians in the sixties desperately wanted programming in their own language. All of these people couldn't speak any English, especially the parents. I remember, I was up and down the streets all the time—you'd go to the door and the kids would speak English but their mothers wouldn't. They were totally isolated. The need was pretty obvious."

In late 1972, they launched a foreign-language channel, Channel 33, carrying Greek, Italian, Portuguese, East Indian, Asian and Croatian programs. They were filling a programming void to attract subscribers. They struck a deal with newly created CityTV to tape its multicultural programming and replay it on a dedicated channel during prime time nightly. "It's about time that people in our nation have a chance for their own kind of programming, whether it be Italian or business news or cultural or sports or whatever it might be. This is what cable is all about," Rogers told *The Financial Post* in 1971. "Hopefully, broadcasting in this country can be the creation of Canadian programming, rather than merely the recycling of American-made tapes. To do this, we need as much exposure for programming as possible. And, this is where cable can help."

They began transforming TV by filling the channels with specific content— what might seem normal today was novel then—commercial-free movies, sports, a ticker tape of stocks trading on the Toronto Stock Exchange, and a nascent version of today's Shopping Channel, then called the Shopping Basket, which listed the best buys for appliances, clothing and even groceries from competing chains. Lind created a channel for westerns—similar to today's version of Lonestar TV. He tried a one-week experiment giving "the man-on-the-street" his say—similar to today's *Speaker's Corner* on CityTV—by erecting a TV camera at the corner of Yonge and Adelaide streets in downtown Toronto for four hours a day, allowing passersby to blow off some steam. He convinced Rogers they should mount a camera on a turntable atop the roof of the city's tallest building, TD Bank Tower, to broadcast shots of Toronto while playing CHFI-FM music in the background. Rogers Cable even offered its subscribers a classic movie channel. They also had other ideas, including specialty channels for weather and business news. Ideas were plentiful. Anything was possible.

Rogers Cable introduced so-called converters, the first to do so, bumping up the 12-channel universe first to 19 and then 22. For an extra $2.50 a month, subscribers could get a bundle of channels that included the multicultural channel, five regular stations, a stock market and a news channel. After adding yet another channel for a total of 23 in September 1974, Rogers was now offering eight homegrown cable, or specialty, channels. Rogers was spending $200,000 a year on programming, more than any other Canadian cable company. Torontonians flocked to their service, making Rogers Cable TV the city's largest cable system with 160,000 subscribers. The more services Rogers could offer, the more he could charge his subscribers.

Rogers aired free movies on a dedicated channel in 1972, a year before the U.S. cable industry's promising pay TV service Star Channel (later acquired by Warner Cable and renamed TMC, The Movie Channel) was introduced and a decade before the CRTC, after much deliberation, finally decided Canada's apparently still-fragile TV broadcasters might be able to withstand six pay-TV services—a national general-interest service (in English and French), three regional general-interest channels, a performing arts channel and a regional multilingual service.

In 1974, Rogers bought a controlling stake in TWC Television Co., which ran pay TV systems in seven Toronto hotels, from an affiliate of Time Inc. in an anticipation of the CRTC permitting pay TV only on licensed cable TV systems in hotels. The company had 11,000 rooms linked to TWC's hotel pay-TV service, making it the largest purveyor of movies to hotel guests in North America. (The CRTC never did regulate hotel pay TV. Rogers sold TWC some 20 years later.)

Phil Lind negotiated the programming contracts, securing the rights for mainstream studio movies for broadcast on hotel-only pay TV. Pay TV had first dibs on them after their theater release and before HBO. Through TWC, Lind had had a hand in helping a budding Canadian film producer named Robert Lantos get his start when he bought a package of erotic films, the best of the New York Erotic Film Festival, in the seventies, Lantos' first major film sale. "At first, we had a lot of problems and so, Ted called it the 'Lind Lemon' but eventually it made a lot of money for us," says Lind. "Ted called a number of things we purchased together over the years Lind's Lemon. If it's really bad, or if it looks bad now, it becomes the Lind Lemon, or Phil's Folly. Even if it's good, it still becomes the Lind Lemon for a while, but if it's bad, it's just the Lind Lemon."

Rogers and Lind exhausted just about every idea to attract subscribers until the CRTC stopped them. Where Canada might have been the leader, it became the follower. Today, Canada's specialty channels are mere knock-offs of their U.S. forerunners: CNN, The Weather Channel, ESPN. "We had all kinds of crazy ideas in the seventies, but they were all prescient," says Lind. "They lasted about four months. We were competing with the broadcasters, and you could never do that as a cable operator. You could never compete. You could never offer anything decent."

At the federal government's request, the CRTC initiated a third inquiry into pay television. In 1980, five years after HBO's satellite debut, the Therrien Committee recommended that a Canadian television satellite service be allowed, a decision the DOC, with a broader mandate than the CRTC's cultural protectionist objectives, applauded. The DOC viewed pay TV as a way of stimulating Telesat's satellite usage. The cable industry hoped pay TV would provide them with another stream of revenue.

As it turned out, the broadcasters had little reason to worry about competition, since the new channels fizzled soon after their launch. Just coming out of a recession, cable TV subscribers were reluctant to pay an extra $16 per channel for old movies and aging Canadian film classics like *Goin' Down the Road*. "Having just seen previews of the programming to be offered through the various new pay TV channels," one viewer wrote to the *Toronto Star* in a letter, "we have opted instead to increase substantially our donations to the original quality, commercial-free alternatives, TVOntario and PBS." Ultimately, Astral Bellevue Pathé Inc., an unsuccessful first-round pay-TV applicant, controlled by the Toronto Bronfmans and Montreal's Greenberg family, bailed out First Choice and turned it into The Movie Network. In 1984, the CRTC then neatly split

Canada into East and West to create a movie-channel duopoly that remained intact for the next 22 years. There would be no homegrown HBO.

Initially, the CRTC was cool to cable. By refusing to permit the importation of distant signals by microwave, the CRTC tried to prevent the cable industry from expanding into unserved regions—geographically disadvantaged Canadians living too far away from the U.S. border to pick up signals with ordinary rooftop antennas. The Prairies (except Winnipeg), the Atlantic provinces and the northern regions of all the other provinces were cut off. The public outcry forced the Commission to reverse its ban in 1971.

The broadcasters, meanwhile, were furious when the cable owners began airing U.S. channels, not because it competed with their domestic programming, but because they were already airing the more popular American programs during prime time to attract viewers. They continually played the culture card, casting cable as the "Trojan Horse menace" to the entire Canadian broadcasting system. Their motives were far from altruistic. They were more interested in their bottom line than developing quality Canadian content. (The two do not necessarily equate.)

By the early seventies, no fewer than 23 U.S. border TV stations were drawing substantial advertising dollars out of Canada, with six stations, including three Buffalo network affiliates, deriving some 40 percent of their gross revenues from Canadian advertisers. In dollar terms, the six U.S. stations shared as much as $20 million a year in gross Canadian advertising revenue.

The CRTC then restricted the industry's rediffusion of American signals to two channels, one commercial and one non-commercial. Well, needless to say, that did not sit well with either TV viewers or an industry intent on growing.

W. Edwin (Ted) Jarmain, son of cable pioneer Ed Jarmain, and Bob Short, the industry association's president, proposed the idea of simultaneous substitution, or signal substitution, to get the CRTC to back off of its proposal to limit the carriage of distant U.S. signals. In signal substitution, cable systems replace the U.S. signals, including their commercials, with the local Canadian channels' programs if both air identical programs at the same time. The CRTC embraced signal substitution, but also limited the carriage of distant U.S. signals to three commercial networks (ABC, CBS, NBC) and PBS, also called the 3+1 rule, which was later expanded to 4+1 to include Rupert Murdoch's Fox Network in 1994. "I believed the consequences of our not having made that give would have been pretty steep," says Jarmain.

Initially, the broadcasters were opposed to signal substitution because it meant they would have to give up the advance release they had negotiated with the U.S. networks. Ultimately, they were handed a powerful economic incentive to flood prime-time viewing hours with American programs that were virtually guaranteed to be popular with audiences and advertisers alike. It's signal substitution that prevents Canadian TV viewers from seeing the much-ballyhooed U.S. commercials during the National Football League's Super Bowl.

In 1973, Rogers Cable was the first Canadian cable carrier to begin deleting U.S. commercials, sparking a 15-year war between the United States and Canada that was fought in the courts and spilled over into the free-trade talks of the eighties. Rogers—the "defender of the Canadian way of selling soap"—began randomly deleting U.S. commercials from programs carried into the 142,000 homes of his customers and substituting them with plugs for his own cable services. He wasn't compelled to take action because his licenses had already been renewed; Rogers, showing his patriotic plumage, just believed it was the right thing to do. He was proud to have been a part of CFTO and didn't want to be regarded as an enemy of Canada's broadcasting industry. By taking the subsequent body blows on behalf of the CRTC, which hadn't mandated stripping out U.S. commercials, he also ingratiated himself with the regulator. The three big Buffalo affiliates sued Rogers Cable and the CRTC.

In 1976, Ottawa finally sought to stem the outflow of advertising dollars with Bill C-58, which disallowed advertising expenses deductions for tax purposes if the expenses were incurred on border stations. In 1977, the Supreme Court of Canada rejected appeals from the U.S. networks. But, that didn't end the dispute.

The United States used the "television border war" in the mid-eighties to pressure Canada into putting cultural industries on the free trade negotiating table. Ottawa agreed to amend Canada's *Copyright Act*—as part of the 1988 Free Trade Agreement—thereby forcing Canada's cable companies to start paying for the rights to retransmit distant signals, ending the free ride they had enjoyed ever since they first began plucking distant signals out of the air for free and retransmitting them to their subscribers for a fee.

In 1990, the cable television industry was ordered to pay $50 million annually in copyright fees, of which 85 percent went to U.S. networks. "Whereas the border stations elevated the economic issue [of Bill C-58] to one of free trade and free flow of information, Canada elevated the economic issue to one of cultural protectionism," wrote Barry Berlin in his book *The American Trojan Horse*.

It all boiled down to ad revenue. Seeing cable's threat, CTV's Murray Chercover led the assault before the CRTC. "… [M]ultiplicity of program choices inherently infers fragmentation … there won't be a single audience large enough to use as a marketing instrument, so that source of revenue is gone. Now, that means we're gone," he predicted, "unless some magical fairy godfather appears in the clear blue."

He did not need to worry. The indomitable Pierre Juneau was the industry's magical fairy godfather. "I think it would be a bad move for cable companies to get involved in production in an industrial way," Juneau said in 1974, reiterating his opposition to advertising on cable. "I think advertising is already too widespread."

Oddly, the CRTC did encourage local program production, although it wasn't mandatory. Lind latched on to that faint glimmer of light. On its local community station, Rogers Cable aired CNN-like coverage before Ted Turner launched CNN. In 1977, when a gunman held 13 people hostage in a National Bank of Canada branch at King and Yonge streets, a shocking occurrence for a city then nicknamed "Toronto The Good," Rogers Cable—a mere two blocks away—raced over and broadcast the drama non-stop for 11 straight hours. CBC, CTV and CBS all sought to air Rogers' footage.

In an effort to protect the more politically powerful broadcasters, the regulator ordered Rogers Cable to pull its novel broadcasts off the air. With a few rare exceptions, the CRTC, kowtowing to the broadcasters, kept the cable TV industry shut out of the content game for virtually the next three decades. "In the '50s, we were enthusiastic idiots. Nobody thought it could succeed. In the '60s, we were local boys that made good," former Premier Cablevision chairman Garth Pither told an industry publication. "Then, when we got around the CRTC in the '70s, we were a threat to the Canadian way of life for fragmenting the local audiences."

If the cable companies couldn't develop content, or own channels outright, they pushed for carriage access to the new cable channels emerging in the United States to offer their subscribers more programming choice. By 1980, some 28 national cable channels had emerged in the United States, including HBO, the first national cable TV service, Ted Turner's WTB (later just TBS), Christian Broadcast Network's CBN (later the Family Channel), the Showtime movie service, Warner's Nickelodeon, TMC, Getty Oil's Sports Programming Network (later called ESPN) and Turner's CNN. Finally, in 1984, the CRTC approved five specialty channels—MuchMusic, TSN, Chinavision, Cathay and Telelatino—with Canadian content requirements for cable distribution along with 17 approved U.S. signals. The regulator required the cable companies to link them to the U.S. channels to ensure distribution of the new Canadian channels. U.S. channels such as music video channel MTV and sports channel ESPN weren't allowed in Canada because of MuchMusic and TSN. The commission's "banana republic" policy was, to say the least, highly controversial and created a whole new cast of programming monopolists in the guise of cultural protectionism. The CRTC gradually granted more specialty channels licenses, all the while banning U.S. versions of channels that were "deemed too subversive for Canadians to watch in their original form—unless, of course, the same programming passes through the hands of a Canadian middleman or monopolist who will culturally sanitize the programming by skimming off a fat profit," *Globe and Mail* columnist Terence Corcoran succinctly stated. (The CRTC still bans HBO.)

Just as the broadcasters felt besieged, the cable guys felt constrained. The broadcasters "hated us for bringing in Buffalo and they hated us for bringing in more channels. The whole time the broadcasters, the CBC, but mainly CFTO, complained to the commission and the commission would come down hard on us. They had 'whining' departments. Nobody else was doing it. So, why couldn't we do it? We were an absolute anathema to existing broadcasters and they pinned us down for many, many years," says Lind. "They're still pinning us down."

"It's a symbiotic relationship between the broadcasters and the commission," he says, cursing under his breath. "The commission has protected the broadcasters, whereas in the U.S., almost all the specialty channels are owned by cable companies; in Canada, almost none—for that very reason. We were well ahead of the broadcasters. But, the commission was unsure."

Rogers wasn't allowed to produce content. He was prevented from introducing pay TV, a new lucrative revenue source. Rogers already boasted more than 82-percent cable penetration of the homes in his monopoly territories. The only way to grow the business was by acquisition. In the seventies, Rogers audaciously began to stalk Canada's two largest cable TV companies: Canadian Cablesystems Ltd. and Premier Communications Ltd. Rogers, along with Lind, proceeded on parallel tracks, unsure if they'd succeed in snaring either one.

CHAPTER 8

Predatory Strike

"Ted's style is not given to fifty-fifty partnerships."

—Trevor Eyton

"WHY STOP AT FIVE PERCENT?" TD Bank's Robin Korthals quipped to Ted Rogers. Rogers had just told Korthals by phone that he intended to buy a 5-percent interest in Canadian Cablesystems Ltd. (CCL), a company four times the size of Rogers Cable. The year was 1974. Korthals recalls that he was just trying to smoke out Rogers' true intentions towards CCL. Instead, Rogers took it as a vote of confidence. Emboldened, he bought 350,000 CCL shares—or 9 percent of the stock—on a Friday afternoon in mid-February. "I would have been incredulous if all he wanted was five percent," says Korthals. "When we did credit arrangements with Ted, a deal was no sooner signed than he would want more."

CCL was created three years earlier when Famous Players, controlled by multi-billion-dollar U.S. conglomerate Gulf & Western Industries Inc., underwent a major restructuring to comply with the federal government's new foreign ownership rules. The cable assets were spun off into a widely held public company, while a new subsidiary, Famous Players Ltd., was created to house the movie theater and real estate assets. Gulf & Western held a 51-percent stake in Famous Players and the newly created CCL owned the remaining 49 percent. CCL, at the time, had about 4,000 stockholders. Unable to finance a buyout, cable pioneer Ed Jarmain, who merged his systems with Famous Players, became a small minority owner. Jonlab Investments Ltd., privately owned by John H. (Jake) Moore of Brascan Ltd. and his associates, received a big chunk of treasury shares when it provided the cable company with much needed funding. Jonlab held an 8-percent stake.

Brascan, with its roots in Brazil's power industry, was Canada's sixth-largest company, with assets of more than $3 billion from mining, beer (John Labatt), real estate, chocolates (Laura Secord), merchant banking and insurance (London Life). Jake Moore, a London, Ontario native, was its chairman and chief executive officer, one of the "unofficial triumvirate" at the apex of Canada's financial establishment—the others being Argus Corp.'s Bud McDougald and Power Corp.'s Paul Desmarais. Moore was also a close friend of Phil Linds' parents and knew Linds' late ex-wife Anne. Together they shared a passion for the arts.

In 1972, Moore had hired Anthony F. (Tony) Griffiths, a Harvard MBA, to manage Jonlab. Griffiths, a Burmese native schooled at Ridley College and then McGill University, came from Consumers Packaging Co., where he had been president. Griffiths not only decided to invest in CCL—getting its initial equity stake in return—he left Jonlab to become the cable company's president. It wasn't long before he was fending off Ted Rogers.

Two days later after Rogers' purchase, on Sunday night, Griffiths received a phone call from Robert Smith, a Rogers director and president of Slater Walker, the Canadian unit of a U.K. merchant bank that had acquired UNAS. Smith informed Griffiths that a consortium had acquired the CCL shares and planned to buy more with the intention of making a "friendly proposal" to management. Smith recalled that he bet Rogers a case of champagne that Rogers wouldn't be able to pull off a merger. He was right. Griffiths turned to his former employer for help. Jonlab responded to the overture by raising its stake to 23 percent from 8 percent, part of Moore's plan to incorporate the cable company's earnings into Jonlab's, which were highly leveraged at the time. Stymied by Jonlab, Rogers sent Smith a case of Dom Pérignon. Griffiths took it for granted that Jonlab would always be there to support the cable company. He would come to misread Jake Moore and underestimate Rogers.

Rogers had long admired Ed Jarmain and his son, CCL president W. Edwin (Ted) Jarmain, who held three university degrees—an engineering degree and Master of Science degrees in both electrical engineering and industrial management, all from the acclaimed Massachusetts Institute of Technology in Boston. Ted Jarmain had taught university courses in industrial management at MIT and the University of Western Ontario, London. Both men were well known and highly regarded in the cable industry for their commitment to excellence and innovation.

"I have always been a great admirer of very talented people, and Ted Jarmain was such a person," says Rogers. "I thought, boy, I would love to be a partner with this guy. I kept talking to Ted about why don't we merge our companies and get rid of Famous Players.

"I didn't quite know how but somehow we could do it, and he would, at least, encourage me to come to dinner to talk about it, but nothing came of it, and my problem is that once I've got a project going, I don't let go."

Unable to get anywhere with CCL, Rogers wanted to pursue Premier Cablevision, a Vancouver-based company that was even bigger than CCL. He also wanted to keep his position in CCL. He was still highly leveraged. He couldn't afford to build a position in Premier using debt with potential cash sitting idle in CCL stock. Rogers weighed his options with directors Robert Smith and John A. Tory and his Toronto-Dominion (TD) banker, Ernest Mercier. He was told to make up his mind. Rogers eventually blew out his CCL position and used the proceeds to buy stock in Premier.

Premier's founder, Sydney Welsh, had branched out from his father's plumbing and heating business in 1952 to sell TVs and antennas. He and two partners, Bud Shepard and Garth Pither, managed to secure pole attachment rights from B.C. Telephone and bought out their main rival George Chandler's Tru Vu Television System to create Vancouver Cablevision Ltd. In 1963, Shepard met CBS vice president Harvey Struthers on a trip to Seattle, a meeting that led to CBS buying a 75-percent stake. (Struthers had followed Shepard into the bathroom at a Seattle cable conference, neither noticing until inside that they had sauntered into the ladies' room. They shared a laugh and got talking. Shepard bemoaned the difficulty of getting financing from skeptical Canadian banks.) CBS invested some $18 million, enabling Vancouver Cablevision to expand to Victoria, to Toronto with York Cablevision (and later Keeble Cable), and places like Hawaii and Dublin, Ireland. CBS was then forced to divest all but 18.5 percent of its stake to comply with the 20-percent foreign ownership cap on cable companies.

In 1971, the company, renamed Premier Cablevision, became publicly traded. Shepard was Premier's president until May 1975 when he and his partners hired lawyer Stuart H. Wallace to manage the company. Then, eight months later in January 1976, Shepard died at age 46 of cancer in Houston, where he had been hospitalized receiving special treatment for an illness for several months. His tragic death put the company into play. In March, Rogers spent $5.8 million to amass 20 percent of Premier's shares on the open market in the span of less than two weeks. Rogers sent Stuart Wallace a telegram expressing his "complete faith" in the industry. "If it is just an investment, of course, we are delighted that Mr. Rogers shows his enthusiasm in such a financial way," Wallace replied.

In his four years at the helm, Wallace rebuffed three overtures from Rogers. Broadcaster Frank Griffiths (no relation to Tony Griffiths) also courted Premier, but had more success. Griffiths, who owned the Vancouver Canucks NHL franchise, was transforming Western Broadcasting Ltd. into a radio station powerhouse. The company was later renamed WIC Western International Communications Ltd. He managed to persuade the Premier ownership group to sell to him, only to have the CRTC quash his bid for control in late July 1977. The regulator argued that the merged entity would create too much debt, an ironic statement in light of its future decisions. It also expressed concern the stock purchase primarily benefited the principals rather than the public. The unexpected ruling threw Premier wide open again to other bidders. CCL immediately jumped into the fray. Rogers couldn't. He had already agreed to sell his 21-percent block in Premier to Frank Griffiths, although he refused to complete the sale after the CRTC rejected Western's bid, prompting Griffiths to seek an interim injunction to prevent Rogers from tendering the shares to CCL's offer. By then, Rogers had already trained his sights on the next best prize, CCL, the one he wanted all along.

But Rogers was about to get a major break.

He found a willing seller of CCL shares in Royal Trust Co. CCL had two major shareholders: Jonlab—now controlled by Jake Moore's Brascan through a highly controversial and self-enriching sale involving Moore as both buyer and seller—with a 25.7-percent stake; and Royal Trust, which also owned approximately 25 percent on behalf of its clientele. The Jarmain family owned just 8 percent. CCL management owned another 1.3 percent. Rogers' broker, Peter Legault, at MacDougall, MacDougall & MacTier, a boutique stock brokerage, facilitated the transaction. Since the trust company was slowly pulling together its paperwork, Legault says he decided to call Brascan "on a whim" to see if Jake Moore might consider selling Jonlab's position in CCL. He rang Moore at four-thirty in the afternoon.

"Funny you should call now. Why don't you come over around 6 p.m.?" he recalls Moore telling him.

Legault arrived at his office promptly at six and told Moore he had a buyer for the CCL block. He outlined the basic terms without disclosing the buyer's identity. His firm, known as the 3 Macs, was based in Montreal and widely known for representing brewery giant Molson Cos., which made no secret of its attempts to diversify out of beer. The next morning, Moore called Legault. They verbally agreed to the terms. Legault then told him who the buyer was: Ted Rogers.

"He was quite shocked," recalls Legault. "He thought my bidder was going to be Molson Companies."

Rogers backed out of his deal with Royal Trust, opting to buy Jonlab's share block. He was buying the stock through RTL, the family holding company. He couldn't buy both stakes without first seeking the regulator's prior approval.

The CRTC had a 30-percent threshold. Investors owning less than 30 percent of a regulated company did not have to disclose their shareholdings.

On Friday, September 2, 1977, before the Labour Day holiday weekend, Rogers, Bob Francis—his unflappable chief financial officer, Legault and Lionel Schipper, a Brascan lawyer, met at the helipad at Toronto's waterfront. Rogers had chartered a helicopter to fly them to Jake Moore's farm in London. Francis was carrying a check inside his briefcase for $4.3 million, the down payment for the Jonlab block, but the weather wasn't cooperating. Grounded by fog, the group trekked to the offices of Brascan's merchant bank Triarch Corp. in the Richmond-Adelaide Centre in downtown Toronto.

In the building's lobby, Rogers stopped at a pay telephone to call Tony Griffiths to let him know he was about to buy Jonlab's stake. Griffiths urged him not to buy the block because management was working on a plan to take CCL private for $64 million. It was all too little, too late. The company was vulnerable to a hostile takeover. The Jarmain family couldn't afford to build up a controlling position and Griffiths had mistakenly trusted Jake Moore. Rogers replied that if he or Jarmain were to buy the Jonlab block "without further delay," he wouldn't proceed. Griffiths, apparently, didn't offer to buy the Jonlab block from Rogers.

Rogers ended the call, and took the elevator up to Triarch's 11th-floor offices, where he signed an agreement to buy 25.6 percent of the CCL shares held by Jonlab for $17.2 million, or $16.75 a share—a 24-percent premium from the previous day's closing price. By quarter to seven that evening, with the fog lifted, Rogers flew to Tobin's island cottage, where he made it in time for dinner. He had just set into motion the industry's first hostile takeover.

The next day, John Graham rang the outgoing CRTC chairman, Harry Boyle, to advise him of the purchase. Boyle also received a telex from Griffiths, imploring the CRTC "to do everything in its power to prevent Rogers" from buying more CCL shares. For the next 10 days, Rogers and John Graham made, and took, calls from Jarmain and Griffiths.

J. Trevor Eyton, a corporate law partner at Tory's and the empire's overseer, was a friend of Rogers. The two men had shared a cramped office in their articling days together at the Tory law firm. Eyton recalls that he and Jack Cockwell were killing time at John F. Kennedy International Airport in New York, waiting for their delayed flight to Rio de Janeiro, Brazil to board, when they began discussing ways of diversifying Edper, which had mostly real estate holdings. Cockwell, a tough, no-nonsense accountant who had emigrated from South

Africa, managed Edper for Edward and Peter Bronfman, the disenfranchised nephews of liquor baron Sam Bronfman. Cockwell would gain renown in the eighties for masterminding the transformation of Brascan into Canada's largest conglomerate through an intricate web of companies, worth an estimated $100 billion at its peak.

The cable industry was attractive; it was garnering a lot of press. The cable and broadcasting owners were on the prowl in the seventies, trying to consolidate. In the United States, the city franchising wars were just heating up. The two men initially viewed cable TV as a rapidly growing tax-protected business that spun off regular cash flow. They reckoned it was a good fit for them.

Eyton called Rogers from the terminal to tell him that Edper planned to go after CCL. He knew Rogers was in Bermuda, visiting his in-laws at Romay House off Elephant Walk in Tucker's Town, a beautiful hillside estate with a championship croquet lawn. Eyton remembers ringing him just as the family was finishing dinner. Since it was considered poor form to ring during the dinner hour, Eyton was curtly told Ted Rogers was unavailable and to call back later. He insisted, saying that it was important to talk to him now because he was flying out of the country and would be out of touch for some time. Ten minutes later, Rogers came to the phone.

"Jack and I are here, and we know that you're at twenty-five percent, and you can't buy any more, but we're buying it," Eyton recalls telling him. "We've bought a few shares, and we thought we might buy a few more. We're not sure how many, but we just wanted you to know, as a courtesy. We're not asking for anything, but we thought we'd buy significantly more shares."

Eyton recalls a pause on the other end of the line before Rogers said in his booming voice, "I'd think that'd be terrific."

By month's end, an unidentified buyer—not engaged in cable TV—scooped up $5.9-million worth of CCL shares in the open market, representing 10 percent of the stock, in two big block purchases. The name of mystery buyer—Edper Investments Ltd.—didn't hit the newspapers for another week.

Edper, through Jimmy Connacher's Gordon Securities Ltd., amassed a 24.2-percent stake in CCL on the open market. Upon their return from Brazil, Eyton and Cockwell met with Rogers and John Graham. They reached a verbal understanding that each would support the other in its efforts to put three men on CCL's 15-man board of directors, and if either of them decided to sell their stock, they would give the other first shot at buying it. Rogers proposed the "shotgun," a mutual buy-sell provision giving either of them the right to offer their stake to the other at a specified price, subject to the CRTC's approval. If approval wasn't forthcoming, they included a "slingshot" provision, permitting the joint sale of the shares to a third party. Combined, the two groups now owned 50.01 percent of the cable TV company.

"It was all over then, and Tony Griffiths and Ted Jarmain knew that. There was no room for debate," says Eyton. "They were looking to [the CRTC], but the fact is we had the shares and the fact is we were going to sell them to somebody. Ted was always nervous on that shotgun, that we'd have more firepower."

In early October, the CRTC blocked Rogers and Edper from buying more shares on the open market, pending a review. The rules of the regulatory game were that a cable company's license couldn't change hands without the CRTC's prior approval. In private meetings with the regulatory body, Rogers and Edper claimed they weren't after control, but merely investing in a growth industry. In later public hearings, Rogers emphasized to the regulator that he was seeking "to do a joint venture" where "several different ownerships each have minority interests and work together, with no party having control." Barely a week later, the regulator lifted its order, seemingly satisfied that a transfer of control of CCL hadn't taken place. The regulator was highly criticized for meeting with Rogers and Edper behind closed doors rather than in a public forum.

Meanwhile, Ted Jarmain and his father sought a rapprochement of sorts with Rogers. Jarmain proposed to create a holding company structure in which Rogers and Edper would each be offered 24-percent stakes with appropriate board representation. However, once the Jarmains learned of the shotgun arrangement, they immediately withdrew their offer. "Quite frankly, I now feel, and my father now feels, we were misled," Jarmain later told the CRTC. Feeling lied to, and cheated, they refused to accept either party as a shareholder or director. Knowing that control of a cable company's license must not change hands without the CRTC's prior approval, Griffiths argued that Rogers and Edper broke the rules with their shotgun arrangement. On the advice of outside counsel, he refused to register the transfer of shares to Rogers and Edper until the CRTC ruled that a change in control had occurred.

Griffiths demanded a public hearing, a wish that was granted. The CRTC called for a public airing of the dispute in January. A week later, Rogers canceled lunch with his idol, John Diefenbaker, to accommodate Griffiths' schedule. He hoped to make peace while breaking bread. It just wasn't in the cards.

The CRTC held not one, but rather three, hearings to resolve the control issue: the first, to consider if the shotgun arrangement constituted a change in control; the second, to sort out procedural matters before the actual takeover hearing; and the third, to decide the fate of the CCL licenses.

The first hearing, held over two days at the Downtown Holiday Inn in Toronto in mid-January 1978, was high drama. The hotel's Commonwealth Centre Room was filled with tension and hostility that only mounted as the months passed.

Sitting in the front row with Loretta were two of the Rogers children. The lawyers and spectators crammed into the room were surprised to see children there. Charles Dalfen, lawyer, former professor and Departmant of Communications (DOC) legal advisor, who at 35 was serving as a CRTC commissioner, witheringly remarked to Rogers, "Maybe, at the next one, you can bring your grandmother." The children weren't there the next day.

"I knew we were going to get some flak," said Rogers later. "And I think it's [good] for children to grow up knowing the world is not always a nice place. It prepares them for life." Lisa, the eldest, was 10 years old. Edward was just eight; the same age his father was when Velma issued his marching orders. "I remember just sitting there, not a whole lot besides that," says Edward. Just as well.

CCL was fighting mad. Donald J. Wright, the company's outside counsel, spewed against Rogers a tirade of accusations of distorting the facts and misleading the CRTC to cover his tracks, and called the shotgun "a very subtle, very clever corporate maneuver which is so admired in certain circles, centered around Bay Street." He accused them of working "together in concert" to guarantee effective control and questioned if such a "predatory" tactic was in the public's interest. "This is perhaps a classic confrontation between rampant and unrestrained free enterprise on the one hand, and the Commission's publicly announced policies on the other," he said. He repeatedly reminded the CRTC that Rogers didn't seek the CRTC's approval first before acquiring a control block. Ted Jarmain spoke of the company's *esprit de corps* and commitment to excellence and professionalism. "It was," wrote *Toronto Star* columnist Jack Miller, "the most caustic personal attack on one major operator by another in the annals of the CRTC."

"I was very upset," recalls Wright. "I took the position that they were saying something that wasn't true or even if it was technically true, it wasn't true in a matter of substance. I remember John Graham getting up at the end of the argument and saying that, until that point, the hearings before the CRTC had always been gentlemanly affairs, implying that I hadn't been a gentleman. I must say, I was really quite embarrassed. However, I got over it. I get pretty aggressive when I'm representing a client. If I was doing it again, I'd probably handle it much more diplomatically."

On February 9, 1978, the CRTC ruled that the share purchases did constitute a change of effective control. So, a new hearing—the real takeover hearing—was called to decide if the control group should be awarded the cable TV licenses. The date was set for September 12. Before the main event, nearly a dozen lawyers for the three groups appeared before the Commission to squabble over the hearing's format, who the applicant should be and who should be allowed to appear. The CRTC decided Rogers was the sole applicant, and granted CCL, the effective licensee, the right to make a full presentation.

•

With the hearing date set, Jarmain asked Rudi Engel, who was working at London Cable TV, to use his many community contacts and compile an anti-Rogers petition. At the time, he was producing the *Peterson Report* for the local community cable channel on behalf of David Peterson, who was then a Member of Provincial Parliament for London Centre en route to becoming Ontario's 20th premier. Engel, who wanted to stay neutral, begrudgingly asked a few people to sign the petition, including Peterson. "No, I won't do that," Peterson told Engel. "Ted Rogers is an important guy and I may have to deal with him in the future."

In April, barely two months after the CRTC's ruling, Edper agreed to sell its CCL block to Rogers for $17.4 million, or $18 a share. Peter Bronfman had grown uneasy in the regulatory spotlight. Edper also realized it would have to commit substantial capital resources to the company, especially with a partner like Rogers.

"Ted is the visionary and wants to be on the leading edge of technology," says Trevor Eyton. "He wants the best equipment, the best system and all of that costs money. We liked cash flow. Suddenly, we realized we had this investment that we would have to double or triple to keep going. Ted had a different vision and a way of managing. Ted's style is not given to fifty-fifty partnerships."

Trevor Eyton recalls Peter Bronfman saying, "I know we have the shotgun, and we'll make a little money if we sell the shares, but Ted, this is his heart's blood. This is important to Ted. It's not important to us. So, we won't exercise the shotgun. We'll just tell Ted we're prepared to sell to him and give him time to arrange his financing and buy us out." Eyton went on to say, "[Peter] liked and respected Ted and didn't want to put him in a corner. So, we did that and really at Peter's direction.

"I'm not sure what Jack or I would have done," Eyton laughs, but he and Cockwell would develop a more calculating, cut-throat reputation. "Peter didn't interfere very much, but on things like that, and that was a big decision, he would be the person to make the call. He would lead mostly with his heart."

The CRTC put the onus on the applicant, in this case RTL, Rogers' private holding company, to demonstrate that approval of the transfer of ownership would be in the best interest of the public, the communities served by the licensee and the Canadian broadcasting system as a whole.

Rogers' right-hand man, Phil Lind, made sure they left no stone unturned. In what would become his hallmark at Rogers, Lind ran the equivalent of a political campaign to get the job done. He made sure the Rogers team knew every last detail about the decision makers. Since every applicant before and after always presented the Commission with a grab bag of promises, it was important to know the commissioners' interests and beliefs. Rogers made note of being told Charles Dalfen was opposed to commercial deletion and had a "distrust of people making money." Dalfen was also in favor of more distinctly Canadian programs. Rogers spent $16,000 to prepare for the three-day hearings. Lind commissioned 10 consultants' studies, mostly on policy subjects. His team did their due diligence on their opponent's expert witnesses to the extent that they learned one of them had a drinking problem. Unbeknownst to Rogers, someone left a bottle of whiskey outside an expert witness' hotel room door the night before he was scheduled to give testimony before the commissioners. His muddled presentation surprised all but a handful of spectators.

Both sides overwhelmed the Commission with paper. In all, there was a stack of 23 CRTC volumes 30 inches high. CCL rounded up 1,200 interventions, while Rogers mustered up 90. CCL mounted a smear campaign against Rogers, flooding the regulator with anonymous letters of complaints. In Cornwall, Ontario, fictitious names of subscribers appeared on petitions supporting CCL. Lind, who needed someone he could trust implicitly, brought in John H. Tory, the son of John A. Tory and like his father a lawyer by training, to help him formulate responses to the interveners filing on behalf of CCL. The two connected initially in politics, when Lind worked for Robert Stanfield, the former federal Progressive Conservative leader. Lind packaged the responses in the "green book" for the Commission's convenience, a small deed sure to engender goodwill among the commissioners.

The growing enmity between the two sides was such that Lind's close friend Colin Watson, a CCL vice president who was running Metro Cable, angrily remarked, "Rogers is treating this whole thing as if it were a takeover of Acme Screw & Gear." Lind would later caution his friend to lie low. He didn't want any bad blood to fester between him and Rogers if they emerged the victor, especially since Rogers hoped to keep the management team intact. Lind walked a delicate line between the two camps, caught between his friendship with Watson and his loyalty to Rogers. He rarely associates with the enemy—a deliberate decision that leaves him free of any emotional ties that might otherwise cloud his judgment. (For instance, he doesn't know BCE's Michael Sabia and prefers it that way.)

Andrew J. Roman, a partner at law firm Miller Thomson, was representing the Public Interest Advocacy Centre during the hearings when Trevor Eyton sought to hire him. "Everyone has a price, Roman, what's yours?"

"My price is amusement, and I'm afraid you have nothing to offer me," replied Roman dryly.

The only takeover defense CCL had was the CRTC. The licenses were public property. The government, through its quasi-judicial regulator, is the guardian of those licenses. The argument was made—and ignored—that the transfer of ownership should be determined through a public process and not through private or public stock purchases. But, since the regulator refused to hold competitive hearings whenever licenses came up for renewal, the only way to gain a license was to take over a company that already had one. The CRTC essentially was abdicating its licensing authority. It allowed the transfer of the license, or the transfer of effective control over a license, permitting trafficking in licenses. On paper, they were licenses but, in fact, they were corporate approvals to carry on business. If a holding company held 20 or 30 licenses, the regulator was not going to cancel one or two of them. *Globe and Mail* columnist Geoffrey Stevens raised the issue in two columns, "Who's in Charge?" and "The Empire Builders," pointing out that private stock dealings and other corporate maneuvers should have no bearing whatsoever on who had the right to apply for or to control cable licenses. For its part, the regulator maintained it wouldn't accept competitive applications on transfers or renewals because it would constitute "an unwarranted interference in the market." What market? asked Stevens. "The market, presumably, for second-hand broadcasting licenses. It's a busy and expensive market."

Herschel Hardin, a public interest advocate and former NDP candidate, wrote *Closed Circuits: The Sellout of Canadian Television*, a 1985 exposé of Canada's broadcasting system. Hardin says the regulator should have stopped the takeover. "The Commission should have simply required Rogers to put its stock back into the market, or held a competitive hearing, where all parties could have bid on the license, and then sort out the assets later on. The Commission never established a structure consistent with its regulatory licensing mandate. It allowed private purchases of assets, instead of licenses, virtually undermining its own licensing authority," he says. "We wanted the Commission to make the license primary and stock-market purchases, or private company sale, subsidiary to the logic of public licenses. They never took that step."

Hardin ran up against the system when the regulator rejected his group's application to take over cable TV licenses in British Columbia. The Commission later awarded them to Rogers. He says his time in the industry made him "totally cynical about the process."

On September 12, 1978, the parties gathered at the Auberge de la Chaudière in Hull, Quebec for the first of the three-day hearings. Both cable companies carried the proceedings live over satellite. CCL replaced Don Wright with his more temperate brother, Robert, who later became Ontario Securities Commission (OSC) chairman. CCL went into the hearings with the attitude that they were the better managers, indeed, the better stewards of the public cable TV licenses than Rogers. "A lot of people inside the company at the time really didn't think Ted was going to be very good for the company either to help employee relationships or the service record," says Tony Gooch, CCL's former chief financial officer. "His service record with subscribers was pretty awful and ours wasn't that much better, either."

CCL, with annual revenue of $26 million, had 460,000 subscribers, more than 117,000 of which were in Toronto through Metro Cable. Rogers Cable, a privately held company, had 195,000 customers. If CCL was regarded "cautious" and "conservative," Rogers Cable was considered "imaginative" and "innovative." On sheer financial strength, CCL had a better record, which was one of the key reasons Rogers wanted to buy it. The company had an amazingly low debt-to-equity ratio of 0.17—which, while commendable, also meant, from Rogers' viewpoint, it was underleveraged and, as such, was missing potential opportunities to boost earnings by financing projects that could earn a higher return than the cost of debt. Unlike CCL, RTL was carrying 1.7 times more debt than equity. CCL had 12 professional engineers on its payroll; Rogers Cable had none. CCL was regarded as a "superbly run" company with a decentralized style of management and an engineering expertise that was far superior to Rogers Cable. Whatever he might have lacked, Rogers fielded a team that had—and displayed—more charisma, wit and ambition. Faced with the prospect and ignominy of losing the company, the CCL team displayed no sense of humor and had even less sense of theater.

"The two words 'charm offensive' come to mind," says former Globe and Mail business reporter Barbara Keddy, who covered the hearings. "I can't remember the other side [CCL], but I do remember Rogers. Rogers had more charm, and I think it was natural. They were fun, energized and they had a vision and they were going for it. They were better [at] PR."

In his intervention, Ed Jarmain painted Rogers as an amateur who would jeopardize the effectiveness of his tight-knit team if the CRTC permitted the takeover. He focused on his company's management philosophy, its quality of service, its emphasis on research and development, and quoted liberally from two management-consultant articles, one outlining the reasons corporate marriages fail, and the other, detailing the evils of corporate takeovers. He never once mentioned Rogers by name; he merely implied it with every statement he made. "Cablesystems has developed a superior management, whose accomplishments attest to its quality. I do not believe that the proposed takeover would enhance, or even maintain, the level of professionalism that has been achieved by the Cablesystems team.

"Even more disturbing to me, the proposed CEO would own or control half of the company. I believe that this is totally inappropriate in any public company. Obviously, Cablesystems would be stronger, and more effective, under a Board and management where there could be genuine interaction among peers.

"Cablesystems' management has the quality seldom found, even among engineers, namely, an innovative flair, tempered with a sense of good engineering and economics. ...The proposal before you would transfer the control and management of this sensitive operation to a new Board and management, which has heretofore shown no interest in research, and which is obviously deficient in the essential qualities I have just described; and furthermore, is lacking in both training and experience for R&D management.

"At worst, this valuable Cablesystems' asset would be destroyed. At best, it would be seriously jeopardized."

Phil Lind recalls that Rogers was upset and hurt by the remarks. When asked to respond the next day, Rogers replied, "I admire and revere Mr. Jarmain as a pioneer in engineering, as I do my own father. And, I'd ask him to accept that I have the same commitment as his son. I don't have the same knowledge in engineering, but I have the same commitment.

"I think that if you're looking for an applicant who will be able to understand the problems of the industry, that's the group of people that you see here, and we will go that last mile and do everything possible to make it work, and we know each other, and we respect each other." He stressed that apart from "the share thing," the two antagonists agreed on 95 percent of everything else. Whenever he or John Graham spoke too long, Lind kicked them under the table to get them to wrap it up. Rogers managed to throw a few punches: "CCL management just doesn't have a strong entrepreneurial thrust."

Rogers pledged some $3 million in social dividends, including a Metro-wide community programming service in Toronto, a special channel for Canadian programming for children, multicultural and French educational channels, a program studio for East York, and a commitment to devote 1 percent of annual revenue to a fund to support Canadian programming. Rogers also offered to spend $2.4 million over two years to transmit the federal House of Commons broadcasts across the country via satellite. He felt it was a waste of time to have Canada's Anik satellite sitting up there in space with unused capacity. It was the only promise the CRTC rejected.

Ted Jarmain said his plans for CCL's future were "more substantial and innovative by far" than anything Rogers could possibly propose. He added that there wasn't anything that Rogers has proposed that CCL couldn't do without a change of control. When he finished, he cursed the Rogers team under his breath: "Fie Upon Them."

"I don't think anyone understood what he was saying," laughs Tony Gooch, who was sitting next to Jarmain. "Ted [Rogers] outmaneuvered Ted, Tony and myself. He didn't win by clout; he won it by his skill in putting together a deal."

The commissioners were unmoved by CCL's management philosophy vis-à-vis their interpretation of how they thought Rogers might run the company. Pierre Camu, the CRTC chairman, described both companies as "probably the best in the country" in terms of service and programming, saying that the hearing characterized them as "two antagonists in the ring trying to protect [their] own interests."

On January 8, 1979, the CRTC approved Rogers' purchase of a 50-percent controlling interest in CCL. The decision hoisted Rogers from fifth to first place among Canada's cable TV companies. He tripled his subscribers to more than 600,000.

Rogers now had 17 percent of Canada's cable TV subscribers, while Vancouver-based Premier had a 14-percent market share. Montreal-based National Cablevision Ltd. was third, with 10 percent; and Maclean Hunter Cable TV Ltd. was the fourth largest, with 9 percent. In Toronto, Rogers Cable now controlled 37 percent of the cable TV households. By contrast, Premier dominated 67 percent of the Vancouver market and National Cablevision served 56 percent of Montreal's cable subscribers. Moffatt Communications Ltd. controlled 68 percent of Winnipeg.

The losers privately griped, blaming their loss to partisan politics: "Rogers is a well-known arch Conservative, and the Liberals don't want to be perceived to be interfering with business just before an election." With the country buckling from the strain of big budget deficits, high unemployment and high interest rates, Pierre Trudeau and his Liberal party called an election for May, which they lost to Joe Clark's Progressive Conservative party.

In the aftermath of the regulator's ruling, Ted Rogers, 46, sought rapprochement. Tears flowed at the CCL offices the day the CRTC's decision came down. For the past year, the executive team at CCL had been in a state of denial, confident the Commission would pick its bench strength over Rogers'. Jarmain had lost the family business against his will. Rogers, sensitive enough to the atmosphere, didn't storm in the next day. When he did visit their 26th floor offices at the Commercial Union Tower in the TD Centre, a black funeral wreath was hanging on the door to greet him.

Rogers met with the key CCL managers individually at his Adelaide Street office. "Let's talk, just the two of us," Rogers told Graham W. Savage. In the midst of the rancorous takeover fight, Rogers penned a note to Savage to congratulate him on his promotion to vice president. Just 29, Savage was the youngest vice president in the 58-year history of Famous Players-CCL. Rogers' thoughtfulness touched Savage.

Still, heading into the meeting, Savage fully expected to be fired. The people he had been working with—Ted Jarmain, Tony Griffiths and Tony Gooch—were all going to be fired. Gooch, who was negotiating their severance packages, asked Savage if he wanted to be included so that he would at least exit with some cash. He agreed. "I was not sure what the future would hold and had heard so many terrible things about [Rogers], and he's such an intimidating personality to a person not yet thirty," he says. "I wasn't sure if I wanted to join Ted or not. I sort of did and I sort of didn't."

Rogers wanted Graham Savage onboard. He refused outright to negotiate any severance package that included him. "God knows why he did that because I was not a senior person at that time. He seemed to know who I was," said Savage.

In the middle of the meeting between Rogers and Savage, the telephone rang. Rogers answered and was told that one of his relatives just died of cancer. Caught off-guard, Rogers was overcome with grief and began to cry. Savage was taken aback. He was seeing the compassionate side of Rogers that doesn't make it onto the business pages. "Wow, here's a side I hadn't heard about," he thought.

"I've been told about this terribly aggressive, absolutely flamboyant, take-no-prisoners kind of guy, and here he was shedding a quiet tear for a fairly distant relative. I thought, there's a real human being in there. I thought I should give this guy a chance."

Neither of them knew just how vital Savage would become to the company's growth. He was the financial alchemist who enabled Rogers to turn his bold rhetoric of competing with Bell into reality. He was one of a small coterie of lieutenants with a Young Turk mind-set in the new executive suite that helped keep Rogers in—and ahead—of the game. In a cast of hundreds, they included Phil Lind, 37; Bob Francis, his 43-year-old CFO; Jim Sward, 34, overseer of the radio assets; Savage; Lind's pal, Colin D. Watson, 38, who became head of the cable company; and engineer Nick Hamilton-Piercy, 41, who pioneered the use of fiber optics in the cable industry.

Colin Delacourt Watson, Graham Savage and Nick Hamilton-Piercy were all born in the U.K., although Hamilton-Piercy was in his twenties when he immigrated to Canada. Watson was born in Kattering, England in 1941 to a British schoolteacher and Princess Patricia Canadian Light Infantryman, the family settling in Vancouver in 1947, where Watson was raised. He went to the University of British Columbia before receiving his MBA from the University of Western Ontario and getting a job at Triarch. Watson became president of Metro Cable TV in 1974. Graham William Savage was born on the Isle of Man in 1949.

He had just turned six years old when his family docked in the port of New York in March 1955 en route to Canada. Savage did his undergraduate degree and his MBA at Queen's University in Kingston, Ontario. He lasted a year in the investment department at National Trustco—he found it "boring"—before joining Burns Bros., later Burns Fry and now BMO Nesbitt Burns, as a communications, steel and special situations analyst. Jarmain hired him after hearing him testify before the CRTC on how its policies impeded cable industry's ability to raise capital. Juneau still held court then. "We were arguing that if you wanted to [build] a strong communications sector, you needed an efficient capital market for them to raise money in," recalls Savage.

Jarmain remained with the company for several months to smooth the ownership transition. He, like Griffiths, prefers not to discuss the takeover. Rogers invited Jarmain's father onto the merged company's cable board. Years later, the late Ed Jarmain told *The Globe and Mail*'s Gordon Pitts that he liked Rogers, but added, "If somebody is battling you and trying to take over your company, you don't foster very much love for him." Rogers was hurt by his comments. "It saddened me. I think he's done well since we did the deal."

With his team in place, Rogers immediately reorganized the company's capital structure to ensure that no predator would ever do to him what he did to Jarmain and Griffiths. He intended to secure ironclad control over the company with the best takeover defense imaginable: dual-class shares—creating two classes of common stock, one with voting rights and one without—a structure that, while still controversial today, was then regarded as highly unusual. Rogers vested his family's control of the company in the voting A shares. The B shares were non-voting but offered their holders dividends. Having spent $36 million for a 50-percent position in CCL, Rogers then folded into CCL his own cable assets—valued at $34.6 million—for $9.5 million in cash and 2.26 million new class A treasury shares.

Rogers' next big break came three months later. In April 1979, Premier's president Stuart Wallace—Rogers' main roadblock—retired. Premier replaced him with George Fierheller, a Rogers' Sigma Chi frat brother. Fierheller, 46, a month older than Rogers, had spent 13 years at IBM Canada before co-founding Systems Dimensions Ltd., which he and his partners grew into Canada's largest independent computer-services company. Fierheller tried to make *Instant World* a reality in the seventies when he wanted to buy Ottawa Cablevision Ltd. to use its coaxial cable as a pipe to its data center and to provide two-way computer services to the home and office. CRTC president Pierre Juneau killed that idea. "They just couldn't get their minds around the fact that cable could be used for something other than watching *Anne of Green Gables* or whatever they thought Canadian content should be," says Fierheller.

Fierheller knew that Sydney Welsh, 66, wanted to retire and get his money out of the company. Welsh finally conceded that he would have to accept an offer from an Eastern-based company after the CRTC vetoed his four previous attempts to sell Premier to, or merge it with, his friend Frank Griffiths' Western Broadcasting. Their last merger attempt was aimed at preventing the two companies from being taken over by Toronto-based Torstar Corp., the publisher of the *Toronto Star*. Combined, Premier-Western owned 51 percent of Premier's stock. The other big shareholder was CBS, with 18.5 percent. "It wasn't long before I realized that the owners were getting up in years, and they wanted to sell. So, I said, 'Have I ever got the guy for you,' because Ted was ramping up his interest in cable," Fierheller says.

In the span of 10 days in November, Rogers made three offers to buy control of Premier before he finally sealed the deal. "I'm never surprised by anything Ted Rogers might do," Welsh told *The Globe and Mail* after Rogers made his first unsolicited bid. "He's a pretty versatile guy." Welsh would know.

Just days before, Rogers and his broker, Peter Legault, had met with the Caisse de dépôt et placement du Québec in Montreal to acquire its sizeable chunk—about 11 percent—of Premier shares. They were lunching afterwards at the Beaver Club restaurant in the Queen Elizabeth Hotel when Legault advised Rogers to let Welsh know about the share purchase. Rogers sent Welsh a telegram from the hotel.

Welsh scheduled a board meeting where Rogers could present his offer. Rogers, through CCL, had accumulated a 14-percent stake for $8.28 million. Two days later, Rogers, Legault and Lind flew to Vancouver aboard Canadian Pacific Airlines. As part of the promotion for its Toronto-Vancouver-Hawaii flights, CP Air had a three-piece Hawaiian band and four hula dancers onboard providing entertainment. Lind decided to hire the troupe. They preceded Rogers and Lind into the Premier boardroom, to the utter astonishment of the directors. "I wanted to show them the cable business was now show business," boomed Rogers. They apparently were not impressed.

Rebuffed, Rogers raised his initial offer of $20 a share to $22 a share. When the late Israel (Izzy) Asper tried to butt in, Rogers returned with a new $42.5-million proposal, offering one of three options: $25 a share in cash, one CCL preferred share, or one-and-a-half non-voting class B shares. He clinched the deal by offering to pay the going rate of interest on the dollar amount offered until the CRTC ruled on the takeover application. "As soon as there was some indication that Ted was interested, Izzy Asper came and made a run for it, and there was a bidding war," says Fierheller. "So, they were delighted. I was a hero in the West Coast as far as they were concerned, and I agreed to stay on and run the western cable systems. I thought I'd retire out there. But, it never works out that way." He'd be back east before he knew it.

Rogers called industry icon William S. Paley at CBS in December to buy CBS' 18.5-percent stake in Premier. Paley, who turned the failing CBS radio network into a vast broadcast empire, was Ted Rogers' father's contemporary. Rogers Sr. had negotiated an arrangement with Paley to broadcast CBS's weekly musical programs on CFRB, laying the seeds of a relationship between the two companies that endures to this day. Rogers, who says he had a spirited negotiation with Paley, who remembered his father, agreed to buy the CBS stake for $25 a share for a total of $15.4 million along with a $1.5-million non-refundable fee to cover its regulatory application costs and for the loss of control over its block of shares while the regulator made up its mind.

Rogers and Lind flew to Ottawa to meet with lawyer Robert Buchan, a former DOC staffer who helped navigate them through the pay TV and the CCL hearings.

"Bob, I think you'd better sit down for this one," they told him.

"What is it?"

"We've acquired Premier Cablesystems," Lind said.

Buchan was astonished. Just a year earlier, Rogers ranked fifth in the industry's bigness stakes. He worked the reverse takeover of CCL—in which the smaller company devours the larger one—to create Canada's largest cable company with 700,000 subscribers, pushing Premier to the number two slot. Acquiring Premier would bump up Rogers' subscribers to 1.25 million, a third of the national total and roughly two-thirds of the Toronto market, which was then the world's largest. He inherited 73,000 subscribers in Ireland. For a final price tag of $86.5 million, Rogers lassoed 63-percent control of Premier's stock. He arranged to borrow $65 million—60 percent from TD Bank and 40 percent from CIBC—to finance the acquisition. With the 14 percent of CCL he already owned, Rogers had 83 percent of the stock tied up. He just needed regulatory approval.

In March 1980, Rogers brazenly declared at the annual shareholders' meeting that the cable TV industry will "murder" the telephone companies in the supply of two-way communication and information retrieval services if it were to be allowed to develop the strength to compete with them. He was setting the stage for the May regulatory hearings in Vancouver.

For the past decade, the CRTC and the DOC had been constantly at loggerheads, each trying to exert control over communications policy. They sparred openly in the seventies over pay TV, Manitoba Telephone Systems (MTS), satellite operator Telesat Canada, and CNCP's interconnection request. Just to complicate matters, federal-provincial jurisdictional wars broke out. In 1977, the Supreme Court upheld the federal government's exclusive authority to license cable TV carriers, a jurisdictional battle that arose after Quebec created its own licensing and regulatory authority, forcing cable companies to hold both federal and provincial licenses. The Prairie governments also asserted jurisdiction because their phone utilities wanted a piece of the cable TV business.

In the seventies, rapidly advancing technologies—fiber optics, word processing and satellite transmission—once again stoked Canada's anxieties about national identity and sovereignty. Jeanne Sauvé, the federal communications minister, appointed a seven-person committee to assess the impact of telecommunications on sovereignty. Chaired by J. V. Clyne, the former B.C. Supreme Court judge and lumber giant MacMillan Bloedel Ltd.'s CEO, the committee, which issued its report in March 1979, emphatically supported the separation of carriage and content, a position advanced by the telephone companies. Significantly, the report endorsed the consolidation among the 400-plus cable companies and called for a new *Telecommunications Act* to replace the 1906 *Railway Act* in part to enable the CRTC to regulate cable companies as telecom carriers, as well as broadcast receiving undertakings, especially if they were going to deliver two-way connectivity—meaning the cable guys would undergo the same rigorous process as the telephone companies before any rate increases were approved. The cable industry dodged that bullet. The report, released two months before the Trudeau Liberals lost the federal election to Joe Clark's Tories, was shelved to collect dust.

The CRTC was eager to develop a strong broadcasting presence for larger cable TV companies as a defense against Bell Canada, which wanted to own the cable TV connection. Bell was actively working behind the scenes circulating discussion papers, particularly within the DOC, to promote its position of one integrated network for the transmission. Up until 1977, Bell Canada built and owned the coaxial cable it installed for the cable companies. It leased only that part of the spectrum in the cable that sent radio and television programs. In 1977, the CRTC ordered Bell Canada to allow cable companies to build and own their own coaxial cable networks, a major victory for the cable industry. The decision prompted Bell Canada to move toward an emerging technology—fiber optics.

Fiber optics—then in the experimental phase—revolutionized the world of telecommunications. These strands of optically pure glass as thin and flexible as human hair use light pulses to transmit information over long distances at frequencies a million times higher than is possible over copper. One hair-thin fiber could deliver both telephone and television signals. It would be the information carrier of the future.

By decade's end, Canada was not just the world's most wired country; it was also a hotbed of fiber-optic pilot projects. In November 1978, CCL applied to the CRTC for permission to test a two-way TV system to offer subscribers burglar, fire and medical alarms. In London, Ontario, CCL had already buried an experimental eight-kilometer fiber-optic line with the backing of Maclean Hunter Cable, Rogers Cable and premier Cable, a revolutionary, yet expensive, undertaking since fiber wouldn't really become affordable for another decade. MTS and SaskTel were paying close attention to CCL's endeavors.

A month later, in December 1978, at a luncheon for its inauguration of a fiber optics system in Toronto's Yorkville district, A. Jean de Grandpré, Bell Canada's chairman, declared that Bell intended to replace the existing cable TV system with its own network. He questioned the need for constructing separate cable and telephone networks, since new technologies were bound to remove any justification for separate facilities. "I believe that the public interest would continue to be best served by one carrier in a given area, providing, for shared use, a single integrated network capable of transmitting all voice, visual and data communications," he said.

There are growing indications, he continued, that competition and regulation make strange and indeed incompatible bedfellows, and that there is no way they can co-exist in effective and equitable harmony.

"Either you're going to have a natural, regulated monopoly, or you're going to have competition … so we're going to have either a monopoly situation and offer a portion of the pipe [fiber-optics cable] that we've built, or we are going to have a competitive system, in which case I'm going to build it. But I will be given the opportunity to deliver a cable signal to the same degree that the cable operators are delivering a cable signal," he said.

De Grandpré grew red-faced—whether impassioned, angry or both it was never reported—while talking about his plans to build an integrated fiber-optics network. Seated next to him while he spoke was DOC minister Jeanne Sauvé. She nodded often in support of his remarks, but when it came time for her to speak, she left no doubt about her position that the marketplace, not Bell, would decide if there would be two fiber-optics systems, adding that if indeed any monopoly might develop, it would be regulated. She cautioned that the replacement of copper wires with fiber optics would take place over time, up to 50 years from then.

Rogers characterized de Grandpré's speech of the telephone industry taking over the cable guys as sounding like *Mein Kampf* and the road to extermination camps, which not unsurprisingly drew the ire of Bell.

De Grandpré's remarks riled the broadcasters, CNCP and, naturally, the cable industry. "One gets the distinct impression that Bell management have never forgiven themselves for the strategic blunder in not seeing the potential of cable TV some twenty years before," Colin Watson imparted in a letter published by *The Globe and Mail*: "Advocating that such a monopoly is in the public interest should leave even Mr. de Grandpré somewhat red-faced."

His new boss, Ted Rogers, responded in kind. "The most important priority is the war with Bell," he said. "We must mobilize and close ranks, develop a national cable system."

CHAPTER 9

Taking on America: Part I
Urban Oil Wells

*"We know how to build cable systems in cold climates.
We don't string cable from palm tree to palm tree."*

—Ted Rogers

BY THE LATE SEVENTIES, when Canada was virtually wired for cable television, the scramble for franchises to wire America's biggest cities was just revving up. In the United States in the sixties, cable TV had evolved in the hinterlands between cities where rural Americans could get little but snow on their screens.

In bowing to pressure from the Big Three broadcast networks—ABC, CBS and NBC—the Federal Communications Commission (FCC) slapped a "freeze" on cable's move into the hundred largest TV markets. The FCC lifted the freeze in 1972 only to put new restrictive and expensive rules in its place, such as limiting the number and types of distant signals that cable networks could carry and requiring them to carry signals from the nearest network affiliate. At that time, the biggest cable systems had just five thousand subscribers, but "The Thrilla from Manila" blew the lid off.

On September 30, 1975, Time Inc.'s Home Box Office (HBO), founded by cable pioneer Charles Dolan, used a satellite to deliver the Muhammad Ali-Joe Frazier fight, where Ali decked Frazier after 14 rounds, from the Araneta Coliseum in Quezon City, Philippines to paying customers on UA/Columbia Cablevision's Vero Beach-Fort Pierce, Florida cable systems. Satellite transmission turned cable operators from isolated systems into part of a national network. Soon after, the FCC legalized small receiving dishes or earth stations, allowing cable operators to pick up signals from satellites.

Then, in 1977, a federal court threw out most of the FCC's anti-pay-TV rules. The FCC then repealed most of its remaining restrictions on cable television, unleashing fierce battles for the exclusive rights to wire America that many compared to the Klondike Gold Rush or Oklahoma Land Rush. Suddenly, cable content providers sprung up, such as HBO, Showtime, Cable News Network, Pat Robertson's Christian Broadcasting Network (Family Channel), Entertainment and Sports Programming Network (ESPN), Nickelodeon, Public Affairs Network, Spanish International Network, and Bravo. Baseball teams, emulating Ted Turner, who was distributing Atlanta Braves games via satellite to cable systems across the country, were rushing to sell their cable rights. Customers were actually chasing cable trucks to get hooked up. "We're drilling for oil down there," Rogers told the *Toronto Star*.

Unlike Canada, where cable systems are federally approved, U.S. city councils award the licenses—15-year monopolies—resulting in a highly politicized franchising process.

In the five-year "franchise wars," the cable companies made outlandish promises that were neither technologically feasible nor financially realistic—and were not remotely related to TV broadcasting—in their attempts to win votes from city councillors. It was the only time the cable guys turned on one another. They lost their minds. They offered to fund art museums, new municipal offices, libraries, drug-treatment facilities and tree-planting programs. In a small town in Illinois, after bids for the local cable franchise were in, the mayor reopened the bidding and awarded the franchise to the applicant that proffered a million-dollar interest-free loan for a new water system. Bribery was often suspected, yet rarely proven.

By the time the Federal Bureau of Investigation (FBI) initiated a nation-wide investigation into corruption over cable, most of the franchising was over. Cable companies routinely loaned politically connected individuals money to buy as much as 20 percent of the equity in the franchise in exchange for their support in lobbying city council votes, a practice called "rent-a-citizen." While not illegal, it was highly criticized. Some politicians eagerly latched onto this get-rich-quick scheme, brazenly approaching the cable companies first and attempting to extort payment from them. "It was an unsavory time," recalls John P. (Jack) Cole, co-founder of esteemed law firm Cole, Raywid & Braverman LLP in Washington DC, who helped the pre-Rogers CCL win the Syracuse franchise for 68,000 homes in 1978. "If you were going to get the franchise, you had to puff and puff and puff. You had to blow up your proposal to be more appealing. The game became 'can you top this.' It was like bidding up a poker pot. If you came in with a practical nuts-and-bolts good business proposal, you didn't stand a chance of getting the franchise. The cities would go out and hire 'consultants,' independent consultants that told them how to put the screws into the cable operators."

CCL had won Syracuse, beating U.S. rivals, because of its technical expertise. The company also had an edge over its U.S. rivals because of its experience in building urban systems. In Syracuse, which became the company's flagship system in the franchising process, CCL-Rogers offered two-way capability, with medical-emergency and burglar- and fire-alarm services to subscribers in 1979—services the CRTC ironically denied to Canadians. In awarding a 15-year monopoly to "aliens," American-elected city councillors acknowledged the company's engineering expertise when Canada's federal authority would not. "It's the same old grey Canadian policy that kept us from having our own TV stations first," Rogers told the *Toronto Star* in 1979. "The regulators in this country always have been afraid to try something new, but once they see something works in the U.S., they first allow it, and then encourage it here."

In granting field-trial licenses only, the CRTC stated it first needed to assess the "economic, technological, cultural and social impact" of home security services, a process that took seven years—almost but not quite as long as pay TV. Seemingly innocuous, burglar alarms sent the policymakers into hiding. Lumped in with video games, computer-software downloading, energy meter-reading, videotext, telebanking and futuristic information services, burglar alarms fell into the category—or black hole—of so-called "non-programming" services that had the potential to alter cable's traditional role of simply providing clear reception of conventional TV signals. Still immersed in the unfolding pay-TV fiasco, the regulator was caught in yet another quagmire, attempting to "regulate" an industry within the confines of inadequate legislation that failed to deal with hybrid broadcast/telecom entities. So, the CRTC called a hearing for 1981, then postponed it for two years, canceled it and then held it in October 1985, delays that left Telidon and Nabu, taxpayer-subsidized groundbreaking precursors to the Internet, stuck in field-trial limbo, assuring their speedy demise. Prevented from offering Telidon in Canada, Rogers rolled it out to subscribers in Minneapolis and Portland.

In 1983, the year Bell Canada morphed into BCE, Francis Fox, the Liberal government's communications minister, anointed the cable industry as its champion to deliver the "information revolution" to Canadian homes, a watershed statement. Finally, in February 1986, the unelected lawyer-bureaucrats of the CRTC and their federally appointed masters, having filled in the political black hole, ruled that non-programming services "generally have little direct relationship or impact upon the objectives of the *Broadcasting Act*." In its infinite wisdom, the CRTC decided the cable companies didn't need licenses for non-programming services after all and urged the services' distribution "rapidly in light of market and competitive requirements." It took them seven years to catch up to Syracuse.

Led by André Bureau, the CRTC's new chairman, the Commission deftly stuck to a do-nothing policy under the guise of doing something—it deregulated cable rates. In its new "supervisory" approach, the CRTC failed to create a framework to deal with non-programming services, content to give the cable industry free rein with the caveat that basic cable rates didn't subsidize their development and TV programming had spectrum priority on the pipe. Regardless of what Fox said, the CRTC considered cable a frill, not a common carrier. "We have to realize that cable service is not considered an essential public service like that provided by a telephone company," Bureau said. The issue garnered little mainstream press. Instead, the nation was gripped by a deeper, more pressing concern: Canadianizing the boob tube. With tax receipts earmarked to reduce the colossal debt left behind by the Trudeau Liberals, the impoverished CBC, led by Pierre Juneau, was airing *Dallas* in primetime. Television in Canada was in a crisis.

Fed up with the delays, the Canadians headed south. Maclean Hunter, David Graham's Cablecasting Ltd., CHCH TV's owner Selkirk Holdings, Jeff Conway's CUC Broadcasting and even Conrad Black's Argus-controlled Standard Broadcasting owned slices of America. Selkirk won the franchise for Fort Lauderdale. David Graham, through Cable America, picked up Atlanta from Cox Communications. Graham also owned Valley Cable TV in the west San Fernando Valley area of Los Angeles, selling part ownership to Standard to raise money to fund construction. For the most part, they acquired their franchises; they didn't fight in the trenches like Rogers did.

Nick Hamilton-Piercy, a British émigré who satisfied his boyhood fascination with explosives by blowing up school toilets, revolutionized TV transmission with fiber-optic ring architecture, which is now the standard for cable TV backbones worldwide. His team built the first hybrid coax/fiber cable TV networks. "He's world class technically, and was an ombudsman for us in many ways," says Dr. Richard Green of Cable Labs, which elected Hamilton-Piercy chair of the company's technical committee for eight straight years. In 2002, Hamilton-Piercy was inducted into the Society of Cable Telecommunications Engineers Hall of Fame. Rogers twice refused to let him retire. He remains a part-time consultant for RCI.

Hamilton-Piercy grew up watching the dogfights between Spitfires and the German Luftwaffe flying over his hometown of Crowborough, Sussex in southern England. To his mother's dismay, the seven-year-old boy played with the gear the army left behind after the war, hurling mortar shells from a long rope against the cliff face and then diving quickly behind the rocks, shielding himself from the falling stones and shrapnel. He also avidly tinkered with discarded military electronic equipment and old radios his mom would pick up for him at jumble, or yard, sales. By the time he was 12, Hamilton-Piercy was building single-valve radio receivers and crystal sets from kits and his own design.

Before he was 20, Hamilton-Piercy apprenticed for aviation and electronics maker Elliott Automation at Rochester, Kent, in southeast England. He bypassed conscription because he was involved in work considered vital for defense— classified equipment designs associated with nuclear weapons. He worked for engineering consultants Spembly Ltd. for a year before immigrating to Canada in 1962. He landed in Montreal, where he joined Canadian Marconi Co. and became involved in the development of microwave equipment, giving him his first exposure to cable TV entrepreneurs. At Marconi, he designed HF/VHF/UHF transmitters and receivers for tactical radio systems for the U.S. Army Signal Corps, tools still in use today.

He first met Rogers in 1970 while working for Marconi. He was pitching microwave technology to cable owners and met with Rogers at his Adelaide St. offices. "It wasn't a satisfactory sales meeting," chuckles Hamilton Piercy. "All he was interested in was telling us about his latest pitch. So, we never got a chance to give him our sales pitch. But, we heard all about his vision and what he wanted to do."

He thought the cable pioneers were all "a bit flaky." Technically, they weren't sophisticated and he just couldn't see how they'd ever evolve from a television-repair shop mentality to telecommunications systems operators. His brother-in-law, though, had defected to the cable TV industry. Kevin Hancock left Marconi in the early seventies to become vice president of science and engineering for the Canadian Cable Television Association. When Ted Jarmain asked Hancock for possible candidates to fill the head-engineering job at CCL, Hancock suggested his brother-in-law. Jarmain phoned a decidedly reluctant Hamilton-Piercy and pressured him into meeting his, as Hamilton-Piercy says, "secret weapon"—his father, Ed Jarmain. "He is just the perfect Canadian gentleman, a visionary. He saw fiber optics, forty-plus channel distribution and two-way long before any of us thought it could be possible," said Hamilton-Piercy of his meeting with the CCL founder. "He just sucked me right in."

Hamilton-Piercy proved invaluable to Rogers, who more than anything wanted to be at the forefront of technological change. "Nick is the dean of North American engineers," says Robert B. Clasen, chairman and CEO of Starz LLC, a Liberty Media Corp. unit that offers pay movie channels, who ran the

Syracuse cable system before Lind co-opted him for the franchising team. CCL had hired the Ohio-born psychology professor from Continental Cablevision Inc., co-founded in 1963 by Harvard MBA graduates Amos B. Hostetter Jr. and H. Irving Grousbeck. "We always had some wrinkle in our bid that was well engineered and all the other cable companies would smack their heads and say, 'They one-upped us again,' and it was because Nick really had built a well-regarded research facility. It was just a great group of engineers. Ted was very focused on technology, and the detail, and would keep Nick close to him."

Rogers spent a great deal of time with his engineers. With unwavering regularity, he had dinner with seven or eight engineers virtually every quarter, rotating the venue among their homes. The participants included Rogers, Hamilton-Piercy, Nick Kauser (who joined Cantel), Bob Berner (who came from Bell Canada to Cantel in January 1985 and is now RCI's chief technology officer), Ted Chislett (now president of Primus Canada), Carl Scase (Primus Canada), Roger Keay (now retired) and Sture Ostland (former president of Ericsson Messaging).

In a relaxed atmosphere over a home-cooked meal and several bottles of red wine, they discussed the latest technical innovations and their potential impact on business. Rogers, peppering them with questions, was always thinking about how the technology might translate into new customer services or improve network efficiencies. While Rogers and his technicians talked about where the wired and wireless worlds might be in 10 years, the mandarins in Ottawa debated how they could deliver more "Anne of Green Gables" content into Canadian homes. "Ted had a tremendous interest in the technology, and in many ways, the technologies defined the capability of the company," says Roger Keay, Rogers' longtime technology advisor, who retired in 2004 after nearly 25 years at the company. "Once he sees a business purpose to it, he'll be a strong promoter. He'll put a strong push behind it, and a lot of the things that happened have been through Ted hearing about it, often through these engineering committees."

It was at one such dinner when a technician, no one quite recalls who, happened to mention that he had been speaking to CN Rail and learned the railway company wanted to lay fiber-optic cable across the top of Toronto but because it didn't have the budget allocation, planned to bury copper wire instead. CN told him it was willing to plough in fiber cable for Rogers in exchange for some of the fiber rights. What did everyone think? Without hesitation, Rogers said, "Well, let's do it." It was a key decision.

"We'd talk technology, and in fact, those meetings have sometimes been referred to as the real decision-making within Rogers, and there's some truth to that," says Rogers. "The engineers were always key to it all. Technology always has been driving the business."

Phil Lind ramped up the franchising program Ted Jarmain began. Graham Savage, vp of investments, had already short-listed several cities based on population size, demographics, and potential revenue. Then, they relied on gut instinct. In mud-slinging contests for what former New York City mayor John Lindsay described in the late sixties as "urban oil wells beneath our city streets," it boiled down to which cities might be the most receptive to a foreign applicant. For city councillors, awarding the cable franchise was the most important decision of their political lives, since the water and gas lines had long since been laid and the telephone and power grids completed.

Rogers Cablesystems was up against some of the biggest U.S. corporate names: Time Inc.; Storer Broadcasting; Warner Cable, part of Warner Communications; American Express; Viacom; TelePrompTer; Westinghouse Electric; *Times-Mirror*; the *New York Times*; Cox; Cablevision; and Hearst Publishing. Tele-Communications Inc.'s John Malone stayed out of the fray, flying under the radar to gobble up small, independent cable systems. Names now legendary in the cable TV business, such as Amos Hostetter, Gus Hauser, Bill Bresnan, NBC's Bob Wright (wearing pink-framed glasses), Charles Dolan and Jim Robbins, competed side by side with Rogers in the franchising wars. There was a wave of young talent flowing into the industry. They all cut their teeth on it at the same time. Lind suspected but never truly knew which companies the franchising team would face until the applications had been filed.

Lind, Colin Watson and Savage tried to narrow the odds in Rogers' favor by carefully selecting cities that they believed "were relatively clean [of corruption] and didn't have any anti-Canadian or anti-British bias," says Lind. For these reasons, they scratched off their list Boston, New York, Dallas, Houston and even Nebraska's capital, Lincoln (half the population of London, Ontario). Instead, they sought franchises in and clustered around Minneapolis, Portland—northern U.S. cities—and in Orange and Los Angeles counties in southern California. Rogers inherited a difficult 50-50 partnership CCL had with Dickinson Pacific Cablesystems in California.

Rogers wanted to apply for as many franchises as possible. Says Lind, "There were forty to fifty cities that were actively franchising and Ted said, 'Let's apply for every one of them and we'll win a couple.' He was absolutely wrong because every one was contested, hugely." All of the competing cable companies hired franchising teams—many with impressive political credentials—to set up camp in a city and work it until the award was made. Warner Cable's Gus Hauser and his boss, Steve Ross, hired Richard Aurelio, who used his extensive political experience to win cable franchises (Aurelio had engineered John Lindsay's re-election in New York City, became deputy mayor and managed Lindsay's unsuccessful 1972 Democratic presidential nomination campaign). Aurelio set up a 30-person "boiler room" in New York to prepare applications. Warner Cable, then Warner Amex, had as many as one hundred franchise applications pending in 30 different states at any given time. "We were at a terrible disadvantage. We were foreigners. It was next to impossible to do what we did," Lind says.

CCL competed for franchises in Miami and Clearwater, Florida and Erie, Pennsylvania, losing all three. The snowbird set on Rogers' board insisted that Lind compete for Miami against his better judgment. He had been dead-set against Miami, where corruption was suspected but never proven. [Decades later, the cable entrepreneur that Miami chose fled the United States to escape prosecution for fraud and tax evasion. He was extradited from Australia and stood trial, pleading guilty in 2006.]

RTL later formed a joint venture with Tribune Co., the parent of *The Chicago Tribune*, to seek the cable franchise for Montgomery County in Virginia, but pulled out of the application process because, by then, Rogers had other priorities, not least of which was dealing with his company's mounting debt.

To win votes, Lind couldn't just rely on his company's engineering prowess. Warner Cable, later Warner Amex Cable, introduced something called QUBE, a glorified two-way interactive TV system, in Columbus, Ohio in 1977. With QUBE as bait, Warner Amex dazzled city councillors to win more franchises than any other company. But QUBE never made it out of Columbus and was folded in the mid-eighties. It promised burglar alarms, home shopping and home banking, all of which were duds. QUBE couldn't compete with the comprehensive package of two-way services that Rogers offered.

In Minneapolis and Portland, Rogers built two-way networks—sophisticated for their day—using, of all things, Telidon, which was superior to QUBE and another service, Cox's two-way INDAX interactive system. The Telidon terminals, priced at $1,000 apiece, were too expensive for subscribers, so Rogers attached terminals to utility poles, enabling subscribers to connect to the communal terminal from their homes. "It was simple applications like question of the day, or educational type questions. It was like a mini-Internet. It was quite primitive by today's standards but it had a lot of 'wow' factor," says Hamilton-Piercy. Rogers also used Telidon at the head-end for high-quality pictures and graphics on its information/community channel, something no other multiple systems operator—industry jargon for cable companies with more than two systems—had.

Lind entered each U.S. city with the mindset of a political campaign manager. He spent countless days just sitting in city hall auditoriums where he listened to the public debates, getting a feel for each councillor's concerns and ideologies. "I would sit there and listen," Lind says. "Everybody thought I was nuts." He and his team scrutinized their contribution records. He spared no expense in hiring the best local talent—lawyers, former political aides, and public relations consultants—from both political stripes, Republican and Democrat, even though U.S. local politics tends to be Democrat. The team tapped support from local luminaries and affluent local businessmen, who not only might be able to exercise moral suasion at city hall, but also provide the necessary financial support.

"Phil carried the load," credits Rogers. Unfailingly polite, Rogers is more generous in his praise for the people who never left his employ, although it really depends on his mood at the time he's asked. "My job then was to get the money and to go and pitch when we made the pitches."

In California, Lind hired Stuart K. Spencer, a close advisor to U.S. president Ronald Reagan when he was California's governor, and Dennis E. Carpenter, a former state senator. In Portland, Lind teamed with Larry Black, founder of Black & Co., a prominent retail brokerage in the northwest. In Minneapolis, to Lind's relief, Savage had already retained law firm Popham, Haik, Schnobrich & Kaufmann; Wayne G. Popham, a Republican, had served in the Minnesota senate.

"You wanted to hire the people who had the best connections," says Lynn Wickwire, who ran the grassroots campaign in Minneapolis. Wickwire, a political aficionado with a degree in city planning from Yale University, knew the inner workings of local politics after 13 years with the state of New York, mostly under Governor Nelson Rockefeller, the last five of which he spent overseeing the state cable TV commission, an entity he helped establish. "The people who were making the decision would look around and see who represented each of these different firms and all things being equal—since the applications tended to look the same—they'd say, 'I'm going to give it to somebody who has helped me in the past.'"

For a Canadian company in virgin territory, Rogers was both an asset and a liability. He was not scriptable and usually impatient. He called it like he saw it. He didn't care what people thought. On road shows, he'd baldly tell investors that there was "no fucking way" he'd ever pay a dividend, not exactly the best language or way to entice people to buy the company's securities. Unlike equity investors, bond investors typically shun flamboyant, bombastic gamblers. Rogers was then an unknown quantity in the United States. Companies and their representatives had to make an immediate favorable impression, or risk losing buyers.

Lind, Watson and Savage—whether in franchising, or raising money—were articulate, intelligent and polished lieutenants speaking the language of their respective constituents, the elected officials and all-powerful debt-rating agencies and Wall St. financiers. For Rogers, his most important constituents were not public stockholders, but ultimately, the debt-rating agencies. Bond investors assess risk and return. They look beyond the CEO to the hard numbers. Savage, usually the first man in, rounded up the local partners, and structured the limited partnerships and then the public debt financings that kept the company afloat.

In Minneapolis, at a cocktail reception held at the Windows on Minneapolis restaurant on the 50th floor of the city's tallest skyscraper, the IDS Center, Phil Lind introduced Ted Rogers to city councillors and influential local business leaders. "We know how to build cable systems in cold climates," boasted Rogers proudly before taking what he considered a good-natured swipe at his Miami-based rival, Storer: "We don't string cable from palm tree to palm tree."

He thought he was being clever. Lind, overhearing the smart-ass remark, "almost sank through the floor," recalls David Jones, a former Popham Haik attorney working on the franchising team. Jones later became the in-house counsel for Rogers U.S. Cablesystems. "Phil was afraid we had not been 'nice' in the classic Minnesota sense, or somehow [the comment] was going to screw up our relations with certain council members."

Rogers was up against three other applicants: ATC, Warner Amex, and Storer. In September 1979, the city council awarded the franchise to Rogers' Minneapolis Cablesystems and instructed the city staff to negotiate the franchise ordinance, essentially the contract between the city and cable company. The losers, however, recognized that until the contract came before council, the franchisee could still be overturned. With an election imminent, the losers worked to sway votes in a politically charged atmosphere, attacking the victor's Canadian roots in the press.

In late November, when the ordinance came before council, a substitute motion was made to replace the name on the contract from Rogers to Storer's Northern Cablevision of Minneapolis. Alderman Zollie Green, who had supported Rogers, switched his vote to Storer. His vote cost Rogers the franchise. Lind's team was stunned. They had already shifted gears from franchising to the construction mode. When the shock and disappointment wore off, they were beside themselves with anger. Minnesota had a reputation for clean, progressive politics.

Lind struck back through the courts. A flurry of lawsuits ensued. "It was in the newspaper every day; it was the subject of network news on [a] fairly regular basis, the franchising wars were all covered extensively, there was an article every single day—all of your actions were scrutinized. We had regular sweeps on our phones to make sure they weren't tapped," says Jane Bremer, a Minneapolis-based communications lawyer, who was part of the Storer's legal team at Larkin Hoffman Daly & Lindgren and then became the city's cable officer.

Lind maintained Storer had wrongfully interfered with its contractual right by lobbying against them between the first and second votes. Through the law firms, Lind hired private investigators to investigate the team's suspicions of bribery. Nothing ever came of their investigation. In a separate matter, the late Zollie Green, described in the press as a "lame duck alderman," was charged and subsequently acquitted for taking bribes related to city bus-shelter contracts.

From start to finish, the controversial process lasted 45 months—beginning in September 1979 when Rogers won the franchise by a one-vote margin and ending in June 1983 when rival Storer finally bowed out. Rogers spent millions of dollars in lobbying and legal fees. "The strongest supporter by far was Ted. He was fantastic. Even in the depths of Minneapolis, when we won it and then lost it and it took two years, we were coasting around doing nothing except spending oodles of money every month, the guy that should have said, 'That's enough, Phil' did just the reverse: 'Look, if [you] think you have a chance there, go for it.' It was unbelievable," says Lind. "He stayed the course."

"That kept people in the field going," adds Vernon Achber, a South African native who became Lind's right hand in the U.S. franchising wars.

With the battle for Minneapolis tied up in the courts, Rogers bid for the suburbs around the city. Rogers won the five communities to the southwest, while Storer won the 10 communities to the northwest. "The battle for the suburbs became incredibly heated. Those were, in many ways, as ugly or uglier than the Minneapolis battle because they were all designed to influence Minneapolis," recalls Bremer. "It was a real interesting game of gender politics, of old versus young, in-town versus out-of-towner, technical merit versus political punch—all of those things got tossed into the cauldron and at the end of the day, the elected officials were called on to make the decision."

In the end, the two feuding parties reached a peace agreement. They split the city in half. Storer took the north and Rogers the south. The former adversaries met in Anaheim, California, during the Western Cable Show to discuss the great divide.

Lind, who was concerned about possible antitrust charges, retained Philip L. Verveer, the lead antitrust lawyer at the U.S. Justice Department, to oversee the proceedings. He had just entered private practice after making his mark by crushing the world's biggest monopolist, AT&T. This was his first private case. "The first thing he said was, 'No notes,'" recalls Achber. "We were in a different league."

"This was for real," says Lind. "You had to tell your counsel what you were going to say before you said it. So, I would say to Verveer, 'I'm going to say this,' and he would say, 'Okay.' The other side did the same. We thought the FBI would break in at any time. We had to be absolutely clean because if we weren't, then both of us would be out and someone else would win the franchise."

The victories came in fast and furious. In January 1981, the same month Rogers replaced the "Canadian" in the corporate name with "Rogers," the franchising team won licenses for the Californian suburbs of Rossmoor and La Mirada. In February, they won five Minneapolis suburbs. In March, they secured the franchise for Portland, followed by Stanton, California in May. In June, they won licenses for the contiguous cities of Downey, Pico Rivera, Santa Fe Springs, Bell Gardens, Paramount and Lynwood, all in southern California. In six months, they won franchises for 303,000 homes. The city of Garden Grove, a big win, came later with 41,000 households.

"For two and a half years, we were very hot," recalls Starz CEO Bob Clasen, who had been a member of the Rogers franchising team. "We won more than we lost. We were growing. We were very appealing to people. We had strong local management. I was actually disappointed when we changed the name to Rogers [Cablesystems] because Canadian Cablesystems had some real pizzazz."

Clasen left in 1984 to become president of Comcast Cable when Rogers, now focusing his energy on cellular, began to unwind his U.S. cable business. He declined an earlier offer from Westinghouse, then the largest U.S. cable company, to run its cable business to stay at Rogers, although dealing with the founder wasn't always easy. "We had fifteen people in the boardroom and I'm making a presentation and it goes on for an hour and a half, and it's only Ted and me debating the issue and everybody else is kind of nodding and finally Ted says, 'You know, I've had enough. We're doing it my way,' and he storms out. Phil looks at me and says, 'That's not bad, Bob, you only lost by one vote.'"

He met his future wife, Liane Langevin, at Rogers. Lind recruited the former special assistant to the federal Liberal minister of justice Ron Baseford, from the CBC to lead the southern Californian franchising team. The core franchising team included Lind, Watson, Savage, Hamilton-Piercy, Clasen, Wickwire, Achber, Steven Moss, who wrote their franchising proposals, Langevin and young William (Bill) Craig, then in programming. John (Skip) Ciero, the former executive assistant to the mayor of Syracuse, also joined the team.

"The first meeting we had in Toronto, I thought, 'Wow, what energy there is in this room.' You felt you were on a wonderful team in a political campaign but with a business focus," says Langevin. "I was really honored to be recruited into that group.

"We weren't just talking a good story. We actually had put our money where our mouths were. I think that helped a lot and gave people a comfort level that they knew we were there to stay and not [to] just blow in and get the franchise and do nothing with it for years," she says.

They were parachuted into cities where they didn't know a soul, apart from perhaps the recently hired lawyers. Lind wanted his team to all be on a first-name basis with the mayor and city councillors in a matter of months. "It was like the last two weeks of an election campaign the whole time," says Lind. The way they dressed, how they spoke and their comportment all made a difference. Just as in politics, they were acutely attuned to the local sensitivities. Lind had Clasen lead most of their presentations because he "didn't speak Canadian yet." Langevin, who had tremendous success in southern California, made a concerted effort to tone down her "aboots."

The small city franchises were just as difficult, if not tougher, to win. The in-the-field teams worked local community events. Depending on the city's demographics, they gathered support for their proposed local community channels from artists, blacks, Hispanics, Asians, religious groups, the hearing impaired and environmentalists. The parade of special-interest groups prompted one official to joke that if somebody proposed an access channel for unicorns, they'd likely see one testify on its own behalf.

Jane Bremer believes they might have had greater franchising success had the core team reflected the diversity of urban America. "There was always an aloofness, or a failure, or a refusal to recognize that ten white men walking into a room isn't necessarily going to be compelling in urban America," she says.

"The American companies understood they were walking into a rough-and-tumble environment that was not a meritocracy. It wasn't going to be the best companies that won because they were all good companies. It was just degrees of separation between them, and to assume that elected officials who had no background in this industry could discern those subtle differences was naïve. I'm sure [Rogers] would have been even more dominant in the United States if they had made that assessment earlier and invited people who were a little unlike themselves into the inner fold. They probably would have been the Comcast."

With so much at stake, Rogers' U.S. rivals began to play the Canadian card. The opposing bidders started to refer to the Rogers Cablesystems team as

"The Canadians." In Portland, when rival Liberty Cable made its pitch to city council, the late Monford A. Orloff, a prominent local businessman, arts patron and Liberty Cable director, urged city councillors to keep the franchise in American hands. He went so far as to slander all Canadians, calling them untrustworthy, according to those present. His words carried tremendous weight in the community. Orloff had built Portland-based Evans Products Co. into one of the state's largest publicly traded companies with tentacles in home finance, forestry, home hardware stores, rail car manufacturing and equipment leasing. "He said you couldn't trust Canadians. It was very mean spirited," recalls Skip Ciero, who witnessed the presentation. Orloff's remarks rankled Ciero enough to make him stop drinking Henry's, a famous Oregon microbrew, because of the local titan's affiliation with its brewmeister, Blitz-Weinhard. He'd rather drink Budweiser than Henry's. He warned his associates that if they ordered Henry's, he'd make damn sure it wouldn't be on the company's tab.

Right after Orloff's speech, Lind left the council chamber to call Thomas M. Waterland, the B.C. forestry minister. Orloff's Evans Products held valuable timber rights in B.C.; enough, in fact, to make it one of the province's top 10 timber and plywood producers. Lind told Waterland that Orloff was badmouthing Canadians. By the time Orloff returned to his office he had a message waiting for him from Waterland demanding he immediately fly to Victoria, the provincial capital, to explain himself. After all, he had a lucrative business in Canada at the government's pleasure. If he hoped to stay in the minister's good books, he had better start making amends fast.

Soon after, Orloff stood before city councillors retracting his earlier anti-Canadian statements. Lind had silenced the propaganda war. "You don't take it personally," says Lind's right-hand man, Vernon Achber. "We were moving towards one event, getting the majority of the votes from a particular council. That was it. That was all that mattered."

The Rogers team, helped by investment banker Larry Black, rounded up enough partners to split ownership of the limited partnership in the cable system 50-50—a move allowing it to emphasize its local partners in its advertising campaign and downplay its Canadian roots. Rogers' cast of community and business leaders prompted one rival to remark, "I wish I had some of the people they've got."

The cable companies used the press to promote their strengths and point out their opponents' weaknesses. In Minneapolis, Storer whipped up an anti-Canadian furor by handing out flyers and running advertisements depicting storks carrying bags of money flying back to Canada. The ads appeared during the 1979–80 hostage crisis in Iran when 70 Americans were taken captive in the U.S. embassy. After Canada's ambassador Ken Taylor spirited six American

Edward Rogers Sr. in Florida (circa 1937).
(Courtesy of the Rogers family.)

Velma Rogers holds her newborn son Ted.
(Courtesy of the Rogers family.)

Ted Rogers at five years old.
(Courtesy of the Rogers family.)

An 11-year-old Ted Rogers stands in the backyard of the family's home on Glenayr Road.
(Courtesy of the Rogers family.)

DETENTION OF two University of Toronto students by immigration authorities in Florida was termed a "mistake" by U.S. officials yesterday, but before their release, protest signs, such as this, were carried before U.S. consulate in Toronto

University of Toronto students protest in front of the U.S. consulate in Toronto. (*Toronto Star*)

DEMONSTRATION BY U. OF T. students in front of U.S. consulate in Toronto is shown. Immigration official in Miami said incident was "a case of mistaken identity of individuals and not political parties." The students are on their way home. Rogers' mother in Toronto said they will arrive by Thursday at the latest

UNIVERSITY OF TORONTO STUDENTS DETAINED IN FLORIDA

THE STUDENTS will be "paroled" later today and permitted to return to Canada, immigration service said. Rogers, left, talks to Toronto on phone from hotel room in West Palm Beach, Fla. Boultbee is at right. Both are active in Young Progressive Conservative movement at U. of T. They were both detained yesterday

Ted Rogers, with Bill Boultbee, calls home from a hotel room in West Palm Beach, Florida in 1954 after U.S. Immigration detains them for allegedly being communist sympathizers. (*Toronto Star*)

The Bank of Nova Scotia

ESTABLISHED 1832

SPADINA AND LONSDALE ROADS
FOREST HILL VILLAGE
TORONTO 10. ONT.

November 20th,1959

Mr.Edward S.Rogers,
405 Glenayr Road,
TORONTO, Ontario.

Dear Ted:

We advise your Current
Account is overdrawn $28. following
payment of your rent cheque for
$155. We would also draw your
attention to the overdraft in the
"Cousin's" account amounting to
approximately $72. Your attention
to these matters would be appreciated.

Yours very truly,

J. D. Allan,
Manager.

Ted Rogers receives his first notice from the bank that his account is overdrawn.
(Courtesy of Rogers family.)

Ted Rogers and Canada's prime minister, John Diefenbaker.
(Courtesy of Rogers family.)

John Bassett, Joel Aldred, Foster Hewitt (standing) and Ted
Rogers at BBG hearings for the CFTO-TV licence in 1960.
(Courtesy of Rogers family.)

The wedding party. John Graham and Velma Rogers-Graham are on the far left. Loretta's parents Lord and Lady Martonmere are on the far right. (Courtesy of Rogers family.)

Ted and Loretta Rogers are married at St. Margaret's Church at Westminster Abbey, London, England in 1963. (Courtesy of Rogers family.)

Loretta's parents John Roland and Maysie Robinson, Lord and Lady Martonmere, outside Buckingham Palace. (Courtesy of the Rogers family.)

(l. to r.) Loretta Rogers, Vaughn Bjerre, CHFI station manager, Velma Rogers-Graham and Ted Rogers at Christmas party in the mid-1960s. (Courtesy of the Rogers family.)

Ted Rogers and Ron Turnpenny in CHFI's control room. (Courtesy of Rogers family.)

Phil Lind in Rogers Cable TV studio. (Courtesy of RCI.)

Ted Rogers in his cable TV studio in 1972. (CP)

(l. to r.) CRTC hearing for Premier Cablevision in 1980. Front: George Fierheller, John Graham, Ted Rogers, Phil Lind. Back: Gord Keeble, Pat Douey and Colin Watson. (Courtesy of RCI.)

John Graham and Ted Rogers.
(Courtesy of Rogers family.)

Robert Francis. (Courtesy of Marilyn Francis.)

Graham Savage. (Courtesy of Graham Savage.)

Marc and Samuel Belzberg.
(Courtesy of Samuel Belzberg.)

Vernon Achber and Phil Lind flank Minneapolis mayor Don Fraser. (Courtesy of Phil Lind.)

Minneapolis lawyer David Jones, Rogers' U.S. regulatory vice president in the 1980s, displays his Rogers Road Warriors T-shirt at a cable franchising party. (Courtesy of Phil Lind.)

(l. to. r.) Kip Moorecroft, vice president of programming, Phil Lind, Bob Clasen, Frank Nuestle, Rogers' cable system manager for Portland, and Colin Watson in Portland. (Courtesy of Phil Lind.)

diplomats out of Iran on fake Canadian passports, Lind saw an opportunity to neutralize Storer's brazenly anti-Canadian ads and capitalize on the outpouring of U.S. support for Canada in the wake of Taylor's heroism by taking out full-page ads in the local Minneapolis newspapers that said, "Thank You Canada. You're the Greatest." No one ever knew Rogers Cablesystems placed the advertisements. They created a dummy organization whose name was used instead. He "really nuked that whole campaign [of the stork ads]," says Achber.

"We were capitalizing on international politics," says Lind. "Believe me, it was really important. [Pierre] Trudeau had been stiffing the Americans in the Midwest with his National Energy Policy. U.S. cable companies had been kicked out of Canada, so they were furious that Canadians were coming down to their country and bidding against them."

With the onset of the recession, the protectionist sentiment in Congress only deepened. Canada–U.S. relations, abysmal in the Diefenbaker and Pearson eras, steadily deteriorated during Trudeau's almost unbroken 15-year reign. The Liberal Party's new National Energy Program and the expanding role of the Foreign Investment Review Agency fueled a growing U.S. backlash to Canada's discriminatory trade policies. U.S. policymakers were so incensed that there were as many as 53 pending pieces of legislation aimed at curtailing U.S.–Canada trade in areas ranging from trucking to electronic technology to auto-making.

The U.S. cable titans had long and bitter memories. Just a decade earlier, Pierre Juneau, carrying out the wishes of the Trudeau government, booted out Famous Players and CBS, which financed the early cable pioneers when the banks wouldn't. Dallas-based Sammons Enterprises, a top 10 cable operator that had diversified into insurance, construction and power industries, was still livid. Sammons had two prospects for its cable properties in Trois-Rivières and Shawinigan, both in Quebec, and sought permission from Pierre Juneau to sell. "The answer was—and listen to this—that neither of them are acceptable. Isn't that a hell of an answer?" recounted William B. Strange Jr., who oversaw the sale for Sammons, in an oral history for The Cable Center in Denver.

Juneau's decision enabled the properties to fall into the hands of Henri Audet, a Canadian Broadcasting Corporation vice president who started the Société Radio-Canada station in Trois-Rivières. Cogeco Cable was born. Sammons ended up getting $1.9 million for properties that it originally had a firm deal to sell for $3.7 million until Juneau vetoed it. "We did the deal and then couldn't get the money out of Canada. So I am telling you I was just crushed. Here I worked the best deal I could get, which was highway robbery. I told them that if we didn't get the deal done I was going to hold a press conference, call the Wall Street Journal, and accuse Canada of being another Chile. I knew that they had us over a barrel. There wasn't any question about that. Well, sir, a light went on and our people started leasing Boeing 737s. We formed a company called Adventure Tours with the money that we had in Canada. We filled up those airplanes and took them to our hotel in the Bahamas in the winter, but we made them pay us in St. Louis and that is the way we got our money out of them. Later on, Adventure Tours paid [Sammons] the $1.9 million for our Canadian properties, which gave birth to a very successful company here in Dallas called Adventure Tours. Why our government permits unequal treatment of its American businesses is unbelievable," says Strange Jr.

Rogers' success in the franchising game ignited a foreign ownership debate in Congress. The FCC rejected two earlier pleas to restrict foreign cable ownership in the past four years. Then, in 1982, the U.S. Senate Commerce Committee passed a bill sponsored by Barry Goldwater, the influential Republican senator from Arizona and a 1964 presidential nominee, containing an unprecedented provision to bar foreign ownership of cable systems to the extent U.S. companies are barred abroad. It was aimed directly at Canadian companies, which then served 4 percent of the U.S. cable market. "I am tired of playing with a stacked deck supplied by our Canadian friends," William (Bill) Bresnan, the chief executive officer of Westinghouse Electric's Group W Cable unit, told a Washington UPI reporter. Bresnan, who spent 16 years with Jack Kent Cooke, had been forced to sell Cooke's two cable TV systems, one in Sault Ste. Marie, Ontario, and the other in Edmunstun, New Brunswick, at 10 cents on the dollar. Bresnan recalls that the buyer was predetermined. "We didn't have a free-market-type sale. We had to sell it for whatever the buyer was willing to pay. So there were hard feelings because it's one thing to sell your business, but to sell it for less than it's worth was a pretty raw deal."

The Senate provision was the first instance that the U.S. government ever demanded that an ally divest itself of U.S. holdings. The bill, which passed 13 to 3, included a grandfather clause allowing existing Canadian investment in the U.S. cable industry. The bill was en route to a full senate vote.

In the run-up to the 1984 Cable Bill, the U.S. cable titans and the National Cable Television Association (NCTA), their Washington DC-based trade group, began exerting their influence over policymakers to include measures in the proposed cable bill to prohibit Canadian cable companies from owning U.S. cable properties.

Howard H. Baker Jr., a Republican senator from Tennessee and a close friend of Barry Goldwater's, was then the senate majority leader, one of the most powerful positions in Washington. The senate majority leader helps set the floor agenda, controls what comes to the floor for a vote and brokers key compromises to move legislation. Baker, who served on the senate committee investigating the Watergate scandal, famously asked, "What did the President know and when did he know it?"—a question given to him by his legal counsel and former campaign manager, Fred Thompson, who at the time was relatively unknown. Thompson later became a Republican senator from Tennessee and gained fame as the character Arthur Branch, district attorney on the TV show *Law & Order*. (Thompson has declared as a 2008 Republican U.S. presidential candidate.)

With the anti-Canadian furor building in Washington, Lind struck pre-emptively, retaining Thompson, Baker's trusted advisor, to monitor the legislation's progress in order to protect Rogers' interests. When the NCTA also sought to hire Thompson, it was stunned to discover that Lind already had him locked up. The NCTA wanted Thompson so badly that Lind offered to relinquish him if the NCTA agreed to withdraw any reference to Canadians or Canada in the cable bill. The NCTA agreed and Thompson became its chief lobbyist.

"It was quite a divisive issue," recalls Thomas E. Wheeler, the former NCTA president, who cast the tie-breaking vote on the NCTA board to scrap the foreign ownership rules. Lind had tried to hire him before he took the NCTA job. Wheeler later became the head of the Cellular Telecommunications Association industry trade group. "It's the only time in twenty years of experience of running trade associations that I ever cast a tie-breaking vote, which is not a healthy position for an association executive to be in. It was a tough decision, but the right decision."

Lind, who had sought a seat on the NCTA board for years, was granted his wish in 1984. NCTA members finally decided, in the words immortalized by Lyndon B. Johnson, that it was better to "have him inside the tent pissing out than outside pissing in." Lind is the first—and only—Canadian to ever be elected to the NCTA board. "Phil could play on this side of the border like the natives," says Lee E. Sheehy, a former Popham Haik lawyer and Minnesota's chief deputy attorney general.

Lind kept a toehold in America right up until 2001. RCI had a mere 7,300 subscribers in Alaska, the perfect locale for Lind, who founded the Sierra Club of Ontario. He hiked the fabled Chilkoot Trail, a grueling 53-kilometer route from Alaska to the Klondike Goldfields that 30,000 gold seekers trekked to their death or glory in the winter of 1897–98. Lind befriended the powerful Republican senator for Alaska Ted Stevens, a fellow angler. Stevens was his insurance policy just in case the U.S. cable TV barons attempted to revive any anti-Canadian-type laws that might impact Rogers.

"We out-Americaned the Americans," says Lind.

William Bresnan, now 74, a respected U.S. cable-TV pioneer and CEO of Bresnan Communications Inc., recalls being extremely impressed by the way Colin Watson and Phil Lind ran the company. "How do you do it? What's your secret?" he asked them.

They explained to him their managerial grid approach, where managers learn to achieve results by changing their behavior. Bresnan embraced their advice wholeheartedly. Over the next three decades, he consistently sent his lieutenants for leadership training in the highly acclaimed managerial grid program developed by Drs. Robert R. Blake and Jane S. Mouton, two world-renowned organization development pioneers. "That was something that we learned from Rogers," says Bresnan. "It's really worked."

Turns out, Lind and Watson were not talking about the Blake Mouton Managerial Grid but their own. They had devised their own four-point grid not to manage the company, but instead to manage Rogers: "Too little. Too much. Too early. Too late."

"That's how you feed information to Rogers," says Lind. "It's too early, or it's too late. Nothing is ever right. It's remarkably accurate, and it's true to this day. We still feed information to Rogers and he'll come back and say, 'it's too much information, or it's too little, or I only received it at the last minute, or if it were sent last week, it came too early for me to deal with it.'"

One day, Rogers said to Lind, "I don't think we're doing real well. Take me down there."

"In those days, Rogers was really into Ronald Reagan," Lind grins, remembering the sheer anxiety he felt over Rogers' proposed visit to the United States because of his boss' penchant for speaking his mind and his unbridled enthusiasm, which often bowled people right over.

Rogers, a lifelong Conservative, greatly admired the former actor who was sworn in as the 40th president of the United States on January 20, 1981. Reagan, who survived an assassination attempt 69 days into his first term, reawakened a sense of pride in Americans after a decade of political scandal and military defeat. Along with his own unique brand of budget and tax cuts called Reaganomics, the president also boosted defense spending. In March 1983, he unveiled the controversial Strategic Defence Initiative, which heightened already frosty tensions between the United States and the USSR. The initiative, dubbed "Star Wars" after the popular George Lucas sci-fi movie, was meant to destroy missiles from space.

"We had five of the twelve aldermen turn out [for a dinner meeting]," Lind recalls. "And Rogers talked about why Star Wars was so important. He lectured them … on and on …"

Rogers, who sincerely believed he was winning their votes by voicing support for the U.S. president, didn't realize that local politicians are almost always card-carrying Democrats. "We lost all five," sighs Lind.

He tried to keep Rogers at home after that. "He rarely wanted to come," admits Lind. "He came on voting day, and that was very important because he needed to make the call on some things."

"Phil was able to tell Ted that at critical times either I need you here or stay out. He was able to say, 'Thank you for your input; now go away.' For him to have had that kind of support and trust from Ted was really quite amazing," says lawyer David Jones, general counsel at St. Paul, Minneapolis-based Hubbard Broadcasting Inc.

On the day of the vote to award the Portland cable franchise, Mildred Schwab, described as a firm Jewish spinster aunt—a "tough old broad" who was one of the most forthright and popular city councillors—pointedly asked Lind if he would be willing to freeze the company's cable rates for seven years on the Tier 2 buildout. Lind croaked out, "Um …" He looked immediately at Ted Rogers.

"I wanted to say, 'Yes, of course,' but if Rogers had been in Toronto and heard that I had frozen rates for seven years, he'd have had a shit."

Rogers' outside counsel whispered to Achber seated beside him, "Is he going to do it?"

"Do bears shit in woods?" Achber whispered back.

Rogers quickly assessed the situation. With the entire chamber focused on him and waiting for his response, Rogers said, "Yes."

"So I said, 'Yes, I'll freeze rates for seven years,'" recalls Lind.

"Of course, that was great because I never sold that Tier. It worked out fine, but I could've been portrayed as an absolute lunatic, freezing rates for seven years. Rogers was there to be in on that caper."

Rogers lost its bid for the five suburbs east of Portland, known as Multnomah County, to Viacom after the New York-based company (acquired in 1987 by mogul Sumner Redstone) promised "the moon, the sun and the stars," including a 150-channel universe that just wasn't technologically feasible, recalls David Olson, who worked briefly for Lind's franchising team. Olson, a lawyer who worked for former governor Vic Atiyeh, became Portland's director of the Office of Cable Communications and Franchise Management in 1983, a position he's held ever since. "It was a real, wide-open, wild and woolly bidding process. During that period, Rogers was considered 'best-in-breed.' They were a darn sight better than any of the American-based companies—in terms of quality, representation, system experience and in local programming."

He recalls Ted Rogers meeting with the franchising team in the banquet room at the Thunderbird on the River Inn on the Columbia River just days after Rogers lost the franchise bid. After various presentations aimed at bringing the corporate team from Toronto up to date, Rogers joined the table where the demoralized members of the franchising team were sitting. "We were feeling just horrible," recalls Olson. "We told him, 'We just feel we've really let you down.'"

"You know, it's a beautiful day out there. The sun is shining. The trees are green. This is going to come out just fine," Rogers told them.

"It was a huge morale booster," Olson recalls. "And he was one hundred percent right."

Six months later, Rogers captured the suburbs after original winner Viacom broke off negotiations with the city. Commenting on the character of the victory, Olson says, "Rogers was very much missed from the moment they left," says Olson. Portland's post-Rogers cable providers included TCI, phone giant AT&T, which then acquired TCI, and Comcast, which purchased AT&T Broadband. "If there were a snowstorm, or an outage, we'd work with them. They always kept us in the loop. They worked with us on notices. They answered their phone. I can't say that about a number of their successors. We knew the trucks would roll. We knew repairs would be made generally on time. There's no cable company in the world that's blemish-free, but Rogers was definitely one of the leaders of the pack in how they just ran the system. They also cared a lot about local programming here and making their own community programming. They really believed in it and if they didn't, they wouldn't have won and continued to win awards for quality local programming.

"There's no question in anyone's mind down here. We look back on the system Rogers built and managed as the glory days of [the] cable TV system. We were very, very proud of the cable system. We sometimes look back wistfully, and say, 'You know, if we could get another Rogers in here, we'd be in a lot better shape than we are.' The systems have never been as well built, well managed and well run subsequently as they were under Rogers."

But in Portland, Rogers crossed the "Maginot Line" that Ottawa erected between the cable and phone companies in Canada. Over its network, Rogers was transmitting voice and data traffic to local bank branches and supermarkets at lower-than-telephone costs, raising the telephone company's hackles. Pacific Northwest Bell sued, charging that Rogers should be forced to register with the public utility commissioner as a local exchange company. Rogers prevailed in court.

And Rogers wasn't the only one making waves in telecom. Chuck Dolan's Manhattan Cable TV in New York was also providing data transmission. Even Warner Cable rolled out data transmission, in Milwaukee, although it didn't offer voice services, and unlike Rogers or Dolan, the company looked at it as a side business rather than another service or revenue stream.

In Minneapolis and Portland, Rogers built advanced, dual trunk, two-way networks that enabled the head-end (control center) equipment to sweep the system every six seconds—primitive people meters, reporting how many households were tuned to each channel at any given time. Not even Nielsen's Television Ratings were as yet that sophisticated. Lind began sharing viewing pattern data with TCI's John Malone, who was busily acquiring cable channels, the beginnings of Liberty Media. "I would just fascinate Malone with these numbers," Lind says. "He would just be in bliss because it would show, for example, that HBO was number three after ten o'clock. No one would believe anything like that. Everyone thought HBO was a pay network down at the bottom, but after ten or eleven o'clock at night, HBO climbed near the top. Everybody thought BET [Black Entertainment Television] was terrible, yet it showed up quite well. Malone then went out and bought BET.

"We were proposing things that even today they haven't done in Canada, and we were doing them in the States in the seventies. We had ratings surveying every six seconds in Minneapolis that they still can't do today. We were the best pay-per-view operator in the U.S. by far," he says.

CHAPTER 10

Taking on America: Part II
A Hell of a Marriage

"Ted and I were just like oil and water."

Robert Rosencrans

IN MAY 1981, Ted Rogers, 48, was in Quebec City at the Chateau Frontenac. He was seated in the Café Canadien, reading *The Wall Street Journal* while waiting for Phil Lind to arrive for breakfast. They were in town for the cable industry's annual conference. Rogers was catching up on the latest twist in the bitter fight for control of UA/Columbia Cablevision Inc., the 10th-largest U.S. cable company, with almost half a million subscribers in 15 states.

Dow Jones & Co. and Knight-Ridder Newspapers Inc., two of America's most powerful publishing companies, had surprised UA/Columbia with a per-share takeover offer of US$72 in February when the stock was then trading around $56. United Artists Theatre Circuit Inc., which owned 28 percent of UA/Columbia, had lambasted the offer and threatened to go to court to block it. The price had ratcheted up from there. United Artists—no connection to the movie company—had countered with a partial takeover bid at $90 a share, eclipsing the improved $80 offer from Dow Jones and Knight-Ridder. The management of the company at the center of this maelstrom was telling stockholders to tender to the lower offer.

If it hoped to win, United Artists desperately needed a partner to help fund an offer for the entire kit and caboodle. When Lind appeared for breakfast, the two men ordered a light breakfast of toast, orange juice and coffee. Rogers blurted out, "Let's buy UA/Columbia." Lind nearly choked on his OJ.

"Why not?" he replied. Lind was game. He loved the United States. He also needed to gain much-needed clout in a rapidly consolidating industry.

Westinghouse Electric Corp., a U.S. industrial heavyweight, had just acquired the number one U.S. cable company, TelePrompTer, for US$646 million, the biggest merger in the cable industry's history. TCI was gobbling up the mom-and-pop operations that started the industry. Several cable companies had already teamed up with major corporations in order to get the huge capital outlays necessary to bring in new subscribers and develop programming for television. "Cable TV is into the big money era," TelePromTer chairman Jack Kent Cooke told *Time* magazine. "Without a very rich grandfather, you can't keep up."

UA/Columbia, based in Westport, Connecticut, had 467,000 subscribers in 15 states from New York and New Jersey to Florida, Texas and California, with a potential audience of more than 1 million. Many of its cable systems were fully developed, while those Rogers controlled, with the exception of Syracuse, were still in the construction stage. Rogers had just 50,000 paying subscribers, and hoped to have 250,000 by 1985. UA/Columbia was adding new subscribers at the rate of 5,000 to 8,000 a month, making it one of the industry's fastest-growing companies.

With the explosion of cable-funded content and pay television in the United States, the U.S. cable industry was simply far more lucrative than in Canada, given its cultural hang-ups. UA/Columbia took in US$55 million in revenues in 1980 from one-third the subscriber base that Rogers Cablesystems required to earn US$70 million in revenues. The American company earned US$4.8 million, more than three times the US$1.4-million earnings of Rogers' cable operations. The cash flow from UA/Columbia's mature systems would help pay for the completion of Rogers' immature ones. That was the plan, anyway.

Rogers would also gain a U.S. management team that was widely regarded as one of the industry's best. Robert Rosencrans, the company's president and CEO, and his partner, Kenneth J. Gunter, merged Columbia in 1972 with UA Cablevision, an entity spun off from UA Theatre. They had pioneered pay TV with HBO at their Vero Beach-Fort Pierce, Florida cable systems. San Francisco-based UA Theatre, the nation's number two movie theater chain, was 51 percent controlled by Robert Naify, 59, and his older brother, Marshall, 61, the sons of a Lebanese immigrant who founded United California Theaters in 1920 and merged it with United Artists Theatre in 1963.

Rogers flew to San Francisco to meet the Naifys after the conference. Four days later, Ted Rogers had a deal. On May 19, 1981, through his family company, Ted Rogers and United Artists bid US$215 million or $90 a share, for 72 percent of UA/Columbia, a deal only eclipsed by Westinghouse's takeover of TelepromTer. (UA Theatre already owned 28 percent.) Fêted as a white knight, Rogers made front-page headlines north and south of the 49th parallel.

In a hallmark move, Rogers appeared to come out of the blue, but in reality, he had been contemplating a bid for UA/Columbia since the summer of 1980. He had met with Rosencrans, who was also a substantial shareholder, several times that summer to discuss their mutual objectives. He even turned down a Knight-Ridder proposal for a 50-50 joint venture in the autumn because he had wanted control. Indeed, Rogers was now gambling that Knight-Ridder and Dow Jones would fold. He was right. They did. "When Knight-Ridder decided last fall to go for a 50-50 joint venture, that said something. It wasn't as essential to them as it was to us, or they would have bought it all," Rogers told *Forbes*.

Rogers was now the world's biggest cable TV company, with 1.9 million subscribers, leapfrogging over Westinghouse-TelePrompTer, which had 1.5 million customers. That's not all. Rogers planned to cross the pond. He told Toronto's *Globe and Mail* that the United States fit with a three-region growth strategy that also embraces Europe—lessening the company's exposure to one constrictive regulatory regime. He intended to expand beyond his base in Ireland into other parts of Europe in the second half of the decade. Indeed, Vidéotron, Maclean Hunter and Cablecasting all expanded by the decade's end into the U.K., although with decidedly mixed results. In his daily organizer earlier in the year, Rogers jotted that he wanted to "strategically position ourselves—Fortress Cable—to defend ourselves against predatory telephone companies—buy our own cable."

Rogers, through Rogers Telecommunications Ltd. (RTL) paid US$185 million for a 51-percent stake of a new company that owned UA/Columbia. UA Theatre paid the rest, increasing its stake to 49 percent. Under the terms of the deal, Rogers Cablesystems, the public company, agreed to buy the 51 percent in UA/Columbia from RTL at cost within three years, including carrying charges. The family company would not profit from the related-party transaction.

To fund the acquisition, RTL took a one-year US$150-million loan from a TD Bank-led bank consortium by pledging as security his five radio stations and his stock in the public company. He had hocked the family assets. TD Bank refused to lend him money unless he took out extra life insurance as collateral. He renewed the $8-million policy on his life and purchased another $24 million in temporary, or term life, insurance. Rogers Cablesystems also increased its founder's life insurance policy by 60 percent to $25 million. If he keeled over tomorrow, their risk was greatly minimized.

The stock fell on the announcement. Equity investors wrung their hands. Rogers was already paying close to $7 million in annual interest costs. Now, he was taking on more debt at a time when the economy was slipping into the worst recession since the Great Depression. Inflation soared to an all-time high of 12.5 percent and the prime lending rate, which banks offer to their best customers, climbed steadily, peaking at a painful 22.75 percent in August before declining to a still high 17.25 percent by year's end. Rogers made no attempt to reassure investors, either. With interest charges eating into profits, Rogers told *Forbes* he intended to trim or cancel the company's dividends. Indeed, stockholders wouldn't see a dividend again for another 20 years.

To pay back his bankers, Rogers sold preferred shares; the 49-percent stake in Famous Players; his non-cable assets; and, importantly, the U.S.-franchised subscribers he had acquired to UA/Columbia. Rogers also shed the 12.5-percent stake in Northwest Sports Enterprises Ltd., owner of the Vancouver Canucks NHL hockey team that he inherited from Premier.

To reduce the bank loan, Rogers had committed to shed Famous Players, something he really didn't want to do. Rogers inherited the 49-percent stake from CCL. Gulf & Western, the owner of Paramount Pictures, held the remaining 51 percent. Rogers enjoyed being on the movie theater company's board with the iconic Charles G. Bluhdorn, an Austrian émigré who arrived in America in 1942 and Wall Street cotton trader who founded Gulf & Western, building it into one of the largest U.S. conglomerates.

For a while, Rogers was chairman of the Famous Players' audit committee, at a time when Bluhdorn flew everyone to Paris to meet the theater company's French partner. (The company owned 50 percent of a French company that had 34 French theaters.) They were having a wonderful lunch in Paris when Rogers began to ask the French partner questions; he had a list of 43 questions with him. He got through three questions when Bluhdorn stood up and left. "I didn't move. I kept going and went through all of the questions, and there was just a couple of us there," says Rogers. He had a feeling something just wasn't right. He later spoke to Bluhdorn about it. "Charlie, I can't prove it but there's something wrong. Who is this guy?"

Bluhdorn replied, "He did some work with the Nazis during the war, but he's been a friend of mine and he's a good guy. Why don't you enjoy Paris? The rest of us are."

Rogers didn't let it go. Eighteen months later, Rogers went back to Bluhdorn, insisting this French partner was stealing from the company. "Charlie, this guy has been stealing from us. He's taken money out and here's the papers to prove it. Even though he's your friend, you've got to call him up and get our money back," he told him. "He was mortified," Rogers recalls.

"Haven't you got better things to do with your time?" Bluhdorn retorted.

Rogers was not thanked for his efforts. A year passed. At their next meeting, Bluhdorn, who had once chased Rogers' predecessor, Tony Griffiths, around the boardroom table in a fit of anger, yelled at Rogers. "You bloody fool!"

"Charlie. What is it now?"

"The guy stole the money to make movies and the movies were a hit, you idiot."

"What do you mean, Charlie? We didn't own the movies."

"Yeah, but we could have recovered the movies."

Rogers pounded the table with his fist, laughing heartily at the anecdote. "We were blood brothers," he reminisces.

His so-called blood brother didn't mind taking him to the mat. In the negotiations to buy Rogers' stake in Famous Players, Bluhdorn insisted on paying mostly stock, not cash. In July 1981, Rogers Cablesystems sold its 49-percent stake in Famous Players to Gulf & Western (G&W) for the bargain price of US$47 million—receiving just US$2.5 million in cash, a half-interest in a Toronto's Skyway industrial park, 600,000 shares of G&W-controlled pinball and video game company Williams Electronics Inc., and 1 million G&W treasury shares held in escrow until December. In order to guarantee a floor price on the G&W shares, Rogers, through RTL, his private family company, purchased the G&W stock in December for US$20 million to provide liquidity for the public company. He put the risk into the family company to protect the public company.

In return for bearing the risk, he received a two-year option to buy half a million class A voting shares at $11.87—a move enabling Rogers to increase his stake in the public company to 59 percent from 57 percent. The cotton trader got Famous Players for a song. Rogers and his team underestimated the value of the movie theater's real estate assets. Just a month after the sale, the movie theater exhibitor hived off its real estate assets into a stand-alone company that had an estimated asset base of $170 million.

Rogers held the G&W shares until February 1983, hoping the stock, which had languished in the mid-teens, might retrace its losses. With the stock trading at US$17, Rogers called Bluhdorn, offering to sell at $17.50 a share. Bluhdorn bid $16.625 net. They settled on $16.87. The family company absorbed a $3.12-million loss. Rogers used the proceeds to pay down the public company's burgeoning U.S. debt load.

Just weeks later, the Austrian-born U.S. industrialist was dead. Bluhdorn, 56, suffered a fatal heart attack in late February 1983 aboard his jet flying home to New York from a business trip in the Dominican Republic, where G&W had vast sugar plantations. "I cried when he died," says Rogers. "I enjoyed him. He was intimidating. Bluhdorn was an emperor, much more than Bassett. Bassett wasn't like that at all. But, they were both sure of themselves."

On the UA/Columbia front, Rogers rolled out the red carpet. To build bridges, Rogers invited nine of the company's key executives to his Tobin island cottage in Muskoka, north of Toronto, to mingle with his Canadian team before the transaction closed. Rogers had stated in public, as well as offering private assurances, that the UA/Columbia management would continue to run the U.S. holding. He said he was sensitive to their concerns because it irritated him when Canadian companies are run from U.S. head offices, with little priority given to local concerns. He also named Bob Rosencrans to the RCI board. Filled with optimism, Rogers hoped the two teams might forge close bonds by mixing business and pleasure. "They had a fabulous time, but they couldn't understand why they had to work all day. They had a golf-centric management style that drove Rogers absolutely bananas," recalls Colin Watson, adding, "The only downside to my tenure at Rogers is that I was never allowed to play golf, so I didn't become a golfer until I left Rogers."

In November 1981, Rogers and UA Theatre sealed their "marriage"—that's what they called it—by completing their acquisition of UA/Columbia. Rogers now had two U.S. cable companies—the 51 percent of UA/Columbia, renamed Rogers UA Cablesystems Inc. (RUAC) and 100 percent of Rogers U.S. Cablesystems Inc. (RUSCI), which housed the franchised assets. To keep them straight, insiders called them by their acronyms, pronounced phonetically as "Roo-ak" and "Rus-kee."

The new partners agreed right at the start to divide the venture if a dispute ever arose. In the marriage documents, the Wall St. lawyers, having already dealt with several U.S.-Canadian corporate breakups, set out the potential policy disagreements that permitted either party to terminate their partnership and spelled out the terms of their divorce with uncommon specificity. Skadden Arps and Loeb & Loeb, two New York law firms, represented Rogers, while Wachtell, Lipton, Rosen & Katz acted for United Artists. The shareholders' agreement— "prenuptial agreement" might have been a more appropriate description—filled three hard-backed volumes, each six inches thick.

Their foresight proved prophetic. On paper, the two companies were a perfect fit. But they could not have been more different in style and philosophy. Paradoxically, Rogers wants his managers to act like entrepreneurs, but only so long as his word is final. Here, he had a management team who were the genuine articles—strong-willed, independent-minded entrepreneurs—and he treated them not as equals but subordinates. UA/Columbia had a conservative financial philosophy, moving ahead with capital investments as needed. Rogers was far more aggressive. UA/Columbia wanted to upgrade its 12-channel cable systems in Arkansas, Oklahoma and Tennessee before pouring money into rebuilding the almost-complete 35-channel San Antonio, the crown jewel.

The tenor was set from the start. At the first management meeting of the two companies, someone, not Ted Rogers, arrogantly said, "What are we going to do about these dogs in Florida?" in reference to the revenue-generating Vero Beach-Fort Pierce systems, where cable TV history was made when HBO was launched. The systems apparently weren't performing to the levels the Rogers management team desired. It was proposed they either get rid of them or change their managers. "It just floored us. It was as a frontal attack. That's the way we took it," recalls Marvin Jones, then 44, part of the UA/Columbia team who had turned around the Florida systems. Jones became TCI's chief executive officer in the nineties. "Things went from bad to worse."

"We trusted middle management. We picked those middle managers and divisional vice presidents and divisional engineers carefully but when we did, we assigned to them quite a lot of authority and discretion," says Ken Gunter.

Rogers was exactly the opposite. He ran a highly centralized operation. Rogers ran a multi-million-dollar enterprise as if it were a small family company. No decision was made without his approval first. By virtue of his intellectual acuity, curiosity and drive, Rogers devoured every report. He had the mental capacity to retain its contents right down to the page number. Unlike most CEOs, Rogers delved into the minutia, which meant he often failed to see the forest through the trees. For example, Rogers would demand to know from Ken Gunter why those four-dollar refurbished converters hadn't been delivered yet when Gunter was dealing with the bigger problem of microwaves malfunctioning in the rain.

"I like Ted Rogers, but on the other hand, I disagreed with him quite often. He can be fairly heavy handed," says Gunter. "Ted was always very much a gentleman, but Ted, even being a gentleman, I can't tell you how raucous some of those board meetings were in Toronto, and he would conclude the meeting as chairman by saying, 'My goodness, what a wonderful meeting we've had'—and, everyone's walking out of there with their tails between their legs.

"In many ways, he's a very agreeable and diplomatic man but, when you get right down to the nut-cutting, you either click your heels and say, 'yes sir,' or there's trouble. Ted is very much an autocrat. He would tolerate the discussion, but Ted would not tolerate his edict not being followed when the discussion ended. Colin Watson would say certain things, but he was also careful to be sure that Ted approved. Colin was a nice guy, but he operated very much under the umbrella of Ted Rogers.

"Phil Lind would actually take Ted on at times with us. Phil was probably the greatest diplomat and mediator that Rogers had. He mediated through several serious disputes between UA and Rogers by just his style and his ability to see through both sides of the story and try to work a compromise. Phil either had it, or simply claimed it. But, even then, he finally had to cave in to Ted because once Ted had his mind made up he just wasn't negotiable. He had a lot of pressure on him."

"Phil is not the least bit afraid to poke fun at Ted," says Marvin Jones. "He and Colin used to sit in meetings, cracking jokes about Ted right there, while Ted was talking away. It was insider stuff. Ted can get full of himself and start going on. They did that to poke fun at him all the time."

"Ted and I were just like oil and water," says Bob Rosencrans. "Maybe it was my fault. I think I failed to come to a stockholder meeting. I was in Aspen and I didn't feel like flying in the middle of February and the weather was terrible. Colin made it and I didn't. I always regretted that. Ted wasn't happy, and I don't blame him. I should have made it."

"Ted never forgave him for that either," recalls Jones. "That started the whole split; I really do believe this. Ted was never able to control Bob or Ken. Bob is a gentleman and a very nice human being. He refused to be a puppet of Ted's. It wasn't fun. It was very stressful."

"He's very insensitive, and keeps pushing and pushing, irrespective of what the hell he's pushing. We just couldn't work together in a way that was productive. Ted was totally centralized. He would have been much better off if he had said to Ken and me, 'Look, you guys have a little experience. Give us your plans, give us your budgets and you guys, go ahead and make it work.' But, instead, he micromanaged everything, and we said, 'What do you need us for? Go ahead; you don't need us.' That was what we felt. But listen, the guy's been successful," says Rosencrans.

"Ted had a different approach than I did. I felt that anybody that worked for the company should be an owner. Ted looked at it that he and UA were the owners and everybody else was an employee. It was a totally different approach to running a company, and that created some tension between us. Just to tell us that 'you guys are management; you run the systems and don't worry about anything else' was just not the way Ken and I had grown up. And, maybe they were right, but that created tension."

Ron Harmon, a former UA/Columbia regional manager, recalls, "If you look at it and ask, 'What could have made it work?' it would have taken Ted Rogers having to stay out of it for the most part and act more like a board member more so than getting involved in day-to-day operations with daily phone calls. That was too much. You couldn't plan your future because you didn't have any idea what Ted was going to come up with the next morning. It really wears on you, especially when you're not accustomed to it. Ted ran it with an iron fist."

Indeed, one UA insider likened Rogers to a "charming Adolf Hitler," and as offensive as this characterization might be, it illustrated that there was no love lost between the two groups. When the San Antonio gang gave Rogers his first tour, they took him up on one of their Cessnas. After a loop around the city, the pilot suddenly keeled over, scaring Rogers half to death. The prank did not go over well with a man who felt blessed just to make it beyond 39.

The tension escalated when UA Theatre became involved. Five months after Rogers and UA/Columbia married, Rogers broke their wedding vows, if not contractually, in spirit. In a memo to the Naifys, Salah Hassanein, the Naifys' right-hand man, referred to a memo Rogers sent to the staff of UA/Columbia and Rogers Cablesystems that he found "disquieting" since it appeared to "relegate [Rosencrans] to a subservient position, makes his employees responsible to their counterparts in his Canadian organization" and "totally emasculates the management which we sought to perpetuate." Rogers also forced UA/Columbia to channel all of its insurance needs through his school pal Toby Hull regardless of prior commitments, a decision that annoyed U.S. management. Rosencrans resigned from the RCI board.

The Naifys iced Rogers' plans to fold his franchising properties into UA/Columbia until he backed off. In a letter to Rogers, Marshall Naify reminded him that they had mutually agreed to keep the present management team intact and had in fact embodied that sentiment in their final shareholders' agreement. He wrote.

> With this in mind, why, then, do you demoralize these very executives into whose hands we have placed this valuable asset? How can we expect them to work for our best interests when they are unhappy and disquieted? You have a partner who is vitally concerned and has an agreement with you as to how we should run this entity. If our cable company is to grow and prosper, it can only do so with sound management. If this matter of management is not resolved, we would be foolish to consider any long range plans. We must move quickly to get the staff back on an even keel. There is no business as pressing as this.

Perhaps not for him, but Ted Rogers had hocked virtually everything. Months earlier, Rogers warned shareholders at the company's annual meeting not to expect any significant earnings until the "harvest year"—1985. Turns out, he was overly optimistic by about two decades. When 1985 rolled around, he bluntly told shareholders, "This company is like the *Queen Mary*—hard to turn around." Indeed. Rogers was trying to stay afloat in a sea of debt.

At its August 31, 1982 fiscal year-end, Rogers Cablesystems' long-term debt had more than tripled to $574.9 million in one year. Its cash flow was a mere $26 million. Just three years earlier, long-term debt had been only $15 million. The company posted a loss of $13.3 million, compared to a year-earlier profit of $3.4 million. The non-voting class B shares dipped as low as $5.25. Soaring interest rates were skewering the company. The annual cost to service its ever-increasing mountain of debt rose to $64 million in fiscal 1982. The banks ordered Rogers to fix his lopsided balance sheet.

As if things couldn't get any worse, Ottawa's price-restraint program, dubbed the 6-and-5 rule, limited cable rate increases to 6 percent or less just when RCI was hit with labor strife and a 17-percent jump in wages at its Vancouver system. Cable rate increases were held to 6 percent in 1982 and 5 percent in 1983. Pay TV, another revenue stream, had not yet arrived. Rogers sold its 50-percent stake in the USA Network. The company froze salaries and fired 175 employees after its applications for rate increases of more than 20 percent—some of which were filed in 1981—were slashed by Ottawa's 6-and-5 rule. The CRTC initiated an investigation into the staff cuts and Rogers' capital spending to determine if the company had contravened its licensing conditions.

The single biggest drain was Rogers' UA/Columbia loan. And, he had yet to see any benefit from that partnership. The main premise for the UA partnership was to fold Lind's franchising efforts into UA/Columbia, but the two sides were deadlocked.

Rogers couldn't get anywhere with the Naifys. "The Naify brothers "were like 'Heckel and Jeckel'—the two old crows; that's what they were like," says Lind. "They were incredible, in-cre-di-ble. They were weird, weird, weird people. They would yell at you all the time. They would storm around. UA was really a movie distribution company, and apparently, everybody yells at everybody in that business all the time and that's all they did—yell at us."

The Naifys appeared to run the publicly traded company as if it were their private domain. In a 1978 lawsuit, Georgette Naify Rosekrans accused her brother Marshall of collecting a large salary for negligible work, abusing his executive perquisites and operating the theater company in violation of federal securities laws. She portrayed her brother as a religious fanatic who had indulged in drugs. The lawsuit, settled out of court, led to an SEC investigation of company practices that was eventually dropped, but not before Marshall Naify resigned as chairman for a few years. He became a California horse owner and breeder, and a prominent one at that up until his death. "[The Naify's] were wonderful when they were passive investors," says Rosencrans. "I would much prefer Ted over the Naifys."

Marvin Jones offers this assessment: "They were like Ted incarnated ten times over without Ted's background. They had no knowledge of the cable business."

Rogers and the Naifys just were not able to reach an agreement on fair market value. They were haggling over subscribers worth an estimated US$75 million, but UA/Columbia didn't want its relatively pristine balance sheet torpedoed by Rogers' capital-hungry U.S. projects, some of which weren't expected to break even until 1987.

"We disagreed on the valuation," says Rosencrans. "I guess I was the one who said the prices were too high and that didn't create goodwill. In retrospect, Ted was probably right. They turned out to be good."

The marriage lasted 14 months.

On February 4, 1983, Rogers and UA Theatre publicly announced their divorce. The stock market appeared relieved. Rogers' class B non-voting shares rose 25 cents to $11.25, while the class A voting shares climbed 12 cents to $11.12. The shareholders' agreement laid out the divorce proceedings with so called "unlocking" provisions that split the company in half between the two owners. The lawyers called it the "split off."

According to the prenuptials, if one side wanted a divorce, the other would divide the assets and liabilities into two equal parts and give the instigator first pick. Rogers pulled the plug. The Naifys ordered UA/Columbia to split the assets into two lists. Rogers had three months to choose between the lists or forfeit the rights to the Naifys.

Rosencrans, Gunter and Jones divided the assets into two groups. They wanted San Antonio. The city had just 53,000 subscribers but once the company finished laying down the cable, they'd pass 330,000 homes, the largest of any of the cable systems. So, they compiled in Group A all of the southwestern systems, which had fewer subscribers, but greater cost efficiencies and revenue potential. It had places like El Centro, Yuma, Alamogordo, San Angelo (Gunter's home town), Gainesville, Laredo, Fort Smith, McAlester, Tennessee, East Texas and San Antonio, the crown jewel.

They strategically included in Group B cable properties in the northeast—New York and New Jersey—that were mature and generated a higher cash flow. Indeed, the New Jersey systems were the company's cash cow. Rosencrans, Gunter and Jones were gambling that cash-hungry Rogers needed the higher-revenue generating systems. They included the Florida "dogs" because of their profitability and that old snowbird connection. For bait, they added Aspen, Colorado because they knew Colin Watson and Bob Classen were avid skiers. Similarly, they included the northwest cable systems in Oregon and Washington because Phil Lind loved to fly-fish.

They totally misread the RCI team. Rogers, a shrewd businessman, does not make business decisions out of sentimentality, even if he's emotionally engaged. Phil Lind wanted San Antonio. He was adamant that Rogers take San Antonio. Only Bob Francis, the CFO, lobbied hard for Group B. The team scattered across 15 states to visit 22 cable TV systems to perform their due diligence. They were thorough and meticulous.

"To his credit, Rogers forced a discipline on making sure that was the right decision," says Classen. "He was always looking for hidden assets. When we sold off Famous Players, we had gotten burned by underestimating the value of the real estate and we didn't want to make that mistake in this case, so we were looking at what they owned versus what they leased, how many physical assets they really had, where was the hidden value. It was a good lesson for me later when I was at Comcast because we always drove down to the minute level to be sure that we weren't missing any assets when we were making our bids."

In March 1983, Rogers flew to San Francisco to tell the Naifys his decision. It was Group A. He picked the southwest group, which promised higher revenue generation and the greater cost efficiencies. Then, he carried on to Los Angeles to visit Michael Milken, Drexel Burnham Lambert's junk-bond wizard. The UA/Columbia team had gathered in San Antonio to await the call. Rosencrans was in Connecticut, patched through by telephone. They were shell-shocked—totally floored—when they heard Rogers picked Group A. The atmosphere was as if someone had died. They retreated to a nearby restaurant for the wake. The companies completed the transaction on August 30, 1983.

"I lived through all of it and I still don't believe it," says Gunter.

CHAPTER 11

Taking on America: Part III
Hell on Wheels

"We've got to get back many of the promises we made and, if we don't, we're toast."

—Phil Lind

ROGERS INHERITED A 15-YEAR IRONCLAD CONTRACT with the San Antonio Spurs, a National Basketball Association team, to televise their games. In awarding its first cable franchise, the city forced UA/Columbia to sign a lopsided contract that paid the Spurs millions of dollars each year before it even finished wiring the city in return for the right to broadcast a few home games—nearly a decade before multimillion-dollar television sports agreements were even contemplated.

Soon after RCI closed the acquisition, the first payment of US$1 million to the Spurs came due. Rogers was furious when he saw the contract. He withheld payment. Despite the fact there were 10 years left on the contract, Rogers knew he would never be able to honor the terms given the company's financial condition. He had to renegotiate the contract. "How could anyone have signed this deal?" he said. "I've got to get out of this. This is crazy." He instructed Missy Goerner in San Antonio, the vice president of programming, production and regulatory affairs, who managed UA/Columbia's relationship with the Spurs, to arrange a meeting with Spurs owner Angelo Drossos. She was one of the few UA/Columbia employees who remained at Rogers. She would become indispensable to Phil Lind in negotiating cable content deals. Goerner was not hopeful about the forthcoming meeting between Rogers and Drossos.

Drossos, half blind in one eye, was born in San Antonio to Greek immigrants. The six-foot-three Shearson Hammil stockbroker and former Ford salesman had a reputation of being unconventional and an often-ruthless negotiator with a penchant to sue and win. He led the intense merger discussions that resulted in four American Basketball Association (ABA) teams, including the Spurs, joining the NBA in 1976. He was the lead negotiator for the NBA team owners against the players' union and had pushed for a player salary cap. He also pioneered the use of contract incentives tied to franchise win-loss records. Drossos had also been part of Storer's failed bid to prevent UA/Columbia from getting the cable franchise. He told Goerner he had absolutely no intention of making any changes to the contract, but he did agree to host a luncheon in his office.

When Rogers and Lind arrived at the hotel in San Antonio, they both had messages from their people urging them—no matter what—to be on time for lunch since nothing made Drossos angrier than lack of punctuality. Goerner arrived first and she attempted to make idle conversation with Drossos, but it was evident his mood was souring with each passing minute. Finally, Rogers and Lind arrived 27 minutes late and exactly 24 minutes after Drossos had removed the warming covers from their plates of food. He was as hot as the plates were cold. He was certainly no longer in the mood to meet them. "It was then, in the next few minutes, that Ted so classically illustrated what makes him a genius at times and sets him apart from the rest," Lind said.

Rogers rushed in and grabbed Drossos' hand. He apologized for being late explaining that he wanted to bring him something for their first meeting and that it had been late in arriving. All of this was delivered in one breath and Drossos had yet to utter one word. While they were still standing in a virtual face-off, Rogers said, "Angelo, I asked to meet with you because I want to talk about your contract with the previous owner."

Drossos visibly stiffened and replied, "Your lunch is cold and you owe me one million dollars."

The money was six months overdue. That was Rogers' cue. He said—in a louder than necessary voice—"That's what I want to talk to you about. That's why we're late."

The door opened and in walked several armed security guards pushing carts loaded with bags of US$10 bills, totaling $1 million.

Rogers was beaming. Drossos was speechless, as the guards stacked bag after bag of money on the table. For a moment, Drossos was quiet and unreadable, and then he burst out laughing. The transformation was remarkable, says Lind. Drossos warmly shook Rogers' hand.

Then, Rogers said, "Oh, do you mind if we take a picture?"

The three men stood behind the pile of garbage bags full of money, beaming wide smiles at the photographer. By the end of the lunch, Drossos said: "You know, we don't have a fair contract. It really is one-sided and I think I can do business with you. If you will come back, then we'll talk about changing the agreement." They met a month later—and Drossos gave concessions to Rogers that amounted to millions of dollars over the remaining life of the agreement.

"It was Ted and me," recalls Goerner, who became instrumental to Lind in negotiating highly coveted sports-content deals. "We didn't even have an attorney in the room. It was Ted, me and Angelo and my counterpart with the Spurs. We sat there for three hours and went over [the contract] clause by clause by clause. Angelo's guy is writing down these clauses and sending them out to the secretary, and when we left that day, we had a three-page legal document that had replaced [the old, voluminous] one. It saved us about five million dollars over that four-year period. The only thing Angelo said was, 'Let's start with this, but if I've given you back too much, I'd like to call you and we can talk about it.' And, so for the next two to three years, they'd talk over the phone and make minor changes. That doesn't happen in sports deals anymore."

For as long as Drossos owned the Spurs, he hung the photograph of himself, Rogers and Lind surrounded by bags of money on his office wall. When people asked Drossos, why he would willingly change a deal that cost him millions of dollars, he would always say, "Because Ted Rogers knew the art of making a deal and nothing is better than that."

"In all the years we've been together, what truly amazes and impresses me the most about Ted is his uncanny ability to walk into situations, where you know going in that you are in deep trouble. Where mere mortals, like myself, know you simply cannot win—and where Ted, not only survives, but will pull victory out of almost certain defeat," Lind said. "It's not just his relentless optimism; it's much, much more than that."

Bob Francis, Rogers' unflappable CFO, took a drag on his du Maurier cigarette. He was hot, tired and frustrated. He was standing on the side of a road in Oregon near the parked rental car watching Ted Rogers, Phil Lind and Lind's right-hand man Vernon Achber bent over maps of Multnomah County splayed across the car's hood. He listened in disbelief as they animatedly discussed the company's 80,000-home franchise adjacent to the city of Portland when, just like Mount Hood three years earlier, he erupted. "We can't do this!" he hollered.

The three men straightened up to stare at him. They had never heard him yell before. Robert Morley Francis, a heavyset broad-shouldered man, who at five-foot-ten—shorter than the others by several inches—still cut an imposing character. He smoked about a pack of cigarettes a day, and had a sweet tooth.

His somber demeanor belied the ever-present twinkle in his eyes. He had been the finance chief at Canada Cycle and Motor Co. (CCM) and the president of Double Diamond Electronics Ltd., a subsidiary of Philips Electronics Industries Ltd., before joining Rogers in 1976 thinking that at age 40, after he helped the small family company sort out its financial difficulties over the first six months he'd been there, he'd had a nice, easy nine-to-five job with minimal overtime. Francis, whose word was like gold with the bankers, was always forthright but never volatile. It took a lot to ruffle his feathers. "He was quiet, but you always had the impression that he was the enforcer," says Bob Classen. "In a way, he was almost Ted's alter-ego."

Each time Lind went after another franchise, Francis told him: "Phil, we just don't have the money." Lind always responded: "Just this one; then there won't be any more."

Lind now sought to reassure Francis. "Bob, we can do this."

"You people don't understand!" Francis yelled. "The bankers!"

"It was one of the few times that Bob ever yelled at anybody," recalls Lind.

They ran the bank ratio tests every week, wondering how many of them they were going to miss at the end of every month. Lind had burned through $3 million to $4 million a year just on the bidding process. The expense reports left KPMG auditors aghast. "The auditors were just going crazy. There were no procedures, nothing. It was just Vernon and me. We signed it and it went through. The auditors would say, 'Ten thousand or twenty-five thousand for entertaining in Portland? What is this?" recalls Lind.

Lind had to be careful that he didn't bid for too many cities simultaneously. If his team competed for seven cities and won five in rapid succession, he might sink the highly leveraged company. To win, he had to make commitments— whether it was free basic cable or planting trees—which they knew just weren't economically feasible to deliver. Cable systems require heavy capital investments. Revenue only begins flowing in when subscribers have signed on and begun paying their monthly fees. The various cable systems were in numerous stages of development. "You're out there working away, and by the time the lawyers have the papers done, we are in default," says Rogers. "The numbers weren't quite as we forecast. This happened six times. But, we made it. And, all the people who loaned us money got every cent of interest. Nobody lost a nickel. Nobody lost a nickel of principal. We had a lot of people in those communities who invested. They all made money."

Rogers and Francis worked through restructuring the labyrinth of agreements with the U.S. bank consortiums, while Savage designed the limited partnerships. Rogers made the most of corporate tax law by using offshore jurisdictions to reap interest deductions in Canada and the U.S. With the debt accumulated from UA/Columbia, both the acquisition and the liabilities inherited from the divorce, Rogers' access to capital was rapidly running dry. The banks either wanted out of the consortiums, or desired less exposure. Rogers was on the brink of losing everything yet again.

Enter the Wizard of Oz: Drexel Burnham Lambert Inc.'s Michael Milken.

Milken was able to create and deliver money out of thin air to the Munchkins. With his high-flying junk-bond empire, Milken revolutionized corporate America by "democratizing capital"—opening a half-trillion-dollar pool of capital to mid-size companies and corporate raiders that before had been only available to the Fortune 500 and utility companies. Junk wasn't considered respectable. It carried the stigma of the fallen angels—industrial-strength companies that had fallen on hard times and from grace. He took a retrospective academic study and showed that junk bonds defaulted only slightly more often than investment-grade, or blue chip, bonds, yet paid interest rates 3 percent to 4 percent higher. "It's profound," says Rogers. "I'll never forget what [Milken] said: 'If you go back to the twenties and list the leading corporations of the day and then you list the ones that weren't proven, you'll find that twenty-five years later, there's not much difference in the default level.'"

In the late seventies, Milken, with near-messianic zeal, persuaded big investors—insurance companies, pension funds, college endowments, banks and other institutional investors—that the bonds were safe, ultimately developing a network of money managers that made him one of the world's most powerful financiers. Bond buyers were willing to take the extra gamble on mid-size-growth companies because of the higher yields. The issuers of junk could afford to pay the higher rates out of their future earnings because, unlike dividends on stocks, the interest is tax deductible. Though Drexel didn't invent the leveraged buyout, the junk bond market spawned the eighties' corporate buyout craze. The firm began raising predatory junk money for corporate raiders, including Rogers' Cantel partner First City Financial. In 1983, the "king of junk bonds" had not yet reached his zenith.

"I admired him a lot," says Rogers. "These guys were unique."

But his admiration didn't stop him from arguing with Milken over the best way to sell his junk-bond issues.

Rogers was one of Drexel's first cable clients and Canada's first junk-bond issuer. It seemed an odd match: Rogers, of Establishment stock, doing business with Drexel, a Wall Street also-ran. He had no choice. Rogers lacked the corporate heft to warrant attention from Merrill Lynch, Goldman Sachs, J.P. Morgan & Co. and Morgan Stanley, the white-shoed bulge bracket financiers to blue-chip giants. In Toronto, the investment banking clique, never known for seeing, let alone thinking, beyond their parochial four corners of Bay and King streets, lacked the ingenuity and incentive to help the maverick cable guy out of his difficulties. Bay Street typically lagged Wall Street by years. The cable TV industry just wasn't taken seriously.

Canada's glorified investment dealers were rich, fat, risk-averse and quite comfortable feeding off the spoils of Canada's oil, timber, beer and mining giants. They were also busy wooing Ma Bell. "Drexel was more of [a] blue-collar firm than we felt we were," says Savage. "We weren't Exxon. We were an up-and-coming fast-growing company and that's what they were." Using high yield, high-risk bonds, Drexel, through Milken, laid the foundations for the new information economy by funding Ted Turner, Craig McCaw, John Malone, Sumner Redstone, Gerald Levin, Rupert Murdoch and Bill McGowan.

Graham Savage headed to New York to work on the debt-refinancing package with Albert Gnat, a holdover director from CCL. Since Rogers did not have an in-house counsel at that time, Gnat was the legal go-to person. He retained Skadden Arps, which put a young lawyer Matthew J. Mallow on the file. The point person for Drexel was Leon Black, now best known as the founder of gigantic private equity fund, the Apollo Group. Milken occasionally participated via conference call from Beverly Hills, where the Los Angeles native had relocated Drexel's high-yield trading group.

Savage spent nearly six months working on the eventual three junk-bond issues. "We were all digging in new ground," says Savage, who corrected Milken when the "grand sorcerer" of finance actually erred on a technical aspect of the structuring.

In February 1983, the month when the junk-bond market exploded in size, Drexel sold US$181 million-worth of high-yield, or junk, bonds for Rogers—$30 million more than anticipated—through three sophisticated debt instruments: $75-million senior debentures bearing 13 5/8 percent interest; $75 million of senior subordinated debentures with a 14 ¼ percent coupon; and, $30.9 million from two zero coupon notes, due in 1988 and 1989. Zero-coupon bonds—Wall Street's in-thing until the tax rules changed—are sold at deep discounts to their face value and mature at their face value. They pay no interest but, if held to maturity, the bonds Rogers sold yielded 13½ percent. For a company like Rogers, that was cash-strapped and constructing franchises, the zero-coupon notes meant they didn't have to pay any coupons until five or six years later. It also meant they could deduct their annual interest costs without actually having to pay them. Savage was getting the bankers off their backs by attracting equity-like money from bond investors without sacrificing any of Rogers' equity ownership.

"The one unpardonable sin in business is to run out of money," says Craig O. McCaw, the Seattle-based multi-billionaire widely regarded as wireless industry visionary. "There's a time to stretch, and then there's a time to pull back and be more careful. It's the street term, 'bears make money and pigs get slaughtered,' and those of us, who have gone to the brink before, know how painful it is when you're the guy on top and you're the one that goes to bed at night knowing the buck stops with you. I had wonderful people who helped save me from myself many times. Graham did some wonderful work for Ted.

"Graham was the guy they said looked like me—of all the funny things. I met him after I was told that. I didn't think he really looked like me. Ted had beaten him down. He was trying to keep the money flowing for Ted [and that made] your shoulders slump faster than some ..."

Rogers used the proceeds to retire the company's bank debt. He threw a party—dubbed the "Paydown Party"—at the Toronto Club, the power elite's most exclusive club and domain of Argus Corp's Bud McDougald. Surprisingly, few people recollect the event because Rogers held "so many" paydown parties. They do remember that champagne flowed. Bob Francis presented a cheque to the Royal Bank of Canada's Rowland Frazee. Graham Savage handed one to CIBC's Russell Harrison. When Ted Rogers presented the third cheque to TD Bank Chairman Dick Thomson, Thomson quipped that he wouldn't stash it away because Rogers would be banging on his door soon enough.

To commemorate Rogers' 50th birthday just months later, TD Bank's Robin Korthals presented him with a black-framed calligraphically penned loan document, which still adorns Rogers' office:

We are pleased to inform you that the TD Bank on the occasion of your fiftieth birthday is prepared to make available the following line of credit for your personal use, subject to the terms and conditions generally as outlined below:

Borrower: Ted Rogers.

Amount: $50 billion.

Lender: TD Bank.

Purpose: to help promote and prolong the state of good cheer and good health.

Availability: in amounts of $1 billion per year on demand subject to normal bank conditions, margin requirements and other security, interest rate to be negotiated in an amount consummate with risk.

Security: 1. one cottage

        2. other considerations as appropriate

        3. co-signature of Loretta Rogers with John Graham

Maturity: May 27, 2033, when you reach a hundred.

We are pleased to have had this opportunity to express our appreciation and look forward to continued utilization throughout the terms of this loan. Happy Birthday.

Out of necessity more than anything else, Rogers blazed a trail for other Canadian companies by using innovative financing tools not available in Canada. Inevitably, he became exposed to some of the high-profile debt swashbucklers of the time, notably Michael Milken and his merry band of junk-bond acolytes. Milken invited Rogers and Savage to attend Drexel's four-day symposium in Beverly Hills, which later became immortalized as the Predators' Ball, an evangelical happening noted as much for its guest list as the entertainment. (Savage skipped the gala dinner for a courtside seat at a Los Angeles Lakers basketball game.) The event was frequented annually by the titans of industry, corporate raiders, arbitrageurs and deal lawyers, such as Carl Icahn, the Belzbergs, Sir James Goldsmith, T. Boone Pickens, Nelson Peltz and Ronald Perelman, who rubbed elbows and plotted their next corporate conquests—men with big egos and appetites.

In her book *Predators' Ball*, Connie Bruck portrayed the gala event as a typical high-testosterone evening, capped off with "extremely attractive young women" who were paid to keep the high rollers entertained. In the early years, Drexel used the women as bait to attract well-heeled Wall Street clients to the firm. Drexel, which helped shape corporate America in the eighties by bankrolling billions of dollars of corporate takeovers, became well known on Main Street after earning US$522 million in 1986, more than any other investment bank. Publicly, Milken, whose take-home pay topped US$550 million in 1987, came to embody all that was wrong with the go-go "greed is good" decade. "They had a great business, a great idea, but then greed took over and destroyed their power," Malon Wilkus, president of American Capital Strategies, a Maryland investment bank, told *Newsweek*.

Things became to unravel for Drexel in 1986 when the firm became caught up in the scandals that swept Wall Street after the fall of Ivan F. Boesky, the undisputed king of Wall Street arbitrageurs. He paid US$100 million to settle insider-trading charges with the SEC in exchange for testifying against Drexel and Milken. In 1989, Drexel pleaded guilty to six felony counts, agreeing to pay US$650 million, a financial settlement that ultimately proved to be its undoing. Caught in the crosshairs of the politically ambitious U.S. attorney Rudolph Giuliani, Milken was indicted on 98 counts of insider trading and securities fraud. For the time being, America's love affair with junk bonds was over. "They had parties and beautiful women, and all that sort of stuff," Rogers recalled. "The whole thing was super. Everything good has to end, I guess."

Rogers' hopes to expand into Europe were dashed when his board of directors vetoed his plans. The company needed to sell assets, not amass more. "I could have made it 14 votes against one controlling vote, but I knew in my heart of hearts that they were right. I've come to realize that we are a fragile company compared with other world firms. We can't sustain big write-offs," Rogers told business reporter David Olive.

On April 7, 1984, Ted Rogers agreed to sell its 75-percent stake in Dublin Cablesystems Ltd., serving 110,000 subscribers in Dublin and Waterford, to RTÉ Relays, the Irish government's broadcasting arm. Irish Allied Banks held the balance. Rogers sent Graham Savage and Albert Gnat to Dublin to complete the transaction. Rogers expressed concern to Savage that they might have difficulty getting their money out of Ireland.

"Don't come home without the money," Rogers warned him.

In Dublin, before his meetings to finalize the sale, Savage met with Chase Bank Ireland (now J.P. Morgan Chase) to arrange the wire transfer of an Irish government cheque in the amount of roughly £10 million to New York.

Chase reluctantly agreed to transfer the Irish punts but refused to stay open beyond 5 p.m. With the five-hour time difference between Dublin and New York, there should have been no problem completing the wire transfer that day. "You couldn't get anything more gilt-edged than that, but Chase said, 'Okay, okay, we'll take it and wire it, but you've got to be here by five because we're not staying open,' which is absurd, because if it had been New York, there's no question they'd stay open," recalls Savage. He persuaded the bank to stay open an extra half-hour, knowing that closings always take longer than expected.

Now well past five o'clock, Savage and Gnat dashed out of the lawyers' offices. The streets were already empty. They broke into a run. Gnat, 45, a decade older, struggled to keep up to Savage, at the time a marathon runner. Realizing he was holding Savage back, Gnat stopped after half a block. Gasping for air, he panted: "Just go. Just leave me for dead. Go."

"I was literally running in a business suit down High Street in Dublin, trying to get to Chase," says Savage.

Just minutes past 5:30 p.m., Savage skidded to a halt in front of Chase. The bank manager stood behind the locked glass door, glaring at him. He tapped his wristwatch, shaking his head in admonishment. Savage banged on the door, pleading with him to open up. Finally, the banker opened the door, and without permitting Savage to enter, grumbled: "What do you want?"

"You know why I'm here. I've got a cheque that needs to get to New York."

Savage heard Ted Rogers' words echoing through his ears: "Don't come home without the money."

The banker disdainfully examined the Government of Ireland cheque, which had two signature lines—one signed by a government official whose name he claimed he didn't recognize, and the other, blank. He refused to process the cheque, even though only one signature was required. Expletives were exchanged. Then, the banker slammed the door in Savage's face and locked it. He flipped over the "Open" sign to "Closed" and walked away.

Aghast, Savage stood there slack-jawed, holding in his hand a £10-million cheque. Then, Albert Gnat arrived; tie loosened, panting and sweating even more profusely than Savage. "What happened?"

"Well, the cheque just bounced."

Stunned, he said: "What are we going to do?"

They went to the cocktail reception Savage organized to thank the Irish government. They didn't have time to return to their hotel to change their attire. By the time they arrived—late to their own closing—the Minister of Communications, the RTÉ head, various dignitaries and the deal lawyers had already consumed several cocktails. The Minister appeared sloshed. As host, Savage recalls beginning to address the gathering. "'Thank you all for coming but, by the way, Minister, your cheque bounced.'

"I was making a joke," says Savage, "but he didn't think it was very funny, and said, 'What are you talking about?' I said, 'Well actually, Chase wouldn't accept the cheque, but we'll sort it out.' But he went red and got quite angry. This was kind of embarrassing, and I hadn't realized this would be such an offensive thing."

When the reception ended, the Minister said to Savage in his lilting voice: "Me and the boys are going to have dinner with the wives. Would you and Albert like to join us?"

Off they went. They joined 14 people at a long rectangular table in a private dining room in one of Dublin's finest restaurants. The Minister was sitting beside his wife directly opposite Savage. Gnat was seated beside Savage, one person removed. "The Minister had been drinking steadily," says Savage. "I'm not drinking at all because we've got to get on a plane tomorrow for London to New York to Toronto and it's going to be a long, long day and I didn't want a hangover. So, I'm stone cold sober, and he's absolutely drunk. He looks at me partway through the meal and, honest to God, he looks at me and his eyes completely glazed over and he went face down right into his mashed potatoes. Nobody even stopped talking. His wife leans over and picks him by the scruff of his neck and takes his face out of the potatoes and plops it down on the table beside his plate, and doesn't even clean off the peas and mashed potatoes off his face. I am absolutely stunned. This is not like any closing I've ever been at. He's unconscious with mashed potatoes and peas on his face. I look over at Albert, and we sort of shrug our shoulders. Then, we have our little speeches. So, I made a little speech and then, the government's lawyer gets up, and if this is a New York closing, he's going to make another speech, but it's not a New York closing, it's a Dublin closing, so he sings two songs from *Oklahoma*."

"I am just stunned. He sits down and then the woman beside him stands up and starts to sing an Irish ballad and she sits down and the man beside her got up and starts to sing. I'm thinking, 'Holy shit. It's coming around the table.' I lean around the woman beside me and said to Albert, 'What are we going to do?'"

"I don't know, but it gets to you first," Gnat quipped.

Savage, unable to think of anything but the national anthem and a few nursery rhymes, passed up the opportunity to croak out a tune. So did Gnat. The only other person who didn't stand up and sing was the Minister, who was still passed out. When dinner ended, two other ministers dragged him out, one arm around each shoulder. His wife, with her purse in hand, trailed behind nonchalantly.

The next day, Savage left the cheque with their lawyers in Dublin, while he and Gnat boarded their flight to Heathrow en route to Toronto. The lawyers were given instructions to sort out the signature issue and deposit the cheque that morning. The two men prayed the money would be wired out of Ireland by the time they landed at Heathrow. If it wasn't, they intended to return to Dublin. While they were in the air, the Government of Ireland lambasted Chase. When Savage called his lawyers from Heathrow, he was relieved to hear that the proceeds had been wired to New York. "We were free and clear to go home," he says.

The story didn't end there. The Government of Ireland punished Chase by ordering the central bank to cut Chase out of its weekly bond auction for the next six months.

Phil Lind's connections in Washington yet again proved invaluable for Rogers just before the 1984 *Cable Communications Policy Act* became law. The *Cable Act*—described as either a Magna Carta for cable owners, or a *carte blanche* to print money—limited franchise fees to 5 percent of gross system revenues annually and deregulated rates for basic cable services, effective January 1987 for most existing franchises. Significantly, it also barred telephone companies from entering the cable TV business.

Through his contacts on the Hill, Lind learned the lawmakers intended to freeze basic rates for two years, which would be disastrous for Rogers, which was teetering on the financial high wire as it was. However, Lind was informed that the bill included a provision that opened a window of six-to-eight hours in which cable owners, if they were savvy enough to spot the loophole, could hike their rates before it closed again for two years. For a bill to become law, the Senate and House of Representatives must agree to identical versions of the bill. If they don't, the differences between the two versions must be reconciled in what's called a conference committee, an ad hoc committee comprised of both senators and representatives who typically worked on the legislation when it came before their own committees. If Lind could ascertain when the bill was to make it through the conference between the two houses, he could increase rates system-wide before the loophole closed.

Since Rogers and Chuck Dolan's Cablevision, then busily wiring the Bronx, were the industry's two most financially shaky companies, knowledge of exactly when the bill made it through conference was critical to their survival, says Lind. Both companies had their cable system managers on standby, the equivalent of DEFCON 1, maximum readiness. When word came down, both companies instantly jacked up basic cable rates by as much as five dollars per month in one day. According to Lind, they were the only two cable companies that were informed of the provision and took advantage of it. "They left it open for one day, and we drove Brink's armored trucks through it," says Lind. "The company was on the edge. It saved us. If we hadn't have gotten those rate increases, we would have been toast."

Rogers was teetering on top of a mountain of debt. In just four years, Rogers had amassed a long-term debt of $762 million—six times 1980 levels. In trading bank debt for public bond debt, he opted for security, not savings. Four years after Lind's ambitious U.S. expansion program, Rogers Cablesystems was generating nearly half of its revenue from the U.S. The time had come to retrench. To reduce debt, Rogers put on the block its cable TV systems in Syracuse, New York, and in Orange and Los Angeles Counties in California. "It has been hard to keep this company one that you can be proud of," Rogers admitted at the time. "I certainly look forward to the day when we don't have this embarrassing lack of profits, but I'm never going to run my company only for money. I won't do anything foolish—I think we've passed that—but I also won't hesitate to spend money on things that will propel RCI into the future. ... If you're going to grow, you've got to create excitement. And, you know, I've got a belief, and a faith, and an ego, that tells me, we can succeed no matter what we try."

The franchising days were over. Or, so Ted Rogers thought.

Then Phil Lind, accompanied by Vernon Achber, broke the news to him that he had another franchising project. "What's that?" Rogers asked.

"We've got to get back many of the promises we made and if we don't, we're toast."

"Christ," said Rogers, "you've got to do that."

It was a humiliating task, although not entirely unexpected. Bob Francis had been sounding the alarm bells for some time. Achber, Lind's point-person with the city cable officers, found himself in the unenviable position of negotiating relief packages with the cities. He coined the "eco-techo" term Rogers has since used regularly. Is it technically and economically feasible? Achber couldn't just ask the cities to tear up their franchise contracts. When Drew Lewis, Reagan's former Secretary of Transportation, the new Warner Amex CEO who replaced Gus Hauser, tried to play hardball with the city of Pittsburgh, the city kicked Warner out. "We didn't want to do it that way," says Achber.

"For almost two years, we 'eco-techoed' all our franchises," says Lind. "Rogers always talks about how we were in default seven times before we got that done."

"We really had to watch our covenants," adds Achber. "We worked with the financial people. The company needed huge amounts of money. Revenues weren't coming in fast enough. It was somewhat embarrassing but in the end, we did it.

"It was hell on wheels."

From 1984 to 1987, Achber criss-crossed America revamping the city franchise contracts. The U.S. cable giants were doing exactly the same thing. "It was like Chrysler—there's a point in time when you've just got to save them," says Minneapolis' former cable officer Jane Bremer. "The bailout that occurred on the part of major U.S. cities to benefit cable television companies were largely because they didn't have a choice. At that point, either the systems were built, or partially built. The entire industry was in a downturn, so it's not like you can turn around and say, Rogers, you're in violation of your contract and we want Storer back, or we want Warner back. They were all in deep do-do because they had all been on this feeding frenzy of franchises. They had all overbid and they were all in the process of scaling back. Everybody was in the same boat."

Since the cities had the right to buy back the cable systems at the end of 15-year franchise at book value, Lind and Achber fought to rework the contracts to ensure that if they ever sold the franchises, they'd receive fair market value for them. "It didn't take me long to figure out that this thing was being groomed for sale," says Achber. "Phil may have known, but he didn't tell me."

"I knew, but I didn't want to sell. I didn't want to. To this day, I never wanted to sell," says Lind.

Rogers wryly sums up Lind's franchising era: "He was paid a bonus to make all of these idiotic promises, and then paid a bonus to get rid of these idiotic promises. My word, being 'idiotic.' Listen, he did well. He beat a lot of American companies. Not too many Canadian companies go down and compete like that."

Indeed. Most Canadian companies—from hardware retailer Canadian Tire Corp. (twice), coffee retailer Second Cup, book retailer Coles, clothiers Danier Leather and Marks Work Warehouse, pharmacist Shoppers Drug Mart, investment banker Wood Gundy, the banks, CIBC, the Royal Bank of Canada to the Bank of Montreal—went down to the United States with high hopes and returned to Canada humbled and embarrassed.

"Having competed in the U.S., and having sold the U.S. properties, was the defining moment of our company," says Lind. "Our ability to come up against the Americans and beat them added—a sort of toughness—a dimension to this company that no other company had in this country. We've managed to persevere."

They worked hard and played hard. Underneath the intensity of their work, the non-stop travel and the omnipresent threat that the company might implode, there was a comedic subtext. They filled colleagues' hotel beds with shaving cream. It was all *Animal House* stuff. Pranks were played on newcomers. Philip R. Ladouceur, Rogers' new CFO and a particularly favored target, was hit hard. He'd arrive at hotels to find his reservations mysteriously canceled. "Terrible. I wouldn't have approved. He didn't deserve that," says Rogers, discovering their antics afterwards.

Lind handed out T-shirts to the franchising team that said: "This body is a temple: 24 hours a day."

"We used to say: 'It may be Ted's money, but it's my body,'" laughs Lind.

They were "Ted's Ninja turtles"—referring to the four wise-cracking pizza-obsessed adolescent superhero reptiles fighting the forces of evil. Named after Renaissance painters, the *Teenage Mutant Ninja Turtles* were popularized in the comic book-turned-animated children's TV series and hit live-action movies. Lind and Watson, known as the Bobbsey Twins or Golddust Twins, earned various nicknames. One city councillor, as irreverent as they were, jokingly referred to them as "Twiddle Dum & Twiddle Dee." Best friends, they hung out together and dressed alike. They looked more American than Americans in their Brooks

Brothers attire with navy blazers, blue or white buttoned-down shirts and pink, yellow or khaki-colored pants. They were walking advertisements for Brooks Brothers. Clasen typically packed several trousers as a precaution so they didn't look as if they were wearing uniforms.

In this era before cellular phones, email and Blackberries, Rogers had his lieutenants provide him with their schedules a year in advance. For the current month, they prepared "week at a glance" itineraries that they updated every two weeks to reflect their ever-changing schedules to keep Rogers informed as to where they could be reached, or so that he knew, for example, if they were giving a speech at the Western Cable Show in Anaheim, California. In their year ahead calendars, they clandestinely chose one day of the year where they'd collectively meet up to play golf or tennis—a "get-away trip" to relax, given their hectic schedules. They deliberately wrote down some bogus trip in order to prevent Rogers from finding them. "It was a real camaraderie in those early years," says Clasen. "The camaraderie of that core group—Vernon, Graham, Phil, Colin and myself I never captured again. There was a lot of male bonding and a lot of successes on the business front."

For his part, Rogers, who loves a good practical joke, studiously ignored theirs if he happened to discover them. He claims he didn't know the corporate jet was secretly christened "Quiz Air." For one flight, Lind and Watson were late and raced up the ramp in breakneck speed, shoulder to shoulder, for the seat farthest away from Rogers, knowing that if they ended up sitting beside him, they'd be interrogated for the entire flight. Running up the stairs, they hit the open door together and bounced off it. "Quiz Air," grins former cable boss John H. Tory. "You don't get frequent flyer points; you get aspirin."

"I remember I went on a flight to Vancouver with him [once] and he asked me questions about business from the minute we took off, and as we came into view of the mountains, I remember the sun was setting and he looked outside and said, 'Isn't that pretty' and then he started talking about something else. It was unreal. It was just a business discussion but it went on for five hours. I was hoping I would fall into a coma, or something. Ted, he's just like a machine."

The boss was not part of the franchising clique.

"Ted worked late every night," says Kevin Shea, the former Sirius Satellite Radio CEO, who was Roger' marketing guru, overseeing the lengthy licensing process for specialty channel YTV before becoming its president. "It'd be seven or eight o'clock, and Ted's office was about four down from mine and I'd saunter down and say, 'Ted, why don't we go downstairs and have a beer?' And, he'd look up from his desk and say, 'By God, that sounds like a good idea.' And, we'd just go downstairs in the TD Centre and have a beer or two. No one would do that with him because they were afraid of him. And, he wanted to be, every now and then, just one of the boys."

Rogers' frailty in childhood would shadow him all his life. He was vigorously arguing at a board meeting of fine china maker Josiah Wedgwood & Sons (Canada) Ltd. when he was overcome by a wave of nausea. He got up, excused himself and went to the washroom.

"I'm sitting on the toilet, and I suddenly remembered that my friend Don Hunter [of Maclean Hunter] had this happen to him, and he had passed out on the toilet and they took an hour or so to find him and get him to a hospital, so I thought, 'Oh, oh, I'd better get up and not be in here,' and the meeting was sort of over by the time I got back, and Loretta was arriving with the car because the wives would be there for dinner. I said to Loretta, 'I just feel terrible,' so she said, 'Well, the car is still there, you take the car and go home, and I'll go to dinner.' So, I went home and got into bed and went to sleep.

"Now, that's a mistake. 'Course, I knew nothing, because twenty-five percent of the people who have this on average don't ever get up. You normally go between three in the morning and nine—that's the high-incidence period—but I didn't know that at the time."

When Rogers awoke the next morning, he still felt unwell, but had a full day ahead of him. He was expected to hand out a prize that afternoon at Bishop Strachan School, a prestigious all-girls private school in Toronto which his daughters attended. His stepfather, John Graham, was there along with their family friend, Ontario's lieutenant governor John Black Aird. Aird commented on Roger's sickly pallor. His stepfather mentioned it to Rogers the next day: "John said you looked absolutely terrible yesterday."

"I was a bit annoyed at this," recalls Rogers, "and I said, 'Well, he didn't look damn good either!' "

Rogers didn't know it at the time, but at age 52, he had suffered a silent heart attack, suffering no pain apart from the nausea, but his heart muscle had been irreparably damaged. He underwent a battery of tests, showing an irregular heartbeat during the stress test. He jotted in his personal organizer, as is his wont, to take his medication, limit his alcohol consumption to two drinks a day, take aspirin, and exercise five days a week, and to not drink coffee or tea, a regime he's since maintained, discounting his continued enjoyment of fine wine and champagne.

Later, while at a Sigma Chi fraternity function in San Diego, Graham took Rogers to the Scripps Clinic for a checkup. "I'm getting dressed afterwards, and we're leaving, and they come running down the hall and the doctor yells my name. 'Don't leave! Don't leave! You've had a heart attack.' That's when I first knew I had a heart attack a couple of weeks before.'"

Upon returning to Toronto, he stopped in at a bookstore en route back home. "I bought three books on heart attacks and stayed up most of the night reading them, and underlining, so I knew a fair bit by the next morning."

It was a beautiful sun-filled Sunday morning at Lyford Cay on February 16, 1986. Ted Rogers was having breakfast with his lieutenants. The only person missing was Bob Francis.

Graham Savage recalls, "We had come down for breakfast. Bob hadn't come down. Ted disappeared for just a moment but wouldn't go up. So, I got up and went to take a look. I opened the door. And Bob was lying on his back on the bed. He looked quite peaceful but I could see that the blood had pooled in his arm, which was hanging down the side of the bed, and I knew in an instant he was dead. I checked his pulse, and no pulse. No breathing. I went out and told the group. There was just shocked silence. I called the police and an ambulance. It hit Ted very hard."

Bob Francis, who had quit smoking and was taking HCG injections to lose weight, was dead at age 50. He had suffered a massive heart attack.

Loretta was in Toronto. "Ted called at about eight-thirty in the morning and said, 'I think Bob's dead.' Ted was upset, obviously. He was quite affected. He really liked him. I said, 'Do you think Bob's dead?' He said, 'Well, the doctor's coming, but yeah.' I said, who the hell is going to tell his wife? I didn't particularly want it to be me, so I called John Graham. He always went to church to either the early or the eleven o'clock service. He remembered Bob had a brother who was a lawyer and called him, who went to see Bob's wife and two kids.

"Ted told me that Nassau wanted a relative to identify the body. It was a Sunday and there aren't many planes and Air Canada had already gone. I knew there was a Thomson charter flight in the afternoon. I thought, How do we get tickets? The charter's probably booked up. So, I tried to call John Tory Sr., but he wasn't home. He was in Collingwood skiing. Finally, I got someone to get John off the ski hills and I explained to him why I needed two tickets. So, we took him down there.

"Ted luckily had been very bright. Ted was pretty sure the CID [Criminal Investigation Department] sent a junior to come and do the [preliminary investigation]. So, when all the staff had been asked questions, and at the end, the fellow said, 'Would you sign? and Ted said, 'I want a copy.' 'Why do you want a copy?' And, he said, I just do.' So, he made a copy. The next morning, we were there, the CID comes back and wants to go over all the same questions because it was done by juniors and Ted just said, 'They've all been answered; here's a copy.' Then, we had to go identify the body and there's a real backlog on Monday mornings because they don't do too much on Saturdays and Sunday."

The funeral was held that Friday at St. Aidan's Anglican Church in Toronto's Beaches neighborhood. The turnout of Bay St. bankers to pay their respects shut down Kingston Road.

Rogers took it upon himself to make sure the family was financially secure and offered to pay for the funeral, but his widow Marilyn Francis, who never remarried, graciously declined his generosity. Andrew Francis, whose father took him and his sister to the office when they were growing up, called Rogers, "Uncle Ted." He joined RCI in the 1990s as a technical writer.

Rogers, only three years older than Francis, was devastated. "We were like brothers."

"Francis was a great soldier for Ted," says former RCI director David Wilson. "He went the extra mile."

Rogers pulled double-duty, while seeking Francis' replacement. His heart wasn't in it. Francis understood him. With just a three-year age-gap between them, they shared a special bond. Furthermore, he wasn't ready to give the nod to Graham Savage, who at 37 was 16 years his junior. Just like a mourning period, it took him 11 months to hire a new financial chief, who didn't last long. In the aftermath of Francis' death, Rogers had added more bank debt on top of his junk pile to buy back foreign-held stock to keep his cable licences Canadian.

In Canada, some financial relief appeared on the horizon when the CRTC, led by André Bureau, deregulated basic cable rates, bowing to the industry's rhetoric over the competitive threat from satellite dishes and VCRs. Rogers also rolled his five privately held radio stations into the newly re-christened public company, Rogers Communications Inc., of which he owned 71 percent. The name change heralded bigger things to come. He was no longer just the cable guy. He was becoming deeply immersed in cellular telephony. He also hoped to build a national multicultural TV network after rescuing ethnic TV broadcaster CFMT-TV, founded by the late Italian-Canadian Daniel Iannuzzi, from bankruptcy. But, the CRTC, which reluctantly permitted Rogers to save CFMT, thwarted his shared ambition with Iannuzzi to create a national TV network.

Buying CFMT was a fluke. Lind just happened to call Iannuzzi, who invited him for lunch. That's when he learned that the receivers intended to seize possession of the TV station. Lind returned to the office, told Rogers and, by Sunday night, Rogers and Lind had carved out a deal with Iannuzzi. Rogers then parachuted in Jim Sward, his broadcasting head, to fix the ailing TV station.

With shop-at-home TV sweeping America, Rogers leapt onto that bandwagon. In Minneapolis, Lind had been working with Peter Barton, who TCI's John Malone had sent to Minnesota to set up Cable Value Network Inc., a rival to Home Shopping Network, then Wall Street's hottest IPO. Now, they worked to bring CVN to Canada, where the Canadian Home Shopping Network (CHSN), an HSN offshoot, was getting off the ground. Anticipating high startup costs, Rogers—declaring the home shopping idea to be just another one of Phil's follies—sold the infant network, which never made it to air, to CHSN in exchange for a minority stake and then worked his magic to seize control. He hung on to the money-losing network, although nearly a decade passed before it turned a profit, coincidentally almost the exact amount of time it took the CRTC to permit the network to show moving pictures.

It was a big deal for Canada to permit its citizenry to shop at home on their TV sets. The regulator didn't even want to licence a home shopping network. Frightened by the phenomenal success of U.S. home shopping networks, the CRTC fretted that an equally successful network in Canada threatened the advertising base of the conventional broadcasters, the chosen guardians of Canadian culture. The regulator only allowed still photographs, or graphics, with voice-overs. No sexy TV hosts hawking jewelry or furs on Canadian TV. The CRTC did its damnedest to kill home shopping, while Rogers just rode it out.

In the U.S., Rogers had become a full-fledged member of the cable club when he joined the consortium John Malone organized to bail out Ted Turner who had impulsively overloaded TBS with junk bonds to buy Kirk Kerkorian's ailing Hollywood studio MGM. Milken, representing both the buyer and the seller, concocted a complex scheme under which Kerkorian would loan Turner US$2 billion to buy MGM and then Turner would repay the sum by issuing junk bonds. If Turner failed to make the payments, he had to surrender stock in his company. To avoid losing everything, Turner—in a now famous anecdote—turned to John Malone, calling him at home late one night to tell him that Time Inc. had offered to buy 51 percent of CNN. "Ted, you can't do that. That's the crown jewels," Malone told him. "Well," Turner replied, "either it's that or it will be the KNN [Kerkorian News Network]." Malone pulled together a consortium of cable companies. In exchange for a cash infusion of more than half a billion dollars, Turner ceded more than one-third ownership of TBS to 31 cable companies.

Rogers just happened to be with Phil Lind in Hawaii for HBO's Superbowl party, where the two men were relaxing, talking shop with TCI's Stewart Blair at 2 a.m. when Blair explained Turner's predicament. Turner was another of Lind's occasional fly fishing companions. Though he himself was strapped for cash, Rogers instantly told Blair to count him in. "Everyone was a little tipsy," recalls Lind. "Stewart was explaining [the bailout] and Ted said, 'Sure, I'll do it.' Everyone else was doing it too at that time, and Ted was there. We did not have the money. But, we did it. We invested to help keep Turner afloat."

The cable industry in the U.S. underwent tectonic shifts in the eighties. The companies engaged in the franchising wars either merged, swapped systems or exited the business altogether. Malone's TCI kept getting bigger and bigger. Once the largest U.S. cable operator, Rogers was now the 25th largest. Through Cantel, he knew he could compete with BCE, which had grown complacent. While Canada chose not to shatter the nation's telephone monopolies like the U.S. did to AT&T, the winds of change were blowing north and Rogers wanted to position RCI to take advantage of it. He began to plot his next big move. He already had his sights trained on a stake in CNCP, the railroad companies' telecom joint venture. Through RTL, Rogers accumulated a 21-percent stake in Moffat Communications Ltd., a family-owned Winnipeg-based cable TV company and radio broadcaster. With an already highly leveraged balance sheet, Rogers had to prioritize. His choices boiled down to selling U.S. holdings and focusing on Canada, with a regulatory and political climate where he was the most comfortable, or risk being marginalized in both countries. If nothing else, he hates being a bench player. He's not one to watch the game from the sidelines. Being the 25th biggest in the U.S. just wasn't good enough. To be a bona fide player, he needed to get bigger, or go home.

On a Sunday morning in April 1988, Rogers summoned Colin Watson and Phil Lind to Frybrook to inform them that he had instructed Graham Savage to sell the U.S. cable properties. Rogers made a pivotal decision that set the company on a new course. His lieutenants weren't surprised; they had been expecting as much for months and had tried to persuade him differently for months. "I hated leaving the U.S. Just hated it," says Lind. "Sometimes it can take quite a while to recognize the genius of Rogers' ways. I would agree now that the sale of the U.S. was probably the right thing to do. I don't know if it was right at the time but we certainly couldn't have done everything.

"Ted has all of these other things going on at the same time," he says. "As everyone has found out over the years, mostly Ted listens, but then at some point, he decides, and he's going to do it no matter who the hell is in favor or against."

Seven suitors later, Rogers agreed to sell the U.S. cable properties to Houston Industries Inc., the parent of Houston Light & Power, the eighth-largest U.S. power utility, in August 1988 for US$1.26 billion, a near-record price of US$2,400 per subscriber—three times the going-rate just five years earlier.

To transfer ownership of the franchises, Rogers needed approval not just from the FCC, but also from each individual city, a time-consuming process. There were 69 franchises to transfer in five major metropolitan areas, including San Antonio and Laredo, Texas, Minneapolis, Portland, Oregon and Orange County, California. Their drop-dead deadline was February 28, 1989 when either side could call off the deal.

The city of San Antonio nearly derailed their blockbuster deal.

According to the original contract, San Antonio had right to buy the cable TV system at a 5-percent discount to market value after the system's tenth anniversary, which was in late 1988. Lou Fox, the city manager, had astutely inserted the highly unusual buyout clause into the franchise when negotiating with UA/Columbia a decade earlier. Since San Antonio already owned the electric gas utility, Fox thought that the city might one day want to get into the cable TV business. Plus, Fox knew a thing or two about negotiating cable franchises since he wrote the cable contract in Overland Park, Kansas where he had been the assistant city manager.

In 1988, before Rogers even put the For-Sale sign up on the U.S. properties, Fox began maneuvering to buy the cable TV network. The city council considered buying the system and operating it through its electric utility company, then flipping it at a substantial profit to another cable company, or becoming an equity partner with Rogers. Fox, who favored the latter, proposed that Rogers make a flat payment to the city for the right to own and operate the system through the full 15 years of the contract, prompting howls of greenmail from Rogers. Normally, buyout clauses are included in franchise agreements to protect a municipality against a cable company that fails to provide services as stipulated in its contract. The other cities weren't even aware of their buyout clauses until the dustup with San Antonio.

Ranked No. 4 in the U.S., the San Antonio franchise had 225,000 subscribers, representing 42 percent of Rogers' total U.S. subscriber base. It was the centerpiece of its U.S. business. The city was so proud of its cable TV system that San Antonio Mayor Henry Cisneros, the country's first Hispanic American mayor, made Ted Rogers an honorary mayor. (Cisneros later became U.S. president Bill Clinton's housing secretary. Cisneros' extra-marital affairs cost him both jobs.)

Rogers maintained that the buyout clause was unenforceable. Rogers sent in lawyers to deal with the problem to no avail. Then, Rogers himself went down.

"His first response was, ah, they're bullshitting. I'll just go down there and tell them a few things, and we all went down and we sat there for two hours as Rogers read them the Riot Act. Everyone from the city said, he can talk all he wants, but he can't get the system," says Lind. David Edwards, Rogers' San Antonio cable systems manager, then publicly admitted the city had Rogers in a tough spot. "He acknowledges, in the crass Marine Corps vernacular, that we've got them by the balls," Fox, a six-foot-two former Marine, summed it up in the press.

Cipriano Guerra, a former assistant city manager, who was working as a consultant for Rogers, approached Cisneros, whom he knew quite well, offering on Rogers' behalf to pay the city $250,000 if it just dropped the matter. Upon learning of the low-ball offer, Fox suggested to Cisneros to let him handle it. He held firm. Investment banking estimates pegged the cable TV system's worth at US$400 million. That meant the city could realize a profit of about $25 million. The local press was all over the story. Guerra and Fox were waging a war of words on radio stations. The impasse deepened when RCI jacked up monthly basic cable rates by two dollars to US$14.45, which the city regarded as retaliatory move.

Then, Houston Industries emerged with a firm takeover offer in August 1988. Within months, the entire takeover process ground to a screeching halt. The other cities stopped their due diligence, waiting to see what San Antonio would do. Houston Industries, which didn't appreciate the complexity of the city franchise regulatory approval process, became nervous. The power company was a passive 50-50 partner with Time Inc.'s ATC in Paragon Cable but had gone it alone in this transaction. The deal came close to blowing up. "It's all on my shoulders at this point. Everything centers on my office because Graham can make the deal but if it can't get turned over ..." sighs Lind.

"Phil's about to have a fit because things were not moving forward," recalls Missy Goerner, sitting in Lind's office located down the hall from Rogers'. Though based in San Antonio, Goerner remains a consultant for Rogers. In the 1990s, working with Lind, she negotiated the cable industry's first National Football League deal, breaking the satellite-exclusive barrier to the NFL Sunday Ticket package. That made Rogers Cable the world's only cable company capable of offering a year-round sports package of NFL Sunday Ticket, NHL Center Ice and MLB Extra Innings. (Caught napping, BCE's ExpressVu cried foul and sued.)

Goerner arranged for Lind to meet Lou Fox privately. They met at a hotel for breakfast, where Fox, 44, an athletic marathoner, was taken aback at the sheer quantity of food Lind, a year older and just as trim, consumed. Lind was widely known for never missing a meal and sometimes eating two in one sitting. By the time they'd finished, Fox felt that they might be able to hammer out a solution. Now, well into November with the regulatory process in limbo, Goerner anxiously called Fox to set up another meeting only to learn he was heading to Miami for a city managers' conference. She told him that Lind would fly to him, regardless of his location. That day, Lind was on a flight out of Toronto. The two men met in Fox's hotel room. They quickly got down to brass tacks. Lind scrawled in his trademark purple felt pen the terms of the franchise renewal agreement on one sheet of foolscap. He left a blank cheque for the amount of money it would take to release Rogers from the buyout clause. Lind then asked Fox what amount he wanted. Fox replied US$25 million. Fox initialled the paper and then called up a bellboy to go make a photocopy of it. "I gave the guy a hundred-dollar tip. I said to Phil, 'This was the most expensive copy that you will ever make in your life,'" recalls Fox.

"The whole damn deal turned on that one piece of paper," reflects Lind. "The whole damn deal."

Houston Industries had given RCI a finite sum to pay the cities to secure the transfer approvals, which Lind had just blown on San Antonio. Before Fox had a chance to inform San Antonio city council, thereby making it public knowledge, Lind called Houston Industries. He volunteered to handle the San Antonio transfer if the power utility picked up the US$10-million tab that he had negotiated for four Californian cities—Huntington Beach, Fountain Valley, Westminster and Stanton—which represented some 55,300 subscribers. (Huntington Beach was the largest of the four franchises with 34,300 subscribers.) Even though their buyout clauses, substantively different from San Antonio's, didn't kick in until 1999, Lind knew that when push came to shove he'd have no choice but to pay them to win the transfer approvals. Houston Industries agreed, believing Lind would never succeed in San Antonio. If he failed, the company wouldn't have to fork out any money if the whole deal failed. Similarly, the Californian cities almost instantly accepted the US$10-million offer, believing it might end up with nothing if San Antonio didn't transfer. Just days later, the news broke that San Antonio had settled its dispute with Rogers. With his horse-trading tactic, Lind managed to save Rogers a bundle of money.

Back in San Antonio, the city council was beyond thrilled. "When I told the council, I thought everybody was going to die. I earned my salary obviously for a thousand years," says Fox. The San Antonio city council used the cash windfall to set up the Texas Research Park, a world-class center of bioscience research and medical education, and create an affordable housing commission.

On March 15, 1989, RCI completed the sale of its U.S. cable systems to Houston Industries for US$1.37 billion in cash, much more than originally expected. Rogers had cleverly structured the deal so that the final price depended on the total number of subscribers. Once he had a better idea when they might actually complete the transaction, Rogers ordered his U.S. cable managers to sign up as many subscribers as fast as humanly possible. They ran commercials advertising free cable TV, hoping to spread the word. Rogers had his employees embark on a door-to-door sales offensive much like an Avon Calling campaign. In San Antonio, they promised free cable TV service for three months plus free groceries to people in predominantly low-income Hispanic neighborhoods just to jack up their numbers. The campaign was so successful that Rogers had signed 42,000 new subscribers. Furious, the power company had to fork out an extra US$110 million. Rogers would need every last dime.

Rogers, his battle-hardened team, accountants and lawyers all went to celebrate with champagne at Winston's, the upscale Toronto eatery for Canada's corporate titans, political wags, and Bay Street power brokers. Later that day, Rogers flew to Lyford Cay, where the next day he socialized with Prince Philip.

Selling the U.S. business netted Rogers a profit of US$800 million. He immediately announced an ambitious $1.1-billion capital-spending program to take the company into the 21st century before a standing-room only crowd at Roy Thomson Hall, home of the Toronto Symphony Orchestra.

With the passage of time and a damaged heart slowing him down, Rogers is said to have mellowed. He's not the tyrant that he used to be when he was younger, although he still attempts to intimidate with piercing glares, employs sharp tones and refers to his father's legacy either to implore or impale his executives if he feels they're not moving fast enough, or not following his commands. In years past, each week, when he held court with his divisional heads, Rogers inevitably singled out one of them, and callously, ferociously railed at him for no apparent reason. There was considerable nervousness and tension among the divisional managers until the "goat of the week" was chosen. Then the others breathed a bit easier. For the person who had the misfortune of being that week's victim, life became miserable. There was nothing that manager could do that was right until Rogers focused his attention elsewhere. While some of the faces changed as the years unfolded, "the goat" phenomenon endured.

At the poolside breakfast meetings at 3 Frybrook, his lieutenants—those who figured it out anyway—strategically sat wherever the carved heron on the table wasn't pointing—since after careful observation over countless meetings, a pattern seemed to emerge: Rogers would unfailingly upbraid whoever happened to be seated coincidentally where the heron's beak pointed. The longest-serving executives learned to cope with his explosive tirades. They absorbed it, letting it roll off their backs and trying to shelter their subordinates as best they could. The only problem was when the divisional head, middle manager and Rogers were all together in the same room. Rogers, a detailed-oriented taskmaster, took on the subordinate, prompting the lieutenant to intercede to defend his man. Inevitably, subordinates witnessed Rogers tongue-lash their direct report.

Rogers' style of management is one of creative dissonance. Only the strong survive in Ted Rogers' world. "An awful lot of people went through the revolving door over twenty years, and a lot of people who stayed had the character, or force of will, or personality to be able to stand up to him," reflects one long-time lieutenant. "Sometimes, it got to daggers at ten paces. People would be shouting at each other and often, these things are a question of interpretation, and there are alternate ways to do things and Ted's way was not the only way, so these things were often pretty vicious and pretty tough at times." Says Marilyn Francis, Bob Francis' widow: "Bob would just sit back and listen to it. He felt he didn't have to yell back in kind. Ted would have these blowups, and Bob always told us, 'Don't react. Act. Don't react to a situation, but listen. Listen to it."

Colin Watson bore the brunt of it because he was the operational head for cable TV, where Rogers directed much of his energies. Rogers' lieutenants traveled heavily in the franchising days, and so were physically separated from him in what became a much-needed cooling-off period for everyone to calm down. Things would return to normal and then it would start all over again. "You just learn to live with him," says Watson. "You started with the supposition that Ted never held a grudge. He never meant any harm by any of his behavior. We used to laugh that if Rogers wasn't yelling at you, you didn't matter any more. I am being a bit facetious. It is kind of his way of caring. He is just very intense, and that is the way he manages. You don't let it get to you. If you did, you'd go crazy. I suppose a lot of people did let it get to them, now that I think about it."

"But, that was Ted. The trouble is that he'd be right most of the time," says Graham Savage. "I was lucky because I got left alone probably more than anybody for which I was eternally grateful. I like to believe he had confidence in me, but that's utter bullshit, I think it's because I wasn't in operations, and it certainly wasn't because he didn't know about investments or mergers and acquisitions stuff. He knew that stuff cold."

The operational heads—radio, cable and wireless—were based in different offices throughout Toronto. Lind, Savage and the RCI team were headquartered with Rogers—although Lind had escaped to the United States for much of the eighties—at the Commercial Union Tower, one of the six black steel TD Bank Centre buildings. They were known as the Black Tower Group; they were closest to the throne. Initiatives emerged from the Black Tower that often blindsided the operational heads. They built their personal schedules around Rogers. They always carried his detailed itinerary with them. It was a template for their lives.

Rogers was constantly stirring people up with provocative ideas, theories and initiatives. For every brilliant idea Rogers had, there were four or five more that were duds. The people around him consequently spent a lot of time guiding him along the path of useful and constructive initiatives, while steering him away from the less productive and potentially destructive ones. Rogers always surrounded himself with people who were able to manage, deflect, or tear him away from his nine dumb ideas of the day, and it was his own raw tenacity that allowed him to develop the one brilliant idea for which he developed a legendary reputation as an unstoppable and formidable Canadian business leader. Unwaveringly loyal (to this day), they appeared initially skeptical to his initiatives only because they cared enough about him and the company not to see either blown asunder. They were like the band of brothers in Shakespeare's *Henry V* who were battle-tested and bloodied but unbowed.

To outsiders, there appeared to be smugness within the band that they ran the company and not Ted Rogers. RCI chairman John Graham, a lawyer, who did not have an office on site, and RCI director John A. Tory—the two men who carried the most influence with Rogers—acted as steam valves for lieutenants. Without betraying confidences, they helped pull Rogers off the pedestal and get his feet back down on the ground. While a valued advisor, Gar Emerson, in being protective of Rogers, upset the dynamics of this tight-knit group when he joined the RCI board in 1989 as vice chairman and five years later, replaced John Graham as chairman. Emerson was not part of the band. Nor was he John Graham. He could not dispense fatherly advice to Rogers the way John Graham could. He didn't appreciate their battle scars at the time, nor realize he was about to develop some of his own. "People like Graham Savage paid the price. His first reaction to Ted's initiatives was suspicion and he was the one that Gar locked horns with first," says a former insider.

Emerson had left his esteemed legal practice to become an investment banker. His job was to put Rothschild Canada on the map. Compared to other firms, Rothschild was a niche player on Bay Street, providing corporate finance advisory services. Though the firm lacked the capability to underwrite and distribute securities, Rothschild took a "ton of fees" out of RCI, most of it based on Emerson's advice. That became a bone of contention inside the band of brothers. Rogers began to listen to Emerson's advice over Savage's, even though his CFO had the less conflicted position. Savage didn't like it.

Emerson, risk-averse, framed his advice to Rogers in conservative wrappings to the point of just blocking ideas that had any whiff of risk associated with them. Savage, on the other hand, was equally conservative but he could manage the risk by distributing it, while safeguarding the empire from becoming a house of cards. Though the company carried enormous debt in the form of bank loans and debt financings, Savage spread the risk without ever allowing cross-guarantees, cross-defaults or cross-indemnifications across the empire's assets. In other words, while the legally trained Emerson shunned debt, Savage was prepared to assume debt to grease the company's growth, in keeping with his boss' aggressive style, as long as it was properly managed.

For the next decade, Rothschild Canada became involved in virtually every acquisition and divestiture involving RCI. "Ted Rogers made Rothschild," says one former lieutenant.

The U.S. investment bankers had them pegged this way: Lind was Mr. Outside. Savage was Mr. Money. (He held the place together.) Rogers—known as just Ted in Canada—was Mister Rogers to the Yanks, the eternally jolly feel good guy from the beloved PBS kids show *Mister Rogers' Neighborhood*. They regarded him warmly since they reaped incredible fees from his account.

Rogers commanded respect and unusual loyalty from his lieutenants. They were privy to a side of the man that was also charming, fun and compassionate. While working for Rogers undoubtedly took its toll, they loved the business. There was no other company quite as exhilarating as Rogers. "You can always tell a Rogers man," says Pierre Morrissette, founder of the Weather Channel, who served on the Rogers Wireless board. "Pride. Confidence. Integrity."

ACT THREE

WIRELESS

CHAPTER 12

Cutting the Cord: The Birth of Cantel

"He heard 'licenses' and 'telephones' and said yes. We asked him to put up $200,000, and he said yes on the spot."

—Marc Belzberg

ON A COLD, BLUSTERY DECEMBER AFTERNOON IN 1900, Reg Fessenden sat before a microphone in a makeshift shack belonging to the U.S. Weather Bureau on Cobb Island in Maryland's Potomac River. Having been rejected for the position of chairman of McGill University's electrical engineering department, Fessenden was asked by the U.S. government agency to build a speedier system for transmitting weather forecasts from remote stations along the Atlantic seaboard.

In his spare time, an hour or two each day, he worked on his boyhood dream of besting Alexander Graham Bell's invention of the telephone by transmitting words over the air without resort to wires, despite being warned that he'd be fired if he so much as dared to experiment with speech transmission. "We want nothing to do with that sort of quackery," U.S. Weather Bureau chief Willis Moore told him. "My superiors would laugh me out of the bureau, yes, right out of the country if they found me wasting taxpayers' money on such tomfoolery." Fessenden ignored him.

Speaking clearly and loudly into a microphone, Fessenden said, "Hello. Test: One—Two—Three—Four. Is it snowing where you are, Mr. Thiessen? If it is, telegraph back and let me know." He had barely finished speaking when he heard a telegraphic reply crackling in his headphones: It was indeed snowing. The two men were, after all, only 1,600 meters apart. In spite of the short distance, the "old man," as his engineers called the bearded, bespectacled professor when he wasn't looking, had just proven that the human voice could be transmitted across radio waves, almost a year before Guglielmo Marconi's celebrated trans-Atlantic transmission of the letter "S" in Morse code. At age 34, "old man" Fessenden had achieved the impossible, bringing together two technologies—wireless and telephony—that would be the earliest seeds of the modern cellphone industry.

A century later, more than 2 billion people—almost a third of the world's estimated population—now use cellphones. More people in the world are using wireless phones than fixed landlines. "This is the most popular product known to man," Chase Hambrecht & Quist analyst Ed Snyder told *Time* magazine in 2000. "More cellphones will be sold this year than all the computers, TVs, personal digital assistants and pagers combined."

No longer is the cellphone the status symbol it was in the eighties when only the very rich could afford to pay US$3,995 for the "Brick," the world's first truly mobile phone from Motorola that weighed 758 g (28 ounces)—about the same as a bag of sugar—and measured 300 x 44 x 89 mm (13 x 1.75 x 3.5 inches), gigantic by today's standards. It had just one hour of talk time and eight hours of standby time. Motorola spent a phenomenal US$100 million to develop the Brick—a phone that prompted people who remembered the hit sixties TV show *Get Smart* to pull off and cup to their ears their shoes, mimicking the inept Secret Agent Maxwell Smart who contacted the luscious and smart Agent 99 on his Shoe Phone. Officially called the DynaTAC, the Brick was a huge improvement over the aptly named "luggable" phone that came with its own immensely heavy, lead-acid battery and cellular transceiver housed in a briefcase-sized bag.

Cellphones are now so small they can fit inside the palm of a child's hand, or be worn attached to your sunglasses. They weigh next to nothing, and offer an ever-increasing multitude of bells and whistles from voice-activated dialing (now passé), text and picture messaging and Internet browsing to celebrity voice mail, musical ring tones, video recording, 3D video games, and real-time TV. The cellphone has woven its way into the fabric of our lives so completely that it's hard to imagine what our lives were like before it. Students use their cellphones to play music, text friends, film fights or tantrum-throwing teachers—and then post the videos on YouTube—and browse the Internet to cheat on tests. It's become such a problem that some schools are banning cellphones altogether. Some of the most intimate images of the July 2005 terrorist bombings in London's transit system came from citizen shutterbugs, using cellphones equipped with cameras and video recorders. In 2006, two years after introducing a so-called wallet phone that's embedded with a radio frequency ID (RFID) chip, Japan's mobile phone giant NTT DoCoMo has more than 10 million mobile wallet phone customers who use them to download digital money—virtual cash—to pay for train tickets, shop for groceries, rent movies or buy a drink from a vending machine.

There's a cellphone for everybody. It's become an appendage. While cellphones are ubiquitous, they still carry a certain cachet—only now it's all about the type you own: the camera phone, the videophone, the ultra-sleek Moto RAZR and its limited edition hot-pink sister, Apple's iPhone, and for the fashion conscious, the PRADA phone. There are waterproof cellphones with global positioning systems for wandering pets. There are Fireflys for children, BlackBerrys for executives and Pearls for the masses. A Canadian invention, the BlackBerry, a palm-sized email pager, was quickly coined the "CrackBerry" by addicted users. "It is the heroin of mobile computing," Salesforce.com CEO Marc Benioff told *USA Today*. "I am serious. I had to stop. I'm now in BA: BlackBerry Anonymous."

No one—except perhaps its inventors— ever imagined these miniature Star Trek-like devices—or the impact they'd have on the way we live, work and play—when the first clunkers debuted in 1983, a full decade after Toronto-born inventor Martin Cooper made the first private call from a portable, handheld cellular phone the size of a Kleenex box. While walking in midtown Manhattan, Cooper, then a Motorola executive, called Joel Engel at rival AT&T's Bell Labs on a chunky plastic DynaTAC prototype—that weighed a hefty 1.3 kilograms (2.5 pounds)—just to prove it could be done. "Even those jaded New Yorkers stopped and stared," Cooper told the Toronto *Globe and Mail*.

How did we get from there to here? Since the licensing of cellular technology in 1982 in the United States and a year later in Canada, we've gone from analogue to digital and beyond in less time than it took for the concept of cellular radiotelephony to become a reality.

The need for safety—on the seas, in the air, on the battlefield and on the road—fueled the growth of wireless communications industry. It wasn't until the sinking of the *Titanic* in 1912 that the role of wireless as a safety tool was thrust into the spotlight when the *Carpathia* answered the Marconi operator's insistent pleas for help, steaming 85 kilometers in the frigid North Atlantic to rescue hundreds of frightened, freezing passengers who would otherwise have died. Up until that tragic event, the wireless telegraph, patented by Marconi in 1896, was considered mostly as a profit source: passengers aboard ocean liners were encouraged to send and receive personal news and greetings via so-called "Marconigrams," just as they would via telegrams.

In the twenties, the police were among the first who sought to use in their patrol cars the technology that had improved the safety of ocean-going vessels.

The Detroit police department used the first car-mobile radios in 1921—but only one-way transmission was possible, from dispatcher to car, so policemen had to pull over and find a telephone if they wanted to reach headquarters. Two-way communication appeared in 1933 when the Bayonne, New Jersey police department employed the first two-way push-to-talk system.

Many engineers and ham radio operators around the world were attempting to build portable, two-way voice radios in the thirties. Toronto-born Al Gross, raised in Cleveland, Ohio, was just a teenage radio ham when he built a two-way radio in 1938 that caught the attention of the U.S. Office of the Strategic Services (now the Central Intelligence Agency), which recruited him to develop a ground-to-air battery-operated radio that could transmit up to 50 kilometers. Motorola, erroneously credited for introducing the first truly "portable" two-way communicator, came out with its "Handie Talkie" in 1940 for the U.S. Army Signal Corps. A year later, Motorola followed that with the first two-way AM police radio, an FM model with greater range, and then, in 1943, a two-way FM portable radio, called a "Walkie-Talkie" with a range of 20 to 35 kilometers.

But long before these renowned advances, bush pilots in Canada's hinterland were already using portable two-way voice radios. In 1937, Donald Lewes Hings, living in Rossland, British Columbia, about halfway between Vancouver and Calgary, developed the world's first truly portable two-way voice radio while working for Consolidated Mining and Smelting Co. (now Teck Cominco Ltd.). The mining company outfitted its pilots and geologists with the radios in case they became stranded in the Canadian wilderness. If there was an emergency, they could call for help and give their location. The radio had a range of more than 200 kilometers. Featuring a folded antenna, the radio was encased in an easily identifiable yellow-painted container that was both waterproof and buoyant—just in case a floatplane sank. Seven years earlier, in 1930, Hings, an inveterate tinkerer, had successfully devised an airplane two-way radio, using Morse code, not voice, to communicate between ground and air. In 1939, Hings approached his employer about taking out a patent for his portable two-way voice radios. While the mining company wasn't interested in communications patents, it allowed him to patent the device. So, in September 1939, Hings traveled across the border to Spokane, Washington, the closest city with an authorized patent attorney. On September 10, 1939, the day Canada declared war on Germany and four years before Motorola's Walkie-Talkie, the U.S. government awarded Hings a patent for his portable two-way voice radio.

Hings, who emigrated from Britain to Canada at age three with his mother, was seconded to Canada's National Research Council, where working as a civilian with the Royal Canadian Corps of Signals he designed the C-58 walkie-talkie that was widely considered superior to any other used by either friend or foe because it was substantially lighter, more durable and had a longer signal range. Manufactured in Toronto, the radio sets were used throughout Europe and Asia. Hings called his wireless radio a "packset," but it was dubbed a "walkie-talkie" in a 1941 article published in the *Toronto Star*. According to Hings, as recounted by his grandson, the reporter had asked a soldier about the device strapped onto his uniform during a demonstration Hings was giving for an enlistment drive in downtown Toronto. The soldier answered, "Well, you can talk with it, while you walk with it." Motorola is said to have coined the same name independently.

The walkie-talkie revolutionized battlefield communications, saving countless lives. "To infantryman, the walkie-talkie is like giving a football team a quarterback," an article in the *Toronto Star* declared in 1943 when the security ban was lifted on Canada's C-58 walkie-talkie, a "closely guarded, hitherto secret war weapon." Indeed, the British Army was so impressed with the Canadian sets that it took them away from the Canadian soldiers and gave them to its own troops for the D-Day invasion of Normandy on June 6, 1944. The Canadians were given the lower-quality British models on which they hadn't been trained. Years later, Hings would tell his grandson that he always felt the swap contributed to the unnecessary loss of Canadian lives on D-Day. Hings became an honorary colonel of the Royal Canadian Corps of Signals. In 1946, he was made a Member of the Order of the British Empire, but the government of Canada—engaged in (and losing) a postwar patent dispute with him over his invention—failed to acknowledge his vital wartime contributions until 2001 when the country finally awarded him the Order of Canada, its highest honor, although he was made a Member, the lowest of the three available ranks: Companion, Officer and Member. He was then 94 years old. He died three years later.

If the walkie-talkie hadn't fired up the public's imagination, then the creator of comic strip hero Dick Tracy certainly did. In 1946, U.S. cartoonist Chester Gould created a new crime-fighting tool for his square-jawed Chicago private detective: the 2-Way Wrist Radio.

As children clamored for toy replicas that year, AT&T's Bell System began offering mobile phone service for automobiles in 25 cities, starting in St. Louis, using newly licensed radio spectrum from the Federal Communications Commission. The phones, built by Motorola, used the same push-to-talk technology like the police mobile-radios of the twenties and thirties. Callers pushed a button to connect to a local operator, who in turn dialed a regular phone to connect the call. These early radio-phone systems depended on a single powerful antenna, blasting away on 25 channels, so the service area was extremely limited and the number of possible users small.

Each conversation tied up one whole channel of radio spectrum for more than 125 kilometers in every direction, depending on the terrain. (A channel is a pair of frequencies, one to transmit on, and the other to receive.) Since taxicab dispatchers, the police, fire departments and the military were considered essential services—and therefore, far more important than the casual mobile-phone users—the spectrum was quickly used up. With only a limited number of channels available, few people could actually use the mobile phone service. In a city like New York, the system could handle just 12 simultaneous calls, and even then, the sound quality was horrible.

In an effort to use the airwaves more efficiently, AT&T's research arm, Bell Labs—winner of an astounding 11 Nobel Prizes—not surprisingly introduced a revolutionary new concept in 1947 called "cellular" communications to solve the spectrum shortage. They divided every population region into dozens of smaller areas, called "cells," to greatly increase the number of available mobile telephone channels. Ingeniously, they used small, low-powered transmitters in each cell, instead of one centrally located powerful transmitter. With this new "low and soft" design, each radio channel in a given area could be extensively reused, dramatically increasing capacity to handle thousands of calls. Aided by the newfound power of computers, callers and radio channels could be switched from channel to channel seamlessly and instantaneously, making the cellular system feasible. This technology is the one used today. As the caller moves from one cell into the next, a specialized switching computer "hands off" the call from one transmitter to the next, automatically selecting the stronger channel without the customer noticing. Since the transmitters are all linked to the regular telephone network, anyone using a cellphone can call any telephone anywhere in the world.

The scientists at Bell Labs toiled away on making cellular a reality, only to be stymied in their efforts when the FCC refused to make available the necessary requested spectrum, preferring instead to safeguard it for the burgeoning television industry. Faced with this roadblock, Bell Labs worked on improving the existing mobile system, trunking together separate blocks of radio channels, and developing tiny computer circuits that would automatically find an open channel or connect callers to the phone company. Then, in 1964, the Bell System introduced a new mobile telephone system, Improved Mobile Telephone Service, or IMTS, which eliminated the need to "push to talk," while retaining backward compatibility with older systems. Car phone users no longer had to go through the arduous task of going through each channel separately to find an open one—mobile car-phones found the open channel automatically. Instead of connecting to a switchboard operator, customers could do their own direct dialing.

In 1970, with the technological pieces falling into place, the FCC agreed, albeit tentatively, to allocate 75 MHz in the 800 MHz region, requesting industry proposals detailing how a commercial "cellular system" might be constructed. AT&T, which had proposed a broadband mobile phone system operating in the 800 MHz band a full 17 years earlier, was the only respondent. Four years later, the FCC made a firm allocation of channels in the 800–900 MHz range.

Initially, the Commission intended to grant the whole block of spectrum designated for cellular to AT&T, a move vigorously opposed and prevented by the U.S. Justice Department, which had just launched an antitrust lawsuit against the company based on its monopoly of the wired phone systems. In classic bureaucratic fashion, the FCC—buffeted by industry lobbyists, equipment operators, paging companies and the Bell System companies—then spent the remainder of the decade trying to figure out "who" would get the spectrum licenses and "how" to award them.

Just what is spectrum? Spectrum is the lifeblood of a wireless company. To the physicist, it's a way of measuring and defining energy as it moves through time and space in any of its many forms—light, sound, x-rays, or TV or radio waves. It refers to the entire range of frequencies over which electromagnetic signals can be sent. Every wireless device—as diverse as toy airplanes, baby monitors and garage-door openers to pagers, radios, TVs and satellite dishes—runs, so to speak, across it. Once a certain frequency band like a station on the radio dial—is assigned for a specific use, it's unavailable for anything else.

In the United States, the FCC is responsible for distributing spectrum licenses. The Department of Transport managed Canada's spectrum until the Department of Communications (DOC) was created in 1968. The job then fell to Industry Canada when it absorbed the DOC 28 years later. In 1994, the FCC began auctioning spectrum licenses to the highest bidder; Canada followed a couple of years later.

Spectrum is a highly prized, closely regulated and scarce resource. That makes it enormously valuable. It's the equivalent of real estate, without the picket fences. Ted Rogers has always understood the importance of spectrum. As wireless technology has evolved, the price of spectrum has skyrocketed. "I want as much spectrum as I can get. That's the key, really. You can never own enough spectrum," he says. His early years in FM radio taught him that. He's a veritable spectrum gourmand. "Ted has yet to meet a spectrum, or MHz, that he doesn't like," jokes Michael Binder, assistant deputy minister in Industry Canada's spectrum branch.

By the mid-seventies, waiting lists for car phones were forming. As many as 20,000 people in the United States were on five- to 10-year waiting lists for car phones. In New York City, just 545 customers had AT&T car phones, with 3,700 customers on the waiting list. One in seven U.S. cars had a citizens' band—CB—radio. Even so, the FCC regarded the CB craze as more of a blue-collar fad—spurred by the hit song and eventual movie *Convoy*—than proof of pent-up demand for mobile phones. However, unlike citizen band radio users, who could only talk with one another, cellular phone customers could call anyone anywhere in the world. Former FCC staffer Tom Gutierrez admitted to *Wireless Nation* author James B. Murray that the Commission viewed cellular as a "niche" issue. "We all missed the boat big time," he said.

In 1977, seven years after AT&T first requested it, the FCC permitted the construction of two experimental cellular systems—one in Chicago and the other in the Baltimore–Washington DC area. AT&T was granted the right to build the Chicago system through its Advanced Mobile Phone Service (AMPS) subsidiary. Motorola teamed with a local paging and mobile operator called American Radio Telephone Services Inc. (ARTS) to build the Baltimore–Washington system.

By then, countries such as Japan, Sweden, Norway, Denmark, Finland and even Saudi Arabia—all with comparatively less bureaucracy—became the world's first to get their commercial cellular networks up and running. For its part, Canada's DOC, which was following events in the United States closely, felt it really couldn't do anything until the FCC got its act together, given the proximity of the two countries. Even so, Canada seemed content to watch the drama unfold down south before embarking on its own unique cellular giveaway.

Alberta accounted for roughly half of Canada's mobile phone market. Alberta Government Telephones (AGT)—now Telus—began developing a "cellular" network in 1976, a year before the FCC authorized field trials, to meet demand from oil and gas exploration companies for portable phones.

Compared to New York, Toronto was a mini hotbed of mobile users—no thanks to Ma Bell. Bell Canada had a 100-percent lock on the city's car phone market in 1969 when a small entrepreneur named Sheldon Kideckel began selling and servicing push-to-talk mobile car phones. By 1977, his aptly named company, Challenge Communications Ltd., had snared most of the market away from Bell—about 1,200 customers to Bell's 324. Challenge, whose annual sales rarely exceeded $1 million, boasted better service and hands-free phones and even hand-painted the sets if their customers wanted a color other than black.

Bell's phones were plain black and "looked like a great big tank." For seven years, Bell did nothing to improve its service.

Granted, the market was limited. A mobile phone cost almost as much as a brand-new car. Only sales or real estate agents, the odd businessman and the Rogers cable technicians had their cars or vans equipped with the units. Bell was content just collecting the monthly service charges from its customers (and Challenge's, since all mobile users went through a special Bell operator whenever they made a call).

Who cared if car phone users in Canada were using a technology their American counterparts had discarded 13 years earlier? Bell apparently didn't— not until 1977, coincidentally the same year the United States finally moved a step closer to adopting cellular mobile networks. In one fell swoop, Bell sought to quash Challenge and re-establish its monopoly with its Automatic Mobile Telephone Service (AMTS), a system similar to IMTS. The new system changed the mobile phone market overnight by permitting direct dialing and making more channels available to users.

Bell was clever, although perhaps too clever. It designed the system to work only on its own equipment, which meant the existing U.S. phone hardware wouldn't be able to work on its AMTS service. Bell also refused to reveal the specifications for its new equipment, effectively shutting out would-be competitors. Canada's biggest and most profitable company evidently believed it had the right to do whatever it wanted. "Our customers wanted to deal with us, but they wanted the new equipment that Bell wouldn't let us sell," Kideckel told *Canadian Business* in 1978. "Bell told me flatly, 'Shelley, you'll never get auto dialing.' Just like that, we were out of business."

Not for the first time, Bell would misjudge its opponent. Kideckel, a stocky and dark-haired man who wore heavy gold jewelry, wasn't about to let the country's most powerful company crush him. He hauled Bell in front of the CRTC, which the year earlier had assumed regulatory control over telecommunications. "Bell had an entourage of about 25 guys—vice presidents, corporate lawyers, and people like that," said Kideckel. "Hell, I'd never been in court before and there they were laughing and joking. Throughout the hearings, the Bell top brass slouched in their seats with little smirks on their faces."

In December 1977, the CRTC not only ordered Bell to allow Challenge to interconnect its own AMTS phones and to make available its specifications but, in an unprecedented move, the Commission also awarded costs to be paid by Bell. Kideckel had won. (Ironically, CNCP, which had asked for permission to interconnect to Bell's network the previous year, was still awaiting a decision from the CRTC.)

Stunned, Bell retaliated through the courts. For Bell, the issue wasn't so much control of the Toronto car phone market as it was its right to control interconnection—that is, the physical linking of its network with someone else's. Bell had always been able to keep other people from interconnecting with its service by arguing that other people's equipment would destroy the "integrity" of its communications network. The cable guys had run into the same problem when they wanted to string their cable lines on telephone poles.

Bell feared the Challenge ruling would become the Canadian equivalent of the FCC's "Carterfone Decision" of June 1968, which had resulted in virtual universal access of interconnected devices. Texan Tom Carter had complained to the FCC after the telephone companies refused to allow him to connect the coupler he had invented to tie mobile phones to their networks. The FCC declared that the Carterfone could be attached to the telephone network and ordered the Bell System (and other wirelines) to revise their tariffs to make such attachments possible.

The ruling, which became effective in 1969, ended the Bell System's monopoly in the telephone equipment business, although the phone giants mounted a rear-guard action that delayed the consumer's right to connect privately owned and manufactured terminal equipment for another eight years. Bell, through its subsidiary Northern Telecom, ironically benefited from open interconnection in the United States, while back home, just like the U.S. monopolists, Bell tried desperately to defend its turf.

Bell lost in the federal appeals court and in the Supreme Court of Canada. While the Challenge ruling didn't have the same sweeping repercussions of Carterfone, the CRTC had fired the first of many salvos at Bell to break its monopoly. "The Challenge decision broke through the idea that the phone company had some kind of absolute right to determine who could, or could not, use its network," says Ian Angus, a telecom expert and consultant.

Nevertheless, Challenge didn't survive, having used all of its resources fighting Bell's lawsuits. Ironically, after Kideckel started a new mobile phone company, he received a $75,000 order from Bell for 14 car phones for Bell executives.

On May 4, 1981, the FCC announced its decision to split the 40 MHz blocks of spectrum designated for cellular into two equal blocks for each market—one, to a local telephone ("wireline") company, and the other, to a non-telephone ("non-wireline") company.

The idea was to give the phone company one franchise, then let the other go to auction. If more than one company applied for either block in any given market, the FCC staff would turn the competing applications over to an administrative law judge, who would then conduct a "comparative hearing" to decide who was best qualified to receive the license. The local phone companies were allowed to apply only for licenses within their own geographic area. If just one company met the qualification in a particular market, it would be awarded the license outright. But in other markets, where local providers overlapped, their cellular applications would go to comparative hearings, just like the non-wireline companies. With the final rules still to be ironed out, the FCC did not call for applications until March 1982, when it announced it would distribute cellular licenses in "rounds," beginning with the top 30 markets.

On June 7, 1982, the deadline for Round I applications, FCC staff were inundated with filings. A total of 85 companies had filed 190 applications: 55 applications for the wireline block of spectrum and 135 for the non-wireline block. One ambitious non-wireline applicant, vying for all 30 markets, filled two semitrailers with 1.5 million pages of supporting documentation.

If FCC staff imagined themselves snowed under then, they were further shocked to see trucks lined up outside their building on November 8, the deadline for Round II applications for the next 30 markets. Round II resulted in a stunning 353 applications, nearly twice as many as Round I, an average of 12 applications per market. Fearing the licensing process would be bogged down for years in comparative hearings, the FCC decided to switch to a lottery system for markets below the top 30, in an equally controversial licensing process. In the end, the United States wound up with a hodgepodge of various cellular systems that, more than two decades later, the marketplace is still trying to sort out through consolidation.

While some of the markets had only one wireline applicant, usually AT&T or General Telephone and Electronics (GTE), the largest independent local-exchange carrier, every market had multiple non-wireline applicants—and surprisingly, the least attractive markets tended to have more. Ironically, the non-wirelines all bid for the smaller markets where they expected the least competition. As a result, places like Tampa, Florida ended up with 11 non-wireline applications, while Boston and Chicago each had just two. The non-wireline applicants were now facing the prospect of vying for licenses at public hearings in front of local judges, which would drag on for months, costing them valuable time and money. Even after a decision was made, appeals were made. Litigation often ensued. For a company like MCI, which was forced to compete for licenses like all the other non-wireline bidders because it ran only long distance and not local service, it would spend the next two years fighting for licenses before it could build out a service competitive to the phone companies.

Worse, AT&T and GTE, the two industry wireline heavyweights, did an end-run around the non-wirelines to ensure that they had that all-important head start in the marketplace. Having agreed to split ownership of the top 30 markets, they intimidated the local phone companies into standing down in exchange for minority stakes by convincing them they didn't have the expertise nor the ability to raise the capital to build cellular networks. On June 8, the day after the Round I deadline, AT&T and GTE issued a joint press release, announcing that AT&T would run 23 of the 30 wireline cellular systems, and GTE would run seven.

Whenever new technologies are introduced, companies fight hard to be first out of the starting gate, because the first customers tend to be the heaviest users. These customers are also the easiest and, consequently, the cheapest to attract. Cellular players were well aware that the first systems to get on the air in any particular market could easily expect to capture 70 percent or more of the early adopters, underscoring the importance of having a head start.

Four months after the FCC launched its process, on October 15, 1982, Canada's DOC called for license applications for 23 cities identified as cellular markets. To promote competition, it copied the U.S. model of awarding two licenses for each city: one to the local wireline company, and the other to a non-wireline. February 28, 1983, was set as the deadline for submissions. By virtue of its dominance in Ontario and Quebec, Bell Canada would automatically be given licenses in Ontario and Quebec for 12 cities, roughly half of the designated cellular markets. Just as in the United States, the non-wirelines had to duke it out.

Applicants had four-and-a-half months to pull together their bidding consortiums. Canada had its own mini-version of the great U.S. spectrum rush as everyone, however remotely connected to the telecom industry, raced to form alliances for some or all of the 23 licenses. Global TV's then-co-owner Seymour Epstein and Toronto cable pioneer Geoff Conway joined forces with Western Union Telegraph Co. of New York to form Honeycomb Telephone Corp. Bell Canada's long-time telegraph and long-distance foe, CNCP Communications, teamed with U.S. cellular phone maker Motorola Inc. Winnipeg-based Inter-City Gas Corp. partnered with the Toronto Bronfman family's merchant bank, Hees International Corp., and the rebel Toronto securities firm, Gordon Securities Ltd. (the now-defunct Gordon Capital Corp.). Inter-City, which was aligned with New York-based Millicom Ltd., called its consortium Roam Communications. Millicom had recently been awarded one of the two U.K. national licenses and was vying for U.S. licenses. Radio and TV network owner Selkirk Communications and pulp-and-paper company Abitibi-Price teamed with Cellular Canada Communications Inc., a consortium of radio common carriers (RCCs).

Less than a month before the deadline, Cantel was created. It was backed by three of the unlikeliest partners, each having stumbled into this new uncharted world of cellular radio communications purely by happenstance, uniting to bid for what would become the most politically charged licensing process Canada had ever seen either before or since.

King Margolese was a young, cocksure Vancouver native anxious to win the license for his hometown. The 23-year-old, who later changed his given name to David, was so enthusiastic about wireless communications that he had dropped out of university to focus on his small, yet prospering, paging business. In June 1980—more than two full years before Ottawa finally acted—he tried to rally his fellow RCCs into forming a partnership to apply for cellular licenses in their respective provinces. "Cellular radio has the potential to become all-pervasive," he prognosticated in his 1980 position paper. "Tomorrow's mass market will use the cellular market for much more than simply voice traffic." But, the other RCCs lacked his vision.

After the call went out for applications, a despondent Margolese bemoaned their continued lack of interest to a family friend, David Huberman, a partner in the law firm that represented entrepreneur Samuel Belzberg. "How about Rogers?" suggested Huberman. Too small to make a solo bid, Margolese realized his most logical partner was indeed the city's biggest cable provider, Rogers-owned Premier Cable. It was a brilliant idea. He approached its CEO, George Fierheller, who knew zilch about cellular, but nonetheless was willing to hear his proposition. Exuding confidence, Margolese gave him a quick tutorial on the workings of a cellular network, information that an intrigued Fierheller, after brushing off the young man, then passed along to Rogers.

"If he can do it, why aren't we doing it? We're the cable company," Fierheller recalls telling Rogers. Fierheller even sent Rogers photocopies of a cutting-edge book, *Future Developments in Telecommunications* by computing guru James Martin, to educate himself about the industry and circulate to his directors.

There's nothing Rogers embraces more than new ideas if he is convinced they will make his company stronger. Rogers thrives on championing new innovations. But, he's not rash. He does his homework. His mother drilled into him that some of his father's best ideas were borrowed from others. If he has been told he really needs to read something, he'll stay up that same night until two in the morning to read it. He's not shy about cold-calling strangers in his eagerness to learn as much as possible about a new technology before making the commitment of time, energy and resources. He seeks the views of industry experts, and sometimes even from his competitors, on the feasibility of a new technology before formulating his own opinion. When he does commit, it's total—sometimes to the point of clouding his judgment as to a project's continuing viability. And, once he's made up his mind, then irrespective of what others may think or say, he cannot be swayed from his decision. This time was no exception.

In December 1982, while on a layover at Miami International Airport on his way to his home in Nassau, Rogers walked over to the bank of pay phones to call Ottawa lawyer Bob Buchan, who advised Rogers through the CRTC hearings on CCL. Once on the line, Rogers cut to the quick: "What do you know about this cellular thing?"

Buchan hesitated. He was mindful that neither Lind nor Watson—his primary contacts at the cable company—wanted him to encourage Rogers to go into cellular. They didn't want their boss pouring his diminishing resources into cellular when the debt-laden company was barely meeting the banks' stringent loan ratios. On the other hand, he heard through the grapevine that Rogers was asking others the same question.

He decided that he should better tell Rogers what he knew, which wasn't much. He related a conversation he had with Dr. John deMercado, the DOC's director-general of regulation, over lunch a couple of months earlier. An eccentric yet brilliant telecom guru, deMercado, who was then retiring from his post, began prattling on about cellular, telling the lawyer that the technology would be "the next big thing." Buchan recalls that he was initially dubious, fearing it might ultimately prove not much more successful than the previous decade's Telidon text terminals.

"It is not a hula-hoop technology," deMercado insisted. Buchan repeated those exact words to Rogers.

Buchan ultimately had been so impressed by deMercado's conviction that, upon returning to the office, he recounted his conversation to his partners, Christopher Johnston and Charles Dalfen, and urged them to prepare a briefing book so at the very least they could appear knowledgeable if and when a prospective client called. Before long, their phones started ringing. Ultimately, Dalfen would play a critical role in arranging the marriage of Cantel's founding, if dysfunctional, triumvirate: Marc Belzberg, Philippe de Gaspé Beaubien and Ted Rogers.

At 55, Philippe de Gaspé Beaubien was restless. Through Telemedia Inc., the suave, soft-spoken moustached Montrealer owned radio and TV stations in Quebec, and publications including the Canadian edition of *TV Guide* and a national family magazine, *Canadian Living*. He had taken the company he had bought from his close friend Paul Desmarais as far as he could. He was anxious to explore new opportunities for growth.

A charismatic, sophisticated man, de Gaspé Beaubien is the closest thing Canada has to French aristocracy. His family's roots run deep in Quebec, where his fur-trading ancestors emigrated from France in the seventeenth century. (The original land title deed signed by King Louis XIV, passed on through the generations, hangs framed behind glass on his office wall.) He comes from a family of entrepreneurs, although his forebears never managed to maintain their businesses beyond two generations in their entire 350-year history in Canada. Consumed with a desire to break that tradition, de Gaspé Beaubien defied his father's wishes by going to Harvard Business School. His father, the owner of a wholesale electrical supply business, feared his son would fail because of inadequate schooling in English. Nor was business a popular career choice for a Quebec francophone in the fifties. But de Gaspé Beaubien not only succeeded (Harvard MBA, 1954), he also met his future wife, Nan-b, a Bostonian studying psychology at nearby Smith College.

He earned enormous respect in both business and political circles in French- and English-speaking Canada for overseeing the phenomenally successful 1967 World's Fair in Montreal, known as Expo '67. The following year he was made an Officer of the Order of Canada. Called the "mayor of the fair," de Gaspé Beaubien formed valuable contacts. "He is great at networking," says former Telemedia CFO Pierre Morrissette, who started Canada's *The Weather Network*. "Philippe can go anywhere and he would know everybody that he needs to know within a few days."

The following year, de Gaspé Beaubien became president of Telemedia when it belonged to Paul Desmarais' Montreal-based conglomerate, Power Corp. of Canada Ltd. In 1971, de Gaspé Beaubien acquired the then-ailing division, using money lent to him by its parent. In 1976, he teamed with the venerable newspaper chain Southam Inc. to buy the Canadian edition of *TV Guide*, a highly profitable magazine with newsstand sales of more than 1 million copies a week. *TV Guide*, a veritable cash cow, became his launchpad into the world of publishing. In 1979 he picked up one of Canada's top-selling magazines, *Canadian Living*, from brewer John Labatt Ltd. Over the next five years, Telemedia acquired and turned around (at a slower pace) money-losing radio stations and consumer magazines outside of Quebec to surpass both CHUM and Standard Broadcasting in annual revenues. Telemedia would eventually own as many as 76 radio stations across Canada, including Toronto's the FAN 590 and the EZ Rock network. If de Gaspé Beaubien had one weakness in business, former executives say, it was that he was too trusting and often gave away too much just to complete a transaction. He was not inherently a good deal-maker.

As the seventies drew to a close, de Gaspé Beaubien began weighing his options. How was he going to generate growth? He realized he needed to expand, or diversify, from his base in the secessionist-led province of Quebec. To that end, in September 1982, he hired a gung-ho young marketer-turned-management consultant, David Lint, from McKinsey & Co. as his corporate development officer. Lint hired his former employer to identify new growth opportunities in media or broadcasting that were emerging in the United States but hadn't yet hit the Canadian scene. Cellular radiotelephony topped the list. Shortly thereafter, de Gaspé Beaubien hired Charles Dalfen.

Marc Belzberg was lunching with William B. Ginsberg, a former FCC official-turned-private investor, at the Regency Hotel on Park Avenue in Manhattan, discussing the possibility of investing in propane distributors. As they were finishing their coffee and waiting for the bill, Belzberg, as taught by his father, Sam, asked one final question: "What else do you like?"

"Have you heard of cellular radio?" Ginsberg asked.

"No, what's that?"

"Marc, look around this restaurant and imagine everyone's got their own phone," Ginsberg answered. "Just imagine. You can be in constant communication wherever you are."

"You're kidding?" replied Belzberg, whose ear was practically glued to a landline phone when he was in the office. The notion of being able to call anyone from anywhere at anytime fascinated him.

Just 28 years old, Belzberg was the point man in New York for the family's Vancouver-based conglomerate, First City Financial Corp., after spending almost four years at Salomon Brothers and Oppenheimer & Co. Founded and controlled by his father, Samuel, and two uncles, Hyman and William, First City speculated in oil and gas, developed real estate properties and owned what became Canada's seventh-largest trust company, First City Trustco. The brothers had amassed $2.2 billion in assets, and were gaining a fearsome reputation for their profitable run-ins with companies, including Bache Group Inc., the parent company of major New York brokerage house Suburban Propane Gas Corp. of Morristown, New Jersey, and Toronto-based Canada Permanent Mortgage Corp. They had made a pretax profit of more than US$40 million alone on the sale of its Bache stock to Prudential Insurance Co. of America. As one of Canada's wealthiest families, they drew such publicity that Hyman, the eldest of the three brothers, was kidnapped and held for 24 hours in December 1982. Heading into 1983, the Belzbergs would make a run at a Maryland propane maker and distributor called Pargas Inc.

As the eighties unfolded, First City would become so feared as a corporate raider that two U.S. states passed anti-takeover laws to thwart its possible surprise attacks. Indeed, the company became so legendary that there are two veiled references to the Belzberg brothers in Oliver Stone's 1987 movie *Wall Street*. But, at the time, in 1982, the Belzbergs were not even remotely involved in the telecom industry and, like most people back then, Marc Belzberg had never even heard of cellular telephony.

Born in 1954 in Edmonton, Alberta, Marc Belzberg was the only son of four children raised in an affluent secular Jewish household. His father moved the family to Vancouver in 1969, drawn by its beauty and temperate climate after a year-earlier fishing trip there with Marc. Kicked out of middle school, Belzberg was developing into a problem kid. He spent his junior high school years in Vancouver organizing parties. His parents sent him away to Israel for a year, which he spent carousing. He was heading for disaster until a young Baltimore-born rabbi, Pinchas "Pinky" Bak, took him under his wing. Belzberg astonished his parents by becoming a religiously observant Orthodox Jew. His parents were strong supporters of Zionism, but they only attended synagogue for Yom Kippur and Rosh Hashanah. Although immensely proud of their son, they thought he was just going through a phase. He wasn't. In Grade 12, the formerly unruly youth became president of the National Conference of Synagogue Youth's (NCSY's) Vancouver chapter. "Had I not discovered NCSY and Pinky Bak, I might be dead—from OD'ing, drunk driving, AIDS, who knows?" Belzberg told the magazine *Jewish Action*. "Instead, my life has meaning. Every day is significant. I wake up in the morning and ask, 'What do the Jewish people need? What should I do for the Jewish people today?"

After lunch, Ginsberg took Marc Belzberg to his office in the General Motors Building, where he had a small factory running to prepare applications for the FCC's upcoming Round II filing deadline on November 8, 1982 for the next 30 U.S. cities. Ginsberg had mountains of thick binders, and presentations strewn everywhere.

Retuning to his own office, Belzberg mulled over the possibilities. "I walked out and said, 'Wow. If there's such a thing as being able to walk around with a telephone in your pocket, I'd be the first guy to have one,'" says Belzberg, blue eyes brimming with his recalled enthusiasm over cellular's possibilities. "I thought, okay, this is a brilliant idea. I don't want to start competing with him in the United States. This guy just told me about it, and it wouldn't be fair to turn around and compete with him. I wouldn't do that, so I said, 'Okay, let's see what's going on in Canada.'" As the son of the family business patriarch with his cousins already proving themselves competent managers, he was under enormous familial pressure to prove himself. First City had focused on real estate, energy and finance. Cellular was outside the family's sphere of knowledge. He assigned a recently hired junior analyst, Oliver Bush, to go to Ottawa to find out what was happening in Canada. He liked what he heard back from Bush.

He asked his dad for the money to bid for the cellular licenses. He had been sent to the world's most powerful financial center to carve out his own path, and the very first idea he brings home is cellular! His father said he was nuts.

"Who wants a phone in their car?" Samuel Belzberg asked. "Nobody wants a phone in their car. They don't work anyway. I have a phone in my car, and I never use it."

"Number one, if you had a phone in your car that worked and had excellent reception, maybe you'd use it, and number two, the next step is going to be a light, hand-held model that you can carry with you everywhere. It doesn't have to be a big, heavy thing. This is going to replace the telephone company, Dad."

"You're dreaming. No way. You think you're going to replace a big company like Bell Canada? You're dreaming," Sam Belzberg said.

But seeing his son's earnest belief in cellular, he asked, "How much are you going to spend?"

"We're going to spend $1 million on the application, and either we win, or we don't win. And, if we win, it's worth a fortune, but if we don't win, the money's gone, but the risk-return ratio is fabulous."

"Yeah, but if I spend a million dollars and build a building, when it's finished, even if I don't rent it, I still have a building. Eventually, I'll rent it," his father told him. "But, this. You spend a million dollars, and if you don't win, you have nothing. You're throwing away money."

"But, it's worth a lot of money in the future if we win this," his son persisted.

"Write down on a piece of paper what this company will be worth in five years," said Samuel Belzberg, caving in to his son's enthusiasm. "Put it in an envelope. Don't tell me what it says. Put it away in a safe, and we'll open it up in a couple of years."

He did as his father instructed. As he sealed the envelope, Marc Belzberg told himself that if he invested $1 million, the licenses would be worth as much as $100 million in five years, not a bad investment by his reckoning. All he needed was partners.

Samuel Belzberg, a Liberal party backer, put his son in touch with Jim Coutts. A former McKinsey consultant, Coutts served as the principal secretary, or chief of staff, to then-current prime minister Pierre Trudeau for six years until he resigned to run unsuccessfully for a parliamentary seat in a 1981 federal by-election. A powerbroker in the federal Liberal Party, Coutts had all the necessary connections to put Belzberg in touch with the right people in Ottawa. He retained Charles Dalfen on Belzberg's behalf.

In Montreal, Philippe de Gaspé Beaubien was also becoming intrigued with the concept of cellular, but he was no fool; he knew it would cost him dearly to erect a network and he'd be competing against mighty Bell Canada. He just didn't see how he could do it on his own. Two of his key executives, meanwhile, had crunched the numbers, done the legwork and, recognizing a potentially explosive new growth market, urged him to go for it. Pierre Morrissette, his CFO (who later served as a Rogers Wireless director), and David Lint attended a trade show in Toronto, where U.S. and U.K. firms were jostling to form alliances with Canadians. They took note of the players, including Marc Belzberg and Oliver Bush. Lint had already trekked to Chicago and Baltimore to check out the U.S. field trials firsthand.

The three men agreed the best way to proceed was as part of a consortium. De Gaspé Beaubien received an unexpected telephone call from an American company seeking a Canadian partner for the DOC's cellular application. In his recollection, de Gaspé Beaubien says he eventually discovered that the U.S. company was also talking to the Belzberg family, seemingly playing one party off the other to extract more favorable terms. Annoyed, he directly contacted Samuel Belzberg in Vancouver. "I don't know you, and you don't know me, but I want to talk to you about cellular radio," he told Belzberg. Before he could get any further, Belzberg explained that cellular was his son's deal and gave him Marc's number in New York. In Belzberg's recollection, Dalfen, who de Gaspé Beaubien also sought to hire, brought them together.

Belzberg and de Gaspé Beaubien connected. They decided to divide the country between them. Belzberg would own 75 percent of the company that held licenses for western Canada, with the remaining 25 percent held by de

Gaspé Beaubien, and vice versa for eastern Canada. "The immediate challenge was getting the applications written," recalls Marc Belzberg. "I was hoping to find one body that knew what the hell they were doing, where I could basically say, 'You write it for us.'"

With that goal in mind, Belzberg called a ballsy telecom upstart: MCI Communications Corp. MCI, which originally stood for Microwave Communications Inc., had spent the past 14 years fighting corporate monolith AT&T, one of the world's greatest monopolies, to become America's first alternative long-distance telephone carrier. In 1974, when MCI unveiled Execunet, which used private lines and customer-owned switches to offer long-distance service to business customers, AT&T tried to crush the fledgling service by tripling the access fees it charged MCI to let customers connect to Execunet. MCI sued, accusing the world's largest corporation of violating antitrust laws. Led by its maverick leader, Bill McGowan, who hated AT&T, MCI hired a battalion of lawyers and relocated the company to Washington DC. The cigar-chomping McGowan, a voracious reader who despised bureaucracy, once told his employees that they wouldn't succeed in the long-distance business until they succeeded in the litigation business. MCI won its case, and the U.S. Supreme Court refused to hear AT&T's appeal in 1978. MCI was awarded US$600 million in damages, which under U.S. law was trebled to a stunning US$1.8 billion, the largest monetary award in U.S. history. The case paved the way for the U.S. Department of Justice's antitrust case to break up the Bell System.

On January 8, 1982—two months before the FCC set June 7 as its deadline for receiving the first cellular applications—U.S. District Court judge Harold Greene issued the now-famous landmark consent decree that shattered AT&T, forcing the world's greatest monopoly to divest itself of its 22 local telephone companies, about two-thirds of its US$120 billion of assets—a mammoth undertaking that would take two years to complete. Just as Carterfone broke Bell's monopoly in equipment, MCI razed the barriers to entry in the long-distance telephone market. With the taste of victory still sweet, McGowan viewed cellular as a way for MCI to compete in the local phone business.

Belzberg arranged a meeting with two key MCI executives at the company's head office in Washington DC, flying down with his hired gun, Jim Coutts, and lawyer, Charles Dalfen. They met with MCI's corporate development head, H. Brian Thompson, another McKinsey man whom Coutts knew from Harvard Business School where they were classmates, and a McGowan protégé, Gerald (Jerry) H. Taylor, who was overseeing the company's push into cellular. Taylor became MCI's president 12 years later. The corporate development team under Thompson's leadership laid the groundwork for MCI to become one of America's fastest-growing companies in the eighties, all in anticipation of a huge financial payday that never materialized. But on appeal of the Supreme Court's decision, MCI's award was reduced to a disappointing US$113.3 million in 1985, forcing McGowan to sell 18 percent of the company to IBM for cash and a year later unload its hard-won cellular licenses to Craig McCaw to reduce its mammoth debt-load.

Just as Belzberg had initiated talks with MCI, de Gaspé Beaubien concurrently phoned Bill McGowan. De Gaspé Beaubien knew McGowan from their Harvard days together. They were "poddy buddies" in residence, roommates in the adjoining suites that shared a bathroom. "When they talk of a perfect storm, this was kind of the perfect storm," laughs Thompson.

Thompson assigned Herman "Whitey" Bluestein to work with Belzberg on the application. An engineer by the name of David Ackerman, whom Belzberg tried to hire away from MCI, was also lent by MCI to work on the file. In a flurry of meetings, they crafted a plan of action with their lawyers and traversed the country in search of potential partners for the various cities. In Vancouver, Belzberg had already teamed with Margolese, who approached him after Fierheller had sent him packing. On one of their frequent trips, Bluestein and an MCI associate had caught the first flight out of Washington's Dulles International Airport to Toronto where they met Belzberg for back-to-back meetings. The threesome were heading to the airport for an early afternoon meeting in Ottawa with Mitel Corp., a potential partner, when a famished Bluestein asked Belzberg, "Can we stop for a sandwich, or get something to eat?"

"No, we've got to catch this flight," Belzberg replied. "We've got to keep on pushing."

They raced through the airport to board their flight. Once in the air, Belzberg reached into his briefcase and to their astonishment pulled out a kosher sandwich. He ate it right in front of them. "I think we were ready to eat our shoes at that point," chuckles Bluestein. "He was quite focused. He knew what he wanted to do. It was reflective of the high energy that we had, and just working hard and going nonstop."

In the end, MCI balked after learning that Canada would restrict MCI to a maximum 20-percent ownership of any company that won a cellular license because of its foreign-ownership limits. "It was important to McGowan that we have control wherever possible," recalls Bluestein. "We concluded at the end of this adventure that we would take a pass because we just couldn't take a large enough stake. I was disappointed, but at the time, we were up to our ears in applications."

Without MCI, Belzberg and de Gaspé Beaubien were left scrambling for another partner. Recognizing they had a gap in Ontario, Charles Dalfen suggested bringing in Ted Rogers. They needed a partner who could bring an engineering component to the table if they hoped to be perceived as a serious contender against the likes of telecom heavyweight CNCP.

Dalfen had already run the idea past Bob Buchan, who told him Rogers had contacted him before Christmas to inquire about what he thought of this new-fangled technology called cellular radiotelephone. He told Dalfen to call Rogers if he wanted to, but not to hold his breath. Rogers had a lot on his plate already. He was in Los Angeles on a road show with junk bond financier Michael Milken's Drexel Burnham Lambert to raise US$181 million in public debt in a near-desperate attempt to restructure his crushing debt load and finance the buildout of his ever-expanding U.S. cable franchises. The company had just reported its quarterly loss was now $4.25 million, up from just $500,000 a year earlier. He was also on the brink of divorcing UA/Columbia less than 18 months after their celebrated merger.

On February 2, 1983—two days before officially terminating the UA marriage—Rogers was in San Antonio, Texas, home of the jewel of his company's U.S. cable assets, for the annual Texas Cable Show. His focus was entirely on his cable business. Rogers admits the impending bust-up of AT&T, and its possible implications in Canadian telecom, didn't even register on his radar screen.

Rogers was striding into the Marriott Riverwalk Hotel just as Canadian cable pioneer Israel "Sruki" Switzer was leaving. Rogers recalls Switzer grabbing his arm and asking, "What are you doing in cellular?"

"I'm certainly looking at it," Rogers replied.

"Look, didn't I advise you to go into cellular? Why don't you just go and get at it?"

Switzer, a respected cable TV engineer, was working as a consultant to MCI once a week in Washington DC when his client asked him if he could recommend a partner for the Belzbergs now that it had decided not to pursue cellular licenses in Canada. The first name that sprang into his mind was not Ted Rogers, but rather Fred Metcalf.

Switzer, a second cousin of Samuel Belzberg, spent 13 of the previous 16 years working for the late Fred Metcalf at Maclean Hunter Cable in Toronto. He was the company's first cable employee, in June 1967, after Maclean Hunter Ltd. bought Metcalf's southern Ontario cable systems. Switzer still felt a sense of loyalty to the company. He emphatically believed cellular radiotelephony was a natural fit for Maclean Hunter, especially given the venerable company's early success in paging, a business into which he had spurred the company. He felt that if Maclean Hunter, one of Canada's longest surviving and most prestigious companies, could compete successfully against the telephone companies in paging, they could certainly take them on in cellular.

Led by its redoubtable chairman Donald Campbell, Maclean Hunter took a pass, choosing to wait and see if cellular would be, as one DOC staffer told *The Globe and Mail*, "a cash cow or a bust." Campbell recalls that he talked with Philippe de Gaspé Beaubien several times about making a joint application, but ultimately he and the Maclean Hunter board felt the timing just wasn't right for them. The company, hurt by advertising cutbacks during the recession, was focused on paying off the debt it had accumulated from buying a controlling stake in the Toronto Sun Publishing Co., a newspaper company. Metcalf, a cable pioneer, also was not particularly enthusiastic about cellular. "He didn't see cellular as we see it today," says Campbell, now 81, "but we were very busy. Our plate was full. We decided cellular was not for us at that point. We were just getting back into a very healthy cash position, so we weren't about to start all over again in cellular. We decided to stick to our knitting." Ted Rogers was to ultimately benefit from Maclean Hunter's strategic miscue.

According to Switzer, Metcalf believed the spectrum licenses would be awarded to several "independents" who would inevitably go broke, after which time Maclean Hunter could then sweep in and scoop up the licenses. "I was quite disappointed they rejected my suggestion," recalls Switzer. "I had no particular relationship with Ted other than acquaintance. I don't think I went looking for Ted. I could have called him, but seeing him in that hallway in the San Antonio hotel triggered the idea in my mind that he might be receptive to the suggestion." Later, Switzer again would urge Metcalf to join the Belzberg-de Gaspé Beaubien–Rogers consortium "while there was still time." "I told him he was mistaken [to wait], but he didn't listen."

Rogers admired Switzer. If this renowned engineer was so insistent that cellular radio systems were going to be the communications networks of tomorrow, who was he to doubt him? He had already been mulling over the idea, but this accidental meeting was the clincher. "He focused my thinking," says Rogers. Later, he sent Switzer a cheque for $10,000 to thank him for the referral.

On Friday, February 4, 1983—24 days before application deadline—Philippe de Gaspé Beaubien was in his company's Toronto office on Merton St. with his partner, Marc Belzberg, and their lawyer, Charles Dalfen. David Lint, who had done the initial legwork on cellular for de Gaspé Beaubien, was also present, as was Jerome Redican, another former McKinsey consultant and co-founder of The Canada Consulting Group. De Gaspé Beaubien picked up the phone and called Ted Rogers in Nassau at his in-laws' home, El Mirador House.

Rogers hesitated. He was enthusiastic over the technology's promise, but he didn't think they'd be able to pull together a winning application within three weeks. In Redican's recollection, they had to persuade Rogers it could be done. Redican's presence certainly helped since he had worked on the pay-TV applications for Rogers, as well as the takeover of Premier. Rogers was comfortable with him and his firm's abilities. Belzberg noticed no hesitation. "He heard 'licenses' and 'telephones' and said yes. We asked him to put up $200,000, and he said yes on the spot."

Belzberg and de Gaspé Beaubien each owned 40 percent of the equity. As third man in, Rogers was the minority partner, with a 20-percent stake. Belzberg represented the money; Rogers, the engineering; and de Gaspé Beaubien, the political angle. Each agreed to contribute manpower from their firms to work on the applications.

Later that day, Redican met with his business partner, Sheelagh Whittaker. They spent the rest of the day strategizing and developing what ultimately became a close blueprint of the application. Of the three owners, Marc Belzberg was the most closely involved in the application. Margolese flew in from Vancouver to help work on it, too.

Because of a commitment in British Columbia, Redican was unable to attend the project team's first meeting that Sunday at The Canada Consulting Group offices above the liquor store near Toronto's popular farmers' emporium, the St. Lawrence Market. Whittaker led the team of Belzberg, the other partners' proxies, and some 25 consultants, lawyers and pollsters. There were plenty of donuts but not nearly enough chairs.

The owners brought in top guns to work on the application. There was an American management consultant, Kas Kalba. His firm, now known as Kalba International Inc., would prepare the financial models. Liberal Party pollster Martin Goldfarb's consulting firm (now part of U.K-based WPP Group Plc's Millward Brown) would gather consumer demand data. Calgary-based NovAtel Communications Inc., jointly owned by Hong Kong tycoon Li Ka-shing's Nova Corp. of Alberta and provincial carrier AGT, pulled together the engineering specs. AGT had just introduced NovAtel's Aurora-400 system to Alberta's booming oil patch, some nine months before U.S. pioneer Ameritech offered a commercial service in Chicago. Nova and AGT hoped to build NovaTel into the next Motorola, Nokia or Samsung in the nascent mobile phone industry.

Rogers' CFO Bob Francis and Telemedia's CFO Pierre Morrissette met with TD Bank to get financing letters to show that the application had financial support. Ultimately, the Belzberg's First City wrote a letter attached to the application, giving a guarantee to finance the buildout of the cellular system to the tune of $100 million.

They had everything except a name. As the project team worked literally around the clock, the days flew past and still no one could agree on what to call the new entity. Finally, at one meeting, the owners batted around ideas when Margolese suggested "Cantel." He didn't realize until later that he was subliminally contracting the name of his small B.C. paging company, Canadian Telecom Inc. Everyone approved until the lawyers discovered it had already been incorporated by several other companies, including one based in the DOC's own backyard of Ottawa. Whittaker, who had a strong bias against three-letter acronyms, such as the proposed moniker CCT (Canadian Cellular Telephone), pushed for the name Cantel over the lawyers' quibbles. Since she and Redican had final edit, they went with Cantel. Two months later, in late April, the lawyers incorporated Cantel Cellular Radio Group Inc.

Redican and Whittaker were the two point people, shepherding the work and writing the applications. Halfway through, with nine days left, they were stricken with food poisoning after dining out together with their spouses. They nevertheless went in the next day, a Sunday; feeling wretched, working on the application between frequent visits to the loo. Everyone was working flat out. Despite two ill participants, the energy level was high.

The owners might not have been there physically, but they held almost daily conference calls with the project team. Their respective employees were tasked with various duties. They began divvying up lobbying duties. The Belzberg family and de Gaspé Beaubien were both well-known supporters of the Liberal Party, while Rogers was Tory. There was a sense of history in the making, from the owners to the typists. There was the feeling they were all working on something "revolutionary," a service that would change the way that people communicated.

"It was a colossal effort," remembers Whittaker. "Jerome and I did not sleep for the last three days of production. I remember sitting with Kas Kalba and Jerome in the bar at the Four Seasons [Hotel], trying to write the Executive Summary at about 2 a.m. on the Friday night before the Monday [deadline]. The French translations were always done at the end when the English was finalized, and the young woman who was typing the French translation sat at her word processor typing, and crying from exhaustion, for hours."

Desktop computers—used so skillfully today to design and produce documents with graphics—were then still rarities, and Canada Consulting wasn't equipped with desktop publishing equipment. They used word processors and printers in a small shop in the city's west end. "I remember being told in the middle of the night that we had thirty hours of printing backed up and only twenty hours to get the documents over for photocopying and binding," says Whittaker. They found a small Xerox printing shop that was willing to stay open all night. The printers arrived with their Saturday night dates in tow, all dressed up. Their dates whiled away the hours sitting on top of the copiers, chewing gum and smoking cigarettes until their boyfriends sent them home in cabs at about two-thirty in the morning, when it became clear that they weren't going to be finished before dawn. Whittaker, Redican and Lint spent the night inserting maps and tabs and triple-checking the documents.

They managed to complete applications for 17 of the 23 markets, which they categorized into four regions: Quebec, Ontario, the Prairie provinces and British Columbia. Each of the four books was a good eight centimeters thick. The executive summary on each listed all the licenses (west to east) for which they were applying. The applications were all identical, except for their thickness (depending on the number of licenses per region) and the color of their cover. The map of each region was illustrated on the lacquered cover of its respective application. The regional covers were color coded. The cover for Ontario—Rogers' stamping ground—was fittingly Tory blue. Quebec was also an easy choice: blood red, the color of the Liberal party, symbolizing the territory to be controlled by de Gaspé Beaubien. The colors for British Columbia and the Prairies were also symbolic, albeit a less blatantly political green and yellow, respectively. Copies of each regional application were provided in French, even though it wasn't the de rigueur standard it is today. By making that additional effort, they were hoping to curry favor with the Trudeau government, which the previous year, in the country's Charter of Rights and Freedoms, had just guaranteed the use of French.

"We went as fast as we could and as hard as we could until the deadline came, and all we had was seventeen done, and that's what we applied for," says Belzberg. "It was like a marathon. Everybody was fabulous. There was no fighting. It was a whole team effort. It was elegantly executed. It was fun. It was a challenge. It was a great time."

On February 28, 1983, the applications were hand-delivered—not couriered—to four DOC offices. The multiple copies were delivered by truck to Ottawa. An exhausted Jerome Redican flew to Vancouver where he and Brent Belzberg, Marc's cousin, presented the books to the regional DOC head. Sheelagh Whittaker, accompanied by a NovAtel salesman, flew to Edmonton. Telemedia's Pierre Morrissette and Canada Consulting's office manager Madeleine Rogers (no relation to Ted) delivered the document to the DOC's regional office in Montreal. Laurence Dunbar from the law firm Buchan & Johnston delivered it to the departmental headquarters in Ottawa.

Rogers wasn't confident that the board of his publicly traded company would back him in this bleeding-edge endeavor. Philippe de Gaspé Beaubien was using his own money after his board withheld its approval. Rogers wanted the public company to invest $500,000 into his cellular radio venture. But, there was a minor hitch: an empty till.

Rogers Cablesystems was barely subsisting on borrowed money. The company had amassed more than $560 million in long-term debt, six times equity. If that sounds bad, its debt-to-cash flow ratio was worse: 8-to-1. The company was spending eight times more than the cash it was getting from its cable TV subscribers. Interest charges alone that year exceeded $80 million. As fast as Graham Savage was pulling in money from junk-bond issues, Bob Francis was whittling down the bank debt. The cable guys were burning through millions of dollars south of the border, where they were not only building cable TV systems, but were still locked in a bitter legal fight with Storer over its Minneapolis franchise.

Rogers was relying on the cash flow from his company's Canadian cable TV systems to fund its losses in the United States and he intended to hit his Canadian subscribers with huge rate increases, up to 38.5 percent in Vancouver and 51 percent in Victoria. But the rate hike was stymied when Ottawa introduced a 4 percent price guideline in its budget, a move that extended its controversial 6-and-5 price-and-wage restraint program. Later in the year, the CRTC approved increases of up to 20 percent in cable TV bills.

The bankers had Ted Rogers in their sights. In no uncertain terms, they warned Phil Lind and Colin Watson what would happen if they didn't stop him. "We'll have a new guy in the corner office," Lind recalls being told. "I thought, I don't want that; despite the fact that I want to wring his neck sometimes, he's the greatest guy. It wasn't that we were against cellular, per se. We just didn't want the corner office to be displaced. Now, as it turned out, that was all bullshit. It was all B.S. The bankers [different men, same banks] were in Ted's office a week later signing financing for the cellular deal." Colin Watson remembers, "We both thought it was cuckoo to go into the cellular business. That's how smart we were."

At the board meeting, the directors backed Lind, not Rogers. Even his wife voted against him, although reluctantly so. The vote was 16 to 1. Stung by their decision, but undaunted, Rogers told them he'd do it on his own. As the controlling shareholder, he could have overruled their decision. Instead, he took the advice of one of the company's directors, Gordon Gray. A chartered accountant, Gray helped build Canada's largest real estate brokerage, Royal LePage. He remembered that the company had granted Rogers an option to buy $5.94 million worth of Class A voting shares. But, he also knew Rogers didn't have the money to exercise the option before its expiry date. Gray proposed extending the expiry date if Rogers agreed to give the company the opportunity of acquiring any cellular licenses awarded by the DOC from him at cost. Rogers readily agreed. "By sheer coincidence, Ted had these stock options expiring that he wasn't ready to exercise," says Gray. "The idea just flashed into my mind as we were about to see the thing fly out the window."

The first time Marc Belzberg met Rogers was at his Frybrook home. He was walking into the dining room just as all of Rogers' top lenders, in their drab business attire, were filing out, each one sullen and somber-faced. Rogers greeted Belzberg warmly. The two men sat down to talk cellular.

"A license, Marc," Belzberg recalls Rogers telling him, "is always a wonderful thing to have! You own a certain amount of something for a period of time, and you own a monopoly on a line of business, in this case, a piece of spectrum for a period of time.'

"I was amazed at this guy," says Belzberg. "I was really amazed. Here's a man down on his luck, doesn't have a penny to his name, almost bankrupt, and he called and said he'd put up more money on the spot. This guy is under extreme financial pressure, and here he is thinking about the future, taking money out of his own pocket and throwing it into a whole risky venture that I had to go and pitch my family on. One of the ways I explained it to my family is, I said, 'Ted understands this. Ted's willing to just …' (he snaps together his middle finger and thumb) 'chuck money two seconds flat into this. It's got to be something good. You imagine the pressure he's under, and he's going for this!'"

Two days before the February 28th deadline, Rogers signed a memorandum of understanding with Belzberg and de Gaspé Beaubien, sealing their partnership. "You know this deal that Dalfen's putting together," Rogers told Buchan. "We've got a Jewish guy from Vancouver. We've got a French Canadian, and we've got a WASP from Toronto."

"All you need is [the Yukon's] Rolf Hougen," jested Buchan.

"Sounds too Liberal to me!" Rogers sprightly rejoined.

On February 28, 1983, the DOC received more than 50 applications, mostly from mom-and-pop radio common carriers—local businessmen with paging companies. Unlike as in the United States, where the non-wirelines tried to outsmart one another by applying for the least attractive markets to ensure a "win," the Canadians went after the two most attractive markets: Toronto and Montreal. "Nobody wanted to go to Charlottetown," recalls Vincent Hill, the DOC policy director, who chaired the department's cellular licensing committee. The DOC winnowed the list to seven contenders: Cellular Canada Communications; Cantel; CelTel; CNCP; Honeycomb; Roam; and Time Cellular. Only two of the seven—CNCP and Inter-City's Roam—submitted applications for all 23 cities. As for the wirelines, the department received nine applications, including a bid from city-owned Edmonton Telephones, which applied to compete against the provincial government's AGT.

While Canada may not have bungled its cellular giveaway as the United States did, its process engendered no less controversy. There were no public hearings or public interveners. After canvassing the applicants for their opinions, the DOC chose to hold private half-day meetings with each applicant, much like judicial in-camera sessions. Watching the debacle unfolding in the United States, the applicants welcomed a process that promised to expedite the awarding of licenses. If left in the CRTC's hands, they feared a protracted public debate. They also reckoned they'd have a better chance of influencing the outcome. The CRTC had been effectively shut out of the process when the federal government decided to exercise the ministerial licensing power—as permitted under the Radio Act—to award licenses. Since 1968, when it replaced the BBG, the CRTC had been defiantly usurping the government's policymaking role by updating and reinterpreting the *Railway Act* of 1906, which served as Canada's only guide to telecom policy for 87 years until the 1993 *Telecommunications Act*. With the arrival of cellular radiotelephone communications, Ottawa seized the opportunity to wrest control over telecom policy away from the CRTC.

The fate of Canada's cellular industry lay with the eight bureaucrats who comprised the department's licensing committee. They would give a shortlist of potential winners to the Minister of Communications, Francis Fox, who would recommend to Cabinet a victor for each of the 23 markets. According to Hill, the committee set firm ground rules to immunize itself from the onslaught of lobbying that ultimately occurred at the Cabinet level. None of the applicants were made privy to the details of the other submissions. The committee also didn't allow the applicants to submit comparative analyses in their presentations. Each meeting was held in-camera. Each application was to be kept secret. Fox was kept fully informed throughout.

Midway through, the federal government changed the process, deciding that it was going to award a national license to one non-wireline "made in Canada" applicant—raising suspicions that it revised its policy to favor certain applicants. Indeed, the lack of a transparent process coupled with the fierce political lobbying that occurred contributed to the lingering belief that the eventual victor didn't win on the merits of its application, but rather on politics.

The applicants met separately with the DOC's licensing committee in three-hour, closed-door meetings at the old Grand Truck Railway station (now the Government Conference Centre) across from the Chateau Laurier Hotel. Everyone was crammed into a small upstairs conference room with the windows thrown wide open to alleviate a mid-July heat wave. The building didn't have central air-conditioning. Precisely at ten in the morning, the presenting applicant was drowned out by the horns and drums of the marching band heading towards Parliament Hill for the Changing of the Guard ceremony. A moment of levity rapidly dissolved into fury as the applicant complained that the disturbance cut into their presentation time. "All hell broke loose," recalls Hill. "I said, 'Don't worry. We'll take that into account.'" All of the other applicants consequently were forced to take a 10-minute break while the sentries in their scarlet tunics and bearskin hats marched past.

Unlike the other presentations—all the standard corporate fare—the Cantel team milked the partners' deep familial roots in Canada. At their presentation, masterfully led by Charles Dalfen, Cantel's owners took turns waxing eloquently and passionately about their storied forebears. Belzberg spoke of his grandfather, a poor Polish fishmonger, who immigrated to Canada in 1919 and worked on a farm outside of Calgary before moving into the city where he carved out a living for his family by opening a secondhand furniture business that became Cristy's Arcade. Rogers could go back as far as the nineteenth century to his Quaker roots in Canada. De Gaspé Beaubien was next up: A descendent of French fur traders and merchants, he could claim the oldest lineage of anyone present in the room. His forebears, who traveled with French explorers Médard Chouart des Groseillers and Pierre-Esprit Radisson, were among the founding fathers of the city of Chicago. When they finished, DOC panel member Richard Stursberg stood and bowed, quipping that he was regretfully only a second-generation Canadian. "It was a slick presentation," says Hill, adding that the panel wasn't mesmerized by what he describes as their "razzle-dazzle." "It wasn't their personal appearances that sold the decision. It was the application, the paperwork itself."

The DOC's criteria for selecting winners changed substantially after the private meetings. The government wanted to avoid the potencial embarrassment of one of the regional winners going bankrupt. And because both CNCP and Roam—the only two of the seven applicants to vie for all 23 markets—actively promoted the idea of a national cellular network, the small paging companies, which lacked the financial wherewithal to build a national network, lobbied vigorously to ensure that the government mandated their inclusion in a national consortium.

On August 18, a month after the presentations, Fox called for a national carrier, one with a decidedly Canadian bent. The new deadline for re-submissions was October 14. The applicants were told to: 1) make room in their consortiums for equity participation from radio common carriers; 2) ensure they fostered and promoted Canadian technology and research; and 3) prove they had begun negotiating interconnection agreements with the telephone companies.

The applicants immediately began to court CelTel and Time Cellular. Fierheller negotiated a deal to bring Time Cellular into Cantel's tent. Michael Kedar, a Swiss-trained engineer, Paul Lloyd, a Hamilton, Ontario-based entrepreneur, who had taken over his mom's answering service business, and Harley J. Murphy, a Wood Gundy corporate finance banker, co-founded CelTel with $100,000 from roughly a dozen investors. Abitibi-Price dangled a 10-percent stake to CelTel to persuade them to join its consortium, while Cantel tabled the worst offer, 4 percent. Surprisingly, CelTel chose Cantel. "We heard through the grapevine that four percent was better than nothing," recalls a CelTel investor.

Indeed, Philippe de Gaspé Beaubien, a strong supporter of Canadian federalism in the face of Quebec's separatist movement and the Expo '67 mayor who made Canada sparkle on the world stage, had been working hard behind the scenes to lobby federal politicians. His friends in the highest reaches of governing federal Liberal party would not forget his efforts.

Cantel reconfigured its ownership structure for local RCCs, allotting up to 20 percent, with CelTel and Time Cellular, owning 4 percent and 2.5 percent, respectively. Ted Rogers' stake was now reduced to 20 percent from 25 percent. The two original partners—Belzberg and de Gaspé Beaubien—split the remaining 60 percent equally.

Until now, foreign investment in telecom had been a non-issue. Indeed, an American company, GTE, controlled the provincial wirelines in British Columbia and Quebec. But, this new emphasis on being "Canadian" underscored the political fragility of Trudeau's government. Led by Trudeau, the Liberals were perceived as the party of national unity. Just a year earlier, in April 1982, Trudeau had "patriated" the Canadian constitution from Britain and enacted the Charter of Rights and Freedoms—in an attempt to unite a country deeply fractured by Quebec's separatist movement. In his almost unbroken 16 years as prime minister, Trudeau moved towards a command economy to reduce the country's dependence on the United States, most notably with his much-despised National Energy Program. Facing a backlash from voters, a continentalist faction began emerging within his caucus. Cantel's emphasis on being an "all-Canadian" application would hold great appeal among the nationalist faction, providing just the right optics at a time when the Liberals wanted to show a nation united, not divided.

Of the applicants, CNCP-Motorola was considered the most formidable candidate. Because of its established national microwave network, CNCP already had the necessary support staff and resources for billing, diagnostics, engineering and customer service to compete with the wireline companies. It also had the necessary interconnection agreements with Bell Canada and BC Tel. Failing to note the political climate, CNCP continued to boast of its supplier affiliation with Motorola.

Under intense petitioning from the applicants, Fox gave them one more opportunity to make their pitch before the committee. Each applicant trekked to the DOC's Slater Street offices in November. Cantel pulled out all stops, lining up the "Father of Cellphones," former Motorola executive Martin Cooper, to speak on its behalf, even though his former employer, one of the world's leaders in cellular technology, had aligned itself with CNCP. "We brought in everybody we could think of," says George Fierheller, whom Rogers lent to the Cantel project team late in the process.

Cantel, perceived by its rivals as the dark horse, met all of Ottawa's new suitability tests. Wrapping itself in the flag, Cantel assured the bureaucrats and politicians alike that it would use Canadian expertise to build a cellular phone network, a promise it would later by necessity break. Cantel also pledged to locate its head office in Fox's home province of Quebec, although not in his political riding. Just like the Royal Bank of Canada and the Bank of Montreal, Cantel officially would be headquartered in Montreal, but its executive suites would be based in Toronto.

The licensing committee's choice was kept a closely guarded secret before the Cabinet meeting. Francis Fox, his deputy minister Robert Rabinovitch and Vincent Hill went into the meeting with a gigantic six-foot-high chart of poster board sheets taped together. The applicant names were down the left-hand side and the criteria headings were along the top. The rest of it was deliberately blank to ensure absolute secrecy. "We didn't want to print it up ahead of time," says Hill. "That's how secret it was."

Fox made the presentation to Cabinet, Rabinovitch handled the chart, and Hill stood by to answer any technical questions. Hill passed around an exact replica of the Brick that Motorola had given him to show the politicians. To his irritation, someone broke off its antenna. Fox "checked off" the boxes beside the applicants' names according to their fit with the chosen criteria. Applicants with foreign affiliations weren't checked off in the "Made in Canada" box. Cantel met every single criterion. The fact that Cantel was astute enough to have cross-country ownership simply defused the political outcry that might otherwise have erupted inside the Cabinet room. Toronto-area Liberal MPs, who didn't like Rogers, griped about the $540,000 fundraiser he recently hosted at the Toronto Harbour Castle Hilton for Brian Mulroney's Progressive Conservative Party, a dinner-and-dance event aired live on Cable 10, Rogers' community cable channel. Others pushed hard for their respective friends. The then-minister of transport Lloyd Axworthy strongly advocated Roam because Inter-City was headquartered in Winnipeg, the riding he represented. While Cantel from all accounts undoubtedly tabled the best application, the overlay of Quebec politics helped to shape the outcome.

On December 14, 1983, Fox announced the winner: Cantel. The awarding of a national license for cellular radiotelephony service was "the electronic equivalent of the federal giveaway that accompanied the building of the CPR," Peter C. Newman wrote in *Maclean's* magazine later that month. Cantel's rivals were stunned. CNCP was floored. How could it have lost? "CNCP were an embarrassment to us for many years. Many times, I told them to go away and play with their trains," says Hill. "Telecommunications wasn't a big deal with the railway guys."

Cantel didn't walk away from the beauty contest scot-free. The company paid—and continues to pay—annual license fees based on complicated formulas, which have changed over time. Likewise, the regional wireline carriers were also required to pay annual fees. From Cantel alone, as of mid-2007, Ottawa has earned $500 million on that original spectrum. In its application, Cantel also offered to invest 2 percent of its annual revenues a year into research and development, which Ottawa later made a condition of its license. The wirelines were not required to make a similar R&D investment until 1991, when their licenses came up for renewal.

Fox phoned Fierheller to give him the good news. The next call Fierheller received was from Philippe de Gaspé Beaubien. "George, what the hell are we going to do now?" asked de Gaspé Beaubien. "Now, we've got to build a telephone company."

"That's not my problem," laughed Fierheller. "You only asked me to get the licenses."

CHAPTER 13

Twelve Months to Launch

"It was like catching lightning in a bottle."

—Tim McChesney

CANTEL, THOUGH, DID QUICKLY BECOME George Fierheller's problem. After some cajoling, Fierheller agreed to help the owners organize Cantel until they hired a president. Or so he thought. Instead of his planned semi-retirement in Vancouver, Fierheller wound up relocating to Toronto where he would spend the next decade alternatively as the company's chairman or its chief executive.

Originally, the owners each intended to put up cell sites and manage Cantel within their respective territories. Rogers would be responsible for Toronto; de Gaspé Beaubien, Quebec; and Belzberg, western Canada. They planned to expand slowly, doing just enough to keep the licenses. "They didn't have any idea of the magnitude of what they won," recalls Fierheller.

Cantel rung in the year of 1984 with just one asset: its national license. No offices. No infrastructure. No management. No engineers to select the cell sites. No supplier contracts. No financing. For weeks, Fierheller carried around everything that pertained to the company in his tattered black legal case, working away at whatever desk at the Rogers' offices happened to be vacant that week because someone was on the road in the States. Each night, he took Cantel home with him, usually to the King Edward Hotel, where he lived out of a suitcase until more permanent digs could be found.

The contrast with Ma Bell could be no starker. The previous year, A. Jean de Grandpré gave Bell Canada a corporate facelift. He reorganized the company's sprawling interests, which spanned the globe, into Bell Canada Enterprises Inc. (BCE) to pursue profits in non-regulated fields without the CRTC's continual interference. Fêted on Wall Street as the "Belle of Bay Street," BCE was Canada's biggest, wealthiest and most powerful company. The new multinational conglomerate was on track to becoming the first Canadian company to report $1 billion in annual profit. Bell Canada, with its landline monopoly, had been reduced to a mere subsidiary of its omnipresent parent. The telephone company, holding the cellular licenses for Ontario and Quebec, intended to introduce cellular service in September. Since it didn't have to compete for its licenses, Bell Canada was ready to go. It had already installed a $5-million cellular switch and other technical equipment in Toronto.

One of Fierheller's first priorities was to persuade the DOC to set a specific date so that all of the licensed carriers came out of the starting blocks at the same time. Fox agreed. On March 14, 1984, Fox announced that Bell Canada must delay the start of its service until Cantel was ready, throwing a wrench into its plans. He set the starting date as July 1, 1985. Annoyed at the delay, Bell Canada was particularly irate with Fox when he attached a new condition to its license: Fox informed Bell Canada president Raymond Cyr in writing that BCE must create a separate subsidiary that could not rely on its parent's resources.

In this way, Fox was ensuring both Cantel and Bell were on equal footing when they introduced their service. The new entity would have to build its own marketing, accounting and engineering departments. "If [Bell] had been given a head start, Cantel would never have gotten off the ground," says Vincent Hill, the former director-general of the DOC's national telecommunications branch. "Well, they might have gotten off the ground with somebody like Ted Rogers running it, but they would have been under a fantastic disadvantage. That was so obvious to us. I had people bleeding all over my floor about what we were doing to them with that head start policy, but it was just not negotiable."

Bell considered the decision unfair. It was just one of the many rulings, notably the 1982 interconnection decision permitting non-Bell Canada equipment to be hooked up to Bell's telephone lines, aimed at chipping away its monopoly piecemeal. "It was just one more thing," says Raymond Cyr. "It was an annoyance more than anything else because we still operated the telephone company. It's not like we were going to die. The government would never do anything that would have killed Bell. We were the largest single taxpayer in Canada and remained so for many years. So, they would never kill that, but we felt we were being had."

"That was my first sort of real experience of the power of Ted Rogers in Ottawa," Cyr says. "We were a monopoly, so obviously we never got much of an ear in Ottawa. Ted was a newcomer in these fields and that was always better both in media and in government. The incumbent is never in grace."

Fox also fired off a warning to the other provincial phone companies. He told them that even though the official start date was July 1, 1985, they were not allowed to use their frequencies until six months after their regulator, the CRTC, approved an interconnection agreement with Cantel. Ottawa would no longer tolerate their continued intransigence on negotiating with Cantel interconnection agreements, which were so critical to a working phone system. The province of Manitoba had, the previous summer, proclaimed a law preventing Cantel from interconnecting with the provincially owned Manitoba Telephone System, a move that would block Cantel from providing service in Winnipeg. "We had a hell of a time with Manitoba and Saskatchewan. They wanted to get going, and they would not let Cantel in," recalls Vincent Hill. "They just didn't want Cantel out there." (Three years after its launch, Cantel was offering service in every province except Saskatchewan, where SaskTel didn't introduce cellular service until 1989.)

The war was just getting started. Bell and the other provincial telephone companies wanted to treat Cantel as a customer rather than their equivalent, a distinction that would enable them to charge the upstart exorbitantly more when it connected to the public-switched telephone network. Bell also demanded $1.50 a month from Cantel for each telephone number assigned to a Cantel customer—extortion compared to the monthly 3 to 30 cents charged by U.S. wirelines. As well, Bell sought to charge Cantel for calls made by Cantel customers to Bell customers and vice versa. Cantel insisted each company bear its own costs up to the point of connection. The newcomer wanted cellular numbers to be allocated to it in blocks of 10,000 without charge and as needed through the central allocation body in Kansas City. Rogers and de Gaspé Beaubien were asked to complain behind-the-scenes to their political friends.

After negotiations fell apart, the companies asked the CRTC to settle the disputes. Although the regulator reaffirmed Cantel's status under federal law as a telephone company, the CRTC sided with the wirelines, ruling it wasn't in the public's best interests for monopoly telephone subscribers to assume the costs of cellular interconnection and ordered Cantel to pay Bell for telephone numbers assigned to its subscribers.

Cantel urged the CRTC to monitor closely BCE's relationship with its subsidiary, Bell Cellular. For its part, Bell felt that Cantel was employing a strategy of "fear, uncertainty and doubt" to influence the CRTC into forcing Bell Cellular to be as far removed from its monopolistic parent as possible. The company wasn't allowed to use its parent's name in its promotional and marketing materials. "We had to make sure that everything was on the up and up. They were constantly watching us to find any transgressions that they could take to the CRTC," says Robert Latham, Bell Cellular Inc.'s former president and chief executive officer.

Fierheller submitted a budget of $1.5 million to cover Cantel's start-up expenses. The owners reckoned the cost to build a national network over the next seven years might be in the vicinity of about $200 million. By 1990, when they could claim national coverage, Cantel spent more than $700 million, well in excess of what the owners had imagined.

Since none of the owners had that kind of money at their disposal, they sought bank financing. Canada's biggest banks—with the exception of BCE's banker, the Bank of Montreal—agreed to loan $60 million on the condition Cantel first raise $40 million from the sale of equity. Cantel hired two prominent investment dealers to get the job done: Austin Taylor's white-shoed McLeod Young Weir Ltd. (later acquired by the Bank of Nova Scotia) and the U.S.-owned heavyweight Merrill Lynch Canada Ltd. They proposed selling Cantel stock directly to institutional investors, half in the United States and half in Canada. They figured it would be a slam dunk. But the two biggest names on Bay St. couldn't find a single investor between them in Canada to invest in a new company in a new industry with no proven market. Rival applicants, sore at having lost the beauty contest, declined their overtures. Public pension funds, such as the Ontario Teachers' Pension Plan, among Canada's biggest reservoirs of investment capital, weren't allowed back then to invest in anything other than safe, secure government bonds.

From the get-go, Marc Belzberg immediately sought financial backers. "I was a complete kid," says Belzberg. "I had never done this in my entire life. It was a brand-new industry, a lot of risk. So, we said, let's find a major partner to put in some money, and who believes in us. Merrill Lynch, on the spot, represented us, and said, we think you can raise $20 million on a $100-million valuation. So, the license became worth $100 million overnight."

Merrill took Belzberg to see Motorola and American Information Technologies Corp., one of the seven U.S. Baby Bells, better known as Ameritech. Through its subsidiary, Ameritech had inherited AT&T's pioneering cellular radiotelephone company. Motorola arrogantly sought a 20-percent equity stake in Cantel at no cost in exchange for providing 80 percent of the equipment financing, Belzberg recalls. "And, then we went to Ameritech, and they, on the spot, said we want this. We want more than you want to give us." Ameritech was willing to invest US$30 million for a 30-percent stake.

Belzberg was focused entirely on Cantel. He even bought himself Motorola's Brick, becoming the first person in Canada to own one. Even though Canada didn't have any cellular networks, Belzberg was able to use the Brick in Toronto because it connected to the system in Detroit. "I was at the Toronto airport on my Brick, roaming the Detroit system, and everybody walked over to me. I mean, everybody walked over and asked me, 'What is that?' and 'What are you doing?' It was a real conversation piece."

Cantel needed a CEO, and the founders' first choice was John McLennan. At 38, the Cape Bretoner spent eight years alongside co-founders Terry Matthews and Michael Cowpland building Mitel Corp. into Canada's high-tech darling. He left just before it ran into financial difficulties, and was enjoying life as a stay-at-home dad and part-time consultant. Although he declined their eventual job offer, McLennan offered his consulting services and became a director on Cantel's board. The next person on their shortlist was Walter F. Steel, 52, a Vancouver native, who spent most of his career in the U.S., including a decade at Chicago-based Bell & Howell Co., a movie-equipment maker renowned as a training ground for entrepreneurs, working with CEO Peter G. Peterson, who became U.S. President Richard Nixon's Commerce Secretary. In 1975, Steel and Eric Baker, the co-founder of Innocan Investments Ltd., acquired a struggling Montreal company called AES Data Inc. from its founder Stephen Dorsey, a MIT-trained engineer, who married a typewriter with a TV set to create the world's first general-purpose personal computer, years before Microsoft and Apple were created.By the time Innocan sold its AES shares in 1978 to Crown-owned CDC—where present-day Quebecor Media Inc. CEO Serge Gouin ran it into the ground—Steel had built it into a money-maker with $200 million in annual revenue.He retired at age 47 to enjoy a life of fly-fishing and big game hunting.

Telemedia's CEO John Van de Kamer knew Steel as a friend and called him at his home in Vermont to see if he would consider joining Cantel. Steel already knew de Gaspé Beaubien and was acquainted with Sam Belzberg, but he had never met Sam's son Marc, or Ted Rogers. He was asked to meet with each of them as soon as possible. First, he flew to an Arizona resort, where the Belzbergs had congregated with New York's Jewish elite for the Jewish holidays. "I knew from the day I met Marc, he really would have been happier in a kibbutz in Israel," says Steel. Instinctively, he also sensed that Marc had taken an instant dislike to him. It was also clear to him, as it would become to others, that Sam Belzberg was only ever interested in flipping the license, while his son wanted to build the business, although to his credit the family patriarch, even with his own doubts about the business' viability, was willing to stand behind his son.

His next meeting was with Ted Rogers in Toronto. Rogers, the minority partner, was clearly preoccupied with his cable woes. "It was almost as if he didn't care," Steel recalls. After meeting everyone, he had deep reservations about the commitment of the founders and their ability to work together. He met one more time with Sam and Marc Belzberg in New York. The conversation went something like this: "I've talked with all three of you. Here you are, a western Canadian Jewish New York greenmailer. Philippe is a Catholic French Canadian who became an agnostic and a Harvard Business School graduate, and here's the greatest WASP in the world, Ted Rogers. Sam, I don't think this is going to work."

"Of course, it's not," Sam said.

"That's not true. That's not true," retorted Marc. "No, we're going to work together. It's going to be wonderful."

For better or worse, Walter Steel took the job. He was intrigued enough by the challenge of building another bleeding-edge company. It would become the worst experience of his previously stellar career.

The co-founders desperately needed an engineering head when venture capitalist Stephen Kauser, a Telemedia director and an Innocan co-founder, mentioned to de Gaspé Beaubien in passing that his younger brother was an engineer who might be interested in a job. Nicolas (Nick) Kauser, an ex-Marconi Wireless engineer and McGill University graduate, left Montreal in late 1964 when he was 24 for a job in Caracas at Venezuela's National Telephone Co. He thought he'd go for a year or two and stayed for almost 20. He and his brother spent their formative years in Caracas. His family fled Hungary in 1944 for Austria just before the Soviet Army invaded. They lost their nationality when their parents refused to return to the Communist-occupied country. In a circuitous route, they immigrated to Venezuela, one of the few countries then accepting displaced persons without quota restrictions. At 13, Kauser went off to boarding school in the Barbados, where after receiving his Oxford and Cambridge school certificates, he followed his school chums to McGill and graduated with a degree in electrical engineering.

Kauser spent the first six years in Venezuela working for state-owned National Telephone Co. before starting his own business, designing, installing and servicing telecom equipment and networks. He and his family were planning to return to Canada after their eldest child graduated from high school in 1984, but they fast tracked their plans when the super-charged petrodollar-fueled Venezuelan economy of the late seventies began unraveling, collapsing to near depression levels. He had a standing job offer from Nortel anytime he wanted to return to Canada.

On a Thursday afternoon, with the movers in his Caracas home packing the family's belongings for an unknown destination in Canada, Nick Kauser received a telephone call from Cantel's headhunter, wondering if he could fly to Toronto to meet Ted Rogers for dinner on Monday. That evening, Kauser, Rogers, George Fierheller and his cable engineer Nick Hamilton-Piercy, who knew Kauser from Marconi, met at the King Edward Hotel for dinner. Over pre-dinner drinks, Kauser discussed his background. His peers already respected him, and he would go on to become a world-renowned expert in the wireless industry. Once seated for dinner, Ted Rogers raised his wine glass and looking at Nick Kauser, said: "Welcome to Cantel." As far as he was concerned, he had heard enough. George Fierheller explained the daunting challenge ahead of them. They had less than 12 months to build from scratch a workable cellular network. "Do you think you can do it?" Rogers demanded to know. Not missing a beat, Kauser responded: "Are you giving me a choice?"

Kauser would play an instrumental role in the building of Cantel in the eighties and again in the nineties. He wasn't expecting to be hired on the spot. The next day, he canceled his flight back to Caracas and went out to buy some clothes. He decided to stay the week, get the lay of the land, return home, get the family organized and come back. For the remainder of the week, he worked with Roger Keay, loaned by Rogers from the cable company, reviewing Cantel's situation with NovAtel. The company was designing what they promised would be a revolutionary system, based on multiple small switches, each controlling a limited number of cell sites. While theoretically the system could grow to any size by the aggregation of small systems, in reality it was only practical for low-capacity systems for rural areas needing wide area coverage, but it couldn't deliver the capacity that an urban system—with many small cells—required. Previously NovAtel had developed the Aurora-400 system, which operated at 420 MHz, using 86 cells but featuring no handoffs. The technology didn't allow handoffs between the large-size cells. Cantel needed to build what everybody else would be erecting, the standard of the day, an analogue AMPS system operating in the 800 MHz frequency band. NovAtel neither had the equipment, the resources, nor the expertise to build what he needed. Prior to Kauser's arrival, Roger Keay and the team prepared and sent out request for proposals to six suppliers. In order to meet the condition of Cantel's licence—remember their promises to be the all-Canadian solution—they chose six companies that were either domestic firms, or had enough of a Canadian presence to be considered Canadian. As a result, Sweden's L.M. Ericcson Telephone Co. was not even invited to participate.

The clear-cut winner was BCE-controlled Northern Telecom Ltd. (now Nortel Networks Corp.). The negotiations however dragged on over the summer, even though the contract was worth as much as $120 million to Nortel. It was customary to have three levels of access to the switching technology within telecom contracts: 1) the right to use, 2) the right to know, and 3) the right to modify the software. Kauser wanted the rights to know, so that they could judge the extent and reasonable cost if they wished to request a modification that could distinguish Cantel from its competitor.

Nortel had a few issues, which were worked through, but the company refused to include the right to know. The two parties, and their legal counsel, argued over this one point for weeks until Kauser, in frustration, demanded an explanation. Kauser had acted as a Nortel agent in Venezuela. He knew the company well, and had negotiated a countless number of telecom contracts, which included the right to know, on behalf of Nortel for customers in that country. Nortel had never before been so intractable. "Having lived overseas and having dealt for twenty years with every major international telecom equipment manufacturing company, I kind of said, 'This is nonsense,'" says Kauser. "Eventually, they came back and said, 'Not in Canada.' In those words." It became instantly clear that Bell had a preferred customer status.

On a warm spring day in 1984, Philippe de Gaspé Beaubien was making his way by water taxi to the Royal Canadian Yacht Club, a two-storey Southern-styled clubhouse on the Toronto Islands. He was joining his partners for a full day of back-to-back meetings with Cantel's new executive team. It was their first meeting together as an entire group. Their wives would join them later for dinner. He was impeccably dressed in a navy blue suit with a blue-and-white pinstriped shirt accented with a white collar, white cuffs and a pastel green tie. Outwardly, he was the suave French gentleman he is. The last to arrive, he made his apologies before they got started. The only sign something was amiss was his deepening frown. He was battling a migraine headache. It was a bad omen for how the rest of the day would unfold.

Marc Belzberg brought along Oliver Bush, his accounting minion. Ted Rogers came alone. George Fierheller was present. Walter Steel and his top five vice presidents—Joe Church (corporate development), Marc Ferland (eastern division), Paul Kavanagh (sales), Nick Kauser (engineering) and David Perks (finance)—were also in the room. The meeting started off cordially enough.

As president, Walter Steel led the proceedings. At-six foot three-inches, he was slightly taller than Rogers with a will to match. Unlike Rogers, Steel was an avid reader of management guru Peter Drucker's books, the most influential business consultant of the 20th century. Steel began explaining to the owners how he intended to organize the company, using the words "matrix management." Ted Rogers, who had been reading through the stack of faxes and reports he'd brought along with him, sprang to his feet, gesticulating. "This sounds like communism to me!" he proclaimed loudly.

"Matrix," said de Gaspé Beaubien, interrupting Rogers' tirade, "that sounds like motherhood to me!"

Steel glanced over at Marc Belzberg. He was sitting back in his chair, smirking. "I thought to myself, oh boy, we're in trouble here," Steel recalls. "My mandate is a high-tech start-up. We had to grow very, very fast. The technology was on the bleeding edge, and nobody knew if people, other than people who owned Cadillacs, would buy a phone. I thought this was the beginning of the end."

Paul Kavanagh was up next. He recalls presenting his idea of a cross-country network of authorized franchised dealers, to be known as Cantel Service Centres, to facilitate car phone sales, installation, activation and subscriber training. It was the fastest—and least costly—way of setting up a national distribution network. They needed to sign on subscribers before the July 1 start date, a task all the more difficult because they were also striving to educate the public about this new service. The owner-dealers would bear all of the up-front risk by buying the car phone units, and in turn, be richly compensated for each subscriber they signed up. For their efforts, they also would be rewarded through a bonus plan of Cantel shares that were to be vested over three years. The service centers would therefore fulfil the company's licensing commitments to support the small RCCs.

Rogers was deadset against the plan; he didn't want anyone sharing the company's revenue stream, Kavanagh recalls. According to the recollection of several people present, the ensuing debate over how best to organize and market the company degenerated into a yelling match between Steel, Rogers and Belzberg. With his head throbbing, de Gaspé Beaubien, who is known to seldom raise his voice in anger, also joined the fray. The group watched, aghast, as the owners flung wild accusations at each other and their managers.

The atmosphere turned so acrid that the five vice presidents were asked to leave the room. Shell-shocked, they walked around the island for two solid hours before a battle-wearied Fierheller was sent to find them. This was the first time the management team had met with the founders as a group. They had spent hours preparing and rehearsing their presentations. They didn't think Cantel would survive the day.

"Look," assured Fierheller, "it's not as bad as it looks. Things are calming down. It's alright. We'll start again after lunch."

Nick Kauser was the first to present after lunch. He started to explain their designs for the Toronto and Montreal cell sites and the type of equipment they would use. He was almost finished when Steel casually interjected that their supplier likely wouldn't be Northern Telecom, but rather Sweden's Ericsson. The owners erupted again. "We were nowhere near ready for me to expose this to the owners. I wanted to package it up and have some certainty, and he throws this bomb right in the middle of the room," recalls Kauser. "We were almost asked to leave again."

He quickly sought to make his voice heard above the roar. "Let me finish, let me finish," he recalls, saying. He managed to calm everyone down by stressing to the owners that he and Steel were only chatting with Ericsson—nothing had been finalized. There was no formal agreement. According to Steel's recollection, Kauser had triggered the outburst when he imparted the news that he estimated the cost of erecting a cellular phone network linking Toronto and Montreal to exceed $100 million. The owners just weren't prepared to spend that kind of the money. Either way, the damage had been done. Says Kauser, "We were admonished."

Steel, the Bell & Howell veteran, was a manager-operator accustomed to dealing with bleeding-edge companies, presenting before what seemed like the Canadian equivalent of Larry, Moe and Curly: Ted Rogers, an investor with no patience for his managers; Marc Belzberg, a trader with seemingly no empathy; and Philippe de Gaspé Beaubien, a pacifist with little capacity that day to focus. "It was a horror. It was an absolute horror," recalls Steel.

The meeting created deep fissures between the owners, and the owners and their managers. The owners disagreed from the get-go. They also sweated over the cost of the network build out. Who was going to foot the bill? Rogers and de Gaspé Beaubien didn't have the cash resources available at their disposal. Could Marc Belzberg pry more money out of his father?

Indeed, the first cash call blindsided minority investor CelTel. Cantel sent CelTel a cash call demand of US$5 million, the amount proportional to its 4-percent ownership. That's when CelTel's Harley Murphy and Mike Kedar called RCI's Graham Savage. Over lunch, Savage proposed RCI acquire CelTel's stake in Cantel for 100,000 RCI class B shares, then trading at $22 a share, on the condition that the decision to sell was unanimous among its 15 investors. Faced with a hefty cash call, the CelTel investors readily accepted the offer. Many of the investors, mostly Hamilton, Ontario businessmen, had contributed either

$2,000 or $4,000 to fund the original $100,000 application. CelTel sold its 4-percent stake for $2.2 million in RCI stock. Most of them did extremely well by holding RCI shares. Murphy and Kedar immediately sold their RCI stock, using the proceeds to co-found Call-Net Telecommunications Ltd., an alternative long-distance carrier, with a passive investor, Dundas, Ontario-based furniture manufacturer Robert Crockford.

Rogers lost the skirmish over the Cantel Service Centres, but five years later, he had Jim Sward, who had moved into the Cantel hot seat from the radio division, begin dismantling the network of owner-dealers, which was responsible for fueling the company's growth. Rogers "never bought into it," says Kavanagh. "He did not like the concept of not owning anything." He couldn't buy the owner-dealers out fast enough, since by then cellular values were skyrocketing. According to the owner-dealers, the company even disguised its overtures through third parties in fear of driving the price higher if they knew he was the buyer.

Ironically, Rogers was rushing to buy the shares out of the very hands that were helping him become successful. They might not have liked the way it was handled, but he had his reasons. The independent dealers who didn't sell were eventually squeezed out. "No one should ever try to take anything away from Ted," Cantel Service Centre owner Tom Ungar told *Canadian Business* in 1994. "He's a visionary, a bright guy, and he works enough for three people. But once he took over, it was clear that things had to be done his way."

Ted Rogers may have been the minority partner but he sure didn't act like it. "Ted would from time to time write me letters," recalls Steel. "I get a letter. I read the letter, and hey, I'm not stupid. I can read. I didn't know what he was saying. He would go on and on. He had obviously whipped off this memo. So, I would ask George, 'What does this say? What does he mean? What's he trying to say? Tell me.' George would never answer. He would never speak for Ted. None of Ted's people ever spoke for Ted. I said, 'George, let's have a meeting with Ted and ask about this; I need to understand what he's saying.' So, he would arrange a meeting with Ted in his office. Ted would ask me to do things, and I would say, 'Well Ted, we have to get the board's approval for that. We have to get the approval of the other two partners.' That ended the meeting. And, George said I was stupid as hell to talk to Ted like that. George rarely ever gets mad. I'll never forget it. In one meeting I had with George, he stood up and shouted, 'Walt, you don't understand!'"

Rogers walks into most meetings with a pile of faxes, reports and all sorts of documents. "I was really focused on what was going on, and Ted had a stack of papers a foot high, and he's signing, he's reading, and he's paper clipping and he's underlining," says Marc Belzberg. "There was never a meeting where Ted didn't walk in like this and wasn't doing fifty things at the same time. I admired that. This guy is multitasking. He's running a cable business. He's running an empire. He's a very busy guy. You had to be on your toes all the time. You never knew why he was saying what he was saying. What was he pushing? You could see [the wheels] were turning. So, you were always concerned. He was confrontational, but the main issue was, where's he going? What's the real endgame here? What's he trying to push towards?"

Cantel still had no financing in place. The company blazed through $5 million, of which the founders contributed $3 million pro rata based on their ownership. The remainder came from Canada's banks without the usual paperwork. Cantel, as a corporate entity, had not yet negotiated formal lines of credit, Steel recalls. Whenever it needed cash, Cantel just asked the founders for more money. It helped that Cantel co-founder Philippe de Gaspé Beaubien also happened to be a director of TD Bank.

The underwriters couldn't seem to whet people's appetite for cellular telephony. No one believed the business was viable. Who was going to pay on a per-minute basis for the privilege of talking on a phone when local landline calling was free? Who would spend a couple thousand dollars on a cellular phone and then pay 60 cents a minute to talk? If the market was limited to just CEOs and diplomats, cellular was bust. Skeptics abounded. Kenneth Cox, the chairman of New Brunswick Telephone Co., jokingly predicted that cellular wouldn't have a place "until a phone is literally small and cheap enough to be surgically implanted in someone's head."

At one investor sales pitch at McLeod Young Weir's downtown Toronto headquarters, Paul Kavanagh recalls how one analyst, whose name he can't remember, made mincemeat of him before a roomful of potential investors. "I was to present the pro forma subscriber projections, basically the business case," he says. "I kept whittling down my projections, because they said they were too aggressive, to the point where we almost couldn't have a business. I remember saying, 'We will have 100,000 subscribers within five years,' and there was an analyst sitting halfway down [the] table, who was as anal as can be, and he totally pricked my balloon when he said, 'I have never heard such a load of shit in my life.' And, that was the end of it. That's what ruined that investment."

Cantel was enthusiastically optimistic in its forecasts: it predicted 60,000 subscribers within the first two years following the July 1, 1985 launch and 110,000 within five. Bell was much more conservative, guesstimating a mere

10,000 customers by 1987 and 40,000 by 1990. (Both companies were far off the mark. No one anticipated the industry's meteoric growth once mobile phone prices plummeted. By the end of 1990, Cantel had 265,700 subscribers—more than double its forecast, and Bell had 209,000 subscribers.)

Cantel was strapped for cash and pressed for time. It needed to start building a network. It needed to finalize the contract with Ericsson. It needed a sugar daddy to pay for the supplier's contract. Steel decided to take charge. He and Nick Kauser put out a few feelers with their contacts at Ameritech, unaware that Belzberg had initiated talks with the U.S. giant. They sought Ameritech as much for its money as for its expertise in building out a cellular network.

Steel flew to Chicago to meet with Ameritech's chairman and chief executive officer, William L. Weiss, and its chief operating officer, James J. Howard. As part of the AT&T break up, the Baby Bells weren't allowed to do their own research and development. That remained the domain of AT&T. To whet Ameritech's interest, Steel stressed that Canada didn't have such R&D restrictions. Ameritech could work with Cantel and Ericsson in Canada to develop new cellphone applications, such as voice mail, call waiting and call forwarding, now considered basic features but which at the time didn't exist. It quickly became evident to Steel that Ameritech knew as much (or less) about cellular phone technology as they did. By the end of their meeting, Steel knew he had a deal. They all shook hands on it.

No sooner had Steel reported back to the owners' surrogates about his trip than Ted Rogers went to Chicago. Steel was appalled at the interference, the undermining of his position. But then, Rogers had his own agenda. He didn't care about protocol. He was thinking ahead, and thinking about himself. He was cozying up to Ameritech, laying the seeds of a possible sale of his U.S. cable assets to the American giant. "Ted has got a nose for these deals like you can't believe," says Steel. "He did the same thing with Ericsson."

Talks moved into high gear. Rogers and Belzberg together flew to Chicago to meet with Ameritech Mobile's president, Dennis (Denny) F. Strigl, who had overseen Ameritech's move into cellular. Strigl was keyed up for the meeting. Ameritech was being given an opportunity to invest in, and maybe even eventually buy, a company that could run its wireless right across Canada. Ameritech would be making history if the decision were made to invest in Cantel, by becoming the first U.S. telephone company to make an international investment. The meeting lasted more than an hour with both men trying to persuade Strigl to buy a 19.9-percent stake in Cantel—the maximum allowed under Canada's foreign ownership laws. "I can tell you, when both guys left my office, I don't think I liked either one of them," remembers Strigl, now the president and CEO of Verizon Wireless, an industry behemoth with 62 million customers (more than Canada's entire population) and 2006 annual revenue of US$38 billion—virtually three times more revenue than Canada's largest wireless providers combined.

"After hearing the original business plan and meeting two seemingly very aggressive individuals, I thought I really don't want my company taken complete advantage [of] here. While I thought this was a tremendous opportunity, I really questioned whether I could get along with either of these individuals."

Strigl says Rogers ultimately persuaded him onboard. Rogers returned to Chicago alone for more face time with Strigl. They talked about how they would operate the business and the technologies they would use if they partnered. "I decided after [the meeting] that this is a guy I can get along with," says Strigl. "Of the three partners in the business, it was clear to me that Ted had a sound basis for how to run a wireless company. There weren't many people running wireless companies in those days, but his cable background lent itself very well to how to run a wireless business. I didn't know whether Marc or Philippe could operate a wireless or cable business, but I did know that Ted Rogers had a good vision of where he would take the business."

Steel and his executive team were taken off the deal. Belzberg's proxy, Oliver Bush, who wasn't even on the Cantel payroll, was put in charge of closing the transaction. When Steel demanded to know from the owners who intended to pay for Bush's services, he was appalled to be told in no uncertain terms that Cantel would bear the cost, not them. Steel interpreted the message: The managers were there solely to construct a network. The owners didn't trust one another, let alone the hired help, if it involved their equity ownership positions. In essence, they had stripped their executive team of its corporate duties. "This was like a spear in me," says Steel.

With less than nine months before the July 1, 1985 launch, Cantel still didn't have a supplier. Nor did it have any money. RCI had just announced a loss of $26.5 million for its fiscal year ended August 31. Rogers put the for-sale sign up on his showcase cable system in Syracuse, New York and the southern Californian franchises. De Gaspé Beaubien, who was investing in Cantel personally, not through his public company, was considering going after a license to operate a second private French-language TV network in Quebec. The Belzbergs, among the year's leading deal-makers in the same league as British industrialist Sir James Goldsmith, the Texan clan Bass Brothers and financier Carl Ichan, were spending tens of millions of dollars amassing shares in potential takeover targets, including apparel maker Blue Bell Inc., life insurer First Executive Corp. and household product maker Scovill Inc. Belzberg's First City had the cash, but the family still had its doubts about Cantel.

Nick Kauser was becoming increasingly concerned that if they used the same switching equipment as Bell, Cantel wouldn't be able to distinguish itself from the competition. And, as negotiations deteriorated with Northern Telecom, Kauser called a contact at Ericsson, who arranged for Steel to meet with the company while he was in Europe. They were lucky. Ericsson was game.

But, as Kauser had stressed to Ericsson, there was just one hurdle: Cantel needed Canadian content for their alliance to pass muster with Ottawa, otherwise they risked losing their license. Steel made two requests: one, Ericsson commit to a research lab in Canada; and two, Ericsson team with NovAtel. Ericsson would market NovAtel's mobile telephones abroad, and NovAtel would supply Ericsson switching equipment to Cantel. NovAtel didn't take too kindly to Cantel's plans, feeling betrayed, yet another example of Easterners breaking their promises. Neither Cantel nor Ericsson were confident that NovAtel could deliver the switches—the heartbeats of a cellular system. Nonetheless, the Swedish giant agreed that if NovAtel couldn't do the job, it was prepared to tell Ottawa that it would establish a manufacturing subsidiary in Canada to build all of its radio base station equipment for the North American market.

Cantel didn't firm up its deal with Ericsson until early 1985, more than a year after winning the coveted national license. Says Kauser, "There were times when the whole thing almost fell apart. We would go late into the night, and then we would go back to the King Edward Hotel and have a couple of drinks, and come back the next day and try again."

For their part, the owners were divided over the choice of supplier. In Kauser's recollection, Belzberg wanted to bring in Motorola, Rogers was adamant that they do a deal with Northern Telecom and de Gaspé Beaubien backed the hired help. "Once I did have a deal in principle from Ericsson, I did go back to the owners and explained it to them. I got support from Telemedia, and then I had a meeting with Ted. Ted looks at me, and says, 'Nick if something goes wrong with Nortel, I pick up the phone and I call [Nortel's CEO] Wally Light, and if I have something go wrong with Ericsson, I don't even know which direction Sweden is in.'"

Kauser recalls Rogers giving him a steely eyed, penetrating look. "But, I'll roll the dice and I'll back you," Rogers told him. "Ted would latch on to one particular thing and then explore it to the very end," says Kauser. "By doing that, he actually uncovered a lot of things that didn't have good explanations. It's like pulling a spaghetti on a spaghetti plate—the whole thing eventually moves and many unexplained items emerge."

Kauser didn't receive Belzberg's support. "Marc was always pushing for Motorola," says Kauser. "He fought me to the end. He felt we were going to get sued because we had this letter of intent with Nortel and because of the seeming likeness between the two contracts." As it turned out, Nortel didn't sue and Belzberg later conceded to Kauser he had erred in his judgment.

In September 1984, Brian Mulroney and his Progressive Conservative Party had just walloped the governing Liberals in the federal election in a massive landslide victory. Marcel Masse became minister of communications, replacing the outgoing administration's Francis Fox. Masse, a former high school teacher and cabinet minister in Quebec's provincial government, was an avowed Quebec nationalist. He would excel in his new portfolio, balancing the many interest groups attempting to curry favor with him to do what he felt was right for Canada.

Cantel needed to keep Ottawa apprised of its progress, or rather lack thereof. In October 1984, Walter Steel wrote Marcel Masse to inform and assure him that the proposed alliance between Cantel, NovAtel and Ericsson was beneficial to everyone involved, including Canada. Steel recollects there being enormous political pressure on them to go with Northern Telecom. The losing applicants were also making waves, hoping to persuade the minister, his aides and the bureaucrats to revoke Cantel's license. It was time to go to Ottawa. "Ted didn't want to go because he thought that was being pushy. Philippe didn't want to go because he was a Liberal and had done most of the government [lobbying] when it was Liberal. Marc had no stature," says Steel. After much debate, they convinced Sam Belzberg to go.

Steel and Belzberg promised Masse, among other things, that the head office would be an enlarged office in Montreal and a research and development facility would be located, once again, in Montreal—a bone to the Quebec minister. So far, so good.

The two men had one more request: to bring in Ameritech, an American company. Masse was concerned Ameritech might end up with control over Cantel. Worse, the optics didn't look good. The three Cantel owners appeared to be back-pedalling on their earlier promises of an all-Canadian solution. There had been two critical elements in the government's decision to award Cantel the license: first, the company was supposed to be owned by Canadians; and second, it was to build a network relying on a Canadian design. Cantel now was proposing to sell 30 percent of its equity to a foreigner, tapping into not only its capital, but also its expertise. If the founders didn't put up as much as Ameritech, if not more, it would seem as if the government had been duped into awarding, arguably, the country's most important national license to a group of seemingly Machiavellian entrepreneurs.

In the end, Masse signed off on Ameritech's investment, with some conditions. In typical Canadian fashion, Ottawa insisted that the Canadian owners match Ameritech's investment on a dollar-for-dollar basis. Masse set a maximum ownership limit of 20 percent, which was already applicable to broadcast and telecom industries, but also demanded the founders put hard cash into the deal.

Ameritech was allowed to invest $14.8 million only if the founders guaranteed that Cantel had a minimum of $25 million in Canadian equity. Once they met that threshold, Ameritech then could invest the remaining $6.2 million for a total equity investment of $21 million. (Ameritech sidestepped the problem by purchasing a $6-million debenture from Cantel.) The founders, who had already coughed up $9 million (on a pro rata basis) had to raise at least another $15 million from Canadian investors.

Masse then cut them a break—they had until December 31, 1985, or one year, to come up with the additional $15 million in Canadian equity. For its part, Ameritech cleared its own regulatory hurdles, receiving permission from the U.S. Department of Justice and AT&T antitrust judge Harold Greene to invest in, and market, cellular radiotelephone service outside of the United States.

On December 14, 1984, Ameritech acquired a 19.9-percent equity stake in Cantel, through a newly created subsidiary, Pan-Canadian Communications Inc. For one-fifth of a stake in Cantel, AT&T's baby ultimately provided 80 percent of the capital that got Cantel off the ground. Instead of breathing easier, the founders were still faced with rustling up money.

Denny Strigl's first board meeting in Montreal astonished the veteran Bell System man. "I remember sitting at the table with these three phenomenally successful Canadian businessmen thinking, 'What am I doing here?'" says Strigl. "I thought, 'I've just invested Ameritech's money in this business and the very first thing we do is we sit down to talk about hiring a new CEO.' It was a crazy set of circumstances."

Walter Steel's head was in their guillotine.

"I'd like you to come to my house after work," Steel recalls Ted Rogers asking him. It was Valentine's Day—February 14, 1985. Steel had never previously been invited over to Frybrook. He picked up Rogers at his office in his Jaguar. They chatted pleasantly during the short 15-minute drive to Rogers' home in Forest Hill from his downtown Toronto office in the Commercial Union Tower (now the Canadian Pacific Tower). Upon arriving, Rogers asked him to take a seat in the atrium just off the entrance hallway. Loretta Rogers walked past but she didn't stop and she wasn't introduced. Steel knew then something was wrong. Looking at Steel, Rogers then quietly said, "Well, I think you should quit."

Steel was taken aback. Rogers was the minority owner. He was treating Steel as if he was his employee. He didn't offer an explanation. He just expected him to fall in line with his wishes. Steel's temper flared. He demanded to know if the two majority owners also wanted him gone. Rogers skirted his questions. He refused to be drawn into a discussion.

"Are you going to quit?" Rogers bluntly asked.

"No, Ted. I'm not going to quit," Steel tersely replied. "I've got a contract, and you have to meet the terms of my contract."

"What?"

Steel was the only Cantel executive with an employment contract. The owners, consequently, sicced their pit bulls on him. Each founder brought in his own attorney, three against one. It turns out that the owners didn't want to honor his stock options. Steel wanted to sue them, but eventually was forced into settling. No law firm aspiring to service Canada's parochial and closeted business elite would dare take on three of the country's highly vaunted and connected business families. Why would they risk possible future business for a small fee today? Steel left behind options that, at the next valuation date, were worth as much as $17 million. In hindsight, he says he probably would never have been able to exercise the options anyway. He was more irked over how he had been treated. He never once received an explanation. "But, I knew," he says. "from Marc's point of view, he wanted John McLennan. From Ted's point of view, I was a thorn in his side, and Philippe went along with the other two."

His team at Cantel were shell-shocked. His firing went down in Cantel lore as the St. Valentine's Day massacre, reminiscent of infamous Al Capone-Bugs Moran Prohibition Era shootout in Chicago. He was a good leader. He was good at managing down, but unfortunately, not up. "Walter was an extremely clever marketer," says Nick Kauser. "It's a pity that his character was such that he would not take orders from the owners. Eventually, they got fed up with him."

A reluctant John McLennan replaced Steel as an interim president for a 12-month commitment, long enough to see Cantel through the July 1 launch. "The three original owners were very, very, very nervous because all the pundits in the telecom industry were saying cellular was not going to be very big. Don't forget, it was a big, clunky telephone and you had to almost rip your car apart to get it installed. There were no handsets. You didn't walk around with a little handset in your purse or back pocket. It was a big three-watt phone in your car. And, people would say, who the heck would pay $100 a month for that? So, there was a lot of nervousness about raising the money, even amongst the three owners in the early days," says McLennan.

At the end of McLennan's 12 months, from that point on he chose to contribute as a consultant, rather than an employee, a decision that turned out to have far-reaching implications on the battle for control. The owners turned to the avuncular and mild-mannered George Fierheller, whom they felt they could trust, even though he clearly was a Rogers man. McLennan later swapped titles with Fierheller to become chairman, a position he held for four years until 1989. He remained a consultant, deliberately choosing to stay just outside the sphere of Rogers' control. "He is one of the most gracious and warmest men I've ever worked with, and at the same time, he's also one of the toughest, one of the most impatient and sometimes, not always fair in his comments, although he never ever was that way to me," says McLennan.

In 1990, when he decided to accept BCE's offer to become chief executive officer of Cantel's hated rival, Bell Mobile Communications Inc., McLennan was petrified of telling Rogers that he was joining the "dark side." McLennan rang him in Nassau, where Rogers was meeting with his cable team. "Ted, I've decided I'm going to do something, and it's going to be announced tomorrow, and I want you to hear it from me and nobody else," McLennan recalls saying. "I'm going to join BCE Mobile."

He heard Rogers gasp. "What's your job?"

"I'm going to be president and CEO."

There was another audible gasp and, under his breath a baby swear. But, he recovered quickly. "Well, at least I'll have somebody on the other side that I can talk to." (They didn't really speak for the next couple of years, although at McLennan's invitation, Rogers attended the black-tie dinner BCE hosted to welcome McLennan to Bay Street.)

Fierheller held the operational helm until Rogers convinced his broadcast head Jim Sward to take over in 1989. "I remember thinking right from the beginning that this is some kind of a power play on the part of Ted here [when Fierheller came in]," says Strigl. "It was interesting to see these three guys interact. Marc Belzberg, of course, was very interested in the financial side, how do we make money quickly. Philippe, I think, was just interested in being part of it and representing Quebec, and Ted, being the operator in the bunch, in wanting to see that the whole business succeeded long term. He'd ask, what's the technology we're going to use; where are we going to build out; how do we strap this thing together so it's nationwide coverage. It was very interesting to see how three entrepreneurs could partner together, and at the same time, try to kill each other in these meetings. While the owners tended to slug it out with each other, it was remarkable to me how John and his management team were able to make the business viable and a tough competitor."

Rogers and Belzberg locked horns frequently, with the burden of conciliation falling to Graham Savage. There were innumerable board meetings that often dragged on for hours, with squabbles over money or management propositions. Initially, the partners totally underestimated the enormous amount of capital that would be needed to build a cellular network. The capital requirements wouldn't diminish, either. According to a 2006 report, Canada's wireless players together have spent almost $20 billion cumulatively in capital expenditures since 1985. And, the industry has yet to recoup its capital investment.

As well, the more estranged the partners became, the more reluctant they became to put up their pro rata share of the capital, especially after Ameritech's money ran out. "It was like a ship with three bows. You might be able to get some forward motion, but not a hell of a lot," says Fierheller. "The arguments that went on amongst the three shareholders were really horrendous. Board meetings went on for a couple of days trying to hash things out. I'd be there saying, 'We have the opportunity to go into Alberta, let's go for it.' They'd say, 'Well, whose going to put up the money? Who gives a damn about Alberta?' New Brunswick, Nova Scotia—forget it. I mean, there were constant arguments."

Paul Kavanagh continued to sign distributors across the country to market Cantel phones, including Charles Sirois, an ambitious 30-year-old paging supernova from Chicoutimi, Quebec, who became one of Canada's telecom gurus before burning out with the bursting of the technology stock bubble in 2000. Sirois owned the Cantel franchise for Quebec City, eventually selling it and merging his rapidly growing paging empire with the enemy, Bell Mobility, to create BCE Mobile Inc. Two months before the July 1 start date, Cantel had 15 Service Centres. Less than two years later, the company had 300 authorized agents at 37 Service Centres, of which 32 were independently owned and operated.

Belzberg helped develop the ads, promoting Cantel prior to the launch date: "Announcing the End of the Line for the Telephone ... Now the Phone Can Go Anywhere ... So get ready Canada, for a revolution in mobile communications. Get ready for Cantel." He still has that poster hanging on the bathroom wall in his Manhattan home.

David Parkes, who a decade later became Sprint Canada's CEO, came on board in October 1984 as Cantel's general manager of central Canada. He remembers how at the start all they had was a wooden phone and a theoretical explanation of how it worked. "I walked in the door one day thinking this is really going to be fun and within four hours, I was so busy that I didn't look up for a year," he says.

He was charged with building a team, a mandate that included hiring engineers to help Kauser build the cellular network within nine months. Cantel's office space in the Cadillac Fairview building beside the Eaton Centre was crammed with desks and employees, just like a trading room, with no private offices. This lack of privacy proved to be a problem when interviewing prospective hires. Parkes converted the walk-in closet into a makeshift interview room, with two chairs, a "wee" table and a lightbulb. "I'm one of the few people who worked out of a closet for about three or four months until we moved into the next space," he laughs. He changed offices 11 times in the 10 years he was with Cantel.

"I met quite a few talented people, who said, 'You guys got a really good plan but it can't be done in the time frame you're talking about doing it. You need another six months to a year to implement this.' I said, 'Gee, thanks. It's been nice talking to you.' I needed to find people that are crazy enough to think it can be done, and that's what we did. We had some very talented people who had that adventuresome spirit, that 'I can do it despite the odds.' That's who I went after."

Cantel's mantra was "ready, aim, fire." Bell initially was in "ready, aim, aim, aim mode," Parkes says. Cantel's culture resembled Rogers' early days in radio and cable. "We started out with a slightly irreverent approach to the market, everywhere from our advertising to our approach to pricing our products and services," says Parkes. "We were known as an organization that could figure what we wanted to do, go out quickly and get it done, and damn the torpedoes, and if we made a mistake, we'd circle back and fix it quickly rather than sit there analyzing until the cows came home and never do anything."

With the clock ticking, Cantel had to find the appropriate cell sites for its antennas to enable calls between Toronto and Montreal. Eight months from launching, Cantel still didn't have a site for its switch in Toronto, the all-important device connecting the cellular service to the public telephone network. Parkes suggested the CN Tower. He had contacts there from his previous job at food caterer Cara Operations Ltd., which ran the CN Tower's gift shop concessions. Cantel quickly signed a lease for space in the basement for its switch. It also leased space on the rooftops of buildings for its towers. Kauser says he never spent so much time as that year craning his head skyward.

Because Cantel didn't have the luxury of time to go through the municipal hoops of getting zoning approvals and building permits for cellular towers on open land, Kauser came up with a novel solution: Cantel would house the cell site equipment in standard metal sea-going containers. The containers made it possible to install and test the transmitting, receiving and signaling equipment without having to wait for the permits to available land sites to build the concrete blockhouses typically associated with base stations. The company ordered 18 of these sea-going containers built to their specifications at a cost of $17,750 apiece. It scoured the countryside between Toronto and Montreal, looking for the appropriate cell sites, bought parcels of farmland, dug the holes, and then dropped in the containers. Says Fierheller, "We just had to scramble in those days to get whatever we could get."

On July 1, 1985, during the Canada Day celebrations at Toronto's city hall, Toronto mayor Art Eggleton direct-dialled his Montreal counterpart, Jean Drapeau, on a Cantel cellphone. Drapeau took the call inside the Egyptian pavilion at the Expo '67 site. Making a big marketing splash, Cantel's name was draped from the top of Toronto's CN Tower. Much to Bell Cellular's astonishment, Cantel not only managed to get its Toronto-to-Montreal network operational in time for July 1, but the owner-dealers had actually been using the network since the last week of May.

Cantel trounced Bell. Cantel initially had more customers than Bell did in the Toronto market. Given its rival's financing and supplier issues, Bell adopted a lackadaisical and arrogant attitude towards Cantel, never truly believing that the upstart would survive, let alone amount to a serious contender. It also underestimated market demand so that within three months of the launch, Bell, which had boasted that it had been ready to go the year before, was already receiving complaints from customers about busy signals in heavy-traffic areas.

"We out-marketed them, but what thoroughly irritated Bell was that we out-engineered them," says Fierheller. "If anything irks Bell, it's being out-engineered. They might say somebody could out-market them maybe, but to out-engineer them, it's just unheard of, and they poured mega-bucks into [their network] after that, which just put more pressure on us."

"Ted would always ask, 'How do we beat Bell Canada?'" recalls Verizon's Denny Strigl. "That was always the main subject. 'How can we do better than the telephone company?'"

Bell fell so badly behind that in August 1986, BCE installed Robert Latham, a Bell Canada veteran, to reclaim lost ground. "One of the best things we did was to create a 'shadow marketing plan,'" recalls Latham, who in his five years at the helm built Bell Cellular into a tough, vibrant competitor. He hired outside consultants to pretend they were Cantel — to think, act and make decisions just as Cantel might, using available industry statistics and trends, known financial results and the company's previous sales and marketing strategies. They pored over Cantel's product and price offerings, looking for patterns. "We were very often able to anticipate, or be right with them, or be ahead of them on the stuff they were thinking about," says Latham. "They used to accuse us of having moles in their organization. We used to laugh about it, saying, 'Oh yeah. Yep. Yep.' We never had anybody in there."

Cantel and Bell Cellular raced to get their service up and going in cities and towns first. Take, for example, London, Ontario. This mid-size wealthy university city between Toronto and Detroit had an estimated initial market of 800 car phone sets. Both companies were spending in excess of $500,000 to establish their service. Both were planning to introduce their services on January 1, 1986. Bell broke ranks, changing its start date to December 1. Cantel then moved up its launch date to November 1. Bell countered, going live on October 1. Only it wasn't live. Bell faked the call because it wasn't able to get its system up and running for the new start date. The only reason the call appeared to work was because it had been wired into a landline.

Bell built a system running north from Montreal up into the Laurentian Mountains where BCE's chief Jean de Grandpré had a summer home; Cantel erected a network from Toronto alongside Highway 400 north into the Muskoka cottage country where Ted Rogers had his summer home. "The name of the game was 'Coverage, Coverage, Coverage.' How much red is on their map and how much blue is on our map," Latham says. "It was a continual competition."

In July 1987, two years after starting, and a year ahead of Bell, Cantel had completed its network, providing continuous cellular telephone service along the main highway corridor between Windsor and Quebec City, the world's longest cellular phone corridor, stretching 1,200 kilometers. Bell Cellular counterattacked by saying it preferred to wait until it could supply quality service before forging in.

It wasn't easy rolling service out across the country. In Vancouver, Cantel, burning through Ameritech's cash, was in talks with BC Tel to build a network together. "We were in no hurry to spend money that we didn't have," says Kauser. "So, eventually we found out that BC Tel were already testing their switch. They were stringing us along." Having been duped, Cantel raced against time from

November 1985 through January 1986 to build the Vancouver system. "It was one of those winters where it actually snowed in Vancouver," recalls Kauser. "Today, you could do it with one arm tied behind your back."

According to its license, Cantel had to build cellular networks in 23 cities. City number 23 on the list was Chicoutimi, 225 kilometers north of Quebec City on the Saguenay River, the home of Canada's future prime minister Jean Chrétien. "I will never forget that. Why would you go to Chicoutimi?" sighs Kauser. "How could we afford it? We were still trying to get the NovAtel equipment, and wondering if we could put a very small system in Chicoutimi to meet our license obligations. But, we ended up racing with Bell to see who could get there first. Instead of putting up one cell site, we put up seven! Those were the early days of competition."

Cantel and Bell attempted to outsmart each other with marketing schemes to win customers. In its sales campaigns, the upstart enlisted retail help from Imperial Oil Ltd., Canadian Tire Corp. and Budget Rent-a-Car. Esso gasoline stations gave away Cantel phones as prizes in contests; Canadian Tire stores sold and installed them; and Budget put them in their luxury Lincolns. Kavanagh created the *Cantel Club*, a precursor to the customer loyalty programs so prevalent today. Based on their usage of phone minutes, subscribers earned points that could be redeemed for merchandise, including Mitsubishi electronics, Wilson sports gear and Budget car rentals. Subscribers received a monthly catalogue, *Cantel Club*, which debuted in December 1985. It was short-lived. Rogers killed it. Loyalty programs, aside from Canadian Tire money, weren't accepted as effective customer retention tools in the mid-eighties. But Air Canada introduced its frequent flier program, Aeroplan, in 1984; Zellers introduced Club Z in 1987.

"I had a real battle with Ted over it," says Paul Kavanagh. "It was absolutely unbelievable how many people wanted to be in this catalogue, giving us free TV sets and free nights of hotels, golf clubs. It just went crazy. I had to hire more people. The moment I started to hire more people, that's when it became an issue, even though we didn't put up any money. We had people to administer it, and it became almost a joke that I've got this program where we are not generating any revenue. We are contributing to loyalty and, of course, only time would prove that that was the right thing to do. So, [Rogers] canceled it. I said, 'It's just a matter of time that Bell's going to wake up and we will start to lose subscribers. We have got to have some hooks in here.'"

Elsewhere, politics, not competition, played a role in how soon Canadians received cellular service. In New Brunswick, it took almost 18 months after the 1985 start date before cellular service was introduced. Frank McKenna, then the provincial premier, used the province's interconnection agreement as a bargaining chip with Cantel to attract jobs to his province, even though the delay meant that New Brunswick Tel couldn't provide cellular service either. By the end of the eighties, the wireless carriers blanketed 95 percent of the country's population. By 1991, with cell sites located less than one kilometer apart, Toronto would have the world's most concentrated urban cell network. It was an exhilarating time. "It was like catching lightning in a bottle," says Tim McChesney, the marketing head at Bell Cellular from 1986 until 1991.

CHAPTER 14

The Put

"How could we lose that battle?"

— Marc Belzberg

AS THE DECEMBER 31, 1985 deadline neared, the founders still hadn't met Ottawa's demand to match Ameritech's investment. Earlier in the year, they had retained yet another eminent investment banker, Wood Gundy Inc.—later dropped for Lawrence Bloomberg's more aggressive trading house, First Marathon Securities Inc.—to help McLeod Young Weir reel in potential equity investors. No one would bite. Their only prospect, and a lukewarm one at that, was a whisky maker.

Hiram Walker Resources Inc., the maker of Canadian Club Whisky, about as old as Canada itself, was controlled by the then-mighty Reichmann family's Olympia & York Developments Ltd. O&Y had that summer set the oil and gas industry buzzing with takeover speculation after revealing, as was considered at that time, a monster $3-billion acquisition of Chevron Corp.'s 60-percent stake in Gulf Canada Ltd. However, the Reichmanns felt Cantel's $7-a-share offering price was too rich, particularly since it didn't even buy them any influence on the board. They'd be passive investors holding a minority stake that they judged they wouldn't be able to unload all that easily.

Fierheller proposed that the founders invest the $15 million themselves on a pro rata basis, or agree to have a single dominant shareholder. Belzberg, facing doubts from his family, mainly cousin Brent, about the risk of putting up more money, lobbied for more time to find outside buyers. But Ted Rogers was fed up. After securing a loan from TD Bank, he offered to buy the entire $15-million private placement on December 11, 1985, 20 days before Ottawa's deadline. Rogers' offer set into motion a bitter contest for control of Cantel. As the deadline neared, Fierheller managed to get a two-month extension until February 28, 1986—buying everybody extra time.

Philippe de Gaspé Beaubien decided to make his own bid. He recalls working with Marc Belzberg at a New York hotel through the night to iron out an agreement whereby Belzberg would support him. On February 12, de Gaspé Beaubien made a $15.9-million counteroffer. Rogers paid TD Bank a visit. Then, four days before the February 28 deadline—and eight days after Rogers' CFO Bob Francis' sudden death—Rogers raised his offer to $21.1 million. He also offered to buy 400,000 class A shares from both Belzberg and de Gaspé Beaubien for $5.15 apiece, a $2.1-million cash inducement for each of them to concede.

To de Gaspé Beaubien's astonishment, Belzberg backed Rogers. He recalls feeling betrayed. He never understood Marc Belzberg. He says he could not comprehend how a man so committed to his faith could be so cold blooded in business, until one evening over dinner, de Gaspé Beaubien's wife, Nan-b, asked Marc about his religious and business philosophies. In de Gaspé Beaubien's recollection, Belzberg simply said, "Religion is religion. Business is business." A deeply spiritual man himself, de Gaspé Beaubien was simply not cut from the same cloth.

"I was young, arrogant. So, were there moments …" reflects Marc Belzberg. "I was strong-minded. I knew what I wanted, and I was not a pushover. On the other hand, I knew what I knew and what I didn't know. I think I was a reasonable, good partner, but was I cocky? I'm sure I was cocky. I'm more of a fighter."

Belzberg didn't like the situation any more than de Gaspé Beaubien did. He discussed it with his father. Ultimately, the whole family, as it typically did then, became involved in the decision-making process.

"Marc, you want to put up money to keep this thing?" his father baldly asked him.

"Yes."

"You want to go full time to run this yourself?"

"No."

"You've got a choice. If you love it so much, let's see if we can buy it. You stop doing this stock business in New York and move to Toronto."

"No. I want John McLennan to run the business."

"Alright, if John McLennan will run the business and you trust him to run the business, then that's fine with me, I'll put up the money. If John McLennan isn't going to run the business, and you do it, then I'll put up the money. But if you don't have anybody else to do it, then we should let somebody else put up the money," Sam Belzberg told him.

McLennan, though, didn't want the job, a decision that "was a very big disappointment to me because I really liked him a lot," says Marc Belzberg. "If he had said yes, I want to run the business, we would have put up all of the money. I said to myself, I've never run a business in my life. I don't know anything about engineering. I don't know anything about cellular. I don't know who to hire. I was twenty-something years old. I'd be managing a humongous business I know nothing about, and I was scared out of my pants. So, I said, no, there's no way I'm doing that. I'm not going to risk my family's money. I'm not going to risk my reputation. I'm not going to fail."

The Belzberg family, as a unit, decided to back Rogers, not de Gaspé Beaubien. The crux of their debate centered on Rogers' inimitable reputation as a gambler, able to build big but often at the risk of losing it all. "We basically said, on the one hand, with Ted, we're taking more of a risk. When you weigh the pros and cons, we can count on Ted more than we can on Philippe to actually get the job done. He's built out systems. He's got a reputation. He knows what the heck he's doing. Yes, he might blow it up at some point in the future because he'll over-leverage, but on the other hand, he's built big companies," says Marc Belzberg. "Philippe, on the other, he's a nice guy. He's a gentleman. He's never done this. So, Dad said, 'Okay, I want my money back. I want to own whatever I can own for close to nothing, and now, we're taking a ride. If Ted makes it work, he makes it work. We're betting on Ted to make it work and if not, we're out, and I want future liquidity.'"

First City not only recovered the money it put into Cantel, but because it actually sold stock to Rogers, it also made money. Belzberg sums up Rogers' victory: "If Ted wouldn't have been always jockeying to get control, we certainly would have gone along with our pro rata share, and so would have Philippe. Ted forced the thing into his hands by saying, 'I'm not going along with you guys. Either you put it all up, or I'll put it up.' And, he's smart enough to know that Philippe wouldn't have done it, and we could have done it, but he didn't know how much I wanted to do it. I would have loved to do it, but I didn't have the confidence to do it. So, he played all the cards right and won. If McLennan had said, 'I'm in,' we'd own the company. If I had said, 'I feel confident in myself as a manager to do this,' we'd have owned the company. Neither of those two things occurred, so we said, 'Okay, we'll own a small piece of the company and ride with it and see what occurs.'"

For his part, Ameritech's Strigl also backed Rogers. "Philippe was very angry with me over giving my vote to Ted," he remembers. "But, when push came to shove, and I was asked, 'Who can run this business?' I said, 'I think, it's Ted Rogers.' It was a very uncomfortable feeling because I had very high regard for Philippe. He was truly a gentleman and very successful in his own right."

"We were all prima donnas," reflects de Gaspé Beaubien, asked to recall events he says he'd rather forget. He says he's blocked out a lot of what transpired back then. "Ted is a good friend, but he is not a good partner. He's very forceful. He wants things his way. It was not an easy partnership for me. I'm not of that culture. It was a painful time for me. I was very upset. I felt they had let me down. I felt wounded, but then, who wouldn't? But, you go on with life."

He's not the only one who has tried to erase memories from that period of time. "It was two years of my life," reminisces First City's then-lawyer Morley Koffman, "but it's two years I'd like to forget. It was fun, but when entrepreneurs disagree about how to go forward, it gets a little ugly. One of them had to take over. Ted had bigger guts than the others."

"Philippe and ourselves never had any problems, and Ted had problems with both of us," recalls Samuel Belzberg. "In retrospect, Ted probably wanted to control it all from day one, and that was his game at all times. We didn't realize it at the time, and it wasn't as much [him] micromanaging, as it was keeping the partnership off balance."

The partnership proved difficult for everyone. As for Loretta Rogers, she barely tolerated the young Belzberg. She recalls her husband inviting him over for breakfast one day. "He had my staff in tears, he was so rude," she says. "He wanted cereal. We had ten or twelve types in the house. Each one was not one he wanted. We didn't have the milk he wanted. Oranges? No. There was nothing he ever liked.

"Once Ted forgot to tell me who we were having over for dinner, and we were actually having ham, and then he tells me! 'Oh shit,' I said to the help, 'go into the village and buy a steak, and while you're at it, buy a baked potato,' because we were having scalloped potatoes, and you can't put in milk or dairy. I think we were having milk in the dessert, so I said, 'Get some strawberries.' It was not an easy meal. Then, he arrives ten minutes after we should have sat down for dinner, of course, and I said, 'Would you like a drink?' No. 'Would you like a Coke or a ginger ale?' No. 'Would you like a glass of water?' No. I finally said, 'How do you like your steak cooked?' I don't want one. I thought, 'You're going to be dead meat yourself by the end of the meal.'

"He was not an easy person. His father was charming. He was a lovely guy. Marc was just different. I finally said to Ted, 'That's it, he's not coming here anymore.'"

Loretta may have misinterpreted Belzberg's personal adherence to a strict kosher diet. Belzberg, who remembers that evening, ate melon, the only kosher food Loretta could scrounge up. "The rules aren't easy. It was the first time Loretta experienced that, and she had a rough time with it."

By the end of May 1986, the battle was over. In a stunning role reversal, First City and Telemedia became minority partners, not only diluting their stakes, but also selling into Rogers' offer, each ending up with 12 percent of the equity and 6 percent of the votes. Ameritech's stake remained unchanged. Rogers then immediately sold the stock, including most of his own, to his public company at cost. RCI bought 38 percent of Cantel's fully diluted shares (66 percent of the votes) from the Rogers family for $34.6 million in cash and stock, or just over $6 for each potential subscriber, or "POP" in cellular parlance. (Later, RCI raised its stake to 40 percent when others failed to meet Cantel's capital calls.) "We gave it to them too cheap," grumbles Loretta Rogers. "We held it the first few years [because] they were nervous, and then they said, 'Well, we want it.' I felt like saying, 'Well, go stuff yourself.'" Her husband continued to own 12 percent of Cantel's equity personally through RTL, the family's private holding company. Rogers and Belzberg attended the signing of the new shareholders' agreement at the Tory law offices; de Gaspé Beaubien sent his emissary, Harold Nickerson.

In ceding control to Rogers, First City and Telemedia negotiated what they believed to be an ironclad exit strategy if they wanted to liquidate their Cantel shares. They decided the best way to liquidate their holdings was for RCI to take Cantel public, which would enable them to sell their shares on the secondary market. If RCI failed to take Cantel public, they had the right to get Cantel appraised and exchange their Cantel stock at the appraisal price for RCI's class B non-voting shares. In securities industry lingo, it's called a "put."

In their accord, known as the "share exchange agreement," dated May 29, 1986, the founding triumvirate and Ameritech, through its Canadian subsidiary, set December 1, 1988 as the "start date," the earliest date by which any of them, including RTL, could put their Cantel stock to RCI for its B shares. The put was exercisable until either its expiry on May 31, 1991, or the date on which Cantel became publicly traded, whichever came first. "It was the most complicated, trying agreement ever created by man or beast," says First City's Morley Koffman. "I always tell the story that if you want to see a shareholders' agreement that wouldn't work and was doomed to failure, you take a look at that one."

The terms of their pacts—the shareholders' agreement and the share exchange agreement—were never publicly disclosed because, as a privately held company, Cantel was not subject to the disclosure laws, such as they were, governing publicly traded companies. (Canada's disclosure laws for public companies were then woefully deficient and far less onerous than in the United States.) Sparse details emerged two years later in Cantel's preliminary prospectus, a document for prospective investors that's required by securities regulators to be filed whenever companies seek to raise money from the public. Even so, the dynamics of what transpired next were never fully revealed and illustrate the lengths to which Rogers sought to secure control of Cantel.

On September 15, 1987, almost a month before the Black Monday stock market crash, Rogers called Craig McCaw. Just like Rogers, McCaw was defying conventional wisdom by borrowing billions to build what would become the nation's largest cellular-phone company. At 38, he was quickly becoming a cellular kingpin. Just the previous year, he completed the acquisition of MCI's cellular and paging business for US$122 million. Relying on junk-bond financing from Drexel, McCaw had amassed a veritable gold mine of spectrum licenses, covering 35 million POPs in 94 markets, nearly twice as many POPs as the second-biggest non-wireline rival, LIN Broadcasting Corp., which had 18 million. In August, two months before the market's horrific crash, he took McCaw Cellular Communications Inc. public, raising more than US$280 million, considered one of Wall Street's hottest initial public offerings of the year and dwarfing the US$58.8 million that Microsoft had raised a year earlier.

"Should I buy these guys [Ameritech] out?" Rogers asked McCaw. He was trying to figure out what Ameritech's stake in Cantel was worth, recalls McCaw. "I thought they were a complete bargain," says the quiet-spoken Seattle-based billionaire. "But, Ted always checks all angles, and it was a big step for him. I think I told him it was a good deal."

With so much buzz about cellular offerings on Wall Street, the Cantel suits began preparing a prospectus for a public offering, although Rogers had other reasons, entirely unrelated to the then favorable market conditions, for getting the ball rolling. As it was, Rogers was also trying to dampen McCaw's interest in Cantel, attempting to limit the potential damage his two senior Cantel executives inflicted the night before when they suggested to McCaw that he buy Ameritech's stake in Cantel. Over dinner with McCaw in Toronto, George Fierheller and Nick Kauser had animatedly talked up Cantel, broaching the subject of McCaw replacing Ameritech. The next day, the two men, chuffed at having found the perfect partner, proudly recounted to Rogers their conversation. Rogers was aghast. He immediately called McCaw and told him to forget it. "He did not like it at all, because of course he had intentions of buying it himself," recalls Kauser.

"I may have been my own worst enemy," chuckles McCaw. "We'd have been thrilled to have a piece, but there was plenty for us to do."

The misstep of his executives, though, helped forge a closer relationship between Rogers and McCaw, who earlier had crossed paths in the cable business. Thereafter, Rogers, Fierheller and Kauser met as often as three times a year with McCaw and his right-hand man, Wayne Perry. In 1990, when Kauser resigned, he joined Craig McCaw—a demoralizing loss for Cantel and a personal blow to Rogers. Indeed, Rogers and his wireless CEO Jim Sward convinced McCaw, who felt guilty for stealing Kauser, to permit him to work at Cantel three to four days a month, an arrangement that continued until Sward left.

Rogers stayed in close contact with McCaw, getting together every six months or so. They shared the similar misfortune of their fathers dying suddenly and leaving their estates in shambles. McCaw's mother, a trained accountant, liquidated everything to stave off the creditors, except for a small cable TV system, which her husband fortunately had registered in their sons' names. Craig, the second oldest of the four McCaw boys, ran the cable company from his college dormitory at Stanford, building it into America's 20th largest before he jettisoned the cable TV assets to focus on cellular.

"We had lots of good times. We'd go down to Lyford Cay and chat about what to do. There was tremendous sharing back and forth about technology," says McCaw.

Out of one of their meetings came the idea to integrate their cellular networks. In 1990, Kirkland, Washington-based McCaw Cellular upgraded its switching system to provide seamless cross-border coverage with Rogers Cantel, eliminating roaming or access codes. (Cellular carriers typically charged exorbitant access fees and higher per-minute airtime rates to cross-border customers for the ability to use, or "roam" onto another cellular company's system.) "We created a wonderful roaming arrangement, something that has never really been duplicated to this day," says McCaw. "We allowed our customers to have truly seamless high-quality service, which I would say to this day Nextel and Mike don't have between them, for instance. The other operators never did quite the same thing, where the customer didn't just end up on the wrong system arbitrarily, or accidentally roaming—one minute he's on one system and the next minute, he's crossed the border but he hasn't moved. We were able to control the border area very well without interfering with each other. I'd have to say that it's almost unprecedented in the world. Today, I don't know many places where anybody's done anything that worked so well for the customer and yet, kept everything straight.

"Rogers was the only truly national Canadian operator. The phone companies were cobbled together, and while it worked, it was not as seamless as Rogers. He had a huge advantage. Canada had a national network way before the United

States. Most countries had that and the United States didn't, and we saw a kinship with the national Canadian network," says McCaw. "We found them to be kindred spirits."

The stock market crash on October 19, 1987 was thought at the time to signal the end of a five-year surging bull market. In its aftermath, investors shunned cellular stocks, fearing cost-conscious subscribers would drop their phone service in the expected recession—an economic downturn that didn't actually materialize for another three years.

Although the crash scuttled several U.S. plans for cellular stock offerings, Rogers fast-tracked plans for a Cantel public offering, totally baffling Bay Street analysts since the purpose of an initial public offering, known as an IPO, is to raise as much public money as possible. There really couldn't have been a worse time for an unproven cellular upstart to tap the public equity markets. Furthermore, Rogers certainly didn't need to raise equity, since his bankers were tripping over themselves to lend Cantel money. On the one hand, here he was repatriating foreign-owned RCI class B shares, largely under duress to stay onside of the broadcast rules, and on the other hand, he was preparing to issue stock in his wireless carrier. The irony was not lost in the media.

However, Rogers had his reasons. He really had no intention of taking Cantel public. Rather, he was setting into motion the mechanics to thwart his co-founders' ability to trigger the share exchange—that is, the "put"—in a year's time, when they'd have their first crack at exercising it. The earliest any of them, RTL included, could exchange their Cantel shares for RCI's class B non-voting stock was on December 1, 1988. It was anyone's guess what the exchange ratio might be in a year's time, because it all depended on Cantel's appraised worth and RCI's share price. But, with share prices currently reeling in the wake of the crash, and little expectation at the time of a speedy recovery, the put was looking extremely attractive to Rogers' co-founders. Why? RCI was trading at a hefty discount to its private market value, or breakup value—meaning its parts were worth more than the whole. If Cantel was ascribed the same value as its high-flying U.S. cousins, it would be, hands down, his most valuable asset. Under those circumstances, if the put was exercised, First City and Telemedia would not only dilute Rogers' stake in RCI, but they'd also own a good chunk of his coveted cable TV assets for virtually nothing. And, certainly, the last thing Rogers needed was a greenmailer as RCI's major shareholder, irrespective of the share class. Says Sam Belzberg, "If he had issued stock in the parent to us, he probably would have lost control of the company."

The put had two expiration dates, a fixed date of May 31, 1991, and a so-called "public distribution date." Rogers hated the idea that his co-founders might exercise their right to exchange their Cantel stock and become large shareholders of RCI. The only way he could nullify the put was to make the expiration date occur before the start date—the earliest date on which his co-founders could request that their Cantel shares be exchanged for RCI's—by creating a "public distribution date" before December 1, 1988. By closing the window between the start and expiration dates, he would effectively ensure that the put would never be exercisable.

The public distribution date was defined as the date when Cantel was publicly traded with a $12.5-million public float and First City's and Telemedia's shares were freely tradeable. The put would only be completely nullified if both conditions were satisfied. In retrospect, the size of the public float was ridiculously low, although no one anticipated that cellular would become such a valuable asset so quickly. Remember, Cantel was selling car phones. Portable hand-held cellphones wouldn't become a mainstream consumer product for another 15 years. "We thought we'd be happy with a float like that," recalls Robi Blumenstein, a former Tory lawyer who was Belzberg's right-hand man.

The second condition emanated from the "hold provisions" under Ontario's "closed system" of securities regulations, which prevented shareholders from selling their stock to whomever they wanted, whenever they wanted—in Cantel's case, one year after becoming a reporting issuer. To become a reporting issuer, Cantel needed to file a prospectus with the Ontario Securities Commission. Ergo, Cantel had to become a reporting issuer before December 1, 1987 for Rogers to start the clock running on the one-year time period. To end the period during which the put might be exercised, he still had to fulfil the two aforementioned going-public conditions, but here's the kicker: if he missed the December 1, 1987 deadline to become a reporting issuer, the put, as contemplated in the share exchange agreement, would at least be exercisable on the December 1, 1988 start date, no matter when Cantel eventually became a reporting issuer.

Rogers was in a jam. December 1, 1987 was mere weeks away. He instructed his Cantel team to prepare a "shelf," or non-offering, prospectus, a document that expedites the process of selling securities to the public. It permits companies with no immediate plans of selling stock to the public to pull their prospectus off the metaphorical shelf to take quick advantage of favorable market conditions. So called shelf filings shortened an otherwise lengthy regulatory going-public process. As soon as the shelf was filed, Cantel would become a reporting issuer—and that's all he really cared about because then he would start the clock ticking on the one-year period necessary to create that all-important public distribution date. All he needed now was Cantel's board of directors to approve the shelf.

In November, Cantel held a board meeting to approve the shelf prospectus in Halifax, the venue for its annual meeting. First City's Robi Blumenstein recalls taking the directors through the prospectus paragraph by paragraph in excruciating detail to stall the process, either by forcing the meeting to end early without the board approving the prospectus, or to convince some of the non-Rogers directors that the proposed shelf was so defective that they couldn't possibly exercise their fiduciary duty by approving the filing. At typical board meetings, management presents the prospectus, and then the directors are asked if they have any questions. If not, they approve the prospectus. It's a straightforward, cut-and-dry process that might take under an hour, maybe less. Here, they spent an entire day going through the shelf prospectus, word by painful word. The company's bylaws required a minimum 48 hours' notice to convene a board of directors meeting. If the prospectus was not approved at this meeting, Rogers wouldn't have enough time to properly convene another meeting to approve the prospectus and file it by November 30, the following Monday. If his co-founders had succeeded in delaying the shelf one week until Tuesday, December 1, they would have locked in their option to exchange their Cantel shares for RCI shares one year later.

Rogers, anticipating a filibuster, did an end-run around his co-founders by having his wife deliberately stay behind in Toronto. Loretta Rogers, a Cantel director, joined the meeting by telephone from the Tory law offices in Toronto, although the other directors, aside from her husband, were unaware she was ensconced at Tory's with Cantel's lawyers, who were quietly waiting with pencils sharpened to make any agreed-upon changes to the prospectus. The co-founders, almost half a continent away in Halifax, had no idea the Tory lawyers were listening in on their meeting. "I would repeat things several times, and they all understood this because Loretta is not that experienced in business. I'm making sure [the lawyers] get it all in Toronto exactly, and if they didn't, they'd give Loretta a hand signal, and she would say, "I don't understand. What did you say?" laughs Rogers. "It never dawned on them that I would be able to get it filed by the end of the day.

"I teased Robi later, because he should have picked up on it, and he didn't," says Rogers. He recalls telling Blumenstein, "You guys certainly blew it."

"That's a disgraceful way to behave with your partners," Blumenstein answered.

"Well, it takes one to know one," Rogers rejoined.

According to Marc Belzberg's recollection, Ameritech aided Rogers either by permitting Loretta to cast her vote *in absentia* by telephone, something not permitted by the company's bylaws, or approving the filing of a shelf prospectus. Cantel's corporate bylaws clearly stated: "Upon a vote by a show of hands, every person who is present and entitled to vote shall have one vote." There was no mention anywhere in the bylaws about voting by telephone. Although Rogers controlled the board, if the directors didn't show up in the room, they couldn't vote. "It came down to the people in the room," says Marc Belzberg. Ameritech's decision to allow Loretta to vote was, therefore, critical.

Belzberg was furious at the outcome. He remembers heading to the airport stunned at the turn of events. "Wow, we lost that battle!" he recalls saying. "How could we lose that battle?

"It was a sham way of getting around the put, because the idea was for us to get liquidity or get the put, and here, we lost the put and we had no liquidity," says Belzberg. "It was a complete violation of the spirit of the agreement.

"We thought we had this down pat. It was a major, major, major disappointment and a letdown. He needed something for the shelf that really wasn't appropriate and shouldn't have passed, and the board went along with it because Ameritech didn't want to fight. That's all it was. They didn't have the balls."

First City had attempted to delay the shelf by filing a formal complaint with the OSC, alleging that portions of the prospectus breached securities regulations by failing to spell out the purpose of the offering, and the degree to which Cantel relied on RCI's management. The OSC decided not to interfere, siding with RCI's position that the securities regulator wasn't responsible for resolving private shareholder disputes, even if they affected a reporting issuer.

In an attempt at levity, Rogers' pal George Fierheller marked Rogers' victory in the time-honored manner of securities underwriters by having a few mock tombstones made for a few select Cantel executives, including Rogers and his stepfather John Graham. The tombstones, carved out of black marble, resemble legitimate ones, with the words inscribed in gold inlay:

> No securities commission or similar authority in Canada has in any way passed on the merits of the securities referred to therein ... This prospectus is filed as a shelf prospectus.
> NO SECURITIES ARE BEING OFFERED HEREUNDER. $000,000,000.
> There is no market for the securities of Cantel Inc.

The game wasn't over yet. The put wasn't dead just because Rogers eliminated its start date. Belzberg and de Gaspé Beaubien might have felt as if they had lost, but on paper, the put didn't expire until Cantel was listed and they could sell their stock freely into a secondary market, which meant Rogers still had to take Cantel public. Only now, the ball was in Rogers' proverbial court. He might ultimately decide to do an IPO if demand rekindled for cellular issues. If RCI shares recovered, the put would become far less attractive for all of them. Rogers had to weigh the options of taking Cantel public, possibly before it was ready, versus what the exchange ratio might be for RCI. Keep in mind, Rogers also benefited personally from a share exchange because of his investment in Cantel through RTL, the family holding company. In the back of his mind, he was always considering how he could, when ethically and legally permissable, improve his own position vis-à-vis the public shareholders of RCI.

On Tuesday, November 24, 1987, the date of the shelf prospectus, Cantel became a reporting issuer, subject to all of the securities regulations governing publicly traded companies. As it now stood, Rogers was halfway home—Cantel would now be a reporting issuer for at least one year by the time the start date rolled around. In fact, he was more than halfway—now he had a whole year to sell a paltry $12.5 million to the public and that small amount of stock could always be priced to sell.

Ameritech Mobile's 36-year-old Richard (Dick) C. Notebaert replaced Denny Strigl as president, when he was parachuted into his parent company's ill-fated acquisition of money-losing Applied Data Research Inc. Notebaert, now chairman and CEO of Qwest Communications Inc., the fourth-largest U.S. local-phone provider, oversaw the sale of Ameritech's stake in Cantel to Rogers.

"Ted was trying to drive everything as if he did have control. That was totally the point of contention, with all of the board members—not just me, with everyone who was there. And there were some bruised people," Notebaert says. "I remember looking around the room one day and I said to myself, 'Good gracious. Everybody has their own lawyer [here] but me.' People actually brought their lawyers to the board meetings. It was rough and tumble.

"The question was: Was the asset being optimized for one investor, or for all of the investors? And, that's really where the rub came."

Born in Montreal but raised in the United States, Notebaert, like Strigl, is a Bell System man. In 1969, as a college student, he swept garages and washed trucks for Wisconsin Telephone Co. before becoming a pole-climbing technician and later a manager. In 1983, a year before the AT&T divestiture, Notebaert joined Ameritech, eventually becoming its chairman and CEO in 1994. Five years later, he engineered its sale to SBC Communications Inc., another Baby Bell, for US$8.4 billion in stock. In June 2002, he came out of semi-retirement to repair Qwest's debt-laden balance sheet. In 2005, he lost a heated bidding war for MCI to Verizon.

Notebaert distinctly recalls Rogers' business philosophy. "I remember one classic quote: 'We don't ever want to have a profit because then we'd have to pay a dividend, and once you start, you can never stop,'" says Notebaert, now laughing at his dumbfounded reaction. "I just looked at him. I can remember sitting there in awe. I just shook my head.

"I was part of a company that was part of an earnings model, and here's a guy who said, 'What do you mean, make money? Never make a penny, because then they'll expect it.' I can still remember him saying that. He just never wanted to get off the cash-flow model. 'You know, positive cash flow, what's this profit stuff?' It was fascinating," he chuckles, adding, "I always liked Ted."

In early 1988, First City discovered that Rogers had made a lowball offer for Ameritech's shares. First City's Robi Blumenstein recalls convincing Ameritech to reject the offer, urging the U.S. giant to extract more money from Rogers. Armed with this knowledge, First City began salivating over the possibilities. If Ameritech exited the picture, the foreign ownership slot would open up, allowing the Belzberg family to sell its stock in the United States, where cellular values were skyrocketing. Wireless guru Craig McCaw kicked off 1988 by paying record prices for key cellular markets, stunning the naysayers and only serving to underscore the value of Cantel's national license. Fund manager guru Mario Gabelli didn't help matters either by talking up Cantel's worth in Barron's greatly anticipated annual Roundtable. First City and Telemedia filed the requisite notices stating that they wanted to sell their Cantel holdings for $60 a share, giving Rogers first right of refusal. He took a pass.

Then, in March 1988, Ameritech, exasperated with its quarrelsome Canadian partners, agreed to sell its stake in Cantel to RCI for $106 million, or US$85 million, four times its original investment. On a per-share basis, the Chicago giant made roughly $28 a share. "Ameritech sold out way before it should have," says Ameritech's former general counsel Allan Arlow, explaining that, among other reasons, the parent company wanted to smooth out its earnings to offset Applied Data's losses. Notebaert, following orders from upstairs, ordered Arlow to make the sale. "I was plainly told that if I didn't sell that company I would be out on my duff, so I had to make the deal. I was tempted to go and find some bank and buy it myself. Ted was given this great opportunity to pick things up, and he did.

"There was a great deal of friction and a lack of cordiality among the three Canadian partners, and that was always difficult for us," recalls Arlow. "Ted was treated as sort of the weak sister of the three because of the fact that the stock value of RCI wasn't that great. There was a certain fragility to his position. It was always a situation where I felt Ameritech's money probably was the most moderating force allowing them to stick together."

The foreign ownership slot held by Ameritech was now vacant, and Rogers was able to thwart his co-founders' plans. He was a step ahead of them. He had his lawyers incorporate a holding company in Nova Scotia to fill the Ameritech slot. How can a company incorporated in Canada be considered foreign? According to one of the CRTC's foreign ownership tests, a telecom company is deemed Canadian if at least 80 percent of its directors are Canadian citizens. However, the province of Nova Scotia just happens to be the one jurisdiction in Canada that permits U.S. residents on corporate boards. Rogers appointed three Americans to the board—his aunt, Patricia McAllister, and two former directors of his U.S. cable subsidiary, Dick Roberts and Harry Moore—thus stacking the deck. From the CRTC's standpoint, Rogers' newly incorporated Nova Scotia company was a foreign entity.

Through a quirky, arcane piece of provincial corporate legislation, Rogers stymied the Belzbergs, who in turn appealed to the DOC for an interpretation. With a favorable ruling, First City could have sold their shares as part of a private placement in the United States, where cellular values were skyrocketing. But, its petition was denied. "I remember thinking, why Nova Scotia?" says Robi Blumenstein, who admits the maneuver caught him off guard. "He's so brilliant. He's unbelievable. He was smart.

"He's just a guy who's really on top of what's he's doing. People take this stuff way too personally. They demonize the person just because he's advancing his own interests. It's okay as long as it's legal. You don't want it to be unethical either, but I wouldn't consider what Ted did to be unethical. It's not like it's forbidden.

"Rogers is a great entrepreneur," he says. "You just have to know what you're getting into, and make sure that your interests are aligned as closely as possible with his, or that you otherwise protect yourself. He's a loner kind of guy. That's why he's so successful."

In April, a month shy of his 55th birthday, Rogers underwent a series of medical tests to prep for surgery after an angiogram detected an aneurysm just below his kidneys. In the back of his mind, he always feared that he might suffer a similar fate as his father, whose life was cut tragically short by a ruptured aneurysm. Even so, he did not become fastidious about getting regular checkups until after learning he'd had a silent heart attack. He really didn't have a family physician until the mid-eighties when he became a patient of Dr. Bernie Gosevitz, who was already his sister's and Loretta's family physician.

Rogers had a second heart scan done the morning of Loretta's birthday before taking her out for a celebratory lunch at Winston's, a restaurant where all the corporate titans, politicians and Bay St. power brokers lunched so regularly they had their own select tables. The results came back better than expected: his heart was pumping blood pretty darn good for a damaged muscle. Surgery was a go.

He wasn't about to put the business on the backburner. In between medical appointments, he was attempting to raise his stake in the Canadian Home Shopping Network, tangling with his Cantel partners, meeting with his bankers and pursuing talks with CN and CP over their telecom company, CNCP.

Four days after announcing in mid-April the sale of his U.S. cable TV systems, he jotted notes in his personal organizer from Peter Hanson's book, Joy of Stress: "Heart attack is not bad luck, but bad management ... senility—not enough stress—keep working; need stress to stay young ... Stress can produce excellence." He reminded himself to follow the Pritikin Principle, a low-fat diet based largely on vegetables, grains and fruits.

The stock market was none the wiser about Rogers' precarious health. Applauding his decision to ditch his cash-draining U.S. assets, investors drove the class B shares 25 percent higher—more than $8 on the day—to $42. His lieutenants always kept their boss' medical maladies closely guarded secrets, lest word leak out and impact the share price. They were also protecting him, just as they will circle the wagons and protect the family after his death. It's an odd sense of loyalty they feel toward him. Such were the characters of the men who built his company. They carried as much pride as Rogers—maybe even more so because of the bond they shared in enduring him as their boss. Their pride swelled as they rescued the company from one near disaster to the next. They would do well at the company so long as their egos didn't outstrip their boss'. Before going in for surgery at Toronto's Wellesley Hospital, Rogers wrote a checklist of everything he needed to do:

1. Get organized for the hospital—clothes, toilet articles, books, seven magazines, TV—Radio (which he underlined), water cooler, eyeglasses.
2. Purchase of TD block RCI convertible preferred shares.
3. Offer to purchase balance of RCI convertible preferred shares.

4. Employment contract—sign.
5. New shoes, haircut, suit.
6. RTL bank loan closed.
7. Offer to Shaw, re: CHSN.
8. Chagnon, re: CHSN.

Five days before his surgery, Rogers did what he always does on May 6, the anniversary of his father's death—he visited his father's inconspicuous grave at Toronto's prestigious Mount Pleasant Cemetery, a world-renowned arboretum and one of the city's most heavily trekked green spaces. Assuming a businesslike approach to his surgery, he methodically wrote: "Mortality risk—2%; loss of limbs—one in 300/400; paralysis—1 in 10,000/20,000. Graft infection—would be disaster."

Rogers is usually the one to divulge his surgeries to the business press. He is so jubilant that he has yet again cheated death it's almost as if he's compelled to share his triumph. He has a reputation of being hard at work hours after surgery, although depending on the operation, that's a bit of an exaggeration. This surgery was an ordeal.

Waking up in recovery, he moved one leg, then the other, to check if he could move them. He was in intensive care for a couple of days. Four days later and off painkillers, he wrote he could have champagne. On the seventh day, he spent an hour with Graham Savage catching up on company business. RCI was about to close the Ameritech deal on Cantel.

Released after eight days in the hospital, Rogers had dropped 10 pounds. He felt awful and was tired. Not allowed to go into the office for three weeks, he continued to work from home. His lieutenants, already accustomed to his frequent breakfast meetings, simply marched to his house.

"I thought I was very lucky to get where I am and I still do, so when I have a fall, or a problem, it's within that context. I've got this far and I'd love to keep going. Of course, you say your prayers and you're scared, but it just goes on."

Reminded of his mortality, Rogers decided to secure his family's control over RCI by buying more non-voting B shares, especially given the backlash against dual-class share structures. For $88 million, he bought most of the company's convertible preferred shares, a move that effectively raised his family's stake to 47 percent fully diluted, up from 37 percent. He explained to *The Globe and Mail* that with "all the fuss about voting and non-voting shares" he was concerned the Ontario government might order all non-voting shares be given the vote, a development that would rob him of "absolute control" over the company. "People like me can't work without absolute control. I don't get motivated that way."

After buying Ameritech's stake, Rogers began picking off the Cantel owner-dealers, through RTL, just before their start-up anniversary dates, when they had the right to subscribe for more Cantel shares. In April, he paid $41.72 a share—one and a half times more than what Ameritech received—to buy out one Cantel Service Centre dealer. In May, he bought out another owner-dealer at $51.92 a share. As he approached the put deadline, Rogers was increasingly shelling out more and more money to take out Cantel's minority shareholders. In August, soon after finding a buyer for his U.S. cable TV assets, he set into motion a plan to take out his Cantel co-founders before it cost him even more money.

After three years of shareholder wrangling, Rogers felt his co-founders were blocking him from building Cantel. Even though they were reduced to minority status, they still wielded veto power, a demand they extracted from Rogers to protect their investment just in case Rogers' penchant for debt threatened to bankrupt the fledgling company. They still had a voice in the company's activities—something Rogers couldn't live with, even though, for their part, his co-founders contend they were only doing what they believed was in Cantel's (and consequently, their own) best interests. According to the 1986 shareholders' agreement, the founding shareholders could restrict specific corporate actions, including, among other things, paying dividends, capital expenditures, acquisitions and contracts with RCI or RTL. Their veto power would cease to exist—again—only when Cantel was publicly traded on the Toronto or Montreal stock exchange with a market value of not less than $12.5 million, and the stock held by First City and Telemedia became freely tradeable under Ontario securities law. The earliest date on which these requirements could be met was November 25, 1988, when the hold provisions were finally lifted.

"I remember [that] once, we needed more money," says Rogers. "We needed another $5 million from Belzberg, and he said it just wasn't worth it, and his rationale was that the $5 million he had in was now worth $20 million, so he had a 4-to-1 hit, but if he put in another $5 million, his hit would be reduced to 4-to-2.5. Can you believe it? Here I am, trying to get the towers up. They were very, very competent legally and played every game. They'd vote for every project as a director and then veto it as a shareholder.

"This is what happens when you have vetoes on shareholders' agreements," he fumes. "The Naifys from UA/Columbia had vetoes too. Nobody was in charge, and I don't like that. You have to make decisions. You can't be having board meetings all the time, and others would say, negatively, that that's a bunch of bull. 'Ted just likes to run everything, and he's too hands on and he doesn't want to share power with anybody.' That's what they would say, but there is a certain truth to that. You can't build a business by committee."

On August 23, according to his personal organizer, Rogers met separately with his co-founders, inviting Marc Belzberg over for breakfast, and meeting Philippe de Gaspé Beaubien for dinner at the York Club about the prospects of buying them out. Two days later, on August 25, RCI filed a preliminary prospectus for a Cantel IPO.

Rogers didn't want to take Cantel public; instead, he planned to fold Cantel into RCI as a wholly owned subsidiary to take advantage of its substantial tax losses, counterbalancing the huge gains anticipated from the sale of the U.S. cable TV assets. He used the filing as a tactic to force his partners to the negotiating table. Indeed, the proposed public float would be so small there wouldn't be enough liquidity for either First City or Telemedia to sell their entire holdings publicly without disrupting the market, and certainly not at the price they felt Cantel was worth. (According to its final prospectus, Cantel planned a public float of just shy of $50 million—not even a quarter of what First City's interest was worth.)

With the clock ticking, Rogers turned up the heat on his co-founders by hiring investment bankers—ScotiaMcLeod, Burns Fry and RBC Dominion—to embark on cross-country and European road shows to pitch the Cantel IPO to investors. Frustrated, de Gaspé Beaubien caved first. "I agonized over it," he says. "I had a proprietary interest, and my reputation was on the line with the people, the government, the community and the company. I didn't want the money. I wanted to run it. I wanted to build it. I'm an entrepreneur. I'm a founder. I'm very proud of what I built." He pauses in reflection. "But business is not everything. It is one aspect of life. It was a disappointment to me, but maybe, it was the best thing that happened to me." Indeed. He left the party $146 million richer. Rogers paid him $50 a share for his stake. Flush with cash, Telemedia went shopping, spending almost half of its windfall over the next year on publishing acquisitions in Canada and the United States.

Rogers had a tougher time with the Belzbergs. They demanded $60 a share. Rogers refused to go above $50. He finally agreed to pay First City $59.99 a share, one cent below their asking price, for a total of $225.6 million, half in cash and half in promissory notes.

Rogers secured the deal on October 7. Back in Vancouver, Sam Belzberg opened the safe to remove the envelope his son had given him four years earlier. Inside was the sheet of paper on which Marc had confidently predicted in the face of his father's skepticism that their cellular investment would be worth $100 million. It turned out to be more than double that amount.

Just when Rogers thought he had a firm deal, at the last minute, Marc Belzberg stunned him by changing his mind. "The family had made the decision. They were all thrilled with it. Everybody was very happy, but me. I was the only guy who didn't want to sell," says Belzberg.

Belzberg went to his father. "You're making a big mistake. We shouldn't be selling this."

"It's your deal," his father told him. "We're all proud of you. We all think it's a great sale, and we're all very happy with this. If you don't want to sell, you think you can get more money, call Ted. You're responsible for this piece of the portfolio."

The family finally persuaded him that if he agreed to sell, they'd give the additional money he could pry out of Rogers to charity. Belzberg called Rogers back. "You know Ted, I'm not sure we want to sell. We'd like to have $10 million more, and we'll give it to a foundation, a charity."

Rogers, with the taste of victory so close, hollered, "You're out of your mind. You're crazy."

"He went completely nuts," Belzberg recalls. "He was going to be out of touch because he was leaving the next day for Japan. I said, 'No big deal. We'll talk when you get back.' But he wanted this thing wrapped up and done. He pretended to leave. He basically put off his trip to get this thing done. He was ticked off because legitimately, I didn't have to sell. I didn't want to sell."

A cooled-off Rogers called him back a day later. "Okay, fine, we'll put $10 million into a charity account, but we're going to split it. I'll go on the board and you'll go on the board, and you give away half the money, and I'll give away the other half."

"Wait a minute; these are my shares, not yours. We get to decide where the money goes," Belzberg retorted.

Outraged, Rogers shouted into the phone that the deal was dead. Belzberg informed the family of this turn of events. His family, primarily cousin Brent, was angry because he had botched the deal by playing around for an extra $10 million on top of the $225 million. Says Marc Belzberg, "My dad said he was fine with it. I was fine with it, but it was a lot of pressure because I'd screwed the whole deal, and it was the most profitable deal the company had ever made in terms of rate of return and size. So, when it was back on the next day, everybody was fine."

Rogers relented, agreeing to Belzberg's terms. On October 11, they signed the agreement. RCI's Graham Savage hurriedly called the underwriters to pull Cantel's 1.1 million stock offering. They aborted the IPO just hours before they were to file Cantel's final prospectus with the OSC. (Rogers didn't take Cantel public until August 1991.)

"There was no reason to buy Philippe and me out. He could have left it the way it was. We didn't come at this by having to own it all. He did. He said, 'It's mine and nobody else's.' He couldn't have had nicer guys. I would have deferred to him. What did I know about engineering? It wasn't about not getting along. He has no problem getting along with people. It's about needing to own it all. It's about empire building. It's about financial greed. It's about power. It's a matter of him wanting to own it all—at great risk. He took on $600 million of debt to own it all," says Marc Belzberg. "It's a certain megalomania."

For his part, Rogers admits he only ever feels comfortable when he's in control. "If you've got a vision, never give up control. If you're lucky enough to get somebody to put up some money, they'll want to share control and their idea of sharing control is to have vetoes on you, and you're just a serf in your own business. Don't sell control," he advises, "even if it means you have to stay smaller than you might otherwise be."

"The personalities didn't click—and, it wasn't just the personalities. Ted had his own game plan," says Sam Belzberg. "You've got to respect him for it."

"I came in as the third man," says Rogers, "and that's always a difficult situation, and I'm uncomfortable. I like to have partners, but I like to have us running it. I like to be accountable for it. All my life I've been that way, so I'm very difficult when I'm the third man—and I don't feel good about it."

Relinquishing control of Cantel to Rogers hurt. "That was a significant disappointment, and it was a result of my youth, my immaturity and my fear of taking on the responsibility of being a loser," says Marc Belzberg. "Ten years ago, I was filled with hostility towards Ted, which I'm not anymore. I was filled with hostility for all the battling that went on, and it wasn't over the business and the build out. It was for the tricks he engaged in along the way to get control the first time around, and not participating in the group. It's you or me, and looking at it objectively, the guy played the game. You can't complain. In retrospect, he did a good job. He played a tough, tough, nasty good game."

Rogers brought much needed stability to Cantel. He had a long-term vision of where he wanted to take the company, and the management team would no longer be pulled into multiple directions. "Ted wasn't as concerned with how much cash you were going to spend in the next quarter as he was that you were spending it on the right things," says Cantel's then-general manager of Central Canada, David Parkes.

Rogers wasn't finished consolidating control, though. In early 1989, RCI purchased Rogers' personal stake in Cantel for $267 million, or $58 a share, in cash and preferred stock. Rogers said he was using the cash proceeds from the sale of his Cantel shares to reduce, but not eliminate, the debt he accumulated in his family's private holding company. RCI now owned 97 percent of Cantel. But, it needed to own all of the equity to access its cash flow and tax losses.

RCI made a separate $58-a-share offer to buy out the remaining 3 percent of the stock held by employees, friends and Cantel owner-dealers. Shortly after making the offer, a committee of independent Cantel directors hired RBC Dominion Securities for advice. RBC Dominion put a fair market value on Cantel's stock of between $92 and $105 apiece—significantly higher than RCI's $58-a-share offer. RCI initially refused to improve its offer. And, for their part, the independent directors merely offered dire warnings to shareholders that the cellular bubble might burst and consequently they should take RCI's lowball offer. While half of the shares had already been tendered, RCI planned to force the others out by way of amalgamation. The offer was to expire on February 17.

Belzberg was right. First City sold too soon. To Rogers' annoyance, cellular valuations were soaring. The analysts "have been promoting cellular as if it was God's gift to the world," Rogers complained to the *Toronto Star* in February 1989.

In March, he raised his offer to $93 cash, or one RCI class B non-voting share for each of Cantel's. Less than two weeks later, after the B shares traded as high as $108.25, Rogers changed the terms yet again. Now, he was offering $98.50 a share in cash for each Cantel share, the midway point in RBC Dominion's valuation. Cantel shareholders no longer had the option of picking up RCI B stock. In total, RCI dished out a hefty $24.5 million to buy out the remaining 248,232 shares shrewdly hung onto by the savvy Cantel Service Centre owner-dealers and Rogers' friends, family and employees. From his perspective, Rogers viewed the windfall to his employees as bonuses. Phil Lind, who had opposed Rogers' decision to go into cellular, made almost half a million dollars from the improved all-cash offer. TransCanada Glass International, owned by the Skidmore family in British Columbia, who—unbeknownst to Rogers (and later to his fury when he found out)—had been given a favorable side-deal with a Cantel sales representative—made a cool $9 million.

Cantel's Paul Kavanagh remembers asking Rogers one evening over dinner, "How can you sleep at night with all of your debt?"

"Well, you've got to understand," replied Rogers, "it's not what you make, it is how much you can borrow that determines your real wealth."

In the late eighties, over at Bell Cellular, President Robert Latham was eyeballing the latest projections with his marketing expert Tim McChesney and engineer Joe Sarnecki. What they saw scared them. The market was going to virtually double in size over the next year, and with a capital budget of just $40 million, they wouldn't be able to keep apace with the expected growth. They reckoned they needed $200 million. "We were in deep doo-doo because we didn't have a capital program that was even close to the market's potential growth," says Latham.

Latham flew the following morning to Montreal where he knew BCE's directors were gathering at Bell's stately headquarters on Beaver Hall Hill for a board meeting. He worriedly examined their crammed agenda with the secretary, managing to secure a spot just before lunch, hoping the timing would induce the directors to approve his request quickly. He knew they were running behind schedule, and would really want to break for lunch, which was typically the high point of their quarterly confabs.

He was asking for a five-fold increase in his budget to expand and convert Bell Cellular's network to digital cellular technology to meet the explosive growth his team anticipated in customer demand for true portability. "If anybody had come into a Bell Canada meeting looking for $200 million worth of capital, they'd have binders coming out of their ying-yang," says Latham. "I had five slides."

The first slide explained the company's current position; the second detailed the growth projections; the third outlined the reasons behind the expected explosive growth; and the fourth revealed his request for $200 million based on the average cost to acquire a cellular customer. "I'm going to stop right here because if you don't believe these first four slides, then the last slide is redundant," he told them. They hesitantly said, "Okay."

He unveiled the fifth slide. It simply read, "Ted Rogers."

"You have a choice," Latham recalls saying. "We know that Ted Rogers is going to go and do this. You either do it now and it'll cost you $200 million, or we wait. We fall behind. You lose market share. The marketplace loses confidence in you. Your customers start dumping you. Ted is going to have you guys. He's going to be looking down at you, and it's going to cost you twice as much to get caught up."

Done. The directors nodded their consent and went to lunch.

"That was a big thing for Bell. We can't be the second guy," Latham says.

"The 'Ted Factor' was always prevalent," adds McChesney. "He kept you on your toes, and it felt pretty good when every once in a while you could trump him. I think he made the industry better. I think Ted made us better. I think that's why we have such a flourishing wireless industry in this country today.

"Historically, Bell did not have a reputation for being a fast-moving marketing company until we created the wireless group against Ted, who had been an entrepreneur all of his life. It's part of his DNA. It was often challenging to get some of the folks on the board at Bell to understand the reality of this emerging opportunity. So, Ted actually helped us in that regard because he saw them and talked to them."

Indeed, BCE was perpetually surprised that RCI didn't just implode under the weight of its crushing debt load. BCE's former chief Jean Monty kept shaking his head, saying, "The guy's going to fall apart." Monty was later to add, "Everybody was wondering if Rogers wasn't betting too much on wireless. It turned out to be a hell of a good bet, probably one of the best one's he's ever made in his life."

Bell Cellular let it be known that it intended to introduce a $39.95 a month package before Christmas that included a phone plus airtime, the first-ever wireless bundle. Once word leaked out, Bell rolled out the intended package three months early at $29.95, the price it intended all along. "Rogers didn't have time to react, because back then, you couldn't just plug a rate into your billing system. It took time," recalls McChesney. "We just rocked that year. We took probably 60 to 65 percent of the market that was available in those two months. That was one of the highlights for me, where you actually trump an entrepreneur. It wasn't likely to happen again, but we certainly revelled in it for some time."

Bell teamed with cellular subsidiaries of the telephone companies to form CellNet Canada to compete against Cantel's national marketing campaigns. "It was guerrilla warfare," says Latham.

Rogers is the only one of the three original Cantel founders still standing. Cantel became his savior. In the aftermath of the corporate bloodbath, Rogers and Fierheller raced to Germany and China, attempting to win cellular licenses. TD Bank, which carved out a profitable niche for itself in wireless, rewarded Rogers with a seat on its board, one ironically vacated by Jean de Grandpré, who resigned after BCE acquired Montreal Trustco.

By 1993, revenue from Cantel had overtaken cable. Indeed, Cantel became his savior. If not for the wireless, RCI wouldn't be the company it is today. Wireless has become RCI's growth engine, accounting for more than half of the company's total revenue for 2006, and 68 percent of its operating profit.

First City, at its peak an $8-billion empire, doesn't exist anymore. By the end of the eighties, the company collapsed in ignominy under the weight of its debt and amid charges the Belzberg family had amassed their wealth through greenmail. Sam Belzberg was ousted from the company. First City and Marc Belzberg, 36, were convicted of evading securities disclosure laws. Cousin Brent picked up the pieces.

Like a phoenix rising from the ashes, Sam Belzberg, now 79, built Second City Capital partners and sister company Gibralt Capital Corp., which provide mezzanine debt and equity financing to mid-market and real estate companies, respectively. He co-founded Action Canada, a private/public partnership, to help develop Canada's future leaders.

To this day, Marc Belzberg's co-founders contend First City was only ever involved in Cantel to flip the licenses, a charge he vigorously denies. "There's no truth in that," Marc says.

"Marc never wanted to sell," asserts his father Sam. "He had started it." Without Marc Belzberg's initial impetus to form Cantel, the company would never have been created.

In 1991, Marc Belzberg moved his family to Jerusalem, where he pursued, unsuccessfully, a cellular license with one of Israel's largest companies, Koor Industries Ltd., when the government opened the market to a second carrier in 1994. He again tapped Canada Consulting's expertise, hiring Jerome Redican and Sheelagh Whittaker. A flourishing venture capitalist, Marc Belzberg followed in his father's philanthropic tradition, becoming an activist for families victimized by anti-Israeli terrorism.

Telemedia—once Canada's largest publisher of consumer magazines with titles including *Canadian Living, Harrowsmith, Coup de Pouce* and *Elle Québec*—is a mere shadow of its former self. Philippe de Gaspé Beaubien, who had the political wherewithall the others lacked to deliver Cantel its national license, and his wife began devoting more of their time in the nineties to their Institute for Family Enterprise (now the Business Families Foundation), a non-profit organization that aims to help entrepreneurial families cope with succession issues. In 1998, at age 70, de Gaspé Beaubien handed the reins to his children. Four years later, his children shed the magazine and radio assets their father had spent 30 years accumulating. His cherished dream of the family business enduring more than two generations wouldn't be realized, although in the process, his children made the family considerably richer.

David Margolese sold his paging company, Canadian Telecom, to a publicly traded Vancouver outfit that re-sold it in 1989 to Rogers, becoming the nucleus for Cantel Paging. He also sold his Cantel shares to RCI when Ted Rogers began consolidating his ownership in Cantel before taking it public. Now a wealthy young man, Margolese set off on two ambitious quests: satellite radio (which no one thought would ever amount to anything), and convincing the Israelis to open their cellular monopoly to a second competitor. Just like Marc Belzberg, he formed a consortium, approaching big-name U.S. carriers and Israeli high-tech companies in his pursuit to persuade Israel to allow competition. When Israel did license a second carrier, Margolese's consortium didn't win. With his hopes of developing the world's most sophisticated wireless system in Israel dashed, he returned to New York to devote all of his energies to CD Radio, which became the hugely successful Sirius Satellite Radio. Margolese was inducted into NASA's Space Technology Hall of Fame in 2002. He and Marc Belzberg remain close friends.

Ericsson ultimately provided all of the switches and radio base station equipment for the Cantel network. To this day, RCI maintains a close, collaborative relationship with the Swedish company. After having virtually no presence here, Ericsson employs more than 2,000 people in Canada. Its Montreal research lab is the largest R&D facility outside of Sweden. NovAtel, bought, sold and revamped, designs and sells high-precision global positioning systems in Calgary.

Ameritech Mobile's Dick Notebaert climbed into his parent company's chairman and CEO seat and orchestrated the U.S. Baby Bell's 1999 merger with SBC Communications Inc. As part of the merger, Ameritech Mobile, by then renamed Ameritech Cellular, was sold to GTE, which is now part of Verizon Wireless, run by Denny Strigl. SBC merged with AT&T in 2005, and adopted the AT&T name.

Rogers put Francis Fox, the former minister of communications, on the wireless payroll in 1997, giving him various executive roles while he continued to serve as a senior counsel at his law firm, Fasken Martineau. Fox left both positions in 2003 when he became principal secretary for Prime Minister Paul Martin. Martin later appointed him to Canada's Senate.

In 2006, 21 years after the birth of cellular in Canada, the wireless industry surpassed the traditional telephone business in both revenue and profit. By licensing a single national carrier rather than several regional ones, Canada avoided the chaos and ensuing shakeout that occurred over the next two decades in the United States and left Americans with unreliable networks, abysmal service and high costs. In 2002, Verizon astutely lured subscribers, not with low prices and free minutes, but by emphasizing network reliability, something Canadians had already enjoyed for years, in its "Can you hear me now?" TV ad campaigns that featured a "test man" roaming across snowy mountains, alongside highways and through wheat fields, asking a question that resonates with anyone who has ever tried using a cellphone south of the 49th parallel. Canadians can make calls easily right across the country's vast geographic terrain. It's in odd pockets of our urban jungles where the service still annoyingly fails. "Population for population, I'd rather have Cantel than one of the U.S. operators," reflects McCaw. "It's not a direct comparison, but I like the Canadian market better, personally. I think the service provided in Canada does happen to be better on average than in the United States. A recent survey gave the U.S. operators a D-plus for service."

CHAPTER 15

Ownership Gambit

"He's not someone I want to invest with."

—Salvatore Muoio

TED ROGERS FACED ANOTHER PROBLEM: he had more fans stateside than in Canada. By the mid-eighties, in the wake of its junk-bond financings and cable franchise wins, the company's profile had soared south of the border. Even TCI's John Malone says he owned Rogers stock, however briefly, and albeit preferred shares. His stockbroker mistakenly bought more than Malone had ordered in 1982, resulting in an unexpectedly large windfall when he sold two weeks later. From the sale of his Rogers shares, Malone, then 41 years old, was able to afford his first sailboat, a custom-built 59-foot Hinckley Sou'wester, which he named after his wife Leslie Ann. And, unbeknownst to him, Rogers helped safeguard jobs for a few Maine shipwrights, who otherwise might have been unemployed during the depths of the 1982 recession.

U.S. investors regarded RCI as a play on cellular, which was becoming a hot Wall Street investment trend, despite the skepticism on Bay Street. The stock had also just become margin eligible, which meant U.S. brokers could lend customers cash to buy the stock. In 1986, the price of Rogers' class B shares jumped 25 percent, to $27, within the month of October alone. In the previous years, the stock had never traded above $18, the price Rogers had paid Brascan for its CCL block, falling to a low of $5.25 in 1982 and rising, however fleetingly, to a high of $15 in 1983 when the CRTC finally permitted pay TV, a lucrative new stream of revenue for the cable companies.

Like any astute businessman, Rogers desired, and needed, foreign investment, but U.S. investors held so much of the company's float—89.6 percent of the class B non-voting shares in 1986—that he feared he might lose his coveted broadcast licenses. Canadian rules restrict foreign ownership to 20 percent of voting stock and 20 percent of the paid-up capital. Was he offside? And, if he wasn't technically in violation of the foreign ownership limits, was Rogers breaking the spirit of the law?

Rogers wrestled with possible solutions. His lawyers and their regulatory counterparts clashed over their differing interpretations of paid-up capital and the seemingly innocuous conjunction "or" in the phrase "effectively owned or controlled." Paid-up capital, a technical legal and accounting term, generally refers to the consideration received by the company of the issue of its shares, although it wasn't defined in the *Broadcasting Act* or in any other piece of federal legislation. While there was no doubt Rogers controlled RCI through his majority ownership of the class A voting shares, did he effectively own the company if non-Canadians held most of its equity? Rogers' stepfather John Graham, a skilful conciliator, who was respected and well liked at the CRTC, argued that "or" meant either-or, while the CRTC's legal eagles countered that "or" was meant by legislators in this context as "and."

When the first alarm bells sounded after he acquired Canadian Cablesystems, Rogers took steps to deal with the level of foreign investment by delisting CCL's class A shares from the Nasdaq, the U.S. national market system, hoping to encourage investors into the B stock, a move that subsequently proved too successful. Now, with so many Americans owning the B shares, the foreign-ownership issue was threatening to unravel into a full-blown crisis.

The ensuing imbroglio was embarrassing to Rogers, who is enormously proud of being Canadian. He was keenly aware of the inherent, although inadvertent, hypocrisy of his situation. While he uses his patriotism adeptly to strike just the right chords with the CRTC and the politicians—as every other broadcaster does when they're defending their turf—no one has ever disputed his fidelity to country. But now he couldn't even call his company Canadian.

In December 1986, Rogers took his first major step to reduce the level of foreign ownership by delisting the company's stock on NASDAQ, an unexpected move that sent the stock reeling. Buyers of the stock also had to fill out forms disclosing the citizenship of the ultimate beneficial owner.

Fearing the CRTC might not renew the license for his recently acquired ethnic TV station CFMT-TV, which was coming up for review in the spring of 1987, Rogers sought advice on his foreign-ownership conundrum from his cousin's husband, H. Garfield Emerson. A senior partner firm Davies Ward & Beck, where he gained renown as the "King of M&A" working for, among others, the prominent Reichmann family, Emerson was already becoming much sought after for advice in the then-emerging field of corporate governance and fiduciary responsibilities. In 1964 he married Melissa Taylor, the daughter of Velma's younger brother Dr. Alan Taylor, a family practitioner in Windsor, who had taken his distraught sister and her son into his home after her husband's death. Emerson's wife was a favorite of Velma's, frequently summering with their toddler at her aunt's Muskoka cottage. The young couple often dined with Velma and John Graham, and maintained close ties with Graham when he remarried after Velma's death. In 1989, Rogers invited Emerson onto the RCI board after he left Davies to head the Rothschild family's new merchant bank in Canada, and in 1993 Emerson became RCI chairman when John Graham, in his 80th year—and still enjoying his scotch, albeit with a straw because of Parkinson's—decided to retire.

In late April 1987, during the licence renewal hearing for CFMT-TV, the CRTC's general counsel Avrum Cohen raised the ownership issue, asking to examine the company's shareholder registers. Within a week following the hearings, Rogers heeded Emerson's advice to impose transfer restrictions, which essentially prevented Americans from selling their shares to anyone who wasn't Canadian. Instead of imposing them on both share classes, the RCI board prohibited the transfer only on the class A voting shares, most of which Rogers owned to control the company. Both A and B shares tumbled on the announcement of transfer restrictions, causing the RCI board to form a special committee to figure out ways of resolving the ownership debacle. Cohen remembers that the ownership issue "bothered Rogers as a person and from the point of view of perception. He wanted to do the right thing and looked for ways to be within the law."

The committee's chairman was Claude Ducharme, an esteemed Montreal lawyer and a holdover from the CCL board. Not long after the special committee's formation, Ducharme received a fax from Rogers, who believed that even though he (Rogers) wasn't on the special committee, he should participate in its meetings. Rogers wrote: "I do feel with my background and continuing activity in tax and corporate simplification that I can provide some essential input. Unless there is a conflict of interest in my attendance, it is my intention to attend the meetings of the Special Committee. I will continue to provide liaison with Davies, Ward & Beck to ensure that adequate information is provided between meetings."

Ducharme sent back an immediate reply that amounted to no. He felt the board had made it clear that Rogers was not permitted to join their meetings. The committee had access to him, not the other way around. The ever impatient Rogers fired back:

> You are aware of course that these diversions are beginning to multiply in terms of draining away the Corporation's leadership and resources. There is a danger that if unsolved for many more months it will envelop the Corporation, frustrate all financing and totally tie up all progress. For that reason, the hours that the Committee meet are extremely precious and,

therefore, the more preparatory work that can be done the more progress that will be made. I have already cut back a number of other commitments and am prepared to do everything within my ability to be of assistance.

"I was not saying yes right away, and I don't know if it's because I was brave," recalls Ducharme, "but I could say [to him] 'I don't agree with you.' He was not there to quarrel. He was there to find solutions. He's one of the most intelligent men I ever met. He understood any problem. He knew more than the specialists. He always had a solution to a problem. He'd always find a way."

With the CRTC breathing down his neck—having asked no fewer than three times in July for more details—Rogers felt he needed to do more. While foreign ownership had fallen during the past six months, it had actually risen in the month of July.

At noon on July 31, the Friday before the Civic Day holiday weekend, RCI announced its intention to buy 8 million of its class B shares, at $24.08 apiece in a bid aimed exclusively at non-Canadian shareholders. The company also prohibited the same transfer restrictions for foreigners holding class B non-voting shares that it had in May on the class A voting and preferred securities. When the stock market reopened on Tuesday, investors, furious the bid wasn't open to all shareholders, hammered the stock, sending the B shares down 12 percent from their Friday close of $27.37 to $24.12. In an era where minority shareholder rights were being trampled and the courts were just beginning to take a harder line on fiduciary transgressions, the provincial overseer of the country's largest capital market, the Ontario Securities Commission, refused to permit such an exclusive bid, forcing Rogers to go back to the drawing board.

On October 19, 1987—Black Monday to most financiers—the Dow Jones Industrial Average (DJIA), considered a barometer of the U.S. economy, crashed, precipitating a worldwide meltdown that vaporized $1 trillion of value and marked the end of a five-year global bull market in equities. The DJIA, composed of the world's 30 best blue-chip stocks, plunged 508 points, or 22.6 percent of its value, its largest single-day percentage loss since the October 1929 crash. In Toronto, the devastation erased $37 billion off the value of Canadian stocks. The TSE 300 Composite Index tracked the decline, tumbling 407 points, or 11.3 percent. Rogers class B shares tumbled to as low as $15.75.

Rogers took advantage of the shaky market conditions to re-launch the aborted stock buyback, his fourth attempt to repatriate shares and reduce his level of foreign ownership. On October 30, RCI offered to repurchase 10 million class B shares at $25 cash apiece. The offer, open for a month, was conditional on foreign investors tendering at least 75 percent of the shares. Since it was targeting U.S. investors, Rogers bought a one-third-page ad in the *Wall Street Journal* to publicize its offer, although the stock was already attracting a fair bit of unwanted publicity after the revelation that Ronald Reagan's Supreme Court nominee, Judge Donald H. Ginsburg, owned US$140,000 worth of Rogers stock, while he was the antitrust head at the Department of Justice overseeing the government's effort to reduce the regulation of cable-TV systems. Ginsburg later withdrew his nomination over his alleged use of marijuana.

According to its offering circular, foreigners owned 69.4 percent of the 22 million class B non-voting shares at September 30, 1987. Combined with 5.2 percent of the 4.6 million class A voting shares also held outside of Canada, the company's total foreign holdings amounted to 58.3 percent—a level that wouldn't even be acceptable today. The current law permits foreigners to own a maximum of 20 percent of an operating company and one-third of a holding company for an effective ownership cap of 46.7 percent. (Indeed, Rogers' foreign ownership crisis caused the federal government to remove the contentious phrase "paid-up capital" and replace the innocuous "or" with an "and" in the *Broadcasting Act* of 1991.)

Rogers adjusted the company's paid-up capital to comply with the legal ownership diktats by moving the company's incorporation from federal jurisdiction to British Columbia, which permits the creation of par value shares. Remember, accountants generally define paid-up capital as the total amount of money all shareholders have paid for their shares. By switching jurisdictions, Rogers substantially lowered the stock's par value so that foreigners could still own a lot of B shares without owning a large percentage of the company's paid-up capital. Unlike the federal jurisdiction, B.C. also permits subsidiaries to buy and hold shares in its parent, which meant that if a subsidiary of RCI made the tender offer, the parent could avoid a hefty tax bill.

While shareholders had approved in April the change in name from Rogers Cablesystems Inc.—which was discontinued as a federally incorporated entity— to Rogers Communications Inc., the new entity was officially incorporated in British Columbia on October 20, the day after the market crashed. Technically, the company was now no longer in violation of the paid-up capital rule, although it still had to deal with the high level of B shares in non-Canadian hands. Outmaneuvered on the paid-up capital issue, the CRTC sought opinions from outside accounting experts, only to discover the phrase was open to various interpretations. As the tension mounted, Rogers' temper flared. "If something was bothering your wife and you wanted to remain married, you'd bloody well fix it," he fumed to *The Globe and Mail*. He hoped the buyback campaign would take off some of the heat he was feeling from Ottawa.

The buyback, coming when it did, went better than expected. RCI was flooded with almost twice as many tendered shares as it wanted to buy. Investors tendered 18.5 million class B shares by the November 30th deadline, although Rogers fell short of the 75-percent threshold from non-Canadians. With just 65 percent of the tendered shares from foreigners, Rogers waived its condition and accepted 10 million of the tendered shares on a pro rata basis, taking 54 shares for every 100 tendered. The company sought regulatory approval to take up the entire 18.5 million shares, but the Ontario Securities Commission denied its request, insisting the company needed to have an independent valuation before it could buy more than what it originally sought. The net result: foreigners still owned roughly 60 percent of the class B shares. Rogers was, as CRTC's Avrum Cohen dryly observed, "becoming more Canadian."

Rogers tried again. On December 28, RCI launched another tender offer, open until January 26, 1988. The company planned to buy 5 million shares at $25 a share. This time it was accompanied by an independent fairness opinion from Burns Fry Ltd. The investment dealer discounted the class B non-voting shares by 20 to 25 percent, since no coattail provision existed to ensure the minority shareholders would be treated equally if a takeover bid were made for the family's controlling stake. Based on several factors, including subscriber growth and Canadian- and U.S.-comparable cashflow multiples, Burns Fry valued the B shares at a range of $37.50 to $43.50 apiece—an astonishing 50 percent to 75 percent higher than the $25 a share buyback price. Armed with this data, the company's directors refrained from expressing an opinion to shareholders, apart from stating that the buyback price wasn't intended to represent the intrinsic or fair value of the shares. Shareholders were left to make their own decision.

With the equity markets still twitchy, investors chose to sell into the offer. By the January 26, 1988 deadline, 6.5 million shares—1.5 million more than expected—had already been tendered. Instead of taking up the 5 million shares, Rogers got greedy and tempted fate by announcing on Wednesday, January 27 that it was raising the limit to 7.5 million shares and extending the deadline by another two more weeks.

Unbeknownst to Rogers, two days earlier, in the Monday issue of *Barron's*, an influential U.S. financial publication, Mario Gabelli, a prominent New York money manager who became known as "Super Mario," said the B shares were worth about $110—an astounding four times more than the $25 buyback offer and two and a half times higher than Burns Fry's estimate. Gabelli, a perennial guest in the magazine's annual investment roundtable discussion of the coming year's best stock picks, accused Rogers of doing "everything that they could do to hurt U.S. owners"—first, selling his shares with the CRTC's aid and then, using the "ownership shield" to buy them back at "25 cents on the dollar." He charged Rogers with using the share buybacks to force out minority shareholders as a prelude to going private, a suspicion held by many other analysts at that time. Asked if he would buy the stock regardless of its treatment of U.S. investors, Gabelli unequivocally answered, "I would buy it. I would buy it big, if I could."

While most publicly traded companies don't normally scold analysts for suggesting their stock is undervalued, RCI attempted to discredit Gabelli's remarks. In an angry letter of rebuttal published in *Barron's* the following week, Graham Savage, RCI's senior vice president of investments, cited five examples of the money manager's "misleading and erroneous" statements, each of which he refuted: "... [T]here is absolutely no basis for a statement that such a stock could be worth about $110 Canadian," he wrote. Savage, concerned Gabelli had deliberately interfered with the buyback offer because of his ill-timed remarks, demanded a "prompt retraction."

Gabelli refused to retract his statements. "Let's calm down," his published response began. "My clients are shareholders of Rogers, we are all working to enhance the public market value—aren't we?— as well as the private market value of the company." He fanned the flames of controversy by confidently offering further prognostications, assigning a private market value to the B shares of $104 a share in 1988, $133 in 1989, $165 in 1990 and $202 in 1991.

"Graham put me on the spot," says Gabelli. "That just got me interested in taking on the challenge. We had this little spat with Ted and it really escalated when Graham decided to say I was wrong, and the proof was in the pudding. Ted understands I was speaking for my church and we had a different point of view."

How could his numbers be so radically different from Burns Fry? It all came back to Cantel. Gabelli valued Rogers's 42.1-percent stake in Cantel at $800 million, compared to Burns Fry's estimate of $240 million to $327 million. He based his analysis partly on a comparison with the cellular market in Los Angeles, a market worth US$1.65 billion, based on a population of 11 million people and an average per-capita cellular revenue of US$150. "So, how could a cellular system for all of Canada be worth only $300 million?" Gabelli's research head Salvatore Muoio asked in a *Globe and Mail* article. Gabelli also marked up the cable business, valuing it at about $1.5 billion, versus Burns Fry's $800 million to $900 million. "While I may have made some minor assumption errors, even if I discount my 1991 numbers by 50 percent, my conclusion that the stock is a roaring buy is unchanged." Gabelli tartly added, "... [I]f I had been uncharacteristically diplomatic ... I would have said Rogers was trying to 'freeze out' or 'squeeze out' or 'force out' the minority shareholders, which would have been more proper."

"We did the work, and literally, he was offering like twenty or thirty cents on the dollar," recalls Muoio, a veteran cable investor, who was aggrieved more over Rogers' treatment of his U.S. cable division's public shareholders than the buyback fiasco. "I haven't wasted a single ounce of analytical energy on the company since then. Why spend time? Life's too short. There are plenty of other stocks with people you trust."

Rogers took his U.S. cable division, Rogers Cablesystems of America Inc., public on NASDAQ in the fall of 1985 at US$11 a share. In early 1986, he issued more stock at US$14.50. In early October 1987, two weeks before the market crashed, he made an offer to buy out the 4.9 million Rogers America shares RCI didn't already own for US$22.50 a share. His total cost: US$110 million. After privatizing Rogers America in December, barely four months later in April 1988, he put the U.S. assets on the auction block, agreeing to sell them for a whopping US$1.27 billion. So, in essence, mere months after buying out the 20.9-percent minority stake, Rogers flipped it for US$265 million, 2.4 times more than what he paid U.S. shareholders.

"That was one of the worst instances of corporate thievery I've ever seen in twenty-five years," says Muoio, who founded SM Investors LP, a New York-based money-management firm, in 1997. Though companies will try to squeeze out public shareholders at discounts, "this was so blatant and so obnoxious," he says. "He basically screwed the U.S. investors in that company. He must have had it already in the works. You don't just wake up one day, buy the public out, and then decide to sell it. I don't think he would have gotten away with it if he were a U.S. company, actually. I think the shareholders would have just slaughtered him over it.

"He clearly, clearly, obviously, just had no morals. And, after that event, I said you never want to invest in anything this guy does. I haven't followed him very closely since then. He's not someone I want to invest with."

Given that Rogers was in the midst of negotiating with Ameritech to buy its stake in Cantel, it's hardly surprising that RCI attempted to downplay Gabelli's analysis. For their part, the Canadian analysts played right into Rogers' hands. While conceding the $25 offer was well below RCI's asset values, they derided Gabelli's remarks as "absolutely ludicrous." But the damage had been done. Investors changed their minds about tendering their shares. When the offer expired at midnight on February 9, RCI netted only 4.2 million shares, well below its original goal of 5 million. Americans had submitted and withdrawn some 2.3 million shares. In a year's time, Rogers aggressively reduced the company's level of foreign ownership to a more acceptable 35 percent, repurchasing a total of 14.2 million B shares for the bargain-basement price of $360 million, financed entirely on credit.

Turns out, Gabelli was right. Just as he predicted, Rogers' class B shares surged in 1989 to $133.50, an all-time high. Because of their control premium, the class A stock, owned mostly by Rogers, climbed to a record $156 a share. While the buyback helped boost the shares in 1988, the stock really didn't take off until after Rogers announced he was dumping his U.S. cable assets. By then, Cantel was fueling the stock's spectacular rise. Wall Street was much further ahead than Bay Street in recognizing the potential value of cellular licenses, driving valuations higher just as Rogers was trying to buy out his minority Cantel shareholders.

Commenting on RCI's rollicking stock price, which Bay St. analysts dubbed "Rocky B" because of its stock symbol, RCI.B, Rogers told the *Toronto Star* in 1989, "To those of us who are trying to figure out how to make it profitable, it's almost amusing. The whole thing is an exercise in nonsense, and as I've said before, I hope we're strong enough and live long enough to make the company worth what the stock market says it's worth."

To justify a per-share value of $100, RCI would need an after-tax profit of $189 million, Rogers said. "That would be quite something," he quipped. In 1988, the company recorded a profit before extraordinary items of $1.45 million, its first profit in six years. "It reminds me of Houdini ... These people who don't work for a living, in the sense of running companies. They go around prattling about other people's work. They have this thing called private market value. That is the price if the company sold all of its assets, paid no tax and then distributed all that cash to shareholders and they paid no tax. It's an exercise in absurdity, but it's one that's fashionable for people who observe work, but do no work themselves. It's nonsense."

In March 1991, RCI lifted the self-imposed ban on transferring shares to non-Canadians, hoping to spur U.S. interest back into a stock that was trading at considerably big discounts—as much as 50 percent—to that of U.S. cellular companies, such as McCaw Cellular. Foreigners owned 2 percent of the voting shares and 3 percent of the redefined paid-up capital, low enough levels that Rogers felt comfortable that RCI no longer risked breaking federal laws.

When Rogers took Cantel public on NASDAQ later that year in August, Goldman Sachs & Co., the lead underwriter, insisted the prospectus include additional minority shareholder rights protections specifically because of the lingering discontent among U.S. investors over Rogers' controversial buyback scheme. The IPO was a resounding success. Though also listed in Toronto, the majority of the stock was sold in the United States and Europe, where demand for cellular plays appeared virtually insatiable. To celebrate the IPO, Goldman presented Rogers with a mock tombstone called "The Ted Factor" and Savage with a mockup of *Business Week* with him on the cover as CFO of the Year at a closing dinner fête held at the American Yacht Club in New York.

While U.S. equity investors were so slow to forgive Rogers—and some, like Muoio, never did—he certainly had no problem tapping into the U.S. high-yield, non-investment-grade debt markets—the biggest beneficiaries of Rogers' entrepreneurial daring. With demand high, RCI's debt offerings were oversubscribed. In the next two and a half years, working now mostly with the venerable Merrill Lynch after Drexel's demise, Graham Savage and his RCI team raised a staggering US$3 billion in public debt to finance Cantel's growth and challenge Ma Bell in the looming long-distance wars.

"You have to give him credit for recognizing where to be and not missing those opportunities," says Sal Muoio. "There are plenty of companies that didn't participate in wireless when they could have. There were a lot of mistakes."

After its hard-fought battles to win cellular licenses, MCI agreed to sell its franchises to McCaw Cellular for US$122 million in 1985. McCaw then sold them to AT&T for a staggering US$11.4 billion in 1994. Western Union Corp., once a venerable name of American industry, sold its cellular licenses and 50-percent stake in Airfone Inc. in the mid-eighties as part of a corporate restructuring of its crippling debt. In 1993, Sprint acquired Centel Corp. in a US$3-billion takeover to get back the cellular franchises it had sold to Centel four years earlier.

"Rogers has been in good businesses that have had a lot of growth," says Muoio. "If you were able to be exactly aligned with [Ted's] interests, you probably would have made a lot of money, but you don't want to be a minority shareholder. It doesn't pay." That is, until recently.

ACT FOUR

RIVERBOAT GAMBLER

CHAPTER 16

Unitel: Here We Go Again

"What the hell is he trying to do?"

—Jean Monty

TED ROGERS, 55, held three cards: radio, cable and wireless. Now, the Riverboat Gambler called for a fourth card—telephony. He asked John A. Tory to set up a meeting with William Wade (Bill) Stinson, the head of Canadian Pacific Ltd., a rail, air and hotel conglomerate. Tory, 58, happened to be a close friend of Stinson's, 55, who was five months younger than Rogers. Stinson, a fourth-generation railway man, was highly respected in financial circles.

"Sure," Tory replied.

The three men and CP treasurer William (Bill) Fatt, 37, met for lunch at the Royal York Hotel in December 1988.

The previous month, CP had agreed to buy the 50-percent stake it did not already own of CNCP Telecommunications Ltd. from partner Canadian National Railway, then a Crown corporation. The railway companies had built a national fiber-optic and digital microwave network for its now shrinking telex business that could be used to transmit long-distance (LD) telephone calls, making it a potential rival to the telephone companies.

For the past year, Rogers, encouraged by Cantel's George Fierheller, had been angling to break into Canada's lucrative $7.5-billion long-distance business. Long distance then was the most profitable part of the wireline business. Unlike the United States, where AT&T's LD monopoly had been ripped open, the phone companies in Canada remained entrenched monopolies, leading to LD prices 20 to 25 percent higher than what U.S. carriers, such as AT&T, MCI and Sprint, charged. Unlike Europe, local landline calls in Canada were (and are) free. The telecom regulator's cost methodologies, which became increasingly complex over time, created artificially high LD rates that subsidized artificially low local service. The subsidization of local service was entwined with the issue of universality, which politicized the long-distance debate. In the emerging world of fiber optics, distance ultimately would no longer matter. For the time being, though, LD was the cash cow.

Though the CRTC sanctioned telecom resellers (with just enough limitations to emasculate them), the Commission rejected CNCP's first application to provide an alternative facilities-based LD telephone service in 1985. Former Cantel minority shareholder Michael Kedar, 47, an Israeli-born, Swiss-trained electronics engineer, was the Canadian equivalent to MCI's Bill McGowan, the lone combatant fighting to bring LD competition to Canada. In 1986, Kedar co-founded Call-Net Telecommunications Ltd. with the proceeds from the sale of Cantel stock. Unlike Rogers, Kedar didn't play by club rules. He set up a competitive LD billing system that the CRTC immediately ruled was illegal because it encroached on Bell's monopoly. Bell Canada and the CRTC both tried to put him out of business, forcing the former Israeli soldier to take the issue to the Federal and Supreme courts, where he lost each time. The Mulroney federal Cabinet intervened twice to prevent Bell from disconnecting Call-Net, urging the telecom regulator to reconsider its LD position.

Rogers saw CNCP as a way for Cantel to bypass the monopoly wireline companies, then called Telecom Canada. Ideally, he wanted to combine the two companies. The prospect of going after archrival Bell became exhilarating. In July, with U.S. cable franchises on the auction block, Rogers publicly said he was willing to invest millions in CNCP if CP gave him operating control. "The telecos would like us to use their fiber-optic line into the house for local calls, cable and long distance. Why can't my line be used for all the same services?" he opined to *Business Week*. Rapid changes in technology had begun to blur the boundaries between the cable TV and telephone industries, unraveling the arguments for natural monopolies and allowing competition in once heavily regulated territories. "What I really want to do," Rogers told *Maclean's* Peter Newman, "is establish a Second Force in Canadian communications. Look, you have Telecom [Canada] across the country already and that's Force 1. The Second Force will be whoever is licensed for long distance and data transmission across the country. CNCP already can transmit data—in fact, everything but voice. Then, I have Cantel, which is licensed to carry long distance across the country—so, by combining the two, you'd have the Second Force. All of us one day will have portable phones, and there won't be any need for wires all over the place."

Over lunch, Tory told Stinson in front of Rogers: "Bill, I should tell you that, as a partner, at times you might get really upset at Ted. He might not be your idea of the best partner."

Rogers, taking his words as a compliment, didn't blink. He was trying to buy the whole kit and caboodle anyway. Yet, here again, Tory was imparting good advice, but Stinson ignored his friend's warning. On April 19, 1989, Ted Rogers was beaming when he announced his partnership with CP at a press conference. He had agreed to buy 40 percent of CNCP from CP. Sitting beside him, Stinson, somewhat more subdued, couldn't help but smile when the irrepressible Rogers threw down the gauntlet, promising to put an end to the phone companies' "Soviet-style communications monopolism."

Former BCE chief J. V. Raymond Cyr says he recalls laughing when he first heard Rogers' "self-serving malarkey," as one columnist called it, given Rogers' cable TV stronghold. "He was very good at defending his own monopoly and attacking the other one," says Cyr. Though Bell threatened to get into the cable TV business, the company was just rattling its saber since de Grandpré had traded away that option in the sixties. In Britain, BCE teamed with Montreal-based cable TV Groupe Vidéotron ltée to pipe TV and phone signals over the same network. Cyr had already begun to dismantle the de Grandpré empire. BCE used—some might say wasted—its monopoly profits to diversify into gas pipelines, oil and gas exploration, trust company operations, real estate development, printing and publishing, high-tech products and forest products.

Cyr, a cigar-chomping engineer who started at Bell as a student climbing phone poles, dismissed Rogers' claims that LD competition would lead to lower phone bills. "He speaks with such a large mouth, he drowns out the others," Cyr said at the time. The gloves had come off. Rogers brashly quipped that if he ran The Phone Company, he would have wined and dined and seduced the cable industry, offering to rent video fiber-optic cable at small amounts for the first five years and then gradually increasing the rental to wipe them out and take over their operating profits.

So, Bell tried other ways to make Rogers' life as miserable as he was making theirs. When Rogers asked the CRTC to permit basic cable rate increases to help pay for the construction of its fiber-optic networks, Bell protested that monopoly cable subscribers shouldn't have to pay for upgrades if Rogers planned to use the facilities to compete against the phone company. When Rogers then created Rogers Network Services to transmit data for business customers—brokerage firm Wood Gundy was its first customer—Bell demanded the CRTC regulate it as a phone carrier. Bell lost both times.

Rogers paid $288 million for the 40-percent CNCP stake in cash, using the money he made from the sale of the U.S. cable franchises. His marriage with CP, as with all of his partnerships, began with much enthusiasm. Over the next four months, they ironed out a two-volume-long sharcholders' agreement that gave Rogers extraordinary rights. (John A. Tory served as an intermediary for the two companies, helping bring them together.) RCI secured four of the 10 seats on the CNCP board, 50 percent of the seats on the company's executive and audit committees, and had veto powers over major investments and other decisions, including bringing in other partners. Rogers was named chairman.

CP seemed content to let Rogers have operational control. Bay St. analysts applauded their union, saying it was the last piece of the puzzle for Cantel to get into the telecommunications industry. Rogers then acquired 4 percent of Teleglobe Inc., a monopoly overseas telecommunications carrier, to protect Unitel's access to its facilities and prevent control from falling to BCE. (His toehold in Teleglobe later proved crucial for Quebec telecom guru Charles Sirois.) Throughout, Rogers toured the country, expounding the virtues of competition; only he wasn't advocating full-blown competition. As in the cellular business, Rogers wanted a duopoly: just him and The Phone Company.

"He was willing to go body and soul and capital into joining our industry and fighting Bell," says former BCE chief Jean Monty. "In those days, we had a monopoly on a lot of stuff, if not most of the stuff, and you have to be impressed by him, but at the same time, you have to say, 'What the hell is he trying to do?'

"We were skeptical. He called it a David–Goliath type of struggle, and it was. There is no question that it was. He's been a bit of a lightning rod for change for everybody and that's been healthy. He's been sometimes too aggressive, but you can't be perfect."

CNCP now had two owners with clashing corporate cultures. CP began to perceive RCI as cowboys, while RCI regarded CP as too staid for its blood. "This is CP. First, we have a board meeting, and then we have a nap" was the inside joke at the time. When Phil Lind and lawyer Bob Buchan went into CNCP to join its strategy sessions to prepare for the LD hearings, they were shocked at CNCP's laissez-faire attitude, both men say. CNCP had no fire in its belly.

CNCP's new hire Mark Goldberg, a Canadian with American work experience from Bell Labs and AT&T, dubs the culture the "mmmuffin mentality." Every internal meeting he went to had pots of coffee and the inevitable box of muffins from the Toronto Bregman family's mmmuffins franchise chain. "It seemed to me, it wasn't an official meeting unless there were muffins served. Maybe it's because I spent six years in the States where people had already learned that you needed to be leaner and you don't have the luxury of monopoly profits to pay for these kinds of things. I think the folks from mmmuffins made more money than anything else. I mean, how many muffins could a person eat in a day? So, we shook things up quite a bit." Indeed.

Lind hijacked the application process. Here again, he managed it as if it were a political campaign. He oversaw the production of a brochure—*The Winners Are Everybody*—that was sent to 30,000 people. Politicians and reporters were massaged alike. He parachuted in consultants, political allies and lobbyists, including John H. Tory Jr., 36, then a law partner at his father's old firm and co-chair of the national PC party; Pierre Fortier and Paul Curley from Public Affairs International; Patrick Gossage, Trudeau's former speechwriter; and Allan Gregg, the head of Decima Research and the PC Party's pollster. The Ottawa-based lobby newsletter, *The Lobby Monitor*, likened Unitel's long consulting list to a baseball card collection. Though Buchan had six lawyers on the file, Bell outnumbered them in lawyers four to one. "It was like taking on the Red Army," Bob Buchan said. For his part, Unitel's president George Harvey retained Heather Reisman, then the head of Paradigm Consulting Inc. and now a bookstore mogul, to help him revamp the organization to eliminate deadwood and to foster a competitive mindset.

Worse, CNCP, gun-shy of the CRTC after previous rejections, intended to brush off its original LD application even though the technology was outdated, because the Commission never had an issue with its technical plan. CNCP wanted to propose "line-side" access, which meant that instead of dialing "1" in an LD number, the caller first had to dial a local number, wait for a dial tone and then dial the LD number. It entailed connecting its network to hundreds of local switches. "They were going to use 1970s architectures, and then I arrived on the scene and said, 'Guys, this is not how you design a 1990s long-distance network' and it really forced a full stop on the business plan development," recalls Goldberg, who began working on a technically superior "trunk-access" interconnection plan that required spending more money up front.

Just weeks after sealing their marriage, Rogers and Stinson were suddenly being asked to kick in more money, specifically $400 million. In his first CNCP board meeting, Rogers honed in on the new technical plan. "I'd been on the scene for a month and I'm getting grilled all to hell," recalls Goldberg, then 32. "And, afterwards, the meeting finished up and it was a very cold day, and we're bundling up, going into the elevator, and Ted jumps on the elevator and says, 'That was a good presentation,' and my boss was thinking, 'Man, he was getting grilled—that's a good presentation?'"

Meanwhile, Royal Bank of Canada's chairman Allan Taylor rallied the business establishment to press for competition—full competition. The banks were the country's biggest LD users. Royal Bank was Bell's single largest customer after the federal government. For too long, the business community had been held hostage by Bell's monopolist intimidation tactics. They mounted a revolt that Ottawa could not ignore.

In a watershed decision on March 1, 1990, the CRTC permitted the resale of voice and data services in the business phone market, opening the door partly to competition. After six long years, Call-Net's Michael Kedar had finally won. Two months later, in May, CNCP, now renamed Unitel and flying the Rogers red, filed its much anticipated and overdue application to enter the long-distance fray. Close on its heels, B.C. Rail and Call-Net submitted a joint LD application. For five months in 1991 from February to July, the CRTC held its second LD hearings in seven years, an exhausting and rigorous process that produced more than 10,000 pages of evidence.

Unitel lawyer Michael Ryan and RCI lawyer Kenneth G. Engelhart spent hour upon hour prepping the team in mock hearings, and video recording and transcribing their rehearsals to ensure the owners, the expert witnesses and the engineers delivered a clear message and left the right impression in these historic hearings. The joint appearance of Stinson and Rogers was dubbed "Bill and Ted's Excellent Adventure" after the 1989 comedic film of the same title, *Globe and Mail* reporter Lawrence Surtees wrote. The CRTC intended to make a decision in 1992.

In the meantime, Rogers became an officer of the Order of Canada. Prime Minister Brian Mulroney asked Rogers to join the Senate, but he declined. "I was disappointed, but not fully surprised," says Mulroney. "He loved politics, but Ted made a choice early in life that he wanted to be a hugely successful entrepreneur. Ted had an empire, and he had a lot of financial challenges at the time."

Heading into the nineties, the company's capital needs became voracious just when the Canadian economy, tracking the United States, its biggest trade partner, slid into a severe recession. Rogers was upgrading its cable and wireless phone networks, ploughing fiber into the ground and erecting cellular towers. The recession walloped RCI shares amid concern of falling subscriber revenues, particularly from wireless. RCI shares nosedived from a post-seven-for-one-split high of $20 in 1989 to a 52-week low of $5.25 the following year. Rogers blamed it partly on the "Campeau factor"—referring to real estate and retailing baron Robert Campeau's well-publicized demise. "People are thinking, here's another Canadian entrepreneur who's … going to get blown out," he said of himself half-jokingly on a conference call to analysts. "That's the Canadian way."

For a company with a business model predicated on cash flow, RCI was not generating "free" cash flow. In accounting vernacular, cash flow is defined as EBITDA—earnings before interest, taxes, depreciation and amortization. Free cash flow is EBITDA less capital expenditures and dividends. It's an important distinction that Rogers failed to appreciate (until recently) because of his overriding psychological need to be at the forefront of technological change.

In trying to emulate his father, the inventor, Rogers was determined to be a leader in technology, causing him to make capital expenditures early to ready the cable and wireless networks for future battles. The drawback of spending capital too soon is that it might conceivably be wasted if technology changes, forcing him to reinvest fresh capital. Rogers figured that as long as EBITDA grew, he could just keep piling up the debt.

To equity investors, his business philosophy didn't seem all that different from the government's, where tax receipts keep flowing in without making any discernible impact on the debt load. "Ted runs the business on debt. He believes that as long as as you are within your debt covenants, you can keep borrowing and borrowing. He's always paid the bankers and bondholders off. Nobody's ever lost a nickel. He's proud of that, and he should be. But sometimes, even people with integrity borrow too much and they can't pay off their creditors because there's a little blip in the business, or the regulatory environment changes, or a new competitor comes in. That's why you don't keep the debt up to your chin, says John A. Tory, who straddles boards at Thomson Corp., which he helped build with the late Ken Thomson, and RCI, two companies with distinctly different approaches to business. In trying to protect Rogers from becoming overleveraged, Tory chanted the free cash flow mantra. "It's not always smart to be first. I'm not smart enough to know what's right technologically and what isn't. The only thing I know is that any business that never generates free cash flow while the debt keeps rising eventually runs into trouble. You can't keep betting the farm."

Drexel Burnham Lambert, Ted Rogers' financial lifeline in the 1980s, was becoming unglued. Junk-bond king Michael Milken had been indicted on charges of securities law violations and racketeering. The previous year, in 1989, Drexel was forced to disgorge US$650 million in penalties and sever ties with Milken to avoid being charged under RICO. Drexel, beset with internal infighting and partners pulling their capital out of the firm, began to face its own liquidity crisis. The junk-bond market was in total disarray as defaults, notably Campeau Corp. and UAL Corp., mounted, and savings and loan institutions were barred from buying new bonds and forced to liquidate their holdings. The very survival of the junk bond market at the time was in question.

In February 1990, Drexel collapsed while Graham Savage was trying to raise another US$250 million in high-yield debt. "It was a Monday morning. We were sitting in a presentation in New York with investors and the Drexel salesmen, and halfway through [the meeting], the phone rings. I see the blood draining from the face of the Drexel salesman who took the call. He put down the phone and said, 'We have to go.' They never came back," recalls Savage.

The call was an order to cease and desist all business. The preceding Friday, the SEC and the New York Stock Exchange prevented Drexel from continuing to move money from its NYSE-regulated broker-dealer upstairs into the parent company to pay off its commercial paper obligations, or short-term IOUs. With lenders refusing to roll over Drexel's commercial paper and Drexel now unable to raid its regulated subsidiary, the beleaguered firm faced a liquidity crisis. Over the weekend, Drexel scrambled to raise money, hoping the New York Federal Reserve Bank president Gerald Corrigan might lobby the commercial banks on its behalf. He didn't. With few friends on Wall Street and none in Washington, the poster child for the U.S. government's war on greed filed for Chapter 11 bankruptcy protection late Tuesday, February 13. The firm that shaped much of Wall Street in the eighties and raised hundreds of billions of dollars for its clients went into liquidation for want of a few hundred million dollars. More than a dozen companies slated to raise US$4 billion were left without an investment banker. In the midst of a complete meltdown in the high-yield market, Savage still managed to complete the offering.

Drexel fired all but 500 of its 5,400 employees. In April 1990, Milken pleaded guilty to six felony charges of securities fraud, none of which were related to the junk bond market. He ended up serving two years in federal prison. The employees who stayed behind dismantled the firm, sold its securities positions and finished deals-in-progress to collect the underwriting fees. For months they worked without any pay. Many of them had lost everything because they had reinvested their bonuses in Drexel's now worthless stock. (Before the firm went under, Drexel had begun paying bonuses in stock to reduce the massive capital outflow.) When Savage discovered that they weren't being paid—Drexel claimed the court wouldn't release the funds—he refused to pay Drexel its underwriting fees. "I told them, I'm not paying you until you pay the people who stayed on, or I'm going to take a certain amount of money and give it to them directly and I'll give you the balance," recalls Savage. "They screamed and yelled and threatened to sue me. It got nasty, but they finally relented and paid them, and then I paid the firm."

Savage sought Rogers' approval. "I said, 'I've got to go to the wall on this. Ted, are you going to be okay on this? We might get sued.'"

Rogers backed Savage to the hilt. "It's the right thing to do," Rogers replied.

"To Ted's credit, he was prepared to back me, and it worked out fine," says Savage.

Given the recession and tight market conditions, Savage postponed raising additional funds until absolutely necessary, but before long, he and his team—treasurer Lorraine Daly, who joined from Scotiabank, lawyer David Miller and corporate vice president Bruce Day—began structuring a flurry of financings to sate Rogers' appetite for capital and retire existing debt. The timing was horrendous, however. The deepening recession, combined with a lack of liquidity in the global banking system, made it virtually impossible for a junk issuer to raise money without a great deal of creativity. The hangover from the eighties' lending boom, the U.S. savings and loan crisis, the near implosion of Japan's banking industry, the Basel Committee's stricter risk-based capital rules for banks, and higher oil prices from Iraq's invasion of Kuwait precipitated a credit crunch. Canadian banks, already strained, became increasingly stretched, especially after the Reichmann empire collapsed. Further, the federal and provincial governments were sopping up every dollar in Canada that was available from bond investors.

Rogers was forced to ask cp's Bill Stinson for a loan. RCI borrowed $135 million from cp at prime plus 1.5 percent per annum, using its Unitel shares as collateral. Savage wanted to remove the pledge on the Unitel shares as quickly as possible. He also had to pay off the Cantel note to First City before RCI could proceed with plans to take Cantel public. By mid-year 1991, RCI's long-term debt had climbed to $2 billion, three-quarters of it in bank loans. Interest expenses totaled $113 million—or more than $625,000 a day just to service its debt. Long-term debt was running at 17 times operating cash flow.

Financially, RCI had gained respectability among the U.S. white-shoed investment bankers after the blockbuster sale of its U.S. cable company. The company began using Merrill Lynch and Goldman Sachs. In fact, Drexel's demise became Merrill Lynch's boon. In July 1991, RCI became Canada's first issuer of a Merrill-engineered financial beast, a liquid yield option note, or a "LYON," which is a zero-coupon convertible debenture that's both callable and redeemable.

RCI took Cantel public at $19.50 a share in August 1991, selling 14 million shares to raise $270 million (after underwriting fees), which was used to retire debt. RCI then sold additional stock to reduce its Cantel stake to 80 percent. In less than a year, Savage removed any fears of a cash shortfall by raising $3 billion through more than a dozen debt and equity financings (a third in equity), mostly from the U.S. capital markets. They chopped bank debt to about $140 million and even had cash to spare. "You take the money when you can get it, not when you have to have it," Savage told *The Globe and Mail* at the time. The company also had $2 billion in untapped bank credit lines, fueling hotly denied rumors that Rogers was building a war chest as a prelude to buying out cp's stake in Unitel.

Early in 1992, Rogers surprisingly sold 6 million RCI Class B shares. The sale initially made equity investors skittish until he explained that the family's private company was $75 million in debt, because he had been in the market loading up on his own stock. "I'm 58," he said, "and being out of debt personally is something I think is very important." The need to get his affairs in order would become apparent eight months later.

On June 12, 1992, in a 206-page ruling, the CRTC allowed facilities-based long-distance competition, throwing open the doors to full competition. Though Unitel won its application, the victory was hollow. It was not granted a duopoly. The market quickly became overrun with *resellers*—companies that lease surplus lines from the telephone companies at wholesale rates and attach their own equipment at either end to route and bill calls. Their costs are substantially less than facilities-based players. Unlike Unitel, resellers could slice their profit margins down to almost nothing to attract customers. In the next five years, dozens of newcomers emerged—359 registered, although half were inactive—and many went belly up. Call-Net and Montreal-based Fonorola Inc. emerged as the two largest resellers.

BCE's Jean Monty aptly described the long-distance battle as a "David versus David struggle." The CRTC's decision surprised BCE, he recalls. BCE unsuccessfully challenged the decision in the Federal Court of Canada. The tactic merely garnered bad publicity. "The incumbent is never in grace," adds Cyr. For a monopoly, Bell responded far more quickly than either CP or RCI had anticipated. CP and RCI had been myopically focused on the hearing, not the looming war. They fell prey to their own hype. "We were starry-eyed in the long distance business. We thought everything would work out for us if we could only win this hearing," says RCI's Ken Englehart.

Unitel tried to prepare for the inevitable price war. That meant automating its billing systems. Ideally, it needed a partner to provide network software and manage the installation of the system. Unitel's British-born CEO George Harvey hired Brooklyn, New York native and West Point graduate Nate Kantor from MCI to run the company's newly formed LD implementation team. Lawrence Surtees' book *Wire Wars*, which details the LD fight, tells how Kantor sent out comprehensive Requests for Proposal during the regulatory hearings to all major U.S. LD carriers and telecom vendors in order to find a U.S. partner. MCI, led by CEO Bert Roberts Jr., became Unitel's preferred choice. Harvey took the Unitel board to visit MCI in Washington and Sprint in Kansas City in late November to prod them into making a decision.

Heading into 1992, Unitel finally authorized management to negotiate a deal with MCI. Just months later, before the CRTC's landmark decision, Stentor, formerly known as Telecom Canada, joined MCI in a 12-member international telecom consortium known as the Financial Network Association to provide seamless telecom services to the global banking industry. MCI then turfed Unitel to forge a deal with the Bell-dominated Stentor consortium. Unitel felt that somehow word had leaked to Stentor of its talks with MCI, prompting Stentor to insinuate itself with MCI. Ted Rogers and Bill Stinson intended to fly to Washington DC for a last-ditch meeting with MCI's Bert Roberts in June to salvage the deal, but their meeting was canceled when MCI's chairman and founder Bill McGowan died of a heart attack at age 64.

Two months later, Ted Rogers went under the knife. In August 1992, Rogers had quadruple bypass heart surgery at the Mayo Clinic in Rochester, Minneapolis. His Bahamian physician, a heart specialist, had pestered him to have an angiogram after an examination revealed worrisome discrepancies from his latest medical records. The procedure discovered several partially blocked arteries.

"He's not average. He's like a wind-up toy. I've yet to see anyone recover as fast as him," says his Toronto family physician, Dr. Bernard Gosevitz, who scrubbed in for the surgery. "He's the poster boy for drive. He's one of the toughest people I know when it comes down to sheer will and determination. And, he vocalizes it. He internalizes, but he vocalizes. There are times when he'll just sit and shake his head and he'll just go off on a litany of comments, and it's good that he verbalizes it. But, there are times when he doesn't, and he internalizes it."

In Rogers' absence, RCI chairman John Graham became acting chief executive, backed up by deputy chairman Gar Emerson. Emerson flew to Washington to meet with MCI's Roberts to ascertain how and why their alliance had fallen apart. In the wake of MCI's pact with Stentor, CP's Bill Stinson then called AT&T's Bob Allen to initiate talks. They code-named their negotiations "World Series"—since the Toronto Blue Jays were heading to the Fall Classic against the Atlanta Braves. (In October, Rogers and his wife, Loretta, entertained Braves' owner Ted Turner and Jane Fonda, who were in Toronto for the World Series.)

Bob Allen sent Joseph P. Nacchio to meet with the Unitel owners. Nacchio, 43, a ballsy AT&T vice president, was widely regarded as the frontrunner to succeed Allen. Given AT&T's bitter history with MCI, AT&T was infuriated that Stentor, AT&T's century-old partner, had aligned itself with the hated monopoly buster. AT&T and Stentor shared more than $1.3-billion worth in cross-border telephone calls, making Canada the largest telecom-calling partner with the United States. AT&T would launch a patent lawsuit in Washington against

Stentor and MCI, resulting in countersuits and lawsuits in both countries. Nacchio regarded Bell, the largest Stentor member, the enemy. He intended to show BCE that it couldn't push AT&T around. Emerson recalls that he and John Graham contacted Rogers at the Mayo Clinic by phone from the stateroom aboard the smaller first *Loretta Anne* yacht moored in the Toronto harbor, where the RCI directors were having a night out, to brief him about their meeting with Nacchio. Soon after, talks between AT&T, CP and RCI began in earnest. The negotiations, secretly held in the concrete-walled basement of a hotel in Parsippany, New Jersey, proved difficult. People familiar with the situation recall that talks almost derailed because of CP's CFO Bill Fatt, a fast-rising star, although then a novice dealmaker, whose brusque manner angered the mighty AT&T. Eventually, Rogers and Nacchio ironed out the remaining differences in an all-night negotiation.

During their negotiations, AT&T was sealing a pact with McCaw Cellular, America's biggest cellular telephone company. On November 4, AT&T agreed to take a 33-percent stake in McCaw for $3.8 billion with an option to take majority control at some time in the future. McCaw blanketed 40 percent of America's population and almost all of its cities. Five days later, MCI announced plans to launch a new wireless network with Sprint, who was trying to find an entry point into the cable TV industry.

In early autumn of 1992, after Rogers' bypass surgery, Cantel chief James F. Sward was summoned to Frybrook. Seated in the atrium off the front entrance, Rogers, wearing a bathrobe, basically told Sward to stop arguing with him. He parted the robe and showed Sward his scar, still fairly fresh, running down the length of his chest along the breastbone. "There are ten reasons why I have this scar," Rogers told him, "and you're responsible for six of them."

Sward was slack-jawed. "The scar just scared the heck out of me," he recalls. But, it didn't have the desired effect Rogers was hoping for. Instead of falling in line, Sward quit. In March 1993, RCI announced that Sward, 47, had retired. "I just felt, my God, I've done this to somebody, at least, he believes I've done this to him. I care a great deal about Ted, still do to this day. I'm no saint. If I feel I'm right, I can be a royal pain in the ass, but that was the turning point for me."

"In my defense, I was only six reasons; somebody else was four," Sward chuckles.

Sward had slid into the Cantel hot seat in 1989 after Rogers persuaded him to take the job. He was then 44 years old. Though his knowledge of cellular

Philippe de Gaspé Beaubien at an Expo 67 reception with Queen Elizabeth in July 1967. (CP)

(l. to r.) Bill Neir, vice chairman of Continental Cablevision, Phil Lind, Terence McGuirk, Ted Turner's right hand at Turner Broadcasting, and Peter Barton, John Malone's No. 2 at TCI and founding president of Liberty Media, at the 1994 Goodwill Games in St. Petersburg, Russia. (Courtesy of Phil Lind.)

Robin Korthals in front of TD Bank vault, 1991.
(Tony Bock/*Toronto Star*)

John A. Tory, 1983. (CP/Blaise Edwards)

Peter Godsoe, 2003. (CP/Andrew Vaughan)

Bill Stinson at Canadian Pacific Ltd. 1988
annual meeting. (Allen McInnis/CP)

Richard Thomson, TD Bank, 1990.
(Ken Faught/*Toronto Star*)

(l. to r.) Phil Lind, Ted Rogers, Gar Emerson and Graham Savage. (Ed Regan, *The Globe and Mail*.)

Colin Watson pleads for peace at a Vancouver press conference during the 1995 negative-option fiasco. (CP/Ric Ernst)

Don Campbell and Ron Osborne at a Maclean Hunter annual meeting in 1990.
(Boris Spremo/*Toronto Star*)

Ted Rogers with Blue Jays ace Roy Halladay at a press conference in 2004 to announce the pitcher's four-year, $42 million contract. A smiling Phil Lind is the background. (CP/Aaron Harris)

Craig McCaw. (Courtesy, Eagle River)

Ted Rogers listens to Nadir Mohamed during a 2004 press conference. They just completed the Microcell transaction. (CP/Paul Chiasson)

John Zeglis, Alfred Mockett and Ted Rogers at a press conference announcing RCI's sale of one-third of Rogers Cantel to AT&T and British Telecom in 1999. (CP/*Maclean's*/Peter Bregg)

Ted Rogers swaps cable assets with Jim Shaw in 2000. (CP/Frank Gunn)

Ted Rogers and Larry Tannenbaum, MLSE chairman, hold a Toronto Maple Leafs hockey jersey at a 2006 press conference where MLSE named RCI its preferred telecom supplier. (CP/Nathan Denette)

Ted and Loretta Rogers at their 40th wedding anniversary celebration in 2003.
(Courtesy of Rogers family.)

Ted Rogers meets with his son Edward and daughter Melinda in April 2000.
(CP/*Toronto Star*-Ron Bull)

Phil Lind and Ted Rogers pose for the camera after Lind inducted Rogers into U.S. Cable TV Hall of Fame in Denver in 2002. (Courtesy of the Cable Center.)

Ted Rogers celebrates 10 years on the NYSE in 2006 by ringing the opening bell. (l. to r.) William Linton, RCI CFO, Phil Lind, John Thain, NYSE CEO, Ted Rogers, Alan Horn, RCI chairman, and Bruce Mann, RCI vice president, investor relations. (Courtesy, RCI and NYSE)

Ted Rogers salutes the crowd at the WTA Rogers Cup in August 2004 in Montreal. (CP/Jacques Boissinot)

amounted to the phone's on-off send button, Sward was a trusted lieutenant with a 12-year track record at Rogers Broadcasting.

Cantel, under Sward, experienced phenomenal growth. By the time he left, annual revenue from wireless surpassed cable's, though the cable company was still more profitable. In the midst of a recession, Cantel, which added 465 new cell sites, offset monthly subscriber revenues (from sharply lower phone prices) by signing new customers. In four years, Cantel's subscriber base almost quadrupled to 573,000 subscribers. "We were hiring people by the hundreds. We were spending $1 million a day in the field. It was an intense, very intense period," says Sward.

A month after Sward "retired," Izzy Asper hired him as CanWest Global's president and CEO to replace David Mintz, 63, who had decided to retire. Though he had acquired broadcast interests in Australia and New Zealand, Asper had yet to build his national dream TV network in Canada, where he had four stations outside of Ontario. To fund the dream, Asper had taken CanWest public in 1991, right in the middle of a recession. With the stock languishing, Asper brought in Sward to inject fresh ideas, new energy and the drive to take CanWest to the next level.

"Izzy Asper was brilliant, and I don't think he worked ten percent of the amount of time that Ted did. But he didn't accomplish all that Ted accomplished," says Sward.

"Ted and Izzy shared one common trait: They were both Dicta terrorists. They used that Dictaphone and they were just friggin' terrorists with it. I mean, the bullets that would fly out of Rogers' office Rogers wrote usually in the early morning and sober, and Izzy's best were after his gin cocktails about one o'clock in the morning. You'd come in, sort of feeling good about yourself and feeling organized, and one of these friggin' bombs would land on your desk. Well, they just came short of saying bad things about your mother. They were soul-destroying, and the whole world would get copied," laughs Sward.

Rogers admits he will use tough love techniques if he thinks it will motivate. While not involved in team sports as a young man, Rogers seemed to adopt a managerial style that approximated the great American football coaches of the 1960s—Vince Lombardi of the Packers, Paul William "Bear" Bryant of University of Alabama and George Halas of the Chicago Bears. To wit, if the coaches weren't yelling at you, you weren't important. Years later, when his son, Edward, wanted to take a more conservative cable telephony tack than his dad, Rogers said he'd turn over his father's framed photograph so that it faced the wall, saying that their namesake would be ashamed of Edward if he dared sacrifice quality. Though he didn't do it, Rogers said he would if he thought it might help. "I'm going to take the picture and face the wall because that's an outrage because that sort of thinking will destroy our brand. It's a great line, isn't it? And, [Edward] says, 'Oh, that's a terrible thing to say,'" laughs Rogers. "He'd be horrified [if I did that] because I'd be saying his plan would be unworthy of his grandfather's and father's reputation and heritage and that's about as powerful as you can get."

Rogers has a flare for the dramatic. "I was always fond of Jim and a great admirer of his. I'm sure I said that. You've got to joke about these things." When asked if he truly blamed Sward, Rogers replies, "No, of course not. Nobody is responsible for your medical situation or mine." Even if that's the way it feels at the time? "Yes, but then, it's our inability to handle it," he replies.

In January 1993, AT&T signed on to Bill and Ted's Excellent Adventure. AT&T invested $150 million in exchange for a 20-percent stake and two seats on the board of directors. CP reduced its ownership to 48 percent from 60 percent. Rogers' stake fell to 32 percent from 40 percent. In a decade dotted with industry alliances and breakups, Call-Net brought in its own U.S. heavyweight eight months later. Kansas City-based Sprint Corp., headed by Rogers' friend William Esrey, bought 25 percent of Call-Net, which then changed its name to Sprint Canada. That same month, in August, AT&T unveiled its takeover of McCaw Cellular for US$12.6 billion, the fifth-largest takeover in U.S. history. The wireline giant planned to marry the computerized intelligence of its LD network to McCaw's wireless systems. Their union also gave the wireless company a powerful new way of bypassing local telephone companies. It might well have been a page from Rogers' playbook.

Meanwhile, Unitel became unglued at the board level. It was a three-headed monster with no one in control. The owners, each armed with extensive veto powers, needed to reach unanimous agreement on all decisions, including annual business plans, capital expenditures and compensation policies. That proved difficult given that Ted Rogers tried to exploit his position as chairman. After joining the Unitel board, James Meenan and William Catucci, both from AT&T, were stunned by Rogers' blatant attempts to push through his agenda without giving balance to either Unitel's interests or the interests of the other parties. Rogers pulled a Belzberg. He began vetoing decisions as an owner—after approving them at the director level.

The owners lacked the will to work together to fix Unitel, which was haemorrhaging a million dollars every business day. "Stinson and Rogers never reached a level of mutual admiration for each other's abilities, strengths and expertise. They were worlds apart," one person close to the situation recalls.

Unitel was no longer as important to CP as it was to Rogers. CP, a sprawling cash-rich conglomerate, tended to give its divisional managers a lot of flexibility and autonomy. If the divisions failed, CP tended to shut them down rather than fix them. Unlike those at CP, Rogers wanted to be involved in every managerial decision. "The simple solution is not to fix it, but to sell it," says Rogers. "It reminds me of the people who say, if you have a pain in your leg, amputate it."

Unitel, the largest alterative long-distance carrier among the six new national players and more than 150 small resellers, would win 7-percent market share, but at enormous cost. The company's business plan—based on a duopoly, not open competition—was fundamentally flawed and its ownership group adrift. Inertia kept customers tied to the incumbents. Canadians were overwhelmed with a confusing array of discount LD plans and rates. Faced with cutthroat competition, Unitel's profits evaporated. The company was better at signing up customers than keeping them happy.

Unitel finished 1993 with a loss of more than a billion dollars, which included a massive one-time restructuring charge to eliminate almost one-fifth of its workforce over a three-year period. Job losses mounted. "In a dieting contest, the fat man wins," sums up Richard Stursberg, the former Department of Communications assistant deputy minister and Unitel's point-man on government and legal matters. "The only thing we had to sell was lower prices, and every time we lowered our prices, they would go to the Commission and say, 'You have to let us lower our prices to compete.' The Commission would say yes, which was completely insane on its part. It was impossible to get any traction."

For his part, Rogers initially blamed AT&T for not sending its A team to Canada to manage Unitel and then the CRTC for failing to establish the proper rules of engagement. Unitel and other newcomers were required to pay the incumbents so-called contribution payments amounting to close to half of their long-distance revenues to compensate the landline carriers for the use of their local lines and switching services. In the United States that amount was only about a third, they complained. The Commission reduced the contributions from LD to local exchange service by increasing monthly local rates to telephone customers by two dollars a month for three successive years, a measure the federal cabinet overruled and then didn't bother to fight when the Commission reinstated it later.

"We were too focused on the goal of getting the CRTC to license competition," says RCI's Ken Englehart. "We thought, if we got permission to get into this business that, if there are problems, the CRTC will fix them for us once we're in the tent. It didn't happen. The lesson I learned is to be careful what you wish for. Don't be satisfied with the regulatory win if there's not a business case for it, and if the regulator won't create the necessary conditions for competitive success, don't think they are going to change the rules once you're in the game. You'd better be darn sure that this is a business you really want to go into."

When the dust settled, Bell maintained its business customers without even having to offer discount rate-plans to low-volume LD users—read, the public. Ten years later, competitors controlled 32 percent of the LD market. "The cost of telephone service has gone up in Canada, not down," says Raymond Cyr. "Some people have benefited [from the 1992 decision], while others have paid for it. Thirty-five percent of the customers in Bell in the 1990 period never made a long distance call, so these 35 percent have been paying more for the Royal Bank and all the others that are now paying less. Now, if that's what you want, well, that's fine. And, Ted was quite successful at promoting that model on the basis that prices would go down, which they did on the long distance, and then went up on the local side to balance it. So, how is that good? But, he was quite good at promoting the idea.

"They dealt with it in the U.S. primarily because the [Federal Communications Commission] is less politicized. Here, they decided not to deal with it. That's life in Canada. We're more socialist."

Unitel ran on borrowed money and time. The company owed $650 million (and counting) to a six-bank consortium. (Unitel had a $700-million credit facility.) In September 1994, with Unitel's bank debt due in December, CP began to reconsider if it still wanted to be in the telecom business. Word leaked in the press that CP had hired RBC Dominion Securities for advice on what to do with its 48-percent stake. That sparked months of speculation in the media and among telecom pundits if CP would indeed sell and if Rogers would make a play for the company. Unitel managed to get a three-month extension from the banks. In the third quarter of 1994, the partners injected $70 million into cash-strapped Unitel. AT&T picked up Rogers' share of the tab and another 2.5 percent of its equity position, reducing Rogers' stake to 29.5 percent. In the midst of completing the hostile takeover of Maclean Hunter, RCI could not pony up more money. And Ted Rogers had more trouble on the horizon.

Just before Christmas 1994, calls from angry Rogers' cable TV subscribers were jamming the switchboards.

Rogers had foisted a reshuffled, higher-priced channel lineup on his bread-and-butter cable TV subscribers with an arrogant "take it or leave it" attitude that led to the biggest consumer backlash in Canadian cable TV history. Though it became known as the negative option fiasco, the problem stemmed from how the brain trust at Rogers bundled seven new cable, or specialty, channels.

The CRTC had meted out seven new cable channel licenses—called specialty channels—in June 1994, largely in anticipation of expected invasion by the U.S. direct-broadcast satellites, which threatened to beam hundreds of American channels into Canada. The seven licenses, two of which went to former CRTC chairman André Bureau, were: Bravo!; Discovery Channel; Life Network; New Country Network; RGI, the French news channel; Showcase; and the Women's Television Network—all but the French channel were modeled on their established U.S. counterparts with the requisite Canadian content fillers. The Commission rejected applications for comedy, cartoons and hockey—channels that might actually sell. The new channels were scheduled to air on January 1, 1995.

Rogers reshuffled its lineup so that subscribers who didn't want the new channels would be deprived of popular existing ones, such as TSN, CNN and A&E. The company then notified subscribers of changes in their monthly statements in late December when people were preoccupied with the Christmas holidays. Customers were told they must either subscribe to the newly assembled packages in their entirety at an extra cost of roughly four dollars a month or lose all specialty services. Rogers customers had until February 1 to notify the company of their decision. If they didn't opt out, they'd automatically be charged for new services—negative option billing. It was marketing blackmail, the *Edmonton Journal* wrote.

But Rogers wasn't the first to bill this way; the cable industry had been using negative option billing for years with virtually no complaint. Rogers used it when it created a tier of services known as Basic Plus above the basic 13-station band in 1992 and automatically billed customers unless they notified the company that they didn't want it. Ninety-five percent of consumers became automatic subscribers to the added service. Here, the grand plan was to bundle the channels together to jack up cash flow. Unlike the phone companies, cable TV companies can use funds from their monopoly operations to subsidize other ventures. Well, the normally docile public decided to fight back. Canadians mounted a cable TV insurrection.

Rogers insisted the packaging of existing and new services was done to comply with new CRTC regulations, stipulating they must offer one Canadian cable channel for every American service in a package. That just didn't wash with the public. Cable TV subscribers were furious about the arbitrary price increases and the lack of choice. The controversy prompted 100,000 calls per week and about 4,000 of Rogers' 2.6 million subscribers to disconnect from the optional services. The CRTC and politicians fielded hundreds of complaints.

The lack of marketing—by a company respected for its marketing savvy—made customers suspicious and cynical. In a matter of weeks, the company was perceived as arrogant, greedy and duplicitous—a lot like other monopolists. Faced with emerging direct to home (DTH) satellite services, the proliferation of the gray market in satellite dishes and the developing urban warfare for condominium TV access, the last thing RCI needed was the loss of customer goodwill. Canadians, fed up with monopolies and furious at the CRTC's Fortress Canada mentality, began buying gray-market satellite dishes in droves. Rogers, the largest cable TV company and based in Toronto, the country's media capital, bore the brunt of the consumer backlash, even though more than 200 other cable companies had launched similar packages.

"That really got people pissed off," recalls Rogers, who was responsible for the channel shuffle. "It was a terrible thing. We reversed it. It wasn't the negative billing that angered people. It's because we took some channels from the second tier and put them in the first tier. So, I was paying for a service and now I have to buy them both." He just wanted people to forget about it and move on. When the negative billing appeared in an otherwise glowing story about Rogers a decade after the imbroglio, Rogers quipped in an interview, "I was going to phone the guy and say, 'What's your problem, man?' I think they've got to say something other than praise us."

Shaw escaped much of the abuse hurled at Rogers because it bundled a couple of the new channels on its first tier and put the rest into a second tier. Neither Shaw nor Vidéotron bundled the new channels with existing ones, though they both fielded complaints from customers who rode the surge of national wrath against Rogers. "We compared plans at the time," recalls Jim Shaw, JR's son and Shaw's chief executive officer. "We said, 'We don't agree with the way you want to do it.' I remember Ted saying to Colin, 'We better not have this launched and JR looking good and me looking bad.' And, that's exactly what happened."

In Vancouver, where central Canada isn't much liked anyway, the backlash was the worst. People hurled stones and made rude finger gestures at Rogers Cable vans. "The beautiful thing about cable is that it's like a utility, only with an upside, because you have to be incredibly inept to lose customers," Colin Watson told business reporter David Olive in the mid-eighties. "That is why you can't really drive a cable company over the edge." Evidently, however, you can try.

In the midst of what rapidly became a major marketing and public relations nightmare, the company swiftly went into damage-control mode. Watson took the arrows for Rogers. Just after New Year's Day in 1995, he flew to Vancouver, where he publicly apologized at a press conference, flashing the famous Richard Nixon peace sign. He announced a revamped, larger channel package at a lower cost and gave subscribers another month of free viewing before they had to notify the company of canceling their service. The company estimated a $30-million to $50-million loss in subscriber revenue from changing its plan. Rudi Engel handled Toronto and southern Ontario. Rogers personally worked on the call centers, putting people and systems rapidly in place to handle the call volume.

"Everybody did it slightly differently, but certainly Rogers led more with our chin and we got our chin knocked harder than anybody else. In hindsight, it was not a good thing to do. Live and learn," says Colin Watson.

"We rescinded the offer and got on with our life," he says. "It wasn't the highlight of the year."

Liberal backbencher Roger Galloway tried to ban negative option billing by cable TV companies through a private member's bill that sailed through the House of Commons before the Senate killed it. The senators—backed by Heritage Minister Sheila Copps and cable industry lobbyists—claimed French-language specialty channels couldn't flourish unless all Canadians paid for them because the francophone markets weren't large enough to make them financially viable. In *Free for All*, author Matthew Fraser explains that André Bureau and his allies—Phil Lind sat on the Astral board and Bureau sat on the Shaw board—cleverly played the Quebec card to get the twitchy Chrétien Liberal government, still in shock after the near defeat in the referendum on Quebec sovereignty, to get the Senate to back off. The Bloc Québécois MPs claimed, somewhat ludicrously as Fraser wrote, that with the Galloway bill French Canadians would be deprived of new TV channels in the French language. (Ironically, Quebec banned the negative option billing.) Francis Fox, Rogers' hired gun, was sent to Ottawa to make sure the Senate didn't pass the Galloway bill. He earned his fee. Galloway's bill died. Liberal prime minister Paul Martin later appointed Fox to the Senate, Canada's chamber of sober second thought.

Rogers just kept racking up bad publicity in Vancouver, where a month later, a fleet of 13 Rogers Cable vans surrounded the Pacific Place condominium complex on the former Expo 86 site on the False Creek waterfront. Billed as Canada's first "smart community," the condos were wired with fiber optics, crucial for the speed-is-everything Internet age. Pacific Place Communication Inc., a joint venture of Hong Kong tycoon Li Ka-shing's Concord Pacific Development Corp. and BC Telecom (now Telus), was providing cable TV service, which was prohibited by law from supplying cable TV in areas already served by cable companies, such as Rogers. Pacific Place Cable offered a 46-channel package for $29.50 a month, compared to roughly $70 for a comparable package from Rogers. RCI had already taken them to court. Rogers even bought a condo to check out the rival offering. When the property manager turned the cable guys away, they went down the manholes outside the tower. The company later apologized to Pacific Place, saying its technicians were anxious to provide service to the condo residents. The press jumped all over the story. The Rogers public relations machine made matters worse when it lied to the media, saying the cable vans had gone to the wrong address.

Just as it tried to protect Ma Bell's monopoly, the CRTC was now trying to protect Rogers' cable TV monopoly. In reality, it was just trying to protect itself. It couldn't have anyone undermining its licensing authority or challenging the way it operated. It twice ordered Pacific Place to stop providing service, to no avail. Finally, the CRTC caved. In June 1996, after a five-year battle for the right to offer competitive cable service, Pacific Place Cable broke the Rogers cable TV monopoly in Vancouver. Fighting for BC Tel was none other than future RCI lieutenant Nadir Mohamed.

The backlash to the negative billing option was so vitriolic the Rogers wanted to re-brand the company, dropping the Rogers name altogether, a move Lind fought. Rogers wanted to go with Cantel, a brand he felt resonated with consumers and employees. "Let's make it Cantel Cable; let's make it Cantel Video," Lind recalls Rogers telling him. Ironically, the one person who wanted to give up the Rogers brand had his name on the building.

"I don't know what got into him," recalls Lind. "In a funny kind of way, he was trying to be modest, but he was, in fact, responding to the B.C. thing. He felt the B.C. thing was just overwhelming for him, and he would never be able to march under the B.C. banner in B.C."

Lind stalled for time. His right-hand, Jan Innes, RCI's media spokesperson, came up with the idea of telling Rogers they should undertake market research in the field, which they did, but also partly as a ploy to buy time until he had a chance to calm down and reassess the brand issue. While he's since wizened to their tactics, Rogers fell for it. Months rolled by. Finally, he grew exasperated and plainly ordered them to change the name. "No, don't do that, "Lind recalls saying, "we'll think about it for a while." Later, Diefenbach Elkins, a prominent New York corporate identity consulting firm was hired to undertake the market research that ultimately convinced Rogers to keep his name on the building.

"I fought back, and fought back, and finally he changed his mind," says Lind.

"The original plan was to jettison the Rogers name and have Cantel Cable," says Edward Rogers, who returned from his stint at Comcast in Philadelphia on January 1, 1995, just in time to witness first hand the negative option fiasco— the single most damaging blow to the company's reputation in its history. "Ted was very supportive of that. It would put a new face on the company."

In January 1995, CP went public with the news that it wanted out of Unitel. It would not sink any more money into the company. Rogers had an option to buy CP's stake for $210 million, cash or stock. The option to buy expired April 28, the day when the Unitel bank loan was due. If it exercised the option, RCI was on the hook to repay an even larger proportion of the ailing company's $650-million debt.

Naturally, Ted Rogers wanted control. He unequivocally stated his intention publicly, a declaration that prompted debt-rating agency Standard & Poor's to place RCI on credit watch with negative implications, a move that affected $1.4 billion of the company's U.S. debt. If downgraded, the company would be forced to pay higher interest rates on borrowed money. The credit-rating agencies are the all-important gatekeepers to the corporate bond vigilantes. They determine the company's ability to borrow and to borrow at any cost, thus they can dictate corporate direction. Throughout 1994, the U.S. central bank's target interest rate on overnight bank loans, the Fed funds rate, soared to 6 percent from 3 percent, which sent the bond market reeling. Even mighty Goldman Sachs was wobbling from substantial losses in its fixed-income portfolio. Bob Rae's New Democratic Party government of Ontario was holding its breath, fearing it might lose its double-A-minus rating after being put on credit watch with negative implications. If dropped into the land of single-As, the Rae government would have triggered a global crisis in the swaps market. James Carville, adviser to Bill Clinton's successful 1992 presidential election campaign, famously reflected that if he could be reincarnated, he'd like to come back as the bond market since it was clearly more powerful than the world's most powerful politician. Clearly, no one sent Ted Rogers the memo. He was blithely moving along with a single-minded pursuit of becoming Canada's Second Force.

"Ted desperately, dearly, truly wanted to do it and it took, literally, eight months to convince Ted that he couldn't afford to do it," recalls Rogers' treasurer Lorraine Daly. "We could have scrounged some humongous amount of money together that we needed, but it would have been rolling the dice on all of our operations. Everything. The entire Rogers empire would have been severely at risk over this decision to buy majority ownership of Unitel. So, finally, Ted had to back off. But, he loves rolling the dice."

The unenviable task of talking Rogers out of betting the company fell to his CFO, Graham Savage. Savage, supported by Daly, had heavy-duty discussions with Rogers that involved yelling matches and came close to fist-a-cuffs.

In April 1995, one week before the loan was due, Ted Rogers disconnected his failed six-year foray into the long distance market, a decision that stunned the industry. Several analysts were convinced the announcement was a negotiating tactic. The bankers knew better. Scotiabank's Peter Godsoe called Rogers on a satellite phone from his room at the Four Seasons Olympic Hotel in Seattle, where he was attending a global bankers' conference. TD's Dick Thomson and Royal Bank's John Cleghorn were with him. Though Godsoe claims the banks were not angry with Rogers, Daly begs to differ. "The banks went nuts, and blamed us," recalls Daly. "We were in the doghouse for two years over that."

The bankers spent the summer ironing out Unitel's rescue package. Scotiabank ended up owning 28 percent, TD, 23 percent, and Royal Bank, 16 percent, with AT&T taking the remaining 33 percent. They completed the bailout in January 1996. Unitel changed its name to AT&T Canada Long Distance. CP terminated its 114-year history of involvement in Canadian telecom. Rogers was out. Immediately, speculation swirled in the press that Rogers was courting Sprint to be his next LD partner. The dream had not died.

Rogers had sunk $500 million into Unitel since 1989. All written off.

"Unitel was a mistake, that's all. I was lucky to not have too many more. And, it wasn't life threatening," says Rogers.

Just like Cantel, Rogers faced two tough partners in CP and AT&T. Unlike Cantel though, he couldn't pull off a coup this time.

"There were three of us, no boss. I hated it. I absolutely hated it. Of course, we lost everything," he says. "I've never had anybody speak to me as tough and shrewd as Stinson did to me. He's a lot more important than I am. He is the head of CP and I'm a little guy. It was very, very, very tough. So, never again. Never again, have three as a partnership. To hell with it."

CHAPTER 17

Blood Sport

*"Mr. Rogers only knows two words when he's negotiating:
'No' means 'Maybe' and 'Maybe' means 'Yes.'"*

—Ron Osborne

TED ROGERS, 60, was studying a map of cable TV franchises in Ontario when he suddenly had an epiphany: all of his cable TV territories were adjacent to Maclean Hunter's. That's when he decided he had to buy Canada's iconic media giant. By combining the cable assets of the two companies, he could gird himself for the coming battle with Bell Canada.

Just before New Year's Day 1994, Rogers reached M&A guru Gar Emerson in Kona, Hawaii, where he and his family were vacationing, to seek his help in mounting what would be the biggest-ever media takeover in Canadian history. It was an audacious idea. He took only two other people into his confidence: his wife, Loretta, and Phil Lind, now an RCI vice chairman.

"Ted, I think it's really risky," Lind said.

"No, I want to do it," replied Rogers.

Through RTL, Rogers quietly built a position in Maclean Hunter (MH) stock on the open market in early January. By using his own money, he avoided having to seek prior approval from the RCI board. (He later sold his stake to RCI at cost.) He hoped to pursue a friendly merger, since MH had adopted a poison pill anti-takeover defense, or shareholders' rights protection plan, five years earlier that coincidentally Emerson helped draft before leaving Davies Ward & Beck. (Poison pills raise the price of acquiring an unwilling target.) Failing a friendly merger, Emerson devised a plan of attack that he named "Project Kona."

Lind was concerned over how their bid would be perceived in Ottawa. MH was the fourth-largest cable company in Canada behind RCI, Vidéotron and Shaw. Buying MH would give RCI control of more than a third of the country's cable television subscribers and 70 percent of the cabled homes in Ontario. For the deal to pass muster with the competition and broadcasting watchdogs, Lind had to frame the takeover in the context of Canada securing its place on the heavily touted information superhighway. He needed to keep the spin simple and the message consistent, because there would undoubtedly be a public outcry. The takeover, if successful would make Rogers an instant print heavyweight.

Maclean Hunter was a Canadian publishing icon. A part of the fabric of Canadian life, MH was almost as old as Bell Canada. When John Bayne Maclean launched *Canadian Grocer* in 1887 to escape his dead-end job as a *Toronto Mail* business writer, a media empire was born. He then partnered with Horace Talmadge Hunter to launch trade publications, newspapers and magazines, including *Maclean's*, *Chatelaine* and the *Financial Post*. The company diversified into radio broadcasting, printing and cable television, though it continued to create and acquire publications. Heading into the nineties, MH had more than 200 publications and controlled the tabloid publishing empire of the *Toronto Sun*. MH had 700,000 cable subscribers, almost all in Ontario, and another 534,000 subscribers in New Jersey, Michigan and Florida.

RCI and MH were a study in contrasts. RCI paid no dividends, fearlessly leveraged its cash flow to leap into brand new businesses, regularly posted losses and took pride in walking the high wire with the banks but never falling off. MH, by studiously avoiding debt and espousing a strong balance sheet, delivered steady profits and regular dividends. But its earlier mistake of rejecting investments in the emerging cellular industry had come to haunt it. While cellular had lifted RCI's shares, MH's stock had flatlined as its growth had stagnated.

MH's parts were more valuable than the whole. Indeed, MH's U.S. cable franchises were worth an estimated $1.5 billion. Even with fewer subscribers, the U.S. franchises were worth more than MH's Canadian cable systems because they generated higher cash flow. Americans paid more than Canadians for basic cable TV service and subscribed to the higher-priced pay-per-view channels, including HBO.

In the wake of the autumn mega-merger between cable giant TCI and Bell Atlantic (now Verizon)—a Baby Bell—Maclean Hunter hired New York investment bank Goldman Sachs & Co. to explore the possibility of selling the franchises or bringing in another partner. Since MH carried the franchises on its books for an estimated $300 million to $400 million, MH was searching for ways of selling without triggering a massive capital-gains tax bill.

With the Goldman report expected to land in mid-January, Rogers had no time to waste. He had a ballpark price tag for MH of more than $3 billion. Going into the battle, RCI had $700 million cash on hand. It was hardly a war chest.

"Can I come down and see you?" Rogers asked Scotiabank's CEO Peter C. Godsoe. Rogers felt that he might put RCI's regular banker, TD Bank's Dick Thomson, in an awkward position if he asked him for a loan because TD was also Maclean Hunter's principal banker. Rogers and the MH chairman, Don Campbell, were TD directors.

Though their wives and children were friends, Rogers had never previously done business with Godsoe. Now he was seeking a $2-billion bridge loan. To pay it down, Rogers intended to sell MH's U.S. cable assets. The sale would be critical to his success. He unfurled a cable map of Ontario and several charts in the conference room adjoining Godsoe's office and explained his company's lack of cable TV overlap and MH's media assets. RCI's cable properties were in red, MH's in blue and BCE's surrounded them. "You just have to know military history to know what will happen. We'll be encircled, and we'll be wiped out," Rogers later summed it up.

"I can't commit completely," Godsoe told him 90 minutes later, "but it makes great business sense."

Rogers kept Graham Savage out of the loop until his CFO completed the road show for yet another milestone public debt offering. Savage had just raised $300 million, more than expected, of 20-year debentures for Rogers' cable division in the U.S. public debt markets, the first time a Canadian non-investment-grade company had raised Canadian dollar-denominated debt in the United States. He was locking in the cost of long-term money, while eliminating the added risk of foreign-currency fluctuations. The proceeds were earmarked to repay debt owed to RCI. Now Rogers was cooking up a multi-billion-dollar leveraged buyout. At 5 p.m. on Tuesday, January 25, 1994, the day the deal closed, Rogers called Savage into his office. "You'd better sit down. I have something to tell you."

The next day Rogers called Ron Osborne, his MH counterpart, to arrange a meeting. Osborne, 47, a British-born, Cambridge-educated accountant, joined the company as its CFO in 1981, becoming its president three years later. In 1986, Osborne succeeded Don Campbell as CEO. They agreed to meet on Friday, January 28 at 7:30 a.m. at MH's offices, just before a regular MH board meeting. One columnist wrote that the two men hardly fit the stereotype of the riverboat gambler meeting the local parson. When Rogers heard that, he quipped, "That's awful. They shouldn't call Ron Osborne a riverboat gambler!" The moniker, however, stuck to Rogers. "I like it," he reflects. "It's true."

Just before 7:30 a.m. on January 28, Rogers and Emerson arrived separately at the Maclean Hunter Building at 777 Bay Street for their meeting with Don

Campbell and Ron Osborne. Campbell, greeting them at the elevators and ushering them into his pristine office, told them Osborne would be participating by telephone. He had been stranded overnight in Calgary after an ice storm closed Toronto's Pearson International Airport. Phil Lind was another no-show. The previous day he had flown to Montreal for a black-tie gala at the Queen Elizabeth Hotel, but when he tried to return that evening, all flights had been canceled. He was desperate to get back in time for the meeting. With his winter coat covering his tuxedo, Lind managed to catch the last Greyhound bus. Around 3 a.m., he woke up in Kingston, three hours away from Toronto. Thinking he'd make it back with plenty of time to spare, he fell back to sleep. When he awoke at 6:30 a.m., he was still in Kingston. The highways had been closed. Freezing rain had made traveling treacherous, causing four reported traffic fatalities. Lind called Rogers from his cellphone to tell him he was stuck in Kingston. He was circumspect, worried that anything they said might be picked up by scanners.

Campbell, 68, a chartered accountant who began his career at Maclean Hunter as its controller in 1957 and became its chief executive officer in 1970, was wearing a light brown suit with a bright flowery tie. The former RCAF WW2 bomber pilot sat upright behind his desk. Pasted on his face was the dour expression of a tough Scot Presbyterian minister. Rogers and Emerson were seated directly across from him.

Rogers was nervous. Though he is a masterful political stump speaker, when he's nervous he tends to read directly from his speaking notes. In his briefing notes, Lind had urged Rogers the day before to make sure he stressed that they were "reasonable people" with a "reasonable and fair proposition" who "admired" their work and sought a "cooperative venture" with "no plans to alter the Canadian assets of the company."

Rogers had to strike the right tone. He began by assuring Campbell that he was not making a formal offer. He had not met with his board, though he had broached the concept of a merger the previous day to their mutual banker, TD Bank. He spoke warmly of his close relationship to the late Don Hunter, the founder's son. Great friends and neighbors, they traded 10-year budgets across their adjoining backyard fences. Hunter had been John Graham's best man at his wedding to Rogers' mother. He had even intended to name Graham the executor of his will until Campbell managed to convince him that giving the "enemy" that kind of power was not a good idea.

Rogers sketched out his plan for a "strategic merger," including the board seats and management hierarchy. He raised the issue of succession at RCI no less than three times, proposing that MH's Scott Colbran had a future at RCI, replacing Colin Watson when Watson retired and becoming his own successor.

Colbran had just been named MH's Canadian cable head after Barry Gage died of cancer earlier that month. RCI's substantial tax losses could be used to shelter future MH profits. "We believe," he warmed to the subject in closing, "that putting Maclean Hunter and Rogers together would significantly enhance cable's ability to compete as the two are such a perfect geographic fit … create a Canadian international communications powerhouse akin to a northern Time Warner … and provide a solution to succession problems at Rogers … The best is yet to come!"

Rogers came close to pulling it off. "I thought when he started out that maybe he was talking a true merger and maybe, there could be some advantages to that in numbers and size and strength," says Campbell. "But, then after a few questions as to the makeup of the board and who was going to run what, it was clear that it was a pure takeover, period. I thanked him very much and said, 'Good luck.'" When Rogers and Emerson left, Campbell talked to Osborne, then briefed the directors on this latest development.

But, it was he who needed luck. The first salvo had been fired. In the corporate blood sport of hostile takeovers, the Rogers conquest of MH went down as a classic textbook example of how to execute an unsolicited takeover. The plan was to strike and counterstrike with rapier-like speed to control the process. MH thought itself above a takeover and was totally unprepared.

Savage and RCI treasurer Lorraine Daly, worked the phones with the Big Five banks on the bridge loan. The only bank that refused outright to participate in the consortium was BCE's banker, Bank of Montreal. Scotiabank, TD Bank and CIBC put up the big bucks, while Royal Bank, put up the least. Scotiabank agreed to the exclusivity term; it would not finance Maclean Hunter if it tried to repel Rogers.

When Dick Thomson heard that Scotiabank was the lead, he had a conniption fit and hastily paid Rogers a visit to ask and then demand a senior position for TD to protect and reflect its reputation as lead banker to the cable industry. Since lead bankers reap fatter fees, there was also a lot of money at stake. Peter Godsoe consequently agreed to share the lead if the deal depended on it. Thomson reluctantly agreed to exclusivity and then as a courtesy called Campbell since TD had been MH's banker longer than RCI, although TD generated more fees from RCI because of its larger credit needs.

"It's a pure business decision," Campbell recalls Thomson telling him. "He said there was some exclusivity regarding the right to borrow funds, so we couldn't. I told him, 'No bloody way.'"

With Royal Bank unwilling to bet on Rogers and BMO not even a player, Savage had to ask the co-leads and CIBC to increase their commitments. (They would syndicate the loan to other banks to reduce their exposure.) In turn,

Thomson forced RCI to drop its exclusivity demand, leaving it free and clear to fund MH. Though the exclusivity had been short-lived, Campbell, a 16-year TD Bank director, was furious. He did not stand for re-election the following year.

Three days later, on Monday, January 31, Rogers ran into Ron Osborne at the Metro Toronto Board of Trade's annual black-tie dinner and mentioned that Lind had flown to Ottawa to brief the CRTC. It was then that Osborne realized Rogers was serious.

The next day, Rogers spoke to 700 delegates at the Information Technology Association of Canada's two-day "Powering Up North America" information highway conference in Toronto. The only thing the industry pundits agreed upon was that they hated the moniker "information highway"—a now anachronistic term to describe the Internet. In pitching their visions of the future, the industry chieftains hoped to influence government policy and shape investor and brokerage analyst perceptions of the winners and losers in the emerging convergence war. Further, the higher the stock price—reflecting confidence in the company's future—the easier it becomes to raise fresh capital, or use it as currency to make acquisitions, or reap huge gains from selling.

Predicting that cable-based interactive service was undeniably the best positioned to offer "broadband to the home," Rogers argued that the cable TV and telephone businesses would remain distinct and separate until the end of the century. "I don't see cable providing voice, or phone companies providing cable television service," he said. He didn't think it was cost effective to build a combined voice-video network with high-powered fiber-optic cables directly into the home—a debate that's still raging.

With more pressing matters on his mind, Rogers left immediately after his presentation, missing the next speaker: Nicholas Negroponte, a high-priced telecom consultant, lauded U.S. media visionary and founder of the groundbreaking Media Laboratory at MIT, who called Rogers' speech "mind-boggling." "Fifty percent of what he said was wrong," Negroponte said. He said the idea that video and voice should be kept separate ran counter to the thrust of emerging technology, arguing that the cost of fiber optics and associated computer technology were rapidly declining. George Gilder, notable U.S. futurist, echoed Negroponte's views, predicting it was only a matter of three to five years before the cable and phone industries collapsed and converged into one industry.

Rogers hurried back for a meeting of the financial advisors. He had retained ScotiaMcLeod's David Wilson, an RCI director, and Burns Fry Ltd.'s Peter Eby, who worked on MH's poison pill. MH sent RBC Dominion Securities' Anthony (Tony) Fell and Wood Gundy's Ed King into the Black Tower to ascertain Rogers' intentions. He told them the RCI board intended to meet on Friday to discuss an offer.

On Wednesday, February 2, 1994, MH issued a press release to disclose that Rogers had accumulated 7 percent of its stock and made an informal unsolicited overture. Emerson was pulled out of an early morning CAE Inc. board meeting to take Ron Osborne's call informing him of the imminent news release. He immediately contacted Rogers. When their call ended, Rogers reached Lind by cellphone in Ottawa. Lind was just finishing breakfast with CRTC chairman Keith Spicer and commissioner Fern Belisle at the Chateau Laurier Hotel. On his way to the airport, Lind called Jan Innes, RCI's spokesperson, to arrange a 4:00 p.m. press conference in the auditorium at Unitel. On the return flight, Lind penned their speeches, tugging patriotic heartstrings to justify the creation of a domestic media giant "to tell Canadian stories and paint Canadian dreams" on a superhighway populated by foreign behemoths: Time Warner, Murdoch's News Corp., and Germany's Bertelsmann. With great flourish, Lind and Innes presented their rationale to reporters and TV cameras. But there was no hint of a firm offer.

The two sides then skirmished over a potentially defensive and costly technical hurdle in MH's unique corporate ownership structure. MH indirectly owned a special subsidiary called Maclean Hunter Holdings Ltd., which held 36 million MH shares, representing 17 percent of the stock. If included in his bid, Rogers was looking at shelling out an extra $600 million that he didn't have and would be hard-pressed to find.

The disputed shares originally belonged to the founder's son, Don Hunter, who died of cancer in 1976. Before his death, Hunter sold almost all of the family's stock to MH to provide stability and avoid a takeover threat. MH management then didn't have to worry if and when Hunter's heirs wanted to cash out.

When asked why he didn't opt for dual class stock, Don Campbell says, "I personally just didn't feel comfortable about putting in voting control. Why should we as caretakers of the company be able to control it, even though we had twenty-five percent of the total stock? I felt, and I persuaded the board to feel the same way, that it was not right and not justifiable, so we eliminated the voting control. If we had not done that we could have told Ted to get lost, as he's in a position to do now. Every other communications company did the same thing, and it's wrong."

Though MH said he didn't need to include the share block, on Emerson's advice, Rogers requested a ruling from the OSC. He also wanted the securities regulator to prevent MH from voting or tendering the stock in any offer that he might make.

On Friday, February 11—the day after the OSC ruled in RCI's favor—Rogers made an all-cash offer of $2.8 billion, or $17 a share, plus one participation right in any proceeds from the sale of the U.S. cable assets in excess of $1.5 billion. The stock had been trading in the $12–$13 range before Rogers circled MH. Hours later, the warring parties, dressed in tuxedoes, mingled at the Brazilian Carnival Ball, a ritzy charity Caribana for the power elite, held at the Metro Toronto Convention Centre. In an attempt at levity, Ron Osborne gave Ted Rogers a spoof poster to rib him for the absence of a formal bid—"The phantom of the offer, a comic opera by Rogers and Emerstein"—but events had overtaken his playful jab.

MH formally rejected the offer on Monday. Osborne cranked up the hunt for white knights, fully aware that Rogers was not a man easily deterred. "Mr. Rogers only knows two words when he's negotiating: 'No' means 'Maybe' and 'Maybe' means 'Yes,'" Osborne said.

While he opened up MH's data rooms to potential bidders, Osborne denied equal access to Rogers, prompting RCI to petition the court for access. Although Ontario Superior Court Justice James Farley, no-nonsense judge, colorfully and pointedly dismissed the application, Emerson continued to keep MH discombobulated. Osborne pressed hired-gun tax and legal experts to get an advance ruling from Revenue Canada for a "purchase butterfly," a complex tax maneuver that would enable MH to spin off its U.S. cable assets into a separate company without paying capital gains tax. A positive ruling was vital to MH if it hoped to scuttle Rogers' hostile bid. Emerson immediately fired off a letter to Liberal Finance Minister Paul Martin, urging the government to remain neutral. (Coincidentally, when he served in federal cabinet, Emerson's father had been executive assistant to Martin Sr.) In its first budget, tabled February 22, the Liberal government scrapped the purchase butterfly, quashing Osborne's hopes of defensively restructuring MH. Then, the FCC ordered cable TV companies to reduce cable rates by 7 percent, on top of a 10-percent rollback ordered the previous year. That was enough of a cut to slash cash flows. All of a sudden, TCI's blockbuster merger with Bell Atlantic blew up. The ill-fated merger stirred speculation over the future of the information highway.

Ted Rogers was in New York, speaking at a Merrill Lynch telecom conference. Before returning to Toronto, *Globe and Mail* business reporter John Partridge reached him on his cellphone. The next morning while having breakfast, Phil Lind read the headline: "Rogers Tempers His Takeover Stand—Canadian Cable 'Really What We Want'; $17 Offer Now May Be 'Too Generous.'" He scanned the article for Rogers' quote: "If they phoned this afternoon and we met at five o'clock and we bought their Canadian cable, we'd go away. That's really what we want."

In one sentence, Rogers had undone the Lind's spin. Lind went ballistic. "I was so fucking mad. We had a line. We were presenting it a certain way and he goes off script. We went on as if it never happened. We calibrated Rogers again and just acted as if he had never said that," he says.

Osborne, who likened Rogers to a "Detroit knee-capper," took advantage of the faux pas, accusing Rogers of greenmail. "To somehow give the impression that he's made a bid for Maclean Hunter in order to put a gun to our head to obtain from us an asset that we think is one of the crown jewels is not the way I would particularly want to do business," Osborne retorted.

"We've gone a long way from creating the Time Warner of the north … to the cheapest, schlockiest greenmail that I've ever come across," he said. "It's appalling. We've gone from the grandiose vision to this kind of greenmail or blackmail, whatever you want to call it. I'm just staggered."

Behind the scenes, Rogers gained the support of the Hunter family, who held 10 percent of MH's stock. The Hunters are great friends of his. It didn't take too much persuading. For his part, Osborne was talking to cable pioneer James Robert (JR) Shaw, 59, trying to bring the third-largest cable TV company into the fray as his white knight. "We spent a lot of time looking at it with them," recalls Shaw, the son of an Ontario cattleman. "We listened to their story and it didn't seem to be totally there. I remember Ted called, wanting to meet. I told him that we just need a little more time and I'd come to Toronto the next week." Rogers, who was flying the next day to San Diego for a wireless conference, said he could swing by en route. "Ted's pretty persistent," says Shaw. "I said we weren't ready for that."

Before flying to Toronto, Shaw, his son, Jim, who runs the cable company, and his daughter, Heather, met at Calgary's Petroleum Club to discuss their options. They agreed that if MH was too big for them "to bite and swallow without choking to death," they would prefer to be in a position to take advantage of an opportunity if it presents itself, JR Shaw recalls. He also didn't want to upset Rogers. "We knew that if we would have come in and tried to buy MH's cable systems in Canada, we would have embarrassed Ted Rogers, because this was a major transaction to him and it's his deal. And, we wouldn't have been friends anymore. I'm sure of that."

"Ted's always been after that Ontario market. He's been aggressive. He's been a leader in this industry his entire life. He stimulates everybody, not only his own people, but he stimulates the rest of us in the industry too," Shaw says.

JR Shaw met Rogers at the Toronto Club for dinner. They had the entire oak-paneled dining hall to themselves, just one white-linen-covered table in the center of the room with two chairs. "I thought I was in Buckingham Palace," says Shaw. "We had, more or less, concluded that we wouldn't be for MH, but

Ted didn't know that. We hadn't declared at that time that we were the white knight, but everybody knew it. I mean, there is no secrecy in this industry. We had already raised $1 billion. We had the line of credit in place."

They struck a deal. "I trust Ted. He gives his word; he sticks to it," says Shaw. They agreed to swap certain cable TV franchises if Rogers' offer for MH succeeded. Rogers traded Calgary and Victoria, where Shaw already had cable systems, and MH's systems in Thunder Bay and Sault Ste. Marie in northwestern Ontario for Shaw's cable TV systems in Toronto and southwestern Ontario, Woodstock, St. Thomas, Strathroy and Tillsonburg. Shaw would also get MH's Toronto FM radio station, CFNY. Shaw picked up 145,000 subscribers.

Rogers had his lawyers begin papering the agreement that night. Shaw returned to his hotel room where he spent the next two hours on the phone, first talking to his son and next assembling his legal team. He couldn't reach Shaw's new in-house counsel, Margo Micallef. She was in Portland, Oregon visiting her family. "Boy, was she upset that she wasn't there!" It was after midnight when he rang Roxanne McCormick, a partner at law firm Fasken & Calvin, now Fasken Martineau DuMoulin, at her Toronto home. "What are you doing tomorrow?" he asked.

"We spent the day getting everything done and signed. I wasn't quite as prepared to move that quickly, but Rogers was," says Shaw.

Rogers promised not to disclose their pact publicly until JR Shaw told Ron Osborne. By four o'clock in the afternoon on Friday, March 4, 1994, Rogers still had not heard from Shaw. Lind alerted the print media to stand by for a major announcement. He wanted their story to headline the Saturday papers. Rogers finally called Shaw and told him, "JR, let's have a 'negative option' here. If you don't call us back within ten minutes, we're going ahead with the press release."

"The toughest call I made in my business career was to call Ron Osborne, and tell him we were going to do a deal with Rogers instead of them," says JR Shaw. "I didn't want to make that call. I really liked Ron Osborne. I really thought a lot of him. I had left it until later in the day and then I wished I had done it earlier on that Friday. I kept procrastinating. I just didn't want to do it."

"Well, that means you're in the Rogers camp," Osborne retorted.

"No, that's not the case," JR Shaw tried to tell him. "We were the last white knight, yet they were the ones who were so big in the industry. It really amazed me," says Shaw.

Not long afterwards, Rogers and Shaw had another dinner together. "Are you dealing for CUC?" Rogers asked Shaw. The late Jeffrey Conway and Liberal senator Jerry Grafstein founded the privately held CUC, which had 350,000 subscribers in Ontario, about half of them in the Metro Toronto city of Scarborough and adjacent Pickering. His wife, Julia Conway Royer, held 44 percent of the company's stock. Rogers' neighbor Larry Tanenbaum, venture capitalist Michael Koerner and businessman James Fleck were minority investors.

"Well, who wants to know?" Shaw parried.

"Well, I'd like to know."

"Yes, we are," conceded Shaw.

"Why in hell would Julia Conway deal with you and not the local people?"

"He was quite hurt and miffed at it," recalls Shaw.

Shaw snared CUC, surpassing Vidéotron to become Canada's second-largest cable company, behind RCI. Through CUC, Shaw gained a 28 percent foothold in cable network YTV. CUC also owned half of a British cable joint venture with Alberta's Telus Corp. "We almost choked ourselves to death, but that's the way it went," says Shaw. "Ted knows what's going on. He reads the signs and signals."

MH conceded defeat. Don Campbell paid Rogers a visit Friday night. "We had other people come to us and talk to us about takeovers and we said, 'No thanks.' We said, 'We like it the way it is. Our shareholders are doing fine. Our employees are doing fine. All but Ted went away," reflects Campbell.

At a board meeting on Saturday, the MH directors voted to accept Rogers' offer, but instructed Osborne to meet with Rogers to squeeze more money out of him. Osborne met with Rogers Sunday evening at Frybrook, where they argued for two hours before Osborne called it a night and left. On Monday, March 7, the day before RCI's annual meeting, the two men met for lunch. They were still at loggerheads. Rogers, feeling exhausted, checked into the Crowne Marriott Hotel for an afternoon nap. Osborne returned to the office to brief his staff. His CFO, Bob Furse, suggested that MH could pay itself a special dividend. Osborne rang Rogers' office only to be told Rogers was at the Crowne Marriott. He called him at the hotel, waking him up. His directors might accept an offer of $17-a-share cash plus a 75-cent dividend paid out of treasury.

"Fifty cents," Rogers bartered. "And, no participating right on the sale of the U.S. cable assets."

That evening, while Osborne presented the proposal to the MH board, Rogers hosted a black-tie dinner for his board and invited guests at the Toronto Club. He took Osborne's call in the foyer. "The board has agreed to recommend the offer plus a fifty-cent dividend," Osborne told him. MH also agreed to not use its poison pill under the amended deal. Rogers replied, "I've got my annual meeting tomorrow. I'd like to be able to announce something."

The lawyers negotiated and prepared the documentation through the night. "My view was once you get an agreement or understanding, get the goddamn piece of paper signed immediately," says Emerson. He made it home at five o'clock in the morning on the day he was to chair his first RCI annual meeting. "He helped us get Maclean Hunter," Rogers credits Emerson. "Without him, we wouldn't have."

On Tuesday, March 8, 1994, RCI held its annual meeting in the sunlit Walker Court of the Art Gallery of Ontario before a packed audience. Entering the room, Rogers shook hands with everyone he could reach. At high noon, the florid organ music from *Phantom of the Opera* filled the room before the voice of the phantom echoed, "My dear Maclean Hunter, resist no longer. Allow your shareholders to accept my offer." The tape was Emerson's comeback to Osborne's poster. The business suit crowd was laughing so hard they missed the little drama unfolding at the podium when a Tory's lawyer rushed up behind Emerson and Rogers with the agreement. They signed the $3.1-billion transaction at the podium. Rogers gave no indication of what had just taken place. "I think all of us are a bit nervous because of the events that are going on," he began, before launching into his prepared text.

"This is Canada. Canadians do things differently. The board of Maclean Hunter has made this a strenuous affair. I respect them very much … Don Campbell has been gracious, Ron Osborne has been a friend for years … Over the weekend, I met Campbell on Friday, Osborne on Sunday night, and we approached this in the Canadian way. The meeting went well. There were offers and counter offers."

Twenty minutes into his speech, Rogers finally shared the news: "Maclean Hunter's board approved the final settlement just minutes before the meeting today." As if they were at a theatrical production, astonished shareholders, money managers and brokerage analysts spontaneously rose to their feet, applauding. He grinned broadly and waved. As soon as Emerson closed the meeting, Rogers jumped off the stage and rushed over to hug Loretta. "Are you happy?" he asked. She smiled. He kissed her on the lips once, then twice.

"We could have either gone off on exploits that were second- or third-level desirable, or we could go for the big one, the one that we've never dared dream of," Rogers later told *Maclean's*. "My experience is that you should go for the big one."

When Maclean Hunter lost, RBC's Tony Fell, who had represented MH, was in Rogers' office virtually the next day, looking for business. After all, RCI intended to dismantle MH. There were fees to be made.

Rogers had done his job. It was now up to Phil Lind to come through on the regulatory side. The takeover required approval from four regulatory bodies:

the CRTC, the FCC, and U.S. state and local authorities. The immediate concern was the FCC, not the CRTC, where Lind had already primed the commissioners. The CRTC hearing was still months away. To repay the bridge loan, Rogers had to sell MH's U.S. cable franchises. His success hinged on it.

Four weeks earlier, when the battle began, Lind had immediately reactivated his U.S. regulatory team. While he massaged Ottawa, his U.S. team—lawyers Lee Sheehy and David Jones and consultant Missy Goerner—almost in subterfuge began the change-of-control process in the U.S. cities where MH had franchises. "I would go in and get all the franchises, unbeknownst to Maclean Hunter," says Goerner. Lind's key go-to person on FCC matters—Wesley R. Heppler, a partner at law firm Cole, Raywid & Braverman in Washington DC—wasn't available because of a conflict of interest. His law firm had previously represented MH, which put him on the sidelines for as long as the takeover remained hostile. Heppler persuaded friend and highly respected former FCC general counsel, Diane S. Killory, to represent Rogers.

In hostile takeovers, the FCC expedites its review process to prevent the target company from erecting barriers to the offer, by permitting the suitor to apply for a special temporary authority to transfer the target's shares to a trustee until hostilities are over. If successful, the acquirer then applies to the FCC for a change of control. It's a two-step process. Killory advised Lind that the FCC would look more favorably upon a person, rather than an institution, as a trustee. Since the CRTC had never before recognized the validity of a trust arrangement, Lind and Ottawa lawyer Bob Buchan needed the perfect trustee, someone the regulator respected. Who would be better for the job than Pierre Juneau, the first CRTC chairman and avowed Canadian nationalist? Over a hastily arranged dinner in Montreal, they convinced the 71-year-old Juneau to take the job.

Then, the hostile takeover suddenly turned friendly. The FCC now had no reason to grant RCI a waiver from the normal review process. This spelled trouble. Since the takeover was contingent on the FCC's prior approval and with the amended offer set to expire on March 31, Lind had less than three weeks to convince the FCC to make an exception and grant the special temporary authority. In normal circumstances, there was no way RCI could secure FCC approval to transfer the microwave licenses before its offer expired. If RCI didn't get approval, MH had the right to walk away from the deal. At seven o'clock in the morning, Lind telephoned Heppler at home to tell him the deal had turned friendly and to get on the file now.

MH's DC law firm, Hogan & Hartson, advised Osborne that Rogers had zero chance of getting the FCC's waiver now that the takeover was friendly. It had never happened before. Furthermore, they needed unanimous approval from the five FCC commissioners. "I remember the FCC kept saying, well, we are not going to do the trust now that it is friendly, and I kept saying, but it is really not friendly. Even though they voted [for it], they really don't want to do the deal, and if you let this time expire, the deal is going to collapse," recalls Heppler.

In a strategy session, the RCI regulatory team briefed Rogers. Things did not look good. "There must be a case somewhere that we can use as a precedent," Rogers insisted.

Heppler explained that he had found only one case where the FCC approved a trust arrangement in a non-hostile situation: The regulator granted the owner of a family business a waiver to expedite the company's sale because he was dying of AIDS. Not missing a beat, David Jones turned directly to Rogers and said, "Ted, are you willing to take one for the team?"

"Ted did not think that was funny at all," recalls Heppler. "We all thought that was hilarious."

They didn't actually use that case for their argument. Both Killory and Heppler knew the FCC general counsel quite well. Justifying it on the basis of a parallel national regulatory process, the FCC general counsel wrote their request as a "purple cow" so that if the commissioners approved it, the case couldn't be used by American companies as a precedent.

On March 31, the day the offer was to expire, the two combatants gathered in the RCI boardroom at Commercial Union Tower. MH's Ron Osborne, Don Campbell and their entourage felt confident, indeed ebullient, that the deal was dead. Their DC counsel assured them that the FCC would never approve RCI's request. They were relaxed, smiling at the discomfiture across the table. The RCI team was sweating bullets. Heppler had been working the phones all day. RCI needed the signatures of all five FCC commissioners on the waiver. To prevent it from getting lost in their in-boxes, Heppler had an inside contact doggedly shepherd it around to each office. With the clock ticking closer to the deadline, the room became deathly quiet as everyone waited for the phone call. "I'm facing my life here," says Lind. "Rogers is just walking around like he doesn't know what's going on. Everyone is in this weird state because Rogers doesn't even get mad anymore. He's stopped being nasty."

Time was running out. Then, the call came in. The receptionist transferred the call into the conference room where everyone was waiting to hear the news over the speakerphone but then all they heard was the dial tone. The call had been accidentally dropped. "That's when I started kicking the wall," Lind says. When the FCC rang back, Heppler went into the next room to take the call. When he heard the news, he gave them a thumbs-up sign through the adjoining window. "I was happy to get that call. You never know until they actually get it signed. It was a good day," says Heppler. "It would have been incredibly hard to put the deal back together if they had missed the deadline."

Osborne stood up and congratulated Rogers. The capitulation was now final. For more than a decade, Campbell didn't speak to Emerson. "I was very much upset," Campbell says. "He put in the poison pill for us and then had the nerve to turn around to the courts and say, the poison pill was worthless. We didn't like it." Campbell also resigned from the TD Bank board, furious at Thomson's lack of support. "We had a great Canadian company and we were proud of it."

"Twenty years ago, the idea that Rogers would take over Maclean Hunter would be given the same probability as Joe's Hot Dog Stand taking over McDonald's," Toronto money manager Ira Gluskin told *Maclean's*.

In June 1994, RCI agreed to sell MH's U.S. cable franchises to Comcast for $1.27 billion. During the auction process, Lind went salmon fishing with Comcast's father and-son team, Ralph and Brian Roberts, in Alaska. For the deal, Comcast partnered with the giant California Public Employees Retirement System (Calpers). On January 2, 1995, they completed the transaction, though there was momentary panic when Comcast stopped the transfer of funds. Goerner, Sheehy, Jones and Albert Gnat were sitting around, pleased at themselves for getting all the FCC license approvals, when someone rushed in to tell them that one small microwave license did not get transferred. "We made some frantic calls," recalls Goerner. Heppler was in a taxi going to the airport. They had a lawyer from Comcast call the FCC, which then agreed to transfer the license, and then Comcast resumed transferring the funds.

The last hurdle was the CRTC.

On September 16, 1994, the day before the RCI-MH hearing, the CRTC surprised industry players by permitting cable and telephone companies to dabble in each other's business. The cable companies could offer local phone services, albeit not until 1998. The phone companies could test market video-on-demand service, and compete with cable in information services—the Internet before it was called the Internet—but they weren't permitted to offer cable TV service. They needed legislative change to hold broadcast licenses. For Bell, that would take another four years.

The decision, hailed as a landmark ruling, offered the promise of telecom competition without delivering it. Two years after permitting long-distance competition, the CRTC deregulated long-distance rates, permitted local phone competition and ended the century-old subsidization of local phone service by long-distance users. Starting January 1, 1995, the phone companies were permitted to hike local rates $2 a month each year—that's $24 a year—for three years, a decision blasted by consumer advocacy groups. The CRTC called it "rate rebalancing." Indeed. The CRTC helped Ma Bell offset lost long-distance revenue. Bell Canada could undercut Unitel on long-distance rates, while replenishing its coffers on local rates. Though the telecom regulator claimed higher local rates were meant to stimulate competition, it didn't actually deregulate local telephone service for another two years. According to the CRTC, the higher local rates were meant to stimulate competition. In 1994, the telephone companies had a 100 percent monopoly on local lines. In 2007, they still control 90 percent.

The next day, when Rogers arrived in Hull, Quebec for the CRTC regulatory hearing, a costumed herald from the Friends of Canadian Broadcasting, a national watchdog group, cried, "Welcome Baron Ted, all cable lands west of the Ottawa are yours, let the hearings begin!" That was just the start. More than 700 groups protested Rogers' takeover of MH, sounding alarm bells over cross-media ownership, the size of the combined company, control over content and access to monopoly cable TV systems.

To win approval, Rogers came with a goodie bag of promises—so-called significant public benefits—known as "siggies" in the industry, though regarded as bribes by the public. Either way, concocting the right package requires a great deal of work and thought—subtly playing to the personal biases of often politically ambitious commissioners, while striking the right chords with the staff.

For example, the now defunct Canadian Cable Labs Fund at the University of Victoria in British Columbia was an offspring of the regulatory benefits process. Lind and Bob Buchan dreamt up the Cable Labs Fund to win regulatory approval in 1990 for RCI to buy the 55 percent of a small B.C. cable company, Western Cablevision Ltd., that it didn't already own. The decision wasn't unanimous—with dissenting opinions from four commissioners, including Beverley J. Oda, a former arts teacher and broadcaster, who served as the Minister of Canadian Heritage and Status of Women in the federal government. Rogers, who inherited the stake through the Premier acquisition, failed on two earlier attempts in 1981 and 1983 to buy the company because the CRTC felt that permitting Rogers to increase his share of the province's cable market to 54 percent from 46 percent would "adversely affect the development of strong, regional cable ownership," even though the founding McDonald family, like so many pioneers, wanted to sell. The future had arrived on their doorstep. They couldn't afford to pay the cost of plowing fiber-optical cable in the ground or retooling their systems to handle the promised brave new world of a 500-channel universe, video-on-demand, high-definition TV and interactive TV.

There had always been a disconnect between the industry, the CRTC and the DOC, says Stuart McFayden, retired business economics professor, who has written extensively on the subject. "In the history of broadcasting, they didn't even understand the business side of things and the structures they put in place was always running counter to the market," says McFayden. "The people looking after broadcasting over the years were interested in the arts. They hired a lot of French Canadians and people with arts backgrounds and they ended up with people who didn't understand what Ted Rogers and Jim Shaw or Izzy Asper were doing. They couldn't figure out the business stuff. All they could see was that the [cable operators] never did what they wanted them to do. They were always mad because nothing was ever working out the way they wanted it."

In the MH goodie bag, Rogers promised to pony up another $2 million into the Canadian Cable Labs Fund to bring its total investment up to $5.5 million. Shaw also offered to put $1.5 million into the Fund if the CRTC blessed its transaction. In spite of its less than altruistic origins, the Fund spawned six new patents, 50 research papers and trained more than 20 graduate students in broadband-related technologies. Its most notable success relates to remote antenna drivers, a PCS-over-cable TV architecture that enables cable companies to extend their wireless coverage from their traditional land-based networks. The original idea came from RCI engineers Nick Hamilton-Piercy and Roger Keay.

"It's a very advanced concept," says Dr. Richard Green, chief executive officer of CableLabs, the U.S. cable-TV industry's R&D consortium, which shares patents with RCI. "It's just beginning to emerge in its importance, but ten years from now, it's going to be extraordinarily important. The yield on basic research takes a long time to get into the marketplace. They had some smart people working on cable problems. That's another contribution Rogers made to the industry that nobody else was making and nobody has made since then."

At 10 a.m. on December 19, 1994, Michael Allen, RCI vice president of regulatory affairs, went upstairs in the Standard Life Tower in Toronto, the CRTC's regional headquarters, to collect the sealed envelope of the regulator's verdict on Maclean Hunter. Downstairs at Druxy's, a delicatessen chain, Phil Lind, Missy Goerner and Bob Buchan waited for him over mugs of hot chocolate. Upon his return, they opened the envelope: "CRTC approves Rogers purchase ..."

"There were smiles all around," Lind says. The smiles didn't last long.

Later that day at the press conference, the team seemed off their game. Instead of toasting their triumph, they appeared somber, tired. Humility was the order of the day. They spoke with "toneless earnest" of how MH was their first step to "harden the cable industry" to compete against the telephone companies, one newspaper account described. Ron Osborne, standing apart from the group, called it a "sad" time for MH employees. For their part, the brain trust at Rogers was beset with more pressing troubles—Unitel, and a growing discontent among its cable-TV customers.

Rogers then began to dismantle Maclean Hunter. To repay the $2-billion bridge loan, Rogers sold the U.S. cable-TV properties to Comcast, the European publishing business to U.K. firm EMAP, the cable-TV systems and radio stations to Shaw, Telemedia and Blackburn Radio, and the printing companies to Quebecor

Printing Inc. and GTC Transcontinental Group Ltd. (He also borrowed another $400 million to help retire the interim loan.) He kept the coveted Canadian cable networks and publishing side. MH hoisted RCI's cable-TV revenue above Cantel's. RCI went back to looking like a cable-TV company again. MH also moved Rogers onto the info-highway fast lane.

Remarkably, Rogers says he no longer lists the MH takeover as "absolutely crucial" to what is today RCI. He was about to move on to bigger, bolder dreams.

CHAPTER 18

WAVE Good-Bye

"It changes the whole soul of the company."

—Ted Rogers

TED ROGERS WAS DRAGGED into the Internet age kicking and screaming.

Just like other cable titans, Rogers believed the television set, not the personal computer, was the wonder box. He simply regarded the computer as a marvellous machine that made secretaries more efficient. He had no idea how to use one, nor the inclination to learn. The killer app making the Internet, or Net, accessible to people other than scientists and researchers was then just being developed. At that time, his cable compadres were fixated on turning the boob tube into this magical box that promised to offer a dizzying array of interactive services, from video games, video-on-demand, banking, email and even telephone service. Fearing a competitive threat from the emerging satellite TV industry, the cable owners ratcheted up the rhetoric, dubbing them the "Death Stars."

The dawn of the digital era renewed talk of telephony and television convergence a decade after the phone and cable monopolies first rattled their sabres. The nineties were a decade of upheaval, dotted with gargantuan mega-deals and seemingly improbable alliances as companies searched for convergence strategies. The investment community would become deeply divided over which industry—cable or telephone—would form the communications backbone of the future. In this milieu, Rogers struggled to find his way.

Inside the company, Rogers' cable technologists forged ahead to the electronic frontier without him. "We did it in spite of him," says Colin Watson, Rogers' former cable head, "and he has been very gracious in acknowledging that."

Fortunately, Rogers had some of the industry's sharpest minds working for him. After listening to then-Senator Albert Gore, Jr., give a passionate address at a securities firm conference in Manhattan in 1991 on the urgency of building a national electronic data superhighway if America hoped to remain an economic powerhouse, Nick Hamilton-Piercy, RCI's respected cable technology chief, and David Masotti, an engineering wunderkind, were inspired to redouble their efforts to build a high-speed broadband network. Gore was the first U.S. elected official to grasp the potential of high-speed telecommunications for economic growth and the betterment of education. At the time, he was trying to secure the passage of the *High Performance Computing and Communications Act*, known as the *Gore Act*, to provide funding and resources for the Internet. Though the two engineers from Toronto didn't have the faintest idea who Gore was, his speech was music to their ears. It was a resounding endorsement of Hamilton-Piercy's earlier work in the United States with Telidon, an early Web browser that had been designed for TV owners (since people didn't have PCs in the early eighties). He had been trying to find a way of interconnecting Telidon with a mini-Web-like system called the Source, a videotex service 80-percent owned by *Reader's Digest*, which provided online information for users. The concept was, nevertheless, directly applicable for PCs. "His speech put more fire into our guts," recalls Hamilton-Piercy.

The Internet, or Net, is basically a network of computer networks, enabling people to communicate with each other. Its roots go back to ARPANET (Advanced Research Projects Agency Network), an effort supported by the U.S. Department of Defense in 1969 to link universities and research laboratories. From there, the Internet grew rather chaotically to connect government agencies, academia, corporations and libraries. By the early nineties, some 15 million users in 10,000 networks across 60 countries connected their personal computers to Internet Service Providers (ISPs) over telephone lines, mainly to send and receive email, to post and read messages on electronic bulletin boards, and to transfer data files. America Online Inc. (AOL), CompuServe, Prodigy and Genie duked it out in the ISP industry, with AOL emerging as the dial-up ISP heavyweight.

To deliver the Internet via the cable pipes, the industry needed a two-way cable TV network, a business model and the equipment, and though he lacked the vision to see a ramp onto the Information Superhighway, Rogers poured billions of dollars into his cable network. This is where Rogers was sitting pretty. Traditionally, cable systems used a tree-and-branch structure, where a single coaxial trunk cable is laid starting at the head-end and tributary cables run off the trunk. The signals traveled one way—downstream, that is—bringing video into the home. Hamilton-Piercy had revolutionized the system with his fiber-ring architecture. By encircling its territories with fiber-optic rings from the head-end and tying the fiber into the neighborhood coaxial system, Rogers could deliver picture-perfect signals using just a few, or no, amplifiers. Customers were happy. Rogers was happy. Rogers, driven by the need to be the first and the best, always wanted the clearest and sharpest TV signals.

Now, with the threat of satellite TV, Rogers wanted to ensure that the network had as much capacity as possible to offer customers more channels. Remember, this was the era of the much-ballyhooed 500-channel universe. In his desire to offer the perfect signal and more content, Rogers unknowingly built a network capable of delivering high-speed Internet. He also permitted his engineers to experiment. His team helped develop the industry specifications for cable modems, which crank up Internet speed. Although the U.S. cable companies provided the funding, Rogers provided the engineering expertise. "It went from being purely a Rogers initiative to being an industry-wide one," says Hamilton-Piercy, who made numerous speeches in the United States and graced the covers of magazines.

The industry formed a consortium, called MCNS, which stands for Multimedia Cable Network Systems, which quickly evolved into DOCSIS, Data Over Cable Service Interface Specification, to create cable modem standards. The U.S. giants—TCI, Time Warner, Comcast and Cox—funded MCNS, while RCI supplied the intellectual firepower. The industry's ability to rally around a common standard, and the early cable modem work from the Rogers engineering team, helped give the cable companies the lead over the telephone companies in the broadband deployment race. (The new DOCSIS 3.0 that's expected in 2009 promises to deliver 100 Mbps of speed.) "Nick's team wrote the cable modem specs and got Cable Labs to issue it," says Frank Cotter, a former Deloitte consultant. "There were a number of challenges on the engineering side and Rogers typically solved them first and made it easier for the U.S. cable guys."

The cable technologists soon realized they had to push fiber closer to the home to make the two-way network fast, reliable and secure—without really knowing if there was consumer demand. "It was a complete chicken-and-the-egg thing. No sensible person would have spent the money based on what we knew, but we did anyway," says Masotti. "It was the wild west and the information superhighway. Most people were spending big bucks on interactive TV. Truth is, we really didn't know what was going to happen other than that there was going to be a big two-way pipe to the home, and whatever we ended up using it for, we can probably find a way to make money."

Fast-forward to 1993 when Rogers, who felt that he needed someone dedicated to spotting new business opportunities, told Colin Watson to parachute David Masotti, 31, into the newly created and rather nebulous position of vice president, business development. Masotti, a former Northern Telecom engineer and Harvard MBA graduate, joined the company in 1990 right out of Harvard. He had written a letter to Ted Rogers asking for a job after hearing him speak at the Harvard Business School Canadian Club. "He came down with Phil and gave his Ted Speech, that starts with 'my father was an inventor.' It is impressive as hell. It gets better every year the company gets bigger," recalls Masotti. "I wanted to come back to Canada and work in a company that is Canadian based and trying to be innovative."

Masotti officially took up his new job on New Year's Day, 1994, just as Rogers began to lay the groundwork to acquire Maclean Hunter. Unofficially, he had assumed the role a few months earlier. That's when Rogers and Phil Lind combined to unload an earful on him. In the United States, Time Warner had just unveiled its plans to test an interactive video "news on demand" service, generating banner headlines. "Their concern was that we were falling behind," he recalls. "Nothing bugs [Rogers] more than thinking he's going to be fifth. If it's important, let's do it. Let's be leaders. Let's be first. I got beat up. That's when the idea of a road show started."

Masotti organized a whirlwind trip for mid-February to see Intel, General Instrument, Scientific America, Oracle, Silicon Graphics, and nearby Silicon Valley neighbor Hybrid Network Technologies. The week after unveiling the details of his hostile takeover bid for Maclean Hunter, Ted Rogers flew with his team to California on his new Challenger jet, emblazoned with the call sign C-ESR—his initials, on its tail. Until then, he had previously flown commercial, or shared a corporate jet, typically booking it so far in advance that his co-share partners had trouble reserving it. He decided to purchase the jet after undergoing open-heart surgery in 1992. Joining him on the trip were his cable head Watson, Masotti, Hamilton-Piercy and Keay.

Since they planned to stop in Redmond, Washington to visit U.S. software titan Bill Gates, Frank Clegg, the head of Microsoft's Canadian arm, accompanied them on the flight. For the past two years, Microsoft had been cozying up to the cable industry to form a corporation, Cablesoft, to develop software standards for interactive television. Microsoft's so-called Tiger software would turn the home cable box into a Microsoft-based PC. The meeting with Gates led Rogers to sign a letter of intent in May to license the Tiger software. The two men proudly boasted they would build Canada's first truly two-way electronic superhighway by 1997, just when Rogers was seeking the CRTC's approval to buy Maclean Hunter. For Gates, the announcement was a significant win.

"This is a very important first step for Microsoft," Robert Alexander, an interactive network consultant at New York-based Alexander & Associates told

The New York Times. "The systems in Canada are among the most technically clean systems in the cable universe."

Rogers later scotched the deal on Masotti's advice. Masotti became convinced that Microsoft's video engineering wasn't top drawer, a criticism over which the software giant flexed its muscles, trying to get Rogers to fire Masotti. Instead, Rogers grilled him and then backed him.

Masotti was skeptical about interactive TV right from the start. Interactive TV was all about delivering high-priced content to passive couch potatoes, while the Internet was about people connecting with other people around the world. The cable industry was wrestling over whether the PC or TV set was the better online vehicle. Was the PC a better candidate for handling convergence than the telephone or the TV set?

Naturally, the cable industry was squarely in the television camp. Canada's André Chagnon from Le Groupe Vidéotron had been working since the late eighties on interactive TV, and in 1991 was offering 120 channels through Videoway, a gizmo his company had developed. In the United States, Time Warner, a devout believer in interactive video-on-demand, planned to spend billions to build the ultimate wonder box. To Masotti, the Time Warner silver bullet made little practical sense and no economic sense. Intel, which believed that the PC, not the TV, was the route to take, inspired Masotti most. Further, the cable TV industry didn't have to buy—read, subsidize—the PC, like they would with an interactive set-top box. People could buy their own PCs.

Then, on March 13, 1994, Colin Watson gave "The Speech"—the come-to-Jesus speech—to the cable industry at a CableLabs conference in Phoenix, predicting that the personal computer, not the TV, would be the future autobahn of communications. Watson predicted that PC penetration would be 70 percent in 10 years, up from just 23 percent in 1993. "We said, 'It's not the TV; it's the PC,'" recalls Masotti, who considered the TV to be a group experience, something that people gathered around, but felt that for the Internet, a one-on-one activity, the PC was more suitable.

"People thought we were off our rockers."

That month, Rogers installed its first prototype cable modem. The company connected a North York, Ontario school via cable to the Internet. Throughout the summer, Rogers continued to connect school computers to the Internet. By the end of June, six suburban Toronto schools and several employees were online. By November, Rogers added 20 IBM employees. CableLink was the umbrella name for the trials: CableLink Work, CableLink School, CableLink Home. Masotti, who was alone when he embarked on this adventure, was joined by Frank Cotter from Deloitte and Rogers' eldest daughter, Lisa.

In April 1994, Bell Canada and eight of the country's largest phone companies in the Stentor consortium proudly unveiled their $8.5-billion plan to create a national information superhighway dubbed the "Beacon Initiative." The bulk of the money, Stentor said, would go towards replacing their century-old copper wires with high-capacity lines much like those used by the cable systems.

Beacon—mockingly called the "Bacon Initiative"—was big, bold and full of baloney. It was—in the words of veteran telecom consultant Liz Angus—a "placeholder announcement" to throw off politicians, regulators, investors and business reporters. If another annoying cable guy said, "We're going to do broadband," BCE—and any other Stentor member—when asked could respond that they had already announced their information highway plans. "They never did any of it," says her partner, Ian Angus. "It was based on bizarre technology that was never going to fly and on promises of delivery that they were never going to do.

"They really figured it would be [automatic teller machines] everywhere—nobody had thought of Internet Protocol yet. Nobody knew what was coming. It took years for the prices of various technologies to drop, for IP to take off in a big way and for DSL [digital subscriber line] to become cost effective to deliver."

The Beacon charade was Stentor's delayed response to the hullabaloo over John Malone's "500-channel universe." Both had the desired effect of lifting their respective industry's share prices. Indeed, in June 1992, Canada's cable TV industry announced plans to spend a massive $10 billion over 10 years to upgrade their existing cable networks to digital systems, called Cable 2001, to deliver interactive TV, new content, and video-on-demand services. They dialed down the 500-channel rhetoric drifting across the border from the United States to mere "hundreds" to prevent the CRTC and the specialty channel clique from going apoplectic over new content, and the threats to Canadian culture and their pocketbooks. The industry promised to deliver digital cable TV by mid-1994 to handle the expected onslaught of new channels. In practise the cable industry wasn't ready to deliver new channels and the regulator took its time doling out licenses.

"Look at this, here's a website," Kaia Kruus, a cable technician at Rogers, excitedly showed David Masotti. The year was 1994.

"What's a website?"

Kruus explained that people were posting electronic "pages" of information—journals and catalogs supplied by everyone from the CERN (Conseil European pour la Recherché Nucleaire) physics lab in Geneva to a florist in Connecticut on a part of the Internet called the World Wide Web. Tim Berners-Lee, a British physicist, had invented the Web in 1989 while working at the CERN physics lab. He originally designed the system to enable the world's physics researchers to exchange information in a form known as hypertext. Users see highlighted keywords and images that point them to related sources of information. "I realized that if everyone had the same information as me, my life would be easier," he said. Having begun as an electronic library for a group of physicists, the Web suddenly became a world bazaar.

Then, along came Mosaic. The world's first user-friendly browser, created by University of Illinois computer students, made surfing the Internet fun even for non-computer nerds. Web surfers could connect to computers halfway around the world with just a click of a mouse on a highlighted word or a graphic button, instead of typing in arcane code. The software program, made freely available by the university, wasn't the only browser available, just the easiest to use. Mosaic increased Net traffic ten-thousandfold, unleashing unprecedented commercial energy in the history of the Net.

"How much work is involved to create a website?" Masotti asked Kruus.

"Oh, I can make one," she said. "Anyone can create one. I could throw one together with a few hours of work."

That's when Masotti had his eureka moment. He realized their skunkworks project was not just some marginal niche service, but had the potential to change the way people worked, exchanged ideas, entertained, educated and socialized with one another. Though people were accessing the Web at the speed of telephone modems, the websites—a kaleidoscope of entertainment, information and home shopping applications—would be far more rewarding at higher speeds. The cable pipes had the potential to be the Internet highway.

"How many websites are there?" he asked, excitedly.

"Five thousand," Kruus replied, "but they're growing by hundreds a day."

By year's end, 10,000 websites had emerged. Cyberspace had taken off. Since then, it's only grown exponentially, expanding to more than 100 million websites today.

Just months later, James H. Clark, a Silicon Valley mover and shaker, called Masotti in Toronto. Clark, then 50, a former Stanford University professor who founded Silicon Graphics Inc., which helped bring dinosaurs to life in the movie *Jurassic Park*, had hired seven Mosaic developers, including cyberprodigy Marc Andreessen, from the University of Illinois' National Center for Supercomputing

Applications, to write an all-new version of Mosaic. In November 1994, seven months after founding Mosaic Communications Corp., Clark renamed the company Netscape Communications Corp. after the university complained over the name similarity.

Clark heard that Rogers was well ahead of everybody else in its broadband trials. He wanted RCI to be his Canadian partner and proposed offering the company a 10- to 15-percent equity stake in the company. Clark flew to Toronto for a meeting. Rogers, who was recovering from eye surgery, which had left him temporarily blind, was in a particularly grumpy mood over channel lineups, slow rebuilds and overspending, all the daily headaches of running his business. Clark made his pitch about the paradigm shift created by the Internet. Rogers nodded politely throughout, took some notes, stood up to thank him, and then left the room. His lieutenants were floored. They explained apologetically to Clark that Rogers had just undergone surgery and wasn't as familiar with search engines as they were. The potential deal died when Rogers left the room.

In February 1995, in the wake of the negative option fiasco and with Unitel hanging over RCI's head, Masotti went to the RCI board to press forward with Colin Watson's vision of a cable pipeline to the home PC. His plan proposed to invest $16.8 million over three years—$5.6 million a year—in their skunkworks Internet project, hoping to recruit 20,000 users in Ontario and British Columbia by the end of 1997. The board shot it down. The company didn't have extra capital to spare. Rogers just didn't think the PC was the way to go. His kids tried valiantly to bring him into the Internet age. They even resorted to asking tech guru Ken Nickerson, the general manager of the Microsoft Network in Canada and former RCI employee, to come over to Frybrook on Saturday mornings to introduce dad to the computer. His efforts failed to impress. "[Rogers] was skeptical, but was supportive," says Masotti. "He said, 'If you can go out and get five percent penetration, I'll give you whatever resources you want.' So, we set our targets on figuring out how to get to five-percent penetration," he says.

Then, in July 1995, Rogers Cable launched a technical trial under a new name, the WAVE, in a middle-class suburb about 70 kilometers north of Toronto called Newmarket, which held special significance for Rogers since his forebears had first settled there. Masotti hired a marketing firm, Sharp Blackmore, to come up with a consumer brand for its Internet service. The marketing firm proposed a potpourri of names: Wave, Misty, Zoom and Rush. "The WAVE just did it for me. It's a powerful force of nature," he says. Masotti thought he had the authority to change the name without his boss' approval. "I was naïve enough to think I could do anything I wanted." Though Rogers set him a flamer, the brand name, quite apt given Rogers' canniness to surf the waves, stuck. They quickly learned that they had to bust up the network, through a now-commonplace practice of node splitting, to make the network more efficient. They went from 5,000 homes to 2,000 and eventually down to 500. (In some places, Rogers is now down to 250 homes on a node.)

The next month, in August 1995, Netscape went public in one of the hottest initial public offerings ever, ushering in the era of Internet mania. In what one analyst called a "nosebleed valuation," the stock opened after a three-hour delay on NASDAQ at US$71, more than double the US$28 public offering price. The stock reached an intraday high of US$75 before closing at US$58.25. The company's market capitalization was greater than Apple Computer Inc.'s. Three months later, Netscape shares rose to more than US$110. "The Internet has gone Main Street," analyst Kathleen Smith of Renaissance Capital, a Connecticut firm that evaluates IPOs for institutional investors, told *Business Week*, which dubbed the investor frenzy "browser madness." That same month, Bell Canada, which came rather late to the party, began rolling out Sympatico, a dial-up service that included a customized version of Netscape. Microsoft Corp., playing catch-up, later superseded Netscape's Navigator to dominate the market.

When Masotti hit his targets, he excitedly returned to the RCI board for more money. Rogers now had his eureka moment. People really loved the Internet. The cable modem, at 28.8 kilobits per second, was a thousand times faster than dial up. It was considered blisteringly fast back then. And for Rogers, there was special significance that RCI was pioneering the third revolution—bringing to the world the information age—in the community first settled by his Quaker forebears. It was all systems go. In November 1995, RCI rolled out the world's first commercial Internet service called the WAVE.

"The WAVE is the most significant event in the history of Rogers cable other than its founding," Rogers told the *Toronto Star* in December 1995.

Masotti later met with Yahoo! co-founders Jerry Yang and David Filo, who were still working out of a warehouse, hoping to make RCI their Canadian service provider. The timing was fortuitous since Yahoo! needed to spruce up its planned IPO. In February 1996, Rogers signed a licensing agreement with Yahoo! Canada. Even though Rogers wasn't convinced, he signed off on the deal. On its first day of trading in August 1996, Yahoo! rocketed to US$43 from its IPO price of US$13.

"David Masotti, more than anybody else in the company, was responsible for Rogers getting into the high-speed modem business," says Colin Watson.

In November 1996, Rogers and the largest Canadian cable companies teamed up to take the WAVE national with the slogan "Tomorrow is going to be amazing." Bell Canada soon followed with a promise that it would unveil its own high-speed Internet service six to eight months later. In celebrating the launch at a local pub, Rogers paid tribute to the WAVE team, singling out

Watson and Masotti for spearheading the project. (Neither of them was there. They had quit months earlier, part of a larger exodus of talent that year.) In a heartfelt gesture, Rogers sent them thank-you notes and invitations to a cocktail party and dinner for institutional investors at the brand-new Rogers Campus in mid-town Toronto. Less than six months after the WAVE's highly publicized launch, Rogers had 4,000 subscribers, up from 1,200, for a penetration rate of 2 percent. The WAVE was on a roll.

"It changes the whole soul of the company," Rogers said in 1996. "If we've made any money for our shareholders, and if we make any in the future, it will be from launching new, innovative services, and the WAVE is a perfect example."

Then, he killed it. In April 1997, Rogers joined the At Home network, over the vehement opposition of his cable technologists. At Home Corp. was the brainchild of John Doerr, a powerful Silicon Valley venture capitalist at Kleiner Perkins Caufield & Byers, which made billions from the overly hyped New Economy dot-com boom. Doerr started At Home with John Malone's Tele-Communications Inc., the second-biggest U.S. cable company behind Time Warner Inc. They intended to deliver high-speed Internet service through the cable pipes. Though the idea was hardly novel, the cable industry desperately needed Doerr's magical elixir. At the time, Wall Street had punished all cable stocks, none more than TCI, which had declined 40 percent in 1996 alone. The cable companies, debt-ridden and facing competition from direct-broadcast satellite operators, had lost credibility on Wall Street by failing to keep promises to deliver interactive TV, the 500-channel universe and telephony. "They have lurched from one delayed introduction to the next over the last few years," Sharon Armburst, a Paul Kagan Associates senior analyst told *Fortune* magazine. "This is the last, best hope for the cable industry to set itself apart from its competitors." In other words, the cable industry had a lot riding on At Home's industry success.

New York investment bank Morgan Stanley & Co., the lead underwriter for At Home, convinced the U.S. cable guys that the upstart company needed some real numbers—and paying customers —behind it before they could take it public. That's when they persuaded the Canadians to come onboard. The prospectus basically read like the tried-and-true business model in Canada. In July 1997, At Home became a high-speed Internet stock, more than doubling at the open from its US$10.50 IPO price. The cable companies agreed to market At Home's services to their customers and the two sides would split the revenues. At Home received 35 percent of the typical US$40 monthly subscriber fee, while the cable companies took the rest. That explains the push to sign up subscribers.

After joining At Home, Rogers unloaded a lot of the talent that had worked on the wave, people familiar with the matter recall, which later proved to be a problem when the company had to transition back to its own network. In July 1998, rci officially changed the name from Rogers wave to Rogers@Home. Rogers was not alone. All of Canada's big cable companies jumped onto the At Home bandwagon and all were at the mercy of the Silicon Valley company.

The technical headaches began almost immediately. The service was plagued by long delays; system crashes, and slow-download speeds. "The worst periods were in December 1998 and October 2000, when the service collapsed," recalls Chris Weisdorf, who formed the Rogers At Home Users' Association (later renamed the Residential Broadband Users' Network) on January 1, 1999. Some 5,000 frustrated Rogers At Home subscribers flocked to the association's web site. "The way they handled the situation in December 1998 was abominable. The service never worked normally unless it was four in the morning.

"The network architecture wasn't good. They really didn't do their modeling or math. They didn't account for bandwidth hogs, which always exist on every network. They didn't account for the expansion correctly. They oversubscribed. They didn't order enough circuits. And, later on, they had major problems getting fiber."

Beverley Reade, a small claims court judge in London, Ontario, had been a long-time happy Rogers cable tv customer—until she signed up for Rogers@Home high-speed Internet service in 1998. Though Rogers promised an enhanced multimedia experience and round-the-clock, seven-day-a-week technical support service, the service was unreliable and the support virtually non-existent. Less than a month later, the nightmare began. She was unable to log onto the server for up to days at a time and was sometimes cut off suddenly in the middle of use. The problems became pronounced over the next few months. Reade called customer and technical support numerous times to complain. The single mom of two, a judge no less, spent hours on hold waiting for her calls to be answered. Instead of the service improving, it only deteriorated. The company continued to operate a shoddy Internet service for more than a year, while promoting the hell out of it to attract customers, blatantly advertising its Internet service as reliable when it obviously was not.

"It really was a hoity-toity attitude towards [their] own customers," recalls Reade. "Part of the problem was they signed up so many people and they weren't really prepared for it, and instead of saying, 'hey, everybody, here's two months free,' and everybody would be happy, they just kept denying that they were at fault."

Judge Reade tolerated the bad service for 16 months. The company offered her a credit, but when Rogers failed to send Judge Reade the promised credit for poor service, she refused to keep paying her Internet bill. She continued to pay her cable TV bill since that service was just fine. Things heated up when her unpaid Internet bill reached $139.50. So, what did Rogers do? In short, the company sicced its collection agency on her and threatened to cut off her cable TV service.

The matter dragged on for a year. The collection agency for Rogers threatened to prevent Judge Reade, who had an unblemished credit rating, from obtaining a mortgage or credit card in the future. The single mom, with a full-time job and a teenage son undergoing serious surgery, was beyond angry. When she contacted Rogers' customer service, she learned that she had not been given a credit because she no longer had an account. Rogers had cut her off. That's when she sued. Her friends dubbed her Bev "Brockovich" after Erin Brockovich, the famed legal clerk, whose fight to expose an energy utility's poisoning of a Californian city's water supply became a Hollywood movie.

Judge Reade offered to settle for reasonable punitive damages and a personal letter of apology from the founder Ted Rogers. The company's crack team of lawyers countered with an offer of free services. The theory being, free service shuts up the complainant. They were shocked when she declined. When her story hit the national news, they settled. The details remain sealed. Reade received letters of apology from Ted Rogers and his newly installed cable boss John H. Tory. She had them framed for hanging—in her laundry room.

"Rogers has lost thousands of dollars from me in business, and will continue to lose my business for the rest of my life. That's how bitter I am about it," says Reade, who now owns a bed and breakfast on Pelee Island, Ontario. "Someone gave me a really nice $450 cellphone for Christmas, but I took it back because it was a Rogers phone. I do not buy any Rogers magazines. I do not buy or rent Rogers movies, and I had been a very good customer of theirs for years. They have lost so much more than what they had to pay to settle, including their legal fees. To lose a customer like me who buys DVDs, who buys magazines, who uses Internet access and cellphones, they've lost thousands every year in commerce from me. I'm not alone."

Reade became inundated with consumer complaints that went beyond Rogers to the banks, insurance companies and other telecom companies. She still hears from people complaining about their service.

"We don't have time to be on hold for two hours to deal with a problem that they have created, and do all of the other things that we have to do in our busy, modern lives. I mean, how many times do you have to call them? Bell called yesterday, and it was an automated computer telling me, first in French and then in English, to call this number, which I called, and then I get someone in India, who then starts asking me for my name, my number, my kids' names and my bill number. I don't know. You called me. Call me back when you know what you want to talk to me about, but that was fifteen minutes wasted. I go up to Owen Sound and I don't have the number for dial-up for Sympatico, so I called Sympatico, which is very difficult to find in the phone book, and then you get some guy in India, and what's your name, address, billing address, account number. All I want is the dial-up number. Fifty minutes to get a dial-up number."

Reade is extremely disappointed with the lack of political will in Canada to support consumers. When she complained to the CRTC, the industry regulator referred her to the now-defunct Canadian Cable Television Association (CCTA), the industry lobby group that Rogers basically controlled. When she lodged a complaint to the federal government's Competition Bureau about false and misleading advertising on 24-hour tech support, her complaint vanished into a black hole. (The Competition Bureau declined to comment.) "I'm not happy with what the government did with my consumer complaints, which I thought were all very valid.

"People have to ask the government to enforce their own laws," she says. "We don't have a Ralph Nader in Canada.

"If some little company was sending out the kind of advertising that Rogers was sending out on an almost daily, but surely weekly, basis in the mail and in magazines about this Internet access being an enhanced experience and twenty-four-hour tech support—if somebody else did that and I complained to the Competition Bureau that none of this was actually being provided, they'd go after him or her. They'd go after me. They didn't go after Rogers. I had a very valid complaint. Why didn't they go after them?"

The politicians apparently didn't care. During the At Home crisis, the federal Liberal government's Heritage Minister Sheila Copps, who had oversight of the CRTC, had other priorities, including spending $19 million in tax dollars for an online museum and another $75 million of taxpayers' money to create and broadcast Canadian culture content on the Internet. "When the Internet began to grow, we promised to connect Canada to the world. We also promised to make Canada the most connected country in the world. We have kept that promise," Copps declared.

She was deafeningly silent on the service actually working.

In an attempt to provide content that would complement its high-speed connections, At Home bought the Excite Web portal for US$6.7 billion in

January 1999, the biggest ever merger of two Internet companies. The new Excite At Home Corp.—billed as AOL on steroids—had been orchestrated by Kleiner Perkins, which provided seed money for both startups.

Months later, AT&T completed its takeover of John Malone's TCI to inherit a 58-percent stake in Excite At Home. The telecom giant then outbid a takeover bid for MediaOne from Comcast Group Following its acquisition of MediaOne Group—topping Comcast's bid—AT&T became the largest U.S. cable provider and immediately began talking about splitting up Excite At Home.

Excite At Home had been perceived as a potential Net powerhouse, but clashing egos, greed and management blunders conspired to run the company into the ground. The company blew millions of dollars on acquisitions, including BlueMountain.com, an online greeting-card company. But the pipes-and-content strategy failed as online advertising revenue shriveled and investors fled high-flying Net stocks. As a result, Excite@Home went through several management shake-ups and strategy shifts, all of which failed to stop the downward spiral.

Cox and Comcast bailed to focus on building their own online service. They sold their voting stake to AT&T in 2000 for US$3 billion, or US$48 a share. That boosted AT&T's control to 74 percent. In a move that angered shareholders, AT&T permitted them to disconnect before their contracts expired. Though also part of Excite At Home, Time Warner wisely never scrapped its highly regarded RoadRunner Internet service.

Rogers might have been best served sticking with the WAVE, where he had a network that worked, instead of following his desire to play with the big boys in the U.S. sandbox. As well, his daughter Melinda 28, who worked for Excite At Home, also backed the decision. However, to many company insiders, the At Home investment didn't make sense.

He already had his own network. He didn't need At Home. Through Maclean Hunter, Rogers had his own content, yet failed to take advantage of it. Excite At Home was, well, just far more exciting. Few people seemed to care that Excite's content was at best mediocre and that At Home's hyped broadband delivery required billions in infrastructure investment. At Home built a parallel network of its own that connected to the cable companies. Emails traveled the continent through unnecessary infrastructure to reach recipients who lived mere kilometers away. From an operational perspective, At Home made little sense. "In Silicon Valley, their egos are bigger than you can imagine. And, it came up that if the email system on At Home went down on a Friday afternoon, or late Friday, people went home, instead of working the weekend on it," recalls a former Rogers Cable engineer.

Five angry Toronto-area Internet subscribers slapped RCI with a $75-million class-action lawsuit, alleging it breached subscriber contracts by failing to provide the level of service advertised. However, the allegations were never proven in court because Rogers Cable, led by John H. Tory, who called the action without merit and vowed to fight it, deftly posted an arbitration clause on its website that effectively crushed potential future litigation. The Ontario Superior Court derailed the lawsuit when it ruled that the online arbitration clause was sufficient to require disgruntled consumers to take on Rogers Cable individually in separate arbitration proceedings. The court said it did not matter that individual subscribers might not bother to initiate costly arbitration proceedings to claim a rebate of, maybe, $240. The decision prompted the Ontario government to pass legislation that renders mandatory arbitration clauses in consumer contracts unenforceable. (Rogers settled with the five plaintiffs. The resolution remains confidential.)

Rogers was still neck deep in Excite At Home when ill-fated company filed for bankruptcy in late September 2001. Unlike Rogers, Shaw, which had no divided loyalties, began building its own network in late 1999, which enabled it to begin moving its 600,000 subscribers in mid-2001, months before At Home failed. Rogers scrambled to negotiate a contract with Excite At Home to keep its connection alive for three more months. The company added 200 extra people just to handle the volume of complaints. John H. Tory took to the airways on Rogers Cable's community to inform subscribers to switch their email accounts from @Home.com to @Rogers.com. (The CRTC later scolded the company for misusing its community channel broadcasting licence in such a manner—the only thing over which the regulator found fault.) "It sort of crept up on us," Rogers says.

Rogers was the last cable company in Canada to move its high-speed services away from At Home. It finally severed its tie with Excite At Home at midnight on January 31, 2002, moving 422,000 customers onto its own network. "The Rogers brand has been hurt. I've been associated with a goddamned company that goes bankrupt, but that's the way it works," he shrugged at the time.

Excite At Home, billed as one of the "flashiest stars of the Internet age," ended in disgrace in 2001. Public investors were left holding the bag. Excite At Home had raised US$210 million by issuing stock and almost US$1 billion through debt issues. The high-flying stock, which topped at US$94.66 in April 1999, was worth 6 cents when the company was delisted from NASDAQ in October that year. Through litigation, the debt holders later recouped 53 cents for every dollar invested.

Rogers also took a hit personally. In December 2001, he unloaded his 2 million shares of At Home for US$68,600, a fraction of the US$189 million he could have sold them for at their peak.

"All the cable boys thought it would be a good idea," explains Rogers, expressing disappointment with the failed continental cooperative. "It wasn't really a convergence play. It was a financial play. It did well for a while, and I was on the board. I was on the board right to the end. I didn't get off, even against the advice of lawyers.

"It was a diversion," he admits. "I think we learned a lot. I certainly did. It was helpful. It was painful."

Even though he alienated his customers, Rogers remained steadfast with AT&T and its embattled CEO Michael Armstrong to the bitter end. Armstrong's image, *Forbes* wrote, morphed from AT&T's savior to sucker. His costly foray into the cable-TV business left AT&T heavy with debt. He faced the daunting task of trying to convince big institutional investors to stop caring about profits and embrace cash flow and growth instead. But, without enough cash flow to pay the debt and fund its cable and wireless divisions, Armstrong had been forced to do a humiliating retreat and bust up the company. At Home was just another black mark against him. The enormous backlash on Wall Street prompted an empathic former U.S. President Bill Clinton to tell Armstrong that he has the toughest job in the world.

"I have been loyal to Armstrong, better than most of his board members," says Rogers.

"I went to a do, where he was honored," recalls Rogers. "He had two vice presidents there out of them all and he had me there. I went up and hugged him, and said, 'I'm loyal to you.' Tears came to his eyes. He didn't have too many people loyal to him. He never did a thing I asked him to do, but that's beside the point. He's a good fellow. I was loyal."

With high-speed Internet, Rogers added another important weapon in his arsenal to compete against the phone companies. He now had cable TV, wireless and high-speed Internet. In his stamping ground of Ontario, rival BCE offered ExpressVu satellite TV, wireline, wireless and Internet service. Though Bell already had the quadruple play, satellite TV wasn't as reliable as cable. Further, the regulator prevented the company from bundling its services together.

Ted Rogers never forgot his debt of gratitude to David Masotti, now at Call-Net Enterprises as chief marketing officer. In April 2005, when RCI finally signed its one millionth Internet customer, he sent Masotti another thank-you letter: "Just a note to recognize your initiative and tremendous hard work at Rogers … The Internet has transformed Rogers Cable and has made it a much stronger and more viable company. You should be proud of your accomplishments and I wanted to take a moment to salute your leadership in these regards."

"We're the first in North America to have high-speed Internet—can you believe that?" recalls Rogers. "First in North America, and I'm proud of it. A little Canadian dwarf company."

In a game of one-upmanship, Jim Shaw (JR's son) bet Ted Rogers that Shaw Communications Inc. could reach 1 million Internet customers first. Rogers gamely accepted. The bet was a dinner where the winner, feasting on steak and nice wine, had the satisfaction of watching the loser eats beans and drink beer. Shaw signed its one millionth customer almost a year ahead of Rogers. To mark the occasion, Shaw ordered prime steak to be served in the company's cafeteria, which had been decked out with life-size posters of Ted Rogers holding tins of beans.

Since their schedules didn't permit them to dine together, Rogers honored the bet by sending Shaw a 900-pound steer.

"I get home a little before 6 p.m. and, next thing I know, here pulls up this steer, right on my front lawn. I live downtown! A couple of cowhands are holding it and a big sign from Ted, says, 'Is this steak big enough?' This thing is spraying manure all over the place. It's wintertime. There's cars stopping and honking. It was pretty funny. Everybody wanted to stop and look. They took it away and had it cut up, and we gave the beef to a food bank," recalls Shaw.

Shaw then commissioned renowned sculptor Joe Fafard to create an iron cutout of a steer to surprise Rogers. "It weighed a couple thousand pounds," laughs Shaw. "I had it shipped up to Toronto, and when Ted was in a board meeting, we hauled it into the middle of his office. I said, 'You want to see Shaw for the beef and Rogers for the bull.'"

CHAPTER 19

The Terrible Nineties

"We can't call ourselves a national cable company if we're not national ..."

—Phil Lind

THE MAGIC CANTEL had in the eighties faded in the nineties.

Rogers began integrating the company's customer service representatives to put them under his control—a decision that from a cost-savings standpoint appeared to make perfect sense, but began to diminish its culture. "The day we learned that Rogers was integrating Cantel's customer service with Rogers' customer service, I think half the company cried. Rogers, in cable, was not known for good service," recalls Tom Unger, a former Cantel Service Centre representative. "He had a monopoly. So, people would wait on the phone. They wouldn't get straight answers. Cable wasn't exactly a mature industry in those days either, but the whole mindset—the framework of everything Cantel was doing and were taught to do for customers—was out the window."

According to former employees, Rogers had the vision, but he got it half right. He built a telephone company from scratch but then, it started to act like one. Through his friendship with McCaw, Rogers grew enamored of U.S. talent. In his desire to always do better, he felt the grass was greener elsewhere and failed to recognize in-house latent talent. "He's the most brilliant person but he still has a certain naiveté about what goes on in his companies compared with others, and he just didn't get it, so he made some big mistakes. If he had realized he was making those mistakes, he never would have made them, because it wasn't what he meant to accomplish," said one long-time Cantel executive.

Rogers suffered the same fate as so many entrepreneurs. They are great at ideas, and building companies, yet when the company gets big, they have trouble managing the entity that was once small and built by the force of their personality. The people he hired to manage the rapidly growing company brought in more middle management, creating a bureaucracy, which in turn made decisions based on what they thought the founder wanted, instead of implementing for the greater good of the company.

In the five years after Jim Sward quit, Rogers Cantel churned through four leaders, including Rogers himself. First, Rogers hired David Gergacz, 44, the former president of the Boston Technologies Inc. and a former Sprint and AT&T executive.

Gergacz launched Amigo in June 1994, Canada's first off-the-shelf, ready-to-use cellular phone for consumers, with two monthly pricing plans, the lowest at $19.95 called the Safety Service. "We were highlighting the 'go' part. It was trilingual and has a friendly feel to it," recalls Peter Francey, the president and CEO of Toronto-based branding agency Spencer Francey Peters, who oversaw the branding effort. Rogers liked the name so much he named a boardroom Amigo.

Amigo was launched in just six weeks. When Ted Rogers says 'Go,' his people press the accelerator to the floor. They don't dawdle. It's only when things aren't moving fast enough that he becomes impatient. "The folks at Rogers were having nervous breakdowns every other day. They hadn't even sourced the hardware yet," recalls Francey. "We didn't even know what the phone was going to look like. We had to come up with a name, the packaging, the whole shebang within six weeks. It was a real effort."

Little wonder. Four months later, BCE Mobile unveiled a remarkably similar phone called Liberti. The press had a field day dumping on Bell for playing catch up.

Amigo was an instant hit. The push to market—coming out before Bell—coupled with shrewd marketing gave Rogers Cantel an enormous lift during a difficult era. In one quarter alone, Rogers Cantel was adding 800 new subscribers a day. Sold through national department stores and retailers, Amigo single-handedly took Rogers Cantel over the 1-million-customer threshold. The company, though, was ill prepared for the deluge of subscriptions and inquiries, and the billing systems were overloaded. Churn rates—the number of subscribers who drop the service—spiked. To stem cancellations, Rogers Cantel moved customers to lease-to-own formats under long-term contracts.

With his telephone savvy, Gergacz may have understood the business but did not know how to deal with the company's driven founder. When Gergacz left in August 1995 to become Cincinnati Bell Telephone's CEO, Ted Rogers stepped into the void until July 1996 when he promoted Irishman Michael Mullagh, the former president of BC Tel Mobility, who joined Cantel four years earlier. Mullagh quit within months of taking the helm. Stan Kabala, another American, from Unitel was up next. Kabala was touted on Bay Street as the prince in waiting. Less than 12 months later, he too was gone. As he walked away with a $1.2-million golden parachute, Cantel announced that it planned to fire 800 employees.

There were other departures. Leonard Katz, Cantel's regulatory head, quit, later to join the CRTC. David Parkes, a candidate for Sward's job, bolted to run Sprint Canada, and John F. (Jack) Cassidy, a Cantel sales executive, left to build Cincinnati Bell's cellular telephone division. Many frontline employees, who began their careers at Cantel, left to take jobs at financial institutions.

In March 1996, Colin Watson, 54, resigned after 22 years in the cable TV industry, 17 of those with Rogers, to become Spar Aerospace Ltd.'s CEO. Watson quit to stretch his wings as a real CEO instead of being permanently consigned to mere wingman status. Spar's timing was perfect, given that it headhunted him on the heels of the negative option debacle, for which he was the fall guy.

Watson insists that he was neither frustrated nor burned out. The move to Spar "gave me the opportunity to run my own show."

Though Rogers had contemplated creating a new position at RCI of chief operating officer—someone to relieve him of his day-to-day responsibilities—he kept putting it off, which meant longtime lieutenants had no opportunity for further advancement. His perpetual succession worries ebbed and flowed with the state of his health. His heart bypass surgery and eye surgery contributed to persistent media speculation over potential successors. The potential candidates mentioned the most included Watson, Lind, Savage, Emerson and John H. Tory, who joined in 1995. His son, Edward, then 26, had just joined the company a year earlier. Rogers, 63, already down a president in wireless, now lacked a cable TV head.

The doors to the executive suites began revolving. David Masotti followed his mentor, Colin Watson, to Spar. Scott Colbran from Maclean Hunter quit. Then, five months later in August, Rogers lost his CFO.

Graham Savage, 47, resigned, ending a 21-year career in the cable TV industry. *Global Finance*, a prestigious financial magazine, had just named Savage one of the world's Top 25 CFO superstars. Just like Watson, he had faithfully served 17 years with Rogers.

A confluence of factors prompted Savage to leave. He was highly frustrated with the machinations at the board level, which impaired his ability to deliver direction as the CFO. He had self-doubts as to whether his advice as CFO was being considered. Though issuing equity at current low stock prices was expensive, he felt it was necessary to right-size the balance sheet. He had set into motion the sale of the Maclean Hunter assets and the sale of Toronto Sun Publishing Corp. to a Paul Godfrey-led management group. He wanted to sell more non-core assets. But, Savage butted heads with Rogers once too often. Being a heat shield for his staff also started to wear him down. Lastly, he felt that if he stayed any longer he wouldn't build the wealth he knew he was capable of achieving. "I was getting to an age where if I didn't create wealth soon I never would," he says.

"It was an exciting period for me. The eighties, with the cable franchising in the United States, and wireless, and into the early nineties with Maclean Hunter and Unitel were a lot of fun. Cantel was one of the smartest things Ted ever did. He created billions of dollars of value from nothing," Savage says, with admiration for his former boss. "I always marveled that I could be part of some of these things at my age. It's not often that you get to participate in a brand new industry, let alone, start a brand new company.

"When we started, we had 400 employees and when I left, we had 20,000. When I started, we had $40 million of assets and when I left, we had $6 billion. I was able to witness, or be part of, an awful lot of change and that was fun and exhilarating, but there comes a time when you have to ask, 'Am I having fun? Am I making money? Am I making a difference?' And I couldn't say 'yes' to any of those questions anymore."

Savage, who since has built a successful merchant bank business, suffered a mini-stroke causing no lasting damage eight years after leaving RCI. He then underwent surgery to clear an artery in his neck that was 85 percent blocked. The head scans revealed a much more serious condition, a brain aneurysm, for which he underwent successful surgery.

Savage's resignation rattled investor confidence. RCI Class B shares dropped sharply, declining nearly $1 on the day to a 52-week low of $9.10, the first time the stock sank below $10 in five years. Rogers stepped into the market, buying stock to buttress the share price. Highly respected, Savage was Rogers' alter ego, the financially conservative counterweight to the founder's infectious enthusiasm. Investors immediately sought reassurance that debt-heavy RCI wasn't going to collapse under its mountain of debt. RCI's long-term debt had climbed to $4.8 billion and analysts were expecting it to reach $5 billion by year's end. Both the cable and wireless division posted weak performances. Nesbitt Burns' Doug Kirk in 1996 estimated that Rogers would not generate enough cash, even with the sale of the *Toronto Sun*, to cover its needs. The company's long-term debt to EBITDA had climbed to 6.5, approaching the maximum permitted in its debt covenants. By comparison, Shaw had a 4.5 to 1 debt to EBITDA ratio. Kirk reckoned RCI had to raise equity or sell additional assets to make up the cash shortfall.

Savage's departure prompted TD Bank chairman Dick Thomson to visit Rogers at the cable company. He urged Rogers to hold a press conference that Friday to soothe investor concerns and quell the media's speculation. He told Rogers exactly what he needed to say. Consequently, Rogers spoke in a voice of financial sobriety. Without releasing any details, Rogers said he intended to curtail capital spending, cut costs and inject equity into the company's cable business, everything Savage wanted to do. He unveiled a deal to sell a 50-percent equity stake in The Shopping Channel to QVC Inc.'s parent, Comcast Corp. He also spun Savage's departure in the context of the company entering a new era of less demanding debt growth. "He's like Moses. His work is done," Rogers said at the time.

"That was a tough time," recalls Rogers. "I've made sure that I remain friends with him. At the time, he wasn't happy at all and he left, and the markets started to go down. It was a real problem. It brought out your friends. Dick Thomson came to see me at the cable office. He said, 'This is the first time I've ever been in the cable company.' Here's a guy who has loaned me billions. He says, 'You're in trouble and we're going to help you. So, we'll have a press conference and here are the things you should say, and we'll say this and rally around.' Isn't this a wonderful story? That sort of stopped the deluge [of calls]."

"The market had to be handheld for a few weeks," recalls treasurer Lorraine Daly. "You had to answer all the phone calls from everybody and say the same thing five thousand times.

'Why did he leave?'
'He left because he wanted to.'
'You're not going bankrupt?'
'No, we're not going bankrupt.'

"You had to take the calls and answer the questions. It went on for weeks. You didn't want to duck the calls," she says. "Then Alan came in and life continued."

Thinking it was just an interim position, Alan Horn slid easily into the CFO's chair. Rogers had handpicked Horn, a lanky six-foot-five native of Kintore, Scotland, northwest of Aberdeen, to manage the Rogers family's private company in 1990. A chartered accountant, Horn first came to Canada in 1978 as a member of Scotland's oldest soccer team, the Queen's Park Football Club, for a whirlwind three-week tour. The following year, the 29-year-old Scottish tax specialist landed in Canada to work at his accounting firm's Canadian affiliate, Thorne Riddell, KPMG's predecessor, for a two-year stint. His very first file was Rogers. He had no idea he'd be on it virtually for the rest of his life. His decade-long tenure as CFO would coincide with the blossoming of the two capital-intensive industries that Savage had put Rogers on the financial footing to enter: wireless and broadband communications. The acquisition of more customers—and therefore greater cash flow—enabled Horn to do everything that Savage would have done had he still been there.

"Graham made a great contribution," says former Nesbitt Burns analyst Doug Kirk. "He brought a level of market sophistication to the table."

In November 1996, for the second time in three years, Rogers forged an alliance with U.S. giant AT&T—one that ultimately proved critical to the company's future success. This time, AT&T Canada's Jim Meenan and Rothschild's Gar Emerson negotiated the details for a 15-year marketing deal that gave Rogers Cantel access to AT&T's services, technology and, surprisingly, its brand—one of the world's most widely recognized names. Rogers Cantel became Cantel AT&T—the first time AT&T co-shared its brand. Financially, RCI gained nothing from the alliance. AT&T brought its name to the table, not its money. There would be no debt relief here. Instead, Rogers issued warrants to AT&T, which were exchangeable for a nominal amount of Cantel stock. Cantel was actually putting out money, paying AT&T royalties to use its name. Industry pundits speculated it was a prelude to AT&T acquiring an equity stake in Cantel.

When AT&T acquired wireless giant McCaw Cellular, America's Ma Bell hoped to use wireless to connect to customers without having to pay monopoly rates to the Baby Bells. Local telephony was at the heart of AT&T's cable strategy. AT&T's research arm had also been experimenting with cable telephony. AT&T intended to muscle into the local phone markets that it lost to the Baby Bells through cellular phone service and by linking with cable TV companies to route calls over the cable pipes. For its part, AT&T's Canadian subsidiary was tracking the same strategy on a smaller scale. It wanted to crack Canada's $7-billion local phone business to challenge Bell Canada directly. Rogers' fibered cable and wireless empire looked darn attractive to the mighty AT&T.

The McCaw connection linked the two companies. Cantel and McCaw already enjoyed seamless cross-border cellular network coverage. From that day forward, the two companies walked virtually lock-step into the new era of digital cellular telephony, the second generation of services otherwise known as PCS (personal communications services) and beyond. AT&T brought back Nick Kauser, who joined the Cantel board as AT&T's representative.

The investment was significant enough to bring AT&T chairman Bob Allen to Toronto to celebrate with Ted Rogers. With the talk in Ottawa yet again of potentially scrapping the foreign ownership rules, AT&T had its sights trained on Rogers. The U.S. giant coveted Rogers' cable and wireless networks. The company had even informally broached the possibility of buying from Rogers his controlling stake, people familiar with the situation say. The overture never went anywhere because Rogers dismissed it. He had no intention of selling. Still, AT&T intended to stick around just in case he changed his mind.

"This deal is important to our future," said Bob Allen, at the Toronto press conference. AT&T Canada, Unitel's reincarnation, was attempting to execute the Rogers playbook of uniting the wireline and wireless businesses to build a telecom powerhouse. The dream hadn't died; it had just been co-opted by someone else.

AT&T was not even Rogers' first co-branding choice. He wanted to partner with Sprint Corp. since he had a close relationship with its CEO, William Esrey. The two men were friends. Esrey always gave Rogers the red-carpet treatment whenever he was in town, while AT&T was, well, the mighty AT&T. The company lacked that personal touch. Rogers made an impassioned speech to the RCI board of directors about what a great company Sprint was, but Phil Lind shot him down. "I led the charge against [Sprint] for AT&T, and ultimately, we did the deal with AT&T," says Lind. "You don't do too many of those things, even if you've been here a long time; it's not a good career move really. Most guys would have thrown the guy out for that not once, but twice. I've only led two or three coups against [Rogers]. Most of the time, Rogers and I are at one. Ninety-nine percent of the time, he's charging for something and I'm backing him up."

With his wireless woes mounting, Ted Rogers was not faring any better on the cable TV side of his business. The company's debt hovered over the stock price like a climatic depression in the nineties. After peaking at $19.07 in 1990, RCI's shares fell to a 52-week low of $8.15 in 1996. Indeed, by the end of 1996, North American cable equities were in the toilet. They were among the worst performing stock categories in the S&P 500 index. The outlook for the industry grew bleaker still when TCI's John Malone told *The Wall Street Journal* in January 1997 that he had been overly optimistic about the 500-channel universe and that his push into telephony and the Internet was not working. His remarks sent Wall Street reeling. On the heels of Malone's comments, Ted Rogers flew to New York to speak to Wall Street junk-bond investors to ease their concerns, explaining that the Canadian cable TV industry was different from that in the United States. A month later, in mid-February, he was back on Wall Street to announce he was spending $400 million to upgrade and digitize his cable networks. But, his remarks did little to boost the company's stock price. Investment analysts had turned against the North American cable TV industry and Ted Rogers was lumped in among them.

In May 1997, the two Teds—Ted Rogers and Ted Turner—spoke at the Canadian cable television industry association conference in Toronto. Turner, who had sold his company the previous year to Time Warner Inc. for US$7.5 billion, compared the cable TV industry's looming battle with satellite TV and telephone companies to Poland in 1939, earning him a swift kick under the table from Rogers, who couldn't believe his ears. "The Germans are on the one side and the Russians are on the other," Turner said. "There wasn't really a lot to be happy or cheerful about." He advised cable TV owners to sell if they could find buyers because it's better to get off the *Titanic* while it's still docked than staying onboard and going down with the ship. "Do it early rather than late," he warned. Rogers likely wished he had kicked him harder. RCI Class B shares continued their downward trek, falling 32 percent in 1997 to finish the year at $6.90.

On January 9, 1998, John Graham, Rogers' stepfather, died at age 86. Graham, called a twentieth-century renaissance man, left behind his second wife of 22 years, Natasha Nikolaevna Popova, his daughter Ann "Rooney" and his stepson. Although he had not been RCI chairman for the previous five years, Graham remained chairman emeritus and had continued to serve as counsel to Toronto law firm Cassels Brock & Blackwell. Graham had been Rogers' most stalwart supporter, guiding the boy into manhood and steering a headstrong young man at pivotal junctures in his career. He had been Rogers' closest confidante apart from his wife, Loretta. "John kept Ted and the company from going too far [over the edge]," says former RCI director Gordon A. Gray. Graham was an important sounding board not just for Rogers but also for Rogers' lieutenants.

"We miss him a lot," says Rogers, his words underscoring the deep sense of personal loss. Then, his sense of humor kicks in. "John Graham," he chuckles, "we did this big thing in 1957, and he used to say he spent a whole month or two on it and he never caught up in his lifetime." Graham helped Rogers, who always feared he might suffer his namesake's tragic fate, organize his first and subsequent trusts. (Striving to keep them current, Rogers changed them at least nine times in three decades.)

When Graham died, Phil Lind unwillingly tried to fill the void that Graham left. Lind, Rogers' longest-serving partner, had for the most part managed to escape his boss' relentless, often capricious, demands because he never had direct operational oversight. As the decade unfolded, he increasingly took a more proactive role in managing Rogers and running interference. His friends say the stress showed. "He had become arrogant, [exhibiting] preposterous arrogance—so unlike Phil—I couldn't believe it," recalls a friend. With no John Graham to rein in Rogers, Lind was left trying to guide him through one of the company's darkest nadirs. He would pay the price for it six months later.

The turnover in the executive suite impacted the business. Though revenues exploded, Rogers Cantel was bleeding. From 1993 to 1998, Rogers Cantel's revenue rose to $1.24 billion from $606 million. During that same period, the company lost $643 million. Rogers again relied predominately on debt to finance the network upgrades. At the end of 1997, the company carried $1.86 billion in long-term debt, up from $841.8 million in 1993. The stock swooned from a 1993 high of $41.50 to a low of $12.70 in 1997.

While the cost of acquiring customers remained extraordinarily high—peaking at $623 per customer in 1997—the average monthly revenue per subscriber, known as ARPU a closely watched measure of financial health in the wireless industry—plummeted, reflecting the new competitive and technological environment. To offset falling ARPU, Rogers Cantel fired up the marketing engines. Thanks to tremendous marketing effort and cheaper handheld digital phones, the company's subscriber base tripled to 1.74 million customers from 573,000 in that five-year period.

For the first time, Ted Rogers, the duopolist, now faced competition in the wireless industry. In December 1995, Industry Canada Minister John Manley awarded Microcell a spectrum license for so-called digital personal communications services (PCS) in Ottawa's second and last beauty contest. (The FCC raised US$7.7 billion from its PCS auction earlier that year.) PCS, considered 2G technology, ushered in the new era of digital cellphone service and data communications, which at the time, meant short-text messaging. The incumbents naturally received licenses. Though Industry Canada received 16 applications from new entrants, Manley allocated digital spectrum to just two newcomers: Microcell Telecommunications Inc. and Clearnet Communications Inc.

Microcell, formerly Popfone Canada Corp., was co-founded by celebrated monopoly buster Michael Kedar in the mid-nineties. Kedar, who waged an often thankless six-year war to open the long-distance telephone market to resellers, hoped to crack the wireless duopoly. He then brought in telecom guru Charles Sirois, who acquired control of the fledgling company. Shaw Communications and Le Groupe Vidéotron also were included in the partnership group. Unlike the incumbents and Clearnet, Microcell intended to build a global system for mobile communications, better known as GSM, which is the world's most popular standard for mobile phones.

David Simmonds, a Bell Cellular franchise owner, founded Clearnet in 1984 to sell two-way radios to taxis and buses. He mentored his son's high-school buddy, George Cope, and named the 26-year-old Clearnet's president in 1987. Cope, who launched the innovative "Mike" wireless walkie-talkie service, built Clearnet into a national, albeit money-losing, competitor with about 7-percent market share before Telus swooped in to acquire it in 2000. (Clearnet was the carrier that featured tree frogs, lizards and disco ducks in its marketing, a tradition Telus continued.)

In January 1998, Ted Rogers hired Charles Hoffman, 48, a straight-talking American who wasn't afraid of a mercurial founder, to turn around the wireless company. Rogers called it the "year of reckoning" for the company. "It was just a disjointed place looking for Ted to tell them what to do," says Hoffman. "It was really a case where he needed someone to come in who, one, knew what they were doing, and, two, wasn't afraid of him."

Hoffman, a St. Louis native, came from Sprint PCS, where he had been president of the Northeast Region. (Sprint Corp., led by Rogers' friend, CEO William Esrey, formed Sprint PCS, a joint venture with three cable-TV companies, TCI, Comcast Corp. and Cox Communications Inc., to provide nationwide local, long-distance and wireless phone services and cable TV on one bill.) Hoffman previously spent 16 years at Southwestern Bell (now part of SBC Communications) from 1980 to 1996 in various senior positions. While president and general manager of SBC's Cellular One division, he revitalized the Washington/Baltimore and Boston, the second- and fourth-largest SBC markets, turning them into market leaders. He was no stranger to working abroad, having spent two years in Mexico, where he ran SBC's wireless division.

Hoffman, a veteran of America's cutthroat wireless wars, brought along eight Americans to help right the listing ship. Under his direction, he began to make changes in marketing, distribution, sales, billing and customer care and network expansions. Hoffman gives Alan Horn a lot of credit for navigating both the company and founder through a difficult era. "Alan is solid as a rock," says Hoffman. "He would sometimes support you during Ted attacks. He'd point out quietly a fact that maybe Ted wasn't aware of it. It often didn't help you, but you felt good that there was someone supporting you."

Four years earlier, Bay Street had crowned Ted Rogers the King of Cable. They cheered and applauded him for his brilliant acquisition of Maclean Hunter. Now, he was being jeered. Bay Street investors regarded his stock as "the equity equivalent of nuclear waste." The securities industry felt that Rogers had lost more than his eyesight; he had lost his business vision. RCI was mired in debt, now hovering at a crushing $5.6 billion, most of it in junk bonds. In fiscal 1997, RCI reported a loss of $540 million. Each business day, RCI lost a staggering $2.2 million. Investors became to question the company's viability. "It was a stressful time. We were fighting to stay alive," says Phil Lind.

Though the financial analysts and the press—and some of his closest lieutenants—were highly critical of him, Ted Rogers brazenly continued to plough more money into the wireless and cable TV networks. He didn't care one iota what Bay Street thought. He repeatedly told securities analysts and investors that the company had enough cash flow to cover its debt, even though he still wasn't generating free cash flow. Lind, Mr. Outside, also known as Rogers' "clean-up guy," tried to tell him that he wasn't speaking Bay Street's language. It's not what they wanted to hear. It didn't matter. Rogers wasn't listening. The stress inevitably took its toll on both men. The world was going digital. The cable TV and telephone companies were colliding towards convergence. Rogers, a man who is perpetually in a hurry, understood that his networks needed to be upgraded for the coming era of digital telephony, high-speed Internet and high-definition TV. If Bay Street didn't get it, too bad. Charles Hoffman, the new Cantel head, recalls being surprised by the degree of animosity on the street. "In the U.S., he would be a huge hero," says Hoffman. "In Canada, because he rocks the boat and he's different, he's vilified. It's interesting to see the cultural difference between the two countries. Down here, an entrepreneur who is a character is a big deal, and for me, at least as an outsider, in Canada, it didn't seem to be as accepted."

On January 21, 1998, less than two weeks after the death of his stepfather John Graham, Ted Rogers took another body blow. RCI shares plummeted to $4.80—the lowest it had been in more than a decade. Michael Binder, the assistant deputy minister for the spectrum branch at Industry Canada, recalls making the rounds on Bay Street at that time. "I remember the dark days of cable stock. Everybody thought that telephone companies would kill the cable people. I didn't understand why the investment people were crapping all over the stock," Binder says. "From a technical perspective, the cable companies had more bandwidth than the telephone companies, so I kept asking, and what they didn't understand [was] that it was all going to be about bandwidth. It's all about bandwidth. It's all about content and the consumer. They didn't get it. I think Ted understood it from day one. He hung in there with huge debts because he believed he had a good business model that would prevail, and he was right."

The lowest point came in March 1998 when RCI was banished from the prestigious Toronto Stock Exchange 100 index, which lists Canada's 100 largest companies, and the blue-chip Toronto 35 subindex. RCI failed to meet the Exchange's minimum market capitalization rules.

Just one analyst remained bullish on RCI stock: Doug Kirk, a former TD banker who had worked on the Rogers account. The respected BMO Nesbitt Burns Inc. analyst was the lone contrarian. In January when the stock hit its low, he raised his rating to a "strong buy" from a "buy" as rival firms screamed "sell." In a March 4 report, he predicted the stock would hit $10 within one year. Indeed the B shares would surpass even his target, climbing to a 52-week high of $38.75 the following year. Kirk felt that the market skepticism, driven largely by the media, was overblown. He had full confidence in Ted Rogers' ability to turn around the *Queen Mary*, as Rogers had once called the company. "That was my stake in the ground. Buy it at five dollars," recalls Kirk. "It's done nothing but get bigger and better since then."

But first, Rogers had to pull the proverbial rabbit out of his hat: MetroNet. His former CFO, Phil Ladouceur, had joined MetroNet Communications Corp., a fledgling, Calgary-based telecom company in 1996. Ladouceur raised the initial $15 million in seed money from the Ontario Teachers' Pension Plan Board and Rhode Island-based Providence Equity Partners Inc. to build the fledgling company's phone and data networks. Providence also contributed by parachuting in Craig D. Young, an American with telephony experience. Ladouceur and Rogers teamed up to pull off a blockbuster deal that gave the besieged cable guy badly needed cash to reduce his debt load.

In May 1998, after working 20-hour days for two straight weeks, RCI and MetroNet struck a $1.05-billion deal that stunned Bay Street. Rogers sold Rogers Telecom, his local telephone subsidiary, to MetroNet for $600 million in cash and 12.5 million MetroNet shares, worth $450 million. MetroNet gained 3,400 km of optic fiber and access to 1,300 office buildings and condominiums in 10 cities across Canada, a network Rogers had used to supply local high-speed data services.

For an entrepreneur, who never wants to sell anything, Rogers realized he lacked the expertise to turn the division into the second force. "I know we have to get the level of debt down," Rogers also acknowledged highlighting his "disastrous" foray into Unitel. Though the financial district applauded the transaction, Bay Street immediately labeled it his "Big Retreat." Rogers appeared to be throwing in the towel on his long-cherished dream of challenging the phone giants in the telecom business. In the wake of this transaction, speculation, fueled by the press, mounted that he was even going to sell Cantel to AT&T. Indeed, that was the furthest thing from his mind.

That same day, RCI also announced that cable president Jos Wintermans had quit after 11 months, hoping to bury the news in the splash of the MetroNet deal. For the second time in as many years, Rogers returned to the helm of the cable company. He requested Wintermans to step down, without the board's unanimous approval, just a week before his stock options came due. Wintermans had joined in May 1997 from Canadian Tire Corp., where he was responsible for the credit card business, gas stations, real estate, construction and information technology. "He's like a lot of Dutch," quips former RCI director Robin Korthals, who is half Scot, half Dutch. "They hate authority." Wintermans cleaned house, eliminated dead wood, simplified the organizational structure and restructured the capital budget. He reduced the number of vice presidents reporting to him from 21 to 12. In his short tenure, he eliminated $56 million from operating costs.

"I knew going in that there was a fifty-fifty chance that I would bite the dust someday but, in the meantime, you still take on the challenge, and there are very bright people at Rogers," says Wintermans.

"At one of my town hall [meetings], the union in B.C. said to me, 'How long are you going to be around?' I said, 'Listen, as long as Ted lets me do what I think is right then I'll be around.' Of course, five months later I was gone," he laughs.

"The operating results weren't important to him because he's always lost money and gotten away with it," he says. "We had books just to keep track of all of his questions and what we'd answered to make sure that we weren't duplicating. We had eight, three-inch binders. It got to be a grind.

"It always struck me that there were a lot of very bright people in that business and it had all the potential to be an outstanding operational environment, but it really never got there because of unpredictability of what the priorities of RCI were at any moment in time.

"In the end, he has a very good sense of where the business is going and how to get the assets in place to do it. I really like his tolerance to invest in the technology and infrastructure. That's paid off for him. And, the other part of it is he convinces a lot of people to lend him money, and he's always paid off [his debts] and paid early. It's quite incredible—and his enthusiasm and his ability to turn on the charm—he's quite a going concern.

"A lot of people mope about losing money or doing something wrong. He doesn't," says Wintermans. "He's always moving forward."

The cable industry's prospects were about to brighten considerably. In June 1998, AT&T shocked Wall Street by plunging the cable TV business. The company, led by AT&T outsider Michael Armstrong, said it planned to buy TCI for US$32 billion, or US$46.54 a share, to use the No. 2 cable company's pipes to deliver local telephone and Internet services. The cable barons were ecstatic. Armstrong, a long-time IBM executive and former CEO of Hughes Electronics Corp., who succeeded chairman Robert Allen, was giving the industry a huge vote of confidence. The hated phone company was admitting that the cable's brawny coaxial pipes outclassed its century-old copper wires. Suddenly, Wall Street gazed with renewed interest on cable stocks. The fact that TCI was technologically the most backward of the major cable companies was, for the moment, lost in the mix.

Armstrong, feted like a rock star, embarked on a bold, but risky, strategy to reinvent AT&T. He made a US$100-million bet on the cable market, figuring he could use the cable lines to sell customers a bundle of television, Internet and local phone service. AT&T already had wireless, the fourth service in the all-important quadruple play, words that had not yet seeped into the industry vernacular. Just like Rogers, Armstrong was collecting assets. Unlike Rogers, Armstrong ran out of money. In dramatic fashion, he would be forced to break up AT&T and sell off its cable wires to Comcast Corp., where, for a while, he was chairman.

Just as the clouds were lifting from the cable TV industry, RCI was jolted again. On July 1, Canada Day, 1998, before lunch, Phil Lind, 54, was at his midtown Toronto condominium just finishing a telephone call when he suddenly felt dizzy and collapsed to the floor unconscious. He had suffered a massive stroke. Fortunately, he wasn't alone. Newly separated from his wife, Lind's companion heard him crumple to the ground and immediately called 911. Had he been alone, Lind says he would have died, because people expected him to be out of town.

The entire company reeled from the shock. Rogers reached John H. Tory in Italy, where he was on vacation, to break the news. "He could hardly speak. He was completely overcome by emotion," recalls Tory, who picked up Lind's duties. "He was having such a difficult time [speaking], I thought he was telling me that he had had a stroke, and I was wondering why is he phoning me to tell me this, he's had a stroke. Then I realized he's telling me that Phil has had a stroke. I just couldn't comprehend this happening to Phil. Phil was Mr. Active."

He suffered paralysis in his right arm and leg.

Asked if he feels the stress of that year contributed to his stroke, Lind replies: "Of course."

In the early stages of recovery, he had difficulty speaking. Jan Innes and Missy Goerner from San Antonio kept watchful vigils. Lind had a steady stream of visitors, friends from the industry and company, who read and talked to him, helping to keep his mind alert. Rogers never expected Lind to make a full recovery. However, though first year of his recovery was difficult, he improved steadily.

The stroke changed him. He lost the arrogance that success brought and power fed. "Phil is now like the guy he used to be twenty-five years ago. He has become a sweet guy again,'" says a close friend.

Nineteen ninety-nine was a year of alliances. With cable-TV and phone companies barrelling towards convergence, Ted Rogers and his long-time foe BCE both sought foreign partners.

"It's a time of tremendous change, and change represents opportunity as well as danger. It's a very key time, a time to be vigilant and not be fatigued by it," says Rogers.

In March, Rogers shrewdly parlayed his small investment in MetroNet into another monster deal. AT&T Canada, Unitel's reincarnation, announced it was merging with MetroNet in a stock deal valued at $4.9 billion, allowing AT&T Canada to break into the local telephone market for the first time. Rogers, who was at the press conference, was smiling broadly. RCI ended up with 17 percent of the combined company, worth almost $1 billion.

"It's a typical Ted deal," says Charles Hoffman. "As soon as he had invested in them, he started working on AT&T to buy MetroNet. He just worked it and worked it and worked in until, sure as heck, AT&T ended up buying MetroNet."

RCI CFO Alan Horn later cleverly used the AT&T stake as collateral to raise almost $1 billion in preferred securities to repay bank debt.

In April, Rogers persuaded John Howard Tory, 45, to take the cable helm, replacing James (Trey) Smith III, a 20-year U.S. cable TV industry veteran. Smith, a Californian in his early fifties, had been lured out of early retirement to join RCI the previous year. The former Cox Cable and Times Mirror Cable executive didn't last even five months.

Tory, the son of Rogers' friend and company director John A. Tory, long-time deputy chair of Thomson Corp., had known Rogers for most of his life. When he was 17, he worked in the newsroom at Rogers' CFTR and CHFI. Tory, the former principal secretary to former Ontario premier William Davis, returned to RCI in 1995 to run Rogers Media Inc., the company's print and broadcasting arm. His arrival at RCI coincided with the negative option billing debacle. For those seven years, Tory also served as chairman of the Canadian Football League and for three years, while at Rogers Media, he served as acting commissioner.

In June, less than a year after suffering his stroke, Phil Lind traveled to Chicago, where the National Cable Television Association, the U.S. industry trade group, honored him at its annual conference for his pioneering efforts in programming, including negotiating the first National Hockey League pay-per-view arrangement and establishing local programming at Rogers as a model for other cable companies. Lind, learning to scrawl with his left hand, gradually worked his way back to a prominent role within the company. He insists that during his long career with Rogers that he never considered quitting. "I've always liked it here for two reasons: one, Ted Rogers always let me do more or less whatever I wanted to do. Now, unfortunately, he would steer me in certain ways and then, I would do it but unlike other people, I had fewer boundaries than others. I mean, I couldn't have survived otherwise, and the second thing, goddamn it, it's the most amazingly interesting business," Lind says. "There is never a dull moment."

Rogers snared another major investor in July when Microsoft acquired 9.2 percent of RCI for $600 million, injecting much-needed capital into the company—the first time the U.S. titan had invested in a Canadian company. As part of the investment, Rogers announced it planned to use Microsoft's software for its digital set-top boxes. Microsoft was, in fact, recycling the set-top cable box plan that Masotti had originally resisted. For its part, Microsoft, through its WebTV, saw cable access to the Internet as a way for the company to wield potentially the same software dominance over millions of set-top boxes as it has over PCs. (Later, when John H. Tory, the Rogers Cable head, continued to endorse the Microsoft plan, Ted Rogers overruled him. Though Rogers' decision proved to be the right one because of Microsoft's software problems, Gates did not invite him to the following year's Microsoft CEO Summit.)

It was the kind of deal that befitted a major celebration. But, instead of a splashy media event, RCI held a conference call to prevent the media from finding out that Rogers' health had taken a turn for the worse. "I was in trouble for that one," says Rogers wryly. "I had a quadruple [stomach] aneurysm, and with that you have to lie flat. I really couldn't stand up. I was lying on a sofa. We used a speakerphone and a [microphone]. That's how we handled it.

"Nobody knew," he now laughs. "So, thank God, I'm better now." At the time he recalled though, "We don't have all of our debts paid off. We're not investment grade, so I can't go yet."

Quips Doug Kirk, the former Nesbitt Burns analyst, "He's got more replacements on him than a '59 Chevy."

In August, less than three weeks after the Microsoft investment, Rogers pulled off another blockbuster deal. He sold a third of the wireless business to his co-branding partner AT&T Corp. and U.K. giant British Telecommunications PLC—two deep-pocketed foreigners—for $1.4 billion. He used the cash injection to reduce debt and expand Cantel's wireless phone network. He also hoped to round out his consumer offering of cable, Internet and wireless with long-distance services. More importantly, BT influenced Cantel's decision to adopt GSM, a strategically critical decision that helped Rogers to leapfrog the competition. According to veteran telecom consultant, Eamon Hoey, Rogers' move from TDMA to GSM amounted to a condemnation of Ottawa's decision in the early nineties to adopt non-GSM standards to favor existing manufacturers.

For their part, the two foreign telecom giants gained a toehold in Canada. Under the deal, AT&T and BT received first rights to bid for control of Rogers Cantel if Ottawa eased its foreign ownership rules. The federal government was at the time once again mulling over its rules. (Foreigners are limited to owning 20 percent of the voting shares in an operating company and 33.3 percent in a telecom holding company.) AT&T had not given up hope of Rogers selling. "You never say never on these things," recalls former AT&T Wireless CEO John Zeglis. "Ted didn't want to sell. He likes the action. Ted likes to run his own company, and Edward coming up right after him. We liked having the equity there that cemented the operational partnerships. We liked the fact that when we went GSM, Ted immediately jumped to GSM."

The two back-to-back deals breathed new energy into the beleaguered company. Rogers bounced back in dramatic fashion to trump the naysayers, who had been predicting his ruin. The company's stock price rocketed to a high of $38.75 in 1999 from a low of $4.80 in January 1998.

Inevitably, the year of wheeling and dealing took its toll on his health.

In December, Rogers, 66, felt unwell while in Los Angeles at a convention. He called his family physician, Dr. Bernie Gosevitz, in Toronto, who ordered him to go to the hospital immediately and get an MRI done. He did.

"What insurance do you have?" he was asked.

"Well, I'm a Canadian. What about cash? Is there a discount for cash?"

"I was just making it up as I went along. The lady came back and said, 'Forty percent discount,'" he says, pleased as punch. "I got forty percent off $1,600." It's one of his favorite anecdotes.

"Anyway, it wasn't good news," he says. The vein in his neck was 90- to 95-percent blocked. Ten days later, on December 27, 1999, he went to the Mayo Clinic to have his neck cut open. "We saved him from stroking out. I just had an instinct," says Dr. Gosevitz.

Rogers soon afterward had melanoma removed from his cheek near his left eye. The surgery had been aggressive, causing his eyelid to droop and his good eye to water, making it difficult for him to see properly. He also suffers from glaucoma, and has only 5- to 10-percent vision in his right eye. More surgeries were necessary to correct the problem.

"I would enjoy not having to go for an operation every six months," Rogers said at the time, clearly exasperated. In spite of his health, Rogers amazingly didn't slow down.

Barely two weeks later, on the morning of January 11, 2000, Ted Rogers was in Palm Springs, California at the annual Salomon Smith Barney media and telecom conference when he flicked on CNBC to learn that AOL was acquiring the venerable old media company Time Warner Inc. for a stunning US$165 billion. The megamerger, conceived at the height of the dotcom frenzy, around the world. Claude Chagnon—the son of Vidéotron founder André Chagnon, dubbed "the French Ted Rogers" for his relentless pursuit of new technologies—was also at the conference. His father, 72, was in Florida on vacation. Rogers, on the prowl, approached the younger Chagnon with the idea of a possible merger.

Jetting home from the conference, Rogers, with his usual characteristic zeal, began to strategize. He dubbed the file Macdonald-Cartier after Sir John A. Macdonald and Sir George-Étienne Cartier, two of Canada's founding fathers of Confederation. The name went beyond the symbolism of an Anglo uniting with a Frenchman. If they merged, the combined company would control a cable network that passed 64 percent of the homes in Quebec and Ontario and nearly 50 percent of the homes across the country. The union of Rogers and Vidéotron would create a network that virtually mirrored that of their enemy BCE.

One week later, with the business world still trying to digest the implications of the proposed AOL-Time Warner merger, RCI unveiled a new corporate identity to unify its cable, wireless and publishing divisions under the Rogers banner. The previous year Rogers dropped the name Maclean Hunter, which had been around for almost a century, from its publishing division, replacing it with Rogers Media Inc. He now jettisoned the name Cantel, rebranding the company Rogers AT&T Wireless. Just five years earlier, in the wake of the negative option fiasco—in which the cable division tried to push a new tier of programming down the throats of its subscribers—Rogers had been prepared to dump his name for Cantel's, prompting Phil Lind to mount an effective rearguard action to prevent the founder from making an impetuous decision that he might later regret. RCI, which spent $41 million to remake its public image, introduced a new "Mobius strip" or "convergence loop" logo and a jingle, similar to Intel Corp.'s, to make its radio and TV ads distinctive. Facing increased wireless competition, Rogers and his top lieutenants then blitzed the nation in a three-day, nine-city promotional tour to trumpet the new Rogers AT&T Wireless brand and the company's alliance with AT&T and BT. Not surprisingly, Rogers kicked off the campaign in Montreal, where tiny Microcell Telecommunications Inc. was starting to set competitive fires.

Once the marketing tour ended, Rogers turned his attention back to Vidéotron, presenting an offer to André and Claude Chagnon. Twelve days later, they had a deal.

On February 7, 2000, RCI offered to buy Vidéotron for $5.6 billion to create Canada's dominant cable TV company and North America's largest, most advanced contiguous cable network. In addition, RCI would become the seventh-largest cable company in North America.

Surprisingly, Rogers used stock rather than his preferred currency—cash (read debt). He had offered to pay cash, but André and Claude Chagnon insisted on receiving stock to ensure their continued involvement in the company's future. The Chagnons would join the RCI board and own 12.8 percent of the company's non-voting B stock, becoming the second-largest shareholder behind Rogers. Although the transaction diluted the Rogers family's stake in the company, Rogers retained control through his voting stock. Claude Chagnon, 45, recently named CEO to succeed his father, planned to share the co-chairman title with Rogers. Their decision to sell surprised the financial district. "This is a deal that still has us shaking our head in amazement," John Grandy, then a Yorkton Securities Inc. analyst, wrote in his research brief. "The Chagnon family, who have built up their business over 35 years, who have sacrificed so much to pursue a vision of competing against Bell Canada in telecommunication services ... have sold their company to Rogers and for non-voting Rogers stock, at that."

It was a bittersweet day for André Chagnon. The son of an electrician, who chose his father's trade for his vocation, bought his first cable system in Laval, a suburb of Montreal in 1963 when Rogers was going after an AM radio license. With the support of pension fund Caisse de depôt et placement du Quebec, Chagnon acquired Cablevision Nationale Ltée, a company five times Vidéotron's size, in 1980 for $14 million. The Caisse became his partner. Just like Rogers, Chagnon was obsessed with competing against Bell Canada. Both men shared an intense desire to compete in telecommunications. "I could not be a consolidator," reflects Chagnon. "We needed the scope and scale to compete with Bell Canada."

Together, they would form an industry powerhouse in cable with $25 billion in assets, $4.4 billion in fiscal 2000 revenue and 3.8 million cable TV subscribers and 280,000 high-speed Internet customers. Shaw, the next biggest player, had 1.8 million subscribers, less than $1 billion in fiscal 2000 revenue and $6.4 billion in assets. (Faced by the prospect of being reduced to a distant second, Shaw bought 10 percent of family-owned Winnipeg-based Moffat Communications Inc., a prelude to acquiring the entire company later that year.)

Still, the combined RCI-Vidéotron entity paled next to BCE. The telecom giant, with $51 billion in assets, was still twice its size. Bell Canada boasted $15.8 billion in 2000 revenue and 21 million customer connections through Internet, wireline, wireless and satellite TV. Further, BCE had an $8 billion war chest from the planned spinoff of most of its 39.2-percent stake in Nortel Networks Corp. and the earlier sale of a 20-percent stake in Bell Canada to SBC Communications.

For Rogers, the merger promised to propel him to the forefront of voice-over-Internet (VoIP) protocol telephony. Vidéotron was farther ahead than any other Canadian cable TV company in its cable telephony experiments and planned to begin offering home phone service to cable TV subscribers in the summer. When asked at the press conference at the Le Picardie Room at the Wyndham Hotel in Montreal if his merger represented a defensive move, Rogers quipped, "I'm not normally known to be self-defensive. I'm usually known as offensive—sometimes in both senses of the word."

One week after RCI and Videotron declared their nuptials, BCE revealed its own megadeal. BCE CEO Jean Monty fulfilled the company's long-held desire to own Teleglobe by sealing a deal with his friend Charles Sirois to buy the 77 percent of the overseas long-distance carrier it didn't already own for $9.65 billion. Ten days later, Monty dropped another bombshell. BCE intended to buy the CTV Inc. television network for $2.3 billion. On March 10, two weeks later, the bubble in technology stocks burst. All of a sudden the New Economy—with its "ROV" (return on vision) metrics—didn't look quite so appealing.

Ted Rogers faced one major hurdle in his takeover of Vidéotron—Quebec politics. He threw his pick into the rock face of Quebec Inc. industrial sovereignty and it broke like the other Anglo-titans before him. Quebec Inc. describes the tight-knit cooperation—some would say, collusion—between the state and the business community originally aimed at turning a backward economy into a powerhouse. The Caisse, which managed $105 billion in pension assets, became the main engine of the Quebec Inc. phenomenon that catapulted many Quebecois entrepreneurs into the Canadian business establishment. Unlike most pension funds, the Caisse has a dual mandate: to achieve financial returns and to use its funds to develop the provincial economy.

The pension fund had a track record of protecting fortress Quebec. In the late eighties, the Caisse backed a local bid for retailer Steinberg Inc. to trump a Toronto consortium that planned to sell the Steinberg grocery stores to grocery magnate Galen Weston's Loblaw Cos. The Caisse's front man won and Steinberg went bankrupt. In the late nineties, the Caisse blocked an American attempt to buy Quebec grocer Provigo Inc. and prevented a hostile takeover of Montreal-based Air Canada by leveraged buyout king Gerald Schwartz's Toronto-based Onex Corp.

The takeover conjured up the old nationalist guards. Former Quebec premier Jacques Parizeau, an avowed separatist, likened Rogers' takeover of Vidéotron to "Toronto buying Montreal." He asserted, "It's not a question of nationalism. It's the character and identity of culture in the marketplace."

Other defended the Caisse. "It is quite logical for the Caisse to look after our economy while being a good steward of the money it is given," wrote Jean-Robert Sansfacon in a *Le Devoir* editorial. "The attempted coup de force by the Caisse de depôt and Quebecor for Groupe Vidéotron will certainly be denounced by the Toronto press with their usual anti Quebec rage."

Ted Rogers and Phil Lind traveled to Quebec City to sell the takeover to Quebec Premier Lucien Bouchard and Finance Minister Bernard Landry, who fervent separatists. Rogers thought he had their tacit approval since neither politician told him outright that they'd block the takeover, but Lind has no doubt the political fix was in.

André Chagnon owned 81 percent of the combined multiple and subordinated voting stock in Vidéotron, while the Caisse controlled just 18.8 percent. Even though the Caisse appeared to be a minority shareholder, the pension fund wielded the real power. When Chagnon pulled off his reverse takeover of Cablevision in 1980, Chagnon had to virtually sell his soul to get the money. The Caisse had extracted extraordinary rights from him, forcing him to seek its consent before embarking on almost every corporate undertaking. In other words, Chagnon needed prior approval from the Caisse before agreeing to sell the company. Even though Rogers was fully aware of the history between Chagnon and the Caisse, he decided to let Chagnon pitch their merger to the mighty Caisse alone, which proved to be a strategic mistake.

"Mr. Chagnon," Michel Nadeau, the No. 2 man at the Caisse, told André Chagnon, "you do not have the right to sell the company without our approval."

Chagnon rebutted, "Michel, you are destroying my life. I built this company and now you are depriving me [of] the right to sell."

"You should have told us that you were willing to sell," Nadeau insisted.

Nadeau then called Pierre-Karl Péladeau Jr., the CEO of Quebecor Inc. "My good friend," Nadeau told Péladeau, "you are living among dinosaurs. You should try to do something."

"And he told me, 'What could I do?'"

The Caisse then orchestrated Quebecor's takeover of Vidéotron. Chagnon appealed to the Quebec premier to no avail. Quebecor entered the fray, bidding $5.7 million in cash and stock. On the eve of the shareholder vote to approve RCI's takeover of Vidéotron, the Caisse sought, and won, an injunction to prevent André Chagnon from voting his stock, which effectively killed the deal.

In September 2000, Quebecor emerged victorious, although heavily debt burdened. "We really tried to end the battle and to try to find a solution with the three players, the Chagnons, Pierre-Karl and Ted, but it was impossible," says Michel Nadeau. "Ted was looking for control. He was not interested in selling or to have Quebecor Press."

Quebecor acquired Vidéotron for $5.4 billion in cash, almost 20 times cash flow, overpaying by almost $1 billion analysts said. The company's financial performance deteriorated under the weight of its debt. Investors hammered the stock. The Internet stock bubble had burst. Suddenly, the much ballyhooed corporate convergence strategies looked suspect and the new old- media deals were being questioned. In the wake of the tech meltdown, the Caisse, overexposed to the communications and technology sector, posted major losses. Michel Nadeau and his boss, Jean-Claude Scraire, were gone. They had invested $2.9 billion of the pension fund's money to help Quebecor outbid RCI. The new chairman wrote down the Caisse's 45-percent stake in Quebecor Media to a mere $435 million.

For Rogers, the failed takeover was a disappointment, yet a blessing in disguise. He wasted no time lamenting defeat over Vidéotron. He shot down media buzz that he would sell the company within three years after failing to buy Vidéotron. "Never," he defiantly declared to the Canadian Club in Toronto. "We lost. They won. Next!"

He was partly consoled by a nice fat consolidation prize—a $241-million breakup fee.

"In hindsight, it's probably good that we didn't buy Vidéotron, especially since we got our breakup fee, which Ted has claimed he's spent five or six times over," RCI treasurer Lorraine Daly recalls. "Every time he wanted to spend money on something, he'd say, 'Oh, that's the money from the breakup fee.' Last count, he was up to $1.2 billion."

André Chagnon used the $1.8 billion in cash proceeds to establish the Lucie and André Chagnon Foundation, Canada's largest charitable foundation.

Two years later, in 2002, Quebecor Media sued Claude Chagnon in Quebec Superior Court for $23.2 million, alleging Chagnon illegally accepted stock options on January 19, 2000, the day he became CEO, while having inside knowledge that the stock was about to soar and failing to inform the board of his talks with RCI. Chagnon denied the allegations and is defending the lawsuit. The trial is scheduled to begin in December 2008. The Québec Securities Commission, which confirmed it was investigating the matter in 2002, declined comment.

Though he enjoys his new philanthropic role, André Chagnon reflects that he misread BCE. Vidéotron had blazed the Internet (IP) telephony trail in Canada, readying itself to challenge Ma Bell on local telephone service. Whe the CRTC permitted BCE to enter the cable TV business, Chagnon fully expected Bell Canada to hit back hard, giving urgency to the merger with Rogers. "We would have covered the same territory as Bell Canada. We could offer Internet or telephony or cable and more all over Eastern Canada. That would have been nice, eh? I still believe that I wasn't wrong about that type of a merger because of the potential competition of Bell.

"But, I was wrong on the timing," he sighs. "I thought Bell Canada would move much faster into the cable industry. Bell didn't move as fast as they could. They went in other directions and lost billions and billions of dollars and they are back at square one, but I thought they would have moved much faster."

Indeed. Bell Canada has yet to deploy a wireline TV service to compete with cable almost 10 years after the CRTC deregulated the industry on January 1, 1998. In that time, Ted Rogers kept RCI from tumbling off the high wire to build a formidable competitor.

On a Tuesday evening in March 2000, Jim Shaw met Ted Rogers and his son, Edward, for a dinner of fine French cuisine at Scaramouche in Toronto. With Edward sipping Coca-Cola, the two cable dons put away three bottles of red wine while they negotiated a blockbuster deal to swap $4-billion worth of cable assets, carving Canada into east and west clusters to better challenge BCE in Ontario, Quebec and Atlantic Canada and BCT-Telus in Western Canada, the latter entity created a year earlier when B.C. Telecom merged with Telus. Shaw was half in the bag by 2 a.m. when they finally left the restaurant, sealing the transaction with handshakes. The transaction was inked by noon.

Rogers was exiting British Columbia, swapping 623,000 customers in Vancouver and B.C.'s Lower Mainland for Shaw's 60,000 subscribers in Southern Ontario and New Brunswick. By clustering subscribers, both companies could lower their operating costs, and achieve greater capital efficiency in terms of revenues per dollar invested in fiber-optic cable and network assets. It would become even more important for rolling out IP telephony services. But, there were other factors at work.

Rogers was, in some ways, conceding defeat in B.C., where the company was still associated even five years later with the negative-option billing fiasco. He was gun-shy of Vancouver. And, with the focus now shifting to bundling cable, Internet and wireless services—the so-called triple play—Rogers was facing an uphill and costly battle in Vancouver to repair goodwill. Shaw, as a fresh face in the market, reckoned he'd have better luck. Plus, he would become the dominant cable company west of Ontario, a feat he ensured by taking out his only significant cable rival, Winnipeg-based Moffat Communications Ltd. for $1.2 billion later that same year. Because he lacked the cellular component, Shaw had already agreed to cross-sell Rogers AT&T Wireless services. Since he was exiting Southern Ontario, Shaw also swapped the company's stake in Cogeco Cable and its parent Cogeco Inc. for Rogers' shares in CANCOM. As part of their accord, the companies also agreed to develop their transmission facilities and their media and Internet assets.

Phil Lind, who has a deep affinity for Vancouver, was stunned when he learned Rogers was swapping Vancouver for Fredericton. He strongly opposed the deal, voicing his concerns to Rogers and the RCI board. "We can't call ourselves a national cable company if we're not national, and my definition of national is Toronto and Vancouver," he says. "I never, in my wildest dreams, would have thought that Rogers would sell Vancouver for Richmond Hill, Scarborough and New Brunswick. I know it was to rationalize the Ontario systems, but I've yet to see the rationale."

No one was happier to see the backside of the nineties than Ted Rogers. The new millennium marked the beginning of a new era for RCI.

With his family still living in New Jersey, Charlie Hoffman, 50, decided he had enough of flying home every other weekend. He wanted to return stateside. With that in mind, Rogers set about hiring his eventual replacement. Nadir Mohamed flew to Toronto to meet Hoffman and in particular Ted Rogers. Mohamed, 44, then president and COO of Telus Mobility, knew Rogers by reputation only. He wanted to make sure he could work compatibly with the legendary founder before accepting the job. In June 2000, on a Sunday morning, Hoffman took Mohamed to Frybrook to meet the legendary entrepreneur, an industry icon, for the first time. No sooner had they stepped inside than Rogers' Labrador retrievers bounded over to greet them. "I'm petrified of dogs, animals. I'm being polite just petting the dog but I'm scared out of my mind. Here I am pretending to be cool and Ted came in and we had an incredibly wonderful conversation for a couple of hours," recalls Mohamed.

Rogers then turned to Hoffman. "Where are you off to next?"

"Well, we're going to spend the day together," Hoffman replied.

"Why don't you write up the contract, and we'll get going," Rogers told Hoffman. He had made up his mind to hire Mohamed, who was rather taken aback. He wasn't ready to sign a contract that day.

"I think Nadir would like some time to talk to me and others," Hoffman replied.

"Well, what are you going to do for the rest of the day?" Rogers repeated.

"We'll probably go back to the office," said Hoffman.

"Great. Can I get a ride with you?" Rogers asked.

"Sure. Absolutely."

"Just give me a few minutes."

Mohamed pretended to play with the dog until Rogers returned, carrying three brown paper lunch bags. "Here's one for you, Charlie, one for you, Nadir, and one for me, because we're going to the office and we'll need something to eat."

Mohamed was stunned. Rogers, an icon of industry, someone whom he had admired from afar for years, was treating him as if he were family.

They walked to Hoffman's BMW 5 Series sedan—courtesy of the company—parked in the semi-circular drive.

"Why don't you go in the front seat?" Mohamed suggested to Rogers, who is almost five inches taller than him.

"No, no. I'll hop in the back. You sit in the front."

Hoffman headed to 333 Bloor St. West in midtown Toronto, the old Confederation Life Building. When Confed imploded earlier in the early 1990s, Rogers swooped in to buy the insurance company's three-building complex at the intersection of three arterial midtown Toronto roads—Bloor, Jarvis and Mount Pleasant—in the liquidation sale. He paid just $1 million for Bloor St. building and $32.5 million for the two new chateau-style towers that Confed spent $130 million to build on Mount Pleasant. Rogers then spent another $30 million on renovations, which included a 2,000-square-foot gymnasium, and built a third tower. His wife Loretta was actively involved in the redesign. The campus is important to Rogers because he can finally house all of the company's employees under one roof—wireless, media and the radio stations—to promote a cross-fertilization of ideas. For the first time, all of his lieutenants were under the same roof, making it easier for him to talk to them. After sprucing up the old Confed building, Rogers honored his stepfather and the late Bob Francis by naming two boardrooms on the executive-suite 10th floor after them.

On the short 10-minute drive to the Rogers Campus, Rogers began to talk excitedly about the donation he and his wife Loretta planned to announce on June 21, 2000, to mark his deceased father's 100th birthday. In a swank black-tie cocktail party at the Royal Ontario Museum the following week, Ted and Loretta Rogers gifted $25 million to the University of Toronto, the largest private endowment in his alma mater's 147-year history. In return, the university permanently renamed the electrical and computer engineering department after his father. The endowment provides annual scholarships to 85 graduate and 40 undergraduate electrical engineering students. The university began awarding scholarships in 2001.

Arriving on the 10th floor, where the executive suites are located, Alan Horn, dressed casually in shorts, appeared to greet them. "I've since discovered that he's always actually there. This isn't a novel thing," says Mohamed.

They sat comfortably on the leather sofas in Rogers' office, munching their brown-bagged white bread and cheese sandwiches. His office features floor-to-ceiling windows, a fireplace, an outdoor patio, and an adjacent bedroom with a washroom and shower—Rogers often works too late to go home. Suddenly, Rogers jumped up, saying "I've got something to show you."

He returned to show Mohamed his business card, which read: "Senior Salesperson."

"He was like a little kid. I thought this was neat. I knew the turnover that Rogers had had and that's why meeting Ted was so important because I actually felt comfortable that I would be treated more than fairly and right. It's one of the things, that I think actually is not known nearly as much as it needs to be, is the whole family value that's part of the brand internally but doesn't get expressed as much externally. You really get a sense of being treated with dignity and grace, and Ted's a gracious person."

Mohamed, born in Dar es Salaam, Tanzania in 1956 and schooled at the prestigious Kelly College boarding school in England, has entrepreneurial blood coursing in his veins. His family roots are in East Africa of the colonial era, when the British brought in laborers and tradesmen from India. His grandmother ran a lumber business at the turn of the 20th century in Tanzania, an incredible feat for an Indian woman of that era. The Indians gradually formed a merchant class in Uganda, Kenya and Tanzania only to be forced to flee in the seventies in the face of government-sanctioned anti-Indian hostility. Mohamed's family left for Vancouver in 1971 after the family's hardware business had been nationalized.

His parents wanted Mohamed to be a doctor; a career path he knew wasn't for him after a bad fetal pig dissection experience in Grade 12 biology. He went through one year of pre-med at the University of British Columbia, thinking he could always become a pharmacist, until a friend persuaded him to study commerce instead. He then joined Price Waterhouse to earn his chartered accountant's designation in 1980 before joining BC Tel (now Telus) that same year. Four years later, he was one of four people launching the phone company's wireless company. When BC Tel refused to provide the funding for a financial system, and the upstart company was unable to bear the cost on its own, Mohamed bought two black ledgers from Wilson's Stationary, a local stationary store, which became the official record for the company now known as Telus Mobility.

When Mohamed joined Rogers AT&T Wireless, he shifted the focus to locking up subscribers on long-term contracts to reduce churn, based on AT&T's experience. He also began to focus on data, not voice, which, when tied to the phenomenal rise of Research In Motion Inc.'s BlackBerry wireless email device, would propel revenue growth. Rogers also created Rogers Telecom, signaling his intention to offer local and long-distance cable telephony service to compete head-to-head with BCE. The stage was set for a new era.

CHAPTER 20

Fido, Heel

"When you're fighting Ted, you don't hold back."

—Craig McCaw

"THEY'RE PYROMANIACS," Ted Rogers declared.

The year was 2004. Rogers, 71, was sharing his opinion of Microcell, an upstart Montreal-based cellular phone company, better known to Canadians as Fido, to his friend Craig McCaw, 54, the wireless visionary, over a convivial dinner at Rogers' Frybrook home. The publicity-shy billionaire and minority investor in fire-bomber Microcell was trying to talk Rogers into rescuing the company from Telus Corp.'s clutches. On May 13, Vancouver-based Telus, the country's No. 2 phone company behind BCE, made a hostile $1.1-billion takeover bid for Microcell, hoping to leash Fido before it inflicted any more damage with its new City Fido plan. Microcell had sparked a series of competitive fires with an American-style flat-rate unlimited local calling plan, which threatened to scorch the Canadian wireless industry's revenue model. (The model closely resembled the country's oligopolistic banking system.)

The company had the temerity to offer Canadians a wireless service that made owning a traditional landline phone redundant. For their part, the big three—Bell, Rogers and Telus—were reluctant to engage in yet another costly price war since lower prices would erode their margins, wallop their share prices and hurt their credit ratings. Not that Fido cared. Fresh from bankruptcy protection, Microcell promised to take City Fido national, striking first in Vancouver, where Telus and Rogers enjoyed a duopoly. In less than three months, 60 percent of Microcell's 72,000 new City Fido customers in Vancouver had switched from their former carriers. Fido had become, as Telus CEO Darren

Entwistle succinctly put it, a "problem child." Entwistle had orchestrated the acquisition of Clearnet Communications, the only other newcomer licensed in 1995, four years earlier. Now he intended to take out Fido, bidding $29 a share in cash, an offer the Microcell board flatly rejected. The pyromaniacs turned to Craig McCaw for help.

McCaw had barely been an investor in Microcell for two weeks when Telus put the company in play. He acquired 7.7 percent for $50 million as part of a rights offering to help the company recapitalize, a move he hoped would protect their six-month old fledgling joint venture called Inukshuk Internet Inc. Inukshuk—which is a stone landmark used in the Canadian arctic by the Inuit—held the licenses to build a pan-Canadian, fixed broadband wireless network. Wireless broadband had become McCaw's passion. The previous year, almost a decade after selling McCaw Cellular to AT&T Corp. for US$11.5 billion, McCaw returned to the wireless industry where he made his fortune to pursue his long-held dream of offering wireless broadband Internet and phone service. Through Eagle River, his investment holding company, McCaw acquired Clearwire Corp., which would become his main vehicle. He intended to build a U.S.-wide broadband wireless network. Once again, he was gambling on an emerging and potentially disruptive technology, just as he did in the eighties when he shed his cable assets for cellular phones.

McCaw's investment in Microcell marked the first time he jumped over the 49th parallel into the Canadian wireless industry. That earned him a call from Rogers, who lectured him for not investing with his friends. Unperturbed, McCaw adroitly shifted the conversation to suggest that perhaps Rogers should buy Fido. Rogers had expressed his disinterest then.

Now, over dinner, Rogers again dismissed outright the idea of buying Microcell. McCaw couldn't believe it. His other dinner colleagues—Clearwire CEO Benjamin Wolff, whom McCaw calls his alter ego, and Nick Kauser, who helped build national networks in Canada and the United States for Rogers and McCaw, respectively—were equally baffled. They collectively thought Microcell was a perfect fit for Rogers Wireless, since both carriers used Global System for Mobile Communications, better known as GSM, which is the world's most popular standard for mobile phones. They never really spoke in depth about Inukshuk because Rogers dismissed it as a competitive, not additive, technology. Rogers' first instinct is to protect his monopoly or duopoly. As the late Ian Sinclair, who built the CP empire that Bill Stinson dismantled, always said, "Anyone who hates a monopoly has never owned one."

The three men weren't sure if Ted Rogers had on his game face or not. They failed to whet his interest in Microcell. "There are times when you just have the most impossible conversation with him. You're sure that he's ignored every word you've said, and then, he does exactly what you told him he ought to do," McCaw chuckles.

Neither McCaw nor Microcell wanted to surrender to Telus. Microcell CEO André Tremblay believed that Telus would kill Fido and lay off most of its nearly 2,600 employees, while McCaw did not want Telus to interfere with Inukshuk. For its part, the board of directors felt Telus had tied too many unreasonable conditions to its hostile offer.

McCaw had the name, reputation and money to counter Telus—just the wrong citizenship given Canada's restrictive foreign-ownership laws. Canada bars foreigners from owning more than a third of the parent company's voting stock and 20 percent of the operating subsidiary. Unable to enter the fray, McCaw's Clearwire team contacted potential suitors on Microcell's behalf, including Québecor Inc. and MTS Allstream Inc. No one showed any interest. Then, BCE CEO Michael Sabia called McCaw, proposing that they unite to make a joint offer for Microcell. Unlike Fido and Rogers, BCE's Bell Mobility—like Telus—uses CDMA, a wireless technology that's dominant in North America only and not compatible with GSM. If it owned Microcell, Bell would add 1.2 million Fido subscribers to its 4.4 million wireless customers, solidifying its position as the country's largest wireless provider. By comparison, Rogers had 4 million subscribers at the end of 2003, while Telus had 3.4 million. More importantly, Bell could then offer its customers worldwide roaming ability. As well, international GSM wireless customers, who then accounted for 72 percent of the 1 billion wireless subscribers worldwide, must roam on RCI or Fido when in Canada, another significant source of additional revenue.

However, Sabia appeared to be more interested in the struggling carrier's $1.6 billion in tax-loss carryforwards than in Microcell itself because of BCE's huge tax bill. Since BCE is Canada's largest corporate taxpayer, Sabia hoped to use Microcell's tax losses to shelter profits, but the suggested terms were unattractive for Clearwire as only BCE could take advantage of them, Kauser recalls. Unable to entice Clearwire, Sabia abandoned the pursuit altogether even though BCE had the financial power to outbid Telus and RCI, if it so desired. It did not need McCaw's help. Indeed, by failing to act aggressively, Sabia made a major strategic error that would come back to haunt BCE three years later.

With the prospect of finding a white knight fading, McCaw proposed to the Microcell board that he fund the company, enabling the board to present to shareholders a palatable option to Telus. The largest institutional investors were ready to accept this solution, promising not to tender their stock to Telus. "We offered to keep the company independent and protected from Telus," says McCaw. "We had enough shareholders who said, 'If you stay, we'll stay.'"

Rogers had to dispose of AT&T Wireless as his partner in Rogers Wireless before making a play for Microcell. RCI owned 55 percent of Rogers Wireless, while the U.S. giant, having acquired BT's stake in 2001, now owned 34 percent. The remaining 11 percent was publicly traded. For its part, AT&T was well aware that Rogers wanted to acquire Microcell. In early 2003, when Microcell teetered on the edge of bankruptcy, Rogers hoped to acquire the assets cheaply through the purchase of its debt in conjunction with Microcell's financial restructuring. But, AT&T Wireless, which had the right to veto acquisitions, exercised its power to stymie his takeover plan, a move that he says made him feel handcuffed. "We wanted to buy Microcell, but our partners at AT&T wouldn't let us and they had the vetoes. We had a rather unpleasant time about it," says Rogers.

Preventing a serial entrepreneur from pursuing an acquisition did nothing to improve their already strained relationship. Just the previous year, in 2002, the AT&T Wireless directors on the Rogers Wireless board lamented that although they had good personal relationships with the directors, the board wasn't independent enough to challenge Rogers, and that Gar Emerson, deputy chairman of the Rogers Wireless board, was one of the few who would. Emerson also chaired the RCI board. Their comments fell on deaf ears. Rogers began to stack the Wireless board with more allies. Wife Loretta and crony Chris Wansbrough, who ran Rogers' private holding company, joined. The next year, he added his sister, Ann Graham, and his youngest daughter, Martha, 31, then studying to become a naturopathic doctor. While he expresses that he feels strongly that his children should understand the business even if they don't work at the company, Rogers also requires security that more than a majority of the votes of the directors can be counted on from family and close friends so that his ultimate exercise of control of the company will not, in the end, be frustrated.

The last straw for AT&T Wireless came in December 2003 when Rogers unilaterally withdrew the "AT&T" brand from its wireless products in Canada. RCI linked the removal of the brand to the disappearance of the "AT&T Canada" name. AT&T Canada, the reincarnation of Unitel, had sought bankruptcy protection in 2002, prompting AT&T Corp. to sever its relationship. When the company emerged from bankruptcy, AT&T Canada changed its name to Allstream Inc. "We didn't get out of the marriage what we thought we'd get," recalls Rogers, who says he expected cost-sharing and joint marketing campaigns to promote the Rogers AT&T brand in the United States. "None of that happened. I thought this huge company could help me a lot, help little ole Ted up here, and they really [didn't]."

As one former director puts it, "With every partnership Rogers has, at some stage, he's used it and milked it as much as he can. He just wants it all himself. And, that had arrived at AT&T. He blamed them for everything that went wrong, just like he did with Unitel.

"Every time they ran an ad in the States for AT&T Wireless, he would say, 'Look at this—they don't even show that they have a relationship with Rogers Wireless in Canada. Can you imagine partners like that? How can I live with people like this?' Then, it builds up and finally he gets himself in such a frame of mind that the only exit from the tunnel is getting rid of a partner, which he always does."

When Rogers dropped the AT&T brand, the strategic and commercial reasons for AT&T Wireless to remain as a minority and non-controlling investor in the company also disappeared. On April 28, 2004, AT&T, which was in the process of being taken over by Cingular Wireless LLC, notified RCI of its intention to sell its 34-percent stake in Rogers Wireless. In accordance with their 1999 shareholders' agreement, they entered into a 21-day period of good-faith exclusive negotiations to see if a price could be settled for RCI to buy the Rogers Wireless shares from AT&T. On May 20, RCI said its final and best offer of $1.51 billion, or $31 a share—a 13-percent discount to the wireless company's previous day closing price of $35.75—had been rejected. AT&T then had 60 days to sell the minority block to third parties at a higher price than what RCI offered. However, there were two restrictions under the shareholders' agreement on AT&T's rights to sell during the 60-day period that significantly limited the liquidity and marketability of AT&T's block of Rogers Wireless. First, AT&T's multiple-voting shares had to be converted into restricted shares; and, second, AT&T couldn't sell more than a 5-percent stake to a single investor. Sixty days later, on July 19, RCI announced that AT&T had failed to dispose of its shares. "To bid for Microcell, I had to get AT&T Wireless out. I had to get them out, but I couldn't show it. So, I was publicly, and even within our board, disdainful of buying their block," says Rogers. "I had to do it because word always gets back. I didn't want to give AT&T Wireless a huge lever to harm me, to extort a lot more money."

On a separate track, Nadir Mohamed and his team continued its due diligence on the Microcell file, code-named Hippo. They had, in fact, spent the past year working on a blueprint for integrating the company if they managed to acquire it, particularly since the acquisition of Microcell's network would reduce the wireless company's capital expenditure program and infrastructure requirements. Initially, Rogers perceived Microcell as just a technology, or network play, says one former director. "Ted had great difficulty in appreciating the fact that his subscribers are the real value point in his company," the director says. Indeed, Rogers, without his board's approval, approached rival BCE, hoping to convince Michael Sabia to make a joint offer for Microcell, their common enemy. He proposed to split off and acquire the network, while BCE would take the subscribers and Microcell's tax losses. "He tried to convince Sabia to come in and Sabia wouldn't," says a former Rogers Wireless director.

If Sabia had accepted Rogers' extemporaneous offer, Microcell would have yielded little benefit to Rogers Wireless. However, Sabia not only declined his offer, but failed to recognize the strategic and commercial benefits of BCE pursuing Microcell on its own—a critical decision that ultimately benefited RCI shareholders. Instead, BCE's Bell Mobility bet on Virgin Mobile to make inroads on the youth-oriented Fido brand. In March, two months before Telus put Microcell in play, Bell Mobility formed a joint venture with Richard Branson's Virgin Group to sell prepaid, non-contract cellphone service to the youth market under the Virgin Mobile brand.

For his part, Rogers says the "gang of four"—Peter Godsoe, John A. Tory, Chris Wansbrough and his daughter Melinda—rejected his initial proposal to buy Microcell for its network only. "We had hours of debate," says Rogers. "I was quite conservative, and the gang of four was pushing me to offer more.

"What changed my mind was that the government took off the spectrum cap," he says.

On August 30, 2004, Industry Canada decided to remove the cap on how much radio spectrum wireless phone companies can hold. The government, which introduced the cap in 1995 to spur the industry's growth, decided to remove the restriction because 94 percent of Canadians now had access to cellphone service. "If I could get Microcell and keep all the spectrum I'd go from being poor in spectrum to being rich in spectrum," says Rogers.

Now Rogers moved into high gear. He left his CFO Alan Horn, who happened to be traveling, a voice mail, telling him that the spectrum cap had been lifted. Horn was in Israel to attend a board meeting on behalf of the Albert Gnat, who had died earlier that year of pancreatic cancer. (Rogers had put Gnat and his family up at the company townhouses near the Rogers Campus to enable them to stay in the city while he was receiving his cancer treatment.) From there, he went on to his native Scotland to spend a short holiday with friends. In his absence, David P. Miller, RCI's general counsel and another longtime lieutenant, who joined the company in 1987, did the heavy lifting with AT&T and the investment bankers. AT&T had retained Goldman Sachs & Co., while Citigroup represented Rogers in the negotiations. The two sides had finally arrived at a range between $36 and $36.50 a share for the Rogers Wireless share block. On September 3, 2004, the Friday of the Labour Day weekend, Horn, in Scotland, had a conference call with Rogers, in Nassau, and Miller, in Toronto, to discuss the latest developments on AT&T. While it appeared the two sides were closer to reaching an agreement, they were still deadlocked.

"I've now got them to agree to this," Miller told them.

"Well this is getting late in the day. We're not going to put out a press release on a Friday before the long weekend," Horn recalls in this abbreviated version of their conversation.

"Of course, we will. We have to get this thing going," Rogers said.

"Well, do we not want to buy this? Why are we helping them to sell it?" replied Horn.

"No, we have to get something going here," Rogers insisted. "David, send the thing out."

"It's the Friday afternoon before a long weekend," sighs Horn, "if you want to bury something or create confusion, do it then. So, the press release went out and of course, I get on the plane and I'm flying back on the Monday—and in the papers from the weekend, people are speculating on what the hell this is all about."

Horn was right. The press release had everyone scratching their heads. RCI and Rogers Wireless hinted that they might pursue Microcell without tipping their hand. They announced that they were considering various corporate initiatives that they might pursue, including the possibility of acquiring, alone or with others, the shares or assets of Microcell. On the first day of trading after the Labour Day holiday, Rogers Wireless class B stock dropped more than 4 percent to close at $36.05. Glen Campbell, an analyst for Merrill Lynch Canada Inc., speculated that there was a "low probability" that Rogers would make a bid for Microcell. Mark Quigley at Yankee Group Canada questioned the value of Microcell's customers, who generally spend less money each month and tend to switch service providers.

RCI also announced that it intended to help AT&T Wireless unload its minority stake in subsidiary Rogers Wireless by the end of September, while retaining the right, but not the obligation, to buy the stock itself if the sale price—net of commissions and expense—was $36 a share or less. RCI, which refused to commit at that level, waived a right of first negotiation, meaning AT&T Wireless could sell the shares without giving RCI another chance to buy, unless the net sale price was $36 or lower.

"Ted always had the next two or three chess moves figured out, and these annoying little things like boards and public shareholders had to be consulted. I say that tongue in cheek. Entrepreneurs tend to grow to accept them, but not always happily," says former AT&T Wireless CEO John Zeglis. "Ted was as tough as nails. No lie. The beauty of it is that, at the tense moment, the breaking moment, one or the other of us, or usually both of us, would laugh. That's the great part of Ted. 'John, you're bleeding me dry, John.' 'Ted, you're killing me. I don't want to get fired over this.' And, then, we'd both laugh. He's a tough negotiator but he never lost his sense of humor. They were tough, tough negotiations, but it was always on principle and it never got into personalities.

"We never once thought that he preferred color and personality to good, hard business decision making. No one should ever be misled about Ted. He is not some sort of an eccentric baseball owner. He is one tough, smart entrepreneurial businessman."

The entire deal stalled over 50 cents.

On the afternoon of September 10th, the RCI board met by conference call—the consensus was to approve a deal with AT&T and for RCI to buy its shares of Rogers Wireless.

Rogers, frustrated with the lack of progress, wanted to walk away from the talks. "We'll look silly if we lost it for fifty cents," Horn told him.

"Why don't you offer him $36.13?" Rogers replied.

When Horn grimaced, Rogers told him, "Just see what you can do."

On Friday, September 10, Horn met with Robert Stokes, his counterpart at AT&T Wireless, in the Library Bar at Toronto's Fairmont Royal York hotel. "It was a lightning rod with Ted," Horn explained to Stokes. "Give me something that I can go back to him with."

"Look, I can take $36.37," Stokes said.

Per-share, the offer was 17 percent higher than the $31 RCI had first offered in May. Horn called Rogers to run the number past him.

"Okay. Less one percent commission, that would net AT&T $36. Okay," Rogers replied.

They finally had a deal. That same day, on September 10, Nadir Mohamed contacted Microcell CEO André Tremblay to request a meeting for Monday. Rogers meanwhile flew to Nassau with Loretta to survey the property damage from Hurricane Frances. Two days later, on Sunday, he spoke by phone to Zeglis, hoping for an indication that the AT&T Wireless board, which intended to meet on Monday, would approve their deal. After their conversation, Rogers felt confident that it was a done deal. "I then raced into action," he says.

He returned to Toronto that afternoon and met with his board that night. By 10 a.m. Monday, September 13, 2004, Rogers and Mohamed were in Ottawa for back-to-back meetings with the Competition Bureau, Industry Canada and the CRTC to discuss a possible merger with Microcell. While on their flight to Ottawa, they learned that the AT&T Wireless board had accepted RCI's $1.77-billion all-cash offer for the 34-percent stake in Rogers Wireless. As well, AT&T agreed that its consent under the shareholders' agreement was no longer required by RCI or Rogers Wireless to acquire Microcell. Rogers was now free and clear to pursue Microcell.

By 7 p.m., they were in Montreal, dining in a private room at posh Italian restaurant Le Latini with Microcell CEO André Tremblay and André Bureau, its chairman. Rogers and Bureau, a former CRTC chairman in the eighties, are good friends. Over a couple of bottles of red wine, the two sides decided they could work together.

On Friday afternoon, September 17, Rogers and Mohamed returned to Montreal to present an offer to Tremblay and Bureau. Rogers offered to buy Microcell for $35 a share. Unlike Telus, RCI did not attach any onerous conditions to its offer. Rogers and Mohamed returned to Toronto when it appeared that the Microcell board needed time to vette their proposal. The Microcell board felt that Rogers' request of a $1.50 a share termination, or breakup fee—the amount that's commonly paid to a prospective buyer if the contemplated transaction isn't consummated –was "a little high," Tremblay says. The following day, on Saturday, Tremblay flew to Toronto meet with Rogers at Frybrook to negotiate a lower breakup fee. When he entered the house, Rogers' dogs jumped all over the Fido CEO. "Everybody went crazy trying to follow these dogs," he laughs. After much debate, Tremblay convinced Rogers to agree to accept a lower breakup fee. He also sought assurance from Rogers that RCI would keep Fido intact, which Rogers promised. "He's not there for the fast buck," says Tremblay.

In just five days, Rogers pulled off what Telus couldn't. He leashed Fido. The next day, on Sunday, September 19, 2004, Rogers Wireless agreed to buy Microcell for $1.4 billion in cash, trumping Telus' hostile $1.1 billion offer. The company agreed to pay $35 a share, 20 percent more than Telus' $29 a share offer. Rogers Wireless intended to finance the acquisition with cash, a $700-million bank credit facility, and a bridge loan of up to $900 million from RCI.

Microcell hoisted Rogers above Bell Mobility to become Canada's largest wireless company, with 5.5-million subscribers. RCI solidly became a wireless—not a cable—company, and for the first time RCI began to generate free cash flow. Fifty-five percent of its EBITDA now came from wireless. (That's jumped to almost 70 percent for fiscal 2006.) "The acquisition of Microcell helped to double underline that wireless would be the biggest piece of the pie for Rogers," says Chris Diceman, a senior vice president at DBRS Ltd. "The company's bondholders and shareholders—all the stakeholders—have benefited from the company's gearing towards wireless."

In the span of one week, Rogers eliminated his partner of eight years, AT&T Wireless, and acquired rival GSM carrier, Microcell. The two multi-billion-dollar deals—using cash, not stock—were strategically important investment decisions to expand in wireless, given the industry's expected growth from deeper subscriber market penetration and new data and video services. Even though he fortified the wireless company, Rogers appeared to be gambling everything yet again. RCI's long-term debt jumped 63 percent to $8.8 billion post-acquisitions for a debt to EBITDA of nearly 5.2. To finance the transactions, RCI returned to the U.S. junk-bond market to raise just over US$2.7 billion—the largest junk bond sale ever completed by a Canadian company and the third-largest junk bond deal on record. "It's a pretty daring step with quite a bit of debt," said Stephen Jarislowsky, often called Canada's Warren Buffett and the country's most outspoken institutional investor, at the time. "Ted has always been daring and, so far, has succeeded, but so was Napoleon for a long time."

The RCI board—well aware of Rogers' penchant for debt—pushed management to make RCI surefooted first. The board—led by John A. Tory, Gar Emerson and Peter Godsoe—insisted RCI raise equity to lessen the leverage in anticipation of acquisitions. In June 2004, RCI raised $250 million in equity. The company had already raised $250 million on a bought-deal basis from the sale of Class B non-voting shares the previous June—over the objections of Alan Horn, who advised against diluting the family's equity and argued that the share price was too low, an RCI director recalls.

In the past, when RCI made acquisitions, investments and capital expenditure commitments, the company relied on bank debt and later sought long-term financing without sufficient equity support. This time, the RCI put the long-term debt financing in place and raised equity to support its capital structure—moves that investors greeted favorably. From August 31 to December 31, RCI Class B shares soared 34 percent.

By contrast, BCE shares climbed a mere 5.7 percent. The company squandered the opportunity of preventing RCI from acquiring a major wireless competitor and blocking RCI's expansion in a rapidly growing industry. In addition to its tax losses, Microcell would have provided vitally needed growth and expansion for BCE outside of its declining wireline business. Without GSM technology, Bell Mobility can not easily provide wireless roaming to its customers abroad, putting it at a significant marketing disadvantage, particularly with the growth of Internet data and the popularity of Blackberrys.

No one was more surprised than Rogers when the financial district and business press *praised* him for his high level of debt. "Can you believe it?" he said. "I'm really proud of the way it worked. A lot of people would say, 'Oh, a family-held company, two classes of shares, Rogers is a very dominant person.' That's one of the worst [forms of] corporate governance, but that's not the way it works. The reason we've been successful is because we can raise money on a very short notice, not because of me but because of that reputation."

The last piece of the wireless strategy fell into place when Rogers privatized the company in November. Instead of using debt, this time RCI used its stock as currency. Based on RCI's share price on the date of the announcement to take Rogers Wireless private, the exchange was worth $50 a share—substantially higher than the $36.37 that AT&TWireless received and almost two times more than Rogers offered to public shareholders in 2001. (In 2001, Rogers proposed a share swap that valued the wireless company at $27.50—a lowball offer minority shareholders rejected.) RCI issued roughly 28 million Class B shares worth $882.6 million in exchange for the Rogers Wireless minority.

On Sunday, October 17, 2004, Ted Rogers was aboard Time Warner Inc's Gulfstream jet with his U.S. brethren for a whirlwind five-day trip to Tokyo and Seoul to meet with the world's leading consumer-electronics makers. On the eight-hour leg from New York's LaGuardia Airport to Anchorage, Alaska, where the plane was scheduled to refuel, Rogers animatedly, and alternatively, probed and chatted with his counterparts from America's cable titans: Comcast Corp., Time Warner Inc., Cablevision Corp., Adelphia Communications Corp. and Charter Communications Inc.

Unlike his cabin mates, from their conversations he scrawled copious notes on legal pads, hurriedly jotting down any ideas that leapt into his mind while they were still fresh. Unexpectedly stuck in Anchorage for an hour layover, Rogers disembarked and disappeared. He left to find a landline phone, and for the next 30 minutes, dictated voice mails to his slumbering executives back home in Toronto—imparting what he considered to be the good ideas he'd gleaned so far on his journey and instructing them to pursue every possible angle for discussion upon his return.

RCI, with 2.3-million cable-television subscribers, pales next to Comcast, the biggest U.S. cable company with 10 times the subscribers—the equivalent of Canada's adult population (minus seniors) and twice the size of its nearest rival, Time Warner. Though RCI might be the smallest cable TV company on this road trip, the wily founder had more than earned his spot among America's all-star team of cable: Roberts, Microsoft co-founder and Charter's chairman Paul G. Allen; Time Warner Cable's CEO Glen Britt; RCI director William T. Schleyer, then Adelphia's CEO; and Cablevision's COO Tom Rutledge. Two years earlier, Rogers became the first Canadian and first international cable TV mogul to be inducted into the U.S. Cable Television Hall of Fame in Denver, joining luminaries such as Ted Turner and John Malone. More than 800 cable executives turned out for the black-tie gala in Denver, honoring Rogers and six other industry pioneers. Phil Lind proudly inducted Rogers into the hall, recounting Rogers' deal-making prowess with San Antonio Spurs' owner Angelo Drossos. Earlier, Rogers had donated US$1.5 million to the U.S. Cable Center to build an outdoor amphitheater, which bears his name.

The trip's only old-timer, Rogers was the only original cable guy onboard— one of the few remaining cable TV pioneers left in North America who hasn't sold out, been forced out or been perp-walked out. At 71, Rogers, with an implanted defibrillator for his ailing ticker, displayed all the esprit and vigor of his youth. For the next seven hours to Tokyo, while the others—almost a generation younger—napped or relaxed, Rogers was plowing his way through his many work-related files. A notorious workaholic, he still runs on two speeds: fast and faster. He was by far the hardest-working delegate. "He's like a sponge. He just soaks up all the information," recalls Brian Roberts, 46, Comcast's CEO and son of its co-founder. "Never once did I see Ted nod off or take a little nap. He's just 'Let's talk technology with this engineer,' and 'Let's talk data over here,' and 'Here is my theory with wireless,' and 'Here is a great chance to talk software and computers with Paul Allen.'"

Roberts recalls one meeting at Comcast's headquarters in Philadelphia with his lieutenants and Ted Rogers when Rogers suddenly began to tell them about the importance of 256 QAM. "Our guys would lean over and say, 'What is he talking about?'" laughs Roberts.

In the mid-nineties, RCI was the first cable TV company to use 256 QAM (quadrature amplitude modulation) to pack more cable TV channels into its existing bandwidth. Since then, 256 QAM has become the industry's standard for high-definition TV signal transmission.

"His knowledge of technology is actually quite extraordinary," says Roberts. "He is a true entrepreneur; a lot of things end up coming from Ted's head. He's not that dissimilar from Ted Turner. He has great vision, willing to bet it all and take some risk; occasionally have some bumps in the night that are pretty scary. But, in the end, they are the best builders. They are sticking true to let's compete, let's win, let's go fast and let's mind every dollar like it is our own. He has helped this industry reach levels that none of us have ever imagined."

"He really understands the technology of the business better than I do," adds Bill Bresnan, a respected U.S. cable TV pioneer and an engineer by training. "He's done it all. [RCI has] really been a model company."

Arriving at Narita Airport on Monday, October 18, 2004 in the late afternoon, the cable delegation boarded a bus to the luxurious Imperial Hotel, where everyone, except Rogers, had a light supper and went to bed. He showered and then met his daughter Melinda, already in Tokyo on a separate business trip, for dinner with two prominent Silicon Valley venture capitalists and a top executive from NTT DoCoMo Inc., Japan's biggest wireless voice and data company.

Rogers thrives on such jaunts. He is a strong believer in getting out of the office to find out what other companies are doing.

"I've always been curious," he says. "You pick things up, even though it's going to cost you five hours and you should be doing other things. A lot of successful people are very focused. I can get focused, but I think by nature I'm not focused. I don't call myself a lawyer, but a lawyer is used to handling ten or twenty files all in the same day. You have to work hard because you're so curious."

In Seoul, South Korea, Ted Rogers watched in amazement as Boston Red Sox centerfielder Johnny Damon drilled a grand slam against New York Yankees pitcher Javier Vazquez into the right-field seats at Yankee Stadium during the final game of the American League Championship Series. The Red Sox went on to crush the hated Yankees 10 3 to win the AL pennant and a berth to the World Series, which after 90 years, they finally won. Rogers, who owns the Toronto Blue Jays, didn't particularly care that he was watching baseball history. He was far more engrossed by the fact that he was seeing the game live halfway around the world on a cellular phone. "That's the future," Rogers later enthused. "We'll have that in [Canada], probably, two years. Isn't that something, eh?"

"It's the third screen," explains Phil Lind after an April 2005 press conference to unveil Rogers' new cellular TV service. "The first screen being TV. The second screen being the computer. The third screen being the handset. So, now we're onto the third screen." Surprisingly, Ted Rogers was not there. He participated by conference call from Lyford Cay, where he had been grounded after one of his pilots fell ill. The event marked a small yet historic moment for the two men. Life had come full circle. They witnessed the melding of television and cellular telephony.

The event had added significance for Lind. His role at RCI had diminished after his stroke. Now, Lind was making his presence felt once again, intervening to negotiate content for the new cellular TV phone. Suddenly, the contacts he made in the United States in the eighties were important again. With a phone call, Lind can reach the executive suites at the big U.S. entertainment companies, bypassing the lower ranks that RCI might otherwise have to go through. "He's playing a huge role now," says Rogers.

Indeed, Lind returned to RCI with renewed vigor and undeterred by his physical challenges. He drives his own car, a high-end Lexus, and still fly fishes. He's back to strategizing and bargaining with mandarins and their political masters. He orchestrated the lobbying campaign, which included a 100,000-signature petition, two demonstrations on Parliament Hill in Ottawa and official state visits from the prime minister of Italy, to persuade the CRTC and the federal government to bring RAI International, Italy's 24-hour public TV service, into Canada. The lobbying effort just for RAI took four years. (The CRTC permitted RAI to enter Canada in 2005.) "It was hell," Lind says. "But, we prevailed. There's things like that going on all the time." He did it all over again to bring a Russian channel and then nine Chinese state-owned channels into Canada.

In May 2005, two years after John II. Tory left Rogers to run a close but failed campaign for mayor of Toronto, Ted Rogers promoted Nadir Mohamed over his son Edward to president and chief operating officer of a newly created communications division to oversee both the wireless and cable units. Edward Rogers continued as president of Rogers Cable, while Robert Bruce, the wireless company's marketing head, became president of Rogers Wireless.

For the first time, Ted Rogers had a COO. It was a defining moment. Although he had mulled the idea of having a second-in-command for more than a decade, Rogers could never bring himself to promote one of his lieutenants. Now he finally acknowledged that he needed someone to help steer the company in a new competitive environment.

"The changes we are making are evolutionary," Rogers told the RCI board, "and recognizes the reality of RCI today—an organization, which is already well on the way on its path from a set of disparate customer, technology and distribution strategies to an organization with a distinctive brand, linked offerings across all of its products, a product roadmap that will lead to further inter-operation of our offerings across our wired and wireless properties and an ability to serve and know our customers in a consistent way at every point."

He was careful to point out to the board that he was not naming his successor. "It is an important step in providing stability ... should I be hit by a bus. If I am not hit by a bus or disabled then I would plan to step down as CEO on June 30th, 2008. At that point, God willing, I would steal a leaf from Bill Gates and seek to be Vice-Chairman and Chief Futurist."

As is his wont, Rogers made an occasion of Mohamed's appointment. In a highly unusual move, Rogers invited Mohamed's wife Shabin to attend the board meeting. Most corporate heads do not invite spouses to board meetings to celebrate promotions. Mohamed, unaware of the invitation, was surprised to find her in the Rockies Boardroom on the 17th floor of the Rogers Wireless tower the next day. "It was an incredibly generous gesture," says Mohamed.

"We felt tremendous amount of support not just from the corporate perspective but from the whole family. It made it a lot easier to know that the family was behind the appointment."

Unlike many of Rogers' previous lieutenants, Mohamed has an even disposition that makes it possible for them to work closely together. "He's a wonderful person," says Rogers.

Rogers and Mohamed spent several months negotiating his contract. Mohamed, well aware of the founder's love of debt, won an unusual concession in his contract, where his pension is safeguarded by a letter of credit from RCI's bankers, a person familiar with the situation says. In other words, if the company gets into financial difficulty, he will still get his pension.

The RCI board had one other major item on its agenda: Call-Net Enterprises Inc. Rogers intended to complete the acquisition of Call-Net, better known as Sprint Canada, for $330 million in stock on July 1—the 20th anniversary of his debut in wireless.

Rogers had debated at length whether to build or buy a traditional landline business. He discussed the merits of cable telephony technology and its associated costs with his son, Edward, and the cable team. Since the father and son disagreed, the father, in his typical fashion, sought outside advice, contacting Dr. Richard Green at CableLabs. "Ted wanted to see where other people were, which is prudent, because you don't want to make expensive capital mistakes," recalls Green. "He asked some tough questions. He asked me questions that I couldn't answer." He put Rogers in touch with the chief technology officers at Cox and Cablevision, the two American leaders in cable telephony. Cox, an early leader, blazed the trail for cable telephony through switch-circuit telephony before adopting Internet protocol cable telephony. Once he dissected their business plans, Rogers overruled his son to make the final decision on the technology and told Edward that he wanted to launch the service on July 1 to mark the milestone of Cantel's 20th birthday.

The rollout wasn't going fast enough for Rogers. Call-Net, a reseller of telephone service, would give him an instantaneous presence in a crucial market. The acquisition would catapult him from having no presence in the telephone market to having almost half a million customers—two-thirds residential and one-third business. He was, in essence, hedging his bets. Rogers reckoned it would take him four years to attract that many customers if he relied solely on his fledgling cable telephony service. In the battle of the bundle, he didn't have four years to wait. Unlike his cable brethren— notably, Vidéotron and EastLink—Rogers had not rolled out a cable telephony service. For once, he had taken the cautious approach, allowing others to take the lead and work out the technological kinks.

With traditional telephone service, RCI became the first cable company in North America to offer four services: the vaunted quadruple play of cable TV, wireless, high-speed Internet and wired telephone service. That put him up there with archrival BCE, which also had four services: satellite TV, wireless, Internet and its century-old landline business.

Rogers then instructed his regulatory team try to persuade Ottawa to create the right conditions for his success in cable telephony. RCI applied to the CRTC to prevent Bell Canada from bundling local phone service with other services such as wireless telephony, satellite TV and high-speed Internet, arguing that Bell's monopoly in local phone service subsidized predatory pricing on its other products. The CRTC denied RCI's application.

On July 1, less than two months after announcing the acquisition, RCI completed the Call-Net acquisition. For the second time in less than a year, Rogers acquired two companies founded by monopoly buster Mike Kedar.

Rogers, providing the common touch like his hero John Diefenbaker, shook hands with each Call-Net employee—all 1,800 of them—to welcome them into the RCI family as they filed out of Toronto's Prince Hotel, where everyone had gathered to be briefed about the takeover. Rogers, Nadir Mohamed, Call-Net's CEO Bill Linton, and David Masotti, who had just joined Call-Net as its chief marketing officer in March, formed the short receiving line, shaking everyone's hand.

Through Call-Net, Rogers also leapt back into the business telecom market, a move that he hoped might eventually broaden as well as balance his customer base. In 1999, when he had sold his stake in Metronet to AT&T Canada, he had agreed not to provide telecom services to businesses for five years. After the non-compete expired in 2004, Rogers formed a unit called Rogers Business Solutions. Call-Net now gave it added heft. Rogers could now sell Internet data, long-distance and wireless services to business customers Canada-wide, intensifying the three-way race between Bell, Telus and Rogers. "It's the battle of the titans," said Brian Sharwood, a Seaboard Group consultant.

Rogers didn't realize until after he acquired Microcell that he inherited potential black gold in Inukshuk. That's when he decided he just had to own it all.

Inukshuk had a short, bumpy history. In 2000, Industry Canada awarded to Inukshuk—then owned by Microcell and wireless TV provider Look Communications Inc.—fixed broadband wireless spectrum in the 2500 MHz band to build a national high-speed wireless Internet network that reached beyond urban Canada into underserved rural areas. When Look ran into financial difficulties in late 2000, the company purportedly sold its half of Inukshuk to Microcell. Both Look and Microcell subsequently restructured under bankruptcy protection. However, because of their financial difficulties, Inukshuk was in danger of having its licenses revoked.

Around this time, Nick Kauser, McCaw's CTO, and John McLennan, the CEO of Allstream Inc., formerly AT&T Canada, the old Unitel, were sailing together in the Caribbean. The two men became close friends from their days together at Cantel. Kauser began to tell McLennan about McCaw's intention to revive Project Angel, which he explained had been their ambitious plan in the early nineties to deliver high-speed Internet and voice services via the airwaves to do an end run around the local phone companies.

"Project Angel was an unfinished dream of ours," says Kauser, 67, who retired in August 2007.

McCaw, who credits his dyslexia for forcing him to be a "conceptual" thinker, and his team envisioned a truly wireless world. They kept the project top secret, fearing the local phone companies might retaliate. Some engineers didn't even know what they had signed on for when they were hired. Then, in 1994, after much deliberation, McCaw, 45, sold McCaw Cellular to AT&T. Nick Kauser stayed behind, becoming AT&T Wireless' CTO. He continued to oversee Project Angel until the parent company's new chief, Michael Armstrong, decided to bet big on cable rather than wireless, a decision that ultimately depleted Project Angel's funding. Kauser left, rejoining McCaw. When the cable strategy failed and the money was gone, AT&T refocused on Project Angel before scrapping it altogether in 2001. AT&T didn't want to commit any more resources to it.

But for the McCaw team, the dream lived on.

In late 2002, they decided fixed wireless broadband—a pre-cursor to WiMax—appeared ready for prime time. McCaw acquired Clearwire Corp., which provides Internet service via airwaves once reserved for instructional television. He began to buy broadband wireless spectrum in the United States and in Europe. His team also zeroed in on Minneapolis-based NextNet Wireless Inc., a pre-WiMax equipment maker.

WiMax acts much like WiFi, the wireless Internet technology that's available for free in cafés and hotel rooms, but has a broader reach, covering areas usually associated with mobile-phone networks. The technology is seen as a cheap and quick alternative to wired service in areas where broadband infrastructure is difficult to build or doesn't exist at all. WiMax has the potential to shatter the cable and telephone duopoly in high-speed Internet and threaten cellular and wireline incumbents with VOIP home phone service.

Kauser told McLennan that he was helping McCaw deliver fixed wireless broadband services around the world. McLennan became so enthusiastic that he suggested they work together in Canada. When McLennan returned to Canada, he quickly discovered that Microcell-owned Inukshuk held the spectrum licenses.

In late 2003, he cut a deal with Microcell CEO André Tremblay. Allstream agreed to contribute money; Microcell's Inukshuk brought its licensed radio spectrum into the joint venture; and McCaw's NR Communications committed wireless broadband plug-and-play technology from NextNet. Customers lease modems that plug into their desktop or laptop computers. The modem receives radio signals from a microwave oven-size base station on existing cellular towers in their neighborhood.

Inukshuk launched successful trials of its service in Richmond, British Columbia and Cumberland, Ontario.

Rogers found himself once more in a three-way partnership, not his favorite set of circumstances. Allstream, though, had a new corporate parent. In June 2004, Manitoba Telecom Services Inc. completed its acquisition of Allstream for $1.7 billion to become Canada's third-largest telecom company. "My job is to do [with Inukshuk] what we did before with Cantel," Rogers says. "There's going to be a real war before we're through."

The newly created MTS Allstream bowed out early. It had no desire to invest in Inukshuk and sold its one-third stake equally to RCI and McCaw. McCaw couldn't have been happier to have his friend as a partner. Rogers spoke warmly in the press of McCaw and Nick Kauser, even complimenting Kauser's wife for her excellent cooking. The warm, fuzzy feelings didn't last long.

Instead of working together, Rogers called McCaw's investment in Inukshuk illegal because of Canada's tight foreign ownership laws. He pressed his point, even though Industry Canada was content to give the new owners time to sort out the ownership situation. His aggressiveness rankled the McCaw team. For his part, Rogers blames their lawyers for escalating tensions between them.

Then, in early March 2005, McCaw brought Rogers' enemy BCE into Inukshuk. He initially sold a small stake, eventually selling his entire 50 percent to BCE. The sale was part of a much bigger deal, in which BCE agreed to inject US$100 million of needed capital into Clearwire. In return, BCE would become the exclusive provider of Internet-based phone services and other Internet protocol applications over Clearwire's wireless network. BCE CEO Michael Sabia would also join the Clearwire board of directors.

McCaw felt he had no other option.

"It was our only defense," says McCaw. "[Rogers] was about to drive a truck over us. I mean, friendship aside, business is business. We can fight and be friends at the same time, but when you're fighting Ted, you don't hold back. He thought he had us and we escaped."

BCE's new alliance with his old friend infuriated Ted Rogers. Although he publicly expressed his disappointment, he was so livid that McCaw, Nick Kauser and Clearwire CEO Ben Wolff returned to Toronto to mend fences. They had a cordial dinner at a restaurant, not Rogers' home as they had before. Wolff had safeguarded the interests of McCaw's NR Communications in the original shareholders' agreement with Microcell. "We protected ourselves very carefully in the original agreement, and I mean, that just irritated the daylights out of Ted because he loves to find the holes in the agreements and use them," says McCaw.

On a pleasant August evening in 2005, Ted Rogers finished a yellowfin tuna appetizer at Opus, an upscale Toronto restaurant, when his ultra slim, black Motorola RAZR V3 cellphone rang. He doesn't have a fancy ring tune. Aside from the extra cost, he'd have to have someone download it for him. He glanced at the call display before flipping it open.

"Credit office," he bellowed into the mouthpiece with a grin.

"Ted?"

"Hi. How are you doing? I'm teasing. Thank you for calling, Ken."

Ken Englehart, his legal regulatory affairs maven, was on the line. He and David Miller were at the Ottawa airport waiting for the next flight to Toronto. Englehart inquired after Rogers' health.

"I'm fine. I'm just out for dinner. But, I'm anxious to know what you guys are doing."

Rogers then listened intently. "A terrible meeting, huh."

The two RCI lawyers and their Bell Canada counterparts spent most of the day ensconced in heated talks with Industry Canada mandarins. They hoped to receive approval for their joint partnership in Inukshuk. But, Industry Canada wasn't making it easy for them. The government was threatening to take back a third of Inukshuk's spectrum in order to auction it off. Several companies, including Telus, MTS and Shaw, were lobbying Industry Canada for a chunk of spectrum. Further, the civil servants flaunted letters from both RCI and BCE seeking to have Inukshuk's licenses revoked after Microcell formed its joint venture with Allstream and NR Communications. Their letters now left the lawyers red-faced.

"Ken, obviously, it was a poor meeting and you're worked up. And, I really appreciate everything that you're doing. The Bell people were very supportive?

Right. Well, what can I say? We just have to continue to play the game. I'm grateful for the update. I'm sorry you had this problem, and we'll overcome this."

Englehart then briefed him on their other request: to change the Inukshuk license to "mobile" from "fixed" WiMax. Mobile WiMax does everything fixed WiMax can but permits the user to roam easily between coverage areas. It also has the potential to offer much faster speeds and capacity than mobile phone data networks. (Though still in its testing stage, mobile WiMax is expected ultimately to replace fixed.) Englehart angrily told Rogers that it appeared highly unlikely that they'd be allowed to switch from fixed to mobile WiMax unless they agreed to return spectrum.

"We shouldn't get mad," soothed Rogers. "We should get even, and say the world has changed. The Americans have authorized mobile with no reference to their licenses, and what the hell are you doing in Canada? Are we such a goddamn communist state that we're [not] doing that?"

After listening to what Englehart had to say, Rogers replied, "Yep. But these things will work out, and you and your guys have done a great job, so don't let it bother you. Look, why don't you go out and have a great dinner? I had to put up with this stuff all my life, so don't get yourself in an anger about it. We'll just come back firing on all cylinders."

Finishing his report, Englehart thanked Rogers.

"No problem. Anytime. And please, thank you and David very much. Bye-bye."

Rogers powered off his cellphone. He reflected that he's had to fight, push, cajole and charm the regulators for almost 50 years. His joint venture with Bell hinged on Industry Canada's approval. Both he and Sabia presented their case to Liberal Industry Canada minister David L. Emerson. If they failed to win the government's blessing, the partnership would collapse, resulting in lawsuits. "When we get this goddamned thing solved, people will say, 'Weren't they lucky,'" says Rogers, shaking his head. "'How did they get that? How did Ted get that?' It's not easy. But it's a lot of fun. I don't get stressed out [by] it. I never have in business because to me, it's a game and I love it.

"I used to play chess. It's better than chess. Here you've got, maybe, fifty things on the move that you have to deal with and make fifty decisions in a day."

Rogers, known for his hot temper, explained that he must now step into the role that his stepfather once played. "I have to be serene and calculating. I was normally the hothead and John Graham was the serene one, the wisdom guy, but I'm now seventy-two and John Graham isn't here. So, I've got to be." He paused. "I've got to mature."

In only a few short weeks, Industry Canada approved the RCI and BCE Inukshuk joint venture. The two companies agreed to spend $200 million by 2008 to bring a high-speed wireless network to more than 100 urban and rural communities. Though the former combatants agreed to work together to build the network, they promised the government to compete aggressively on marketing, promotion and price, something that has not happened. On March 31, 2006, they began offering wireless broadband service based on pre-WiMax standards, the same service Clearwire offers in the United States. There, and in Europe, fixed wireless broadband is seen as an attractive alternative to high-speed Internet cable and phone access. In Canada, the two companies have made no effort to market or promote Inukshuk. Indeed, Bell's high-speed Inukshuk offering at around $60 a month is double Clearwire's price point in the United States.

Industry Canada hoped that Inukshuk would cross the digital divide between urban and rural areas, providing high-speed Internet service to people living beyond urban Canada. "I'm very passionate about rolling it out to remote communities, so we're extracting our pound of flesh out of them. We demanded a very clear, aggressive rollout within five years and they have to reach as many as we demand," says Michael Binder, the department's assistant deputy minister. "If they don't comply, they'll give us an excuse to revoke their license. I'm sure they won't give us any such excuse ever."

Though Industry Canada believes the Inukshuk 2.5 MHz band is a mobile band because that's what it's deemed to be internationally, the licenses, which come up for renewal in 2011, remain for fixed WiMax, not mobile. "If Ted runs it as a fixed service, Industry Canada won't take away the license. If he wants to go mobile, he has to give a piece of it back," says Binder.

CHAPTER 21

A Mug's Game

*"Sports teams are a mug's game. Only a fool would get
into them."*

—Ted Rogers

TED ROGERS COULDN'T TELL YOU THE FIELDING STATS for the
Toronto Blue Jays star center fielder Vernon Wells, winner of three coveted
Rawlings Gold Glove awards, the standard for excellence amongst all Major
League Baseball players, all before the age of 28. All he knows is that Wells is
good, damn good—so he's told—and a fan favorite the Jays might have lost if
they didn't offer him top dollar in an escalating free-agency salary market to
extend his soon-to-expire contract.

In 2006, a week before Christmas, after months of media chatter about the
ballplayer's future with the club, Rogers opened his wallet, permitting the Jays
to sign Wells to a seven-year US$126-million contract extension—making him
the highest-compensated athlete ever in Canada in any sport.

In the lobby of Rogers Communications Inc.'s headquarters in mid-town
Toronto, a smiling Wells, poised, articulate and gracious, sat between the 73-
year-old Jays owner and the club's general manager, J. P. Ricciardi, before about 30
reporters, photographers and cameramen, while curious RCI employees gathered
around, or hung over the second-floor garland-decorated railing to check out
the amicable six-foot-one all-star. In his introductory remarks, Jays' president
Paul Godfrey noted the similarities between Rogers and Wells, their leadership,
commitment to winning, and philanthropic works, before mischievously adding
that "now today, we can add the fact that they are both very rich gentlemen"—a
remark eliciting spontaneous laughter from the crowd that deepened when

Rogers, broadly smiling, instantly thrust out his right hand to congratulate the young man seated beside him.

At the press conference, the CBC lobbed the first question to Rogers: "Is my cable bill going up to pay for this, first of all?"

"First of all, your cable bill is a little behind in its payment!" riposted Rogers, drawing laughter from the audience.

"Do you expect Vernon to lead you now to the World Series?"

"I'm the least experienced ... ," began Rogers, appearing momentarily taken aback by the question. Unlike George Steinbrenner, nicknamed "The Boss" by the New York tabloids for his notorious interference with his club, including changing managers 20 times in his first 23 seasons after buying the New York Yankees from broadcaster CBS Inc., Rogers is a hands-off owner. He shows up for the home opener and closer—the former, a photo op for local media; the latter, to visit the clubhouse, thank the players, and give them a "we'll get 'em next season" rallying cry. A busy man, he squeezed in a few more games in the '06 season. He's not a baseball fan. He's not even a sports fan. He is an owner who understands what it means to be part of the club. As owner of the Blue Jays, he couldn't be in a more exclusive club: Major League Baseball. He might not be a baseball fan, but that doesn't preclude him from sharing with the Yankees owner a passion for winning. As evidenced by his team's swelling payroll, Steinbrenner wants to win at any cost; Rogers just wants to win.

In answering, Rogers suggested asking his lieutenants, either Phil Lind, a baseball aficionado who urged him to buy the Jays, or Tony Viner, the CEO of Rogers Media Inc., the subsidiary that owns the club, who is—like his boss—no baseball enthusiast either. "But, of course, our objective is to do everything we can to have a winning team," Rogers explained. "To win the hearts of, and the support of, people in our community—that's the most important. To do that, you have to look like a winning team, and in the end, if you win or not, it's in the hands of God, but we're doing everything we can to give God a good hand."

The third question was directed to Wells. "Is anybody worth $18 million a year, though?"

"That's a good question," answered Wells graciously. "Once I get out on the field, money doesn't matter. I take great pride in this game, and I'll be the first to tell you when I'm doing poorly, and if I'm doing well, you don't have to say a thing about it. I'll take the good with the bad and hopefully, everybody will do the same. I'm a big man and I can take the criticism."

"Let me add to that," Rogers instantly jumped in. "Our country, Canada, is a small country, but we have to be competitive in the future. We have to be competitive in the world market, in all sorts of goods and services, and to do that, we have to be willing to make investments—investments in education, investments in salaries to attract the very best people we can—as we're trying to do here. Whether it's a manufacturing plant, or a services firm, if we're going to avoid going back to [being] hewers of wood and drawers of water, we've got to make these kinds of investments."

Ted Rogers has spent more than half a billion dollars of his publicly traded company's money on the Blue Jays since buying the ball club in 2000. For a fraction of that, he could have owned their broadcast rights forever. He and his RCI directors never envisioned such a massive cash drain or, as one Toronto fund manager described it, a "sinkhole," when they acquired the Jays from Belgian brewer Interbrew SA.

It all started seven years ago. RCI still thought and behaved like a cable company. While his roots are in radio, Rogers' love has always been in cable, where he could truly stand apart from the famous father he never knew. He had a reliable source of cash flow from 2.2 million captive Rogers Cable TV subscribers in monopoly territories in Ottawa, Toronto, Vancouver and densely populated southwestern Ontario. For a while, he thought he had sealed a deal to acquire Quebec's largest cable company. He traded Vancouver to the Shaw family of Calgary to cluster cable TV subscribers in Ontario and expand in New Brunswick.

His core cable business—high-speed Internet and digital/interactive TV (yet to emerge in any meaningful way)—was all the Bay St. analysts talked about. The company had just dropped the beloved Cantel name, part of a major, and as it turned out timely, rebranding makeover to unite all of its services under one name: Rogers. Only a few years earlier, the company reduced its dangerously high debt load from $9 for every dollar of cash flow—from subscriber cable and cellphone bills—to a more respectable $3. Wireless, shaky after five years and four different men at the helm, was still a voice service. Rogers was just getting ready to overlay his analogue wireless network with GSM, the world standard, and GPRS, which would enable the high-speed Internet browsing and email communications we now take for granted—an initiative hailed as "bold" and one that would ultimately set the stage for the company's astounding growth this decade. Only an hour's drive west from Toronto in Waterloo, a tiny, nondescript company called Research In Motion Ltd. had unveiled its world-famous BlackBerry the year before.

America Online Inc., the mightiest force on the Internet, was taking over the august Time Warner Inc. for a jaw-dropping US$165 billion in stock, setting off the equivalent of an atomic bomb in the communications industry. In the wake of the announcement, Rogers cut a deal to buy Le Group Vidéotron Ltée, Quebec's largest cable company, for reasons totally unrelated to much-ballyhooed old and new world media convergence. Close on his heels, rival BCE Inc. announced its own blockbuster deal to buy broadcaster CTV Inc.

In the midst of all this, the Blue Jays were being quietly shopped around again. Interbrew, based in Brussels, inherited the Blue Jays through its $2.7-billion takeover of John Labatt Ltd. in 1995. Initially, Labatt, one of the original co-owners with Montreal financier R. Howard Webster and the Canadian Imperial Bank of Commerce, bought its stake in the club to help market its beer. As the team grew into a contender, the franchise became much more valuable to Labatt as a broadcasting product for its 24/7 pay-TV sports channel, TSN—short for The Sports Network. It wasn't like Interbrew just appeared one day. In February 1993, a financially stressed Brascan Ltd., controlled by Peter and Edward Bronfman, unloaded its controlling stake in Labatt to a consortium of investment dealers who then sold the shares to the public. When Canada's buyout king, Gerald Schwartz, made a hostile takeover bid for Labatt, the brewer sought Interbrew as its white knight. The Belgians wanted the beer, not the sports franchises. The new owner was forced to spin off TSN, its French sister Le Réseau des Sports, and its 80-percent stake in the Discovery Network to satisfy Canada's tight foreign ownership rules. Stripped of the media assets, they were left with—aside from the beer assets—the Jays, a 42-percent stake in the debt-crippled SkyDome, and the Toronto Argonauts Canadian Football League franchise. They were getting into baseball at the worst possible time, in the wake of the 1994 strike that resulted in the cancellation of the World Series for the first time in 90 years.

An absentee owner, Interbrew left stewardship of the Blue Jays in the hands of Alan Chapin, a New York lawyer who knew more about chardonnay than baseball. He put the club on, and supposedly, off the market over the next five years. The Jays had several tire kickers—the disgraced media mogul Conrad Black; the *Toronto Sun*; former Blue Jays GM Pat Gillick, who led the team to its consecutive World Series wins; and Toronto real estate developer Murray Frum. New York tycoon Howard Milstein never seriously considered making an offer, although the late Eddie Cogan, a fast-talking Toronto real estate developer, bandied about his name, a person close to the former New York Islanders NHL team co-owner said. Gillick's boss, Blue Jays president Paul Beeston, unable to find a comfortable fit with Interbrew, was now ensconced in the president's office at MLB headquarters in New York. A good friend of Phil Lind, Beeston assured Lind the MLB would look favorably on an offer from the cable giant.

So informed, Lind convinced Rogers to go for it. It wasn't a tough sell. They had for decades enviously watched their U.S. cable compadres use sports content to build media assets. Sports draw dedicated viewers to a network. Ted Turner, Lind's fly-fishing friend, used the Atlanta Braves—billed as "America's Team"—to build his TBS into a superstation, a national cable TV network, in the late seventies. Cablevision Systems Corp., controlled by Home Box Office Inc. founder Charles Dolan, acquired from Viacom Inc. hockey's New York Rangers, basketball's New York Knicks, and the stadium Madison Square Garden and TV outlet Madison Square Garden Network. Dolan was then the sole owner of the TV rights of not only the teams he controlled, but also the other five pro sports teams in the New York market. Comcast, controlled by the Roberts family, owned hockey's Flyers and basketball's 76ers. Lind's close friend, the late Peter Barton, John Malone's partner in Liberty Media Co., created and amassed some 20 regional sports networks across the United States that were then merged into Rupert Murdoch's News Corp. to create the Fox Sports Network, a national competitor to Disney-owned ESPN. Murdoch planned to use sports programming as a "battering ram" to rapidly gain a large audience for his upstart Fox television network. Walt Disney Co. had acquired stakes in the Anaheim Angels (now L.A. Angels) and hockey's Mighty Ducks to provide key programming for its proposed southern California cable sports channel, ESPN West, a move that prompted Murdoch to pay top dollar for the Los Angeles Dodgers in 1998. It was only natural that Rogers should join the party.

On June 21, 2000, at an early morning board meeting at partner AT&T's offices before the annual shareholders' meeting at the Glenn Gould Studio in the Canadian Broadcasting Corp.'s downtown Toronto headquarters, Rogers made his pitch for the Jays. He was taking a page out of Ted Turner's playbook. The ball club was just one leg of a tripartite strategy to create a sports-content vehicle, called Sportsco, within the public company that would include a network and equity partners. (The name wasn't very original given that the owners of the SkyDome went by the same name, Sportsco International LP.) The plan was to take over Sportsnet, the regional sports channel that CTV was being forced to sell in order to get CRTC approval for its takeover of rival TSN. Rogers proposed bringing in equity partners to reduce the company's risk. Ideally, Sportsco would own "a collection" of pro sports teams. He specifically named Maple Leaf Sports and Entertainment Ltd., Canada's most coveted sports and business franchise, then worth an estimated $1 billion. The Jays just happened to be available. Rogers also emphasized the collateral marketing and promotional benefits Sportsco would provide to the cable, wireless and media divisions. It all tied neatly into the company's new branding efforts.

The board of directors wasn't quite so enthusiastic. A couple of the more stalwart directors voiced their concern. The economics didn't make much sense. It was cheaper to bid for the broadcasting rights than to buy a money-losing club in a sport without a salary cap and rife with labor squabbles. And the only time owners ever make money from pro sports teams is when they sell them. Ultimately, they relied on the numbers submitted by RCI management: The cash losses were forecast to be $24.1 million in 2001; $20.5 million in 2002; $14 million in 2003; and $7 million in 2004. The capital expenditures were estimated at $1 million and $500,000 thereafter. The numbers would turn out to be wildly unrealistic. But, at the time, the general feeling around the table was that the company was now big enough to absorb such a minor disaster. "If there had been strong opposition by the board, Ted would have caved," recalls Robin Korthals, former RCI director who at the time was also chair of the Ontario Teachers' Pension Plan Board. "He wasn't going to go to the wall for this one."

Bell Canada was just in the process of testing a cable-TV-like service through its twisted copper wire in apartment buildings. If it came down to an equal contest in terms of carriage, the only distinguishing factor would be must-see content. By owning a pro sports teams, Rogers would be able to offer more sports content on its cable systems, and not on Bell's, giving people a reason to choose Rogers over Bell. It wouldn't simply be the pipeline that was valuable, but also the captive freight the pipeline carried to subscribers that would set the two giants apart. In the emerging era of digital TV, watching whatever you want whenever you want, what will people want to watch live? It's a no-brainer: news and sports.

But for all the pieces to fit into place, RCI first needed a sports network. Rogers owned a minority stake in Sportsnet, the sports channel that CTV was being forced to sell to get CRTC approval for its takeover of rival TSN. Ironically, Lind was the impetus behind its creation when Peter Barton asked him one day why Canada didn't have a dedicated network for regional sports. Welcome to Canada. With a few exceptions, the CRTC—perpetually afraid the cable guys would give their own content preference over the broadcast channels—refused to allow cable companies to own the freight in their pipes. Knowing he'd face an uphill battle—he spent close to a decade fighting to get approval for a kids' network, YTV—Lind shrewdly teamed with a broadcaster, CTV, and Canada's other big brewer, Molson Cos. Barton, through Liberty Media, came in as a minority partner. Together, they persevered through one license refusal in 1994 to gain a license in 1997. The CRTC restricted RCI to 29.9-percent ownership. CTV owned the most, 40 percent. Sportsnet went live in October 1998, some five years after Lind's conversation with Barton. Lind was heavily influenced by his experience in the United States and respected Barton, who died tragically of cancer in 2002. Barton once told Connie Bruck, "Owning the team is a way of making sure you don't lose the rights." Not only that, they wouldn't be passively collecting rights fees without building equity.

Once BCE went after CTV in February 2000, Lind redoubled his efforts to persuade the CRTC to drop its antiquated content-carriage rules. For three decades, the regulator refused to allow cable operators to own channels, fearing they would give their own channels preferential placement on the limited analogue cable tier—although it bent the rules most notably for the Shaw family. "They've tended to let Shaw do things that they wouldn't let us do," says Lind. "I don't know why, but when Rogers says something, or does something, it's sort of more menacing than when Shaw does something. Maybe it's because Ted is personally so powerful, or seems to be. Jim [Shaw] or JR is seen to be, sort of, a nicer guy, and undoubtedly he is in terms of his relationships with other cable operators. If you sat with Ted Rogers, he would discuss nothing but business with you. That's what he does. That's Ted Rogers. With Jim, or JR, like most people, he can talk about what happened last night at the baseball game. Rogers couldn't. I think it makes a difference. [Jim's] seen to be less threatening. It's a two-edged sword because when Rogers gets in front of some issue, he would be more formidable than any other communications person because that's the way he is, but at the same time, there's not a lot of small talk with Ted."

BCE was carrying television signals through its satellite TV company, ExpressVu. With CTV, BCE would also become a national broadcasting giant. In addition, through CTV, BCE gained control of TSN, SportsNet's rival. In order to execute its sports-content plan, RCI demanded parity. "If it's good enough for Bell, then it's good enough for Rogers," Lind asserted.

In its March approval of CTV's takeover of TSN, the CRTC gave the broadcaster a full year—as opposed to the more typical six months—to divest its Sportsnet stake. Rogers had first dibs on CTV's stake, and he and Lind hoped to secure a deal with CTV before buying the Jays. Albert Gnat, a respected lawyer and long-time RCI director whose life was cut short by pancreatic cancer in 2004, kept the Jays deal perking along for as long as he could, while CTV, according to Lind, dragged its heels.

CTV's prospective parent was pursuing the same sports strategy as RCI. The broadcaster, through its dual ownership of competing national sports channels, may have been deliberately prolonging the divestiture of its 40-percent stake to its prospective parent's rival to weaken Sportsnet and impede RCI's sports content strategy—a situation the regulator seemed willing to condone given its uncharacteristic laissez-faire attitude. CTV denied the public allegations.

Unable to secure control of Sportsnet right away, Rogers' next preferred option was to bring in an equity partner. He called Israel "Izzy" Asper. A self-made TV tycoon, Asper bought a failing enterprise—the Global Television network—and made it the core of his CanWest Global media empire. He had just won regulatory approval to buy Western International Communications Inc., the last link in fulfilling his dream to own a full-fledged national TV network. The jazz-loving chain-smoker was in the middle of talks to buy Conrad Black's Canadian newspapers. Caught up in his own big convergence deal, Asper took a pass. Rogers had to go it alone.

Paul Godfrey, the CEO of Sun Media Corp., which Rogers had owned before selling it to a Godfrey-led management buyout, had just left the company. He was barely two days out of work when Ted Rogers called him. They met for breakfast on June 30th at Frybrook.

"Look, would you be interested in running my ball team?" asked Rogers over a bowl of Rice Krispies.

"I didn't know you owned a ball team!" Godfrey replied, shocked. "I didn't know you were interested in sports."

"Well, I'm not that interested in sports, but I think it's good based upon everything else that's happened."

Godfrey, the charismatic former mayor of Toronto, was suddenly the president of the ball club he helped bring to Toronto. It wasn't just his love of baseball that won him the job. He's easily the city's most connected power broker. He brokered the deal that saw basketball's Raptors and hockey's Maple Leafs combine into a single business entity: Maple Leaf Sports and Entertainment (MLSE). Rogers felt Godfrey's ties to prominent local real estate developers, including Cogan and Rudolph Bratty, would prove useful for the cable company in the ground war with Ma Bell and Telus for condo access. He also hoped Godfrey could work some of his magic with MLSE.

While this was going on, for most of the summer, W. Geoffrey Beattie, the president of Woodbridge, and his predecessor and mentor, John A. Tory, an RCI director, were helping Steve Stavro to sort out the crippling financial problems at his no-frills grocery store chain, Knob Hill Farms Ltd. Stavro, a friend of the irascible Toronto Maple Leafs hockey owner Harold Ballard, gained notoriety in a fractious battle for control of Maple Leaf Gardens after arranging to buy a majority stake in the Leafs while he was executor of Ballard's estate. Stavro was also a close friend of Ken Thomson. The pair were avid Maple Leafs hockey fans. It was only natural for the genteel art collector and shrewd businessman to want to help out his friend. In return for helping Stavro redevelop his real estate properties and close his Knob Hill stores, Thomson extracted a hefty price. Stavro granted Woodbridge the rights—although not exclusive—to buy his controlling block of shares in MLSE.

In a complicated ownership structure, Stavro controlled the Toronto Maple Leafs, Toronto Raptors and the Air Canada Centre, even though he owned only

31 percent of the equity. MLSE is based on a two-tier structure: 49 percent is owned by the teachers of Ontario, through their pension fund, and 51 percent is owned by MLG Holdings Ltd., of which Stavro controlled 60 percent. His minority partners were Larry Tanenbaum, an aspiring sports mogul, and TD Capital, the merchant-banking arm of Toronto-Dominion Bank. The shareholders' agreement, business reporter Theresa Tedesco reported, entitled each of the partners to the first right of refusal, or the opportunity to purchase Stavro's shares, should he ever decide to sell.

As the NHL began pre-season play in 2000, at a meeting at the Air Canada Centre, MLSE's board met with Geoff Beattie. He discussed the Thomson family's plans to converge its newspaper and publishing holdings with a national broadcaster and Internet provider to form a new media powerhouse. Beattie expressed a strong interest in buying a controlling stake in MLSE on behalf of Woodbridge. His reasoning was not unlike that of Rogers: sports teams would provide endless content for the new media company. He was "politely rebuffed." The directors didn't find out about Starvo's side-deal with Woodbridge until later that month.

On September 1, 2000, at the SkyDome Hotel in front of a packed room of journalists, executives and Blue Jays mascots, Rogers confirmed what everybody already knew: he was buying 80 percent of the ball club, through his public company, for US$112 million in cash and stock. Word of talks between Rogers and Interbrew had surfaced in the press as early as April and had only intensified as the summer wore on. Interbrew was keeping 20 percent, and would bear none of the team's operating costs. CIBC was out at long last.

Rogers met the players before that night's game against the Oakland Athletics. The only question from the team was pitched by David Wells, who asked if they'd be getting free cable TV. He was told it is reasonably priced. Rogers, who had never attended a Jays game before, was joined by family, friends and company confidants, all eager to explain the rules of the game to him. It was a festive occasion. After the third inning, Rogers impatiently stood up, declaring, "I like hockey!" His guests roared with laughter. A delighted Rogers then left. He missed the best part: Jays infielder Tony Batista singled in the ninth to drive in the winning run as the Jays defeated the Athletics 4–3 in front of a crowd of 22,187 at an open SkyDome.

Earlier at the press conference, Rogers, donning a Blue Jays jacket, was ecstatic. He launched immediately into a cross-promotional spiel. "In a few years, you will be able to see the Blue Jays on your wireless phone," he prognosticated. "It's fantastic." Sure enough, five years later, Jays fans only had to flip open their Rogers Wireless phones for real-time highlights of the ball games. Weeks later, the convergence began. Cable customers with premium channels began receiving 10-percent discounts on other Rogers products, including wireless services and game tickets. "We're talking co-promotion and mutual advertising support where all of the Rogers businesses will be supporting the baseball team, selling tickets, promoting it. Likewise, the ball team can be promoting our products with signage, displays of prices, every kind of promotion you can think of," said Rogers, barely a month after buying the team. "Let's put it this way: [attendees will] know they've been visiting Rogers Land, if I can call it that, when they go in there." That year, Ted Rogers topped *The Globe and Mail*'s year-end list of people who had the biggest influence on Canadian sport.

Even if Rogers wanted to bask in the afterglow of being the new owner of the Jays, wife Loretta kept his ego in check. Once he bought the team, she reminded her husband of what he told her after media tycoon John Bassett's Toronto Toros, a World Hockey Association franchise, left hockey central for Alabama: "Sports teams are a mug's game. Only a fool would get into them." Loretta recalls, "He was quite convinced they weren't worth owning. I reminded him of it when he bought into the Jays."

Heeding his wife or not, Rogers declared, a nanosecond after announcing the purchase of the Jays, that he wanted to bring a National Football League team to Toronto. Lind, a long-time Cleveland Browns NFL team season ticket holder, is still waiting—and working hard behind the scenes with Paul Godfrey—for that elusive NFL team to arrive. Lind has a long history negotiating sports contracts deals; he negotiated the first pay-per-view NHL contract in Minneapolis and spent a year putting together a pay-per-view contract with the Portland Trailblazers, which immediately boosted the number of their cable TV subscribers. He more than anyone else is responsible for the company's interest in sports, whether for TV content or as an owner, so much so that Rogers couldn't help but quip at the beginning of Vernon Wells' 2006 news conference that "Phil's got great ideas for the future, and I'm not sure we can afford them." It's a bit of a running joke between the two men, who've been together longer than most marriages, including Lind's. They always understood the value of live content—be it news or sports—which has never been more important than in this emerging era of digital TV. If things work out, Rogers gets the credit. If it doesn't, it becomes "Lind's Lemon" or "Phil's Folly."

On September 14, barely two weeks later, Woodbridge and its sister company, Thomson Corp., unveiled a blockbuster deal with BCE to create a $4-billion multimedia company—the first crucial step in its pursuit of MLSE—and not purchase the storied Montreal Canadiens, which had been for sale for months. "No one gives a s**t about Montreal, or even the Vancouver market," an unnamed source close to both companies told the *National Post.* "There is only one market in Canada that can compete with the U.S. broadcast market—and that's the Greater Toronto Area and south-western Ontario."

Jean Monty was on a track similar to Rogers—only on a much grander scale and at the top of the market. The technology-laden NASDAQ stock market peaked in March, a month after BCE agreed to buy CTV. Monty had been in talks with Woodbridge in December 1999 about going after CTV together, but when the team at Thomson, at the time still in newspapers, was unsure if the CTV route was the right formula, Monty decided to go it alone, while keeping their dialogue alive. He was jolted into action when the news broke on AOL-Time Warner. Nonetheless, he had passed up an opportunity to buy TSN in the fall of 1998 when its owners were shopping it. Investment bankers at First Marathon Securities Inc. were urging him to buy TSN and then CTV, which would, as the *National Post*'s Barry Critchley noted, "put a cramp in the success of CTV Sportsnet," which was getting off the ground.

On December 7, 2000, the CRTC rubberstamped BCE's purchase of CTV, but failed to lift its long-standing ban on cable companies being content providers. The regulator, in essence, said it wasn't concerned about Bell ExpressVu abusing its gatekeeper power because of the satellite TV distributor's "continuing non-dominant position"—which no doubt explains why Ted Rogers was forced to pay his BCE counterpart a personal visit in Montreal to resolve ExpressVu's mulish refusal to carry his 680 News radio signal. That same day, Shaw unveiled its $1-billion takeover of Winnipeg-based Moffat Communications Inc. to solidify its position in western Canada. The regulator finally capitulated to the cable industry on the carrier-content ban in June 2001.

Rogers only secured CTV's stake in Sportsnet for $138 million after CTV ran down the clock and then applied to the regulator for a deadline extension, which was granted, and finally appointed a trustee to oversee the divestiture. The transaction closed in November 2001, 20 months after CTV received regulatory approval to buy TSN. Just after Christmas 2004, RCI acquired the remaining 20 percent from Fox for $45 million. In between, it purchased The Fan 590, an all-sports radio station in Toronto and the Blue Jays broadcaster, as part of a 13-station package from Standard Broadcasting Co. The first leg of RCI's three-pronged strategy was now in place.

Paul Godfrey, ensconced in Blue Jays front office, initially convinced Rogers in one-on-one private sessions to inject more money into the ailing team. "The Blue Jays were broken and needed fixing," says Godfrey. Consequently, the payroll jumped to US$77 million in 2001 and 2002 from US$47 million in 2000. When the RCI board became aware of the massive losses Godfrey was incurring, the board forced Rogers to be accountable for the Blue Jays cash drain, which had no pre-approved budget or business plan. "I wrote the unpopular report that we're going to lose much more than [the board] anticipated," says Godfrey. "I think some of them were stunned." Who wouldn't be? The numbers bore no resemblance to those the RCI board was originally given.

In Rogers' first year of ownership, RCI had to inject $52.3 million to cover "a portion of the operating losses," and plainly stated it expected to inject another $55 million in 2002. The Jays never had massive operating profits even during their glory years. The game's economics, low-ticket sales and a weak Canadian dollar had plunged the Jays into the red. Says Godfrey, "I predicted to Rogers management that, you know what, this is a marathon, it's not a sprint. You have to build the fan base back up."

For all the slick marketing and new uniforms, the Jays—the first franchise in history to draw more than 4 million fans during a single season—couldn't lure them back. Godfrey—and son Rob, whose hire ruffled feathers internally—tried every marketing campaign imaginable—from the former mayor himself to "Baseball North" to the more recent "You Gotta Believe." In 2003, the Jays promoted their season opener against the much-reviled Yankees with clever, cocky newspaper ads, showing bird droppings on a Yankees cap, a pun on the blue jay as a mascot. Some of the ads encouraged fans to boo the newest Yankee recruit and Japanese star, slugger Hideki Matsui. Yankees GM Joe Torre slammed the ads as "tasteless," even though they reminded Jays fans of the incident involving Yankee outfielder David Winfield and a seagull, which he killed with a warm-up throw during a 1983 game in Toronto. Just like Winfield, Matsui plays left field. Instead of the Jays pooping on the Yankees, they might have been better off adopting the motto of NFL Oakland Raiders owner Al Davis: Just win, baby. The crowds were bigger when cheapskate owner Interbrew owned the Jays.

RCI underestimated the difficulty of owning a sports franchise in a city that only supports a loser if the sport is hockey, or fielding a contender in a division with America's two most-storied franchises, the Yankees and the Boston Red Sox, whose owners can afford to pay their players stupendous sums because of fan attendance and robust local TV revenues. The Jays didn't have the equivalent of the Yankee Empire or Red Sox Nation—or, for that matter, the Leafs Nation—behind them. Toronto is a hockey town: the Leafs can put an inferior product on the ice: they have, until recently, the country's highest average ticket prices and still sell out every game. It didn't help that Rogers didn't own the SkyDome, whose American owners had let the stadium deteriorate once their bid with a local group to buy the Jays had been snubbed. Rogers was the only MLB owner who didn't own both the franchise and its ballpark.

The sports-media plan was unraveling fast. Alan Horn did his best to make the Jays look less conspicuous—a move that backfired when the audit committee of the board of directors insisted on full disclosure. In April 2001, RCI sold voting control of Blue Jays Holdco Inc. to its controlling shareholder, Rogers Telecommunications Ltd. (RTL), the Rogers family's private company, for $30 million in redeemable preferred stock—a related-party transaction aimed at primping the company's balance sheet. (The transaction didn't require the consent of MLB because Rogers is the ultimate controlling shareholder of both the public and private companies.)

The accounting move wasn't all for naught. The public company was getting some non-RCI cash from Ted Rogers to cover the ball club's losses. The preferred shares paid an annual dividend that RTL received in the form of the Jays income tax loss carryforwards. So, Rogers bought $30 million of preferred voting stock for which he received $79.4 million worth of tax losses to offset RTL's profits. Plus, he got his $30 million back.

"If, on my report card, it looks like a mistake, it *doesn't look* like a mistake, it is a mistake," Rogers said over dinner in November 2001. "I make a lot of decisions through the year and you have to add'em all up, and some are right, and some are wrong. Do I think it's wrong? As of tonight, I think it's wrong. Do I think it will be proven to be wrong? Who knows? The odds are it will be proven to be wrong. Will it work out to be right? Yeah, I'm hopeful. But, if it doesn't, I'll say, 'Hey, there's fourteen other decisions that were right.'"

In late 2001, Rogers and MLSE explored the idea of creating the equivalent of the YES Network in Toronto, persons familiar with the talks said. Chuck Dolan's grip over New York sports TV rights had ultimately provoked George Steinbrenner to create the Yankees Entertainment and Sports (YES) Network. Dolan tried to buy the Yankees from Steinbrenner in 1999, a year before Cablevision's contract to carry their games on his cable TV network was due to expire. Unable to exact favorable terms, Steinbrenner merged the business operations of the Yankees with basketball's New Jersey Nets, owned by a group of investors headed by philanthropist Ray Chambers, called YankeesNet, to gain better leverage over their broadcast rights. Together, they created YES, their own regional sports network, ending Cablevision's monopoly over New York sports. Dolan initiated litigation to block its creation. They eventually settled and the Yankees bought back their TV rights from Madison Square Garden. Then, when they got into a spat over carriage fees, Cablevision refused to carry YES, blocking 2.9 million homes in the New York market from prized Yankees telecasts. It all was eventually sorted out—after litigation, charges of antitrust violations and failed mediation talks. Today, YES is a powerhouse—the number-one ranked regional U.S. sports network, worth between US$1.2 billion to US$3 billion, more valuable than even the Yankees themselves. In 2006, *Forbes* valued the ball club at US$1.03 billion, making the Yankees the first MLB team to cross the billion-dollar mark.

Rogers was unable to get anywhere in Toronto with MLSE owners. The roadblock, people close to the talks said, was the Ontario Teachers' Pension Plan Board, although it denies this. The fund couldn't see any value to be made and didn't want to take on the Jays' continuing operating losses. Both sides doused plans of creating a YES Network. Given the CRTC's micro-management over specialty channels, it was unlikely that YES could be replicated in Canada. Further, MLSE already owns Leafs TV and Raptors TV, two separate money-losing channels with few subscribers.

By then, Jim Leech, head of Teachers' merchant bank division, put the MLSE succession issue on the agenda, canvassing shareholders about selling MLSE outright or bringing in a new investor, or reconfiguring the ownership structure. Stavro was on his way out. He brought Larry Tanenbaum into MLSE in 1996 because the Ontario Office of the Public Guardian and Trustee took Stavro to court and as a consequence the cost of the takeover increased by several million dollars. Tanenbaum put up the extra money and got a small piece of the MLSE pie. Tanenbaum, an economics major who made his father's road-paving, ready-mix concrete and construction company into Canada's largest, is Paul Godfrey's pal and Ted Rogers' neighbor. He was one of the early investors in the late Geoffrey R. Conway's CUC Broadcasting Ltd. through his private investment company, Kilmer Van Nostrand Co.

Perhaps, Rogers could now get his foot in the MLSE door. The two men have a history. Rogers sat on the board of Maple Leaf Gardens in the early nineties when Stavro was vying for control. Stavro used his clout as Ballard's executor to fire the five independent directors, including Rogers and his friend, Thor Edgar Eaton, the third of the four Eaton brothers, who bankrupted the family's legendary retail dynasty. The board of directors hired Cliff Fletcher as president against Stavro's wishes. The hire turned out to be a brilliant move—Fletcher was lauded a "savior" for rebuilding the team—and was just the sort of lightning rod Stavro was looking for to stage his boardroom coup. "We were just there for cosmetics, but I took it very seriously," recalls Rogers. "I didn't act as if I was there for cosmetics. So, we had a lot of split votes. Thor hired Fletcher, and my job was to play lawyer and keep the game going on the board. We did this for as long as we could."

It played out for months until Gardens lawyer Brian Bellmore put them on notice: the estate "exercised ultimate control over the board and the directors should act accordingly." Rogers shot back: "It would be appreciated if you would take me off your mailing list of people needing legal assistance as to how to behave at board of directors meetings." It was a scathing retort that didn't endear him to Team Stavro.

In November 1991, more than 200 people crowded into the Gardens' Hot Stove Lounge for the company's annual meeting, where a slate of new directors was elected. He who controls the votes wins   usually. No one knows this better than Ted Rogers. This wasn't his fight, though. He had other, more pressing, matters before him. Rogers, who owned 1,000 shares, proudly held up a stock certificate, although he joked that unfortunately it wasn't enough to outvote Stavro and his cronies. Well aware that he was going to be kicked off the board, Rogers had suggested to Stavro the previous week that they set aside any bad feelings and have a post-meeting black-tie dinner of the old and new boards. It is a typical Rogers gesture. "We'll wish you well and we'll go out in style, and we'll split the bill—you and I—fifty-fifty," Rogers had told Stavro.

"We shook hands and did it. You can understand, the dinner wasn't as joyful as I would have liked," says Rogers. "To me, it was a bit of a game, but to some of the others, it was really very important."

Fast-forward a decade. Stavro sketched out a possible sale of his MLSE shares to Rogers. It was a napkin deal that didn't go anywhere. Ken Thomson made sure of that; Stavro had promised first dibs to Thomson. In the end, Stavro exited a rich man. He made more than anything Rogers would have paid to him and, according to a person familiar with the offer, more than any other shareholder is likely to see again.

Rogers is dismissive of the whole affair. "We always talk about putting them together," he says. "We did several things on napkins but there's been nothing serious then or since. I wouldn't focus on that because it didn't happen. I do lots of lunches and deals and chats, but when you come to papering them nothing ever happens."

Then he guffaws. "It's not very practical when we're losing money and they're making money unless you want to donate your company to them."

Toronto sportswriters refer to Rogers as "Uncle Junior" after Tony Soprano's uncle Corrado "Junior" Soprano, the ambitious would-be don who outlasted hailer and heartier foes, portrayed by actor Dominic Chianese in the hit HBO TV drama *The Sopranos*. Rogers had never kept it a secret that he would like to see the city's hockey, basketball and baseball teams share their ownership burdens.

So, does he want to own the Leafs?

"I think everybody in Toronto would like to own the Maple Leafs, but I've never had the ambition to own it. I think the most successful way to do sports is to merge all of them into one unit and lower your costs as much as you can and spread your costs. Utopia would be merge it. Near-utopia would be work closely together, so that we can get the same benefits as if it were commonly owned. I'm hopeful to do other things with them."

The complex ownership structure at MLSE provides grist for the gossip mills every couple of years. Who will step in if and when TD or Teachers bows out? Who will be the first to cash in on their investment? "The timing and the economics and the stars need to line up right," Tanenbaum told the *Toronto Star* in 2003.

Just after the Jays' second season under Rogers' ownership opened, Rogers drew fire from RCI investors. On a conference call with brokerage analysts and shareholders to discuss quarterly financial results, Alan Horn was asked point-blank if RCI would continue to pour cash into the money-losing ball club. "Clearly, from a financial perspective, injecting $55 million … is not something that this company is wanting to do on a continuing basis. If it looks as if it can't be fixed, for whatever reason, then we will have to look at other alternatives. But rest assured, an ongoing commitment of $50 million into the Blue Jays is not going to be the case," he said.

Horn's remarks, coming as they did after the league was threatening to contract two teams out of existence (paying off owners to fold their franchises) and another players' strike loomed, registered with the sports media and hit the fans like a ton of bricks.

"I had great sympathy for Alan Horn's position," says Godfrey. "Look, as much as I love the great game of baseball, I also realize that no entrepreneur is going to want to put up those types of losses. We knew that we would have to bring changes."

At the RCI board's insistence, Godfrey embraced a more frugal approach to the game—popularly known as "Moneyball" after Michael Lewis' book—which focused on the Oakland Athletics general manager Billy Beane's successful record of keeping the A's in contention over the years by finding inexpensive players through statistical analysis. To that end, Godfrey fired Jays veteran and then GM Gordon Ash, replacing him in November 2001 with Beane's assistant and former minor-league roommate, John Paul Ricciardi. They whittled down the players' salaries to $50 million in 2004. Instead of overseeing a playoff contender, the Jays finished 67 and 94 that season, dead last, for the first time in more than two decades.

"Running last and having a shabby area where they play is not really good for the brand," said Rogers in a January 2005 interview. "So, you have a choice. Sell it—which a number of board members and shareholders would love—or, fix it up. I happen to think there's a tremendous upside for us. I thought it would be very, very damaging to lose a sports team to some other city in the United States, as Montreal did moving to Washington, and while I'm not a very knowledgeable person on baseball, I know that people care a lot about their home teams, and if we can put on a reasonable competitive showing, not necessarily win, people will feel good about that, and reward us—give us the benefit of the doubt when buying a service that probably to them looks quite similar to other telecom services.

"On the other hand, if we screw up, then it'll harm us. We'll pay for it dearly. I thought those were reasonable odds. Everybody's yelling 'Sell it,' and 'You can't win,' and all this sort of stuff. And, it's tough. There's no question it's tough. I don't suggest that we'll make any money from it, but if you make a tremendous amount of public-merit points, it's the same thing as spending $50 million on advertising.

"We are used to competing with people much more powerful than ourselves—competing with the New York Yankees is like competing against Bell in communications. And, we ain't done bad," laughs Rogers.

Owning the SkyDome brightened the prospects for the Jays considerably.

Rogers struggled for almost four years to buy the neglected ballpark from Chicago-based Sportsco International LP, which acquired the concrete venue, one of the few remaining multipurpose stadiums in North America, in 1999 for $80 million from a court-appointed receiver. (In 2002, BCE acquired the naming rights for the Molson Centre for $100 million, renaming the Montreal Canadiens hockey shrine the Bell Centre.) Sportsco, a fractious consortium of U.S. and Canadian investors fronted by Jays GM Pat Gillick and Greg Sorbara, now Ontario finance minister, ran into its own problems when it repeatedly failed to buy the Blue Jays and after the Air Canada Centre opened just down the street. The company was ultimately controlled by Harvey Walken, a Chicago real estate developer, and Alan Cohen, a prominent figure in the New York sports scene who once co-owned the New York Cosmos soccer team and was the former head of Madison Square Garden Corp.

Alan Cohen's wife, Carol, contacted Paul Godfrey, setting in motion the sale of the SkyDome. Her husband was then quite ill, suffering from idiopathic pulmonary fibrosis. He died later that year in August 2004. She urged Godfrey to make an offer. Sportsco was on the verge of signing Staples for the licensing rights to the SkyDome—the Staples Dome, when Godfrey pushed to complete the sale. Godfrey met with Cohen's partner, Harvey Walken, at the RCI offices. Godfrey worked him down to $25 million from $40 million. Godfrey went down the hall to Rogers' office for his approval. Walken talked to his partners. They wanted $26 million. Knowing Rogers wasn't going to budge, Godfrey held firm. Walken threw up his hands in resignation. Within an hour, it was all over.

The announcement was made in November 2004. Rogers was buying the SkyDome for $25 million, a steal. He was spending just slightly more on the stadium than what he paid that season on the team's star slugger, first baseman Carlos Delgado. The stadium had cost a staggering $578 million to build—a world-class stadium that created a world-class debt for Ontario taxpayers, who were originally told it wouldn't cost them a dime. It was the second-most costly sports shrine in North America behind Montreal's ill-fated Olympic Stadium. The city went apoplectic. Their anger was misdirected.

Rogers wasn't responsible for the SkyDome fiasco. Ontario Liberal Party premier David Peterson, who later joined RCI as a director, negotiated away the rights to control almost every money-making opportunity at the stadium for 99 years to a 27-member consortium of some of the world's richest companies, including BCE, McDonald's Corp. and Coca-Cola, in exchange for tax-deductible $5-million investments. Four years after its rain-drenched opening in June 1989, the SkyDome was sold by Ontario premier Bob Rae's NDP government (he's now a card-carrying Liberal) at a loss for just $153.4 million to a seven-member private sector consortium of insurance companies and pension funds, chaired by Senator Trevor Eyton, who had pulled together the original consortium, which made all of the money. Not long afterwards, the SkyDome went bankrupt.

Rogers could now hang the family shingle on the SkyDome. Here was a tangible piece of his legacy. With his name gracing all of the ballpark's corners, Rogers spruced up the place. The company put in a new Jumbotron and replaced the threadbare artificial turf with natural-looking FieldTurf. The interior received fresh coats of red paint, blinding the eye. In total, Rogers would spend another $20 million. Rogers Land was now a reality. "It's his new toy," Godfrey said. "He's very, very proud he owns it."

They knew that cosmetic changes alone wouldn't lure fans back into the stadium. Rogers committed US$210 million over the next years to players' salaries—lifting the annual payroll to US$70 million from US$50 million. The fans, while applauding the influx of cash, accused the team of writing off the

2005 season by sticking to a tight payroll and allowing for star first baseman Carlos Delgado to leave town while it finalized the SkyDome purchase. Delgado, who earned US$19 million in 2004, 40 percent of the team's payroll, was offered a pay cut—a two-year US$12-million deal—to stay. The money came too late to the help the Jays in 2005.

Rogers, Alan Horn and lawyer David Miller were overseeing the Jays. Up to now, they had essentially given Godfrey a free rein. In January 2005, Rogers moved the Jays into his media company where the franchise became Tony Viner's problem. Viner isn't much of a ball fan. That's probably a good thing. Usually, executives are given incentives to produce winning results. Even ballplayers have individual performance incentives on top of their salaries. In this case, Viner is immune. Indeed, he has a special deal. When he threatened to quit in the mid-nineties, Rogers persuaded him to stay on by cutting him a special compensation deal, where he's paid 1 percent of the *radio* company's EBITDA as opposed to the entire media division. Viner has no incentive to field a winner—other than pride and protecting the Rogers brand. At the end of the day, it's Rogers' call.

The ball club was never meant to be a stand-alone acquisition.

Investors worry the Jays will eat up more and more of the cash RCI is generating. Ironically, Rogers probably spent more time strategizing over his investment in the Jays than he did when he leapt into Cantel, today the engine of the company's growth. By the end of 2004, the total cash costs—the amount RCI's injected into the Jays—had reached a staggering $435 million, a person close to the team says. "They scratch and claw so hard to generate additional cash flow from the core businesses, yet on the other hand, they seem content to let this stuff leak out the other side," sighs John Zechner, who manages $2 billion of pension and individual assets at J. Zechner Associates Inc. in Toronto. "It's the one thing that's completely out of line with everything else they're doing, where you can clearly see a return on capital for money spent, and here you can't."

Paul Godfrey slashed the ball club's losses with a lean payroll and courtesy of a few fat revenue-sharing cheques. Indeed, the Jays have been one of the biggest beneficiaries of the league's revenue-sharing formula, according to Smith College sports economist Andrew Zimbalist says. With salaries paid in U.S. dollars, the rising Canadian dollar has also been a welcome boon.

The complaints from the board and the financial community have long since toned down now that the losses have been whittled down. Financial analysts reckon RCI now subsidizes the Jays to the tune of about US$30 million to US$40 million a year. But, with the parent company projecting free cash flow of up to $1 billion in 2007, the Blue Jays are now perceived as a "rounding error."

During investor luncheons, Rogers still gets asked the odd question about the Jays. He'll give his usual spiel about how great it all fits together, when his son, Edward, interrupts his dad and innocently asks, "It does?" The investors then ask Edward for his opinion on the Jays. "Maybe my dad was a bit confused when we bought the team," he deadpans. He enjoys ribbing his dad good-naturedly when he can.

"Teams go through cycles," says Andrew Zimbalist. "The Jays, just as a team, are easily worth $400 million today. If they promote the team wisely, and invest wisely, and it becomes successful, that is, being competitive every year in the AL East, and make it to the postseason once every two years, or something along those lines, and have one or two charismatic players, they can plausibly capture thirty or forty percent of households. For argument's sake, let's say one million households subscribe. In the U.S., they'd charge over two dollars per household. Then you're talking about $15 million to $16 million a month, and that's $180 million a year. On top of that, you also have the advertising value. All of a sudden, it's something that's potentially very, very lucrative."

Rogers pointed out in early 2006 that his one-thirtieth share in MLB.com, the online arm of Major League Baseball, was extremely valuable. "Pretty soon our interest in that will be worth more than the team," he predicted over dinner. Baseball, like Rogers, has been on the forefront of the Internet. MLB.com—which includes sections for every team, news, fantasy leagues, and subscription-based audio and video streaming of games—has 1.3 million paid subscribers. Some 1.7 billion—that's right, billion—people visited the site in 2005. The site was worth as much as US$2.5 billion in late 2004, according to the Wall St. bankers MLB hired to look into a possible initial public offering. The league now thinks MLB.com is worth between US$4 billion and US$5 billion. Rogers broke open the vault for pitchers Roy Halladay, A.J. Burnett and B.J. Ryan and outfielder Vernon Wells to avoid any backlash the Rogers brand might otherwise suffer if he didn't. "We used to just drive by Tiffany's," joked Ricciardi, the Jays general manager, when asked about the Jays recent free spending. "Now we can stop and buy a bracelet every once in a while."

When the Blue Jays signed the reigning AL Cy Young award winner, Roy Halladay, then 26, to a four-year, US$42-million contract—a steal as it turned out—in January 2004, Ted Rogers called it a "momentous day" for the team. Indeed. Locking up their ace pitcher—the "cornerstone of the franchise," as Rogers boasted—was the club's first major turning point and signaled his commitment to the fans. Likewise Halladay signaled his confidence in the direction the team was headed, setting an example for his peers. With the media hoard and Rogers' employees gathered in the RCI lobby for the event, Rogers beamed and quipped to his ace, "Congratulations. Can I get a loan?"

Rogers may like to be the hero who brings to Canada another World Series champion, but he's not foolhardy. He's at an age where he will not jeopardize his life's work for a sports team. The cost of winning, paid in ever escalating players' salaries, is one he's willing to bear only up to a point. "The city and the country love sports, and we love sports. That's why we're here. But, we have to have the support of the fans. Without the support of the fans, without the support of the media, it ain't gonna work," Rogers said when he acquired the team in 2000. Six years later, he's once again challenging the fans to come out to the ballpark. It's up to them. They need to do their bit. The "or else" is implicit, though never stated.

Rogers' payment of $25 million for the antiseptic concrete SkyDome in downtown Toronto was less than the underlying value of the land it sits on. (The Province of Ontario still owns the land.) It's not hard to imagine condos in its place. Who is to say the team won't ever be moved? Just as Charles and Edgar Bronfman saw their much-loved Expos leave Montreal, cousins Peter and Edgar will be rolling in their graves if the Jays fly south. If you think a move is unlikely, just look at what happened in the dead of night when Walter O'Malley moved the beloved bums of Brooklyn, the Dodgers, to Los Angeles and convinced pal Horace Stoneham to move the New York Giants to San Francisco.

Ted Rogers passionately believes it's important that the Jays stay in Canada, in Toronto. So does Phil Lind. "Sports really do have a hell of a connection with people, and if the Jays ever left town, it would be a terrible thing. Being here connects, and connects us with them," says Lind. "There were lots of problems at the beginning. It's come a long way. There are no comments now at the board about it being a bad thing. I don't think they think it's a good thing, but they don't think it's a bad thing anymore."

Lind, Tanenbaum and Godfrey continue to lobby for a Toronto NFL franchise, which might once again open the door to the possibility of creating a sports cartel, where RCI could reduce its exposure in the Blue Jays. It's all easier said than done. Godfrey visits the NFL headquarters every time he's in Manhattan on Jays business to lobby for a franchise, considered a long shot by the local media. The NFL prefers a football-only stadium. The Rogers Centre is expandable only to the NFL minimum-required 60,000 seats. Toronto is in competition with Los

Angeles and San Antonia. There's also that $1-billion franchise fee to consider. Rogers called the NFL's price of admission a "harem-scarem thing," a comment made on a quarterly conference call aimed at appeasing investors who are still trying to figure out why he bought the Jays. If he becomes involved, it would be through the family's private holding company, not the public company.

To be sure, Rogers will not use his money to allow other people to live out their sports dreams. Tanenbaum, who has even less authority than Stavro had, needs a loyal ally in his camp against Woodbridge if it chooses to vie for ownership. There's no love lost between Tanenbaum and Woodbridge's Beattie. And, ironically, neither of them wants Ted Rogers as a controlling partner. He has a history of devouring his partners. The world's awash in private-equity money. If and when—and the when is what everyone is waiting for—Ontario Teachers' Pension Plan Board liquidates its majority stake in MLSE, RCI might be able to finagle its way into the ownership group. As Ted Rogers is fond of saying, "The future is unfolding as it should."

Ever the optimist, Ted Rogers pulled on his Blue Jays jersey before Christmas 2006, clasped hands with Vernon Wells and smiled broadly. He truly was the owner of the hour. Physically, he's taller than Vernon Wells. Unlike his star player, he was never much of an athlete. As a boy, he was sickly, thin as a rail and gangly. He wore a black patch like a pirate for a while to correct a lazy eye. Lacking the physique of an athlete, he didn't enjoy team sports. He was the kid who was always picked last. Only his sharp wit saved him from schoolyard teasing. He grew up, much like other boys in Toronto did, a Maple Leafs hockey fan, although he never shared their burning passion for the game. Half blind, Rogers, nicknamed "Bones" by his schoolmates because he was so scrawny his ribs showed, took up the sport of boxing when he was eight and stayed in it until he won his weight class five long years later. His tap-dancing lessons—to strengthen his ankles—undoubtedly came in handy. "I didn't pack the punch the other guys did, but I got more punches in," he quips. "I had longer arms.

He lives by his father's code to this day. Learn from and then forget the losses. Keep driving. If something doesn't work, try a different combination until you're successful. It's the code Ted Rogers has lived by ever since. It's what has made him the business mogul he is today.

CHAPTER 22

The Five Final Years

"You can't rule from the grave, but you can try."

—Ted Rogers

AS A MAN WITH A HISTORY of health issues and a father who died prematurely, Rogers has always been obsessed with his own mortality. "I think, Jesus, if something happens to me, and I've had heart attacks and bypasses and all this stuff, we better get this company survivable," he says.

Ever since 1998, when he first promised to step down in 2003 at 70, Rogers has had two goals from which he's never once wavered: one, creating an indestructible legacy for his family and heirs; and, two, crafting a succession structure to protect that legacy after he's gone. The two go hand in hand. "Mark my words," he told several hundred Canadian Club members—practically every suit on Bay St. turned out—in a luncheon speech before the 1998 annual meeting, "if the Lord allows me to finish my final five years as CEO of the Rogers companies, we will by then be investment grade and paying dividends." Right on track, the cable and wireless companies attained investment-grade status fleetingly, only to be thrown right back into the "junk heap," which Rogers angrily attributed to the fallout from Enron's collapse. The big three U.S. debt-rating agencies—the most powerful arbiters of financial probity—grew much more cautious after being heavily criticized for failing to do their jobs after maintaining investment-grade ratings on Enron until a mere three weeks before the company collapsed.

In 2007, four years late and a few big equity-backed deals later, RCI is finally investment grade. While it's just a notch above junk, Ted Rogers will take it. For the first time in its history, RCI planned to raise approximately $1 billion in low-interest investment-grade debt. "It's amazing," opined Rogers at a June

2007 dinner at Il Posto restaurant in Toronto's fashionable Yorkville district of being investment grade. "We'll pay off higher-yielding U.S. debt." When asked if that's still a problem with the Canadian dollar headed towards parity with the U.S. greenback, Rogers responds with a question: "What about next year and the year after? Everyone's in euphoria these days and Ted's going to bed and waking up screaming. I think it's good. I don't need these private-equity guys," he boasts. He's talking about the U.S. private-equity funds that are bailing out his archrival BCE and had even sought to partner with him in earlier years. "If they don't want to buy our bonds, someone else will." As for paying dividends, Rogers was always dead-set against paying them. Just like most founders, he borrowed as much as he could for expansion and traded off dividends for a salary and bonus. He never paid himself the stratospheric compensation levels other CEOs enjoy.

As promised, he began paying an annual dividend, however minuscule at five cents a share, in 2000 for the first time in 20 years. (He paid a 35-cent dividend in 1980.) Two quarters later the dividend vanished, until, right on schedule, his 70th year. Then, in 2007, Rogers surprised Bay Street—and sparked speculation over what he's cooking up next—by tripling the annual dividend to 50 cents, effective immediately. He had just paid himself $71 million. By paying regular dividends, Rogers, with the bulk of his personal wealth tied up in company stock, ensures that his heirs can live comfortably without a pressing need to sell shares, or for that matter, the company into which he's poured his heart and soul.

"I'm still not satisfied, of course," says Rogers. He now talks of making the company "industrial strength." He postponed retiring so many times that his fourth target date of December 31, 2008 was scrapped altogether. He no longer has a fixed date. He just has to give the board six months' notice. He's not ready to leave; his work is not yet finished. It's his rationalization, of course, to stay on, and he will never willingly step aside. It's not even that he doesn't, in his words, "trust" his children or professional managers to make mistakes because he freely admits he's made plenty of them himself. He has an overarching need to be in control.

Just how does Rogers safeguard the family's grip on the company after he's gone? And, make it "industrial strength" at the same time?

Rogers began laying the groundwork in 2002 to ensure that his family retains ironclad control of RCI if, and when, he negotiates a mega-merger that requires him to use stock, instead of his preferred currency, debt. He converted the class A voting shares, of which he owns almost 91 percent, into so-called "supervoting" shares that carry 25 votes apiece. In 2005, he added more firepower, increasing the votes to 50 per share. When one of the company directors learned Rogers wanted to increase his voting rights to 50, he quipped, "Why not do 1,000?" Take it up a notch from auto parts magnate Frank Stronach, who controlled Magna with stock that carries 500 votes apiece. Rogers apparently didn't appreciate the sarcasm.

He was getting his ducks in order, so to speak, heeding events that were unfolding in U.S. In July 2001, Comcast made a headline-grabbing US$47-billion hostile takeover bid for AT&T's cable division that the AT&T board of directors flatly rejected. Even though the board considered the offer too low, the key issue was the votes controlled by Ralph and Brian Roberts, the father-and-son team who run Comcast. Under the proposed terms, the Roberts family would own no more than 1 percent of the combined Comcast-AT&T cable company, but would control roughly 42 percent of the votes, giving them effective control. The AT&T board, finding the proposal unpalatable, entertained other bidders. Shareholder rights activists have long complained dual-class stock violates the key "one-share, one-vote" tenet, which links economic interest to voting rights and has historically underpinned U.S. public-equity markets. AT&T, moreover, has always been one of the world's most widely held stocks.

Comcast eventually won the bidding war, but only after revamping its capital structure to give AT&T shareholders voting stock. In the new company, they would hold a 56-percent economic stake and a 66-percent voting interest. The Roberts family, entering the fray with 88 percent of the votes, emerged the owners of a combined giant, the largest cable company in the country, wielding control of one-third of the new voting rights which cannot be diluted. For that, the family owns just 3 percent of total equity.

Armed with more votes per share, Rogers could, if necessary, grant the non-voting B shareholders at least a vote to placate a possible merger partner and issue a whack of B shares to fund the deal, all the while ensuring the family retains effective control.

It irritates corporate-governance activists.

"What Rogers has is ridiculous. That's having your cake and eating it too," opines William Mackenzie, former president of Institutional Shareholder Services Canada in Toronto. "He wants to keep it in the family for generations, and it shouldn't be that way. When you buy the stock, you're buying it because you're willing to ride in the back seat and let Ted drive. He's got a structure that allows his kids and his kids' kids to come up and drive. I think it's unfortunate that families think they should have that kind of entitlement."

It all ties into dual-class stock. Dual-class stock is rare in the U.S., except among media and cable companies, generally family founded and, particular to the latter, big users of capital. The reason: for media companies, ostensibly, to preserve the editorial independence of the media outlet; and, for cable, with government-mandated monopolies, to build networks without fear of falling prey to a hostile takeover. Since regulators in both Canada and the U.S. rarely revoke cable TV licences, the only way to gain entry, or expand, is by taking over a company that already has one. As soon as Rogers acquired Canadian Cablesystems, he created a dual-class structure. Rogers, who has long chastised the investment industry for its short-sightedness, argues that dual-class stock shields the family from the market's obsession with short-term results enabling him to create long-term value. He's called the Ontario Teachers' Pension Plan Board "hypocrites" for owning his company's stock, while strenuously opposing dual-class stock. The pension funds "don't like family-run businesses because they can't push us around, but if you only have one class of stock, they can threaten to take you over," said Rogers at a June 2007 dinner. "It's not always popular, but it gets things done."

If investors want exposure to the media and cable industry, they must swallow their disdain for unequal voting rights. While the issue remains hotly debated in the U.S., there's less pressure in Canada for things to change. Virtually all of Canada's best-known business families have unequal voting share structures regardless of their chosen industry: Asper (CanWest), Billes (Canadian Tire), Black (Hollinger International), Bombardier, Desmarais (Power Corp.), Péladeau (Quebecor), Rogers, Schwartz (Onex), Shaw, Sharp (Four Seasons) and Waters (CHUM), to name but a few. It's the surest takeover defence going. They all retain voting control, although those with supervoting powers generally restrain themselves to 10 votes apiece. The two notable exceptions are Thomson Corp. and George Weston Ltd., large, family-controlled enterprises with single-share structures.

Then-Ontario Securities Chairman Peter Dey set the tone in 1984 when, as chairman of the OSC, he told investors to "invest with your feet. Walk away from what you don't like." The Toronto Stock Exchange enacted shareholder protections for non-voting holders only after the 1987 Canadian Tire Corp. imbroglio. The rule applied to new issuers only and those that subsequently amended their corporate charters. It wasn't retroactive. That means companies listed before 1987 are exempt from having a so-called "coattail" provision requiring all shareholders be paid equally in a takeover. So, for example, the non-voting shareholders in CHUM Ltd. were shut out from riding along on the change of control premium when the heirs of the late founder Allan Waters agreed to cash out six months after their father's death. RCI also offers no such protection to its non-voting class B shareholders should the Rogers family sell its controlling block of class A shares. "Ted has been very careful over the years never to do any [charter] amendments that would trigger a requirement that he grant coattails as part of the transaction," says a person close to the company. "If that kind of transaction came up, he wouldn't do it.

"He's never made representations that all shareholders would be treated equally. He hasn't said they wouldn't but he hasn't said they would."

So, if his kids ever wanted to sell after their dad died, or if five or 10 years after his death, they get into a big fight and the only way out is to sell control? The buyer might only be willing to pay a certain amount for 100 percent of the company and would pay more for the voting shares and less for the non-voting stock. Or, a buyer might come along who just wants control and doesn't care about the non-voting B shares.

How does Rogers feel about the possibility of his heirs selling out?

"I wouldn't allow it," he says, although he concedes that "times change. And, you can't rule from the grave, but you can try." He's not laughing.

Dual-class stock drives corporate governance watchdogs crazy. U.S. proxy advisory firm Institutional Shareholder Services calls dual-class structures at publicly traded companies the "single most disenfranchising thing a company can do to investors." It's not just about the control premium, or in the worst-case scenario, corporate malfeasance, which, as evidenced by Enron Corp., WorldCom Inc. and Tyco International Ltd., occurs at publicly traded companies with single-share structures. The concentration of voting power in the hands of the founder, the family or entrenched management means the company may take actions, or fail to take actions without the support of the true majority of shareholders, or which favors the interests of the controlling shareholder.

In the wake of major financial scandals, corporate governance at all publicly traded companies took on new meaning. In 2002, the U.S. Congress sought to deter corporate fraud and restore faith in the public capital markets with the *Sarbanes-Oxley Act*, which imposed rigorous financial controls and compliance standards. Rogers, showing his Baptist roots, embraced the new rules, which Canadian publicly traded companies must adhere to if they're listed in the U.S. Indeed, unlike many companies, Rogers slid into Sarbanes-Oxley requirements reasonably seemlessly because of corporate governance rates already in place. He welcomed the CEO certification of financial statements. He has always taken full responsibility for the company's financials, good or bad. The new rules allowed him to scrub the company's internal financial processes and integrate the books of the four companies—corporate, cable, wireless and media—into one financial system. In the years to come, he knows the processes are in place to protect the company.

Rogers finds the spate of fraud in corporate America this past decade appalling. It's something he can't begin to fathom. "You read the papers, some of these people are crooks and others are just lazy and incompetent," he says. "I just couldn't imagine that sort of stuff, manipulating the stock. I mean, you can have policies to tend to flatten earnings, but that's not pocketing—that's not the books. I'm just stunned. As a guy inside a business, I'm just stunned, so I'm a real convert, not a convert 'cause I've always [been] for it, but we are putting in a new financial system for $20 million; we are throwing out all the stuff we've got, because it's not good enough. We've centralized things. If there's anybody in the bowls of the organization fiddling with something, they'll get caught."

He watched a fellow cable guy who he doesn't know well get handcuffed. John Rigas, a U.S. cable pioneer, used Adelphia Communications Corp., the company he founded, as his own personal piggybank. He and his son Timothy were convicted of looting US$2.3 billion in assets and misrepresenting the company's financial health to investors. The financial chicanery plunged Adelphia into bankruptcy, and the Rigas family has forfeited almost its entire fortune to the company to pay for a US$715-million fund to compensate investors who lost money when the company collapsed.

Former Canadian press baron Conrad Black has come to epitomize everything that's inherently flawed with dual-class stock. Black wielded 73-percent voting control while owning just 30 percent of the equity of Hollinger International Inc. through its parent company, Toronto-based Hollinger Inc. He used his control of the share-voting structure—which gave him 10 times the voting power of the public's shares—to run the NYSE-listed public company as if it were his own private fiefdom. In a 2004 report, penned by a special committee of Hollinger International Inc. director, Black and his associates were condemned for running the company as a "corporate kleptocracy," diverting some US$400 million or 95 percent of Hollinger International's adjusted net income between 1997 and 2003 to themselves and holding companies controlled by Black. The 513-page report was authored by former SEC chairman Richard Breeden, Graham Savage and Richard Seitz. The tome became the basis of a criminal indictment by the U.S. attorney for the Northern District of Illinois.

In July 2007, a Chicago jury convicted Black, 62, of three counts of mail and wire fraud and one count of obstruction of justice. The fallen press baron and three former associates had been accused of allegedly skimming millions from the company through a series of non-compete payments tied to the sale of small community newspapers in the United States. Black, who renounced the country of his birth for a seat in the British House of Lords, intends to appeal the conviction.

Watching from the sidelines, Rogers believes, as many corporate-governance pundits now do, that the pendulum on Sarbanes-Oxley has swung too far. After a lifetime spent dealing with the regulatory mandarins in Ottawa, Rogers has little patience for a whole new set of corporate oversight suits. He feels the endless checklists—propagated by lawyers, accountants and consultants—drain management's time, energy and money and suffocate the entrepreneurial spirit.

"I think it's just a pile of absolute bullshit. It's not real life," he growled. "It's to make it look good; whereas, what's real corporate governance is when you have extensive debate, and sometimes divided votes. Not many boards have divided votes; we do. I'm proud of it."

He admits that his exuberance might have landed him into trouble had it not been for his "mentors"—stepfather John Graham, longtime friend and director John A. Tory, and chairman Gar Emerson. He says, they've all helped to infuse the company with their values.

"One, I was lucky to have John Graham. John was the voice of conservatism, which you will notice is duplicated with Gar. John was the one with vision, tolerance, reasonableness, carefulness, and more of the sober second thought. I learned all of those [traits] from him, and maybe, he learned from me a little bit of the importance of speed. I think it's true in war and it's true in business. I like military examples: If you're going to have tanks out in the desert, keep them rolling. So many people stop and dig in. Don't do that. Just keep attacking. As long as you can get your gas supply lines and trucks keeping up and refueling—keep going. If you're winning, don't stop. That's what I've always believed in, and people say, 'We're going to file something by the 15th of the month.' I say, 'Well, why can't I file in two business day? File now and make an amendment [later].' I was very much into speed, but he had great wisdom and was sensitive to the needs of others. He provided me with what obviously Conrad Black never had. I don't mean to be critical, but I'm just saying Conrad Black never had that. We miss John a lot.

"Second, I was lucky to have John A. Tory from '63 on. I've been lucky in my life. I've sought that out. John A. Tory's the key person. He and I think alike. He's more conservative appearing than me, but he's really quite an entrepreneur. He helped the Thomson family through all of their decisive periods. Then, Gar Emerson. He now is quite conservative and very much into corporate governance. He's invaluable in making sure things get done right, and that's so important. A lot of people like me get into trouble taking shortcuts and things. Conrad, I don't think has ever had mentors. And, he's incredibly smart, probably the smartest guy I've ever met. I think it's very sad."

One is long since dead. One's still there. The other?

At 6 p.m. on March 9, 2006 in his office, Ted Rogers, 73, demanded that his much-respected chairman Gar Emerson resign, without the board's prior knowledge or consent. It was done without preamble or emotion. Rogers, the CEO, unceremoniously and without forewarning, simply handed Emerson a

letter, requesting his resignation from the RCI board for "personal reasons."
Emerson, 65, was the independent chairman of the RCI board for 13 years and
a company director for 17 years, helping to guide the man and the company
through some of its most challenging corporate deals and financial periods.
A lawyer, Emerson is one of Canada's most-respected corporate-governance
experts with experience on many other public and private boards and Crown
corporations. He returned to the legal profession in 2001 as National Chair of
law firm Fasken Martineau DuMoulin LLP after 11 years as CEO of investment
banker NM Rothschild & Sons Canada Ltd.

Persons familiar with what transpired say that Rogers requested Gar Emerson
step down on April 25th at the company's annual shareholders' meeting, where
fewer eyebrows would surely be raised. He also demanded that Emerson—who
is married to one of his cousins, no less—resign as a director of all of the Rogers
private companies and as a trustee of the Rogers family trusts. The meeting
lasted no more than 10 minutes. Sources say Rogers blindsided Emerson. Just
the previous week before their meeting, Rogers had been seen bear-hugging
the man. He had even promised to organize office space for him on the 10th
floor, where the executive suites are located, an arrangement similar to the one
Emerson had as chair before the company moved into the Rogers Campus.

In a publicly traded company, the CEO can't just oust the chairman of the
board, or a director. Only the shareholders can elect and remove directors. But,
the only shareholder at Rogers who matters is Rogers. He controls the votes, the
vast majority of them anyway. It's his name on the building. The owner/operator
calls the shots. He has the right—and feels he has earned the right—to do as
he sees fit.

Rogers didn't bother to wait for an answer from Emerson. He began
calling the non-management directors after Emerson left to inform them of
the chairman's "resignation." Really. What was Emerson going to do? Refuse? It
would be inconceivable for him to initiate a public, and assuredly embarrassing,
proxy fight when the votes are stacked against him. Put in a no-win situation,
Emerson complied with Rogers' wishes, but he didn't wait and tendered his
resignation the next day.

On March 21, the board accepted his resignations, which were to take effect
immediately. The board obediently replaced him with the CEO's right-hand man,
Alan Horn. He was supposed to move upstairs to vice chair at the upcoming
annual meeting after successfully quitting as CFO in December. Horn, 54, a
workhorse, had attempted to resign twice before only Rogers had managed to
talk him out of it on both occasions. Rogers accepted his resignation this time
to make room for Call-Net's Bill Linton. Horn returned to his original job, more
of titular role than anything else, of overseeing the Rogers family private holding

company, whose major asset is the family's RCI stock, although Melinda has been trying to diversify the family's holdings. At a time when boards of publicly traded companies typically have independent chairs when the CEO is also the controlling shareholder, Rogers was moving in the exact opposite direction. "You are asking the fox to guard the hen house," said David Beatty, the head of the Canadian Coalition for Corporate Governance. The board also appointed directors Edward and Melinda Rogers to the newly established nominating committee, which had been part of the corporate governance committee. Bill Linton was appointed CFO. The board named Peter Godsoe, former CEO of the Bank of Nova Scotia, the lead director.

The same day RCI issued a carefully worded news release couching Emerson's resignation as part of several "changes to its board." Rogers paid tribute to Emerson. Emerson paid tribute to Rogers. There was no explanation for his unexpected departure. The story faded from the press as suddenly as it had appeared.

The directors wondered why Gar Emerson quit. It was out of character. Rogers dodged their questions before admitting that he had received complaints about him from his pal Ron Besse, who is a frequent guest on the Rogers' family yacht, the *Loretta Anne*. Some insiders regard him as a Rogers sycophant. Besse, 68, the former president of textbook publisher McGraw-Hill Ryerson Ltd., acquired rival Gage Educational Publishing Co., which became the core of his publishing business, and consumer-book publisher Macmillan Canada. He's since sold all of his publishing assets to Thomson Corp. He's been a director on the Rogers board since June 1984. Rogers was, in turn, a director of Besse's private companies before he sold them.

Besse chairs the audit committee. Emerson, who isn't on that committee, attended a meeting in early February 2006 in his capacity as RCI chairman to review the auditor's report, persons familiar with the matter say. The directors on the audit committee were surprised to discover that the auditor's report, prepared by KPMG, contained allegations of conflict of interest and breach of the company's code of ethics by a senior member of the RCI management team. The external auditors had verbally informed Besse of the allegations some four weeks earlier when anonymous RCI employees had first contacted KPMG with their concerns, sources say. The informants chose to contact the external auditors directly, instead of using the company's vaunted whistle-blowing hotline—which coincidentally Besse had just been quoted boasting about in the January/February 2006 issue of *CA Magazine* as proof of the company's good faith of the internal auditor's independence from management. "We have a strong senior management team and they realize the internal auditor's work is a necessary part of our governance," said Besse. Evidently, these whistle-blowers felt differently.

Besse didn't report the allegations to the audit committee members, or the board chair. They were just learning of the allegations now because of the auditor's report. Sources say Emerson asked questions about the alleged conflict and inquired as to the status of the investigation. The internal auditors were unable to provide a verbal status report, even though four weeks had already lapsed. They promised to complete their investigation and prepare a written report. The person in question, who had knowingly been in this alleged conflict for more than a year, was eventually reprimanded with a letter to file. The alleged conflict was deemed by Besse as a misdemeanor, an "indiscretion," sources say. Emerson, in his capacity as board chair and as the country's foremost authority on corporate governance, was only now being kept abreast of the matter, which prompted Besse to complain privately to Rogers that Emerson had "hijacked" his committee, sources say.

Sarbanes-Oxley mandated sweeping corporate-governance changes and new audit committee practices, which have been largely adopted by Canadian securities regulators. In this era of post-Enron corporate-governance scrutiny, the audit committee function goes well beyond the historical rubber-stamping of an external auditor's work. The audit committee members are charged with the responsibility of assessing and monitoring internal controls, particularly those involving ethics and a code of conduct. They must ensure appropriate and timely follow up to whistle-blowing complaints. The audit committee members are held to a higher standard and must set an example for the rest of the organization. "The audit committee, as part of a system of checks and balances on management and the guardian of shareholder interests, should continually assess whether management has set the 'right' tone and whether that tone is reaching the rest of the organization," KPMG wrote in a 2006 Audit Committee Institute report. "Tone from the top" or "tone at the top" is the latest corporate-governance catchphrase—an ethics infrastructure to create a culture of integrity and transparency throughout the organization.

In light of the breakdown of procedure, Emerson was said to be deeply concerned about how senior management and employees would perceive the company's handling of the internal investigation into the alleged conflict. There was no suggestion of any personal motivation on Besse or Rogers' part to attempt to protect the senior manager involved. Emerson urged Rogers to issue a company-wide statement that would send a clear message to everyone—and reassure the whistle-blowers—that the company would not tolerate anything other than the highest standard of ethical business and personal conduct in everyday behavior. He essentially wanted Rogers to endorse a "tone at the top" statement similar to the groundbreaking one at TD Bank in its 2006 proxy statement, persons familiar with the matter said. Rogers apparently misconstrued his words. He took it as a personal affront. Owners, after all, define the values that shape the company's culture. Since Rogers considers himself to be a gentleman in his stepfather's mold—honest and respectful—he feels everyone who works for him will act in kind. "It's a family company," he says. He regards his employees as part of his family. Only he's no longer in charge of a small cable company. He's the owner/operator of a major enterprise with nearly 25,000 employees, not a handful of like-minded lieutenants.

The end result: While a letter of reprimand for a "misdemeanor" was put in the file folder of some senior-level vice president, Rogers summarily demanded the independent chairman of the board step down for his questioning the matter.

Unwittingly, Besse may well have served as the excuse Rogers used to remove Emerson from the chairman's seat. Rogers is always thinking ahead. It all fits neatly into his succession plans and securing his family's ongoing control. By ousting Emerson, Rogers may be smoothing the way for one of his children to become chairman, emulating the corporate structure at the family-controlled Thomson Corp., strongly recommended to Rogers by John A. Tory Sr., where a family member, David Thomson, Kenneth's son, is chairman and a non-family member is CEO. Alan Horn is a transitional chairman until one of the Rogers children—likely Melinda since she has no desire to be an operational head but wishes to control who is—is ready for the job unless Rogers can persuade Edward, who wants a shot at the CEO job, to take the chairman's title instead, perhaps on a co-chair or rotating basis with Melinda. Rogers always wanted one of his children to follow in his footsteps, only he's made the shoes almost impossible to fill. The son isn't his father, and the daughter is too much like the father. "Edward is doing a great job but he needs to mature. He's like a good wine; he needs some time to mature," says Rogers.

Horn may well be in the job for quite a while. Rogers, who suffered from ill health a couple of years ago, says he's fit as a fiddle now. He's not going anywhere. His children, moreover, have since married and are juggling work while raising newborns. Rogers is ecstatic that he now has a dynasty. He already has one grandchild, a daughter Chloé from Edward and Susan, who finally married in 2006. They have a newborn son—Edward S. Rogers IV—and another son on the way. Melinda, who married a Silicon Valley venture capitalist, also in 2006, has a son, Zachery. She hasn't missed a beat, juggling motherhood and working from home while on maternity leave.

The timing made sense for Rogers. He never does anything without having a couple of backup plans. He needed a spot for Alan Horn. He did not want to lose him. Horn is also someone Rogers can claim he fashioned, a real protégé, homegrown talent that he nurtured, someone he doesn't have to compete with for accolades on building the company. He trusts Horn implicitly to safeguard his family's interests, something he clearly no longer felt comfortable leaving in the hands of Emerson, whom he viewed as too independent. The two men also butted heads over audit and compensation committee processes, committees that are headed by Rogers' close buddies, Ron Besse and Toby Hull, although it wouldn't be the first time Rogers has clashed with one or two of his directors over matters that he feels belongs in the domain of management. "Ted *is* the compensation committee," one former director said, a fact of life that caused friction with several directors who felt they should use more objectively-based criteria, such as performance metrics to determine salaries and incentives.

Rogers began to view Emerson too much as, to use a political analogy, a Member of the Opposition party. Sources say he was also upset with Emerson for sending "disruptive" memos to management requesting information for their board meetings, an ironic complaint given Rogers' well-known propensity for overwhelming his staff with his own memos and Emerson's duty as chair to see that the board had adequate information. He may well have felt Emerson was using the alleged conflict as a possible lever to aggrandize his position in terms of influencing company management in the future. If he hadn't, he wouldn't have removed him from the family's private companies, or asked him to resign as a trustee of his estate that will control RCI when Rogers dies. His trustees are named for life unless they voluntarily resign. They can't just be removed, although that's exactly the effect of what Rogers demanded. The other trustees include Loretta, Horn, Toby Hull, John A. Tory and his son John H. Tory, the former CEO of Rogers Cable and Rogers Media, who quit corporate life at RCI for politics.

Rogers is extremely proud of his board. He considers 10 of the current 17 RCI directors as "independent," although their independence is questionable at best. His newest recruit, John H. Clappison, a retired managing partner at PriceWaterhouseCoopers, and William T. Schleyer, 53, an American whom Rogers met through CableLabs and has served on the RCI board since 1998, are the only truly independent directors. Clappison's appointment was the successful outcome of a Gar Emerson initiative. According to sources, Emerson spent two years pushing Rogers to appoint a financially literate director, someone who had more than just a basic familiarity with financial statements and could beef up the audit committee.

Barrick Gold Corp.'s William Birchall, 64, joined the RCI board in 2005, Rogers was comfortable that Birchall, having spent his business life in companies controlled by Canada's gold tycoon Peter Munk, would understand his role as an RCI director. Birchall, whose wife is a close friend of Loretta's, has a home in Lyford Cay, where the Rogers have owned a home since the seventies. John A. Tory and Peter Godsoe are independently minded enough to challenge Rogers. The Tory law firm has advised Rogers and his family since Rogers articled there under John and Jim Tory in the sixties. Godsoe, like John Tory, is a close family friend, not to mention the retired head of the Bank of Nova Scotia, Rogers' lead commercial lender and investment banker.

The other independent directors include Toby Hull, Rogers' closest personal friend, who handles all of the company's and the Rogers' family insurance; Ron Besse, who, as campaign chair, successfully encouraged Rogers to donate to Besse's alma mater, Ryerson University, and who, while a member of the RCI compensation and audit committees, had Rogers as a director of his private companies, retired banker Christopher Wansbrough, who formerly headed National Trust, the corporate trustee of the Rogers family trusts, and who, as chair of the Rogers private companies ostensibly managed the Rogers' family affairs while Alan Horn was CFO; Rogers' former cable head Colin Watson; and politician David Peterson, the former premier of Ontario, who was invited on the board in 1991 to add prestige when he joined the law firm of Rogers' stepfather John Graham after his party's ignominious defeat to Bob Rae's New Democratic Party—prestige that's since been stained after the YBM scandal. Observers from other boards say he's become a much more diligent and vocal director since narrowly escaping regulatory sanctions in 2003. "His episode with YBM really sharpened him up," says a fellow board member.

"You could get somebody who's absolutely independent but who doesn't know much about the business, or doesn't care much," says Rogers. "You know, [somebody who] loves being a board member, but doesn't give management much of a hard time because he's not much into it."

For years, Rogers maintained separate boards for the cable and media divisions along with their own committees, resulting in superfluous duplication with the board at the publicly traded company. Since the wireless company was publicly traded, it necessarily had its own board of directors. RCI directors pulled double-duty on these sub-boards with the a few outsiders that Rogers handpicked presumably for their entrepreneurial smarts, such as bookstore mogul Heather Reisman, wife of buyout artist Gerry Schwartz, both of whom are close friends of Ted and Loretta's. Reisman spent almost four years on the cable board. Several directors, including Emerson, tried for years to persuade

Rogers to scrap the divisional boards to no avail, sources say. Rogers finally eliminated them once RCI privatized Rogers Wireless.

"When Gar left, I did change a few things," Rogers said in a March 2006 interview. Like any successful entrepreneur, Rogers creates his own version of reality and rationalization of events. He prefers to talk about the here and now, not about what just happened. "We had a corporate governance and nominating committee, and we'd spend an hour and fifty-five minutes on corporate governance, and five minutes on nominating new directors and reviewing the chairs of committees. The board should be subject to the same sort of discipline in review as the management is. Gar was real keen on corporate governance, no criticism. Now, I've divided the two, so that we have a separate nominating committee. I thought about putting myself on as chairman, and then I thought, no, that's not smart. I'll put Edward and Melinda on and make one of them chairman for a year, and then the other, as chairman for a year. Their average age is thirty-five and the average age of the rest of us is sixty-five, so you go in between—fifty—that's what we should look at."

Rogers was dissuaded from joining the nominating committee only after it was pointed out to him that Brian Roberts doesn't sit on Comcast's nominating committee, persons familiar with the situation say. Sources say that left in the hands of his children, the RCI board might well have become populated with their friends—more so-called "independent" directors—people accustomed to family-controlled companies, such as Duncan Jackman, son of Hal, and Belinda Stronach, daughter of Frank, in the hope that they might bring their fathers' entrepreneurial zeal to the table.

"But," continues Rogers, "Alan Horn, being chairman. Now, we've got somebody who [can] spend the time to do all these things to make our company better, bringing it all together, and getting it the hell off my desk. We'll work out all the working plans we need for the year and plan the board meetings around them. [Under Gar] we would have a board meeting, and ten days later, we'd have another board meeting to approve everything. It wasn't organized. Now, under Alan, it's all going to be different. I'm proud of this, the company is going to be a lot better managed."

To imply that Emerson, who has been described as "a consummate professional," is not organized is defensive and reflects Rogers' personal insecurity. In an earlier March 2006 memo to the RCI directors, Rogers praised Emerson for taking over the chairmanship from John Graham, preserving and building upon John's great traditions, and stating that "Gar Emerson is known in Canada as one of the country's premier experts on governance and this is reflected in Rogers' leadership."

Emerson should take satisfaction from his tenure as chair of RCI. He was commended by other outside directors for encouraging healthy debate on major issues and ensuring that decisions by the directors were informed and based on accurate and timely information, especially in the face of pressure from Rogers, who sought to exercise control over the board's role as well as the company's senior management.

The burden of challenging Rogers consistently fell on the shoulders of a few. The rest lacked the spine to voice their opinions, at least to his face. "It's tough. I mean, what do you do on these boards? Either you're a lapdog, or you fight and you only fight so hard, and you're off," says shareholder-rights activist William Mackenzie.

"Ted has always wanted someone in the chairman's role to protect the alter ego. He wants the marketplace to realize that there is common sense, as well as down-to-earth people around him to contain his exuberance. Ted is very skilful and Gar fit the bill perfectly," says one former insider.

No less important to Rogers was the role of the chief financial officer. "He has had three men who have been his right hand on the financial side—Bob Francis, Graham Savage and Alan Horn. And they were all very, very important to him as he built the companies, because raising huge amounts of money with as little equity as possible takes great ingenuity," says David Wilson, OSC chair. "Ted didn't do it alone; he always had a smart financial guy with him."

Rogers felt his age that winter. He may have been less inclined to spend time dealing with issues that aren't related to strategy and impose a degree of accountability on his actions. He lost a lot of weight in the winter of 2005–2006 to take a load off of his heart, which was never strong. Blessed with an iron will, Rogers has a very stoic approach to his health. He goes to Mayo every six months for a checkup. "It's sort of like our quarterly reports. I approach the medical the same as the business, and treat it unemotionally the same way," he says. "You just deal with it. You do everything you can."

For the first time ever, in 2005 he actually took more vacation time, though he still put his staff into convulsions preparing briefing binders for his review while he was away. In addition to his usual February jaunt at Lyford Cay, Rogers spent a whole month aboard the yacht in the south of France that year with his wife and daughters—"the girls"—part of his goal to spend more time with his family. Time with his family has never been more important to him. On the evening of August 14, 2003, Ted Rogers almost died. Earlier that day, Ontario and much of the northeastern U.S. were hit by the largest blackout in North American history when the power grid overloaded. Fifty million people were without electricity. With the city of Toronto shrouded in darkness, Rogers collapsed in his Forest Hill home during a family meeting when tempers flared.

His physician had him flown out that night on Rogers' private jet to the Mayo Clinic. But for the defibrillator within his chest he would have succumbed that night. He had just had a pacemaker and defibrillator implanted in his chest that winter at the insistence of his family doctor, over the advice of the Mayo heart specialists. The family meeting "was upsetting," Rogers recalls, though he's quick to add he could have done a better job reining in his emotions. "It's your inability to handle it, your stupidity in not getting up and just getting some fresh air or even leaving, because you don't want to be rude."

Early on, Rogers installed emergency defibrillator packs in his home, in his office and in the jet. His children have all been trained on them. He insisted that his employees be familiar with their use. The company has 18 life-saving machines, the first in Canada to install them. Most companies are now all equipped with life-saving defibrillators. "I told him, you know, you've got to go easy, and the very next day, he's in the office showing people his scars. 'Touch me, I've got a pacemaker.' That is him. He's got more lives than a cat. Part of what drives him is that he knows he's hit the medical wall quite a few times, and he's worried. He wants to leave his stamp on this company in a very strong way," says Dr. Gosevitz, who manages a medical clinic in the Rogers Campus and is also the Toronto Blue Jays' medical adviser. "If he had continued to smoke, he probably wouldn't be sitting here today in this office.

"Ted is one of the most self-read patients I've got. Every month or so, I get cut-outs—Dear Bernie, FYI—it might be from *The Wall Street Journal* or *Canadian Business*. He's constantly got his ears and eyes open. His ego is an interesting one; at times, it can drive you to drink, and other times, you wished it were stronger."

Because of his sometimes-ill health, Rogers has been obsessed with succession plans for the past decade. He's been trying to figure out a way of keeping his children happy, himself happy and the public stakeholders pacified. It's been a balancing act of what's in the best interests for the family, the company and the shareholders, some of whom have a greater economic, though not emotional, interest than Rogers. He and the board have consistently reassured investors that professional management, not his heirs, would run the company when he's gone.

Many considered John H. Tory the front-runner for the brass ring. Some insiders, at the time, believed that Tory was the only person able to keep the family glued together, given the early uneasy working relationship among the children. Tory's father, John A., lobbied hard on his son's behalf although he was clearly in a conflict of interest. Others, including Rogers, felt Tory just wasn't the right man for the job partly because of his tendency to spread himself too thin. In addition to his duties as CEO of Rogers Cable, Tory chaired the United Way campaign of Greater Toronto and sat on the boards of the Salvation Army, St. Michael's Hospital Foundation, food-service giant Cara Operations Ltd. and Microsoft co-founder Paul Allen's Charter Communications Inc. He also had his turn as chair of the now-defunct cable TV industry association. Unlike Rogers' son Edward, and Nadir Mohamed, who focus solely on their jobs, Tory was at his desk at the crack of dawn, doing his job and then went off to do political or charity work. "John was trying to be all things to all people," a person familiar with the company says. Tory, a political junkie who at 27 was the principal secretary to then-Ontario premier Bill Davis, was well liked at the company, although his managerial style, similar to the way Davis ran his Cabinet, secretive and closed, irritated Rogers, who needs to know everything, sources close to the company say. "He never would have been a real operator like Nadir is," says a person familiar with both men. "He's a decent guy, but John did not hire well. He didn't bring in a team. Nadir brought in a team. He hired good people.

"John was about as straightforward about Ted's interference in the cable company as he could be without being disrespectful. Ted respects John in one way, but John didn't produce the way Ted wanted him to produce."

The media speculated for months that Tory was about to enter the political arena, which became a source of irritation. Was he going to make the leap into politics or not? Finally, he was asked to make up his mind. Since he knew he wasn't going to get the job, Tory left in 2003 to run for mayor of Toronto, an election which he narrowly lost. For months afterwards, the two men didn't speak, each waiting for the other to call. They're now best buddies again. Rogers proudly watched Tory sworn into the Ontario Legislature as a Member of the Provincial Parliament.

While pleased at his son's progress in the company, Rogers worries Edward is too conservative. "He's got more of a financial approach to business, whereas I have a strategic approach. Melinda has a more strategic approach to the business," says Rogers. "You see, you can have a financial approach and be a lot smarter than I am with the strategic. You'll avoid the pitfalls, but you'll miss the big hits."

And, that's always been his strength.

"I keep telling Edward, it's not just harvest time. You have to keep investing new money," says Rogers. "You have to keep planting the seeds to make sure there's a harvest two or three years from now—or seven years from now. I've got all these targets, but they are all part of the vision of being able to watch or be active on things at the time of your choosing.

"Even though you might make mistakes and stumble sometimes, you will survive, and in fact, you could do very, very well because you're on the forefront. You're on the right trend. You can make a mistake of implementation, but you're on the right trend. Instead of being killed, you're just wounded. You scraped your knee, but you didn't lose your knee.

"I thank the good Lord so much that he allowed me to live long enough to be at work when two of our four children are at work at the same time and working with me. I really thank God for that every day when I go to work, and by noon, definitely by six or eight [o'clock], I say, thank God, the other two aren't there!" he laughs.

He's drilled into his children the same stories that his mother Velma inculcated in him. Rogers shared the legacy more with Edward than with the others, although Melinda feels the weight of it more heavily, relatives say.

The heavy expectations of filling his father's shoes no doubt contributed to Edward's stutter, family friends say. The boy, nicknamed Ed-Wide in prep school (weight problem), has grown into a man comfortable in his own skin. When he was a teenager, he started his own business, much like his dad did, only in food: Rogers' Food Services. He delivered food to cottages. "You didn't have to walk up the bloody rocks and everything. It wasn't a business, business. It was just to do something. I made no money at it but it was a good experience," he says. The experience landed him in trouble when the local grocer in Port Carling in the Muskokas complained to Ontario Ministry of Health, something about improper refrigeration, just a ruse to shut down the competition. His dad was not pleased. "He's just lighting this guy up like a Christmas tree," Edward says, recalling his dad's chewing the chap out: "My son's just trying not to sit around on his ass …"

In high school, he began working in the call center, handling customer queries. In his twenties, he spent two years at Comcast in Philadelphia learning the ropes before heading up Rogers Cantel paging, where he was known affectionately as le Dauphin. In his Sigma Chi days at the University of Western Ontario, he earned the nickname "Fast Eddie" after his penchant for practical jokes. He became head of Rogers Cable when Tory left in 2003. He is no longer under the microscope as much as he was when he first slid into the chair. He wears the family name and its legacy proudly. "You definitely must prove yourself a lot more than others and it's something that will always be there," he says. "People will always look extra close to how you are doing and judge you on how you do."

He has his parents' sense of humor. He had a black-and-white photo collage made of the family, his mother's parents and father's parents, all of them between the ages of four and six. What is apparent is that his mother's lineage clearly shines through. "We can call ourselves Rogers, but we're really Gasques," he laughs, loving to rib his dad. "You know the gene structure. It's obvious who won that one."

Almost a decade after the birth of his daughter, he married her mother over the family's objections. He is a potential wild card. He wants a shot at his dad's job, and he's working hard—not to the same degree as his super dynamo dad—to earn it. "I'd like to have a shot at running it," says Edward. If he did, Rogers says he likely would step aside in his mid-50s to pursue other endeavors. Like his mother, he's a talented painter, only he uses watercolors, whereas his mother paints with oil. Her paintings grace the corporate office in what's called the "Loretta Walk."

"I don't see myself at seventy putting in the sort of hours that he is doing."

Would he rather exercise voting control, or be in the CEO's chair?

"Definitely working in the business is a lot more appealing," says Edward Rogers. "It's a wonderful business. It's an exciting industry, and we built an absolute wonderful company. I think we've got a great foundation to continue to grow the company and do great things. I'd love to be a part of that.

"I do love the company. I love my parents and what they've built enough that if I was not capable of doing that, I shouldn't do it. The family is a shareholder of the company, but there are others who are shareholders and bondholders of the company that we have to respect, and the family should always want the management team to do a great job."

Melinda, often called "Ted in a skirt," is vice president of the company's strategy and development, a position her brother held before he moved over to the cable division. "Melinda, who is very sharp intellectually, would really press the others, and press me on points and really try to be as semantically accurate as possible," says Harvard's John Davis, at Boston's Harvard Business School Families in Business Programs, where the family has held meetings since 2002. "The way you express something, how you phrase the issue, is very important. Some people are kind of looser about it, and Melinda, for one, was very focused on that."

"Melinda reminds me of my mom. It's her genes," says Rogers. "She's absolutely a star. Melinda's a star is the good news. Melinda's a star is the bad news because you know, and I would say this in front of her, she's very, very good, but I told her, 'Look Melinda, if I'm going to help you at all, you've got to focus. You've got to start prioritizing. You're off all over the place, and you're a star. You're thoughtful. You're a great person, but you can't be doing twenty-five different things.' "

Isn't that exactly what you were like at her age?

"I know," he admits, "but, John Graham straightened me out. He would say, "Ted, write down at the beginning of the every week the five things you want to do that week. I still do. Only it's not by week. On my daytimer, it's every two months. I tick it off when I'm done."

He's currently annoyed with himself because he doesn't have anything checked off as finished on his to-do list. "At the end of two months, you've got to rewrite it all. This whole book."

His two retrievers, Jack and Riley, gifts from Melinda, bound into the atrium at Frybrook. Rogers loves dogs so much he has a permanent fixture of one in his front hallway. When he was a boy, he had a sheepdog that was twice his size. His dogs, over the years, drove his lieutenants nuts since they spent so much time meeting with him at the house. "We used to go over and get licked by the dogs every morning. We went over with our blue suits on and the dogs would rub their butts against us. We'd have dog fur all over us," laughs Colin Watson.

Melinda Rogers does not want the CEO's chair. She relishes turning around small companies, which she did with Rogers Medical Intelligence Solutions, a New York-based subsidiary that provides information and insights on the latest medical and clinical research. "I enjoy working. It's what I enjoy doing, anything that's challenging me, stimulating me, like building things, fixing things, growing things. I loved working in a smaller company environment. I love working with smaller companies," she says.

Family means everything to Rogers. Dates—birthdays, deaths, anniversaries—hold great significance for him. Perhaps none was more important to him than his 40th wedding anniversary. On Saturday, September 20, 2003, Ted and Loretta Rogers, with 250 guests, family and friends, celebrated two milestones: his 70th birthday and their 40th wedding anniversary. His daughter Melinda, reflecting her parents' joy of entertaining, organized the spectacular black-tie extravaganza—billed as Loretta and Ted's Fantasy Island—at the Miller Lash House, a historic bungalow on University of Toronto's Scarborough campus' sprawling estate. She organized the event with her RCI assistant Melanie Kenrick and Los Angeles event planner Debbie Geller. Guests were asked to return cards to Loretta and Ted Rogers with their thoughts, stories, and photographs, "or anything else that you feel would make them smile"—mementos that Rogers collects. After their speeches, Ted and Loretta invited their bridesmaids and best men from 40 years ago to join them on the stage. The only person missing, apart from her brother and the minister who married them, both deceased, was Rogers' best friend Toby Hull. Rogers was deeply disappointed by his no-show. "[Loretta] said, 'I don't know what Toby is doing and I don't care. But, I'm sorry he's not here today.' She let everybody know about it," says Hull's ex-wife Peggy, a Seagram, and also Loretta's matron of honor. "She was absolutely furious. She looked like a million dollars before taxes, and it was the most beautiful party I've ever, ever been to in my life. I thought my wedding was beautiful, but that party was gorgeous."

Melinda has evolved into the family's go-to person for event planning. "She really is the person who organizes, but she doesn't manipulate like Ted does," says Ann Graham in front of Loretta Rogers, who chuckles at the poke at her husband. "She just organizes."

"Because of Ted's health, we thought, 'Why not do something crazy?'" says Melinda. Let's do something to make him happy. I got a budget and we negotiated to bring in some special performers"—including Motown legend Smokey Robinson and the Spanish flamenco band The Gypsy Kings. The five-by-seven-inch tri-fold straw-weaved invitations, overlaid with fabric depicting green palm trees, had on the inside flap the caption, "Paradise is exactly like where you are right now ... only much, much better," underneath a tiny green silhouette of Toronto skyline sprouting palms.

Putting the event together did not come without stress. Hurricane Isabel stormed through Toronto the Friday before the big day. Out in the torrential rain, attempting to redesign the lavish event at the eleventh hour, Melinda became violently ill, consumed with concern that her parents' big day might be ruined. It turned out to be a spectacular day. Originally, they had planned two separate parties, one for their parents' 40th wedding anniversary and one for their father's birthday, but given their father's poor health and Toronto's SARS (severe acute respiratory syndrome) outbreak, they decided to cancel and combine the two events. They sent out notes reading: Sorry About Rescheduling So Late ...

There was just one glitch: Tony Bennett was to perform at Rogers' birthday party in May. His agents readily agreed to cancel and to reschedule for September, but then when a better gig for Bennett came up that conflicted with Melinda's date, they backed out. They still expected her to pay their fee of roughly $250,000. When she refused, they sued her. "We had to learn entertainment law," she says, sounding like father. "Entertainment law is the same as no law." She sorted the agents out and forced Bennett to agree to show up during the SARS hysteria for her father's birthday. "Meanwhile there was no party and he was coming in two days' time," she says. She pulled off an intimate party for 60 at Frybook.

"Ted was speechless, absolutely gob-smacking speechless," says Ann Graham.

Rogers, who wears his heart on his sleeve, stood up on the stage at the end of Tony Bennett's performance to thank everyone. Graham remembers her brother's words: "I don't know what to say. I am absolutely stunned. I can't believe that this has happened considering that I have done nothing but work all of my life, and for my wife and my children to get together and do this for me is unbelievable. It means so much to me."

"I thought he was going to cry right then and there," Graham says. "I was thinking, 'Ted, get off the stage.' He gets very emotional, but he was just stunned. He looked for the words for a good five minutes."

When asked what the children did for *her* birthday, Loretta Rogers quips: "Oh, I refused to allow them to spend too much money. We had a nice party at a restaurant."

On a late winter night in 2006, Ted Rogers shook hands with each of the 85 electrical engineering students from the University of Toronto and presented them with framed scholarships in his father's name. Since donating $25 million six years ago, he's only missed one reception to bestow the scholarships. "A lot of people give money to charity, have their name put on a building and they never go there again," says Rogers. "I wanted to do something that would be meaningful for the students."

In a drab brown suit accessorized with a slightly worn brown woollen tie, Rogers resembled more of a benevolent grandfather than a billionaire industrialist. His face was sunburnt from his recent Lyford Cay getaway. Though he appeared frail, his enthusiasm was infectious. Alan Horn, recently promoted to chairman, was also there, along with several cable executives—no doubt scouting possible young recruits.

"Well look, I just wanted to thank you for coming. I think it's important to honor you," he launched into his 'Ted Speech.' He stood in front of the podium, not behind, humble and charming, the consummate salesman at work.

"No problem is insolvable," he told the students. "Just believe in yourself and have faith."

After the group photo, Rogers surprised everyone when he firmly insisted the photographer take individual snapshots of him with every student. For a second time, he shook each hand again with a "God Bless," almost a Ted-ism given his penchant for ending conversations that way. "It's an unusually large gift and he's memorializing it in concrete ways that last beyond money. He is very keen to connect to the students. He loves it and they love it. I think he represents the spirit of entrepreneurialism," says Jonathan Rose, chair of the university's Edward S. Rogers Sr. electrical and computer engineering department, who has been encouraging his graduate students to become entrepreneurs. " I think that's really a key part of the Canadian economy that we could do better on."

On an August 2006 evening, Rogers worked his way through a throng of 150 high ranking employees gathered in the foyer of One Mount Pleasant Road. He walked past a humongous green "Welcome to Vancouver" highway sign. Lind, who loves Vancouver, had it mounted in the lobby. He's taking a good-natured shot at his boss. The sign, which serves as a reminder of the negative option debacle, is about as close to Vancouver that Rogers will probably get. Rogers wore his trademark sky-blue suit, this time with a red rose in his lapel. He clasped hands like a politician, charming everyone and introducing himself to employees he's never met, though they all easily recognize him. He has attained something close to a cult-like status in the company that bears his name. Tonight, he's invited key officers from his cable, wireless and media divisions to a "special dinner" with his board of directors "to celebrate our Extraordinary First Half, 2006 results."

In the corporate world, self-congratulatory fêtes smack of hubris. It's unheard of for publicly traded companies to celebrate fiscal year-end results, let alone just the first six months. Then again, Rogers has never been one to follow staid business practices. His daughter Melinda persuaded him to expand a regularly scheduled RCI board dinner to include first-to-third line managers as a gesture of the family's appreciation for their hard work over the past two years.

Rogers typically hosts dinners for the company's directors in the John Graham Boardroom the evening before RCI's quarterly meetings. Although he liked to keep them social affairs in the fireplace-adorned boardroom, Gar Emerson tried to turn them into working dinners by seating the directors at several small tables to facilitate a free exchange of ideas. Sometimes, Rogers invited spouses and guests. Occasionally, in the summer, he would host a dinner for the directors and their spouses at the Royal Canadian Yacht Club on his tab, not the company's.

The cafeteria, on the second floor, was elegantly dressed up for the occasion with white-linen tablecloths, covering tables for 10. The dinner began with laughter and a reminder from Phil Lind that there's still six months left to make it a fabulous year. He then said grace in Latin. After the starter, a chilled mango mint soup, Rogers, his voice already hoarse from talking, went to the podium, where he read from prepared notes. Rogers enjoys a good party, even more so if he's the focus of it. Just like most public figures, he thrives on the crowd's energy. He thanked everyone for the company's "magnificent" results. "God bless; you've worked very hard, tried new things and taken risks and achieved great momentum in the marketplace, and now, there's still lots of challenges for the future and it's not the time for us to become arrogant, or to take our success for granted. We shouldn't be reading our own press clippings. But, it's also time to celebrate with the board, and for every single person here to know how important you are to me."

He thanked each lieutenant by name and their respective divisions for their accomplishments. He thanked his children, Edward and Melinda. He acknowledged Phil Lind as "our company's founder" and saluted Alan Horn in his new role as chairman, *"for making a difference"* (his emphasis), "and for all of his help over the years.

"Finally, I would like to recognize and thank Nadir Mohamed for his leadership and motivation over the last year and bringing together formerly separate working groups more and more into one united fighting force, each helping the other for the whole is stronger than the parts. ... God bless you all and my thanks to your family and their support of each of you. Truly, the best is yet to come."

Mohamed was the first in a parade of seven officers to speak before and after the entrée of honey-ginger-glazed beef and jumbo tiger shrimp. He paid homage to the boss, saying they should really begin by thanking Ted Rogers because he "enabled all of these assets to be put together."

Bill Linton, the CFO, lightheartedly thanked everyone for coming to his six-month anniversary at Rogers, which, he pointed out, also was coincidentally the best six months the company ever had. "We've a shot at nine billion in revenue ..." he began—when Rogers wryly interjected, "Where did it all go?"—a remark that generated a few nervous chuckles from those unaccustomed to his often-acerbic wit. "It makes us," grinned Linton, "the twenty-fifth-largest publicly traded company in Canada, and if you exclude the banks and the oil and gas companies, that are riding a wave, we're eighth largest by revenue. ... The other financial statistic that this company is famous for is debt." He was drowned out with resounding laughter. "We've eight billion dollars of that, which puts us in the number-two position of all public companies in Canada, even including the banks and the oil and gas companies! The way I like to describe Rogers is that it's like a lot of you people in this room—you're smart, you're aggressive, you have blossoming careers, you've got a great future and you've got a really, really big mortgage on your house. You're doing great, but you'll do even better when you start paying the mortgage down." There were smiles all around. Applause.

They had another reason to be cheerful. Linton, 51, regarded as another frontrunner to succeed Rogers, informed them that Scotia Capital analyst John

Henderson predicted RCI class B shares would reach $100 a share within two years. The gathering seemed surprised. Investors had not been this bullish on the stock since the late eighties.

Rob Bruce, the president of Rogers Wireless, a marketing guru from BCE Mobile, continued the theme. "It's a real indication of the fact that we're coming together as one team," he said. "One team that works together against a galvanized vision, and it's a sneak peek that we can look forward to in the future and it's something that we can be very proud of."

Ronan McGrath, RCI's chief information officer, whose IT team bears the burden of stitching together Rogers' acquisitions, gave the evening's most heartfelt thanks to Mohamed and Rogers for "bringing this company together," making it easier for IT to support product launches, customer care and billing applications. "The roadmap is much clearer, much less fragmented than two, three or four years ago. We've moved from a series of disconnected companies to a much more connected enterprise," he says. McGrath, an Irish émigré, joined RCI in 1997 from Canadian National Railway Ltd. where he revamped CN's computer systems to help transform it from a money loser into North America's most efficient railroad company.

Edward Rogers spoke last, poking fun affectionately at his father with nary a stutter. Amid all the pressure of growing up in his father's shadow, Edward, the most conservative and money-conscious of the children, has become comfortable in his own skin. He drew the evening's loudest laughs and biggest applause.

"My father likes to party. I know it sounds kind of funny, but literally, a couple of times a week, he goes, 'Edward, I was at a party.' I go, 'Oh Christ, and there's memos, and there's problems.' I don't know if you've ever seen him in action, but he'll go at a customer, and he'll talk about any Rogers product, but I think cable is his favorite, and he'll say [to the customer], 'Do you have any cable problems?'

"'No, no. It's fine, thank you.'

"'Okay, well, but have you ever had a problem?'

" 'No-no.'

"'Well, do you know of anyone who has?'"

He paused: " 'Well, in 1972, my aunt …'"

Edward had the audience in the palm of his hand. They visibly relaxed. Amidst the laughter, his voice gathered strength. "A few years ago, my dad came in and said, 'It's been a hell of a day. I had this crazy guy come up to me and say, "Ted, it's great to see your stock at seven dollars." And, Dad says, 'What the hell are you talking about? I'm not too thrilled with it.'

"'Well, obviously, you've split the stock.'

"'No, we didn't.'

"I think that really did happen," said Edward. "It shows you how far we've come."

He closed with one final anecdote that occurred on May 27, on his dad's 73rd birthday. The children typically call their father "Ted" at the office, "dad" at home. "It's Ted's big day, and everything's good across the company, and he says, 'Cable had a good month.' I'm waiting for the hug and the handshake …"—knowing chuckles can be heard throughout the room from lieutenants who've been on the receiving end of Rogers' hugs—"… and he looks at me, and says, 'Where's all the money?'"

The audience erupted in laughter. In this room on this night, the past and future eras of this company came together. The new and what's left of the old band of brothers. As one, they are still chasing Bell. Indeed, Ted Rogers told his troops that their top priority was "to conquer as much as possible" in the home phone market before the telephone companies unveil "new initiatives and inventions." The endgame remains to offer innovative bundles and lock up consumers.

While RCI celebrated, rivals BCE and Telus were having a far less jovial time. Telus, led by CEO Darren Entwistle, was on track to convert into an income trust. Then, BCE's Michael Sabia decided to ape Entwistle. BCE, spurred by its aggressively minded chairman Richard Currie, a former grocery executive, and urged by director Tony Fell, chairman of Royal Bank's investment bank RBC Capital Markets, the biggest beneficiary of Canada's $10-billion income trust boom, announced its intention to convert into an income trust. Historically, BCE has always been the nation's single-largest corporate taxpayer. By contrast, RCI never paid corporate taxes because of consistent losses. If it converted, BCE would avoid a future tax bill of $800 million.

BCE's announcement forced federal Finance Minister Jim Flaherty's hand. On Halloween evening, 2006, he stunned the financial district with his decision to tax income trusts, removing the primary incentive for companies to convert from a corporation to an income trust. Subsequently, BCE and then Telus scrapped their conversion plans. Then Sabia—calling BCE an antiquated relic—shed Telesat, the last vestige of the BCE era, for $3.2 billion in cash, a surprising $1 billion more than Bay Street expected. When the board and Sabia appeared to vacillate over how to spend the windfall, investors grew uneasy. Kohlberg Kravis Roberts & Co. (KKR), the famed New York-based leverage buyout titan, pitched to BCE the idea of a friendly takeover. Though Sabia rebuffed KKR's overtures, the tectonic shift was about to occur.

While Sabia dithered, Rogers capped off 2006 with an induction, together with that of his father, into the Canadian Telecommunications Hall of Fame.

CHAPTER 23

Are You Rogered?

"Before I go, goddamn it, we're going to fix some stuff."

—Ted Rogers

TED ROGERS is angry and outraged. In the spring of 2007, he began calling investment bankers "suits" and wireless wannabes "scallywags." He's returned to fine fighting form. Indeed, he hadn't felt this invigorated since acquiring Microcell. Physically, he feels great, courtesy of a new heart defibrillator that he says offers him "better spectrum"—no pun intended. The device that monitors his heart rhythm sends signals via the airwaves. Not coincidentally, it is the airwaves that have him currently riled up.

In 2008, Industry Canada plans to auction so-called AWS (advanced wireless services) spectrum in the 1.7 GHz band, a highly coveted broadband spectrum that's needed to deliver new-age services—ranging from streaming video to video-on-demand, mobile TV, satellite radio, mobile banking and consumer-purchasing services—that are already popular in Japan and Europe. Unlike other auctions, the government for the first time will not mandate how wireless providers can use the spectrum, a move it hopes will create competition. The winners are free to use AWS to roll out voice, video or any future mobile phone services.

Rogers finds himself aligned in wireless with his old enemies, Bell Canada and Telus, in trying to protect the status quo. So Rogers is sounding the rallying cry to his troops for the upcoming war in wireless. His comments add spice to the daily business press. He mocks, cajoles and enjoys stirring the pot. Is he kidding? Well, he says, he is. "You can't take this stuff too seriously," he responds. Just don't criticize him on technology.

In an April 2007 speech to the Canadian Club of Ottawa, Quebecor's CEO Pierre-Karl Péladeau, a reseller of Rogers' wireless services, accused the "triopoly" of Rogers, Bell and Telus of holding back on the development of 3G networks and advanced services they can deliver. He couldn't have broadsided his cable "blood brother" harder if he tried. Three years earlier, Rogers Wireless completed its nationwide rollout of 3G with the EDGE network in July 2004. The company then upgraded the network to cutting-edge HSDPA 3.5G (on 850 and 1900 MHz bands) ahead of schedule in November 2006—a software upgrade that allows users faster Internet service over its cellular networks. The new services—such as video calling, expected to be wildly popular among the key 16-to-24-age group—were being rolled out across Canada in 2007. Two weeks before Péladeau's speech, RCI beamed in world-famous Canadian-born actor William Shatner, best known as *Star Trek's* Captain James T. Kirk, to make the North America's first official wireless video call. Evidently, it wasn't made to Péladeau.

True to form, Rogers wasted no time chastising him. "I am outraged about some of the unfair and untrue criticisms of Rogers Wireless by Videotron and some others," Rogers said testily on a quarterly conference call with brokerage analysts shortly after the Quebecor CEO's speech. "I think it's entirely uncalled for. If people want to apply for licences, God bless them. Let them go ahead. They don't need to trample on others to reach their goals."

In anticipation of the auction, Industry Canada unleashed a torrent of rhetoric from industry players and potential contenders, all of them trying to influence the rules of engagement. Quebecor, MTS Allstream, Shaw—all of which had an opportunity to acquire Microcell—as well as the Canadian Cable Systems Alliance, Cogeco, the Assembly of First Nations and Toronto Hydro (which is building a municipal WiFi network)—among others—argued that an open auction wasn't fair because they couldn't afford to pay top dollar. In the name of competition, they asked for a rigged auction, where spectrum is reserved for newcomers. For their part, Rogers, Bell and Telus called for an unfettered auction process. They argued that anticipated rules, such as spectrum set asides, caps and mandated roaming, would distort the market, impact taxpayers and force their shareholders to bear an unfair burden, since they are the ones who risked billions of dollars to build Canada's wireless industry.

"It's just a rip-off to try and get low-priced spectrum," Rogers still fumed at a press conference before RCI's annual general meeting in May. "These scallywags who are going around saying Canadian firms are inferior, they ought to be put in jail."

The next month Rogers had a tête-à-tête over dinner with Péladeau in the Commodore's Room at the Royal Canadian Yacht Club on Toronto Island to smooth away any hard feelings. They shared a hearty laugh over the scallywag comment.

For the first time in its history, Rogers Wireless became cash flow positive in 2003, 20 years after his initial investment. Just when Rogers can finally enjoy the fruits of his labor—the long-awaited-for and much-promised harvest—pillagers threaten to trample over his fields. Now, his duopoly in wireless is at risk.

Industry Canada's auction is expected to be a huge boon to Ottawa's coffers. In the United States, the Federal Communication Commission's AWS auction in September 2006 drew more than 100 bidders and raised US$14 billion, the largest amount ever raised. T-Mobile USA, a U.S. startup created by U.S. private equity fund Providence Equity Partners LLC, was the biggest buyer among the hundred bidders. The auction was so successful, it captured even mainstream press headlines.

Suddenly, wireless is red hot. Investors are awarding quad-play companies (those that offer cable TV, high-speed Internet, landline phone and wireless phone)—like Rogers—premium multiples on their stocks. In May 2007, CNBC host Jim Cramer touted RCI on American TV on his *Mad Money* program because of the company's phenomenal quad-play lineup that includes the fast-growing mobile-phone business. The stock instantly gained 1.6 percent in New York in after-hours trading.

Unlike the FCC, which auctions the spectrum and oversees its regulation, the Canadian system is divided. In Canada, the CRTC regulates the wireless carrier, while Industry Canada auctions the spectrum. That means Industry Canada's auction rules can be shaped by politics. Hence, the intense lobbying that's occurred behind the scenes. "The decisions that Industry Canada makes are political decisions. The decisions that the CRTC makes are strictly on the merits of the economy and the public," says Michael Kedar, who would like to establish a wireless competitor. He points out that Rogers has 85 MHz of spectrum in Toronto, more than the 65 MHz AT&T has in Chicago or New York, cities significantly larger than Toronto. "The carriers in Canada are just sitting there hoarding the spectrum and reducing their capital costs and we, as Canadians, are not getting good service. If you have lots of spectrum, you never to split the cells, you just have to pump more bandwidth over the spectrum."

Just 58 percent of Canadians currently have cellphones—that's three in five Canadians. That prompted Seaboard Group Consulting Ltd. in Montreal to add fuel to the fire with a report that called the adoption rate a "national disgrace," comparing Canada to the African nation, Gabon. However, the report, which garnered widespread media attention, neglected to mention that Gabon has only three wireline phones per 100 people, less than 5 percent of Canada's teledensity. The high quality and the low cost of Canada's traditional landline system are partly responsible for the low penetration rates, experts contend. Outside of North America, wireline users have an incentive to go wireless because they must pay to make outgoing calls.

Indeed, while the Big Three—Rogers, Telus and Bell—protect their turf, a groundswell of discontent is emerging in Canada's cellphone world. Canadians, faced with exorbitant wireless voice and data charges, are beginning to demand competition. Research In Motion Ltd. and Google Inc. have criticized the wireless carriers for exceedingly high data rates. The Big Three prefer price stability, not price competition. The name of the game, after all, is cash flow—sustainable, replicable cash flow.

"Ted's a realist. If he doesn't have the support of the financial analysts, then the entire empire is less strong than it might appear. With the support of the financial markets and bankers, he can take on the big bullies successfully," says Iain Grant, president of Seaboard. "Just like the Pentagon needed to have a Soviet threat, Rogers' marketing department needs to have additional threats, and you'll find them rising to the challenge easily."

Even as he defends his turf, Rogers looks beyond the 2008 auction to the future. While desirable, AWS is not beachfront real estate. The best spectrum has yet to be auctioned. Why? The television broadcasters, the citadels of Canadian culture, are sitting on it. That's the highly coveted 700 MHz band. Signals in this band can more easily penetrate homes and office building interiors and cover loosely populated rural areas, making it easier and cheaper for wireless carriers to deploy 4G broadband networks that use technology, such as WiMax, that will leapfrog today's 3G wireless services. In rural areas, the network operator needs fewer base stations, which translates into lower capital expenses. In urban areas, wireless subscribers can use their phones for voice, streaming video, data, banking and a score of other services inside buildings.

Consequently Canada will lag behind the United States; when Industry Canada auctions AWS spectrum in 2008, the FCC will auction five portions of 700 MHz that's been freed up by TV broadcasters in the conversion to digital TV. The FCC, which set a February 2009 deadline for TV broadcasters to switch from analogue to digital, is auctioning the prized spectrum as it becomes available. That's not the case in Canada.

The CRTC refused to mandate a shutoff date for analogue TV service—letting the broadcasters switch at their leisure—an ostrich-like position that hinders Industry Canada's auction-planning process. Finally, in 2007, the CRTC, led by

Chairman Konrad von Finckenstein, the former Competition Bureau watchdog, mandated an August 31, 2011 switch, one the CBC coincidentally proposed.

CTVglobemedia (CTVgm)—controlled by the Thomson family, two pension funds, Bell Canada and the *Toronto Star*—claimed it couldn't find the necessary money to convert to digital. And yet, it had no trouble coughing up $1.7 billion to buy CHUM and shaking loose another $20 million for its $100-million benefits package out of sheer terror that the new CRTC chairman might force it to divest the prized Citytv stations.

CTVgm had reason to be concerned over its proposed CHUM acquisition. The CRTC, under von Finckenstein, refused to approve CTVgm's blockbuster acquisition of CHUM unless it sold the five Citytv stations. Rogers ponied up to buy Citytv for $375 million, making RCI in one fell swoop a major player in the television-broadcasting industry. The company had already agreed to buy the regional A-Channels from CTVgm on the condition the regulatory board approved CTVgm's takeover application. However, the Citytv channels were the real prizes in CHUM's stable. Quebecor, which owns SUN TV in Toronto, complained it missed out on the opportunity of bidding. The acquisition makes Rogers the fourth television network in Canada behind CBC, CTV and Global. Life is coming full circle for the founder.

"Margin is twenty to thirty percent, generally. We think we can bring it from nothing to industry average, but it's not going to easy. Most of the time we buy things at a lower end. They were floundering. This one was floundering, but it didn't go for a low-end price. There were four or five people interested so that pushes up the price," says RCI vice chairman Phil Lind.

In television, Rogers has already embarked on an expansion program for OMNI TV with the acquisition of two over-the-air stations in Vancouver and Winnipeg to build a national broadcaster, which had always been his dream. The Citytv stations—in Toronto, Vancouver, Winnipeg, Edmonton and Calgary—represent a youth-oriented network, which is precisely the audience to which Rogers, with proven marketing savvy, wants to market his quad-play services. The acquisition gives Rogers an instant presence in key urban markets.

Lind comments, "It's a big machine. It's a promotion machine, and over and above making money with these stations, we also operate them to promote the Rogers Wireless brand and the Rogers Cable brand. That figures into the equation as well."

Since their early days together, Rogers and Lind wanted to be in the content business. Almost 40 years since Rogers entered the cable TV business and nearly 50 years since his involvement in CFTO-TV, Ted Rogers is finally moving to establish himself on mainstream TV.

As Rogers moved deeper into TV, BCE—after much deliberation—retreated from CTVgm, selling the majority of its stake to a Thomson family-led consortium. After BCE replaced Jean Monty with Michael Sabia in 2002, Sabia disposed of Teleglobe's assets. He then sold the moneymaking Yellow Pages division for $3 billion to American leverage buyout firm Kohlberg Kravis Roberts & Co. and the private-equity arm of Ontario Teachers' Pension Plan to help fund the $6.3-billion repatriation of the 20-percent stake in Bell Canada that BCE sold to U.S. giant SBC Corp. The decision to sell Yellow Pages raised investor ire. Sabia made a "profound mistake" by selling Yellow Pages, according to Burgundy Asset Management analysts David Vanderwood and Richard Rooney. They noted Yellow Pages, which became Yellow Pages Income Fund two years later, had a $5-billion enterprise value. Sabia also sold Bell's rural phone service in parts of Ontario, Quebec and Altantic Canada into income trusts and then satellite operator Telesat.

While Rogers pursued Microcell in 2004, BCE decided once again to upgrade its century-old landline network—26 years after A. Jean de Grandpré officially kicked off the world's first field trial of a fiber-optics system for residential telephones in Toronto's upscale Yorkville district. BCE quietly moved ahead with a five-year $1.2-billion plan to bring fiber-optic lines into neighborhood nodes—within a kilometer or so from a group of homes—to deliver high-speed Internet and TV signals into urban homes from Quebec City to Windsor. In 2007, three years into the project, Bell has spent $400 million—a mere third of its budget—to reach a third of the nodes. The company, which is two years behind schedule, now doesn't expect to complete the upgrade until 2011. The money Bell earmarked for replacing copper was yet again being hived off for other things, such as wireless, expanding its retail presence and customer service. In the meantime, Bell hopes new technologies will emerge to push digital data through the copper wire. The strategy might well change under its new owners.

Still, the telephone companies in North America are taking different tacks. Bell Canada is following AT&T's less costly fiber-to-the-curb strategy, while Verizon is taking the bigger, more expensive gamble of pushing fiber to the home, a decision that hammered its stock. While the race to break speed barriers is just heating up between the phone and cable companies, industry pundits offer a word of caution: "It's extraordinarily difficult to compare phone company bandwidth to cable company bandwidth, because speed is only part of the equation," says telecom consultant Ian Angus. "Architecture is a lot of it, and the architectures of those networks are so different that when somebody says, 'we have this amount of speed,' what does the consumer actually get and what experience is very hard to tell—and a number that is lower might actually turn out to be better for the consumer."

The cable pipes in Canada will remain clogged with analogue television channels that hog bandwidth that might otherwise be used for faster Internet service or more high-definition TV. Likewise, Canadian wireless subscribers won't be enjoying 4G networks any time soon, even though they already exist in China, the world's fastest-growing wireless country. "AWS technology is good, but it's not the best," says Rogers. "The best is TV at 700 and the second-best is 850. We have 850—gets in all these tall buildings. And, the 1.7 is fragile.

"The most valuable spectrum won't come available yet. People better save their money for it."

Rogers has always had an enemy—Bell Canada. In the seventies, he described Bell Canada's A. Jean de Grandpré's speech proposing the telephone companies take over the cable networks as sounding like *Mein Kampf* and the road to extermination camps. "Oh the Phone Company was furious," he happily said at the time. In the late eighties, Bell was "Soviet monopolism."

His archrival is once again undergoing a radical transformation, affording him some much-needed time to knit together his cable and wireless companies to make them more attuned to consumers. In April 2007, the Ontario Teachers' Pension Plan Board, BCE's biggest shareholder, put BCE in play when it notified securities regulators that it had shifted from being a passive to an active investor, signaling its displeasure with management. With U.S. private-equity funds and Canadian pension funds circling overhead, BCE, once Canada's biggest, proudest and most prominent corporation, put itself up for sale. Private-equity money has emerged today as important a financing paradigm as Drexel's junk bonds were in the 1980s. When fee-hungry Bay St. investment bankers had the nerve to approach Rogers to join a consortium to buy BCE, Rogers publicly called them "suits." His George Steinbrenner-like remarks did not sit well with the bankers. "I've had some complaints about my 'suits' comments," Rogers boyishly grins over dinner in June 2007. He says for the time being he has banned them from the Rogers Campus because he doesn't want them interfering with his plans to make over the company. "The suits and their eighty-five-dollar haircuts. I'll never make in twenty years what they make in one," he says.

On June 30, 2007, Teachers, Providence Equity Partners Inc. and Madison Dearborn Partners LLC, two U.S. private-equity funds, tabled the winning takeover offer of $42.75 a share in a cash deal worth $34.8 billion, or $51.7 billion including debt—making it the world's biggest leveraged buyout. (The interest charges from the debt on the LBO will wipe out the company's pre-tax income, effectively leaving nothing for the taxman to collect. When the pension fund sells, its capital gains will be tax-free.) Teachers, the loudest proponent of shareholder rights, decided to snare the largesse for itself rather than wage a public proxy fight to oust the board and replace management. Teachers will end up owning 52 percent, while Providence and Madison Dearborn will own 32 percent and 9 percent, respectively. TD Bank, Rogers' long-time banker, will own the remaining 7 percent. Providence, which prefers to build companies, not tear them apart, said that it regards Bell's struggling wireless business as the company's key building block.

Ironically, Providence broached RCI about making a sizeable investment in the wake of the company's takeover of Microcell in exchange for a board seat, no strings attached, a person familiar with says. In dismissing the overture, Ted Rogers now finds Providence in his archrival's tent.

While huge leaps in technology will provide consumers with a broad scope of services, Rogers, Bell and Telus—the entire telecom industry—face a growing backlash from subscribers for poor customer service and erroneous billing. In their haste to be the first to offer new products, the industry also risks jeopardizing consumer goodwill if those products fail to live up to the expectations promised in the marketing campaigns. Subscribers mistakenly look to the CRTC, even though the CRTC's mandate is not to protect consumers but rather to stand on guard for Canadian culture while safeguarding the financial viability of its constituents: broadcasters, and cable TV, telephone and content providers.

RCI, Canada's largest cable TV and wireless company, receives its fair share of complaints. Susan Drummond, an associate law professor at Osgoode Hall Law School in Toronto, became a *cause célèbre* over $12,237 in fraudulent long-distance calls to Pakistan, Syria, Libya and Russia made from her cellphone which she claimed had been stolen from her Toronto home while she was in Israel. She did not take her GSM phone on her trip and reported it stolen after Rogers Wireless contacted her about her bill. When she understandably refused to pay the charges, Rogers Wireless not only argued with her, but then cut off her 11-year-old son's cellular phone service. Her story became national (and international) news only after her partner learned that the Hezbollah had cloned Ted Rogers' cellphone and everyone inside RCI was too afraid to tell him to turn it off.

Though RCI explained that his analogue phone number had been cloned in the mid-1990s, but not by terrorists, the damage had been done. Drummond became an instant media star, while the company appeared arrogant and intransigent. With her story front-page news, Rogers personally apologized to her, offered to write off her bill and reimburse her expenses. Instead, she took RCI to small claims court for breach of contract and won. Shortly thereafter, RCI changed its customer terms of service contract, including a clarification of its controversial mandatory arbitration clause, something the law professor sought to elucidate was unenforceable in certain jurisdictions, though her point became lost in the noise surrounding her case. The company also no longer bills its subscribers for fraudulent calls.

In cable, Rogers faces a potential $100-million class-action lawsuit for "misrepresenting" its On Demand digital cable services. The lawsuit, not yet certified as a class action, alleged that Rogers misrepresented interruptions to its service that took place between June and September 2006. The suit, initiated by Glenn and Loretta Wilkins, alleges the company unlawfully retained prepaid amounts from customers for the service while it was unavailable. "It may be small amounts of money for individual customers, but Rogers basically charged for a service that wasn't provided," says Todd McCarthy, a partner at Flaherty Dow Elliott & McCarthy, the law firm representing the Wilkins. "It's a matter of principle. We believe that the telecommunications industry should be held to the same standards as any other service industry, and that is, if you offer a service, you should provide that service and nothing less, and if not, you provide a refund. Rogers has never provided the Wilkins with an explanation or credit."

"I think they got too big too fast," says Toronto web designer Adam Sherman, who created the IhateRogers.ca website in 2002 when John H. Tory ran the cable division. "When I was a kid all I remember from Rogers is Rogers Cable 10. Nobody had cellphones. The Internet didn't exist. You had to get your cable from somewhere and since there were only thirty channels anyway and you could get them all through Rogers, who cared? Then, they came out with cellular and the Internet and opened up video stores. They have their hand in so many other pies with radio stations and media and the Blue Jays. How big can you get and still be able to maintain a level of service where you're going to keep your customers satisfied?

"I didn't have major beefs with them, but the errors were just so stupid."

Sherman created the website after a customer service representative, a supervisor and then a manager all refused to apologize for the company's mistake. Upon receiving a notice telling him to pay his cable bill or have his service terminated, Sherman called Rogers Cable to say he'd be happy to pay if they'd only send him a bill. He had moved into his third new house but had not yet received a monthly statement, even though he had phoned the cable company each time to provide his new address. Three months later, he received another termination notice. This time when he called, he had the presence of mind to ask what address they had on file for him. It was from his first home. (He had received bills at his second home.)

While he was annoyed to start with, the conversation escalated into a heated exchange with the manager. "Okay, whatever, cancel everything, and I'm starting a website to tell people how stupid you are," he told her. "She said, 'Go ahead.' So, I went right upstairs to my computer and that's when I found out that Rogers owns IhateRogers.com and IhateRogers.org and .biz, but not.ca. They're a Canadian corporation that operates solely in the country of Canada and the one domain name extension they never bothered to purchase was dot ca. That's typical Rogers. So, I thought, 'Well, if they don't want it, I'll take it.'

"I never really agreed that the customer is always right, but for business, you have to go along with it. If you want to keep their business, you're going to have to accommodate them somehow, but I swear, their mantra is the customer is never right. We are right. The customer needs to be reprogrammed. So many of the rants that I receive about them are that they won't admit that they're wrong. They make a mistake and they won't admit that it's their mistake. They would rather lose your business than say, 'You know what, we apologize. That was our fault. That was absolutely our fault.' It's like 'we're so big; if you want to cancel, cancel.' That's their attitude.

"I get probably ten thousand unique visitors a month. I created a monster. I can't maintain it anymore. It's too much," says Sherman, who self-funded the website. He canceled all of his Rogers services and even switched to dial-up, the only available alternative in his neighborhood.

It's these kind of complaints that drive Ted Rogers crazy. Even at 74, when he's in the office on weekends, which is most weekends, Rogers will often take customer calls himself. Though he is proud of his cable and wireless networks, he says he realizes RCI's future success doesn't rest solely on technology. The industry buzz these days is all about being an "experience" provider, not a "service" provider. For the telecom carriers, that means figuring out how to have a profitable relationship with its customers without alienating them. The winner of the race may well be the company that gains a reputation for providing the best overall customer experience. When asked how he would grade RCI on customer service, he rates RCI a C-plus.

"I'm dealing with it. Yeah, in most cases it's justified, and I'm dealing with it. I'm the entrepreneur, who relates more to the customer," says Rogers. "We're not doing a good enough job, never mind marketing. How do you market stupidity? Do you know the hundreds and hundreds of rules that have grown up since I started this company—hundreds and hundreds of asinine rules? Pardon my French. I'll give an example. The widow phones and says, 'My husband died yesterday.' 'Oh, I'm awfully sorry to hear that.' 'He doesn't need his phone, if you could cancel the phone service.' 'Well, we can't do that. You need to send us a death certificate.' I could give you dozens of [examples of] little dwarfish minds here, which I'm going to rub out and eliminate. I'm now very active in turning everything upside-down, bringing in new management, and hiring new people.

"No, we're going to do it before I go. Before I go, goddamn it, we're going to fix some stuff."

When Rogers visits the call centers, which are located in Canada, not India, he will typically wheedle information off his front-line employees. "I look them in the eye and say, tell me what your problems are? Tell me how we can improve. They're a bit shy. They don't want to be squealers or complainers, so it takes me a little time to get it out of them, but I got a lot out of them."

He offered another example. In cable, customer service agents are only permitted to adjust bills up to $63. In wireless, the limit is $75. "The first bad thing is that it's a different amount for wireless and cable, and I'm trying to run a combined call center," he exclaims.

"I believe that we should push down authority. One of the most important things for customer service is actually solving a person's problem on the first call, not just answering the phone," he says. "The push comes from what I call the rulers. The rulers are the people in corporate that say, 'We don't trust those people [in customer service].' Then I come back and raise hell. Why are we doing this?"

When a newspaper article in January 2007 proclaimed that RCI's market capitalization surpassed BCE's—for all of an hour, Rogers laughs—Rogers decided he had to shake up RCI. This however is hardly a new role for him. In 1994, when he was 61, he declared: "I'm in charge of the department of discontent. I'm discontented with pretty much everything. I like the role. You can really stir it up. It keeps the company moving." Now, he calls himself the Chief Agitator. "People were parading around here like they were geniuses," he says. "I could see the place getting very arrogant, and that's the road to ruin. So, I said, I have to dream up something."

He sure did. In May 2007, Rogers embarked on a two-to-three-year $500-million sweeping overhaul of the entire company, with most of the money earmarked for new customer information and billing systems. He intends to pull 30 key executives—and up to 600 people in total—out of the company and move them offsite, where they can rewrite the company's policies and procedures without work-related distractions. The offsite location isn't far. It's across the street, a stone's throw away from Rogers Campus.

"They will re-pot the company," he says with gusto. "They will review everything we do. Everything is being thrown out for review. They won't have time to be arrogant. They will be so up to their eyeballs in problems."

Rogers put a four-person special board committee together that included John Clappison, Bill Schleyer, Colin Watson and Peter Godsoe, as an ex-officio member, to oversee the effort. His decision to remove the top 30 executives worries some people. Rogers says that one RCI director warned him, "Ted, you're betting the company again."

"We need to reinvent the company to protect us from when the bad times come, when the rains come," Rogers says he retorted.

For years, Rogers has been trying to fuse his silo divisions into one integrated unit that to achieve operational efficiencies and transform RCI into a profitable consumer centric organization. He hopes to have a computer system to enable his frontline staff to call up a subscriber's complete profile in a manner similar to the way the bank customer client representatives can see a customer's profile on one screen. In this way, Rogers hopes to provide not only better customer service but also increase RCI's share of wallet since the frontline person will be more knowledgeable when it comes to selling bundles of services.

In 2000, he talked of re-potting the company. Now, he's at it again. Only this time, he's putting real money behind the project.

"I can afford to do this now," he says. "I never could before. Other guys, who are doing well, they spend it all on other things. They buy back shares—not me. I think we're very fortunate and I think we've got great people and I acknowledge them. Having said that, I'm dissatisfied with almost everything. I'm going to fix up the company now.

"I couldn't get anywhere writing memos. Why don't they do the stuff the memo asks them to do?" he asks, clearly frustrated. "We have to put the whole goddamn company in play to get it done.

"You've got to ride this pony. It's a new challenge for me. Otherwise, we'd be sitting around moping and looking for another big acquisition that we can't afford. Afterwards, we can make an acquisition. Not now.

"It's a hell of a project," says Rogers. "It's Ted's last hurrah."

Somehow that seems unlikely.

Vindication

Ted Rogers is like the great white shark, which tears into its prey and feeds until its needs are sated. Also, like the great white, Rogers usually maneuvers alone and quietly as he hunts his prey, whether they're a technology breakthrough, new assets or investments. Many people describe him as a visionary; he's not. Rogers is a combination of almost unerring instinct and bull-headed tenacity. He has always had good antennas, whether in radio or his work.

In nearly every venture where he initially had to share control, Rogers devoured his partners to satisfy his self-confessed need for nothing less than absolute authority. He's left more than a few egos bruised—or worse—along the way. From the time he was a young man, Ted Rogers went about building his business with unwavering fearlessness. Along the way, he made the hard decisions himself, even the ones he hated to confront. Through it all, if he feared anything, it was his own mortality, dying before he could fulfil what he calls "my father's destiny and my mother's dream." He's gone well beyond what anyone, including himself, ever imagined he could achieve. In part, that's because he had the good sense to surround himself with smart lieutenants to help him test the waters. The rise of Rogers has coincided with the fall of BCE, which barely escaped the clutches of American moneymen. "He's a bloody magician," says former BCE chief Jean Monty. "He's made big bets quite adeptly. He's suffered some blows, but he's come back. I give him a hell of a lot of kudos for the way he's handled this whole evolution of the industry."

A columnist for the now-defunct *Toronto Telegram* described Ted Rogers in 1965 as a "pink-cheeked, boyish-looking chap with an exhausting exuberance and a dangerously deceptive air of naiveté." At 74, he's no longer boyish looking, though Rogers' driving personality has become a force to be reckoned with—and often feared—in the 40-plus years since the *Telegram* singled him out. On the road to becoming a telecom titan, nothing in life worth having ever came easily, whether it was when he and his wife conceived their first child to completing his many and often-numbingly intricate business transactions. He sees—and will seek—solutions to problems more quickly than others. "No problem is insoluble," he says. "Just believe in yourself."

In a video honoring the CHUM founder Allan Waters that was shown during his memorial service on December 7, 2005, when Waters was asked if he had been lucky, he replied, "Well, I don't know if it was luck. I worked hard. I picked good people." Ted Rogers leaned into then CRTC chairman Charles Dalfen, seated beside him, and whispered: "God, if they asked me that question, I'd say I was bloody lucky."

It's been more than luck, though. Rogers mastered the sometimes-treacherous regulatory backwaters, became a catalyst for change in Canada and the U.S., and surfed the technological waves at the right time. "We know about regulation," he once said. "You don't make money quickly in regulated areas, but you've got protection on the downside." He used that to his advantage to take risks that no corporate executive in Canada dared to attempt—taking calculated risks in FM radio, in cable TV, in his U.S. cable foray and in cellular radiotelephony. Rogers leveraged himself on the backs of his subscribers to move from one adventure to another. He never showed a fear of risk. For him, risk greased the wheels of his empire and made the journey fun. "Fear is different from concern," says Rogers. "Some people get all buggered with fear about risk, and they just get into trouble."

The burden of debt, for which he was repeatedly criticized, has exacted a toll on him and his people. Rogers' penchant for debt made everybody's sphincters a little tighter. In the annals of corporate history, debt has never been the hallmark of a great leader.

He has poured billions into his cable and wireless networks. In cable TV, he invested almost $5 billion, or $2,100 per subscriber from 1995 to 2005. In wireless, he invested another $5 billion over the same period. Still, those investments—and debt—have protected him from the threat of competition. In that decade, RCI Class B shares rose 68 percent. In the past two-and-a-half years, the stock has risen 190 percent.

Only now is Rogers being vindicated. RCI's current leverage—its debt to EBITDA—was 2.71 on July 31, 2007, the lowest in its history. That's down from 5.2 in 2004 when he acquired Microcell and privatized Rogers Wireless. In 2007, for the first time, investing fans rewarded Rogers with a higher market capitalization, or value—price tag, so to speak—than Bell, a triumph Rogers only ever fantasized about. He has a business school named after him, the Ted Rogers School of Management, courtesy of a $15-million donation to Toronto's Ryerson University.

Rogers' empire was not built without sacrifice. He forced a frantic pace on his faithful lieutenants, although at least half of them escaped the firm relatively unscathed. Although it may be cold comfort to many of them, Rogers doesn't ask his employees to do anything that he wouldn't do himself and therein lies the crux of the problem: Ted Rogers lives, breathes and eats work—a major reason, perhaps, why the titan had to cheat death five times.

His wingmen, who stayed with him through the swells and shoals in building the foundation for what is today Canada's second-largest telecom company, stayed for one reason above all else: Ted Rogers made things happen. "When Ted walked into a room, it was about as close to a Roman god as you're going to get," says David Masotti, former RCI engineer, an entrepreneur in his own right. "We were young guys and we were very, very inspired by Ted. He really had us going. There are so few Canadians that are in the business of creating wealth."

His wife Loretta has been his staunchest ally and sounding board. Without her moral and financial support, especially in the early days, Ted Rogers might not be where he is today. Phil Lind watched his back. Graham Savage raised the money. Bob Francis, who died on the job, kept the bankers at bay. Colin Watson built the franchises. Nick Hamilton-Piercy made the cable systems work. Jim Sward kept radio humming. They had strong teams behind them. All the while, John Graham, Rogers' stepfather, managed Ted Rogers. Graham, along with directors, John A. Tory, Robin Korthals, Peter Godsoe, and Gar Emerson provided sage advice, alternatively raising caution flags or encouraging him on the right course. Nick Kauser, widely acknowledged as one of the modern-day wireless industry's founding fathers, steered Rogers onto the right track—twice. Alan Horn protected the family's wealth before moving into the CFO's chair. They exhausted their credit officers and their credit lines—and they repeatedly surprised their critics, not to mention their bankers.

In the nineties, a watershed decade for the company, Rogers stopped listening to his lieutenants. The company struggled to remake itself in the frenzied hullabaloo of convergence, all the while continuing to pour capital into its networks. The decision to go into wireless, to secure control of Cantel, to replace the network with GSM, to leash Fido—all transformed RCI into the powerhouse it is today. In his soul, he might be the cable guy, but the reality is that the company's growth engine has been wireless. That's why he's fighting so hard to protect it. Rogers has a new team, with some old faces. He hopes his new team will make the "family company" bigger and stronger.

For much of its corporate life, RCI has been an ego-driven monopolistic company. Rogers hates competition. He would prefer to hold onto his monopoly or duopoly status. He built from scratch a company that has $14 billion in assets and 22,500 employees in Canada. Rogers is no longer the little guy that could.

He faces potentially more competition, not less. Bell Canada's new masters may well fortify it and allow it to emerge stronger. In wireless, Canadians currently have two choices: GSM or CDMA. Canadians can't use their GSM phone on CDMA, or vice versa. As a result, consumers can't switch carriers unless they buy a new phone. (Most phones are locked to a particular provider and cannot be easily transferred.) RCI has a GSM monopoly in Canada, but that is unlikely to last forever. There's also the threat of competition from Internet wireless hotspots.

In television, Rogers' nemesis Bell Canada announced plans to roll out IPTV in 2007, although management (before the Teachers buyout) assured the financial district that it had no intention of engaging in a price war with Rogers Cable.

In the twilight of his career, Rogers's headiest challenge is to transform RCI's culture to ensure that the company wins the competitive wars that lie ahead. In the past, he had to take care of one main customer—the CRTC. The regulator had two mandates: to protect Canadian culture and to ensure the financial viability of industry firms. When the CRTC rebelled against technological innovation, Rogers went to the United States, where he raised industry standards. Much of the company's DNA comes from when it walked the high wire of debt.

"He is good at the technology side, but as [former cable boss and current RCI director] Colin Watson used to say when he was running the cable company, 'What we offer is like a taxi service. You hail a taxi at King and Bay, Toronto's financial district, and let's say, you're asking to go uptown, and the taxi driver says, 'No sorry, we're going to Ottawa.' Here is what we offer you, buy it," one former RCI director says.

RCI was the taxi service. Since it had a monopoly, the consumer had no choice but to take what the company delivered. Rogers, the entrepreneur, understands that he must redirect the company's culture to focus on consumers, not just the regulatory customer. He understands—perhaps more than his vice presidents—that the company can no longer compete solely by being first out of the gate with a new product, or by boasting that it has the best, or most reliable, network.

To win the war, RCI must learn to pick its battles. That might mean not rushing products to market until the sales, marketing and frontline customer-care people are aligned. Rogers, who can be brutally honest, wants his lieutenants to come to him with solutions. He has too many VPs—he calls them "rule makers" in the organization—who overlay the customer service reps with rules. That's why the customer is always wrong, because the customer reps follow the rulebooks of the cable and wireless divisions. Only, the rulebooks do not match Rogers' entrepreneurial roots. That leaves him trying to change the company from one that's driven by compliance with rules to one that's motivated to being consumer compliant.

In his book *Good to Great*, author Jim Collins identifies one of the characteristics of great companies: "All good to great companies began the process of finding a path to greatness by confronting the brutal facts of their current reality ... A primary task in taking a company from good to great is to create a culture wherein people have a tremendous opportunity to be heard and, ultimately for the trust to be heard."

The future is about the customer experience. Products—videophones, PVRS or baseball—do not connect people to companies even if the signage blares their corporate name. It's the customer experience surrounding those products that ultimately wins loyalty. That's why the Fido brand outranks Rogers Wireless. According to an Autumn 2006 JD Power customer satisfaction survey, Rogers Wireless, his growth engine, ranked dead last among its rivals. Fido ranked second behind SaskTel Mobility, although being second best in an industry that's considered the worst for consumer satisfaction is hardly an achievement. It's great to talk the talk, but the company must also now walk the walk.

Just as a coin has two sides, Ted Rogers is a man exuberantly confident in business on one side and filled with deep personal insecurities on the other. He admits he is not a natural delegator. He tries to do everything himself—and, for good reason. It's his baby. He has poured his life and soul into it. RCI is publicly traded, but make no mistake, he controls it. It's not easy for him to share the chase, whatever the task. So, his coterie of lieutenants and a handful of strong-minded directors always planted the seeds of their ideas in Rogers' mind until they took root there and became his own. For example, a few RCI directors spent years carping at him to hire a professional at RCI to oversee human resources. For all these years, Rogers has been doing the job himself with Alan Horn as his fallback, picking up most of the load on top of his regular job as CFO. In early 2006, Rogers finally did hire a "chief human resources officer," an acknowledgement that the company has outgrown even his ability to exact control over every facet. He admits he was doing the job himself before as an "amateur," saying he "could never afford these people before."

On a scale of one to 10, with 10 being the best, Rogers rated himself as a husband, father, pioneer, citizen, humanitarian and corporate leader.

Husband? 6.

Father? He hesitates. He's thinking about all the time he spent at the office while his children were growing up. Five and a half, he replies.

Pioneer? 10. There was no hint of hesitation here.

Citizen? 10.

Humanitarian? Nine … maybe, nine and a half. "Loretta is better than I am!" he laughs.

Corporate leader? He pauses. "It depends," he says. "Do you mean someone like John Tory?" he asks, referring to his former cable head John H. Tory, who was considered to be his successor until he quit to pursue a life in politics when it became apparent Rogers wasn't going to support him. In a matter-of-fact tone, he says: "John Tory would be a great corporate leader in inspirational messages and so on and so forth, but he may not be a great corporate leader in actually leading them into 'over here' versus 'over here,'" demonstrating with his arm pointing right, then left. "In one sense, I would say, I'm a 9.5. In others, I would say, 4.5. I'm nine and a half [as a leader taking the team] to the promised land, and sometimes, I get frustrated and I'm not as good and as motivating as I should be."

When asked what the future holds for RCI, Rogers says, "Well, I'd start by saying, to hell in a handbasket.

"My world is very turbulent. I enjoy that, doesn't bother me for a minute. And I don't pretend to have all the answers," he says.

Asked separately for her opinion, wife Loretta says, "We should be on the leading edge of technology. What it is, I don't know. But, that's where we should be."

The promised land still lies before him. In cable TV, RCI is still not a national company. Phil Lind says he and Rogers still have one more big deal in them. Will it be Shaw? In cable, the CRTC has allowed regional monopolies. In fiscal 2006, Shaw had revenue of $2.5 billion. Combined, RCI's revenue would surpass $10 billion—still a distant second behind Bell Canada, with almost $18 billion. RCI would gain 2.2 million more cable TV subscribers to whom it can sell wireless phone services. The combination of Telus and RCI—with revenue of $16.8 billion—would result in a more formidable rival to Bell Canada.

In the making of a communications empire, Ted Rogers was consistently overleveraged, walking a very high wire with a threadbare safety net below. It left his rivals and critics speechless. They were constantly amazed that he never once slipped off. If he is anything, Rogers is above all else an investor, perhaps one of the shrewdest Canada has seen. He runs his company as if it were an investment portfolio. He's in it for the long term. He bet on the right technologies at the right time and had the intestinal fortitude, even if his stockholders didn't, to borrow heavily for the future payback of a communications network to rival Bell's. He's ridden the growth wave of technology. He's been lucky, and he knows it. In two eras, BCE lost $23 billion. Rogers made one major mistake, Unitel, and lost $500 million. The Rogers brand is now bigger than Ted himself.

In the end, Rogers survived by doing everything that was considered unorthodox and improper by running a highly leveraged balance sheet. He outlasted his onetime partner, the mighty AT&T, and he's witnessed his nemesis BCE metamorphize back into Bell Canada. He is the last man standing, the lone ranger with Phil Lind as his ever faithful Tonto.

It was once said of Rogers that he could "sell snow to Eskimos." He can be domineering, demanding and impatient. He is also to a fault humble, charming, witty and caring. He's been married to the same woman for 44 years. For all of his fighting words, he's a man who just wants to be liked—although he will never allow that to compromise a business deal. He's a tough, hard-driving serial entrepreneur. Rogers remained loyal to his country and worked within the confines of its regulatory system to great success. Yet, for most of his career, he was reviled in his own country for his success. It is only now, when his major rival—Bell Canada—is suffering, that people are jumping on his bandwagon.

Throughout, Rogers constantly agitated for more. He set off on a course, gathered momentum and became unstoppable. He has been in a rush all his life, driven by fear he would suffer the same fate as his father—death at 38. "He's always telling me he's not going to make it another six months, but he's been telling me that for sixteen years," chuckles John Zeglis.

Rogers has been a man obsessed, striving to live up to his mother's expectations by trying to outrun his father's long shadow. His mother wouldn't live long enough to see the son surpass the father's success. Still, she likely wouldn't have been surprised. She would not have expected anything less.

Fifty years later, Rogers is still trying to buy CFRB. In April 2007, he tried to charm Ian Greenberg, Astral Media Inc's co-founder and new owner, to sell his father's old radio station to him over lunch. It didn't work.

Ted Rogers never quits.

A Ted Rogers Q&A

Through a two-tiered share class, Ted Rogers wields control over RCI, while owning just over one-fifth of the public company's total equity. Since 1999, when *Canadian Business* magazine first began publishing its Rich 100 list, Rogers' net worth has more than doubled. In 2006, he was ranked Canada's fourth wealthiest business titan with a networth of $4.54 billion, up from seventh the previous year courtesy of his company's rocketing share price. Still, he doesn't see himself that way.

Q: When did you ever feel comfortable enough financially to consider yourself rich?

ESR: It's not easy to answer; when you have shares in the family company that you don't want to sell, you really don't consider that to be rich. So, I felt blessed and felt we were very fortunate, but I've never felt rich, sort of like rich people do that have money all over the place: liquid securities, bonds, debentures. I've never felt rich in that way because I'm not rich in that way. I mean I owe money. I still owe money.

Q: What is your greatest fear?

ESR: Death. Particularly mine because my dad died at thirty-eight and so it's been mine since thirty-five.

Q: How do you overcome that fear?

ESR: You don't. You just do your best to work at it. Probably if you fear it you are better off than if you don't fear it. You tend to do things to protect yourself more—you go to the Mayo for checkups, you exercise occasionally.

Q: Which historical figure do you most identify with?

ESR: Winston Churchill. John Diefenbaker. My father, of course.

Q: What is your greatest extravagance?

ESR: The plane.

Q: What is your greatest regret?

ESR: Not spending more time with the children and Loretta, and having to work all the time.

Q: When have you been happiest?

ESR: Well, I've been my happiest getting married, having children, because we didn't think we could have children. That was a very important happy time, a very special time. We were very close to adopting our second child, very close [when] this miracle happened. What else? Business—happiness and disbelief. I must be honest and look back and say we started with seventeen employees and how did we get here? It wasn't part of a plan. It wasn't all thought through. It wasn't like, did you do this to make a lot of money? I did this to honor my father. I have been very lucky, so I have been happy many times.

Q: Which living person do you most admire?

ESR: My wife.

Q: If you could change one thing about your family, what would it be?

ESR: I'd have taught my wife better to be a widow!

Q: If you could come back as a person or a thing, what would you be?

ESR: I wouldn't change a thing.

Q: What is your most treasured possession?

ESR: Oh my goodness. That's hard to think of.

Q: What was the first thing that came to mind?

ESR: I instantly thought of my father's ring 3BP, which I gave to Edward and he lost it. He feels badly about it. Anyway, I've lost lots of things, too. Do I have a possession that I'd like to be buried with or something like that? I don't think so. The Order of Canada, maybe.

Q: What quality do you most admire among your adversaries?

ESR: Well, I think being a thoughtful business person is what you admire, versus somebody who is a maniac and does crazy things.

Q: What do you most value in your friends?

ESR: Loyalty. Comradeship. Love. Caring.

Q: Who's your favorite musician or singer?

ESR: Peter Appleyard. Nat King Cole.

Q: What's your favorite drink?
ESR: Gin and orange juice.

Q: How would you like to die?
ESR: At the end of a speech. You know where you finish a speech and say, "Now that's my last word!" Yeah.

Q: What advice can you give budding entrepreneurs?
ESR: The thing that is most important is to have adequate financing. That's number one. Number two, for me anyway, if you really know what you want to do, if you have a vision, never give up control. Third, surround yourself with good people, hopefully better than you are. Fourth is, follow your instincts. The world's getting so that we have task forces and we have committees to study [things], and we have other committees to compare notes and negotiate. We have committees on top of committees. You know why? Because people do not want to make a decision. If you're going to [run] your own business, I think you have to follow your instincts. Now, that doesn't mean to say that if you realize you're running into a brick wall, you don't back off and maybe go around another way where there is no brick wall at all.

Q: What's your weakest quality and how did you overcome it?
ESR: I think dreaming up so many initiatives is a strength, but it is also a weakness. It is a weakness of a lack of discipline. Have I overcome it? Yes, to a certain extent. I'm supposed to focus and concentrate on those [initiatives] that are the best. So—focus, focus, focus. So, I'm always pushing. But I think that's my job.

Q: What are the most important characteristics of an entrepreneur?
ESR: Hardworking, motivated and resourceful. You just never give up.

Q: What do you think of ball players' salaries?
ESR: They get paid a lot, compared to me. I think it's the luck of the draw.

Q: You probably can't hit a ninety-seven-mile-an-hour fastball, though.
ESR: I sometimes think in the office that's what I do—especially on certain days.

Q: What is your favorite motto?
ESR: "The best is yet to come." I say it often and sometimes if I want to have a lot of fun with people and if it's appropriate, then I will add: "Because it can't get any worse!"

Endnotes

All expressions of currency are in Canadian dollars, unless otherwise noted.

CHAPTER 1

3   **light-socket powered radio:** Rogers merged CKOK with a London, Ontario, radio station in November 1933 and renamed it CKLW.

5   **wireless telephony:** John S. Belrose, "Reginald Aubrey Fessenden and the Birth of Wireless Telephony," *IEEE Antennas and Propagation Magazine*, Vol. 44, No. 2 (April 2002): 40.

5   **first-ever radio broadcast:** Fessenden, the chief chemist for U.S. inventor Thomas Edison, invented, among other things, microphotography, a precursor to microfilm; sonic frequency echo sounding for measurement of depth of oceans and iceberg detection, technology which later became known as SONAR (Sound Navigation and Ranging); and the radio compass, known today as the LORAN. Born in 1866 in East Bolton (now Austin), Quebec, and raised in Fergus, Ontario, Fessenden held some 229 U.S. patents. The U.S. Navy honored him for his contributions to Maritime safety by naming one of its Second World War destroyer escorts after him. For his invention of continuous waves, Fessenden received the John Scott Medal of the City of Philadelphia, whose other recipients include Dr. Marie Curie, Albert Einstein, Thomas Edison and Frederick Banting. One of Canada's greatest inventors, Fessenden couldn't get a job in Canada, having been shunned by McGill University and refused financing by the Canadian government. He died in Bermuda in 1932.

6   **bitter court thoughts:** John S. Belrose, "Reginald Aubrey Fessenden and the Birth of Wireless Telephony," *IEEE Antennas and Propagation Magazine*, Vol. 44, No. 2 (April 2002): 38–47.

6   **"public stunts":** Stephen L. W. Greene, "Who Said Lee de Forest was the 'Father of Radio?,'" *Mass Comm Review*, February 1991.

6   **Audion tube:** See: Ormond Raby, *Radio's First Voice: The Story of Reginald Fessenden* (Toronto: Macmillan Company of Canada Ltd., 1970). John S. Belrose, "Fessenden and the Early History of Radio Science," *The Radioscientist*, Vol. 5, No. 3 (September 1994). T. H. Lee, *The Design of CMOS Radio-Frequency Integrated Circuits, A Nonlinear History of Radio* (University of Cambridge Press, 1998). Steven E. Schoenherr, Professor of Media History, *History of Radio* (University of San Diego, 1999-2000). Stephen L. W. Greene, "Who Said Lee de Forest was the 'Father of Radio?,'" *Mass Comm Review*, February 1991.

9   **de Forest's radio patents:** While Armstrong's patent had been issued on Oct. 6, 1914, nearly a year later de Forest filed for a patent on the same invention, which he sold with all Audion rights to the American Telephone and Telegraph Company (AT&T). AT&T mounted an attack to overturn Armstrong's patent in favor of de Forest's. The ensuing battle lasted twelve years, ending when U.S. Supreme Court sided with de Forest through a judicial misunderstanding of the technical facts. The technical fraternity refused to accept the final verdict. See: Lawrence Lessing, *Man of High Fidelity: Edwin Howard Armstrong*, published in 1956.

10   **CFRB's signal:** The station received a postcard from F.E. Seger in Honolulu, Hawaii, saying CFRB's March 14, 1927 broadcast "was heard well by me." Ian A. Anthony, *Radio Wizard, Edward Samuel*

Rogers and the Revolution of Communications (Toronto: Gage Educational Publishing Co., 2000), 56.

11   **sizeable fortune:** Ian A. Anthony, *Radio Wizard, Edward Samuel Rogers and the Revolution of Communications* (Toronto: Gage Educational Publishing Co., 2000), 101.

12   **all the business greats:** Conrad Black's father, George, who was president of Canadian Breweries, accumulated a large stake of Argus voting shares. In 1978, Conrad Black and associates gained control of Argus, which owned 47 percent of Standard. In 1985, Black sold Standard's radio and TV assets for $126 million to media magnate Allan Slaight.

12   **Interesting test:** "Wireless Wizard Has Performed Big Feat: Amateur at Newmarket Establishes Transatlantic Communication—Interesting Test," *Toronto Star Weekly*, December 17, 1921.

12   **Canadian wireless amateurs:** Ibid.

13   **the wireless game:** "Toronto Boys' Wireless Caught Story of Wreck in Ireland: Ten Year Old Experimenters Have Best Station in Province of Ontario," *Toronto Telegram*, July 21, 1913.

13   **mass of wires:** Ted Rogers, in a November 1915 letter to his mother from Pickering College, where he attended school, as recounted in Ian A. Anthony's book *Radio Wizard, Edward Samuel Rogers and the Revolution of Communications* (Toronto: Gage Educational Publishing Co., 2000), 35.

13   **a record for Canadian and British amateur stations:** "Amateur Establishes a New Radio Record— Successful in Holding Conversation with England," *Toronto Star*, December 18, 1923.

13   **the tribute of his admirers:** E. S. Rogers' friend and partner Bert Trestrail in a two-page memorial letter to employees of Canadian Radio Corp., the parent company of Rogers-Majestic. Ian A. Anthony, *Radio Wizard, Edward Samuel Rogers and the Revolution of Communications* (Toronto: Gage Educational Publishing Co., 2000), 100–101.

13   **"that describes Ted Rogers":** Radio broadcaster Gordon Sinclair's comments on a special radio program aired on CFRB to commemorate the station's twentieth anniversary.

17   **zoot suits:** Zoot suits were popular men's suits in the forties with wide-legged, tight-cuffed trousers and a long coat with wide lapels and heavily padded, wide shoulders.

CHAPTER 2

22   **use it for free:** Interview with Clive Eastwood.

27   **archetypal underdog:** Diefenbaker was defeated twice provincially and twice federally when he ran for public office. He was also defeated when he ran for mayor of Prince Albert, Saskatchewan.

27   **UCC pal Henry (Hal) Jackman:** Jackman's father, Harry R. Jackman, built the Empire Life group of financial service companies during the Great Depression. His son parlayed his inheritance, using his father's connections, into E-L Financial Corp., whose subsidiaries included Empire Life Insurance Co., Dominion of Canada General Insurance Co. and the Casualty Co. of Canada. Jackman, through E-L Financial, controlled Victoria and Grey Trust and National Trust Co. In 1997, he sold National Trust to Bank of Nova Scotia for $1.25 billion. The family has deep political roots. His father served two terms as a Tory MP in Canada's House of Commons in the forties. His mother, philanthropist Mary Rowell Jackman, was the daughter of former MP and chief justice of Ontario Newton Wesley Rowell. His sister, Nancy Ruth, was appointed to the Senate in 2005.

CHAPTER 3

29   **a small viewing fee:** *Toast of the Town* was renamed *The Ed Sullivan Show* in 1955.

30   **regular viewers:** Dana M. Lee, Television Technical Theory Unplugged, Version 5.0. (Ryerson University, 2004), http://www.danalee.ca/ttt/index.htm.

30   **private broadcasters:** On October 9, 1931, Canada's first TV station, VE9EC in Montreal, jointly owned by radio station CKAC and the newspaper *La Presse*, went on the air with neon-red pictures, although practically no one had TV receivers to view the images. The station collapsed during the Depression.

32   **a voting trust:** CKLW-AM 800, known as CKLW The Motor City, was, ironically, based in Windsor. The station's 50,000-watt signal meant it could be heard in 32 U.S. states and four Canadian provinces. According to the 2004 TV documentary *Radio Revolution: The Rise and Fall of the Big 8*, CKLW-AM became the most powerful force in U.S. music business in the sixties and seventies.

32   **found another buyer:** In 1970, RKO General was forced by the Canadian government to divest itself of its Canadian holdings. The stations were sold to a consortium of the CBC (25 percent) and Baton Broadcasting (75 percent). Later Baton sold the radio station to CHUM. When the CBC took full ownership of the television station, it changed its call letters to CBET.

32   **what he asked of Diefenbaker:** Peter Newman, in reporting the anecdote in a 1994 *Maclean's* story, said Rogers' request, which occurred in 1961, was over a policy decision.

34   **Joel Aldred:** Aldred won the Distinguished Flying Cross as a squadron leader while attached to the Royal Air Force Bomber Command overseas.

36   **media concentration:** BBG chairman Dr. Andrew Stewart, the president of the University of Alberta, forewarned Thomson it was unlikely the BBG would approve the bid given his extensive radio and newspapers holdings and despite the expertise he might bring to Canadian TV. Thomson had acquired Glasgow-based Scottish Television in 1957. Russell Braddon, *Roy Thomson of Fleet Street* (Collins: 1965), 248–249.

36   **Toronto's powerful business elite:** Timothy Eaton founded the T. Eaton Co. in 1869. Upon his death, his son John Craig, known as "Sir John," ran Eaton's until he died prematurely at the age of 46. His nephew, Robert Young, took over for the next 20 years until the rightful heir, John David, was ready to take over the company. According to Rod McQueen in his book *The Eatons: The Rise and Fall of Canada's Royal Family*, John D. was an alcoholic, who spent most of his time on his yacht moored in Vancouver. He left the day-to-day running of the department store chain to an executive committee, and during the sixties and until his death in 1973, he hired outside management to run the company. When he died, the company's ownership and decision-making power was left equally to his four sons—John Craig, Fredrick, Thor and George. They destroyed in less than 30 years what their ancestors had taken a century to build. Eaton's, the once-proud department store chain, went bankrupt in 1999. The assets were eventually acquired by the Canadian subsidiary of U.S. giant Sears Roebuck and Corp. In their heyday, the Eatons were the closest Canada had to an aristocracy, living more extravagantly than most crowned heads.

36   **buy the *Telegram*:** Bassett, who reportedly paid $4 million, outbid three other bidders, including Jack Kent Cooke. McCullagh, who bought the *Toronto Globe* in 1936 and combined it with *The Mail and Empire* to create *The Globe and Mail*, acquired the *Telegram* in 1948 and turned it into a dynamic attractive paper. Bassett closed the money-losing *Telegram* in 1971. Sources: Robert Fulford, "The dazzling life and death of a press baron," *The Globe and Mail* (April 15, 1998): C1. _____. "Bassett, Associates purchase Telegram, price not disclosed," Toronto Star (November 19, 1952): 1.

37   **"thirty-seven percent":** Susan Gittins, *CTV: The Television Wars* (Toronto: Stoddart Publishing Co., 1999), 19.

37   **Rogers never expected:** Aldred Rogers' shareholding was reduced to 34 percent to make room for the consortium's final partner, Paul Nathanson.

37   **"it takes one to know one":** Susan Gittins, *CTV: The Television Wars* (Toronto: Stoddart Publishing Co., 1999), 19.

38   **Bassett consortium:** Paul Nathanson's father, Nathan, was sent to Canada in 1920 by Paramount Pictures Corp.'s Adolph Zukor to establish the Canadian subsidiary of movie theaters known as Famous Players Canadian Corp. He left in 1938 to create the rival Odeon Theater chain. Charles Dubin is best known for chairing the 1988 inquiry into the use of performance-enhancement drugs after Canadian sprinter Ben Johnson had been stripped of his gold medal at the Seoul Olympics. In 2003, Dubin agreed to serve as one of the two public-interest directors on the board of Paul Martin's family-owned Canada Steamship Lines to ensure the company wouldn't reap any benefits from the country's possible future prime minister.

38   **appear less Tory blue:** The breakdown of common equity among the founders before ABC was: Baton, through the Telegram, 40 percent; Aldred Rogers, 34 percent; Heathcourt, 6 percent; Paul Nathanson, 10 percent; and Foster Hewitt, 10 percent.

39   **show back on the road :** Maggie Siggins, *Bassett* (Toronto: J. Lorimer, 1979).

39   **the hearings set the benchmark:** Pierre Berton, "Mr. Jack Kent Cooke's Amazing, Mystical Conversion," *Toronto Star* (March 28, 1960): 17.

39   **He spent \$4.5 million:** Susan Gittins, *CTV: The Television Wars* (Toronto: Stoddart Publishing Co., 1999), 63–64.

40   **exercised his power:** Nathan Cohen, "How will BBG handle Aldred stock transfer?" *Toronto Star* (August 22, 1961): 20.

40   **ABC agreed to buy 25 percent:** Susan Gittins, *CTV: The Television Wars* (Toronto: Stoddart Publishing Co., 1999), 65.

41   **"how long he has to think":** Interview with Ted Rogers.

41   **"you sons of bitches":** Susan Gittins, *CTV: The Television Wars* (Toronto: Stoddart Publishing Co., 1999), 67.

41   **power under the Broadcasting Act:** _____. *Toronto Star* (March 13, 1962): 6.

41   **violating the spirit:** Dennis Braithwaite, "BBG May Probe Finance Setup of Private TV," *The Globe and Mail* (January 4, 1962): 23.

41   **Joel Aldred:** Maggie Siggins, *Bassett* (Toronto: J. Lorimer, 1979).

41   **a minority owner:** Bassett gave Rogers the option of increasing his stake to a maximum of 17 percent. Rogers cannot quite remember, but he believes he did increase his position to 17 percent.

CHAPTER 4

45   **U.S. media and sports mogul:** Cooke sold CKEY to Shoreacres Broadcasting Co., a consortium of various companies, including *The Globe and Mail* and Canadian Westinghouse. In 1966, Shoreacres sold the station to Maclean Hunter Publishing Co.

46   **elevator music:** Piggott increased it to 9,450 watts the following year. See "Report on FM," in *Canadian Broadcaster*, March 9, 1967.

46   **quality of the sound:** Ray Cook, former CHFI technician.

46   **to acquire CHFI-FM:** Rogers sold the background-music business to Muzak's owner, Associated Broadcasting Co., in March 1961 for \$55,000, more than half of what he paid to acquire CHFI-FM. CHUM became the Canadian franchise holder for Muzak when it bought Associated Broadcasting in 1969, since renamed CHUM Satellite Services.

46   **CHFI's radio and transmission equipment:** Ray Cook owns Toronto-based Starlight Studios, doing audio, video and optical sound transfers for the film industry.

47   **rummies sought shelter:** Interview with Russ Holden.

47   **the building shakes:** Former CHFI technician Ray Cook recalls the building shook all the time; it had a natural rhythm. It was so bad that they brought in University of Toronto consultants to look into the problem.

48   **he spent eight hundred dollars:** Board of Broadcast Governors Transcript (August 22, 1961), 465–466.

48   **most powerful FM signal:** _____. "CHFI-FM Goes All Out With 'Canada's Most Powerful Voice,'" *Canadian Broadcaster* (April 20, 1961). FM antennas differ from AM. Successful FM transmission depends on antenna height above the ground because FM radio waves are line of sight, which means they don't follow the earth's curvature. AM coverage is based on groundwave propagation, meaning ground conductivity is more important than the actual height above ground. FM antennas are comparatively small devices mounted on the top, or sides, of towers, while the entire AM tower

is used as a radiator. Source: John Battison, "Antenna Basics," in *Radio Magazine*, March 1, 2001. See http://beradio.com/departments/radio_antenna_basics/.

48   **revamping 1050 CHUM:** Cooke's CKEY had a 37 percent share of the Toronto audience, while CHUM had just 14 percent before Waters changed formats. After adopting rock, Waters doubled CHUM's market share.

48   **rock 'n' roll:** Jennifer Wells, "Remembering the glory days," *Toronto Star* (July 13, 2006): C9.

49   **FM concentration:** _____. *Monetary Times* (November 1965): 33–34.

49   **an FM radio:** _____. "CHFI-FM Goes All Out with 'Canada's Most Powerful Voice.'" *Canadian Broadcaster* (April 20, 1961).

49   **only one household in six:** Newspaper ad, *Canadian Broadcaster* (April 8, 1961): 9.

50   **FM penetration in Toronto:** _____. *Monetary Times* (November 1965): 33–34. Rogers' cost for the radios was $32 plus $0.95 delivery. BBG transcripts (August 22, 1961): 518.

50   **clinking champagne glasses:** Rogers bought out Joel Aldred in January 1962 to become CHFI's sole owner.

50   **the better buy:** Newspaper ad, *Canadian Broadcaster* (April 8, 1961): 9.

50   **stereophonic sound:** Ottawa didn't allow FM stations to broadcast in stereo until September 1, 1961, three months after the FCC permitted U.S. stations to broadcast in stereo.

51   **he was indeed a director:** Gordon Sinclair, "Glance," *Toronto Daily Star* (May 13, 1961): 21.

52   **parking tickets:** Former CHFI radio technician Ray Cook.

53   **Toronto refused to lease:** Andrew MacFarlane, *Toronto Telegram* (April 25, 1962).

54   **too much interference:** The higher the frequency, the higher the skip distance from the transmitter to the receiver once it's been reflected from the ionosphere. The radio signal would bounce off the ionosphere at night and travel great distances, causing interference with other signals.

54   **existing AM stations:** Board of Broadcast Governors (August 22, 1961): 484–495.

55   **land purchases:** He'd eventually sell 1540.

56   **need for AM stations:** Staff, "3 Seek AM Station In Toronto Area," *The Globe and Mail* (February 12, 1962). 13.

56   **Sunrise Serenade:** Herbert quit years later when, in his new role as CHFI's traffic reporter, the helicopter crashed into Lake Ontario just as it was about to land. He became an insurance agent.

56   **changes in tonal quality:** Marvin Schiff, "CHFI enters AM broadcast field," *The Globe and Mail* (August 9, 1962): 4.

57   **From sunrise to sunset:** Newspaper ad, *Toronto Daily Star* (September 11, 1962): 9.

57   **clear channels:** The usage of radio frequencies was governed by the 1941 multilateral North American Regional Broadcasting Agreement (NARBA), whereby certain frequencies were assigned to super-powered AM stations known as "clear channel" stations, which are protected from co-channel interference from neighboring countries. Most clear channels didn't have another station on their channel at night on the continent, and while class 2 stations could be on a clear channel frequency, they could only co-share the frequency during the day so long as there was no interference. These stations were called "daytimers." The 1981 Rio Agreement superseded NARBA. Source: FCC, Canadian Communications Foundation. See http://www.fcc.gov/mb/audio/bickel/daytime.html#FN1.

57   **burning through a lot of cash:** Newspaper ad, *The Globe and Mail* (October, 20, 1962).

60   **trafficking in radio licenses:** _____. "Radio Frequency Traffic Charged." Canadian Press in *The Globe and Mail* (June 8, 1963): 9.

60   **split frequencies:** Canada had just one split frequency in Saskatchewan, where separate transmitters for daylight and night-time broadcasting were used to transmit French-language broadcasting to the local francophone community.

60   "in the face of adversity": Rogers' daily organizers.

61   Rogers signed the material: _____. "The Young Man Who Gets What He Wants," *Monetary Times* (November 1965): 34.

CHAPTER 5

64   Parson became president of Woolworth: Parson, an accountant by training, lived lavishly. In 1918, he bought the famous Shadow Lawn Estate where U.S. president Woodrow Wilson summered. After it was destroyed by fire in 1927, he hired Philadelphia architect Horace Trumbauer to design a fireproof French-style 130-room mansion styled after the Palace of Versailles. After the stock market crash of 1929, he lost most of his fortune. In 1939, Shadow Lawn was sold at public auction for US$100. Parson died in New York City on July 9, 1940, in debt. His widow paid off their tax liens from the sale of Shadow Lawn's furnishings.

67   "This was inconvenient": Board of Broadcast Governors (October 22, 1963): 31–32.

68   Toronto's most listened to and respected radio stations: Rogers lost his attempt to get the CBC's more favorable 860 spot on the AM band when CBC wanted to convert it into a French-language station after the BBG decided his split frequencies weren't good enough to broadcast French-language programming. Dennis Braithwaite, "French at 1540?" *The Globe and Mail* (January 28, 1964): 31.

68   FM was growing in popularity: _____. "The Young Man Who Gets What He Wants," *Monetary Times* (November 1965): 34.

69   regulatory battles: _____. *Ibid.*

70   He was limited to 1kW: Rogers had applied for 10 kW of daytime power but was scaled back to 1 kW after Rochester complained to the FCC about possible interference.

70   to support his fledgling cable business: Rogers' daily organizers.

72   Rogers had spent more than $1 million: _____. "CHFI Makes Million Dollar Move," *Canadian Broadcaster* (April 7, 1966): 3.

72   almost a letdown: _____. "The Young Man Who Gets Want He Wants," *Monetary Times* (November 1965): 33–34.

73   AM signals are reflected: FCC. See http://www.fcc.gov/mb/audio/bickel/daytime.html#FN1.

73   Maltrite Communications Groups transmitters: Maltz was the driving force behind Cleveland's Rock and Roll Hall of Fame and Museum. An espionage buff, he founded the International Spy Museum in Washington, D.C.

73   move the station: In 1979, in exchange for vacating the 680 frequency to allow Rogers to move its transmitter site to Grimsby, Ontario, on the south shore of Lake Ontario, Maltz' WNYR was granted permission by Canada to move to a Canadian clear channel, 990 kHz.

73   pounded the table: The late Nikita Khrushchev, premier of the Soviet Union, famously removed one of his shoes and began pounding it on the table during the United Nations General Assembly proceedings in 1960.

74   relocated the 680 transmitter site to Grimsby: CFTR 680 boosted its power to 50 kW day from the new transmission site at Grimsby in 1985. Night service continued from the Mississauga site.

74   paying CKGB: In 2002, Rogers acquired CKGB in a package of radio stations from Standard Broadcasting.

75   rush-hour traffic reports: CKEY's Dini Petty was the second announcer. Wearing her trademark pink jumpsuit, Petty was the first female traffic reporter to pilot her own helicopter.

77   confusion: Blair Kirby, "Few surprises in CTV lesson on how the other half lives," *The Globe and Mail* (June 7, 1971): 15.

77   "the new CFTR": *Toronto Daily Star* (June 21, 1971): 5.

77 **Bobby Gimby:** Of all of his accomplishments, Bobby Gimby, who composed the popular "Ca-na-da" song for the 1967 centennial celebrations, is best remembered as the featured soloist and raconteur with CBC's long-running *The Happy Gang* radio program.

78 **obtained in a contra deal:** Interview with Vaughn Bjerre. The invitations naturally read 680 magnums.

CHAPTER 6

81 **3 Frybrook Rd.:** Frybrook, previously owned by media mogul Jack Kent Cooke, was built in 1932 by Robert J. Christie, scion of the Toronto founder of Kraft Corp.'s biscuit maker, Christie Brown & Co. The Christie family considered 3 Frybrook their cottage. They lived at 29 Queen's Park Ave., a Victorian mansion that now serves as the women's residences for the University of Toronto's St. Joseph's College. The Rogers' home is listed as one of Toronto's heritage properties.

83 **CATV systems:** Ken Easton, *Building an Industry: A History of Cable Television and its Development in Canada* (East Lawrencetown, NS: Pottersfield Press, 2000), 135.

84 **delivered via coaxial cable:** Initially a success, the Etobicoke experiment was shut down in April 1965. The service was expensive and the company was too slow to offer varied content. Telemeter had 5,600 customers by the end of 1961, 40 percent penetration of its wired area. By the time it pulled the plug, penetration had fallen to 25 percent.

84 **Leafs away-from-home games:** Dennis Braithwaite, "A Costly Experiment," *The Globe and Mail* (February 26, 1963): 15.

84 **gigantic common antenna:** Jarmain had to remove the antenna after Gerry died of a heart attack during the field trial. Jarmain consequently was left without a partner and insufficient financial support.

84 **to meet Wes Hosick:** David Graham, an Ottawa Valley lad turned Harvard MBA, acquired Hosick Television Co. to form Graham Cable TV Ltd. Graham, one of Barbara Amiel's ex-husbands, is not related to John Graham or Ted Rogers.

85 **1 million feet of cable:** After 1967, Bell limited the total territory of any one applicant to 2 million square feet.

85 **Licensees risked losing their territories:** Ken Easton, *Building an Industry: A History of Cable Television and its Development in Canada* (East Lawrencetown, NS: Pottersfield Press, 2000), 149.

86 **Coaxial Colourview Ltd.:** Rogers bought out the remaining 10 percent stake from Barry Ross and his partner, Melvin Shipman, in May 1975.

87 **"like a son of a bitch":** Stanbury admits he's been credited with having made that remark, although he doesn't actually recall having said it.

87 **"if it wasn't for Ted.":** Goodman interview (2003).

88 **"he went far beyond that.":** _____. "Basic Cable: Mergers and Acquisitions," *Mediacaster* (November 2002).

88 **public's demand for access:** Community Antenna Television, 1970, 8709-817, published by Authority of the Minister of Industry, Trade and Commerce (March 1972): 9.

88 **$18 for the installation:** Ibid.

89 **subsidizing cable:** Robert Babe, *Telecommunications in Canada: Technology, Industry and Government* (Toronto: University of Toronto Press, 1990), 210. Quoted from *Manitoba Department of Consumer, Corporate and Internal Services, Broadcasting and Cable Television: A Manitoba Perspective* (1974), 34.

89 **Department of Communications:** Canada was the first country in the world to launch a commercial domestic communications satellite. Created in 1969, Telesat Canada launched the Anik A1 in 1972. The federal government sold its stake in Telesat in 1992 for $155 million to Alouette Telecommunications Inc., a BCE-controlled consortium composed of the satellite company's original co-founders and satellite builder Spar Aerospace Ltd. The telephone monopolies already owned 41 percent, giving

them a 94 percent lock on the equity. Alouette forced the two remaining minority shareholders—Canadian Pacific Ltd. and Ontario Northland Transportation Commission—to tender their shares under the Canadian Business Corporations Act provisions. CP, at the time fighting Bell in the long-distance wars with partner Ted Rogers, owned 3.75 percent and unsuccessfully tried to prevent the squeeze-out through the courts. In 1998, BCE paid $158 million to acquire full control. Jean Monty fulfilled his predecessor Raymond Cyr's long-held wishes for BCE to absorb Telesat. Eight years later, Monty's successor, Michael Sabia, orchestrated Telesat's sale. In December 2006, BCE agreed to sell Telesat and its seven birds for a stunning $3.25 billion in *cash* to the federal government's civil servants, Mounties and soldiers, through their Public Sector Pension Investment Board and New York–based satellite communications company Loral Space & Communications Inc. Sabia didn't even have a chance to complete the transaction before the pension and private equity funds began hungrily circling Ma Bell. He sold Telesat for almost a billion dollars more than what Bay Street had anticipated. Instead of waging a public proxy fight to oust Bell's board and/or its management, the Ontario Teachers Pension Plan—Canada's most outspoken shareholder rights and corporate governance activist and Bell's largest institutional investor with, ironically, a seat on the board—chose to snare the largesse for itself.

90   **Canadian owned:** Department of Communications, *Instant World: A Report on Telecommunications in Canada* (Ottawa: Information Canada, 1971), 199.

90   **Canada's parliament revised Bell's charter:** Robert Babe, *Telecommunications in Canada: Technology, Industry and Government* (Toronto: University of Toronto Press, 1990), 185–186.

90   **"common-carriers, pure and simple.":** Dwayne Winseck, "Canadian telecommunications: a history and political economy of media reconvergence," *Canadian Journal of Communication*, vol. 22, issue 2 (Toronto: Spring 1997).

90   **controlling CATV:** Robert Babe, *Telecommunications in Canada: Technology, Industry and Government* (Toronto: University of Toronto Press, 1990), 185–186.

90   **retaining ownership of the cables:** Ibid., 215–216.

91   **pole rentals:** The change came in 1977 after the CRTC expanded its oversight to include telecommunications.

91   **coax is a step up:** Coaxial cable's message-carrying capacity was more than 300 times that of the copper pair wire used for telephone local loops.

91   **capacity of coaxial cable:** Ralph Lee Smith, "Wired Nation," *The Nation* (May 18, 1970).

92   **The head-end:** Because each local over-the-air TV network, known today as a broadcast network, as opposed to a cable, or specialty, channel, had its own frequency, the cable TV operator needed an antenna for each channel. These antennas were usually built into a single tower, known as the master antenna. Cable TV systems now tend to pick up local TV programming through a dedicated coaxial line installed between the local station and the head-end. Cable, or specialty channels, such as CNN and TSN, are picked up by satellite dish antennas.

93   **"I'll move it.":** The antennas are now perched on the roof of First Canadian Place.

CHAPTER 7

95   **Blue Circle Industries PLC:** Four years later, Lafarge SA acquired Blue Circle, selling St. Marys to Brazil's Votorantim Group SA for €825 million (C$1.12 billion).

96   **J. Stuart MacKay:** Nicholas Cotter, "Media revolution forecast," *The Globe and Mail* (September 20, 1969): B1.

97   **too much control:** Patrick Scott, "Ottawa orders Bassett to get out of cable TV," *Toronto Daily Star* (July 11, 1969): 1. Leslie Millin, "CRTC orders Bassett to sell his interests in cable TV in Metro," *The Globe and Mail* (July 11, 1969): 1. _____. "Rogers plans to buy out Bassett," *Marketing* (July 21, 1969): 2.

98   **cost to lay cable:** Frank Slover, "Cable TV is called profitable investment," *The Globe and Mail* (October 12, 1972): B2.

98   **at $4.50 a month per subscriber:** Pat McNenly, "Why everyone wants to plug into the cable TV boom," *Toronto Daily Star* (January 3, 1970): 13.

98   **"We're betting we'll get our money back.":** Ron Lowman, "The men who struck it rich in Metro's cable TV market," *Toronto Daily Star* (April 18, 1969): 20.

99   **"It never sleeps."** Matthew Ingram, "TD president announces retirement," *The Globe and Mail* (September 23, 1994): B1.

99   **"last pound of flesh":** Ibid.

100   **family and friends filled the void:** According to Rogers's daily organizers, Loretta pledged $3-million worth of securities; his sister, Ann, pledged stocks and bonds worth $300,000; and, Rogers' best friend, Toby Hull, then married to a Seagram heiress, hypothecated $100,000.

100   **"he's flush today."** Blair Kirby, "Fisher, Hewitt in CHIN sweepstakes," *The Globe and Mail* (August 26, 1970): 12.

106   **Rogers Cable's community channel:** Iannuzzi produced multilingual programming at Citytv from 1972 to 1979 before founding Toronto's multilingual TV station CFMT-TV, which Rogers saved from bankruptcy in 1986 when he acquired it and later renamed it OMNI, now with stations in British Columbia and Manitoba.

107   **Rogers Cable introduced so called converters:** Frank Slover, "Chairman of cable TV association views regulations as a means of providing stability for expansion," *The Globe and Mail* (August 29, 1972): B5.

107   **spending $200,000 a year on programming:** _____. "The Wired World," *The Financial Post* (March 13, 1971).

109   **"Trojan Horse menace":** Matthew Fraser, *Free-for-All* (Toronto: Stoddart Publishing Co., 1999), 72.

109   **Canadian advertisers:** Barry Berlin, *The American Trojan Horse: U.S. Television Confronts Canadian Economic and Cultural Nationalism* (New York: Greenwood Press, 1990), 14.

110   **deleting U.S. commercials:** _____. "Wrong Way," *The Globe and Mail* (November 30, 1973): 6.

110   **cultural protectionism:** Barry Berlin, *The American Trojan Horse: U.S. Television Confronts Canadian Economic and Cultural Nationalism* (New York: Greenwood Press, 1990), 107.

111   **"fairy godfather":** _____. "The Wired World," *The Financial Post* (March 13, 1971).

111   **advertising:** Ian Rodger, "Rate-of-return concept is rejected for TV regulation," *The Globe and Mail* (May 30, 1974): B2.

111   **CNN-like coverage:** Nicholaas Van Rijn, "Drama live on TV thanks to fast action by cable company," *Toronto Star* (March 22, 1977): 1. Blair Kirby, "100 Signatures want CBC reform," *The Globe and Mail* (March 22, 1977): 17.

111   **"fragmenting the local audience":** _____. "Basic Cable: Mergers and Acquisitions," *Mediacaster* (November 2002), http://www.mediacastermagazine.com/issues/ISarticle.asp?id=76453&story_id=136594163354&issue=11012002&PC=.

112   **culturally sanitizing the programming:** Terence Corcoran, "Banana republic broadcasting," *The Globe and Mail* (July 26, 1997): B2.

CHAPTER 8

114   **Brascan:** Immediately following the sale of the Brazilian utility, cash-rich Brascan became the subject of a takeover by the Toronto Bronfman family's Edper Group. Moore tried to make Brascan indigestible by attempting, and ultimately failing, to buy retailer F.W. Woolworth Co. in what went down as one of the nastiest takeover fights ever. Ian Brown, "How Jake Moore lost Brascan," *Canadian Business* (November 1979): 122–150.

114   **Canada's financial establishment:** Ian Brown, "How Jake Moore lost Brascan," *Canadian Business* (November 1979): 122.

115 Shepard died: _____. "Cable Industry Loses Leader," *Cable Communications* (February 1976): 1.

115 "If it is just an investment": Roderick Oram, "Rogers acquires 20 percent of Premier," *The Globe and Mail* (April 1, 1976): B9.

116 had two major CCL shareholders: Peter Legault. Royal Trust owned 18.3 percent, according to January 1979 CRTC documentation. Likely, Royal Trust sold stock on the open market.

117 buy the Jonlab block: John Graham's testimony at CRTC's January 1978 hearings, pages 190–220.

120 "the world is not always a nice place." Jack Miller, "Quiet men dread being devoured by dynamo Ted," *Toronto Star* (January 19, 1978): C1.

120 caustic personal attack: Jack Miller, "Quiet men dread being devoured by dynamo Ted," *Toronto Star* (January 19, 1978): C1.

120 the CRTC decided Rogers was the sole applicant: Barbara Keddy, "CRTC chief not upset with by Rogers proposal," *The Globe and Mail* (September 8, 1978): B4.

121 Edper agreed to sell: RTL completed the share purchase from Edper in January 1979, after the CRTC approved the transfer of control.

122 "distrust of people making money": Rogers' daily organizer.

122 a bottle of whiskey: Interview with Phil Lind.

122 takeover: *Financial Post*, September 16, 1978.

123 ran up against the system: Hardin and the Capital Cable Co-operative, a group of about 500 people in Victoria, B.C., wanted to establish a subscriber-owned cable TV system in Victoria.

124 CCL team: Herschell Hardin, *Closed Circuits: The Sellout of Canadian Television* (Vancouver: Douglas & McIntyre Ltd., 1985), 252.

124 evil of corporate takeovers: CRTC. Transcript of Hearing, Volume 2 (September 13, 1978): 507–518.

125 cursed the Rogers team: Ted Jarmain no longer recalls muttering the curse.

126 "two antagonists": Barbara Keddy, "CRTC chief not upset by Rogers proposal," *The Globe and Mail*, (September 8, 1978): B4.

126 Roger' purchase of CCL: The CRTC's approval of Rogers' purchase of CCL was dimmed by the news of the illness of Loretta's brother Richard Robinson. Loretta adored her older brother, who was four years her senior. He served as an RAF pilot in West Germany in the 1950s before moving with his wife Wendy Patricia Blagden, a socialite friend of Loretta's, to Toronto, where he worked at Imperial Oil as a market research analyst. In 1979, just months after his diagnosis, Robinson, 44, died tragically of cancer. Lord and Lady Martonmere established a bursary in their son's name at Lakefield College School in Lakefield, Ontario, where Robinson's 16-year-old son was in attendance.

126 partisan politics: Ian Brown, "The hoisting of the jolly Rogers," *Maclean's* (January 22, 1979): 30.

126 funeral wreath: Rogers says Gooch left it behind. Gooch does not recall any funeral wreath being left behind. Rogers asked Gooch if he wanted to stay but Gooch, an Australian-born sailor, who had decided to go off sailing regardless of the outcome, replied that Rogers already had one finance chief, so what would he want two for? In 2002, Gooch, 63, sailed solo, non-stop around the world in a record-breaking 177 days, the first person to complete such a trip from a West Coast port, Victoria, British Columbia.

128 "trying to takeover your company": Gordon Pitts, "TV not a priority for the man who brought cable to Canada," *The Globe and Mail* (July 16, 2001): B1.

128 Systems Dimension Ltd.: SDL was sold to Crown Life Insurance Co.

129 attempts to sell Premier: Rod Nutt, "Premier founder 'willing to sell to Eastern buyer.'" *Vancouver Sun* (November 6, 1979): D1.

129 **"show business":** Herschel Hardin, *Closed Circuits* (Vancouver: Douglas & McIntyre Ltd., 1985), 250.

130 **cable TV industry:** Edward Clifford, "Cablesystems prepares to take bid for strength to compete to CRTC," *The Globe and Mail* (March 1, 1980): B16.

131 **they sparred openly:** The CRTC refused to permit Telesat to join the Trans-Canada Telephone System after it had already received DOC and ministerial approval. The Cabinet intervened to reverse the CRTC's decision. In 1979, the Commission then approved CNCP's application to connect with the privately owned telephone companies.

131 **Telecommunications Act:** Clyne recommended the first cable companies to offer non-broadcast services—such as fire and burglar alarm services and Telidon, Ottawa's newly developed Internet-style chat and Web-page system that was ultimately a commercial failure. See "Telecommunications and Canada," Consultative Committee on the Implications of Telecommunications for Canadian Sovereignty, pp. 17–22.

131 **defense against Bell Canada:** Ian Brown, "The hoisting of the jolly Rogers," *Maclean's* (January 22, 1979): 30.

131 **Bell was actively working:** Robert Babe, *Telecommunications in Canada: Technology, Industry and Government* (Toronto: University of Toronto Press, 1990), 186.

132 **CCL's endeavors:** In 1980, SaskTel began constructing the world's longest commercial fiber optic network. It completed the build out in 1984, connecting 52 of the province's largest communities with 3,268 kilometers of fiber optical cable.

132 **competition and regulation:** Barbara Keddy, "Bell seeks to take over cable TV service," *The Globe and Mail* (December 13, 1978): 1.

133 **"national cable system":** Ian Brown, "The hoisting of the jolly Rogers," *Maclean's* (January 22, 1979): 30.

CHAPTER 9

135 **FCC lifted the freeze:** Mark Robichaux, *Cable Cowboy: John Malone and the Rise of the Modern Cable Business* (New York: John Wiley & Sons Inc., 2002), 15–16.

135 **Ali-Frazier fight:** ATC launched its satellite service in Jackson, Mississippi, the next day. Two years earlier in 1973, HBO experimented with putting its signal on the Canadian Anik II satellite to deliver the Ernie Shavers–Jimmy Ellis heavyweight boxing match to the NCTA convention, but the bout only lasted one round. Thomas P. Southwick, *Distant Signals* (Overland Park, Kansas: Primedia, 1999), 113–115.

135 **receiving dishes or earth stations:** Brenda Maddox, "The Wiring of America," *The Economist* (June 20, 1981): 26.

136 **They offered to fund:** United Tribune Cable Co., jointly owned by Tribune Publishing Co. of Chicago and United Cable Television of Denver, which suggested its cable TV system could turn on and off air conditioners to control electricity usage on hot summer days to avoid blackouts, promised to plant 20,000 trees if Sacramento awarded it the city franchise. *See* Peter Kerr, "Cable Notes: Cities are waking up to what were empty promises," *The New York Times* (December 11, 1983): 38.

136 **investigation into corruption:** In 1971, Irving Kahn, the chairman of TelePromTer, which held the Upper Manhattan franchise, was sentenced to prison in connection with a $15,000 bribe paid to the mayor to secure the Johnstown, Pennsylvania, franchise. He also testified, with two other unindicted company executives, about bribery for the franchise in Trenton, New Jersey. He was later heralded by the cable industry as a visionary for recognizing that the future lay in electronic information, not relayed TV signals.

137 **field-trial limbo:** NABU, an AOL forerunner, provided interactive software, including videogames, to home computers by cable TV connections. Its founder, John Kelly, later co-founded SHL Systemhouse and later JetForm Corp. The federal government spent $65 million (with matching funds from the private sector) to develop Telidon, a protocol for transmission and display of graphic information that was technologically superior to European videotex terminals but commercially a flop. Telidon

was developed by the federal government's innovative research lab Communications Research Centre (CRC) and Bell-Northern Research Laboratories (now Nortel). Hamilton-Piercy advised the CRC on the project. Quebec remained a testing ground for interactive TV. In January 1990, André Chagnon's Vidéotron introduced Videoway, an interactive TV service, albeit in a limited, analogue form. The innovative set-top boxes delivered two-way messaging, electronic games, online banking and the ability to monitor hydro consumption. In 1979, Bell trialed Vista, a two-way TV system that was scrapped four years later. In 1988, Bell received CRTC approval for a two-year market trial to test a new Internet-like service named Alex, after Alexander Graham Bell. Alex died in 1994.

137   **Broadcasting Act:** Public Notice CRTC 1986-27. Proposed Regulations Respecting Cable Television Broadcasting Receiving Undertakings. Ottawa, February 13, 1986. On August 1, 1986, the CRTC deregulated cable rates in its first new cable TV regulations since 1976. See Public Notice CRTC 1986-182.

138   **"cable service is not considered an essential public service":** Sid Adilman, "Cable TV fee increases a part of deregulation," *Toronto Star* (February 26, 1986): F1.

138   **owned slices of America:** Standard acquired part of Cablecasting's Valley Cable TV, which had the franchise for the west San Fernando Valley area of Los Angeles.

138   **fibre optic ring architecture:** Rather than running fiber out to subscribers in a standard tree-and-branch layout, Rogers encircled each of its territories with a primary ring that was in turn connected to the secondary tree-and-branch coax networks that fed its subscribers directly. The primary ring architecture brought fiber closer to the home and provided redundancy. Jim Careless, "A path to digital cable," *Communications News* (October 1, 1998): 34.

140   **The participants included:** The tradition continues, although they are no longer the intimate dinners they once were. Now held in restaurants or hotel meeting rooms, the 20-plus group has expanded to include IT and operations in addition to engineering. The dinners are now more of an opportunity to lobby the boss and yak with colleagues than the strategy sessions of days gone by.

142   **He was extradited:** The city of Miami awarded the franchise to Americable Co.'s Charles Hermanowski, a local entrepreneur, who in 2006 was convicted of tax evasion and defrauding the U.S. government and other cable TV companies to the tune of US$50 million.

146   **Liane Langevin:** Liane Langevin wrote the proposal enabling Labatt to win the specialty license for TSN in 1984. Her great-great-grandfather was Sir Hector-Louis Langevin, one of Canada's founding fathers of Confederation.

146   **"core franchising team":** Craig, a former CRTC broadcast policy analyst, years later started the Internet broadcaster iCraveTV, which streamed live television signals, sparking lawsuits from Hollywood studios and Canadian broadcasters that ultimately bankrupted the avant-garde company. He also owned the gay-themed digital channel PrideVision, renamed OUTtv, which eventually sought bankruptcy protection after Jim Shaw at Shaw Cable refused to bundle the channel with other digital channels. The dispute, which began before Craig acquired the channel, lasted almost four years. He is not connected with Craig Media.

146   **former executive assistant:** The former Syracuse Mayor Lee Alexander, now deceased, was convicted in 1988 of taking almost US$1.5 million in kickbacks from city contractors while he was mayor from 1970 to 1985. He served six years in prison. Rogers ended up being drawn into the FBI's probe—called Operation Saltshake—into City Hall corruption because of the 1985 sale of the Syracuse cable franchise to the McCaw family, which Alexander had stalled, prompting the FBI to investigate for possible kickbacks. The probe centered on the role played by Skip Ciero, a former Rogers employee, who worked for the Alexander administration during his 20s and who acted as a consultant in the sale. Both Ciero and Rogers had to testify before a special grand jury into the matter. No wrongdoing was ever found.

147   **"access channel for unicorns":** Mary Don, "Interest groups jam cable TV hearing," *Oregon Journal* (September 25, 1980): 6.

148   **"anti-Canadian statements":** Waterland does not recall this specific anecdote but says it's quite likely that he made the call. "I did that sort of thing all the time," he said in a November 2003 phone interview from his home in Nanaimo, B.C.

148   **community and business leaders:** Charles Humble, "Ad, PR Shops Reap Cable Dollars," *Oregon Journal* (July 3, 1980): 24.

149   **curtailing U.S.–Canada trade:** Russ Hoyle, "Facing a Winter of Discontent." *Time* (November 8, 1982).

149   **"a hell of an answer":** Oral History Collection. The Cable Center. Denver. Interview, 1991.

150   **"10 cents on the dollar:"** Ira R. Allen, "Washington News," United Press International (April 28, 1982).

151   **Cellular Telecommunications Association:** Wheeler left the NCTA in 1984 to become the president and CEO of the short lived NABU Network, a subsidiary of Ottawa-based NABU Manufacturing Corp., which distributes computer programs to owners of personal computers via cable TV lines.

151   **his insurance policy:** Lind, an aficionado of U.S. politics, endowed a substantial sum to his alma mater, the University of British Columbia, in 2004 to create The Phil Lind Chair in U.S. Politics and Representation.

155   **a local exchange company:** Paul Desmond, "Cable firms eye local telecom mart," *Network World* (July 25, 1988): 11.

CHAPTER 10

157   **tender to lower offer:** UA-Columbia management owned 20 percent of the stock.

159   **He intended to expand:** Dan Westell, "Rogers takes risks now and hopes for future renewal," *The Globe and Mail* (July 27, 1981); B3.

159   **mixed results:** In 1990, BCE broadsided RCI by teaming with Vidéotron to enter the U.K. cable TV market. The U.S. Baby Bells, prohibited from owning cable companies, were also investing in Britain, where few homes had cable.

160   **cancel the company's dividends:** Larry Marion, "The Legacy," *Forbes* (July 6, 1981): 81.

161   **increase his stake:** Eric Evans, "Rogers raises funds for U.S. purchase," *Financial Post* (July 11, 1981): 22.

161   **"real estate assets":** Peggy McCallum, "Famous Players forms a real estate division," *The Globe and Mail* (August 25, 1981): B7.

162   **U.S. head offices:** _____, "The Cable TV Empire Built by Rogers," *The New York Times* (July 15, 1981): D1.

165   **"emasculates the management":** Memorandum to Marshall and Robert A. Naify from Salah M. Hassanein, dated April 5, 1982.

165   **There is no business:** Undated letter to Ted Rogers from Marshall Naify attached to an April 5, 1982, memorandum from Salah Hassanein to Marshall and Robert Naify.

166   **violation of federal security laws:** David McClintick, "LSD Messages From God Figure In Suit Against Ex-Chairman of Theater Chain," *The Wall Street Journal* (April 14, 1978): 16.

167   **no knowledge of the cable business:** Jones attended Rogers' 2002 induction into the U.S. Cable TV Hall of Fall. Rogers generously offered to pay his way. "I thought, I can't believe someone would do that," says Jones. "I only came to the guy's dinner to help him celebrate. I sure won't need to be reimbursed for it. He was very grateful, I think, that we all came. He was very much touched by that."

167   **assets and liabilities:** Rogers UA Cablesystems Inc. Agreement of Plan and Split-off. Volume 1 (August 31, 1983): 30–33.

CHAPTER 11

177   **wire transfer of an Irish government cheque:** According to the company's 1984 annual report, Rogers netted $5.7 million in cash by selling its 75-percent stake in its Irish systems. The company repaid a $1.9-million loan to Chase Bank. The systems were sold at a slight loss.

180 **"one that you can be proud of"**: Olive, David. "The High-Wire Act of Ted Rogers," *Report on Business Magazine*. July 26, 1985. p. 26.

183 **overseeing the lengthy licensing process**: Shea was president and CEO of Sirius Satellite Radio, guiding the company through the CRTC licensing and start-up processes. He was also Global Television Network's president and COO and an executive vice president at Bell Globemedia Inc.

187 **Wall Street's hottest IPO**: When HSN went public at $18 (U.S.) in March 1986, the stock skyrocketed to $42 on its first day and within a few months, reached $133 a share pre-split.

188 **companies engaged in the franchising wars**: United Artists Cablevision and GE Cablevision merged in 1984. Times Mirror and Storer Cable swapped 12 systems in 1984. *The Washington Post* bought Capital Cities Cable in 1985. Warner Communications bought out American Express' half of Warner Amex in 1985. Leveraged buyout kings KKR bought out Storer in 1985, and then sold it to TCI and Comcast three years later. Westinghouse's Group W Cable was sold and broken up by TCI, ATC, Comcast, Century Communications and Daniel & Associates in 1986. Heritage bought half of GillCable, the nation's largest independent operator, in 1986. Jack Kent Cooke bought McCaw Cable in 1987, and then sold the systems in 1989 to a consortium of seven companies. Continental Cablevision bought American Cablesystems in 1988; and United Cable Television Corp. and United Artists Communications merged in mid-1989.

190 **in the crass Marine Corps vernacular**: Tedesco, Richard. "City presses to buy major cable system," *Electronic Media*. January 18, 1988. p. 1.

CHAPTER 12

199 **wasting tax payers' money**: Ormond Raby, *Radio's First Voice: The Story of Reginald Fessenden* (Toronto: MacMillan Co. of Canada Ltd., 1970), 86.

200 **most popular product known to man**: John Greenwald, "Do cell phones need warnings?" *Time*, Vol. 156, No. 15 (October 9, 2000).

202 **the radio was encased**: Interview with Hings' grandson, Guy Cramer.

202 **two-way voice radio**: Hings, who held 23 patents, also invented the technology used for the DEW Line (Distant Early Warning Line) operated by NORAD (North American Aerospace Defense Command). In 1943, he was one of eight members of the International Commission of the U.S. National Advisory Committee for Aeronautics (NASA's predecessor). After the Second World War, Hings sued the Canadian government for royalties on his Walkie-Talkie patent. The Canadian government argued his invention became its property the day Canada declared war on Germany which, coincidentally, was the same date that the U.S. had awarded him the patent. According to his grandson, Hings won the case after Canadian military engineers were unable to explain the circuitry.

203 **C-58 walkie talkie**: Tom Hawthorn, "Tinkerer invented the walkie-talkie," *The Globe and Mail* (April 7, 2004).

203 **you can talk with it while you walk with it**: _____. "Signaller 'Hams' Build 'Walkie Talkie' Radios," *Toronto Star* (May 15, 1941): 33.

203 **loss of Canadian lives**: Interview with Hings' grandson, Guy Cramer.

203 **creator of comic strip hero**: In 1964, Tracy traded in his Wrist Radio for a 2-Way Wrist TV.

204 **cellular communications to solve the spectrum shortage**: Bell Labs also invented the transistor in 1947, revolutionizing the entire electronics world by replacing the power-draining, heat-generating vacuum tubes that were the core of every computer and radio.

204 **the transmitters are all linked**: The term "cellular" comes from the honeycomb shape of the areas into which a coverage region, or "cell," is divided. Each cell size varies depending on the terrain. Cell range varies depending on the terrain. Today, the typical range is from about 3 kilometers to as far as 25 kilometers. In the early days of analog, the range was much greater. As the size of cell

phones (and their battery power) shrank, it became necessary to position cell towers every one kilometer apart to prevent dropped calls.

206 **challenge communications had snared most of the market:** Wayne Lilley, "How Challenge bloodied Bell," *Canadian Business* (November 1978): 52.

207 **"looked like a great big tank":** Martin Dewey, "Giant-basher back in business after battle rings up heavy toll," *The Globe and Mail* (May 28, 1979): B6.

207 **we were out of business:** Lilley, "How Challenge bloodied Bell," 52.

207 **the Bell top brass slouched:** Ibid.

209 **non-wireline applications:** James B. Murray, Jr., *Wireless Nation* (Cambridge, MA: Perseus Publishing, 2001), 46, 47.

210 **AT&T and GTE issued a joint press release:** Ibid., 24, 47.

210 **importance of having a head start:** Ibid., 48.

211 **"Tomorrow's mass market":** David Margolese's *Cellular Radio Position Paper* of June 1980.

211 **the other RCCs lacked his vision:** Ultimately, the RCCs went ahead without Margolese to form Cellular Canada. Belzberg's lawyer was Morley Koffman, a partner at Freeman & Co. in Vancouver.

213 **Telemedia acquired and turned around:** Frances Phillips, "Print, broadcast, telecom buys push Telemedia Corp. toward public issue," *Financial Post* (Sept. 21, 1985): 9.

214 **The Fan 590 and the FZ Rock network:** Standard Broadcasting, a privately held company controlled by J. Allan Slaight, acquired Telemedia's broadcasting assets in 2001, some of which were sold to Rogers, which now owns The Fan 590.

214 **the brothers had amassed $2.2 billion:** The Belzbergs were greenmailers before the word became part of Wall Street's lexicon. The tactic typically involves a raider acquiring a large block of a company's shares and then forcing the company to buy the stock at a premium order to avoid a takeover. As First City's reputation as a corporate raider grew, companies would "pay off" or offer the Belzbergs a premium for their shares just to get rid of them. Wall Street eventually called the extracted money "greenmail"—financially legal blackmail—in 1983.

215 **one of Canada's wealthiest families:** Hyman ran their father's secondhand furniture store in Calgary, where the family's business dynasty began. He was released after a ransom had been arranged. His captors were found and arrested.

215 **the Jewish people today:** Toby Klein Greenwald, "Leaders Then and Now, Profiles of NCSY Alumni," *Jewish Action* (Spring 2002).

215 **mountains of thick binders:** Ginsberg, investment banker George Blumenthal and mathematician Barclay Knapp leveraged US$2 million in venture capital to co-found Cellular Communications Inc. (CCI), the first U.S. publicly traded cellular company. In a five-year transaction, culminating in 1996, they sold CCI to AirTouch for US$2.5 billion.

217 **a trade show in Toronto:** Both men recollect running into Belzberg, or Belzberg's representatives, at this conference. Belzberg does not recall attending the conference.

217 **an American company seeking a Canadian partner:** De Gaspé Beaubien could not recall the company's name. According to Lint and Morrissette, it was New York–based Millicom Inc., which had partnered with Britain's Racal Electronics Plc to win one of the two U.K. national cellular licenses in 1983. Racal eventually bought out its minority partners to form the cellular subsidiary Racal Telecom Inc. that became Vodafone Group Inc., now Vodafone AirTouch Plc.

217 **In Belzberg's recollection:** Dalfen no longer recalls which person retained him first, although they came together as a group very quickly.

218 **landmark consent decree:** AT&T agreed in January 1984 to split itself up, divesting itself of its local telephone service, which would fall into the hands of seven specially created "Baby Bells," or Regional Bell Operating Companies (RBOCs). AT&T kept its long-distance business and its

most profitable companies, including equipment-manufacturing subsidiary Western Electric (now Lucent Technologies Inc.). In 2005, MCI—emerging from the throes of bankruptcy and the stigma of fraud from its former WorldCom leaders—ironically chose to merge with the shards of the monopoly it helped create when it spurned repeated takeover bids from Qwest Communications Inc., an independent teleco, for Verizon Communications Inc.'s US$6.7-billion offer. Bell Atlantic Corp., one of the seven Baby Bells, merged with GTE Corp., an independent, in 1998 to create the powerhouse they christened Verizon in 2000.

219 **Canada would restrict MCI:** Belzberg doesn't dispute this. He adds, however, that MCI wanted to charge $2 million to write the applications. "We decided we could do it a little cheaper ourselves in Canada," he says. "They wanted too much money and they didn't want to be a partner anyway, so we didn't go with them." Bob Buchan adds MCI was put off by Canada's "banana republic" style of awarding licenses behind closed doors, which Bluestein puts down to MCI outside counsel just whining over the loss of potential legal fees from a protracted open competition process.

220 **Canadian cable pioneer:** Switzer, the father of CHUM Ltd. CEO Jay Switzer, quit his job as a petroleum geophysicist in the fifties to build CATV systems in Saskatchewan and Alberta. He went on to engineer and build cable systems in Los Angeles, Chicago, Washington, D.C., and London, England. He came up with the idea of creating Toronto's Citytv network, of which his wife, Phyllis, became a founder.

220 **Switzer still felt a sense of loyalty:** Metcalf co-founded radio station CJOY-AM in Guelph, Ontario. In 1952, he established Neighbourhood Television, one of the first cable systems in Ontario. Over the next 15 years, he built and ran 20 small cable systems, which he sold to Maclean Hunter Ltd. in 1967.

221 **"a cash cow or a bust":** Jonathan Chevreau, "Competition Heats Up for Cellular Radio," *The Globe and Mail* (March 11, 1983): B13.

221 **24 days before application deadline:** Canada Consulting's co-founders included Liberal Party powerbroker Jim Coutts; Neil Paget; Jim Fisher and David Beatty, both professors at the University of Toronto's Rotman School of Business; and David Galloway and David Jolley, who both went on to build careers at Torstar Corp., owner of the *Toronto Star* and romance novel publisher Harlequin Enterprises Ltd.

222 **Rogers hesitated:** Belzberg says he does not recall any hesitation.

222 **Redican met with his business partner:** Whittaker later became president of Electronic Data Systems Corp.'s Canadian subsidiary. At EDS, Whittaker went through successive promotions from Canada to Australia to the U.K. She left EDS in 2005.

222 **NovAtel's Aurora-400 system:** Ameritech launched the first U.S. commercial cellular service in Chicago on October 12, 1983. Cellular One made its service available commercially in Baltimore, Maryland and Washington D.C., on December 16, 1983. Both companies began their trials in 1979.

223 **a guarantee to finance the build-out:** Interview with Marc Belzberg.

223 **Desktop computers . . . were then still rarities:** IBM only introduced its "personal computer" in 1981. *Time* magazine broke its annual tradition of naming "Man of the Year" to put the PC on its January 3, 1983 cover as the "Machine of the Year." In the same year, Compaq began rolling out the first PC clones. Apple Macintosh didn't debut until January 1984 and Microsoft Windows wasn't available until 1985.

225 **"signing financing for the cellular deal":** Several cellular executives have a different recollection; Lind and Watson were for years both opposed to cellular, now the company's primary growth engine.

226 **Canada's largest real estate brokerage:** Gray merged A.E. LePage Ltd. with Royal Trustco in 1984. He retired as Royal LePage's chairman in 1993.

226 **"All you need is Rolf Hougen,":** Rolf Hougen is a prominent Whitehorse, Yukon–based businessman, who founded TV station WHTV and in 1981 co-founded Cancom, Canadian

Satellite Communications Ltd., the first satellite delivery network to deliver radio and TV to Canada's north.

226 **DOC received more than 50 applications:** In 1983, Canada had some 600 radio common carriers, makers of paging devices and mostly privately operated mobile radio and other communications devices, doing $80 million worth of business annually.

227 **Ottawa seized the opportunity:** Robert Clendenning, *The Licensing of Wireless Technologies in Canada: An Examination of the Use of Ministerial Licensing* (Montreal: McGill University, April 9, 1999), 34.

228 **only a second-generation Canadian:** Others who were present remember the quip; Stursberg doesn't.

229 **GTE controlled the provincial wirelines:** GTE controlled BC Tel since 1955 and Québec-Téléphone since 1966 through a subsidiary called Anglo-Canadian Telephone Co. In 2004, GTE (now part of Verizon) divested its stake in Telus (created through the 1999 merger of AGT and BC Tel). Telus then acquired QuébecTel in 2000.

231 **The awarding of a national license:** DOC allocated 40 MHz (later expanded to 50 MHz) in the 800 MHz band for cellular mobile, awarding 20 MHz to each of the provincial, territorial and local wireline carriers and a national license for 20 MHz to one non-wireline carrier.

CHAPTER 13

234 **The new multinational conglomerate:** BCE reported a profit of $1 billion in 1985.

234 **BCE must create a separate subsidiary:** Lawrence Surtess, "Bell's cellular radio plans blocked," *The Globe and Mail* (March 15, 1984): B4.

237 **Peter G. Peterson:** Peterson became chairman of Lehman Brothers before co-founding the Blackstone Group, a private-equity fund.

237 **AES Data Inc.:** The AES 90, a programmable word processor with a video screen, was introduced in 1972, three years before Bill Gates and Paul Allen started a company they called Micro-Soft (they dropped the hyphen a year later) and four years before Steve Jobs founded Apple Computer Co.

237 **Innocan:** Eric Baker, who became one of Canada's wealthiest high-tech venture capitalists, joined Stephen Kauser, Paul Loewenstein and Ronald Meade in 1973 to help form Montreal-based Innocan, which evolved into Quebec's largest venture capital company after starting out fully loaded with $9 million of seed money. AES was one of their first investments. Innocan, 40 percent-owned by CDC, which invested $4 million, spawned many of Canada's major venture capitalists. Eric Baker—the mastermind of Memotec Data Inc.'s controversial 1987 purchase of Crown-owned Teleglobe Canada Inc.—and Ron Meade are best known for starting Altamira, the mutual funds company now owned by National Bank of Canada. Paul Lowenstein started Canadian Corporate Funding Ltd., a merchant banker to mid-sized businesses.

243 **Ted Rogers:** Rogers, who has received many honors, counts the Order of Canada and his first honorary degree among his most prized.

John McLennan, who attended Clarkson University in Potsdam, New York on a U.S. hockey scholarship, sponsored Rogers to receive his first honorary degree, a doctorate of science, from Clarkson in May 1989. He was honored along with Jack D. Kuehler, an engineer from International Business Machines Corp., who had just been named IBM's president, Arnold O. Beckman, a chemist who founded Beckman Instruments based on his invention of the pH meter, and poet Virginia C. Clarkson. IBM's Kuehler spoke from a prepared speech to the student assembly before Rogers, who was sitting on the stage beside McLennan.

"Ted leans over to me, and says, 'Jesus Christ, that's good,'" recalls McLennan. "And, of course, Ted has no notes at all. So, he gets his honorary degree and stands up in front of these five or six thousand people. He talked about being an entrepreneur, and a little bit about his father, and then he talked about how when the front door's closed, you go around to the side door, and when the side door's closed, you go around to the back door. He was tremendous and the message was fabulous.

"He just wowed them about being a fighter, never giving up, perseverance, which he truly, truly believes and lived. He's lived it. This man is unbelievable."

243 **CelTel:** Cantel and Bell Canada courted Paul Lloyd to become their franchisee for the Greater Hamilton area. Since Lloyd knew that Rogers was always leveraged to the hilt, he elected to become Bell's franchisee, a decision that worked out well for him. Dennis Whalley, another CelTel member, chose Cantel. Since Cantel paid residuals in Cantel stock, Whalley became a multi-millionaire when he sold his stock and built the Heron Point championship golf course.

243 **things had to be done his way:** Ian McGugan, "Such Good Friends," *Canadian Business* (April 1994).

244 **spend a couple thousand dollars:** Cantel's prices ranged from $2,495 to $6,000. Leasing a set cost $99 a month over a 42-month lease, with a $295 down payment. The monthly service fee was $15 and the charge per minute varied from 25 to 50 cents, depending on the number of minutes the subscriber used per month and whether a call had been made during a discount period. Bell Cellular had similar rates, although subscribers picked among four packages, based on their anticipated monthly usage. Depending on the package, the fixed monthly fee ranged from $4.95 to $49.95 and the per-minute charges varied from 25 cents to 60 cents. Lawrence Surtess, "Cellular phone rivals battling to ring up sales," *The Globe and Mail* (June 29, 1985): B13.

244 **"until a phone is literally small and cheap enough":** Lawrence Surtess, "Cellular phone rivals battling to ring up sales," *The Globe and Mail* (June 29, 1985): B1.

245 **Belzberg had initiated talks:** After his initial meeting with Ameritech, Belzberg says he no longer had any concerns over Cantel's financings. He recalls Cantel running into money problems once Ameritech's cash ran out.

246 **an industry behemoth:** Verizon Wireless was formed in April 2000 by combining the U.S. domestic wireless operations of Bell Atlantic—Vodafone AirTouch Plc and GTE. As president and CEO of Bell Atlantic Mobile, Strigl was the brainchild of the merger that created the largest U.S. wireless company.

246 **Rogers put the for-sale sign up:** Craig McCaw bought the Syracuse system in January 1985, paying just over US$805 per subscriber. Two years later, he fetched more than double that amount per subscriber when he sold his entire cable business to Canadian-born Jack Kent Cooke.

249 **The founders, who had already coughed up $9 million:** Internal RCI documentation.

249 **Pan-Canadian Communications Inc.:** According to Canada's Foreign Investment Review Agency regulations, any acquisition by a non-eligible person of 20 percent or more of voting shares of a private Canadian corporation constitutes control and triggers an automatic review. Cantel was careful to structure the deal so that Ameritech's voting rights didn't exceed 16.3 percent.

250 **St. Valentine's Day massacre:** The shooting of seven people on February 14, 1929 in Chicago as part of a Prohibition Era conflict between two powerful criminal gangs, the South Side Italians, headed by Al Capone, and the North Side Irish/Germans, headed by George "Bugs" Moran, is known as the St. Valentine's Day Massacre. Capone's gang ordered the hit as part of a plan to eliminate Moran. Moran was not killed but the massacre marked the end of his power on the North Side.

252 **According to a 2006 report:** "A Study on the Wireless Environment in Canada." Prepared for the Canadian Wireless Telecommunications Association. Wall Communications Inc., Ottawa. (September 29, 2006).

255 **spending in excess of $500,000:** George Blumson, "Cellular Phones Set to Hit London," *The Free Press* (September 21, 1985): D1.

CHAPTER 14

263 **"POP" in cellular parlance:** "Pop" is cellular slang for the number of potential customers in a cellular telephone franchise area. The financial community used the number of potential subscribers in the carrier's licensed territories as a measuring stick to value cellular companies.

264 **before the Black Monday stock market crash:** Rogers' daily organizer.

264 **he was quickly becoming a cellular kingpin:** In a deal that marked cellular's coming of age, McCaw sold 22 percent of McCaw Cellular in early 1989 to British Telecommunications Plc for US$1.5 billion. After spending most of 1989 in a heated takeover fight with BellSouth for LIN, McCaw acquired a controlling stake in LIN in March 1990. Five years later, in 1994, he sold his cellular business to AT&T for a staggering US$11.5 billion. McCaw Cellular is now part of Cingular, America's second-biggest wireless carrier. Cingular arose when BellSouth and SBC Communications combined their wireless business in April 2000.

264 **two months before [the] market's horrific crash:** McCaw sold more than 11 million shares at US$21.75 each, more than the US$17–$20 that the underwriters had expected. Demand was so heavy that the company could have sold six times that amount, analysts told *The New York Times*.

265 **America's 20ᵗʰ largest:** In January 1987, the McCaw brothers sold their cable TV business to Jack Kent Cooke for US$755 million, or US$1,740 per subscriber, at the time an industry record.

265 **I don't know many places:** Clearnet Communications Inc., which built a digital network in Canada known as Mike, teamed with its strategic partner, Rutherford, New Jersey–based Nextel Communications Inc., to provide similar cross-border services later in the decade. Telus Corp. completed its $6.6-billion takeover of Clearnet in January 2001. McCaw is well acquainted with their networks, having invested more than a billion U.S. dollars in Nextel in 1995, then a struggling carrier that had been rejected by MCI. Nextel and Sprint completed their US$35-billion merger in August 2005 to become Sprint Nextel Corp., with 44 million subscribers, making it America's third-largest wireless carrier behind Verizon Wireless and Cingular.

267 **The public distribution date:** According to the share exchange agreement, Cantel had to be trading on the Toronto or Montreal stock exchange with an aggregate market value of $12.5 million, excluding RCI's and the minority owners' shares.

267 **Ontario's "closed system" of securities regulations:** Shareholders must hold the securities for 6, 12 or 18 months (depending on the nature of the issuer and of the securities) from the later of the date of the purchase of the securities and the date on which the issuer became a reporting issuer. Cantel fell into the one-year "hold period." Therefore, the earliest date on which First City's and Telemedia's shares could become freely tradeable was November 25, 1988, one year plus a day after the date of the shelf's filing. Introduced in 1979, the closed system, since replaced, governed exempt distributions under Ontario's Securities Act. See: "Ontario Securities Commission Task Force on Small Business Financing: Final Report," (October 1996): 105–109.

268 **"That's a disgraceful way to behave":** Blumenstein doesn't recall this conversation.

269 **There was no mention anywhere in the bylaws:** Cantel's bylaws were changed later on December 17, 1987, permitting directors to participate in meetings *in absentia* by telephone. The new bylaw specifically stated: "Any director may participate ... by means of such telephone or other communications facilities ... and a director participating in such a meeting by such means shall be deemed to be present at that meeting."

271 **Craig McCaw:** McCaw paid a record US$81 per POP for the Washington Post Co.'s Miami market in January 1988.

271 **Cantel holdings:** Cantel's preliminary prospectus, dated August 25, 1988. Interview with Robi Blumenstein.

271 **Rogers first right of refusal:** By filing the shelf, Rogers also effectively confounded his partners' ability to sell their Cantel shares privately. If they wanted to sell privately, they not only had to give Rogers first right of refusal, as required by their accord, but also, they now had to seek prior approval from the OSC by giving a 60-day advance notice of their intention to sell.

271 **Ameritech's stake in Cantel:** The sale was completed in May.

274 **CHSN:** Canadian Home Shopping Network.

274 **dual-class share structures:** In the wake of the Canadian Tire Corp. takeover controversy, the TSE adopted new rules in 1987 that prohibited newly listed companies from issuing non-voting shares without including a "coattail" provision that rendered non-voting shares equal to voting shares in the event of a takeover bid. Previously listed companies were grandfathered.

274 **"I don't get motivated that way.":** John Partridge, "Rogers satisfied with new stake in cable firm," *The Globe and Mail* (June 11, 1988): B1.

275 **Cantel publicly traded:** Cantel's preliminary prospectus, dated August 25, 1988.

276 **Cantel IPO:** According to the 1988 prospectus, Rogers, directly through RTL and indirectly through RCI, owned 65.9 percent of Cantel's equity. First City held 16.7 percent and Telemedia owned 13 percent. Rogers, directly and indirectly, wielded 88 percent of the voting power, compared with First City's 5.5 percent and Telemedia's 4.3 percent.

276 **Cantel planned a public float:** Cantel planned to sell 1.1 million shares at around $45 a share for a total of $49.5 million.

276 **Telemedia:** John Partridge, "Telemedia chief takes a break," *The Globe and Mail* (November 9, 1989: B8.

278 **aborted the IPO:** Initially, the underwriters were in a snit over their out-of-pocket marketing costs, for which they were eventually reimbursed. In good humor, they ran a fake tombstone, ads placed by underwriters to boast of their involvement in underwritings, in the newspapers in mid-December for Cantel's aborted IPO, proclaiming they "believed that they may have assisted in the transaction but had no direct involvement."

279 **RCI purchased Rogers' personal stake in Cantel:** RCI announced the offer before Christmas 1988 and completed the acquisition from RTL on January 14, 1989.

279 **the independent:** John Partridge, "Valuation shows Cantel shares worth far more than Rogers willing to offer," *The Globe and Mail* (February 11, 1989): B5.

279 **directors merely offered dire warnings:** Adam Mayers, "Ted Rogers wants long-distance feeling," *Toronto Star* (February 23, 1989): D1.

281 **"God's gift to the world":**Rogers was a TD director from August 1989 to March 2004.

282 **First City:** The U.S. Court of Appeals upheld a lower court decision that First City Financial Corp. Ltd. evaded federal reporting requirements when First City purchased Ashland Oil Co. stock and Marc Belzberg was required to turn over US$27 million in profits from the attempted takeover of Ashland.

282 **the family considerably richer:** The family is ranked No. 98 among Canada's richest 100 families, with $430 million, according to the 2006 Rich List compiled by *Canadian Business* magazine.

283 **NovAtel, bought, sold and revamped:** NovAtel collapsed in the late eighties. Nova pulled out, selling its stake back to AGT for a break-even price of C$60 million. As tangled corporate histories go, NovAtel's ranks right up there. The company became an embarrassment to the Alberta government after faulty financial projections and a bungled sale tarnished the privatization of AGT in 1990. The province ended up bailing it out at a cost to taxpayers of more than $600 million.

CHAPTER 15

285 **Malone, then 41 years old, was able to afford:** Interview with John Malone.

287 **John Graham, in his 80th year:** Retired CRTC general counsel Avrum Cohen evinces that Graham "was a good regulatory lawyer. He would try to accommodate the regulator, and yet maintain the interests of his client. He was smart enough to know what's best for the client is not to continually fight with the regulator when they disagree, don't run to court, don't run to Cabinet, but work it out. He would do that very professionally, very gentlemanly."

287 **Avram Cohen raised the ownership issue:** In September, when the CRTC renewed the CFMT-TV license, the Commission stated that given the evidence before it, RCI hadn't breached the foreign ownership limits.

288 **to do everything within my ability:** Internal RCI manuscript. 1991.

289 **moving the company's incorporation:** RCI is still incorporated in British Columbia, which until recently was one of the least progressive jurisdictions for shareholder remedies.

290 **"You'd bloody well fix it":** Partridge, John. "Rogers tackles its foreign ownership problem," *The Globe and Mail*, November 11, 1987, p. B4.

290 **Rogers was . . . "becoming more Canadian":** Partridge, John. "Rogers satisfied with non-Canadian level in buyback bid" *The Globe and Mail*, December 5, 1987, p. B6

290 **the B shares were worth about $110:** Gabelli was accused in the mid-nineties of allegedly using sham small-business affiliates to win FCC cellphone spectrum licenses at a discount, licenses that were then flipped for a profit. In March 2006, the U.S. Justice Department joined the private civil lawsuit, filed under court seal in 2001. Gabelli and affiliated companies agreed to pay US$130 million to settle the lawsuit in July 2006.

291 **using the "ownership shield":** _____ "Barron's Roundtable 1988: Where Do We Go From Here?—Part II—Here's the Answer from the World's Best Money Managers," *Barron's* (January 25, 1988).

291 **a cellular system for all of Canada:** John Partridge, "Assessment may imperil Rogers' buyback," *The Globe and Mail* (February 4, 1988, p. B3).

292 **"Rogers was trying to freeze out":** "Rogers Communications Protests," *Barron's* (February 1, 1988)

292 **he put the U.S. assets on the auction block:** Although Houston Industries Inc. agreed in August 1988 to buy the U.S. cable TV assets for US$1.265 billion, the Texas-based company ended up paying a grand total of US$1.365 billion when the transaction closed in March 1989.

292 **Rogers flipped it:** Calculated on a pro rata basis. Rogers America had a total of 23.5 million shares, of which RCI owned 18.6 million, or 79.15 percent. Public investors held the remaining 20.85 percent.

292 **they derided Gabelli's remarks:** John Partridge, "Assessment may imperil Rogers' buyback," *The Globe and Mail* (February 4, 1988, p. B3)

293 **analysts dubbed "Rocky B":** Jamie Hubbard, "Analysts Call $24M Deal a Bargain: Package signals end of MH's sale of assets following Selkirk buy," *Financial Post* (January 6, 1989, p. B16).

293 **"The whole thing is an exercise in nonsense":** Adam Mayers, "Ted Rogers wants long-distance feeling," *Toronto Star* (February 23, 1989, p. D1).

293 **its first profit in six years:** Adam Mayers, "Ted Rogers wants long-distance feeling," *Toronto Star* (February 23, 1989, p. D1).

294 **MCI agreed to sell its franchises:** The transaction was completed in 1986.

CHAPTER 16

297 **a fourth-generation railway man:** In 1981, when at age 47 he moved to the presidency, Stinson became the youngest CEO in CP's history.

297 **lunch at the Royal York Hotel:** Fatt was appointed CP's chief financial officer in August 1990.

298 **cost methodologies:** The CRTC added a new cost category called "access service" to include the computerized switches, equipment and facilities to produce a dial tone, all of which was used to make both local and long-distance calls. But the CRTC arbitrarily assigned the access costs completely to local subscribers. Local had all the expenses of maintaining a network that enables LD service, resulting in the subsidy. The access category became a catch-all for marketing, public affairs and lobbying costs. Lawrence Surtees, *Wire Wars* (Scarborough, Ontario: Prentice-Hall Canada Inc., 1994), 159–161.

298 **Kedar co-founded Call-Net Telecommunications Ltd.:** Kedar and some of his partners realized $250,000 from the sale of the stock.

298 **willing to invest millions:** Chuck Hawkins, "A Cable Mogul With a Live-Wire Idea," *Business Week* (July 4, 1988): 39.

299 **he drowns out the others:** Mike Urlocker, "Back to the Future: The return road may not be all easy, but BCE's Raymond Cyr plans to focus again on the phone business," *The Financial Post* (October 8, 1990): 5.

300 **Rogers then acquired 4 percent of Teleglobe:** Raymond Cyr had been hell-bent on owning Teleglobe since the Mulroney government sold the company in a botched 1987 privatization that saw it fall into the hands of tiny Montreal-based Memotec Data Inc., controlled by venture capitalist Neil Baker.

300 **toehold in Teleglobe:** In 1992, Rogers backed Charles Sirois, 37, in his proxy fight to take over Teleglobe, a dramatic boardroom coup supported by minority shareholders BCE and the Caisse. Two years later, they co-founded Telesystem International Wireless (TIW), which invested in overseas start-up wireless phone companies. TIW went public in May 1997. Rogers owned 10 percent of TIW. Five months later, Rogers sold 2 million TIW options, roughly a third of the stake held through his private holding company, at $21.50, earning him $43 million. TIW almost went bankrupt in 2001.

301 **a baseball card collection:** Surtees, *Wire Wars*, 200–201.

301 **"trunk-access" interconnection plan:** The U.S. carriers used "trunk-side" or "tandem" access, where long-distance lines are connected directly to an alternate carrier's toll switch, eliminating the need to dial extra digits.

301 **Rogers' appetite for capital:** Daly and Miller, who both joined in 1987, are still at RCI. Day, who made a fortune in JDS Uniphase stock, retired in 2006 after 15 years.

302 **resale of voice and data service:** At the time, there were just two resellers, Call-Net and Marathon Telecommunications Corp. of Vancouver.

302 **the CRTC held its second LD hearings:** Paul Loong, "Long-Distance Service," *Ottawa Citizen* (June 4, 1992): F8.

302 **"Bill and Ted's Excellent Adventure":** Lawrence Surtees, "Bill and Ted's adventure will be a tough journey," *The Globe and Mail* (June 15, 1992): B1. In 1991, a sequel, "Bill & Ted's Bogus Journey," was released, featuring Bill and Ted, cool, hip dudes, crashing through the past, present and future in a time-traveling telephone booth.

302 **officer of the Order of Canada:** Rogers was appointed to the Order of Canada on October 25, 1990. Lind became a member of the Order of Canada in 2001, a notch below Rogers on the three-grade scale of outstanding achievement, a lifetime of achievement and distinguished service.

302 **"That's the Canadian way.":** John Partridge, "Rogers cites 'Campeau factor' in stocks' plunge," *The Globe and Mail* (January 30, 1990): B11.

304 **He didn't:** Laurie P. Cohen, "The Final Days," *The Wall Street Journal* (February 26, 1990): A1.

305 **Reichmann empire collapsed:** The Reichmann family's Olympia & York went bankrupt in 1992. Many worried the highly leveraged Edper Bronfman empire would be next.

305 **a liquid yield option note:** The company sold US$720–million worth of aggregate principal at maturity in 20 years, resulting in net proceeds of US$132 million. RCI was the first Canadian issuer to take advantage of the new multi-jurisdictional disclosure system between Canada and the U.S. regulators, which permits certain Canadian companies to use their short-form Canadian filings to tap the U.S. capital markets.

305 **RCI then sold additional stock:** Goldman Sachs & Co. led the IPO.

305 **Rogers was building a war chest:** Richard Siklos, "Ted Rogers hasn't stopped growing yet," *The Financial Post* (October 29, 1992): 21.

306 **"David versus David struggle.":** Surtees, *Wire Wars*, 304.

306 **to find a U.S. partner:** Ibid. 239–251.

307 **Financial Network Association:** The 12 members included: AOTC of Australia; RTC-Belgacom of Belgium; Stentor of Canada; France Telecom; Deutsche Bundespost Telekom of Germany; Hong Kong Telekom; Italcable of Italy; KDD of Japan; Singapore Telecom; Telefonica of Spain; Mercury Communications in the U.K.; and MCI in the United States.

307 **MCI then turfed Unitel:** Stentor then forged a deal with GTE and MCI for access to GTE's billing and MCI's advanced network operations.

307 **regarded as the frontrunner:** Nacchio went on to become Qwest Communications International Inc.'s chief executive. In April 2007, Nacchio, 57, was convicted of insider trading related to his sale of $100-million worth of Qwest stock in 2001 before the company's stock nose dived amid accounting irregularities.

307 **cross-border telephone calls:** Surtees, *Wire Wars*, 260.

309 **Sward was a trusted lieutenant:** His uncle, Keith Dancy, had instilled in him a love of radio at a young age. At 24, Sward was managing two Montreal radio stations for Newfoundland's eccentric media mogul Geoff Stirling—an alligator hunter—and had transformed Montreal easy-listening station CKGM into CHOM, Canada's first all-rock FM station. In the aftermath of the PQ's electoral victory, Sward moved to Ottawa, where he based his consulting practice. In 1977, Dancy hired him for a six-month contract to devise a fix it strategy for Rogers' ailing CFTR and CHFI in Toronto. Rogers was growing frustrated with Dancy because he felt the radio stations could be doing better and, immersed as he was in cable TV, Rogers simply didn't have time to devote his energies into radio. Dancy then bought CHAM in Hamilton from Rogers and left. With the top radio job open, Rogers hired Sward to execute his strategies. (Rogers made Sward a part owner in Rogers Broadcasting. When he folded the radio company into RCI, several people, including Sward, made a small fortune.)

When he moved Sward into Cantel, Rogers promoted Anthony P. Viner, 42, an impressive man who had joined Rogers in 1982 to manage CFTR. Unlike Sward, Viner began his career at Sun Oil (now Sunoco), which recruited him from University of Western Ontario business school. His older brother, Peter, happened to be doing so well financially in the media business as a salesman that the younger brother decided to jump into the broadcasting world after four years in the staid oil business. (Peter Viner is a long-time CanWest Global executive.) Tony joined Paul Mulvihill Radio Sales in Montreal as a national sales representative. When separatist politics began to stifle Quebec's vibrancy, he relocated to Toronto to help media mogul Allan Slaight launch Q107. Since Slaight had an heir apparent in son Gary, Viner thought he'd try his luck with Rogers. Sward put him in charge of turning CFTR around. To Rogers' delight, three years later, CFTR cracked the magic one-million-listener mark to bump CFRB 1010 from the top spot. Viner remains president of Rogers Media.

310 **industry alliances and break ups:** Kedar left Call-Net in 1993.

310 **bypassing local telephone companies:** Edmund Andrews, "AT&T Paying $12.6 Billion for McCaw Cellular," *The New York Times* (August 17, 1993): A1.

311 **about a third:** Patricia Chisholm, "Hunting the right number," *Maclean's* (January 23, 1995): 39.

312 **competitors controlled 32 percent:** Wireline Long Distance Service Revenues Market Share, 2003. Telecommunications Service in Canada: An Industry Overview.

312 **RBC Dominion Securities:** Jan Ravensbergen, "CP seeks advice on Unitel stake," *The Gazette* (September 24, 1994): C3.

312 **hostile takeover of Maclean Hunters:** Michael Urlocker, "Unitel a tough lesson for Rogers," *Financial Post* (November 26, 1994): 3.

313 **seven licenses:** When New Country Network (NCN) was licensed, the CRTC knocked off Country Music Television (CMT), a U.S. cable channel that had been available in Canada since 1984. The cable companies weren't permitted to broadcast CMT, which then launched a complaint under the North American Free Trade Agreement. The bitter dispute, which raised the hackles of Americans over Canada's farcical broadcast system, was settled when the CRTC permitted CMT to buy a minority stake in NCN.

313 **marketing blackmail:** "Revolt of the Couch Potatoes," *Edmonton Journal* (January 6, 1995): A10.

313 **automatic subscribers:** Ross Howard, "Rogers caves in on cable channels," *The Globe and Mail* (January 6, 1995): A1.

313 **optional services:** Jenish D'Arcy, "Cable gets zapped," *Maclean's* (January 16, 1995): 26.

314 **gray-market satellite dishes:** From 1994 to 1997, the number of gray-market direct-broadcast satellite subscribers jumped from an estimated 3,000 to more than 200,000. Many of them waited for cable TV competition from Canadian satellite providers, but to the relief of the cable industry, the CRTC mucked up that licensing process.

314 **complaints from customers:** _____, "Seething resentment in television land: a wave of viewer anger hits the cablecos and the CRTC will feel it next," *Western Report* (January 23, 1995): 21.

315 **exactly what happened:** Watson disputes Shaw's recollection.

315 **prohibited by law:** Terry Hui has been president and CEO of Concord Pacific Group Inc. since 1992. His family acquired majority control.

315 **down the manholes:** Antonia Zerbisias, "Whose side is Keith Spicer on?" *Toronto Star* (February 19, 1995): C1.

315 **lied to the media:** Ibid.

315 **CRTC caved:** The CRTC imposed the more onerous class 1 license on Pacific Place Cable, which had applied for the less stringent class 2 license under which small cable companies are classified.

317 **James Carville, advisor to Bill Clinton:** Carville's exact quote was "I used to think if there was reincarnation, I wanted to come back as the president or the pope ... But now I want to come back as the bond market. You can intimidate everyone."

318 **Scotiabank..., TD..., Royal Bank... and AT&T:** Their involvement didn't necessarily translate into new business for Unitel, a fear Bell expressed at the time. The banks continued to award Bell business.

CHAPTER 17

319 **built a position in Maclean Hunter:** To avoid the Bay St. rumormongers, Rogers decided not to use RTL's regular broker, ScotiaMcLeod. Instead, he called Lawrence Bloomberg at First Marathon Securities to arrange a meeting, preferably somewhere discreet. They met on a Sunday at Bloomberg's home near Toronto's famous castle, Casa Loma. As far as Bloomberg knew, Rogers was simply making an investment for the family company.

321 **"we'll be wiped out":** Mark Heinzl, "Two Dreamers, One Dream: To be Media Kings—Ted Rogers' Bid Would Fortify Cable Empire," *The Wall Street Journal* (February 4, 1994): B1.

321 **stereotype of the riverboat gambler:** Rod McQueen, "Rogers: Go-for-it entrepreneur aims for 'best of both,'" *Financial Post* (February 5, 1994): S12.

323 **the bridge loan:** In the original deal, Scotiabank, TD, CIBC and Royal Bank provided $2 billion to fund the acquisition and $148 million to pay associated fees and expenses. The loan was then syndicated to 36 banks. An extra $375-million loan was made to backstop MH's commercial paper after the rating agencies insisted on the higher limit. Barry Critchley, "Put up or shut up," *Financial Post* (August 18, 1994): 5.

324 **"broadband to the home":** Jan Ravensbergen. "Beware of data-highway robbery; Road to information superhighway may be rocky: Ted Rogers," *The Gazette* (February 2, 1994): C1.

324 **"I don't see cable providing voice":** Terence Corcoran, "Rogers strategy at odds with experts," *The Globe and Mail* (February 7, 1994): B2.

324 **thrust of emerging technology:** Ibid.

326 **"Mr. Rogers only knows two words":** John Daly and Luke Fisher. "The surprise play for MH," *Maclean's* (February 14, 1994): 26.

326 **"purchase butterfly":** John Partridge. "Maclean Hunter raises the stakes," *The Globe and Mail* (February 14, 1994): B1.

327 **"put a gun to our head":** Michael McHugh, "Cable War Escalates," *Toronto Sun* (February 26, 1994): 42.

327 **"I'm just staggered":** John Partridge, "Rogers Accused of Greenmail," *The Globe and Mail* (February 26, 1994): B1.

329 **Rogers' neighbor:** Richard Siklos. "Low-Profile Cable Magnate Shakes Media World," *Financial Post* (May 7, 1994): S20.

330 **there were offers:** Judy Steed, "Maverick billionaire does it in style," *Toronto Star* (March 9, 1994): A1.

330 **He kissed her:** Ibid.

331 **in hostile takeovers:** The new rules were adopted after Ted Turner's failed hostile takeover bid of CBS Inc. in 1985. The FCC refused to accelerate its review, giving CBS time to implement a stock buyback scheme to block Turner's bid.

331 **validity of a trust arrangement:** The CRTC only required prior approval for the acquisition of control of 30 percent or more of the voting stock, or 50 percent or more of total equity.

334 **public benefits—known as "siggies":** Typically the benefits package equals 10 percent of the price of the assets. In MH's case, the regulated assets were worth $1 billion.

335 **broadband-related:** Rogers Brown, "Making arcane R&D pay off," *CED* magazine (May 1, 1996).

335 **the regulation's verdict:** Rod McQueen, "Rogers assembles forces for multimedia revolution," *Financial Post* (December 20, 1994): 5.

335 **to compete against the telephone company:** Adam Mayers, "Don't let Ted Rogers forget his customers," *Toronto Star* (December 20, 1994): E1.

335 **gin and tonic:** Osborne became BCE's chief financial officer in 1995 and later its president. He then became Bell Canada's president and CEO until joining Ontario Hydro, where he took the fall for the botched retrofit of nuclear reactors in Pickering, Ontario.

CHAPTER 18

338 **ARPANET:** Vincent Cerf and Robert Kahn, who both worked on ARPANET, invented the Transmission Control Protocol (TCP), which moves data on the modern Internet. Though they have publicly stated that no one person or group of people invented the Internet, they are credited with being its founding fathers. MCI's H. Brian Thompson lured Vince Cerf to MCI in 1982, where he engineered MCI Mail, the first commercial email service to be connected to the Internet.

338 **Internet Service Providers (ISPs):** _____, "Linking Up To A Global Network," *LinK-Up*, vol. 10, no. 6 (November 1, 1993): 7.

338 **a tree-and-branch structure:** George Gilder, "Cable's Secret Weapon," *Forbes* (April 13, 1992): 80.

339 **picture-perfect signals:** RCI's technology architecture is based on a three-tiered structure of primary hubs, optical nodes and coaxial distribution. The company achieves additional upstream capacity by reducing the number of homes served by each optical node by what's called node splitting.

339 **X-Press:** They developed a pre-wave product called X-Press that used a cable modem.

339 **broadband deployments race:** Rouzbeh Yassini, *Planet Broadband* (Indianapolis, Indiana: Cisco Press, 2004), 39–42.

340 **home cable box:** Microsoft predicted the Tiger software would be in homes by 1997, an overly optimistic claim. The company failed to get anywhere with the cable TV industry, which questioned the software giant's video technology and worried about its dominance. Unable to succeed with the cable TV industry, Microsoft switched industry allegiances, teaming with the phone companies to

arm them with interactive Internet-protocol television (IPTV) technology to compete with cable companies. In 2007, Microsoft was still ironing out the IPTV software kinks, forcing partners AT&T and Bell Canada to delay their rollouts.

341 **most technically clean systems:** John Markoff, "Microsoft and Rogers Plan Interactive Cable Venture," *The New York Times* (May 25, 1994): D1

341 **PC penetrations:** Just four years later, in 1998, 45 percent of Canadians reported having a computer, almost twice the proportion from five years before when 23 percent owned one. In 2005, 72 percent of Canadians reported owning a computer. Statistics Canada, *Spending patterns in Canada* (62-202): 44.

342 **replacing their century-old copper wires:** Ian Austen, "Phone makeover in works," Southam News in *Calgary Herald* (April 6, 1994): C3.

343 **world wide web:** Robert D. Hof, "From the man who brought you silicon graphics ..." *Business Week* (October 24, 1994): 90.

343 **"my life would be easier":** John Markoff, "Business technology: A Free and Simple Computer Link," *The New York Times* (December 8, 1993): D1.

343 **unprecedented commercial energy:** Gary Wolf, "The (Second Phase of the) Revolution Has Begun," *Wired* (October 1994): 116–121.

344 **all-new version of Mosaic:** Andreessen was a student and part-time assistant at the University of Illinois' National Center for Supercomputing Applications (NCSA) when he and fellow NCSA employee Eric Bina created Mosaic, which made it possible for images and text to appear on the same page and used hyperlinks so that users could simply click on a link to retrieve a document. Within weeks of making Mosaic available on NCSA's servers, tens of thousands of people downloaded the software.

345 **"nosebleed valuation":** Susan Moran, "Stock market sends Netscape to dizzying heights." Reuters in the *Calgary Herald* (August 12, 1995): D8.

345 **"browser madness":** Joshua Quittner, "Browser madness," *Time* (August 21, 1995): 56.

345 **sympatico, a dial-up service:** Lawrence Surtees, "Bell to launch Internet access," *The Globe and Mail* (November 29, 1995): B4.

345 **agreement with Yahoo! Canada:** The licensing agreement expired in January 1999. In 2004, Rogers renewed its relationship with Yahoo!, signing just months after BCE's Sympatico partnered with Microsoft.

345 **"Tomorrow is going to be amazing.":** They charged between $55 and $65 a month, plus a $150 to $200 installation and setup fee.

346 **"It changes the whole soul ...":** Robert Brehl, "A tough-talking Ted," *Toronto Star* (December 30, 1996): C1.

347 **cable companies lost credability on Wall Street:** Marc Gunter. "The Cable Guys' Big Bet On the Net," *Fortune* (November 8, 1996), 102.

348 **threatened to cut off:** See Beverley Reade's claim against Rogers: http://groups.msn.com/peleeplaces/whoisthisbevanyway.msnw

349 **Canadian Cable Television Association:** In 2004, the industry trade group changed its name to the Canadian Cable Telecommunications Association. It disbanded in 2006 after Shaw withdrew.

349 **At Home crisis and Sheila Copps:** Andrew Flynn. "Web-based museum wires up Canada." *The Spectator.* (March 23, 2001): D3.

350 **AOL on steroids:** Soon after the merger, Kleiner Perkins took company shares worth more than US$1 billion and distributed them privately to its investment partners for them to sell if they wished.

350 **potential Net powerhouse:** Peter Elstrom. "Excite@Home: A Saga of Tears, Greed and Ego," *Business Week.* (December 17, 2001), 94.

351   **costly arbitration proceedings:** J. Gardner Hodder. "Ontario residents denied justice," *Toronto Star* (September 13, 2004), A17.

351   **the debt holders later recouped:** The defunct ISP sued Comcast and Cox, which sold their stakes to AT&T in 2000 for US$3 billion in AT&T stock, a deal that enabled AT&T to increase its voting control in At Home to 74 percent from 56 percent. At Home shareholders had opposed the deal because it gave the two cable giants the option of dropping the service before their contracts expired. At Home claimed they reaped a combined profit of US$600 million from its demise, money it intended to use to repay angry bondholders. The U.S. Supreme Court declined to hear At Home's case in 2006. The previous year, AT&T settled one lawsuit, claiming it breached its fiduciary duties and misappropriated At Home's trade secrets to build a replacement network. As part of that settlement, AT&T agreed to pay US$400 million to At Home bondholders, who were owed US$750 million. Comcast footed about half of the AT&T settlement because it acquired AT&T Broadband in 2002.

351   **he unloaded the last of his stock:** Rogers owned as many as 7.72 million shares, or 1.9 percent, of At Home, which included 2 million held by RTL, warrants held by RCI, exercisable with respect to 5.35 million shares, and warrants held by Rogers Cable, exercisable with respect to 367,904 shares, according to At Home's 2001 proxy. According to Washington Service, which compiles data on transactions by company insiders, Rogers sold 430,000 shares for 5 cents each and 1.57 million shares for 3 cents each.

352   **a humiliating retreat:** Rebecca Blumenstein and Peter Grant. "On the Hook," *Wall Street Journal* (May 26, 2004), A1.

352   **the toughest job:** Seth Schiesel. "Incredibly Shrinking AT&T and the Armstrong Agenda," *The New York Times* (November 8, 2001), C6.

CHAPTER 19

356   **800 new subscribers a day:** Enchin, Harvey, "Rogers trims loss to $27.7 million," *The Globe and Mail* (October 22, 1994): B2.

357   **Top 25 CFO superstars:** Global Finance's select list of world-class CFOs included only one other Canadian, Barrick Gold Corp.' CFO Randall Oliphant. *See* Iain Jenkins and Ellen Leander, Global Finance's 1996 CFO Superstars," *Global Finance* (June 1996), 26.

358   **cover its needs:** Doug Kirk's RCI research report for Nesbitt Burns (June 5, 1996).

358   **its debt covenants:** RCI had to maintain a total debt to cash flow ratio of less than 8 to 1 and senior debt to cash flow ratio of less than 6 to 1 in order to sell more debt. Cable's senior secured notes stipulated that it could not incur more debt if RCI's consolidated debt to annualized cash flow ratio was greater than 7 to 1 or senior debt was greater than 6 to 1. Other notes stipulated a 7.5 to 1 ratio. Doug Kirk's RCI research report for Nesbitt Burns (June 5, 1996).

360   **issued warrants to AT&T:** Cantel paid AT&T royalty payments for marketing and technical support and issued warrants to AT&T for an option to buy $32.5-million worth of Cantel Class B shares over four years, amounting to about 1 percent of Cantel's equity. *See* Lawrence Surtees, "Rogers hooks up with AT&T Cantel alliance and co-branding pact a prelude to larger equity deal, observers say," *The Globe and Mail* (November 14, 1996): B1.

362   **a lot to be happy:** Brenda Dalglish, "'Don't put all of your eggs in cable,' Ted Turner says," *Financial Post* (May 13, 1997): 6.

363   **The incumbents naturally received licenses:** Manley awarded two national 30 MHz PCS licences to Clearnet and Microcell, a national 10 MHz PCS licence to Rogers Cantel and 10 MHz PCS licences to the 11 regional wireless carriers owned by the telephone companies. The new PCS service was launched in late 1997.

363   **a loss of $540 million:** Bertrand Marotte and Theresa Tedesco, "Rogers' dream of media empire fading: Many investors question viability of debt-ridden firm," *Ottawa Citizen* (February 10, 1998): D3.

363 **GSM:** The wireless industry is loaded with acronyms. GSM, which stands for Global System for Mobile communications, is known as second-generation (2G) technology, a digital service that provides email/text messaging at a relatively low bandwidth. General packet radio service (GPRS), a 2.5G service, is an "always on" digital connection to the Internet, enabling high-speed data transmission. EDGE superseded GPRS. Fourth generation, or 4G, would bring 1 billion bits per second to mobile handsets, enough to do videoconferencing.

364 **on one bill:** Sprint bought its cable-TV partners to take full control of Sprint PCS in 1998, ending their four-year joint venture. On December 15, 2004, Sprint and Nextel announced they would merge to form Sprint Nextel Corporation.

365 **RCI shares plummeted:** The stock price is not adjusted for RCI's 2-for-1 stock split on December 29, 2006.

366 **raised his rating:** Investors, who took Doug Kirk's advice in 1998 and acquired RCI shares at its pre-split low of $4.80 and then held on to them can now boast of a 20-fold increase in their investment. That's not the case for BCE stockholders. If they bought BCE at its 1998 low of $39.75 and held it, their investment was below water in June 2007. Unlike RCI, however, BCE paid highly lucrative dividends. That's cold comfort to BCE stockholders who inherited Nortel stock. On May 1, 2000, BCE, led by Jean Monty, offloaded 35 percent of 37 percent stake in Nortel to Bell shareholders. Though it had been in the works for some time, the spin off proved timely given that the tech-fuelled rally in stocks ended in March. Nortel's stock price, adjusted for a mid-2000 two-for-one split, peaked in March 2000 at $105.68. The stock closed 2000 at $48.25. The stock continued its downward spiral, falling to a low of 67 cents in October 2002. In July 2007, an Ontario Teachers' Pension Plan Board consortium offered $42.75 a share cash to privatize BCE. That's 7.5 percent more than the company's 1998 low.

366 **his previous mistakes:** _____. "Rogers admits $5.6B debt is a burden on firm," *Edmonton Journal* (May 26, 1998): E7.

366 **challenging the phone grants:** Theresa Tedesco, "Rogers deal worth $1 billion; Telecom subsidiary sold in move analysts calling the 'Big Retreat,'" *Windsor Star* (May 21, 1998): F13.

366 **cash flow to cover its debt:** "Rogers admits $5.6B debt is a burden on firm," *Edmonton Journal* (May 26, 1998), E7.

366 **throwing in the towel:** Theresa Tedesco, "Rogers deal worth $1 billion; Telecom subsidiary sold in move analysts calling the 'Big Retreat,'" *Windsor Star* (May 21, 1998): F13.

368 **sell customers a bundle:** Rebecca Blumenstein and Peter Grant. "On the Hook," *The Wall Street Journal* (May 26, 2004): A1.

368 **US $100 million bet:** Rebecca Blumenstein and Peter Grant. "On the Hook," *The Wall Street Journal* (May 26, 2004), A1.

369 **a super carrier:** The transaction was completed in June 1999.

369 **repay bank debt:** In 2000, RCI raised a net $937.5 million via an issue of preferred securities backed by RCI's holding of 25 million AT&T Canada Class B non-voting deposit receipts.

371 **deep pocketed foreigners:** AT&T and BT each paid $700 million for a combined 33 percent, or 27.7 million Cantel shares, at $34.70 a share.

375 **the political fix:** Michel Nadeau, the former No. 2 man at the Caisse, denies any political influence.

376 **the right to sell:** The two men spoke in French. This is a condensed version of their conversation.

376 **Quebecor over paid:** Matthew Ingram, "More to Quebecor suit than meets the eye," *The Globe and Mail* (September 20, 2002): B10.

377 **denied the allegations:** Robert Gibbens, "Ex-Videotron CEO denies allegations of insider trading," *National Post* (September 4, 2003): FP5.

377 **deregulated the industry:** The CRTC opened up local phone and cable TV service to competition, but phone companies still require a broadcast license issued by the regulator in order to offer cable television.

378 **cable rival:** Shaw retained 72,500 customers in Nova Scotia. In 1999, Shaw acquired Access Cable, a Nova Scotia cable company founded by Charles Keating, a Shaw director, for $167 million in stock. Shaw then sold the assets in 2001 to Bragg Communications Ltd.'s founder John Bragg, another Shaw director, for $220 million, as part of several asset sales to reduce Shaw's debt after buying Moffat.

381 **anti-Indian hostility:** Catherine Mclean. "Princes in waiting," *The Globe and Mail* (June 22, 2007): 50.

381 **dissection experience:** Mohamed says he snipped off the fetal pig's "unbelievably long" umbilical cord, enraging his biology teacher.

381 **Telus Mobility:** That lasted three months. The company was growing so quickly Mohamed once again asked BC Tel for funding. Stymied again, he resorted to spending $3,000 for Lotus spreadsheets, which became the wireless company's financial system for two years.

CHAPTER 20

383 **customers in Vancouver:** "Fido's bite worth barking about," *The Province* (February 13, 2004): A50.

384 **company in play:** Through COM Canada LLC, McCaw acquired a small 7.7 percent stake in Microcell for C$30 million as part of the company's C$150-million rights offering.

384 **stone landmark:** In the Inuktitut language, "Inukshuk" means "for likeness of a person."

385 **GSM:** In the first quarter of 2007, almost 85 percent of the 2.83 billion wireless customers worldwide used GSM or 3GSM, while 12 percent used CDMA or CDMA EV-DO. Source: *Wireless Intelligence.*

386 **AT&T:** Mark Evans, "AT&T spurns Rogers bid for wireless." *National Post* (May 21, 2004): FP3.

387 **code-named Hippo:** Derek DeCloet, "Let's make a deal," *Report on Business Magazine* (March 2005). 30.

388 **Virgin Mobile:** Tyler Hamilton, "Virgin Mobile dials up teen market; Bell hooks up with youth-savvy firm." *Toronto Star* (August 4, 2004.): C1.

388 **Gang of four:** Of the so-called gang of four RCI directors, Melinda Rogers was not on the Finance Committee that discussed and vetted the Microcell acquisition. According to one director, the Finance Committee did not approve Rogers's plan to buy Microcell for its network.

388 **pancreatic cancer:** Gnat had been a director of Blue Square Furniture Inc., the IKEA store in Israel.

388 **AT&T Developments:** John Saunders, "Rogers to help AT&T Wireless unload stake," *The Globe and Mail* (September 4, 2004): B2.

390 **Microcell:** Dave Ebner, "Telus unfazed by idea Rogers might try to top Microcell bid," *The Globe and Mail.* (September 8, 2004.): B4.

390 **Wireless board:** Importantly, however, the two material restrictions contained in the 1999 shareholders agreement on the ability of AT&T to sell the shares to third parties remained and applied to any sale under the letter agreement.

391 **Rogers free and clear:** They agreed to a $45-million breakup fee.

391 **Rogers and Microcell:** The transaction closed in November 2004.

392 **U.S. junk-board market:** Eric Reguly, "Ted Rogers takes the throne as new junk bond king of America," *The Globe and Mail.* (November 27, 2004): B2.

392 **RCI and Class B shares:** RCI sold 9.5 million Class B non-voting shares for $26.20 a share on a bought-deal basis to RBC Capital Markets.

392 **Rogers praised:** Barry Critchley, "Rogers issue sets Street abuzz," *National Post.* (June 14, 2004.): FP8.

393 **stock as currency:** RCI paid 1.75 of its shares for each of the 15.4 million outstanding shares of Rogers Wireless.

393 **almost two times more:** Goldman Sachs & Co. and CIBC World Markets advised AT&T Wireless.

393 **share swap:** RCI proposed to swap 1.1 RCI Class B non-voting shares for each Rogers AT&T Wireless share. The special committee of the Rogers Wireless board recommended shareholders reject the offer after a fairness opinion from RBC Capital asserted that the stock was worth $31 to $36 a share.

394 **honoring Rogers:** The six other inductees were: Daniel Aaron, co-founder of Comcast Corp., Frank M. Drendel, chairman and CEO of equipment maker CommScope Inc., Joseph S. Gans Sr., chairman of Gans Multimedia partnership, Gene W. Schneider, chairman and CEO of UnitedGlobalCom Inc., Gail F. Sermersheim, former general manager of HBO-Atlanta, and the late Edward M. Allen of Western Communications Inc.

394 **original cable guy:** Adelphia's founder, John Rigas, and his son, Timothy, the CFO, were convicted on multiple counts of securities fraud, conspiracy to commit bank fraud and bank fraud in 2004. Adelphia, the fifth-largest U.S. cable company, collapsed into bankruptcy in 2002 after it disclosed $2.3 billion in off-balance-sheet debt. Comcast and Time Warner Cable acquired the company's assets in July 2006.

398 **three-way race:** Tyler Hamilton, "Rogers buys Call-Net," *Toronto Star* (May 12, 2005): D1.

398 **"battle of the titans":** Mark Evans, "Rogers snaps up Call-Net," *National Post* (May 12, 2005): FP1.

398 The question of there being a joint venture is under dispute.

398 **Look Communication:** In April 2004, before RCI acquired Microcell, Look's parent Unique Broadband Services sued Allstream Corp., Microcell and Inukshuk for specific performance, breach of contract, breach of confidence and breach of fiduciary duty in respect of a Right of Use and Right to Match Agreement between UBS Wireless and Inukshuk for the MCS spectrum licenced to Inukshuk. In August 2007, UBS filed a statement of claim in Ontario Superior Court seeking a mandatory order requiring Inukshuk Partnership to return to Fido Solutions (formerly Microcell Telecommunications) any and all rights or licences to use or exploit the Inukshuk Multipoint Communications Systems (MCS) Spectrum and such other, interim, interlocutory or final relief as may be necessary to enable Fido to comply with any order requiring the specific performance of certain obligations to UBS Wireless. UBS seeks $150 million in damages from each defendant.

399 **top-secret:** Initially christened "Dino," after the Flintstones cartoon dinosaur, McCaw CEO Jim Barksdale changed the name to "Michelangelo" after the Teenage Mutant Ninja Turtle, which then was shortened to "Angel." Keeping the project top secret, McCaw hired a special security director and gave clearance badges to engineers working on the technology.

399 **they were hired:** Erick Schonfeld, "On the Net Without a Wire," *Business 2.0* (September 2000): 122.

399 **sold McCaw Cellular:** The company is now part of Cingular, the largest U.S. wireless carrier.

399 **any more resources:** Project Angel's core technology ended up in the hands of Netro Corp. and eventually SR Telecom in Canada when it acquired Netro.

399 **any more resources:** Monica Alleven, "Aspiring for Big Savings in Small Packages," *Wireless Week* (July 15, 2005): 18.

399 **mobile-phone networks:** WiMax is short for World Interoperability for Microwave Access. WiMax standards were not established until 2005. Wi-Fi, another wireless network protocol, is the acronym for wireless fidelity.

400 **Clearwire's wireless network:** Mark Evans, "Broadband venture makes odd bedfellow," *The Financial Post* (March 14, 2005): FP1.

CHAPTER 21

405 **highest -compensated athlete:** Based on a cash-operating deficit. RCI says it has spent just over $400 million on the team and the stadium, including acquisition costs and cash losses, since acquiring the Jays in 2000.

408 **Toronto Argonauts:** Fed up with the money-losing football franchise, Interbrew forced the CFL to broker a sale of the Argos. Sherwood Schwarz, a New York insurance magnate, bought the club in 1999. Four years later, he sold it to Toronto businessmen David Cynamon and Howard Sokolowski.

409 **Anaheim Angels:** Disney sold the Angels in 2003. A year later, Murdoch's News Corp., which had racked up big losses, sold the Dodgers but kept the programming rights.

410 **Connie Bruck:** Connie Bruck, "The Big Hitter," *The New Yorker*, Vol. 73, Issue 38 (December 8, 1997).

411 **Shaw:** The regulator made an exception for Shaw, permitting it to own specialty and pay TV channels after Shaw and Izzy Asper's CanWest Global divvied up WIC Western International's assets in 1998. Shaw then spun off the newly created Corus Entertainment as a separate publicly traded company a year later. Then, when Shaw acquired Moffat, it sold WTN, an analog specialty channel, to Corus, which then fired the staff and moved its base of operations to Toronto.

412 **Paul Godfrey:** Michael Lewis and Theresa Tedesco, "Rogers pitches Jays deal: Offers US$150-million for money-losing team: Paul Godfrey said to be considered as CEO if sale of American League team approved," *National Post* (July 19, 2000): C1.

412 **Rogers and cable access:** Barbara Shecter, "Rogers faces third and 10 on Sportsnet call: Must decide soon if it wants CTV's 40% stake in channel," *National Post* (June 26, 2001): C7.

413 **Teresa Tedesco:** Theresa Tedesco offers behind-the-scenes details in her book, *Offside: The Battle for Control of Maple Leaf Gardens.*

413 **Stavro's side-deal:** Theresa Tedesco, "Leafs' suitors make their power play," *National Post* (September 18, 2000): C1.

413 **word of talks:** William Houston, "Truth & Rumours," *The Globe and Mail* (April 21, 2000): S5.

413 **operating costs:** RCI acquired the remaining 20 percent from Interbrew on January 5, 2004, for C$39.1 million.

414 **visiting Rogers Land:** _____, "Welcome to 'Rogers Land," *Maclean's*, Vol. 113, Issue 40, (October 2, 2000): 50.

414 **biggest influence:** William Houston, "The top 25 in Canadian sports," *The Globe and Mail* (December 23, 2000): S1.

414 **Greater Toronto area:** BCE was a minority owner in baseball's struggling Montreal Expos. It was one of 14 former limited partners of the Expos alleging that baseball officials and the Expos' principal owner, Jeffrey Loria, conspired to destroy Major League Baseball in Montreal. Loria, who gained control of the Expos when the other partners failed to meet capital calls, sold the Expos to MLB for US$120 million and then bought the Marlins from hedge fund manager John Henry for US$158.5 million. Henry then bought the Red Sox.

415 **go it alone:** Katherine Macklem, "A media colossus," *Maclean's* (September 25, 2000): 34.

415 **CTV Sportsnet:** Barry Critchley, "BCE comes late to the party: Could have bought Netstar, then bid for CTV in 1998," *National Post* (September 19, 2000): D3.

416 **fan base:** The Jays advisory board, to help turn around the team, was composed of Godfrey's cronies: lawyer Herb Solway, who helped bring the ball club to Toronto; real estate developer Rudolph Bratty; former Toronto alderman and federal Liberal politician David Smith, now a member of

506 | High Wire Act

Canada's Senate; lawyer Jeff Lyons, now the head of the Jays Care Foundation; and six people from RCI: Ted Rogers, Edward Rogers, Phil Lind, Nadir Mohamed, Tony Viner and company director and lawyer Albert Gnat. The board was disbanded once RCI took up the remaining 20 percent stake in the Jays from Interbrew.

416 **"You Gotta Believe":** Stephen Brunt, "Endgame," *R.O.B. Magazine* (August 2002): 47.

416 **a seagull:** Charges were later dropped when Winfield convinced the Toronto police the killing was accidental. The same man Toronto vilified nine years earlier for assassinating a bird returned to Toronto as a Jay and was embraced as a hero after getting the winning hit that gave the Jays their first of two consecutive World Series championships.

417 **loss carryforwards:** On April 1, 2001, RTL acquired the class A preferred voting shares of RCI's Blue Jays Holdco Inc. (BJH) for $30 million. While they were outstanding, the class A–preferred shares paid cumulative dividends. BJH satisfied the cumulative dividends in kind by transferring to RTL income tax loss carryforwards, having an agreed value equal to the amount of the dividends. Until July 2004, such agreed value is equal to 10 percent of the amount of the tax losses. Blue Jays Holdco Inc. transferred income tax losses to RTL in the amount of $27 million, $24 million and $27.4 million during 2002, 2003 and 2004, respectively. 2001–2005 Annual Reports.

417 **Cablevision's contract:** Dolan balked when "the Boss" insisted that he run not just the Yankees but also the Knicks and Rangers. Dolan was also pursuing baseball's Mets and the New York Jets NFL team. Had he succeeded, Dolan would have emerged as the single-most powerful figure in pro sports. His brother Larry, a lawyer, owns baseball's Cleveland Indians.

418 **they created YES:** Steinbrenner and the Chambers group own 60 percent of YES. The remaining 40 percent is owned by Goldman Sachs & Co. and Providence Equity Partners.

418 **YES is a powerhouse:** Tim Arango, "Pinstripe PayDay—Goldman Eyes Sale of YES Network," *New York Post* (August 11, 2006): 35.

418 **the ownership structure:** Theresa Tedesco, "Stavro's success is only partial: Ensures succession, loses profile, equity," *National Post* (February 12, 2003): FP1.

418 **Canada's largest:** Tanenbaum sold Warren Paving and Materials Group Ltd. to Lafarge Corp. in 2000.

418 **investment company:** Shaw acquired CUC in 1995 for $626.5 million.

419 **legal assistance:** Theresa Tedesco, *Offside: The Battle for Control of Maple Leaf Gardens* (Toronto: Penguin Group, 1996), 161.

420 **Blue Jays:** Paula Arab, "Media firm balks at Blue Jays loss," Canadian Press in the *Toronto Star* (April 19, 2002): E4.

421 **done bad:** Interview with the author.

422 **team's star slugger:** In 2004, Delgado earned US$19.7 million, or C$23 million.

424 **MLB.com:** Grant Robertson, "The Web's Hottest Player," *The Globe and Mail* (October 26, 2006): B1.

425 **"it ain't gonna work":** Paula Arab, "Baseball team becomes part of media empire," *Expositor* (September 2, 2000): A1.

CHAPTER 22

427 **investment grade:** In early 2007, the debt-rating agencies lifted cable and wireless into the lowest-possible investment grade ranking, which is still better than junk. Fitch and S&P also bestowed on RCI the lowest-possible investment-grade status.

428 **"super voting" shares:** See Management Proxy/Information Circulars, 2003–2006.

429 **Frank Stronach:** According to Magna's 2006 proxy circular, Frank Stronach owns 66.4 percent of Magna International Inc.'s class B voting shares. Each B share carries 500 votes apiece; whereas, the subordinate A voting shares (with a float 100 times greater) carry one vote apiece.

429 **public-equity markets:** For 60 years, from 1926 until 1986, the NYSE maintained a "one share, one vote" rule that prohibited the listing of any shares of a U.S. company that has more than one class of common stock, or stock with restrictions on voting power. It abandoned the rule in 1986 during the greed is good decade. In 1994, the NYSE once again prohibited dual-class share structures for U.S. companies.

429 **voting stock:** Comcast's acquisition of AT&T Broadband was completed in November 2002, the year's biggest M&A deal.

430 **Allan Waters:** In July 2006, Bell Globemedia agreed to pay $52.50 a share for the voting stock the Waters family used to control the radio broadcaster, 11 percent more than the $47.25 offered to non-voting shareholders. Waters died in December 2005.

432 **voting control:** Ownership percentages in 2002. See Report of Investigation by the Special Committee of the Board of Directors of Hollinger International Inc. August 30, 2004. p. 8.

http://online.wsj.com/public/resources/documents/hollingerreport20040831.htm

432 **jury convicted Black:** The jury found Black guilty on three counts of mail fraud and one count of obstruction of justice. He was acquitted on nine other counts, including charges of racketeering and wire fraud. Three co-defendants—Jack Boultbee, Peter Atkinson and Mark Kipnis—were each found guilty on three counts of mail fraud. Black's business partner David Radler, who pleaded guilty on a single count of mail fraud in exchange for a lighter sentence, testified against Black.

432 **non-compete payments:** KPMG was Hollinger International's external auditors, while Torys LLP represented both Hollinger International and Black's private company, Ravelston. Both firms have been named in class-action lawsuits. KPMG was chided by the special committee for initially having "resisted" its requests for information. Torys paid US$30 million—mostly through its insurance—to settle a civil lawsuit launched by Hollinger International's board of directors. Torys was accused of not raising red flags over millions of dollars in non-compete fees that were paid to Hollinger executives. Torys made no admission of guilt in settling the lawsuit.

435 **David Beatty:** Restivo, Kevin, "Rogers ends shakeup by naming Horn to chairman," *National Post* (March 22, 2006), FP4.

436 **governance:** Scroppo, Fina, "Control panel," *CA Magazine* Vol. 139. Issue 1 (January-February 2006): 35.

436 **cheques and balances:** *Shaping the Canadian Audit Committee Agenda* (KPMG LLP. 2006), 69.

439 **YBM scandal:** Peterson served as a director of magnet-maker YBM Magnex International Inc., a company linked to the Russian mob. In 2003, the vice chair of the Ontario Securities Commission, Howard Weston, fined two brokerage firms and five YBM directors, who were barred from serving on boards of other public Canadian companies for anywhere from three years to an indefinite term, for failing to disclose while raising public funds that U.S. authorities were investigating YBM for money-laundering and ties to the Russian mafia. Weston didn't fine Peterson but only chastised him for not offering "more insight and leadership to the board," a mere knuckle-rapping that many Bay Street observers felt inadequate. Weston, now chair of the Ontario Energy Board, was a former federal court trial judge and competition bureau director before joining the OSC.

439 **four years:** *According to Reisman, John H. Tory recommended her to Rogers.*

439 **"part of the vision":** Edward Rogers, Jr., joined the board of Futureway Communications, a small Toronto-based phone and Internet company, founded by the De Gasparis family, who made their fortune in real estate, after Rogers acquired a 20 percent stake. In 2007, Rogers Cable, led by Edward Rogers, acquired the 80 percent it didn't already own. Unlike Bell Canada, Futureway ploughed fiber directly to individual homes.

443 **Nadir Mohamed:** Nadir Mohamed currently is on Ryerson University's board of governors and is active in the Aga Khan Foundation (Khan is the spiritual leader of Ismaili Muslims). He is also a director of Cinram International Inc.

CHAPTER 23

454   Pierre-Karl Péladeau: Péladeau inked a deal in 2005 with Ted Rogers to resell Rogers' wireless minutes under its own label to fill a gaping hole in its customer service package. Finally, in August 2006, a month before the FCC AWS auction, Vidéotron began offering wireless services. To compete with rival Bell, Vidéotron needed–and needs–to offer subscribers the quadruple service play. The company, the first to roll out cable telephony service, was already pilfering Bell's wireline customers with cut-rate pricing, offering tethered phone service to its cable TV subscribers at $15.95 a month, compared to Bell's then-lowest monthly plan of $38. "[Péladeau's] much more of a warrior with Bell than I am," says Rogers "He's really serious."

Péladeau now wants to be an owner instead of a reseller, even though he has never given any previous indication of being remotely interested in acquiring radio spectrum. He made no attempt to bail out or buy Microcell, a company in his own backyard, when the opportunities arose. Ironically, the pre- Quebecor Vidéotron had been one of the fi ve original partners in the Charles Sirois-led Microcell consortium that, through a beauty contest, won a national PCS licence in 1995. Péladeau's brother Érik even sat on the Microcell board. Quebecor planned to unload its stock ostensibly to reduce debt, though it stated in its annual report that being a wireless provider "didn't fit in" with its longterm strategy. Fido's stock collapsed before Quebecor could bail. Shaw, another original investor, cut loose barely two years after Fido launched its service, to make almost a $12-million after-tax gain on its investment say they plan to bid for spectrum at auction, depending on the auction format.

456   Gabon: Mark Goldberg, "Hang up on call for cellphone subsidies," *National Post*. (March 29, 2007): FP19.

458   selling Yellow Pages: Paul Brent, "Buy high, sell low," *National Post*. (February 26, 2005): FP1.

458   fiber-optics systems: Barbara Keddy, "Bell seeks to take over cable TV service," *The Globe and Mail* (December 13, 1978): 1.

458   replacing copper: Catherine McLean, "BCE's land-line upgrade gets backseat in spending." *The Globe and Mail*. (March 30, 2007): B3.

459   they make in one: The bulk of Rogers' wealth has always been tied up in RCI stock. According to *Forbes* and *Canadian Business* magazines, Rogers is Canada's fourth-wealthiest businessman behind the Thomson family, Loblaw's Galen Weston, and the Irving family of New Brunswick. In 2006, for the first time, he was the cable industry's highest-paid CEO, taking home a compensation package worth $16.4 million, two-thirds of which came from exercising options.

461   small claims court: She won $2,000 in punitive damages against Rogers and slightly more than $800 in compensatory damages. Drummond accepted Rogers's $5,000 goodwill-gesture check and declined the company's $10,000 offer to settle out of court.

Drummond kept the media buzz alive by inviting Rogers to tea. He accepted, and then later declined after she informed his public relations staff that TV crews might be there—a surefire way of turning their private tête-à-tête into a media spectacle. Rogers invited her to air her concerns privately at his office. She never accepted the invitation. Instead, she created a "Rogers and me" website counting the days that had passed since he declined her offer to tea. She received funding for her website from taxpayer-funded research grants that York University receives from the federal government. Canada's edition of Time praised her and her partner as Canadian heroes, publishing a photograph of the pair beaming, with teapot raised and plate serving up a cellphone extended.

The tax dollars were made available from Social Sciences and Humanities Research Council of Canada (SSHRC), an Ottawa-based government agency that supports university-based research and training. According to the SSHRC, it requested that its name be removed from Drummond's "Rogers and me" website.

461   Susan Drummond: Chris Daniels, "Harry Gefen and Susan Drummond," *Time* (June 19/June 26, 2007): 60.

Partial Bibliography

Anthony, Ian A. *Radio Wizard. Edward Samuel Rogers and the Revolution of Communications.* Toronto: Rogers Telecommunications Ltd., 2000.

Babe, Robert E., *Telecommunications in Canada: Technology, Industry, and Government.* Toronto: University of Toronto Press, 1993.

Collins, Robert. *A Voice from Afar: The History of Telecommunications in Canada.* Toronto: McGraw-Hill Ryerson, 1977.

Easton, Ken. *Building an industry: A history of cable television and its development in Canada.* Toronto: Nimbus Publishing, 2000.

Fessenden, Helen. *Fessenden: Builder of Tomorrows.* New York: Arno Press, 1974 [first published ca. 1940].

Fraser, Matthew. *Free-for-All.* Toronto: Stoddart Publishing Co., 1999.

Gittens, Susan. *CTV: The Television Wars.* Toronto: Stoddart Publishing Co., 1999.

McDougall, Bruce. *Ted Rogers.* Toronto: Burgher Books, 1995.

McNeil, Bill, & Morris Wolfe. *Signing On: The Birth of Radio in Canada.* Toronto: Doubleday Canada, 1982.

Murray Jr., James B. *Wireless Nation: The Frenzied Launch of the Cellular Revolution in America.* Cambridge, Massachusetts: Perseus Books Group, 2001.

Ormond, Raby. *Radio's First Voice: The Story of Reginald Fessenden.* Toronto: Macmillan, 1970.

Smith, Ralph Lee. *The Wired Nation.* New York: Harper, 1972.

Southwick, Thomas P. *Distant Signals.* Overland Park, KS: Primedia. 1998.

Sterling, Christopher H., & Kittross, John Michael. *Stay Tuned: A History of American Broadcasting.* Mahwah, NJ: Lawrence Erlbaum Associates, 2002.

Surtess, Lawrence. *Wire Wars: Unitel's Fight for Telecommunications Control.* Toronto: Prentice Hall Canada, 1994.

Index